THE CRUSADES AND THE
EXPANSION OF CATHOLIC
CHRISTENDOM, 1000–1714

'A study that is both wide ranging and refreshingly insightful, which pulls together historical episodes that are often accorded insufficient attention and traces the fortunes of a developing political matrix in which piety and greed, loyalty and aggression, self-interest and faith, went hand in hand.'

Professor Peter Edbury, *Cardiff University*

The Crusades and the Expansion of Catholic Christendom is a fascinating and accessible survey that places the medieval crusades in their European context, and examines, for the first time, their impact on European expansion. Chronologically structured, John France provides a comprehensive overview of crusading from the development of a 'crusading impulse' in the eleventh century through to an examination of the relationship between the crusades and the imperialist imperatives of the early modern period. Conceiving of the crusades as a long-running phenomenon, France provides a detailed examination of the First Crusade, the expansion and climax of crusading during the twelfth and thirteenth centuries and the failure and fragmentation of such practices in the fourteenth and fifteenth centuries. Concluding with an assessment of the influence of the crusades across history, France notes that whilst continuities existed into the 'Age of Discovery' and beyond through the impulse to explore and seize territory, the motives behind post-Renaissance European expansion differed fundamentally.

Replete with illustrations, maps, timelines, guides for further reading and a detailed list of rulers across Europe and the Muslim world this study provides students with an essential guide to a central aspect of medieval history.

John France is Professor of History and Dean of the Faculty of Arts and Social Sciences at the University of Wales, Swansea. His previous publications include *Western Warfare in the Age of the Crusades, 1000–1300* (1999).

THE CRUSADES AND THE EXPANSION OF CATHOLIC CHRISTENDOM, 1000–1714

John France

Routledge
Taylor & Francis Group

LONDON AND NEW YORK

First published 2005
by Routledge
2 Park Square, Milton Park, Abingdon, Oxon OX14 4RN

Simultaneously published in the USA and Canada
by Routledge
270 Madison Ave, New York, NY 10016

Routledge is an imprint of the Taylor & Francis Group

© 2005 John France

Typeset in Goudy by
Book Now Ltd, London
Printed and bound in Great Britain by
Antony Rowe, Chippenham, Wiltshire

British Library Cataloguing in Publication Data
A catalogue record for this book is available from the British Library

Library of Congress Cataloging in Publication Data
France, John.
The Crusades and the expansion of Catholic Christendom, 1000–1714/John France.
p. cm.
Includes bibliographical references and index.
Crusades. 2. Church history–Middle Ages, 600–1500. 3. Europe–History–476–1492.
4. Europe–History–1492–1648. 5. Europe–History–1648–1715. I. Title.
D157.F67 2005
909.07–dc22   2004030018

ISBN 0–415–37127–9 (hbk)
ISBN 0–415–37128–7 (pbk)

TO MY WIFE, ANGELA

CONTENTS

ILLUSTRATIONS

Maps

Figures

ACKNOWLEDGEMENTS

I am deeply indebted to an enormous number of people who have helped me in the writing of this book. I have, at various times during its gestation, been awarded grants by the British Academy, by the Leverhulme Trust and by Swansea University. These provided me with opportunities to focus on the issues analysed here and the means to travel to many of the places discussed. Professor Jonathon Riley-Smith, Professor Norman Housley, Professor Jeremy Black and Professor Bernard Hamilton have provided me with much inspiration and I must also thank the latter for kindly reading and commenting on much of the text. My colleagues in the Department of History at the University of Swansea have been entirely supportive, and I must extend special thanks to Professor John Spurr, Dr Hugh Dunthorne and Mr Ifor Rowlands who all read substantial amounts of the text and offered their valuable comments. Professor Peter Edbury of Cardiff University was kind enough to read the whole text and to produce constructive criticisms which I value greatly. I am also indebted to his colleague, Professor Denys Pringle, who has shared his unsurpassed knowledge of crusader monuments. Dr S. B. Edgington of Queen Mary, University of London was kind enough to make available to me her text and translation of Albert of Aachen, while Dr A. V. Murray of the University of Leeds provided very substantial bibliographic help. Professor John Pryor staged a remarkable conference at the University of Sydney on Crusader Logistics in the autumn of 2002, and I can only thank him and all those who participated in what was an immensely exciting occasion. Professor John Haldon of the University of Birmingham is another pioneer of the study of medieval military logistics to whom I am indebted. It is a tribute to the vibrancy of the study of medieval warfare that it has given birth to a society, De Re Militari and its own Journal of Medieval Military History. Many of the leading spirits in this group are people with whom I have had long contact, notably Professors B. S. Bachrach, Kelley Devries, Richard Abels and Clifford Rogers. In 2002, at a critical stage in the development of this book, I was privileged to attend the Kalamazoo Conference and meet up with them once more, and to make new friends, amongst whom I would like to mention Peter Konieczny, the able keeper of the De Re Militari Web-Site. Professors Jean Richard, Michel Balard and J. Y. Tonnerre have all provided me with exciting ideas, as has Luis Garcia-Guijarro Ramos of the

University of Huesca whose conferences have been as remarkable for their lively ideas as for their hospitality. I remain indebted to Yvonne Friedmann and Ronnie Ellenblum for much encouragement and help. I am intensely grateful for the advice and encouragement of all these people, but, of course, responsibility for the material is mine alone.

All scholars rely heavily on learned institutions and libraries, so this is an opportunity to thank, in particular, Professor David Bates and his colleagues at the Institute of Historical Research, the staff of the British Library and, above all, the staff of the library of the University of Swansea.

Finally, I would like to thank Victoria Peters and Philippa Grand of Routledge who have worked so hard on my manuscript and licked it into shape.

FRONTISPIECE

Frontispiece 'The Edge of the World.' Whiston Castle, Pembrokeshire, a simple motte and bailey structure within the earthwork wall surrounding the little town clustered around it. This was founded in the early twelfth century on the northern edge of the Anglo-Norman lordship of Pembroke and peopled with loyal Flemings. Beyond were the bleak Prescelli Hills, the no-man's-land between them and the Welsh.

1

IN THE BEGINNING

The 'Expansion of Medieval Europe' is a recognised topic amongst historians of the medieval period. But this raises the difficult question of what the term Europe meant to medieval people, particularly at the beginning of our period. We tend to envisage Europe as a geographic zone, partly because we have a very wide knowledge of the rest of the world which was not shared by people around the year 1000. Our twenty-first century view is rather different from that of the Greeks and Romans who invented the term, and even now there is by no means unanimity on what countries and peoples should be included. *Europa* remained in the vocabulary of learned men in the early Middle Ages because of their education in Roman literature, but it was rare and only revived towards the end of the eighth century as a description of the dominions of Charlemagne in all their diversity. The Regensberg annalist identified *imperium* and *Europa* when he spoke in 888 of the break-up of 'Europe or the kingdom of Charles'. The word was used in this sense by the Ottonian dynasty of Germany in the tenth and eleventh centuries. A famous sequence of manuscript illustrations dating from the turn of the tenth and eleventh centuries proclaims the supremacy of either the Emperor Otto II (973–83) or Otto III (983–1002) by showing a series of figures representing variously *Francia, Italia, Germania, Alamannia, Gallia, Roma* and *Sclavinia* performing homage.[1] But although we tend to use the term European in a geographic sense, we are also aware that it implies much more than this – it is shorthand for a shared historical experience and a powerful sense of a community of culture. It is important to recognise that this sense of cultural community is much older than our sense of belonging to a geographic zone. It is out of this that our present identity has sprung. Around the year 1000 'Europe' was a rare term and it is doubtful whether anybody felt it to be a part of their identity. But there was a sense of a wider community to which the elites of the peoples in part of our Europe felt they belonged.

---

1 The paintings, from Bamberg, Chantilly and Munich manuscripts, are frequently reproduced, notably in C. Brühl, *Naissance de deux peuples. Français et Allemands (ix–xi siècle)* (Paris: Fayard, 1994) as Plates 5–8, and their meaning is discussed, 260–3.

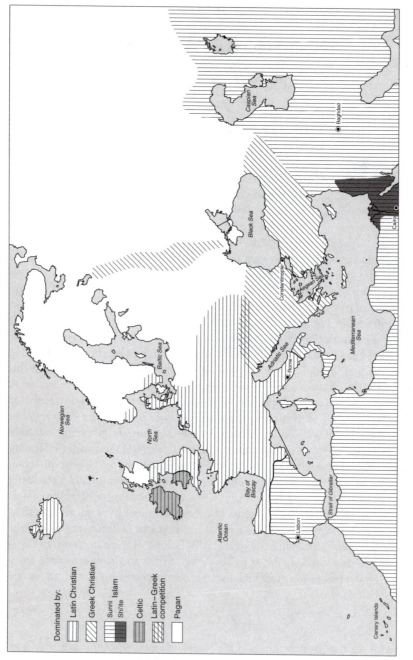

Map 1.1 Three civilisations around a sea: the 'Catholic core' and its neighbours c.1000.

Dominated by:

Latin Christian

Greek Christian

Sunni Islam

Shi'ite

Celtic

Latin–Greek competition

Pagan

Norwegian Sea

North Sea

Baltic Sea

Atlantic Ocean

Bay of Biscay

Lisbon

Canary Islands

Strait of Gibraltar

Mediterranean Sea

Rome

Adriatic Sea

Aegean Sea

Constantinople

Black Sea

Caspian Sea

Baghdad

Cairo

Rodulfus Glaber, writing across the period c.1023 to 1047, felt he was part of the 'Roman' world, but this was clearly not the empire of the Ottonians because he was devoted to the cause of the Capetian dynasty which ruled much of what we call France. What is particularly interesting about this writer is that he set himself to write a history of 'our continent this-side-the-sea'. He never defined this more precisely, but his writing was informed by a deep and explicit hatred and contempt for Greeks, pagans and Moslems. Glaber was consciously identifying what he called 'our continent' with that part of Christianity which looks to Rome. This was probably because he had been brought up in the *milieu* of the great abbey of Cluny which enjoyed a close special relationship with the Roman See, and sat at the heart of a network of monasteries and personal connections which spanned the lands most closely integrated into Roman Christianity. Early in his book Glaber embarked on an interesting excursus in which he debated why it was that Christianity was expanding in the west and north, and not in the place of its birth, the east.[2] In effect, Glaber's 'continent this-side-the-sea' is a religious and cultural construct (and certainly not a primarily geographic one) which can be termed the 'Catholic core', the zone of unequivocal acceptance of the final authority of Rome in spiritual affairs comprising what is now southern England, France, Germany and much of Italy. That is what matters to him and all else is outside.

The primacy of cultural identity should not surprise us. The peoples of the 'Catholic core' were cut off from the rest of the world by the Atlantic to the west, the pagan peoples of the steppe fringe to the north-east and Islam to the east, although its authorities allowed pilgrimage to Jerusalem. In these circumstances their intelligentsia were heavily dependent upon classical writings for geographic knowledge. The ancient world had quite substantial knowledge of the world beyond the Mediterranean. Greek and Roman traders found their way to India, the islands of the Altantic, the Far East and perhaps even ventured down the African coasts. However, the best of their geographic treatises were written in Greek, which was distinctly inaccessible even to most scholars before the later Middle Ages. The very important work of the second century author, Claudius Ptolemy, only became known in the fifteenth century. A great deal of the knowledge of the ancient world was transmitted to the Middle Ages via compilations made in the late Roman period like that of Martianus Capella which contained rather poor geographic material elaborated with fabulous stories of monsters and wonders. The learned tradition was, therefore, confused from the start, the more so because it was handed down in compressed form by writers like St Isidore whose *Encyclopaedia* had an enormous circulation in the Middle Ages. Most of the intelligentsia seem to have inherited from his works and those of others the idea that there were three continents, Asia, Africa and Europe, clustered around the Mediterranean. This gave rise to the 'T-O maps', schematic

2 Rodulfus Glaber, *The Five Books of the Histories*, in J. France (ed.), *Rodulfus Glaber Opera* (Oxford: Clarendon Press, 1989), 1–253.

representations of the three continents which were produced throughout the Middle Ages. This was clearly the basis of William of Jumièges' attempt to describe *Europa*: 'Asia reaches from the south through the east to the north, Europe from the north to the West and Africa begins and stretches from the West to the South.'[3] William repeats the usual belief that Asia was as big as Africa and Europe combined. Rabanus Maurus in his *Commentariorum in Genesim* repeated Isidore's *De Natura Rerum* in putting the boundary of Asia and Europe at the river Tanais, meaning the river now called the Don. Bede certainly understood that the world was round and that this affected the tides and seasons. He was exceptionally curious and observant and others wrote as if the earth was flat.

The Christian religion imbued its followers with a strong sense of the old Mediterranean world, and the popularity of pilgrimage to Jerusalem provided some real geographic information for those who went on it. Sailors who traded with the Greeks and Muslims would have had a similar pragmatic lore. But there was no study of geography and no established body of erudition into which this could be fitted. Furthermore, the biblical assertion that Jerusalem was the centre of the world confused any assimilation of such pragmatic knowledge.[4] In these circumstances even intellectuals believed in wonders and monsters lurking beyond the horizon, an uneasy mix of imagination and half-digested classical knowledge that made 'Gog' and 'Magog' figures of reality in some fantasy-land. In the twelfth century confused stories about a Christian ruler in Central Asia gave rise to the legend of 'Prester John', but the hope of an ally against resurgent Islam led to hopeful stories and legends, so that eventually he became identified with the Christian kingdom of Ethiopia. In the High Middle Ages this compound of classical knowledge, theological ideas, observation and speculation became embodied in *mappa mundi*, schematic representations of the world based on the 'T-O maps' and embodying these assorted ranges of knowledge. For the most part these portrayed the world as a disc, and although some scholars thought the world a sphere, the likelihood is that most did not. Geographical knowledge improved with the passage of time, but only slowly.

Very few medieval people identified with the term *Europa*. The aristocratic elite as a whole would have felt little need because it was not until the later eleventh century that the world outside made much impact upon their concerns. They would probably have reacted with hostility to any idea of a different or dissident religion if it had imposed itself as a reality upon them, but for most it did not. Sharp consciousness of the wider world was limited to a very few amongst the clergy, and was particularly evident at the papal court. The papacy had pretensions to rule the whole Christian Church and, more immediately, was in

---

3 William of Jumièges, *Gesta Normannorum Ducum*, ed. E. M. C. van Houts, 2 vols (Oxford: Oxford University Press, 1992–5), 1. 12–13.

4 A plaque, set into the floor of the church of the Holy Sepulchre, still purports to locate the 'centre of the world' there.

constant contact with Catholics living under Islamic rule in Spain and North Africa. In a letter of 1098 concerning the Spanish diocese of Jaca, Urban II remarked that 'In our days the Turks in Asia and the Moors (*Mauros*) in Europe defeated Christian peoples and captured the cities of their religion.' It was only in the twelfth century that such distinctions became widely diffused as a result of the crusades, so that William of Malmesbury spoke of the First Crusade as an 'Asiatic expedition'. But *Europa* was a vague geographic expression and one that embraced peoples with whom those who occasionally used it would have felt little in common. There was a geographic dimension to identity. Some of those in what we now call France would have objected to the notion that *Gallia* was part of the Empire, but others would not have. In the twelfth century the counts of Hainault did homage to both the German emperors and the French kings with little sense of incongruity. Far more important in fixing identity was religion and the culture inseparable from it.

This was more than simply a matter of accepting the primacy of the Roman See. The churches obedient to Rome had preserved much of the Latin culture of the Roman Empire. The church was the only literate institution, though many nobles could read and some could write. Its higher ranks were colonised by the elite which thus had a clerical wing. The power and presence of the clergy was enormously enhanced because authority in the Church was transmitted from generation to generation by election. This meant that churches enjoyed continuity of policy and development rare in the lay world where wealth and power were transmitted by the random process of inheritance. The Church under Rome was, therefore, an institutionalised cultural unity, intimately integrated into the power structures of the medieval west. When the crusaders arrived in the Middle East the Arab-speaking world called them *franj*, meaning 'Franks' from the name of the dominant group in the 'Catholic core'. Many of them also saw themselves as Franks but the specific notion with which they all seem to have identified themselves was 'Christendom'. For an anonymous knight from South Italy who went on the First Crusade the Turks were 'enemies of God and holy Christendom'.[5] This was a term with a great future, which would be reiterated time after time and represented an identity, at first only for those of the 'Catholic core' but increasingly, as its ideas and institutions took hold elsewhere, for other peoples as well. For Christendom, Glaber's 'continent this-side-the-sea', excluded not only those Glaber portrayed as of other faiths and cultures, the Greeks and the Muslims, but also areas which were at least in part Catholic and owed obedience to the Holy See, yet which were different and clearly regarded as such: these were the lands of the 'Catholic fringe'.

Prominent amongst these were the newly converted lands of what is now called Central Europe. Poland, Bohemia and Hungary had all adopted Latin Catholic

---

5 Anonymous, *Gesta Francorum et aliorum Hierosolimitanorum*, ed. R. Hill (Edinburgh: Nelson, 1962), Book VI, chapter 13, 32.

Christianity by the year 1000, but the process was recent and they were all to some degree influenced by Byzantium and her, as we say, Orthodox Church. Glaber welcomed Hungary into the Catholic fold, but he and others would long continue to see it and the other newly converted lands as being different, though all became more integrated in the course of the twelfth century. Hungary and Poland also had to watch developments on the great Asiatic steppe and this influenced their political priorities and even their social institutions.

To the north were the Scandinavian lands which, at the time Glaber was writing, were only just becoming Catholic. By the year 1000 the people of western Scandinavia had explored the islands of the North Atlantic, settled Iceland and Greenland, and had reached 'Vinland', which can now be certainly identified as America. By the early twelfth century Catholic Christianity was clearly triumphant amongst them, but native paganism had offered a vigorous resistance. Their Atlantic expansion filtered only slowly into the wider consciousness of the peoples of the 'Catholic core' amongst whom it became assimilated to ancient knowledge of islands in the Atlantic. These older stories had already inspired Irish monks, notably St Brendan, to seek solitude out in the Atlantic, and their *Lives* spread this knowledge widely.[6] The eastern Scandinavians had penetrated the river valleys of the western steppe lands and established strong trading connections with Byzantium and the Caliphate. Their settlements in this area became the nuclei of 'Rus', whose peoples would later adopt Greek Christianity.

Then there were the Celtic lands of the British Isles. Wales and Ireland had been Christian at least as long as France and certainly longer than Germany. The Irish converted the Scots and the northern English, and even profoundly influenced the Franks. But the churches of these areas were viewed with suspicion because Celtic Christianity had once sanctioned divergent religious practices that lingered on. There was no such thing as a 'Celtic Church', but the churches of Ireland, Scotland, Wales and Brittany had much in common. Moreover, although the Celtic lands and those of new conversion were very different from one another, they were alike in having much less developed economies than the 'Catholic core'. There was, of course, diversity within the core itself, but the economies of the lands within it were dominated by grain production made possible by a settled peasantry tied to the land. There were major areas of pastoral farming and huge marginal zones, but these were being colonised by a disciplined peasantry in the service of the elites. Everywhere 'Lordship' was emerging as the key social, economic and political institution. This was the result of what elsewhere were regarded as governmental powers, like taxation and jurisdiction, being annexed to private landholding. This pattern of exploitation imposed itself on and shaped the peasant communities who increasingly lived in its shadow. In particular, proprietorial ruthlessness forced the peasantry to be both productive and progressive. This was the motor of the economy of the 'Catholic core', but it

6 D. O'Donoghue, *Lives and legends of Saint Brendan the Voyager* (Felinfach: Llanerch, 1994).

had only just begun to establish itself in the lands of the 'Catholic fringe' where society remained tribal. The elites of the fringe were not as yet so focused on possession of land as those in the core areas where land ownership gave stability to political authority of all kinds and was inseparable from it. Social and economic development was a powerful strand in the commonality of the 'Catholic core'.

And these lands of the fringe were different from those of the 'Catholic core' in another respect: they had not shared the Carolingian experience. Charlemagne had an enormous impact on the peoples over whom he ruled. His 'family of emperors and kings' gave shape to the 'Catholic core' and formed part of the common heritage of the peoples within it. It has to be said that England never succumbed to Frankish power, but its influence on the southern kingdoms of the island was immense. By the time of the First Crusade the myth of Charlemagne was an established part of the consciousness of the elites of the 'Catholic core'. A knight who went on the First Crusade wrote an account of this astonishing event, the *Gesta Francorum*. He reports as history the legend that the old Roman road down the Danube to Constantinople was that travelled by Charlemagne on his way to the great city. More importantly, although this man was almost certainly of Norman descent and had either emigrated to or been raised in Italy, he regarded himself as a 'Frank' and never described himself or his companions in the army from South Italy as Normans. This is the mental world into which was born the epic poem, the *Chanson de Roland*, which portrayed Charlemagne as the great champion of Christendom fighting against the Muslims of Spain. This and its associated stories together form an important element in the great body of European myth.[7] And there was a reality here, for Charles imposed a Frankish aristocracy upon his empire, and their blood ran in the veins of all the leaders and many of the participants on the First Crusade.

Nor had the lands of the 'Catholic fringe' shared another unifying experience. In the ninth and tenth centuries the 'Catholic core' had been thrust onto the defensive by a wave of external attacks, some of them, indeed, launched by peoples of the 'Catholic fringe'. The most spectacular of these were the sea-borne attacks from Scandinavia that have bred an enormous literature. The Magyars (or Hungarians) had imposed a tribute upon much of Germany, and their raids into France and Italy had terrified whole populations. Groups of Slavonic peoples had at times posed at least a local threat to the eastern parts of Germany. Midland and western England were subject to Welsh raiding. Even by the time of the Norman Conquest the frontier between the English and Scottish realms was uncertain. Italy and southern France were exposed to Islamic attacks from Sicily, North Africa, Spain and the islands of the western Mediterranean, which succeeded in planting settlements in these areas. Only a major effort enabled the papacy to eject the Muslims from the Garigliano, about 120 km south of Rome, in the early tenth century, but they continued to rule Sicily and to hold settlements on the

---

7 *Gesta Francorum*, 2.

Italian mainland. The Muslims of La Garde Freinet, near what is now St Tropez in Provence, menaced traffic in the Alpine passes until 972 when their capture of St Mayol, abbot of Cluny, provoked William count of Arles and others to destroy their bases. As late as 1022 the Muslims of Spain mounted a major raid around Narbonne.

The lands of the 'Catholic fringe' were to be the earliest victims, or perhaps beneficiaries, of the expansion of Catholic Christendom. For the elites of these lands there was much to admire in the societies of the 'Catholic core' and emulation was to be at least as strong a factor in their assimilation as conquest. The same was true, up to a point at least, of the pagan neighbours of the 'Catholic core'. Subtle mixtures of attraction and coercion served to bring them into the orbit of the world which looked, in matters of religion, to Rome. Such emulation was as profitable to the noble dynasties of the 'Catholic core' as to the elites who wished to join them, since it was associated with intermarriage and the implantation of their families in new lands. Beyond such peoples, in the north at least, was the open steppe land. In the south were other and alien centres of influence, Byzantium and Islam with their very different peoples and civilisations, which were, from the start of our period, viewed with a degree of hostility by those in the 'Catholic core'.

It must not be thought that because they shared a common religion and culture, rather similar economic and social institutions and recent historical experience, the lands of the 'Catholic core' were homogenous and unified. Indeed, precisely the opposite was true. The wave of invasions in the ninth and tenth centuries were the more threatening because the 'Catholic core' was fragmenting as the Carolingian family fell to quarrelling, or was replaced as it died out by local dynasties, 'sub-kings', as Regino of Prüm scornfully called them. At first sight one is obliged to wonder how dangerous some of these threats were. The 'Catholic core' was richer and enjoyed some technological advantages over its pagan neighbours, notably the steel swords and mail shirts whose export to the 'pagans' Charlemagne had been at pains to prohibit. The ambitions of Slavs, Welsh and Scots were generally localised while the Hungarians seem to have sought a tribute domination over their neighbours.

However, such peoples were dangerous because they could play upon divisions within the elites of the 'Catholic core'. The Vikings were encouraged when western potentates, such as Charles the Bald of the West Franks (840–77), tried to use them against domestic enemies. Regino of Prüm described the coming of the Hungarians in 889 after his account of the confusion attendant on the deposition of Charles the Fat in 887, and the Fulda annalist made much the same point when he remarked that in that same year 'Northmen, hearing of dissension amongst the Franks and the deposition of their emperor, devastated many lands which hitherto they had barely touched.' In 954–55 it was German rebellion which offered the Hungarians another chance to dominate the Ottonian *Reich*. Such interventions could lead on to greater things. In 711 the Muslims of North Africa had been invited to intervene in a civil war amongst the Visigoths and this gave them their opportunity to conquer Spain. The great Danish army of 865 found collaborators in England, notably the 'foolish king's thegn' who held much of Mercia for them, while on the death of Alfred of Wessex (871–99) the Danes were called in to the subsequent succession struggle in Wessex. But the Danish conquest of much of England was quite exceptional, and for the most part the existing elites were quite strong enough to hold off the outsiders, or, in the case of the Norman lodgement in northern France, to assimilate it. The accession to the English throne of the Danish ruler, Cnut the Great (1017–35) was made easier because he was Christian. Accepted as king in 1017 he set about ruling his new lands in the traditions to which they were used. The elites of Scandinavia were targeted by a few zealous missionaries, but above all they were attracted by the society of the 'Catholic core'. The spirit of imitation and emulation did much to protect and extend the 'Catholic core' in the tenth century and later.

The savage struggle of the ninth and tenth centuries against external attack was clearly the result of internal dissent as the Carolingian dynasty became divided, and then died out. But these conflicts did not generate another great political authority. Instead, the leaders of the 'Catholic core', the Carolingian aristocracy, developed articulated dominions resting on the ability of greater landowners to defend them and in addition to coerce others. They achieved this by annexing governmental power to their landholdings, forming the character-istic institution of lordship. They were aggressive, greedy and opportunistic: as early as the tenth century the counts of Flanders were founding castles to encourage the growth of towns and, therefore, taxes. In 1073 Hugh, Earl of Chester, seized Rhuddlan from the Welsh, quickly establishing there a mint and fisheries to generate wealth to sustain this latest advance. This fiercely competi-tive upper class lived and fought within the kingdoms like France and the German Empire which had emerged at the beginning of the tenth century, but except in Wessex and its successor state of Norman England, they were little inhibited by their monarchs. Internecine conflict was a way of life, yet despite this they had a sense of unity. Their success explains the survival of the 'Catholic core' for it was religion and culture that gave these mutually hostile forces a common bond.

Charlemagne had given the Church deep roots amongst his elite. In the depths of political confusion around 900 Berno of Cluny and Gerald of Brogne, who both came from important families, re-established Benedictine monasticism and gave it a new vigour by its association with the great princes. In England, Alfred faced attack by the pagan Danes who were in all respects other than religion very like his own people. He encouraged Church and learning precisely to draw a sharp line between his followers and the Danes. Religious attachment, cultivated by the leading kings and princes as a means of defending and articulating their own power, was a powerful reason for the survival of the 'Catholic core', which was essentially the result of the individual struggles of particular princes. Rudolf of Burgundy had many problems as king of the West Franks, but in 930 he was able to come to terms with Normandy and to rally the nobility to crush a Norse incursion into Aquitaine. It was as dukes of Saxony that the Liudolfing family marshalled the resources which would ultimately enable them to become kings of Germany and 'Emperors of the west'. They ended the Hungarian threat and drove the catholic frontier eastwards into the Slav lands which were increasingly subjected to tribute-domination until the progress of German power was halted by the death in Italy of Otto II in 983. Alfred ruled a kingdom which was very much on the scale of a continental duchy, but he was able to mobilise its resources for war and to drive back the Danes: his successors sustained this and gradually the forces of assimilation converted and absorbed the Norse settlers. On a much smaller scale was the career of Bobo of Noghiers. He was a local lord at the time of the Muslim seizure of La Garde-Freinet in Provence. He built a castle and attacked the Muslim base, apparently with some success. The loss of his brother in battle led him to undertake a pilgrimage to Rome, but he died at Voghera where he was revered as a saint. In northern Spain the tiny Visigothic kingdom of Asturias invoked divine aid against the Islamic threat. The survival of the 'Catholic core' was bound up with the intense localism of most of the attacks, and the generally local response to them.

For what distinguished the people of 'our continent this-side-the-sea' was disunity: the 'Catholic core' was a Balkan shambles of weak states and quarrelling princes. In the year 1000 it was far more fragmented than it had ever been. A degree of unity was imparted by their faith, Roman and Catholic, and by the Latin culture which the clerical elite shared and extended amongst their lay relatives. Everywhere a lay elite ruled over a settled peasantry with which its members had little in common. The major lay lords and their closest followers, the knights, enjoyed great privileges and shared a common and highly militarised way of life. Around the time of the millennium states were barely articulated, and the power of kings depended on personality and drive, on their ability to persuade the noble elite who actually ruled in the localities. Monarchy and its leadership were universally accepted, but monarchs did not have complex administrations which enabled them to command. Western society was driven by a land-owning elite and all major landed proprietors enjoyed de facto important elements of sovereign power. Even minor landowners held aspects of it.

At the very highest level great nobles might enjoy the title of duke, margrave, count or earl, and in the German empire they might be archbishops; these leaders were often described as 'princes'. Such was their power that the papacy itself gave them considerable recognition. Of 152 lay addressees in the Register of Gregory VII, no less than 80 are princes in the sense of ruling persons who are not kings, and the pope speaks of 'king or secular prince' or 'kings and other princes'. In Anglo-Saxon England there were great earls whose power rivalled that of the king, and Northumbria was as yet barely assimilated into the English realm. Throughout our period the princes of Germany waged war on their own behalf with little reference to their king. It has been said that 'German bishops and abbots feuded as a matter of course'. In Italy the power of the German monarchs after the year 1000 was exercised through the bishops in the flourishing cities of the area; this inhibited the emergence of lay princes with a strong territorial base.

However, new social forces in the cities in some places threatened the power of the bishops, and therefore of the monarchy itself. In France the eleventh century was the apogee of princely power, when a duke of Aquitaine could think so little of the monarchy as not to bother to attend a royal election. Aristocratic potentates often used royal formulae to describe their power. Arnulf of Bavaria claimed to be 'duke by the grace of God of the Bavarians and adjacent provinces' and a writer sympathetic to his cause scorned Henry I's claims to rule there 'where neither he nor his ancestors held a foot of land'. William of Poitiers struggled to define the position of his hero, Duke William of Normandy, and explained that 'Normandy, long subject to the king of France was now almost erected into a kingdom.' In the Europe of the early eleventh century, one modern authority has remarked, 'the age of kings seemed to have passed and that of princes to be the future'.[8]

The 'Catholic core' was not alone in generating an aggressive, ruthless, opportunistic aristocracy. But rival elites, such as those of Byzantium and the Islamic powers, existed within a much stronger framework of central authority which provided many opportunities for ambition. The nobles of the 'Catholic core' were fixated on land-ownership and acquisition as the real and virtually the only basis of power and status. There was certainly a concept of the state as an over-arching sovereign authority, but in practice monarchs were merely the most eminent of aristocrats whose domination owed more to personal qualities such as determination, allied to mastery of resources, than to settled structures of command. Landowners were government, a situation not fundamentally altered by the rise of Charlemagne or the disappearance of his line and the dissipation of royal power. But in the absence of a strong central power able to tap the wealth of a whole realm effectively and hand out patronage, or to wage effective and distant war, aristocratic families relied more and more on their estates.

The settled areas of the 'Catholic core' were not overpopulated, but the arms-bearing elite had concentrated their wealth into its own hands. To preserve family lands, inheritance practices became more and more exclusive, so that there was a marked trend in France and England towards primogeniture by which the lands of the father were vested only in the eldest son, though other heirs might have rights, to a greater or lesser extent. The result was a social overpopulation: the children of the elite, unable to count on an inheritance, had to leave home to seek their fortune. In Germany, southern France, Spain and Italy primogeniture was never as widely accepted, but the results were not very different as some children were bound to lose out in the scramble for succession. This process was the greater because intermittently the most powerful of the kings and princes were

8 The quotations are from *L'Estoire de Eracles empereur*, RHC Oc 2.34, translated in J. Richard, *The Latin Kingdom of Jerusalem*, tr. J. Shirley, 2 vols (Amsterdam: North Holland, 1979) 1. 96; William of Poitiers, *Gesta Guillelmi*, ed. R. H. C. Davies and M. Chibnall (New York: Clarendon, 1998), 67; and J. Flori, *L'idéologie du glaive. Préhistoire de la chevalerie* (Geneva: Droz, 1983), 168.

consolidating and beginning to impose their authority. Turbulent young men were unwelcome and obliged to look elsewhere; they were well-equipped to do so because the elite within which they were raised was militarised. In an age when state authority was weak, those who had wealth or who guarded it for others, had to be soldiers. They lived in fortified houses, castles, which guarded the wealth they extorted from the land against both aggressive competitors and the restlessness of its peasant producers. In and around these castles they developed a common style of war based on the heavily armed and armoured soldier who could fight effectively on horseback or on foot. They enjoyed tales of noble warriors narrated in epic vernacular poetry, the *Chansons de Geste*, in which there is a real delight in violence and war. The nature of aristocratic holding was so complex that it is almost impossible to draw maps of the distribution of power. Where a lord held land, he effectively was the government, and in France, Germany and Italy it was unlikely that the king would interfere much with him as long as he was loyal – only in England was royal government to a limited extent interventionist. But land was transmitted by the accidents of birth, death and marriage, so it was not held in great blocks, and where, as was most commonly the case, the possessions of several lords interpenetrated, the locus of authority was much more uncertain. Moreover, rights over land often became divorced from land itself. In this way peasant communities, which formed the units of production, were often divided by multiple units of exploitation of differing kinds. In the absence of powerful central authorities, proprietors of any substance had to be militant and aggressive, or else be prepared to submit to those who were.

The elite of the 'Catholic core' generated numerous young swords for hire, some of whom made spectacular careers in distant lands. Roger de Toeni went to Spain about 1020 and terrorised the Muslims of Spain by pretending to be a cannibal. Robert Crispin joined the expedition to Spain that captured Barbastro in 1064 and later took service with the Byzantines. Roussel of Bailleul was another Norman who became a mercenary in Byzantium and he attempted to set up a principality in Asia Minor in the wake of the collapse of Byzantine power in 1071. Many Anglo-Saxon nobles who fled England after the Norman conquest served in the Varangian guard of the emperor at Constantinople and others settled on the Black Sea. William the Carpenter, Viscount of Melun, went on the French expedition to Spain in 1086, and the First Crusade. But just as important as a motor of expansion was dynastic corporatism. Families on or near frontiers exploited every possibility to enhance their positions. The von Wedels, as Bartlett has shown, came from western Germany to serve the dukes of Pomerania and helped to push his frontier eastwards, in the process becoming highly significant landowners with a network of castles.[9] In England the de Braose were originally a family of secondary importance holding the Rape of Bramber in

9 They and other aristocratic dynasties are discussed in 'The aristocratic diaspora', in R. Bartlett, *The Making of Europe. Conquest, Colonization and Cultural Change* (London: Penguin, 1993).

Sussex. Philip de Braose, (who may have been a crusader) moved to the Welsh March towards the end of the eleventh century and conquered Radnor, which became the seat of a collateral branch. But the real foundation of the family's fortune was the marriage of his son, William (died c.1175) to Bertha, an heiress of the Earl of Hereford. William thus acquired the lordships of Brecon and Abergavenny and set in train a ruthless policy of consolidation and expansion that drove out native lords and replaced them with loyal followers. This brought royal favour, which allowed the de Braose to increase their lands even further, notably by the acquisition of Gower.

Yet this quarrelling, bickering quagmire of authorities and kingdoms was not totally unstable and certainly not chaotic. In an age of poor communications, local power was the most secure and the means existed for determined men to run their lands efficiently. Fulk of Anjou (987–1040) is a remarkable example of a count who built up an important principality. He began with a rich assortment of lands and claims scattered from the mouth of the Loire to some 200 km up its course, of which the most important was the county of Anjou. These holdings were interpenetrated by territories belonging to other important magnates like the lords of Saumur and the counts of Blois who held Tours. Fulk created chains of castles to consolidate his control, and his son, Charles Martel (1040–60) added to his work by seizing Tours in 1044. The subsequent history of the new principality is illustrative; the outbreak of a succession dispute on Charles Martel's death in 1060 weakened his eventual successor, Fulk Requin (1067–1109). The besetting sin was uncertainty, for authority and land passed by inheritance and were subject to the vagaries of personality. It is an apparent paradox that this divided 'Catholic core' was expansive, yet the source of this expansionism was its very violent and competitive nature. The competing dynasties made victims of the weak, and along the frontiers of the 'Catholic core' were neighbours at once troublesome and vulnerable. In North Germany the dukes of Saxony led raids against their pagan and recently Christianised neighbours and in time frontier zones, marches or Marks arose, whose very purpose was expansion. In Norman England the lords of the Welsh march expanded into Wales. Such violent and unstable places attracted adventurers for whom the conditions offered opportunities, and these would be replicated elsewhere. Other forces in turn lent their strength to the outward drive – merchants seeking profit, kings attempting to solidify their grasp on power. Yet if there is one manifest source of the expansive imperative in the 'Catholic core' it was the greed and ambition of the nobility and their followers for land, and this was the driving dynamic of the expansion which created 'Catholic Christendom' and, in turn, modern Europe.

In this, the expansion of 'Christendom' in the Middle Ages was different from that which occurred from the fifteenth century onwards and which is discussed in the later chapters of this book. The 'Age of Discoveries' has long fascinated historians and for a very long time the earlier growth of 'Christendom' was all but forgotten. As medieval expansionism was rediscovered, it was quite natural and reasonable to see in it the roots of the 'Age of Discovery'. There are certainly connections, but the growth of early modern Europe had different roots and took place in a quite different political environment from that of the Middle Ages. Moreover, the assumed connection between the two has tended to distort our perspective of what happened in the period after 1000. We know that the 'Age of the Discoveries' led to the European and later 'western' domination of the globe and this has led to an unduly optimistic view of medieval growth. In fact, the medieval expansion was modest and suffered major failures. Although emulation played a major part in drawing many pagan peoples to the 'Catholic core', its civilisation seems to have had little appeal to the more advanced peoples who came into contact with it. Lithuania developed a pagan society which was just as advanced as that of Catholic Christendom. By contrast, Islam spread into the East Indies, displacing traditional and well-established religions by missionary activity alone. The notion of continuity has given us another false perspective. The European expansion after 1500 has been seen as the result of superior western technology and this idea has been imported to discussions about medieval growth. The notion has taken root that 'Castles, Cavalry and Crossbows' made the whole process possible.[10] In reality Catholic Christendom enjoyed only limited technological advantages over its more primitive neighbours and very few indeed over the Muslim and Byzantine worlds which were its competitors. Moreover, the emphasis on military technology has resulted in a failure to recognise that, at least in its early stages, expansionism owed much to emulation as well as conquest. And in fact discussion of military technology has led historians to underemphasise the significance of maritime development to the medieval expansion.

There was certainly a drive to expansion within the 'Catholic core', but it could only be realised because of the difficulties and preoccupations of the competing centres of influence like Byzantium and Islam. When he referred to 'our continent this-side-the-sea' Rodulfus Glaber laid his finger upon a vital contemporary reality. The Mediterranean was the centre of the world, and around it lived three civilisations. Byzantium was the eastern remnant of the Roman Empire ruled by emperors in an unbroken line from Augustus. But in practice its culture and outlook had evolved in a very different way from the 'Catholic core'. It was essentially a Greek Empire ruled from Constantinople. It was unitary in the sense that it was ruled by a single emperor whose power was conceived of as world-wide and absolute. He was served by a centralised bureaucracy that collected taxes. The immense wealth of this central government made it the focus of competing aristocratic factions. Many of these were important landowners, but such was the wealth of the court that the focus of their interests was control of central power and the person of the emperor. The palace, the bureaucracy and the imperial army offered to the Byzantine elite a diversity of career paths and

---

10 'Castles, cavalry and crossbows' is something of a travesty of 'Military technology and political power', in Bartlett, *Making of Europe*, one of the most important statements of recent years about European expansion.

opportunities for enrichment that simply were not open to western lords preoccupied with landownership. One consequence of the absolute authority of the imperial office was that succession struggles in the Byzantine Empire were particularly bitter. Another pillar of the imperial autocracy was the Church, which was closely integrated into the state. There were minor differences of practice between the Catholic and Orthodox churches, but the essential bone of contention was the authority of the Roman See, for the Orthodox Church looked to the emperor for day-to-day guidance, and to an Ecumenical Council of all the bishops of the universal Church as final authority. Byzantium impinged upon the 'Catholic core' in a number of ways. Its rulers always took seriously their claim to rule the whole Christian world, and they strenuously objected to the pretensions of the German kings who, as rulers of Italy, claimed coronation as Roman Emperors. Otto I had had to fight a war for recognition of the title after his imperial coronation in 962. In a more practical way the Byzantine hold on Calabria and Apulia was deeply resented by the Lombard rulers of southern Italy, by the German Emperors who claimed suzerainty, and by the pope whose southern frontiers were close. Intimately bound up with this were religious tensions over the papal claims to control the churches in some of the Greek-ruled areas, and the autonomy of the Greek Church. Byzantium could pose a real threat. In the mid-ninth century the Emperor Romanus II (959–63) intervened in the affairs of the Italian kingdom and sent a fleet to support Hugh of Arles in his attack on the Muslim settlements in southern France. Later, in 984 and in 997 the Byzantines exerted enough influence in Rome to engineer the election of Greek anti-popes.

Byzantine resurgence at the start of the eleventh century, and her ambition to regain Sicily, tended to intensify these tensions. Basil II (976–1025) imposed a firm domination over Bulgaria, consolidating Byzantine cultural and religious influence in the Balkans and posing an alternative choice to Rome for the areas now called Central and Eastern Europe. In his reign, Orthodox Christianity also penetrated the western steppelands. Here the Rus, Scandinavian adventurers, had established a chain of cities connecting their homelands with the great trading zones of the Byzantine Empire and the Caliphate. Cities along the trade routes, such as Novgorod, Polotsk, Smolensk, Turov, Chernigov, Perseiaslavl and Rostov had all come to recognise the hegemony of the house of Riurik whose chief outpost was Kiev in the south. Prince Vladimir Sviatoslavich (980–1015) had to fight against rivals for the succession to Kiev, and he seems to have recognised that conversion to Christianity would offer a substantial extension of his authority. Emulation was certainly at work here, but it was emulation of Byzantium. The Rus had attacked Constantinople as early as 869, but subsequently they had developed great trading interests in the city where there was a special quarter for them. Byzantine interest in converting these pagans was very strong and it is said that the magnificent rituals of the Orthodox Church at Constantinople impressed the people of Rus. It is likely, therefore, that the two societies were moving together by the time of Vladimir. In 988 Basil II faced a major revolt and he concluded a treaty with Vladimir by which he gave his sister,

Anna, to the prince of Kiev in return for military support, in the form of Russian mercenaries, against his internal enemies. Kievan Russia was now firmly brought into Constantinople's cultural sphere. Constantinople was regarded with great respect and some suspicion in the 'Catholic core', and while we know it would ultimately pose no threat, contemporaries did not. It was clearly an alternative centre of influence and around it there had arisen a 'Byzantine Commonwealth' of countries linked to it by religion and culture, effectively the Balkan region, Bulgaria and Russia whose conversion extended it to the far north.[11] However, from the mid-eleventh century violent political divisions weakened the Byzantine state and prepared the way for the loss of southern Italy to the Normans.

But important as Byzantium was, the central process in the history of the Mediterranean lands was the struggle amongst the successor states and authorities of the great Abassid Caliphate of Baghdad. The rise of Islam had established the Arabs as the ruling force in Persia, Syria, Palestine, Egypt, North Africa and Spain. The new conquerors recognised no division between sacred and secular authority; both were vested in the Caliph, the 'Commander of the Faithful'. In 750 a coup massacred the Umayyad dynasty of Caliphs based in Damascus and established the Abassid dynasty, descendants of the Prophet's uncle, al-Abbas, as Caliphs at Baghdad. The Abassid Caliphate was a world power second only to China, by far eclipsing Byzantium in riches and power. But it had many preoccupations, not least the eastwards expansion of Islam towards India. Although the court at Baghdad had an efficient and well-organised administration based on ministries, *diwan*, the sheer scale of the Arab empire meant that local powers had great autonomy. North Africa was very remote from the centre and by 800 almost autonomous. In *al-Andalus* (Spain) an Umayyad prince who had escaped the massacre of his family in 750 was a thorn in the side of the Caliphs of Baghdad and his house eventually established an Umayyad Caliphate at Cordoba. The Abassid Caliph, Harun al-Rashid (786–809), had been prepared to ally with Charlemagne to curb such independence.

Moreover, this was not the only source of dissent. The Umayyads had seized power in 661 by murdering the Prophet's first cousin, Ali, who had married the Prophet's daughter, Fatima. Many throughout the Islamic world believed that his successors still lived and were the true Caliphs; these followers, the Shi'ites, elaborated a system of law and practice substantially different from that of the orthodox Sunni majority. In 909 the Ismailis, a branch of the Shi'ites, established their leader as Caliph in Tunisia: they took their name of Fatimids from their supposed ancestor, Fatima. This was a serious fraying at the edges of the great Caliphate, and it was in part a consequence of a weakening at the centre. For about a century after its establishment, the Abassid Caliphate maintained control over Islam. However, like their predecessors, the Abassids recruited composite

---

11 D. Obolensky, *The Byzantine Commonwealth. Eastern Europe 500–1453* (London: Weidenfeld and Nicolson, 1971).

armies, made up of mercenaries and contingents from all the peoples subject to them. As a result, court factions found support in sections of the military. Thus the Caliphs fell under the control of a series of court groupings and their military supporters. By 945 power at Baghdad was firmly in the hands of the Buywids, a Persian family who were Shi'ite (though not Ismaili). But their power was localised in Mesopotamia because during the dislocations attendant on court struggles, local governors had taken over their provinces, while protesting their loyalty to the Caliph. The Saminids were a Persian family who dominated eastern Persia and ignored the Caliphs to whom they proclaimed loyalty. The Abassids were, in effect, being treated as a purely spiritual authority; secular power lay with the provincial rulers who fought bitterly amongst themselves for control of the administration and reproduced at a local level the courts of the Caliphs. This dissolution of the Caliphate was accompanied by another great change. The Abassids were Arab, but in their composite army were diverse peoples from inside and outside their empire, prominent amongst whom were Persians and Turks from the Asian steppe. Their leaders were the chief beneficiaries of the dissolution, and by the tenth century Islam was no longer an Arab regime. The weakening of the temporal power of the Caliphs was an event of enormous importance whose consequences would be played out over a period of about 200 years. Its reverberations were felt all across the civilisations of the Mediterranean world.

In 969 the Fatimids of Tunisia, profiting from a wave of disgust across Islam at the corruption of the Caliphate of Baghdad, mounted a military expedition which established their Caliphate at Cairo. They then attacked Syria as a step to destroying the Abassid Caliphate, with the result that Palestine and Syria became a disputed zone between the adherents of the two Caliphs. The Fatimids had come to power to restore Islamic purity, but they recruited a composite army and by the mid-eleventh century they too fell prey to factional struggles which were only resolved by the emergence of an Armenian soldier, the Vizir Badr al-Jamali, and his son, al-Afdal, who took complete military and political control of the Caliphate. The Fatimid schism was a terrible division within Islam because Egypt was enormously rich. At the other end of the Mediterranean the death in 1002 of the Islamic champion, al-Mansur, ushered in a collapse of the Umayyad state of Spain within whose boundaries there arose a plethora of minor kingdoms. The fragmentation of al-Andalus opened the way for the small Christian kingdoms of northern Spain to expand. This was all the more possible because the Spanish Muslims viewed their co-religionists in North Africa with suspicion, a sentiment shared by the Emirs of Muslim Sicily who thereby cut themselves off from their obvious source of military support in Tunisia.

Some of the most important troops in the service of the Baghdad Caliphate were the Turks. They were recruited from Central Asian tribes who had long pressed upon the frontiers of Islam where *ghazi*, zealous young volunteers from all over the Islamic world, had been prominent in defence. Many of these Turks were converted and taken into the service of the Caliphs and their chief magnates, who valued them for their skill as horse-archers. In time whole tribes of Turks adopted

Islam, imbibing from the *ghazi* a spirit of fierce Sunni orthodoxy. In the mid-eleventh century one Turkish group, the Oghuz, loyal to the family of the Seljuks, had come to dominate in north-east Persia. Their leader, Tughrul Bey, established close connections with the Turkish generals in Baghdad. With their assistance he seized Baghdad in 1055 and, under the nominal authority of the Caliph, ruled with the title of Sultan. This great Seljuk empire seemed likely to restore the dominance of Baghdad in the Muslim world, especially as it quickly drove the Fatimids from Syria. The Turks accepted the administrative structure of the old Caliphate, and occupied all the key posts. In essence the Turks were a narrow rural elite, quite alien to the peoples over whom they ruled. In this they were rather like the Catholic aristocracy of the west, but they were drawn into the cities which, throughout the Middle East, were the foci of the money economy. The Turkish nobles were as competitive and aggressive as their counterparts in the west, but the main concern of their internecine struggles was to control the structure of government because this, rather than simple land-holding, was the key to power and influence. The history of the institution known as '*iqta* nicely illustrates the difference between this elite and that of the west. In principle, '*iqta* were very like fiefs, lands allocated by rulers for the support of cavalrymen, and they were much used for this purpose by the Seljuks. However, Muslim armies relied much more heavily on cash wages gathered through taxes by the treasury, which was thus able to control the actual land and merely allocate incomes from it to the cavalrymen. The Seljuks were devout Sunni, but the reconquest of Syria from the Fatimids, which culminated in their seizure of Jerusalem in 1073, accorded much with the expansionist ambitions of their sultans. Not all the Turks were willing to accept the authority of the Seljuks of Baghdad, and several groups, amongst them one owing allegiance to dissident Seljuks, attacked against the Byzantine frontier. The Seljuk Empire appeared to be the most successful successor-state of the old Caliphate now converted into a spiritual authority. The Seljuk promotion of Sunni Orthodoxy and their pressure on Egypt appeared to presage a new unity under Baghdad, but this was not to be.

The great disturbances that attended the decline of the Abassid Caliphate were a primary factor in the expansion of the 'Catholic core'. Islam was immensely rich and highly organised, but had never applied its full power or anything like it against the 'Catholic core'; even so it had often represented a major threat to Christendom. As the break-up of the Abassid Caliphate progressed, the Muslim pressure upon Italy, northern Spain and southern France simply began to weaken, and it became possible to contemplate reconquest in these regions. Indirectly this freed the energies of the 'Catholic core' to turn against the other peripheral peoples. The collapse of the old unitary Arab Caliphate created the basic conditions for expansion. The dynamism and energy of the elites of the 'Catholic core' took advantage of those conditions and was favoured by the imperialistic and militaristic outlook of the Roman Church. This expansion was underway, as will be indicated, by about 950, long before the Crusade.

At first it seemed as if the great beneficiary of the breakdown of the Caliphate would be Byzantium. After the fall of Egypt to Islam in 642, Byzantium was driven onto the defensive for three centuries. In 653–54 the Arabs reached the Bosphorus and in 674–78 besieged Constantinople itself. Crete and Sicily fell to them and they continued to menace Byzantine Anatolia. The first reversal of the tide of war came with the capture of Melitene in 934; then in 969, the same year that the Fatimid Caliphate was established in Egypt, Antioch was recaptured. Under Nicephorus II Phokas (963–69) and John I Tzimiskes (969–76) the frontier was driven deep into Syria, and by 1025 and soon after the Transcaucasus and Armenia were annexed. But under Basil II (976–1025) Byzantium conquered the Bulgars and even attempted a reconquest of Sicily. After Basil's death Byzantium enjoyed a brief term of stability, but succession problems produced a period of uncertainty and factional conflict which proved disastrous for the empire when the eastern frontiers were attacked by the Turks.

Many of the Turkish tribes within the Islamic world refused to accept the dominion of the Sultan at Baghdad, and these dissenters raided the Empire. The Byzantine response was for long uncertain, but under Romanus IV Diogenes (1067–71) a clear and aggressive policy emerged. Romanus was an experienced soldier and he knew that the Sultan of Baghdad, Alp Arslan (1063–72), was preoccupied with driving Egypt out of Syria. Romanus decided to mount large expeditions against Syria in an effort to coerce the Sultan into controlling the Turks on the frontier. The culmination of this policy was the campaign of 1071. Alp Arslan was distracted from his proposed attack on the Fatimids by the Byzantine expedition, but he could not ignore the threat to his lands nor abandon the Turkish tribes. In the event, at the battle of Manzikert, on 19 August 1071, the huge Byzantine army was very badly handled and Romanus was captured during the rout. The Byzantine army was not totally destroyed by this defeat and Alp Arslan imposed only moderate terms upon the Byzantines. However, Romanus' enemies denounced the treaty as shameful because he had agreed to pay tribute to the Sultan, and they deposed and killed him, precipitating a bitter factional struggle within the Byzantine Empire. The Empire fell apart in a protracted series of civil wars during which the rivals for the throne blithely invited the Turks into the cities of Asia Minor which, as a result, fell into Turkish hands. Alexius I Comnenus (1081–1118) managed to establish an alliance of great families and restored a degree of stability, but Asia Minor, the old imperial heartland, was now largely in Turkish hands. Thus Turks controlled garrisons in the cities of the area and dominated the roads, but there remained a large Christian population. The Turks were also divided. In the south-west Smyrna was the centre of an Emirate. A huge swathe of Asia Minor from the Black Sea to the coast opposite Cyprus was held by the greatest Turkish power of the area, the Seljuk Sultanate of Rūm, centred on Nicaea and Iconium. To their east were the Danishmends who held Ankara and Caesarea-in-Cappadocia. Beyond them the Menguchekinds held power around Erzinjun, and the Saltukids dominated around Erzerum further to the east. None of these peoples enjoyed good relations with the Grand Seljuks at Baghdad.

The Byzantine crisis after 1071 produced a development of great significance for the future, though in the short run it was to have no outcome. In response to these troubles of the Eastern Christians, Pope Gregory VII (1073–85) sent out a series of letters in 1074–75 to the potentates of the west appealing for military support for the Byzantines, and even proposing a great military expedition led by himself which would go on to Jerusalem. Gregory may have been acting on his own initiative in response to news of the disasters in Asia Minor, or to an appeal from the Emperor Michael VII Doukas (1071–78), or both. Political circumstances frustrated Gregory's intentions, but although the project failed, it is interesting that the consequences of the collapse of the political power of the Abassid Caliphate stimulated western interest in the East. Although there were tensions between the papacy and Byzantium, these appeals demonstrate a real sense of Christian fraternity – the Orthodox were still seen as part of one Church. This was not the last appeal for military support from a Byzantine emperor to the papacy. In 1095 Urban II (1088–99) set out on a journey into Gaul, but at Piacenza encountered a Byzantine embassy despatched by Alexius asking for mercenaries to be sent to help his war in Asia Minor. No doubt these ambassadors stressed the Turkish threat, but Alexius knew all too well that a new wave of instability was sweeping through the Islamic East which offered the possibility of a Byzantine reconquest of Asia Minor.

In 1092 the Seljuk Sultan of Baghdad, Malik Shah, died. His son, Berkyaruk, succeeded him at Baghdad, but his rule was challenged by his uncle, Tutush Shah, ruler of Syria and of much of Palestine which had been reconquered from the Fatimids. Such succession problems were a commonplace in the Seljuk family. However, this one caused very protracted divisions because Tutush was killed in 1095, and his dominions in Syria were divided between his sons, Ridwan of Aleppo and Duqaq of Damascus. They were hostile to one another, and neither was fully in command of his lands, with the result that important elements, notably the city of Antioch under its governor, Yaghisiyan, went their own way, while Berkyaruk was deeply preoccupied in asserting his authority in Persia. In these circumstances both Fatimid Egypt and Byzantium saw golden opportunities opening up and appear to have concluded a working alliance to dismember the Seljuk domination. These conflicts were bound to enmesh Kilij Arslan of Nicaea (1092–1107) and the other and weaker Turkish lords of Asia Minor. It was to be no accident that the First Crusade entered the Middle East at a time of great political fragmentation. But if the timing of the crusade was the result of the interplay of Seljuk dissensions and Byzantine ambitions, it has to be stressed that this was merely the trigger for the events of the First Crusade, not its cause. For the crusade was not just a mere speculative military expedition, but a complex phenomenon arising from the very nature and experience of the society of the 'Catholic core'.

What was the relationship of expansionism, which is rooted in aristocratic ambition, to crusading? This is essentially the subject of the next chapter, but for the sake of completeness something needs to be said here. The key to understanding this lies in the evolution of papal thinking. The crusade was an attempt by the papacy to make real its long-held claims to supremacy in the universal Church, spurred on by the need to avoid the potential problems which it saw likely to arise from expansion and to capitalise on the opportunities which arose from it. Essentially the crusade was an attempt to enlist the confidence and expectations of an expanding 'Catholic core' behind the banner of the papacy, to impose a degree of unity upon the existing pattern of diversity, and thereby to give Christendom the political leadership of the pope himself. This must have seemed possible because the 'ideology' of the upper class made it responsive to such ideas and because the occasion for the crusade, arising out of events in the Middle East, came at a time when the papacy had achieved a new and impressive, though as yet precarious eminence in Christendom.

SELECTED READING

On the question of European identity and Christendom, D. Hay, *Europe, the Emergence of an Idea* (Edinburgh: Edinburgh University Press, 1957) is still very important. Two excellent accounts of the expansion of Europe are: J. S. R. Phillips, *The Medieval Expansion of Europe* (Oxford: Oxford University Press, 1988) and R. Bartlett, *The Making of Europe. Conquest, Colonization and Cultural Change* (London: Penguin, 1993). Phillips' main focus is the Late Middle Ages, although he also has an excellent introduction to the limitations of geographical knowledge in his opening chapter, a subject treated in many of its aspects by an important collection of essays by C. F. Beckingham and B. Hamilton (eds), *Prester John, the Mongols and the Ten Lost Tribes* (Aldershot: Ashgate, 1996). Bartlett provides a brilliant and highly influential analysis of the dynamics of European expansion. On the definition of Europe, see K. Leyser, 'Concepts of Europe in the early and high middle ages', in T. Reuter (ed.), *Communications and Power in Medieval Europe* (London: Hambledon, 1994) and on the process of conversion R. Fletcher, *The Conversion of Europe. From Paganism to Christianity 371–1386 AD* (London: Fontana, 1998). Charlemagne's influence is admirably discussed by D. Bullough, *The Age of Charlemagne* (London: Elek, 1965). On the period of Carolingian decline see R. McKitterick, *The Frankish Kingdoms under the Carolingians 751–987* (London: Longman, 1983) and G. Barraclough, *The Crucible of Europe. The Ninth and Tenth Centuries in European History* (London: Thames and Hudson, 1976) are particularly valuable. On the kingdoms of Europe in the tenth and early eleventh centuries there is an overview in T. Reuter (ed.), *The New Cambridge Medieval History, c.900–c.1024*, volume III (Cambridge: Cambridge University Press, 1999), which is especially good on relations with central Europe. An examination of Hungarian development and relations with the west was provided by an exhibition, *Bayern-Ungarn 1000 Jahre Passau 8 May–28 October 2001*. There is a catalogue of the exhibition by W. Jahn, C. Lankes, W. Petz and E. Brockhoff (eds), *Bayern-Ungarn Tausend Jahre* and the proceedings of a conference on the subject by H. W. Wurster, M. Treml and R. Loibl (eds), *Bayern-Ungarn Tausend Jahre* (Deutsche Bibliotek: Passau, 2001). On the aristocratic nature of power in early Medieval Europe and the institutional weakness of monarchical authority, see especially M. Innes, *State and Society in the Early Middle Ages. The Middle Rhine Valley 400–1000* (Cambridge: Cambridge

University Press, 2000). There is an excellent collection of essays on the nobility by T. Reuter (ed.), *The Medieval Nobility* (Amsterdam: North Holland, 1978), while a fine study of their values and outlook is provided by C. B. Bouchard, *Strong of Body, Brave and Noble. Chivalry and Society in Medieval France* (Ithaca, NY: Cornell University Press, 1998) whose work has a valuable annotated bibliography. On individual countries, see P. Stafford, *Unification and Conquest. A Political and Social History of England in the Tenth and Eleventh Centuries* (London: Edward Arnold, 1989); T. Reuter, *Germany in the Middle Ages 800–1056* (London: Longman, 1991); D. Waley, *The Italian City-Republics* (London: Longman, 1969); C. Wickham, *Early Medieval Italy. Central Power and Local Society, 400–1000* (London: Macmillan, 1981); J. Dunbabin, *France in the Making 843–1180* (Oxford: Oxford University Press, 1989); R. Collins, *Early Medieval Spain 400–1000* (New York: St Martin's, 1983); J. F. O'Callaghan, *A History of Medieval Spain* (Ithaca, NY: Cornell University Press, 1975). For a study of the rise of a principality, B. S. Bachrach, *Fulk Nerra, the Neo-Roman Consul, 987–1040* (Berkeley, CA: University of California Press, 1993). For Byzantium, see M. Whittow, *The Making of Orthodox Byzantium, 600–1025* (London: Macmillan,1996) and M. Angold, *The Byzantine Empire 1025–1204* (London: Longman, 1984). There is a valuable study of Byzantium and the Balkans by D. Obolensky, *The Byzantine Commonwealth. Eastern Europe 500–1453* (London: Weidenfeld and Nicolson, 1971) and see also P. Stephenson, *Byzantium's Balkan Frontier. A Political Study of the Northern Balkans, 900–1204* (Cambridge: Cambridge University Press, 2000), while for early Russia the indispensable work is S. Franklin and J. Shepard, *The Emergence of Rus 750–1200* (London: Longman, 1996). On the upheavals which beset Islam an excellent summary is provided by P. M. Holt, *The Age of the Crusades* (London: Longman, 1986) and on the Turks C. Cahen, *Pre-Ottoman Turkey* (London: Sidgwick & Jackson, 1968).

2

THE PAPAL MONARCHY
AND THE INVENTION
OF THE CRUSADE

The simple appeal for aid from the Byzantine Empire did not in itself create the crusade. In the years 1086–89 Robert I, the Frisian, count of Flanders (1071–93) went on pilgrimage to Jerusalem. During his passage across the Byzantine Empire he agreed to send Alexius 500 mercenaries. In 1090 he was reminded of this promise in a letter from Alexius, and the troops seem to have arrived in 1091. This was not a crusade, but it was probably the kind of arrangement Alexius had in mind when he sent his envoys to the west in 1095: military aid on a temporary basis for a limited purpose. The First Crusade was clearly much more than that. When, in 1096–97, the great armies arrived at Constantinople in response to Urban's appeal, Alexius clearly recognised that something new had been created, and he was at enormous pains to devise means of submitting it to Byzantine control. It was obvious by that stage that Urban had done much more than send an expedition of western mercenaries, but historians have been divided in seeking to understand how the appeal made at Piacenza in February 1095 was transformed into the First Crusade.

For much of the nineteenth century it was thought that the crusade was generated by the frustrations of a pilgrim, Peter the Hermit. This man, a popular preacher in Berry, was appalled by the sufferings of the Christians of the east under the Turks; the story goes that he promised the Patriarch of Jerusalem that he would return to his own land and recruit a great army to liberate them: the result was the First Crusade which snowballed into a series of expeditions which gathered at Constantinople. Spontaneous combustion of this kind was never very likely. We know that Peter truly was a charismatic preacher in northern France. Another such was Robert of Arbrissel, who attempted to bring the poor into the monastic life by founding the abbey of Fontevraud. In 1095–96 Peter set about recruiting an army which travelled from Northern France to Constantinople via the Rhineland. His charismatic preaching seems to have inspired a series of smaller German expeditions along his route, but given the poor communications of the age it is hard to see how he ignited a desire to undertake the journey in distant areas like southern France, Normandy, Flanders and Italy, from all of which large armies travelled.

For over a century historians have been convinced that Urban II began the crusade at Clermont. Unfortunately our sources about the appeal and how it originated are complex and difficult to use. Most narrative accounts of the crusade date from after 1099, and therefore their focus on Jerusalem may reflect the success of 1099 rather than the original intentions of Pope Urban. Two of our eyewitness accounts of the First Crusade make no mention of Clermont; they assume that Jerusalem was always the objective of the whole enterprise. A third, the account of Fulcher of Chartres, who was probably present at Clermont, says that Urban was primarily concerned to aid the Christians of the east and most especially the Byzantine Emperor, an idea which forms an important sub-theme in almost all our accounts; there was no mention of Jerusalem. To account for this apparent divergence, it has been suggested that while Urban primarily wanted to aid Byzantium, he might have mentioned the Holy Sepulchre as a way of enlisting support; popular enthusiasm then seized upon this to give the expedition a different focus. New evidence drawn from charters and other documents of 1095–96 argues against this. Many of those who took the cross raised money by transfers of land to churches and these were recorded in charters. In such of their charters that survive, most of the participants clearly state that their intention was to go to Jerusalem. From this and other evidence it is now clear that Urban had Jerusalem in mind from the first, though other factors were also involved. Moreover, the idea that spontaneous enthusiasm generated the crusade seems to ignore Urban's very careful preparations for launching his expedition. Even before he made his appeal the pope seems to have been preparing the way for it. After Piacenza, Urban crossed the Alps, then cut south into the lands of Raymond of Toulouse. We cannot prove that the two men met, but Raymond had legates at Clermont who took the cross on his behalf. Indeed the English writer, William of Malmesbury, believed that it was he, not Urban, who inspired the whole enterprise. After that, Urban turned north again and issued the summons for the Council of Clermont from Le Puy, whose bishop was the first to take the cross at Clermont and who was appointed Legate for the journey. From Clermont the pope went to Cluny where he kept Christmas and consecrated the new abbey-church. He wrote letters soliciting support, notably one asking for naval support from the Genoese. After Christmas, Urban travelled across France south of the Loire to recruit forces. He certainly foresaw the need to work with the Greeks and envisaged settlement in the Holy Land.[1] The sense is of a man implementing a plan, not one driven by popular pressure.

The crusade was not a mere military expedition, but the embodiment of a series of ideological and emotional developments synthesised by Pope Urban II. The combination of the institutional power, memory and outlook of the papacy and the fact that it was in the hands of a man with a real sense of vision and an unparalleled perception of the nature of the society of the 'Catholic core', created

---

1 For this controversy, see Selected Reading at the end of this chapter.

the crusade. What is striking in accounts of the crusade is that it was seen as immensely novel, a mighty event without precedent in people's experience. Guibert of Nogent, writing about the year 1109, proclaimed that 'God ordained holy wars in our time, so that the knightly order . . . might find a new way of earning salvation.'[2] It was because of this novelty that the clerical intelligentsia would spend much time trying to find it a place in their perception of the divine economy. This explains why Gratian's famous collection of canon law, the *Decretum*, published in the 1140s, makes little mention of the crusade. It is only necessary to reflect on the extraordinary nature of the First Crusade in comparison with the experience of expansion in the tenth and eleventh centuries to understand how new it was and to recognise that this was a fundamentally ideological phenomenon which transcended all that had gone before.[3]

The expansion of Germany in the tenth century was a piecemeal annexation of regions adjacent to those ruled by its kings. In the north, Otto I's victory over the Slavs at Recknitz on 16 October 955 established a Saxon tribute-dominance over many of these peoples, but this was driven by the Saxon nobility with little royal direction. The loose tribute lordship over the Wends and other pagan peoples of Schleswig and the Baltic coast led to some implanting of colonies of Saxons and a brutal imposition of Christianity. In 983 the defeat and death of Otto II (973–83) in Italy triggered a huge Wendish revolt which drove back the tide of German conquest. Gradually the Germans reasserted their power, largely through the activities of frontier lords of the Saxon march. In the mid-eleventh century Prince Gottschalk, who had been brought up in Saxony, ruled the Wends and seemed to have brought them over to Christianity with Saxon support, but he was overthrown in 1066 by a pagan revolt. Gottschalk was really an extreme example of a local leader who was attracted by the institutions of the 'Catholic core', but it seems that his devotion to the new religion was a step too far for most of his people. In the early twelfth century Count Adolf of Holstein cooperated with Nyklot, the pagan prince of the Wends, in establishing colonies and new towns in the empty lands south of the Baltic, notably at Lübeck in 1143. Nyklot was clearly impressed by the institutions of his Christian neighbours, but he stopped short of adopting their religion. Thereafter the process of German conquest accelerated. The German monarchs inherited from their Carolingian predecessors a deep concern with converting the pagans which was sustained by the obvious connection with pacifying territory. The monastery of Fulda and the arch-bishopric of Magdeburg were powerful centres of missionary activity; in the north Hamburg-Bremen had a traditional concern for Scandinavia. But conquest and

---

2 'Instituit nostro tempore praeilia sancta Deus', in Guibert of Nogent, *Gesta Dei per Francos*, ed. R. B. C. Huygens in CCCM 127A (Turnhout: Brepols, 1996), 87, translated in R. Levine, *The Deeds of God through the Franks* (Woodbridge: Boydell, 1997), 28.

3 For a discussion of how the Crusade was integrated into clerical thinking in the Catholic Church, see below pages 97–103.

conversion were not intimately linked in the way they had been under Charlemagne and as they were to be again in the late twelfth and thirteenth centuries. Imperial control over the border lords, the essential agents of the drive into the Slav lands, was loose, and the greed of these people for land and plunder was often a real obstacle to conversion. In turn, the emperors had so many preoccupations, in Italy and elsewhere, that they were unable to pursue a sustained policy on the northern frontier.

The missionary base for the conversion of Bohemia to Christianity in the tenth century was Bavaria, but it seems to have been the desire of its powerful clans to imitate lordship and stability which drew them into the faith. Poland also became Christian at this time, and the desire of its elites to emulate their western neighbours was fostered by close links to the Bohemian royal house. Thietmar of Merseburg believed that Miesco I of Poland was converted through the influence of his wife, Dobrawa, sister of Duke Boleslav of Bohemia. According to his story, she smoothed his way to the true faith by agreeing to eat meat in Lent, although it was a sin.[4] Hungary was won for Roman Christianity by careful imperial and papal diplomacy directed against Byzantine advances. Essentially the area now called Central Europe was drawn to the 'Catholic core' by the quickening pace of economic development and trade, and by the interest of the local elites in emulating their German neighbours. Imperial rhetoric spoke of advancing the frontiers of Christianity, but this was only occasionally reflected in reality. Henry II (1002–24) was deeply religious, but in the north he found the pagan *Liutici* a useful ally against the Christian Poles, a policy which attracted criticism from Thietmar of Merseburg. Bruno of Querfurt and Thietmar both urged the same emperor to annex these people with a view to imposing the true religion. In France Rodulfus Glaber echoed this call for forcible conversion, for which there was ample Carolingian precedent.[5] However, in reality, forced conversion had an uneven and limited history and cannot be associated with the notion of conquest in the Middle East.

Although the papacy sometimes supported wars within Christendom, the religious element was not usually very significant. William the Conqueror was, famously, given a papal banner when he invaded England, but this was essentially a political arrangement which suited both parties. Thereafter the Normans attacked Wales with vigour, and this began a slow process of conquest that was largely in the hands of local Marcher lords. Although contempt for the supposed separatist practices of the Celtic Church was part of the stock-in-trade of Anglo-Norman clerics, there is little evidence that it fired the process of annexation which was essentially secular in nature. It is often supposed that the Norman seizure of southern Italy and Sicily in the eleventh century had some of the

---

4 Thietmar of Merseburg, *Chronicon*, ed. D. A. Warner (Manchester: Manchester University Press, 2001), 4.55, 191–2.
5 On forced conversion in Carolingian times see below pages 41–2.

characteristics of a *reconquista* because it transformed 'a frontier between Greek east and Latin west, and Christian north and Muslim south' into 'part of the Christian west'.[6] In fact, the Norman intervention in southern Italy was a very complicated phenomenon extending over almost a century. Normans first appeared in the area about 1017, either as pilgrims returning from Jerusalem or as wandering mercenaries. The first of these to come to Italy may have been victims of the process by which the Norman dukes were imposing strong government across their lands. However, after 1035 Normandy suffered from a protracted succession crisis, yet it seems that the flow of adventurers increased. They served anyone who would pay them as mercenaries, and flourished in an area of political fragmentation. The primary power in southern Italy was Byzantium which held the heel and toe of Italy and based its governor in Bari. A network of Lombard principalities, amongst them Naples, Gaeta, Salerno, Benevento and Capua, were nominally subject to Constantinople but in practice were bent on maintaining their freedom of action and therefore often supported rebellion in the Byzantine lands to the south. They also fought amongst themselves and sometimes allied with the German emperors who had claims to the area, or with the papacy which had lands there. There was plenty of work for the Normans who were regarded as able soldiers. By 1026 the first Norman lordship had appeared at Aversa, and this formed a useful base where adventurers from the north gathered. Very large numbers of them seem to have entered Byzantine service for the attempted conquest of Sicily. When this collapsed in 1041, the unpaid and disgruntled Norman troops, in alliance with the Lombard princes, launched an invasion of the Greek lands of Apulia and Calabria. This coincided with a period of increasing weakness at Constantinople that enabled the newcomers to establish themselves.

The Normans were always a tiny minority, who succeeded by a complex process of marriage, political alliance and outright conquest. Their most famous leader, Robert d'Hauteville, called Guiscard, meaning 'the cunning' or 'the weasel', established himself in Calabria by outright terror: 'Robert, supported by many soldiers, ordered them to pillage, burn and ravage all the lands which he invaded and to do everything possible to terrorise the inhabitants.'[7]

But once they had submitted he did not interfere in their affairs. He was first married to Alberada, a Norman woman whom he repudiated in favour of Sichelgaita, a Lombard princess, sister of the prince of Salerno. Robert and his brother Roger were extraordinarily capable and ruthless men. They and the most important of the Normans replaced the native princes, while lesser figures established themselves as local lords or their knightly followers, but Lombards

6 G. Loud, *The Age of Robert Guiscard. Southern Italy and the Norman Conquest* (London: Longman, 2000), 291.

7 William of Apulia, *La Geste de Robert Guiscard*, ed. M. Mathieu (Palermo: Instituto Siciliano, 1961), 151.

and even Greeks remained important in government and administration on the mainland, and its cities, notably Bari, retained much of their old character. Some areas, especially papal Benevento and the borders to the north, remained largely untouched. Much of the south continued to be Greek in language and outlook for centuries. The case of Sicily was rather more complex. Alexander II gave a papal banner to the Guiscard family for the conquest of Sicily which they began in 1071, before Bari had even fallen. In the process of conquest there was extensive conciliation of the Islamic population, many of whom remained in place. Under the Muslim domination, church organisation had totally collapsed and in 1098 Urban II granted to Guiscard's brother, Roger I, legatine powers to re-establish the church there. This restoration of Christ's Church by armed force may well have had a considerable influence on Urban's thinking, however secular the basic motivation may have been.

Sicily was entirely dominated by the Hauteville family because it had been conquered under their leadership. However, the Norman conquest of South Italy was a free enterprise affair which the house of the Guiscards had hijacked. As a result, their rule on the mainland was always bitterly resented by the Norman/Lombard nobility. It was only their extensive lands in the area and the wealth of Sicily that enabled them to maintain an uneasy supremacy. Like the conquest of the Slavs to the east of Saxony, and that of the Welsh, the conquest of South Italy was the result of aristocratic ambition. What was unusual was that the Normans were able to establish themselves far from their native land in an area of acute political fragmentation. Their success in Sicily was only incidentally a Christian reconquest. However, the papacy noted that this conquest ended the jurisdiction of Constantinople in the area which was now returned to Rome and was the indispensable condition for the recreation of the Sicilian Church. Towards the end of the eleventh century Pisa and Genoa were mounting naval attacks against Muslim Sardinia and North Africa, the most spectacular of these being the Genoese sack of Mahdia in modern Tunisia in 1087. Although these formed part of a pattern of sea-borne raiding common enough in the Mediterranean and were clearly motivated by the ambitions of these cities, they were given papal approval because they were directed against Muslim targets.

While Islam was distant and vague for most people in the 'Catholic core', in Spain there was a totally different situation. The Spanish *reconquista* has usually been seen by historians as a major precedent for the crusade, providing Urban with a model and a point of reference for the rest of the Catholic lands. But it is far from clear that the rulers of the Spanish kingdoms and their great followers saw themselves as participating in a Holy War for the reconquest of the peninsula. In the tiny kingdom of the Asturias in the late ninth century the *Prophetic Chronicle* proclaimed that the Visigothic kingdom had been overthrown in 711 because of its sins and that it was the sacred task of its monarch to recover the lands that had been lost: 'Our hope is Christ, that the enemies' boldness may be annihilated and the peace of Christ given back to Holy Church.' A literature which looked to an apocalyptic overthrow of Islam developed, and the sanctity of war for this end was not questioned. But these ideas were short-lived and intimately associated with the court of Alfonso III of Asturias (870–910). They seem to have been developed to assert that Alfonso III was the legitimate heir of the Visigothic kings who, however, would purge the sins of his ancestors and overthrow the Muslims. Expectations of a sudden end to the Muslim domination did not have much currency in the small Christian states of the north in the tenth and early eleventh centuries. Indeed, it seems unlikely that their rulers saw themselves as engaged in an unremitting struggle to liberate Spain from Islam. The Christians were divided: Léon, Castile, Navarre and the counties around Barcelona all had very different interests, and all were reduced to subservience to *al-Andalus* when the Caliphate of Cordoba was under the sway of its chief minister, Muhammad ibn Abi Amir who took the title *al-Mansur bi'llah* (victorious through God). His death in 1002, followed closely by that of his son, Abd al-Malik in 1008, ushered in the collapse of Muslim unity and the dissolution of the Islamic power in Spain into numerous petty kingdoms. Even then many of them remained strong and the Christian rulers needed to pursue cautious policies. The story is told that the Christian ambassadors to the court of Granada in 1009 proclaimed:

Al-Andalus belonged first of all to the Christians until the time when they were conquered by the Arabs who drove them up to Galicia, the region of the country least favoured by nature. But now that it is possible, they want to recover all that was taken from them by force; and so that they may do so definitively, they have to weaken and exhaust you over a period of time. When you have no money or soldiers left, we shall take possession of the country without trouble.[8]

However, this is a very late account which reflects the long experience of war down to the thirteenth century in which Muslim Spain was indeed made to pay tribute, enforced by savage raids, on an immense scale. The piecemeal nature of the fighting and the local nature of politics in the eleventh century often resulted in alliances across the religious divide. In 1073 Sancho IV of Navarre concluded a treaty with Muslim Zaragoza against Aragon with the objective of restoring lands which Zaragoza had lost to Aragon. Rodrigo Díaz de Vivar, the famous El Cid, became embroiled in a feud with a rival Castilian family who had attacked his ally, al-Mu'tamid of Seville, and in 1081 he was exiled by Alfonso VI (1065–1109) of Castile. He took service with Muslim Zaragoza, then returned to Alfonso after his defeat by the Almoravids in 1086, only to be exiled again in 1089. He then exploited the quarrels of the petty Muslim states to seize the city of Valencia from 1094–99, treating the Muslims there well. El Cid was revered as a hero of the Christian reconquest by a later age in which crusading ideas had taken root, but his career is in actuality testimony to a very different world. His sometime lord,

---

8 Quotes from D. Lomax, *The Reconquest of Spain* (London: Longman, 1978), 40, 52–3.

sometime enemy, Alfonso VI triumphed by capturing the old Visigothic capital of Toledo in 1085 after a siege which had lasted four years, but he owed much to skilful diplomatic preparation.

The wars in Spain had relatively little impact north of the Pyrenees until shortly before the First Crusade. The *Mozarabs*, Spanish Christians under Muslim rule, enjoyed a limited toleration, but their numbers were eroded because the civilisation of their rulers was highly attractive and conversion offered excellent career prospects. A group of zealots, concerned about this assimilation, confronted the Islamic authorities and suffered a series of martyrdoms in 851. In 858 Charles the Bald sent monks of St Germain to Spain hoping to find relics of St Vincent, and at Valencia they acquired bones of three of the 'Martyrs of Cordoba' which they brought back, together with the stories of their passions. But their cult was never widely extended and real knowledge of Islam was rare. Adhemar of Chabannes was an Aquitanian chronicler who died about 1029. He was a man of the south and knowledgeable about events in Spain, but treated the wars there with a degree of detachment which leads him to report in neutral terms that, after the Muslims killed Ermengaut of Urgel in battle, they kept his head as a trophy. Rodulfus Glaber, on the other hand, strongly approved of the Christian reconquest which he saw in ideological terms, but he was unusual in that he had a strong sense of Christian identity. At Cluny he met Spanish monks, almost certainly the group led by Paternus and sent by Sancho the Great of Navarre (1000–35) in 1032 to strengthen San Juan de la Peña by forging links with the great Burgundian house; this began a period of strong and sustained interest in Spain at Cluny.[9] We hear of individual northern adventurers trying to establish themselves, but it was only in 1065 that a major expedition occurred. In 1063 Ramiro I of Aragon (1035–63) was killed in battle, rather typically, against an alliance between Muslim Zaragoza and his brother, Fernando I of León (1035–65). This provoked a major French expedition which was encouraged by Pope Alexander II and made up of Normans, Aquitanians and Burgundians. In 1064 they captured Barbastro and, quite contrary to local practice, massacred its inhabitants. All too obviously the northerners wanted booty and cared little for the consequences which were that Zaragoza reconquered the city and killed its Christian inhabitants in revenge. We do hear of later expeditions, but when in 1073 Pope Gregory VII (1073–85) attempted to foster the Spanish wars through an expedition led by the French lord, Ebles de Roucy, his insistence that all conquests from Islam should be regarded as the property of the Holy See caused resistance, and the result was a check for papal policy. The wars in Spain in the eleventh century were very much self-contained and external support for the Christians was only occasional and relatively small-scale. However, it seems that

---

9 Adhémar of Chabannes, *Chronicon*, in *Opera Omnia Pars I*, ed. P. Bourgain, R. Landes and G. Pon (Turnhout: Corpus Christianorum Continuatio Mediaevalis, 129, 1999), 159; Glaber, *Histories*, 114–15.

this changed towards the end of the century. The capture of Toledo in 1085 was noted all over the 'Catholic core' and much of the loot from its fall was sent to Cluny where it helped to finance the building of the enormous monastic church.

These triumphs, so widely trumpeted, were followed by terrible setbacks. The Almoravids were a puritanical Sunni Muslim sect that had seized control of North Africa, the Maghrib, and in desperation the rulers of *al-Andalus* called them in. On 23 October 1086 Alfonso VI was defeated, with huge loss of Christian life, at the battle of Sagrajas, and the whole of Christian Spain seemed to be under threat. In 1087 a large army with elements from Burgundy, Normandy, the Midi and northern France arrived, but it confined its activities to the Ebro valley. However, from this time on Spanish kings and magnates started to conclude marriage alliances with northern dynasties and there was an intensification of ecclesiastical connections across the Pyrenees. As a result, by the early twelfth century the lands of the 'Catholic core' were very keenly aware of the wars in Spain. But in no sense did foreign intervention save Christian Spain. The Almoravids were distracted by events in Africa and their Muslim allies in Spain resented them. It was by supporting Muslim princes against them that El Cid was able to capture Valencia in 1094. Even more remarkable was his victory over an Almoravid siege shortly after. It was only at the very end of the century that people from north of the Alps begin to take a real interest in the *reconquista*. In fact, it can be argued that the real influence of the Spanish wars before then was upon papal thinking and not upon wider opinion. The papacy, for reasons of its own, had long promoted a view of the conflict in Spain as a Holy War but the signs are that this did not make much impact for a long time. The occasional need of Spanish rulers for outside aid, especially in the years after 1186, led them to emphasise the religious divide and the sacred nature of their expansionism. This was accentuated by the influx of northern Christians, notably Cluniacs, into the Spanish Church in the early twelfth century. Gradually the image and reality of the wars in Spain were transformed.

When, in 1095, Urban called for an expedition to liberate Jerusalem he was, therefore, postulating an expedition without precedent in the history of Catholic Christendom. Hitherto, expansion had largely been a matter of propinquity. Moreover, the poor articulation of states meant that in practice it was often, though not invariably, the work of small localised groups: the lords of the Saxon borderlands, the Marchers of Wales, Norman exiles in South Italy, the petty rulers of Christian Spain. No western power was adjacent to Jerusalem, the proposed target, or had any obvious interest in the conquest. Urban II certainly appealed to westerners to save the Christians of the east from subjugation to Islam, but few westerners knew or cared much about Byzantium, and there is no evidence of a widespread hatred of Islam, though undoubtedly almost all would have regarded any non-Christian religion with a degree of hostility, provided it imposed itself sufficiently upon their consciousness. Christian intellectuals regarded Islam as a wicked and particularly obdurate heresy and its spread was rationalised as the punishment of God upon a lax and sinful Christendom but they were a very small minority.[10] Of all the powers of the 'Catholic core' it was only the papacy that was really aware and cared passionately about such remote matters because its prestige and even its own survival were at stake.

The Roman pontiffs had always claimed universal authority over the Church, but their pretensions did not stop there. In Christian thinking the priesthood always stood between God and mankind as the intermediary whose guidance was essential to the attainment of salvation. Such a claim, inevitably, had political consequences. The actions of even the highest and greatest of men were subject to the guidance, even the censorship and perhaps direction of priests. St Ambrose of Milan (339–97) made this very obvious in 390 when Theodosius (379–95) ordered a massacre of 7,000 citizens at Thessalonika in retaliation for the killing of some imperial officials in a riot. In a Christian Empire, Ambrose's threat of excommunication had a clear political implication and Theodosius found it prudent to do penance. The classic definition of the relationship between 'Church' and 'state' in the western experience was that of Pope Gelasius (492–96) in his so-called 'Doctrine of the Two Swords':

> Two things there are indeed, August Emperor, by which this world is principally ruled: the consecrated authority of priests and royal power. Of these, the burden of priests of much the heavier because they will answer even for the kings of men at the divine judgement. Therefore, most merciful son, you may take precedence over the human race, but you bow your head obediently to the leaders of divine affairs and look to them for the means of your salvation. For if the ministers of religion, realising that governance, insofar as it pertains to the keeping of public discipline, obey your laws, you ought to obey those who have been charged with the dispensation of holy mysteries.

The right of churchmen to judge and direct the laity would later give rise to the notion that the pope was the 'Judge Ordinary' of all Christian men and women. Even more political in its objectives was the *Donation of Constantine*, a document of the mid-ninth century which purported to show that when he moved his capital to Constantinople, Constantine the Great gave the whole of the western part of the Roman Empire to the pope.[11] While the authenticity of this donation was challenged, its veracity was always maintained by the papacy and continued to be a source of the ideas about papal authority. But actions were at least as important as ideas. In 751, the head of the Arnulfing family, Pepin, Mayor of the

---

10 On early medieval attitudes to Islam, see B. Z. Kedar, *Crusade and Mission. European Approaches toward the Muslims* (Princeton, NJ: Princeton University Press, 1984), especially 3–41. On Islam as a heresy, see especially Guibert of Nogent, *Gesta Die per Francos*, in Levine, *The Deeds of God through the Franks*, 31–6.

11 N. F. Cantor, *Medieval World 300–1300* (New York: Macmillan, 1963) 95–7, 125–33.

Palace of the Frankish kings, wanted to replace the Merovingian king, Childeric III (743–51). In order to seek a moral legitimacy Pepin asked Pope Zacharias (741–52) to declare the coup lawful, and this was duly agreed. In 800, Pepin's son, Charlemagne (768–814), accepted coronation as Roman Emperor at the hands of Leo III (794–816) and, while Charles might not have agreed, the implication was clear – that the empire lay in the gift of the pope. This was being asserted by popes within a century and would later form a precedent for papal intervention in the affairs of the German Empire. Ultimately the papacy was only the patriarchate of the west, but as patriarchs of Rome the popes had inherited the Roman imperial tradition and something of the belief that the rulers of the City were truly the rulers of the whole world.

Of course, it was one thing to have such ideas and precedents, and even a corporate sense of mission which is one of the most impressive facets of the history of the papacy, and another to give them any reality. By about the year 1000 all of the 'Catholic core' regarded Rome as its spiritual guide, but in practice the affairs of the churches were regulated by local bishops, either as individuals or in meetings of provincial councils. Bishops, in turn, tended to be dominated by strong monarchs in Germany and England who often used them for their own purposes as educated administrators. In France, outside the Capetian dominions, local magnates tried to influence episcopal elections in favour of their own candidates who would side with them in local disputes and enrich them at the expense of the Church. At Auxerre, for example, the death of the bishop was frequently the signal for bitter fighting as the local nobles strove to impose their own candidates. In Rome the nobility of the city and its environs fought amongst themselves to control nominations to the papacy and constrained the actions and focus of the popes once in office. But if the pope in the tenth and early eleventh century was primarily an Italian prince, he was always also something more. From almost its very beginning the great abbey of Cluny was patronised by Rome and amongst its protectors were some of the popes who have been most frequently denounced as corrupt scions of the Roman aristocracy. Every sign of spiritual vigour in the Church was seized upon and supported by the papacy. As a result a new tide of religious vitality began to appear. By about 1000 it was evident almost everywhere that the elites of the 'Catholic core' had fought off the worst of the external attacks and were achieving a degree of stability. This relative peace enabled men and women to consider their spiritual lives. The result was a new and deeper lay spirituality inspired by the example of the reformed monasticism. This displayed itself in the astonishing growth of pilgrimage, in the efflorescence of the cults of saints and in the patronage of new monastic orders like Cluny. So striking was the expenditure by laymen of all classes on new church buildings that one contemporary commented:

> Just before the third year after the millennium, throughout the whole world, but most especially in Italy and Gaul, men began to reconstruct churches, although for the most part the existing ones were properly

built and not in the least unworthy. But it seemed as though each Christian community were aiming to surpass all others in the splendour of construction. It was as if the whole world were shaking itself free, shrugging off the mantle of the past, and cladding itself everywhere in a white mantle of churches. Almost all episcopal churches, and those of monasteries dedicated to various saints, and little village chapels, were rebuilt better than before by the faithful.[12]

The new monastic orders, amongst which that centred at Cluny was the greatest, set new standards of purity by which other churchmen could be judged. The result was not so much a great 'revival' amongst the laity as a whole as a considerable agitation about the behaviour of the clergy as the indispensable guides to salvation and the need to reform such obvious abuses as clerical marriage. Above all, 'Simony', the buying and selling of spiritual office, came to be abhorred. But the new Orders provided more than merely an example of how priests should behave; they also provided a model for a new ecclesiastical organisation. Cluny and other associated orders were directly subject to the Holy See which acted as champions of their rights and lands, and thus became a factor in the lives of many of the elite of the 'Catholic core' – to dispute with a Cluniac abbey was to dispute with Rome. This new climate of opinion influenced rulers; for example, the Emperor Henry III (1039–56) renounced simony and supported proponents of reform in all the churches of his lands.

As western Emperors the German kings ruled Rome, but it was so far from the centres of their power that they exerted their authority in alliance with one of the groups amongst the local nobility. The factional struggles of the Roman aristocracy had often produced dual elections, but in 1045–46 conflict in the city threw up three claimants to the papal throne. The Emperor Henry III deposed all of them at the Synod of Sutri in 1046. He then appointed a number of pious reformers, many of them German, to important posts at the papal court. Amongst these was Pope, Leo IX (1048–54) who undertook a great journey north of the Alps, thereby vigorously asserting leadership in the reform of the Church which laymen and clerics everywhere had come to think was necessary. Even when Leo died the presence of a substantial body of reformers at Rome and the support of Henry III ensured continuity in policy. The death of Henry IIII and the accession of a minor, Henry IV (1056–1106), meant that the reform party at Rome turned elsewhere to assure their position and, in particular, to the rulers of Tuscany and the Norman settlers of southern Italy. Both these parties agreed to support the Election Decree of 1059 which effectively established the right to elect the pope in a college of Cardinals, thus freeing the papal court from German domination. The papacy was launched on an ambitious programme of reform whose key plank

12 Glaber, 3.13, 114–17.

was the stamping out of simony and corruption which were both closely identified with lay control of the clergy. This was to be achieved by centralising control of the Church, which would thus become a papal monarchy presiding over a clerical corporation from whose essential workings the laity would be excluded.

Once he had reached his majority, the Emperor Henry IV regarded the new developments at Rome as a challenge to his authority. The growing centralisation of the Church under Roman authority threatened a political power which was heavily dependent on the support of the bishops, many of whom were deeply dismayed by the new assertiveness of Rome. More specifically, imperial power in Italy depended on key bishops, notably the archbishop of Milan, and the entire imperial position would be threatened if control of these prelates were taken away. The denunciation of the ceremony of Investiture, by which rulers ceremonially gave the symbols of episcopal office, the ring and the staff, to their chosen candidates, not only threatened an important demonstration of royal power but also the strong sense of divine mission and sanction of kingship. When the idea was propounded that the pope had the authority to judge emperors and kings, it must have seemed that a new and deeply threatening order was emerging in the world of the 'Catholic core'. In fact, the vision of the Church as a clerical corporation presided over by a monarchical pope, which emerged more clearly than ever before under Gregory VII, was in principle a threat to all lay influence in ecclesiastical affairs, down to the level of petty local lords who appointed parish priests. However, Gregory VII and his successors were enmeshed in a conflict with the emperor which modern historians have called 'the Investiture Contest', because Henry IV's control of Italy threatened Rome itself and because the emperor had an exalted view of the sacred nature of kingship. From 1080 Henry IV set up an anti-pope, creating a schism in Christendom. This is not the place to chart the course of this struggle, but it made the popes acutely aware of their ambitions and of the real threat posed to them by the contemporary world. At the same time, in the persons of Gregory VII and Urban II (1088–99), two popes of undoubted genius emerged and they personified, though in rather different ways, the aspirations of the institution. The successful, though limited, expansion of the 'Catholic Core' in the eleventh century presented grave and immediate problems to the papacy in this and other connections, especially at a time when it was threatened by the dispute with Henry IV.

We know that the reform movement from the mid-eleventh century led in the twelfth century to a papal monarchy with uncontested authority over the whole Church, but this was not the perspective of the late eleventh-century popes who were faced by grave and immediate problems which threatened to overwhelm them. Their principal concern was that Christians should conform to the models of worship and belief laid down by Rome. This could apply to the most minor details: in 1080 Gregory VII wrote to Sardinia demanding that the local clergy should shave their beards in accordance with Roman tradition. The acquiescence of nations was the measure of papal authority, but the new expansion might be very threatening. The *Reconquista* in Spain brought swathes of Muslims under

Christian control, but with what consequences for orthodoxy and papal authority? Even worse, the liberation of the native Christians or *Mozarabs* brought contact with a people who had been long out of touch with Rome. In the ninth century the Spanish Church had been racked by the heresy of Adoptianism.[13] This was condemned by one of the greatest of Christian assemblies of the early Middle Ages, the Council of Frankfurt in 794, and its strictures were repeated in councils at Friuli in 796, Rome in 799 and Aachen in 800. One consequence of this affair was a deep suspicion of the native *Mozarabic Rite*, although this was purely western and inherited from the Visigothic kingdom which the Arabs had conquered in 711. In 1074 Gregory VII wrote to the kings of Léon and Navarre urging that 'even after long deviations they would at last follow their true mother, the Roman church'.[14] As soon as the Christian kingdoms of Spain began to make headway against Islam, Rome insisted upon the imposition of the Roman Rite which was decreed at the Council of Burgos in 1080. Despite bitter resistance by the *Mozarabs* their liturgy was virtually eliminated. Expansion could, therefore, bring threats and this was why Rome was so interested in events in Spain from the mid-eleventh century onwards. The assertion that this was a Holy War together with the insistence that the papacy had a special standing when land was reconquered from the infidel was a means of control and of self-preservation. This is probably why Gregory VII tried to mount papal expeditions to Spain under a French noble, Ebles de Roucy, and to claim that reconquered lands should belong to the Holy See, even though such actions were inevitably unpopular with the Spanish rulers. This kind of problem was replicated elsewhere. Much of South Italy had long been under Constantinople, so the Norman conquest was an opportunity to reassert papal authority there, especially over the Greek Christians whose ideas might contaminate others. In Sicily too there were Greek Christians, but a Church had to be rebuilt. Hence, in part the alliance with the Normans and the provision of a papal banner for the conquest of Sicily has been noted. In the British Isles the churches of the Celtic fringe were viewed with suspicion, although they were orthodox in belief and displayed only the most minor deviations of practice. However, by the improving standards of the eleventh century they were not well organised. Problems within the Anglo-Saxon hierarchy which seemed to presage a similar weakness may well have persuaded Alexander II (1061–73) to provide a papal banner for William the Conqueror in 1066.

The expansion of the 'Catholic core' provided opportunities and also dangers for the papacy which desperately needed a degree of control over the process. Moreover, the papacy knew that there were many Christians in the east who did

---

13 Adoptianism is the belief that Christ was the adoptive and not the real son of God. For a summary, see F. L. Cross and E. A. Livingstone, *Oxford Dictionary of the Christian Church* (London: Oxford University Press, 1997).

14 Translated in H. E. J. Cowdrey, *Gregory VII 1073–85* (Oxford: Clarendon, 1998), 523.

not recognise their primacy. The Greeks were the most important of these groups, and the popes knew about the Armenians. It is uncertain how aware they were of others like the Jacobites of Syria. In 1054 there was a major incident: Michael Cerularius, Patriarch of Constantinople was excommunicated. It is tempting to dismiss this affair as an aberration caused by strong personalities. Pope Leo IX was appalled by the violence of the Normans and their threat to papal lands, and proposed an alliance against them with the Byzantine Empire. But Cerularius, was deeply hostile to the possibility of western control over the Greek Christians of the area, and took every opportunity to dredge up causes of dispute with the Latins. Cardinal Humbert was chosen by Pope Leo to go to Constantinople to smooth out these problems and to conclude an alliance with the emperor. He was an odd choice, for he was a stubborn and difficult character. Cerularius refused to discuss the issues with him, and Humbert dramatically excommunicated him in the Church of the Holy Wisdom: this sentence was personal to the Patriarch, expressly recognising the orthodoxy of the Byzantine Church as a whole, while Cerularius, in his counter-condemnation, did not impugn the western Church as a whole. But the 'Cerularian Schism' had raised the real issue between east and west, the question of authority. Christians believed that there was only one universal Church, and many of the differences between the Greeks and the peoples of the 'Catholic core' were the result of cultural divergences. However, in the 'Catholic core' Rome was regarded as the ultimate authority in matters spiritual, while in the east it was believed to be vested in a universal council of the bishops. It was unfortunate that this issue was rehearsed at a time when Rome's view of its position was becoming stronger and more confident. The papacy, which considered that it was universally responsible for Christian people, was more disturbed by the existence of Christian dissent than by that of Islam.

This sense of responsibility was by no means confined to the Greeks. Gregory VII conducted a careful correspondence with the remnant of the Christian Church in North Africa, and was prepared to compromise with their Muslim overlords in their interests. More spectacularly, in 1074 he seized upon the need of the Greeks for military help after the disaster of Manzikert in 1071 (when Michael VII may have appealed for military aid) to offer it in return for union under the Holy See. In a series of letters, Gregory VII appealed to the leaders of society to mount an expedition under his leadership to aid the Christians of the east and even to reconquer Jerusalem for Christendom. The vision of a reunion of all Christians and reconquest of the lost lands under the leadership of the Holy See was not invented by Urban II: it was part of the inheritance of the papacy. What Gregory did was develop a mechanism, the offer to the Byzantines of military support, by which that vision could be made real. In a letter to Henry IV, dated 7 December 1074, Gregory proposed that papal military aid would offer an opportunity for all dissenters in the east to settle their differences under the authority of the Holy See. God had punished the pride and sin of the Christian Empire of Constantinople by permitting the Islamic conquest, and it was the task of the pope, as God's emissary, to bring order to the Christian world and to reclaim for the true faith lands lost to Islam. This sense of a divine mission, heightened by the revitalisation of the Holy See in the second part of the eleventh century, was enhanced by the leadership of Christian society which Gregory VII claimed in the 'Investiture Contest' with Henry IV. No other force in the society of the 'Catholic core' was as interested in or as sensitive to the wider world. The emperor was in theory the secular leader of the west, but in practice he was king of Germany and Italy and little more concerned with sacred missions, unless they were to his advantage, than any other king. Thus, arising out of the beginnings of the expansion which offered such challenges and opportunities, the papacy developed an institutional propensity to concern itself with the affairs of the east. This was particularly intense in the case of Urban II, who ascended the papal throne in 1088.

Urban II was a Frenchman who rose to fame as a monk of Cluny where he ultimately became Prior, effectively second-in-command to the abbot, St Hugh (1049–1109), who was one of the greatest spiritual leaders of the century. Cluny, at the heart of a network of affiliated monasteries, was one of the few great centres of communication in a localised world. This gave it an awareness of western Christendom as a whole. In fact his experience at Cluny must have sensitised Urban II to a remarkable degree to the place of the Catholic Church in the world. He was uniquely qualified to lead the Church at a time when its pretensions to universal authority were becoming ever greater. He was also a skilled diplomat and adept politician. Gregory had alienated many of the elite of the 'Catholic core' by the overt nature of his demands. William the Conqueror angrily rejected Gregory's claim that because Alexander II had granted a papal banner for the conquest of England in 1066, he should do homage for the realm. Many nobles feared that the new ideas might threaten their profitable rights over local churches, especially the collection of tithes. Without explicitly disowning anything, Urban simply played down such claims. Alexius Comnenus' appeal in 1095 was virtually a repeat of what had happened in 1074, and the institutional response of the papacy was probably much the same – to think in terms of aid in response for cooperation and obedience. But what had failed in 1074 was participation by the leaders of society. This was in part because Gregory VII was soon after drawn into the long conflict with Henry IV of Germany. When Michael VII was deposed in 1078 Gregory excommunicated both his successors, Nicephorous III (1078–81) and Alexius I Comnenus and the breach with Byzantium caused by this was widened when he endorsed the invasion of the Byzantine empire by his ally, Guiscard, in 1081. Urban inherited the 'Investiture Contest' but saw the relevance of the Byzantine appeal to the dispute. Urban from the first had been anxious lest Byzantium recognise Henry IV and his anti-pope, and opened an active diplomacy which resulted in the lifting of the excommunication of Alexius at Melfi in September 1089, and the inauguration of a period of friendship during which both sides took care not to raise difficult theological issues and laid aside the crucial problem of unity and authority in favour of practical cooperation. There was, therefore, a clear connection between

Urban's policy towards Byzantium and his position in the conflict with Henry IV. At the same time Urban continued to take a keen interest in the conflicts with Islam. The fall of Toledo in 1085 had enthused the 'Catholic core' and the defeat of Sagrajas in 1086 caused widespread alarm. Urban celebrated Pisa's attacks on the Muslims and saw the advance of the Normans in Sicily as part of God's will. In the years 1089–91 he demonstrated his interest in the war in Spain, urging Count Raymond Berengar III of Barcelona to reoccupy Tarragona. The city was made an archbishopric with its rights carefully defined, and in a letter of 1089 Urban offered spiritual rewards to all who helped to fortify it against the Muslims, even as great as those offered for going to Jerusalem. In all this Urban seems to have regarded himself as inspiring a counter-attack on Islam, for after the launching of the crusade in 1095 he wrote to the counts of north-eastern Spain urging them to stay and fight Islam in their area while others went to the east, and in 1099 prohibited Archbishop Bernard of Toledo from going to Jerusalem.

Urban had, to a degree unprecedented, a vision of the rolling back of Islam across the whole of the known world under the banner of universal papal authority. And his ambitions were not confined to attacking Islam. In 1094–95 Urban II wrote to Robert of Flanders urging him, 'for the remission of your sins' to help the bishop of Arras regain lands lost to Henry IV. He undoubtedly owed much to his Cluniac background, but the imperatives of survival in a complex political situation strengthened his resolve. And it is clear that he had no compunction about the use of force. This has been a cause of great difficulty for modern writers looking back on this period. It has seemed to them a terrible paradox that the pope, servant of the 'Prince of Peace', should inaugurate a remorselessly violent movement. But this is to impose modern perceptions on medieval Christianity. The Bible offers no definition of the Christian attitude towards war. The words of Christ himself are ambivalent. He claimed 'I came not to send peace, but a sword' (Matthew 10:34), though at the end of his life he said to Pilate: 'If my kingdom were of this world, then would my servants fight' (John 18:36). The ethic of 'love thy neighbour' was certainly important, but the new religion adopted as authoritative not only the books of the New Testament, but also those of the Old Testament in which vendetta, feud, war and conquest, all in the name of the Lord, appear with great frequency. It is no accident that the triumphs of the First Crusade reminded participants of the divinely ordained triumphs of the Jewish resistance to Hellenistic rule led by the Machabees.

In reaction to persecution by the pagan Roman Empire, early Christians refused to participate in imperial government, whose central purpose was, of course, the maintenance of the army, and this certainly led to some emphasis upon pacifism. However, amongst the early martyrs there were a substantial number of soldiers who saw nothing wrong in fighting for the empire. They were martyred for refusing sacrifice to the God-Emperor, not for refusing to fight. Nabor and Felix, for example, suffered death under Maximian because they refused sacrifice. Under the same emperor Andrew the Tribune fought bravely against the Persians, but took flight when the regime began to hunt down

Christian soldiers, and was martyred. Maximillian the Conscript and Typasius the Veteran were very unusual in that they did refuse to fight. In the case of the former it was pointed out to him that there were many Christians fighting in the army: he was not swayed from his aversion to fighting, but did not criticise the stance of others. Such pacifism, while permissible, though rare, in the days of the pagan empire, was not acceptable when Constantine made the empire Christian. It was now essential that Christians should support the military force necessary for the empire, not least because the establishment of the Church found the coercive powers of the state very useful for subduing their doctrinal enemies.

In practice, Christians made the switch to supporting the Christian empire almost seamlessly. In 314 the Council of Arles threatened with excommunication any soldier who refused service in time of peace. The long years of opposition had evidently left reservations amongst some in the Church, notably Lactantius, Constantine's former tutor, whose *Institutions* insist upon the sanctity of human life. Such ideas would continue to have some currency, but could not be allowed to prevail, and those in the mainstream of Christian development soon found their position strengthened by the ideas of St Augustine (354–430) who turned to the Old Testament and emphasised the absence of any precept against war in the New. He is usually regarded as developing the notion of the Just War, or rather of a series of ideas about the permissibility of war which later writers, notably Isidore of Seville, distilled into the Just War. What Augustine really formulated was a set of circumstances in which war could be waged. It was vital that the state be defended, and, therefore, war launched on the authority of the prince was rightful. In the Old Testament Augustine argued that God spoke directly to his people and directly inspired war; this could be nothing less than Holy War. War, in fact, was holy to the extent that it could be said to be inspired and approved by God. Responsibility for perception of God's approval was vested in proper authority, which alone, in Augustine's view, could wage war. Moreover war should be waged for a just cause (a highly flexible phrase) and in a spirit of correcting the enemy without undue cruelty. Since all Christians regarded the defence of the empire as the sacred defence of the Church, such a war was itself sacred, and in that form Holy War became effectively a doctrine of state in the Byzantine Empire.

The situation in the medieval West was rather more complex because there was no single authority and because the 'barbarian' peoples had a well-developed cult of war which their conversion to Christianity did nothing to blunt. The Canon Law of the Church continued to regard killing, even in war, as a sin deserving of penance, and this position is found in the early eleventh-century canonical collection of Burchard of Worms. However, there were very serious modifications in the Church's formal position during the early medieval period. Carolingian penitentials made a very clear distinction between killing for private interest, and killing in 'public war' at the command of the approved authority, although both called for penance. The *Penitentiary of Bede* of the eighth century imposed a penance of four years on those guilty of murder for gain. But if the killing was vengeance for the murder of a brother, the punishment was one full year only and substantial periods in the following two years. In the case of killing 'in public warfare' the penance was only forty days. In the *Ecclesiastical Discipline* of Regino of Prum written *c.*906 wilful murder incurred a penance of seven years, accidental killing five years, vengeance for a relative one year and forty-day periods in the following three. But for killing in war the penalty was only forty days. The warrior ethic of the Germanic aristocracy penetrated very deeply into the thinking of the Church. Edwin of Northumbria, as the story is told by Bede, promised to convert if God gave him victory over his enemies, and God duly obliged. But the force which, above all, inclined priests to take a positive view of violence was the need to maintain the social and political order in a world where stability was seen as fragile and deeply valued. Throughout the early Middle Ages, the prohibitions against priests and monks participating in war were renewed as part of Canon law. But St Germanus of Auxerre, who led the Britons to the 'Alleluia victory' against the Anglo-Saxons at St Albans in the fifth century, was amongst the most honoured of saints. His successor, Gerannus (910–14), rode out in full armour at the head of the city levies to defeat the Vikings. Udalric bishop of Augsburg (923–73), whose life is unusually detailed, refortified the city and fought at the battle of the Lech in 955 in which his brother and nephew were killed; they were buried with honour at Augsburg. Archbishop Hincmar of Rheims in the ninth century was proud to have contributed troops to the armies of Charles the Bald. A century later the biographer of Bruno of Cologne asserted the need of higher churchmen to fight:

> If anyone who is ignorant of the divine dispensation objects to a bishop ruling the people and facing dangers of war and argues that he is responsible only for their souls, the answer is obvious: it is only by doing these things that the guardian and teacher of the Faithful brings to them the rare gift of peace and saves them from the darkness in which there is no light.[15]

Western churchmen had been deeply impressed by the achievement of Charlemagne. He had brought stability and order in which the Church flourished. His conquests led to the conversion of pagan peoples. In the life of St Boniface, Carolingian armies are seen as a great asset in converting pagans while in that of another Anglo-Saxon missionary, Lebuin, active in the 770s, he is portrayed preaching to the Saxons and threatening that unless they convert, 'there is ready a king in a neighbouring country who will invade your land, despoil and lay waste, will tire you out with his campaigns, scatter you in exile, dispossess or kill you'. This life was probably written a century after Lebuin's death, but the same approval of forced conversion is found in sources of the eleventh century. In fact,

---

15 Ruotger, *Vita Sancti Brunonis, Coloniensis Archiepiscopi (953–65)*, PL 134: 937–77 or MGH SS 4: 252–6.

during the early Middle Ages a very clear distinction seems to have emerged between war against Christians and war against others. Charlemagne pursued brutal war against the Saxons, yet took great pains to justify his conquest of his fellow-Christian, Duke Tassilo of the Bavarians. A little later, Nithard was at pains to portray Charles the Bald as forced to battle against his elder brother at Fontenoy. This does not mean that war against fellow-Christians could not be perfectly proper, as the career of Charlemagne and later the Ottonian emperors shows, but it needed more careful justification. The Scottish bishop, Gervadius, was present as battle was about to be joined between an invading English force and the Scottish army. One of the English invaders asked him for absolution, concerned for his soul because he was partaking in a war of aggression. He received it and his body was later found on the battlefield because it had a white bird (not black like the rest) upon it. St Fintan had a vision of a forthcoming battle in which most of those who fought were evil men, but he distinguished them from those 'who lived well and fought only from necessity', and it was for their souls that he prayed when they had perished. St Tigernach felt he had to bless the offensive military expedition of his patron, King Fiarchrius: but the savagery of war was ameliorated because the victorious king, as Tigernach had asked, returned not as tradition demanded with the heads of the enemy dead swinging from his saddles, but with mud and straw imitations.[16]

There is, in fact, a certain queasiness about wars between Christians, perhaps because of the position of canon law which ultimately saw all killing as murder. But no such inhibitions existed in the matter of wars against others. In the ninth century, when the quarrels of the Carolingians opened their empire to external attack, southern Europe was exposed to the Muslims. These were more than mere raids. Muslims established military settlements in South Italy, and from bases on the river Garigliano threatened Rome itself. In 847 one of their attacks sacked the shrine of St Peter, which was then outside the circuit of the walls. As a result Pope Leo IV (847–55) extended the defences around the Vatican and appealed to the Franks for military support, recalling their past glories and military successes, adding that any who died in battle as a result would 'not be denied the Heavenly Kingdom'. In September 878, Pope John VIII (872–82) replied to a letter from the bishops of eastern Germany, who asked if soldiers who fell fighting against the pagans would be damned. He ruled that they would not be damned, and that indeed war against the pagans was to be equated with other kinds of good deeds as a form of penance. He invoked the authority of St Peter to assure the Germans that such men would be saved. The precise intention of the popes in these passages has been much debated. Erdmann suggested that these were 'assurances of everlasting life'. J. Flori has argued that John VIII was merely excusing those

---

16 *Vita Lebuini*, in MGH SS 30. Chapter 6, translation in C. H. Talbot, *The Anglo-Saxon Missionaries in Germany* (New York: Sheed and Ward, 1954), 231–2. For the eleventh-century writers, see below page 46.

who died from the need to do penance. But it can be argued that Flori thereby fails to note that penance is being equated with military service. What is striking is that these letters were not addressed to kings whose position as defenders of the Church was by now well accepted, but to others. Leo IV was apparently seeking Frankish soldiers to help in the defence of Rome, while John VIII was responding to a letter from the bishops, articulating the concerns of their flocks. These were novel statements, and it seems unlikely that they were intended to be understood in a narrow and technical fashion. The importance of these texts is surely that the Church defines a righteous cause and that individual lay people are asked to act, without the notion of royal authority intervening. We are here very close to the Crusade Indulgence, in which penance was remitted if a soldier promised to go to liberate Jerusalem.[17]

But these two letters represent very rare occasions when some definition was attempted. In general we can see that although the Church maintained the prohibition on monks and clergy participating in war, this was primarily to mark their status and position of apartness from the merely secular world. And in practice it was really only monks who stood aloof. Churchmen saw violence as something that could be used for moral ends, most spectacularly the defence of Christian people and the conversion of the infidel. However, there was no real formulation of when this was permissible. Augustinian ideas survived the early Middle Ages only in attenuated form. In practice a number of notions of 'Holy War' grew up in the centuries before 1000. There was a widespread conviction that fighting infidels was good and that those who did it were praiseworthy. There was the belief, quite elaborately developed in Ottonian Germany, that the Christian Empire had a universal mission to defend and expand the holy religion. There was only a weak notion that the reconquest of Spain from the infidels had become a Christian duty for the remnants of the Visigothic régime there. None of these developments really prepared the way for the idea of crusade. The German experience was heavily pragmatic in practice, while before the First Crusade the war in Spain had attracted only limited attention north of the Pyrenees. But if there was a predisposition to be hostile to infidels of any sort, it was hardly something that Urban II could count upon to rally people to his appeal, because it would only come into play when there was a perceived threat. Urban II, in fact, as he turned his mind to Jerusalem and the papal policy in the east could not appeal to any well-defined ideology of Holy War widespread in the lands of his obedience. Rather, the notion was accepted and applied in different places at different times. There were many kinds of Holy War and circumstance called them into being. In the same way Urban could count on no political force with a real interest in his goal of conquest.

Looked at in this way we can begin to understand just how difficult a task

---

17 For the debate up to 1977 the translators of Erdmann provided a very good short guide, Erdmann, *Origin of the Idea of the Crusade*, 27, n.66; Flori, *Guerre sainte*, 50–4.

Urban II faced, and how great his achievement was. From his predecessor, Gregory VII, he inherited a dynamic notion of the papacy as the supreme authority in Christendom, whose role it was to fix the objectives and determine the means by which Christian society reached them. Gregory did not establish what has been called 'the Papal Monarchy', but he laid the necessary foundations upon which it was based. Very significant work in centralising and regularising papal administration was done by Urban II himself, and his was a major contribution to papal development. That overwhelming sense of responsibility for the good of Christendom as a whole undoubtedly was a moving force for Urban. He was deeply sensitised to the perils posed by Islam, partly by his Cluniac background which gave him a deep interest in Spain. In the years after his accession he did much to encourage the Spanish reconquest, as we have seen. This profound sense of responsibility and fear of Islam converged with self-interest to press him to a *démarche* with the Byzantine empire, whose eventual outcome, after friendly exchanges, was the lifting of the excommunication on Alexius I at the council of Melfi in September 1089. There is no doubt that this was part of his strategy to strengthen his position in the contest with Henry IV. This progressed well, and by 1095 Urban's cause was in the ascendant and Henry IV was in grave difficulties, trapped in Italy, although his partisans continued to hold parts of Rome and its area for the anti-pope. Urban seized this opportunity to re-establish his position in northern Italy and France, and this was undoubtedly the purpose of the journey of 1095. The first major council of his reign was arranged at Piacenza, 1st–7th March, and it was on this occasion that Byzantine ambassadors were allowed to appeal to the assembled clergy, asking for their aid in recruiting mercenaries to assist the empire against the Turks.[18] This was the trigger which set off the appeal for the crusade which he would launch in November 1095 at Clermont.

Urban had a vision of what he wanted to do, and the Investiture Contest gave him every incentive to stage a spectacular coup to demonstrate papal leadership. But the problem he faced was how to involve the laity. Urban needed soldiers, above all those most effective of soldiers, the *milites*, a word usually translated as knights. *Miles* actually means no more than soldier, but by the end of the tenth century armies are described as consisting of *milites et pedites* (horse and foot), presumably because the mounted armoured cavalryman was so effective that he was seen as the soldier *par excellence*. Knights were the paid servants and bully-boys of the aristocracy and constituted a functional group united only by their military role. Many were relatively poor men, hired for short periods into the households of the great, while others were substantial landowners or even off-

---

18 Bernold of St Blaise, *Chronicon*, in MGH SS 5.161 is the only source to mention this appeal, and because of this some historians have doubted its authenticity, but there seems no reason to do so because Bernold, a highly prolific writer, was a contemporary who was strongly interested in the papacy and its doings.

shoots of noble families. Some made their way by war, others were concerned with their own property and many administered that of others. But all were militarised because in an age of precarious political stability it was vitally necessary to be able to defend their own property or that of their employers. Whatever their wealth, such men were intimately associated with the aristocracy. They lived in their houses and castles, ate at their tables, equipped themselves in the same way for war with armour, sword, shield and horse. They shared the concerns of their lords for the well-being and integrity of the estates which supported them, and the petty landowners amongst them must have felt this particularly strongly.

All landowners at this time faced a particular problem. In an age of rising living standards more of their children were surviving into adulthood. If the father tried to provide for all his adult sons he would fragment the family lands and so threaten all with a decline into the ranks of the peasantry. Concern for the integrity of landholdings is evident in the gradual decline in enormous grants of land to churches and monasteries, and the requirement that when they were made all members of the donor's family should clearly consent to them. More significantly, the custom of *gavelkind*, the division of lands amongst all the heirs of the dead father, was gradually abandoned in favour of devices that concentrated the inheritance, and especially the land, in the hands of the eldest son. This was far from universal, but it was very marked in northern France and England. The effects of this process were most dramatic amongst petty landowners like the knights. Wealthy aristocrats could afford to help their younger children, but others could not. Robert Guiscard was one of the twelve sons of Tancred d'Hauteville, a Norman knight. His emigration to southern Italy and his ruthless career there can be understood in terms of his social origins. Such rootless young men, trained in war, needed an outlet for their energies and a goal for their ambitions.

Any serious force needed knights as its backbone. The key to enlisting them was to persuade their masters, the lay aristocracy. They, again, were a very varied group, ranging from petty landowners to great princes who effectively were kings in their own lands. They too were militarised, because it was essential that they have the potential to defend their lands. They too had surplus younger sons with their way to make. Urban II was born Odo of Lagery, the child of just this kind of people, in the region of Chatîllon-sur-Marne about the year 1042. He was, therefore, well qualified to persuade them to follow his ideas. But this was no easy task. As a group they were quarrelsome, selfish and aggressive, and above all their values and their interests were localised and narrow. They had little history of response to ideological concerns. The good of the eastern Christians and the fate of Constantinople were not promising as motives for their concern. Rootless knights with their way to make or adventurous young men might take service with the eastern emperor, but they were not the kinds of people who could create a great army to liberate Jerusalem, albeit they might form a vital element in its ranks.

Jerusalem was certainly at the heart of Urban's appeal. The Canons of the Council of Clermont have survived to us only in a twelfth-century copy, but the second canon informs us: 'Whoever, for devotion alone, and not for the purpose of gaining honours and wealth, shall set out for the liberation of the Church of God at Jerusalem, that journey shall be reckoned in place of all penance.'[19]

What is on offer here is an indulgence, the transformation of a person's normal penance for his sins, into another form: in this case into an act of war, a pilgrim journey to liberate Jerusalem from the infidel. This certainly resolved a major problem for the Church: Gregory VII had proclaimed holy war against his many enemies, but the gap between the high causes he championed and the all too obvious narrow, selfish and worldly interests of those upon whom he depended to fight was eminently patent, indeed at times, scandalous. There was discussion in reform circles of the idea that fighting in a righteous cause might be seen as penance and the Pisan attack on Mahdia in 1087 was spoken of in these terms, but such ideas seem to have had little currency. The insistence on 'devotion alone' in the Clermont decree is very striking: this spiritual benefit is available only to those who first confess, then take a vow to go on the journey, and then conduct themselves in a proper way. Those who went would have a special status, symbolised by the cross they would wear, comparable to the staff and scrip of the pilgrim as a sign of status. In fact they would be pilgrims and their penance was attached to the pilgrimage itself. The crusaders referred to themselves in just this way. Their army was, said a participant, the 'pilgrim Church of the Franks'. Urban also proclaimed the 'Truce of God' in order to protect the lands and property of the crusaders in their absence.

There were other elements in Urban's speech which were designed to appeal to the aristocracy, as we shall see, but this was the heart of it, and a very shrewd appeal it was. Not only was Odo of Lagery a French aristocrat who knew his own people, he had risen to be prior of Cluny before becoming a cardinal in 1078. The foundation of Cluny's greatness lay in its careful appeal to aristocratic piety. From Carolingian times laymen had seen the prayers of monks, the purest of men and in contemporary estimation the closest to God, as very important to supplement their own efforts to escape from the burden of sin. Cluny had been founded by William I of Aquitaine in order that its monks might pray for his soul, and it was in this spirit that rich and poor made donations to the abbey. In return Cluny offered prayer and confraternity, remembrance in life and after death in the devotions of the monks. Cluniac abbeys deliberately cultivated splendour and richness of decoration, and they developed an extraordinarily elaborate and impressive liturgical day. The Cluniac abbey was constructed as a gateway to heaven. The grandeur of such great churches, the richness of their decoration, the power of their glorious rituals supported by sweet music and clouds of incense were all calculated to impress those coming in from the work-a-day world. Today, St Hugh's great church at Cluny lies in ruins: the best impression of it, on a much

---

19 Mansi, 20: 816, translated by P. F. Palmer in *The New Catholic Encyclopaedia*, 15 vols (New York: McGraw-Hill, 1967), 7. 483.

reduced scale, is probably provided by the rather later Paray-le-Monial, in the apse of which, over the high altar, presides the figure of Christ the Judge. For always Cluny reminded men of death and judgement, whose horrors they could not escape, but might ameliorate by generosity to God's poor, the monks of Cluny. Medieval men and women were gripped by a profound sense of their own sin. This was an age in which there was a profound acceptance of the fundamental truths of the Christian religion. Heaven and Hell were facts of eleventh-century life and their opposition was made the more real and more personal by the observable gulf between the way most aristocrats lived and the lives of monks which represented an ideal. They were urged to penance for their sins, but the penitential system was complex and its virtues uncertain. The prayers of good men, of monks, seemed more certain a way of escape than anything an individual could do for himself.

But there were other means of escape. God the Father, God the Son and God the Holy Spirit, the central beings of the Christian religion, might be unknown and unknowable, but the saints were much more accessible and they had direct access to God. In the eleventh century the cult of saints becomes much more visible in our sources. Major cult-centres, like St Martin of Tours, St Faith of Conques or St Gilles du Gard seem to have boomed, and we hear a lot more of journeys by the faithful to these places. This was not a new phenomenon for collected miracles of saints have a long history. The aggressive marketing of some saints produced a spectacular literature, notable amongst which is Bernard of Angers *Miracles of St Faith of Conques*. What such works and the growth of the cults they propagate suggest is that much of the new wealth of the expanding 'Catholic core' was being poured into these devotions. One aspect of the cult of saints was the development of pilgrimages to their sacred precincts, often very consciously undertaken as acts of penance. Gradually a very clear hierarchy of pilgrimages emerged. Everywhere there were the local saints, but above them were centres of regional importance, notably Tours and Conques. Beyond them were centres with enormous international appeal: St James of Compostella in northern Spain, above all Rome. These enjoyed special prestige which offered greater spiritual benefits. But of all the pilgrimages, one was always seen as especially outstanding and offering special benefits to the penitent – Jerusalem.

Pilgrimage to Jerusalem had a great pedigree dating back to the fourth century when many of the sites of the life of Christ were publicly identified and the Constantinian basilica was raised over the place of Christ's Passion and Entombment. Jerusalem was a long and dangerous journey from the west, but pilgrimages to it persisted throughout the early Middle Ages. About the year 1000 two developments made the journey much easier: the Byzantine expansion into Bulgaria and Syria meant that for most of the journey pilgrims would pass through the lands of a single well-ordered power; the conversion of Hungary under St Stephen (1000–38) established a Christian kingdom between Germany and Byzantium. The Burgundian writer, Rodulfus Glaber, saw that the upsurge in pilgrimage to Jerusalem owed much to the conversion of Hungary, and that thereafter there was an increase in the scale of journeying to Jerusalem. About the time of the millennium of the Passion in 1033 he noted:

> An innumerable multitude of people from the whole world, greater than any man before could have hoped to see, began to travel to the Sepulchre of the Lord at Jerusalem. First to go were the petty people, then those of middling estate, and next the powerful, kings, counts, marquesses and bishops; finally, and this was something which had never happened before, numerous women, noble and poor, undertook the journey.[20]

This was a sustained movement. In 1027 Richard, abbot of St Vannes in Verdun, led a substantial party, while in 1035 Robert the Devil, duke of Normandy died at Nicaea on his way back. The difficulties of the pilgrimage seem to have been increased by the relatively weak hold of the Fatimids on Palestine. In 1055 Bishop Lietbert of Cambrai and a sizeable group of French pilgrims were forced to turn back because of political instability in the area. In 1064 the archbishop of Metz and the bishops of Utrecht, Regensburg and Bamberg led a very large group, the 'Great German Pilgrimage' which was ambushed by bandits near to Jerusalem and besieged in a deserted village before being liberated by the Fatimid governor. Thereafter the Holy Land became the frontier between the Seljuks and the Fatimids. Even so pilgrimage continued: Viscount Boso I of Turenne died at Jerusalem in 1092 while the First Crusade encountered a returning pilgrim at Antioch in 1097. Moreover, in the course of the eleventh century, Jerusalem and the Holy Sepulchre began to become increasingly important in the ritual of the Church, and relics of the life and Passion of Christ were highly valued. Some churches were built in the form of architectural imitations of the Holy Sepulchre, like those at Paderborn (1036) and Neuvy-St-Sépulcre (1042). There was a vogue for rotundas in imitation of the one at the Holy Sepulchre: a fine example was the church of St Bénigne at Dijon, completed by St William in 1018. At the same time religious art was becoming more and more naturalistic, and the new representations of Christ focused attention upon Jerusalem. There is evidence of a deep preoccupation with the city and the Holy Sepulchre, its greatest relic. A modern authority has suggested that 'the attitude of eleventh-century Christians towards Jerusalem and the Holy Land was obsessive'.[21]

Urban knew the spirituality of the lay aristocracy intimately, and he would have known of their anxieties. There can be little doubt that laymen grasped that there was a huge gap between what the Christian message preached and the way they behaved. And they were well aware of the savage punishment which God could meet out. The *Annals of Hildesheim* for the year 1059 record:

---

20 Glaber, *Histories*, 198–201.
21 J. Riley-Smith, *First Crusade and the Idea of Crusading* (London: Athlone, 1986), 21.

The blessed Cuono, bishop of Trier was martyred; he was thrown thrice from a lofty crag on a wild and lonely mountain by count Theoderich; in that place God, through him, made many wondrous signs to appear. This count afterwards did penance, and went to Jerusalem where he died, and all those who conspired with him came to a bad death.[22]

Fulk Nerra (987–1039) was a notorious and savage predator who built up the county of Anjou in the lower Loire valley by any means that came to hand. Yet he went at least three and perhaps four times to Jerusalem. These were ruthless men, but they knew their own sinfulness and saw Jerusalem as the symbol of absolution from sin, for of all places it was the most powerful and charismatic. They knew death could come at any time and in mysterious ways, and for the good of their souls they were prepared to found abbeys, pray to the saints, and undertake the terrible journey to Jerusalem. The force of this is evident from the story of the appointment of St Anselm to Canterbury. William II Rufus of England (1087–1100) had resisted making an appointment to Canterbury when Archbishop Lanfranc died in 1089 because he wanted to enjoy the incomes of the see; it was only when he was seemingly dying in 1093 that he appointed Anselm. This was an age of deep anxiety about the burden of sin, and if we are right to think that piety was increasing, so must the anxiety have been. This is not to say that all nobles were pious all the time. Moments of emergency, such as Rufus faced in 1093, must have heightened such tensions. Some individuals and some families were more pious than others. It has been shown that many of those from south-western France who went on the First Crusade were already patrons and friends of monasteries. Sizeable numbers of the aristocratic families of the eleventh-century enjoyed special relationships with monasteries and other great churches. On 25 October 1095 Urban consecrated the high altar of the new abbey-church at Cluny and went to the important Cluniac house of Souvigny where Maiol of Cluny (1049–94) was buried. Subsequently he passed through a number of abbeys, spending much time at St Martial of Limoges. Almost everywhere the monks supported Urban II and the reform party for which he stood, so that it is not unreasonable to expect that their influence would have been put behind the papal appeal.

That appeal, it is important to recognise, was by no means universal. The numbers who went on the crusade were large, but they were not as big as has sometimes been imagined. The army which gathered at Nicaea in June of 1097 was some 60,000 strong, of whom about 6,000 were mounted men – aristocrats and their followers. Many who had taken the cross dropped out or turned back. Substantial numbers died on the way, like the French who drowned as their ship left Bari harbour. Thousands died in the destruction of the 'People's Crusade'. Therefore we can guess that something approaching 100,000 people of all classes

22 PL 141. 584.

and groups were stirred into action by the appeal. Medieval population statistics are unreliable, but an approximation for the populations of the 'Catholic core' from which the crusade was drawn suggests a total of 20,000,000, therefore about 0.50 per cent of the population were drawn to the appeal. In the early 1980s a vigorous European anti-war movement could mobilise well over a million for protests across broadly the same countries with a population of 251,000,000, which produces a comparable percentage. These figures are offered to combat the notion that the crusade was a *Volkwanderung*, a journey of entire peoples, partly inspired by the Greek princess, Anna Comnena, who suggested that 'the whole of the west' was on the march in 1096.[23] In fact, crusading always had a particular constituency. It was in essence a religious exercise and it seems likely that it appealed first and foremost to the more pious, who in turn influenced others. The notion of salvation through slaughter which Urban propagated at Clermont had an obvious appeal to a warlike aristocracy within which there is evidence of a deepening piety. Only rarely did laymen leave us some clue as to why they responded to Urban's appeal. Many of those who went on the crusade entered into land transactions, and in the charters that have survived they speak of their motives for going on the journey. It must be said that the clergy of the beneficiary institution usually wrote these charters, but we can assume that they would hardly have dared to put unacceptable ideas and objectives into the mouths of their beneficiaries. In many cases penance is clearly mentioned, but in others it is not, and one of the great leaders, Robert Count of Flanders, announced his intention in a charter to Saint-Thierry, saying that he was going at the instigation of the pope and by divine inspiration to liberate God's Church and to glorify his own name. Others simply spoke of the liberation of Jerusalem or of conquering the pagan enemies of God. In addition, the anonymous knight who went on the crusade and wrote the *Gesta Francorum* believed that those who died on crusade were martyrs who would enter into the kingdom of heaven, which implies that he believed their sins would be forgiven. This range of evidence clearly points to the strong religious appeal of the crusade with a special emphasis upon hopes for the remission of sins.

Other elements in Urban's speech may have had their attractions. A number of accounts, especially those of Robert the Monk and Guibert of Nogent, suggest that Urban appealed to the racial pride of the Franks, invoking memories of their glorious past; indeed the Anonymous does refer to the legend of Charlemagne's journey to Constantinople. Urban certainly pitched his appeal to seize Jerusalem in terms of a property that was to be recovered for the Lord, something which was comprehensible to a land-owning aristocracy. Urban offered a heady cocktail of spiritual benefits to those who undertook the journey. They were to be pilgrims, signed with the cross, *milites Christi*, soldiers of Christ and those chosen by Him to recover his Holy Shrine in a war which would be reckoned as freeing them from

23 Anna Comnena, *Alexiad*, tr. E. R. A. Sewter (Harmondsworth: Penguin, 1969), 309.

the burden of sin and opening the gates of heaven. And yet we have to ask, are we missing something with this analysis – were there other factors at work? In his letter to the people of Flanders, Urban announced that the date of departure would be 15 August 1096, yet long before then a wave of enthusiasm for the expedition had swept across the 'Catholic core', and by 1 August 1096 Peter the Hermit and elements of what we call the 'People's Crusade', some 20,000 strong, had already reached Constantinople. They penetrated Asia Minor and were destroyed by the Turks of Nicaea before the end of October. The name 'People's Crusade' is misleading. Because of the failure and disasters of these expeditions it suited contemporaries to write them off as a rabble, and even to portray them as heretics and mad men. Albert of Aachen suggests that some of them were led by a goose and a goat, while Guibert of Nogent was deeply hostile. Modern writers found particular fascination in these doomed expeditions of the poor and alienated. In reality they were reasonably well organised and composed of much the same kind of people as the other expeditions, except they were not led by a prince. They put up quite a good fight against the Turks. Guibert describes Peter as an evangelising preacher and it would appear that he advocated the crusade as a continuation of a preaching campaign he had begun some time before. Is it possible, therefore, that northern France was in the grip of a religious revival? We know of other similar enthusiastic preachers such as Robert of Arbrissel at about the same time. This suggests that Urban's appeal fell upon an already excited public opinion. It was once fashionable to see millennial echoes in Urban's preaching – that the call for the liberation of Jerusalem perhaps deliberately invoked the Jerusalem of the apocalypse and the coming of the end of the world. We know that the prophecies of the Tiburtine Sibyl had become remarkably popular at the end of the eleventh century, so it is possible that there was a current of apocalyptic expectation, but it is not really discernible in the sources.[24]

It is likely that a whole range of religious factors came into play, but we need to recognise, perhaps above all else, the sheer force of Urban's preaching and preparation. Before he even proclaimed the crusade Urban II seems to have secured the support of a great prince, Raymond IV of Toulouse, and of a great magnate of the Church, Adhémar, bishop of Le Puy. He then called together a council of the leaders of the French Church and charged them with preaching his great expedition, arming them with the assurance that these great men were already committed. He provided a message which, as we have seen, was appealing at least to the more pious in his target constituency. He then set off on a long

---

24 The Sibyls were oracles of the ancient world, and their prophecies were collected and written down. They were copied by Jewish and Christian writers who often drew upon their own apocalyptic traditions: Cross and Livingstone, *Oxford Dictionary of the Christian Church*, 67–71. These collections were revived in Rome and the west in the eleventh century, partly as a result of knowledge of Byzantine traditions: P. J. Alexander, 'The diffusion of Byzantine apocalypses in the medieval west and the beginnings of Joachism', in A. Williams (ed.), *Prophecy and Millenarianism. Essays in Honour of Marjorie Reeves* (London: Longman, 1980), especially 67–71.

journey which took him into the Loire valley – he had quarrelled with Philip I of France over the king's marriage and so dared venture no further north – before moving west and south, returning to the lands of Raymond of Toulouse before passing the Alps for Italy only in the summer of 1096. He wrote various letters inviting support – those to the people of Flanders of December 1095 and to the Bolognese in September 1096 have survived, but we can surmise that there were plenty of others. We know of a special embassy he sent to Genoa, a city which eventually sent an important fleet to support the expedition. Urban was the first pope to travel north of the Alps since Leo IX 50 years before, and that papal journey caused a sensation and left a trail of papal charters and confirmations. Urban was far more ambitious and far more pressing. He had his failures: Fulk of Anjou met him, but refused to join, while Duke William IX of Aquitaine (1086–1126) similarly was not interested – though large numbers of Aquitanians did join the army and after the fall of Jerusalem William went on the 'Crusade of 1101'. The impact of all this activity on the Church was very great, and we may suppose it was especially felt through the Benedictine monks, for Urban often stayed in great monastic houses such as Sauxillanges, St Maixent, St Jean d'Angély and Moissac. In distant England St Anselm was faced with a scandal when the abbot of Cerne tried to sell the property of his house to finance his journey to Jerusalem. Many clergy did join the crusade, but the pope had always made clear that they needed the agreement of their bishops. Urban wanted to persuade the military classes to join his enterprise; though his target was relatively narrow, through the Benedictines his impact must have been immense.

There is little doubt that Urban offered very appealing spiritual rewards to those who undertook his journey, and that he couched them in terms flattering and comprehensible to the aristocracy and the knights. But how far were men impelled to go on the crusade for these religious reasons, and how far were there other factors at work? This is a controversial issue which has long divided historians. Gibbon thought the crusaders longed to grasp 'the golden sceptres of Asia', and more recently Marxist ideas pointed in the same direction. Runciman's highly influential three-volume account of the crusades condemned the greed of participants in the roundest terms. Yet the influence of ideology was always self-evident and never totally denied. A very strong school of historians now argue in the clearest terms for the primacy of religious feeling, and especially for the power of the ideas of penance and indulgence discussed above. Moreover, it has been pointed out that crusading was expensive: a man might need as much as four or five times his income to sustain a year on crusade. And of course it was a risky business. As one of the foremost proponents of this view has argued:

> In the light of the evidence it is hard to believe that most crusaders were motivated by crude materialism. Given their knowledge and expectations and the economic climate in which they lived, the disposal of assets to invest in the fairly remote possibility of settlement in the East would have been a stupid gamble.

But can we be so categorical in dismissing material motives for participation in the crusade? In the twelfth century experience would have taught people that crusading was expensive and a terrible gamble. But those to whom Urban appealed, would not have had such a precise appreciation of the risks before them. Moreover, this was an age of expansion when risk-taking was common; we only have to think of the Normans who went to South Italy. The percentage of those who really made good was probably low, but they went. People do things in hope: it is the principle upon which every national lottery is run, precisely the spirit of 'a stupid gamble'. Now these are generalisations, and it is against just such generalisations that the proponents of spiritual motivation have propounded their ideas. Strong evidence to show that religion moved men and women to take the cross has been examined earlier in this chapter. The counterargument is not that religion did not move people, but that it was not alone and that other factors had influence. We need to recognise the enormous diversity of motivation. Without religious feeling there would have been no crusade, but it does not on its own explain support for the crusade. [25]

As has been said before, those who went on the crusade rarely speak directly to us. The only group of whom we know a great deal were the leaders, the great 'princes' who led the armies. They, along with kings, were the leaders of society, and a number of them took the cross in 1095–96. It is difficult to discern 'crude materialism' in Robert of Flanders, who ruled a rich principality, fought nobly in the east and clearly was anxious to return when he had done his duty. He was perhaps influenced by family tradition: his father, Robert the Frisian, had been to Jerusalem and later sent 500 knights to help Alexius in his wars. Another unlikely to have been moved by mere avarice was Stephen of Blois, an enormously rich prince who would, for a time, become the commander of the crusader army: however, his letters to his wife suggest that she may have driven him to take the cross. Eustace III of Boulogne, an important magnate in England and Flanders, can have had little financial incentive. But what of Eustace's younger brother, Godfrey de Bouillon? Though duke of Lorraine, he was in the gravest difficulties in 1095 and might well have seen the crusade as an escape; he seems to have sold most of his lands as if not intending to return. Robert of Normandy's position as duke was challenged by his brother, William II Rufus of England, to whom he mortgaged the duchy for 10,000 marks to finance his journey to the east. At first sight, we might take Count Raymond IV of Toulouse to be the most disinterested of crusaders. He was the greatest in wealth and power of all who took the cross and he enjoyed the confidence of the pope. Born in 1041, he was elderly by the standards of the age and might be thought to be chiefly concerned for the good of

25 The quotation is from Riley-Smith, *First Crusade and the Idea of Crusading*, 47, who has so eloquently urged the case that men were moved to go on the crusade primarily by religious considerations. For proponents of other views, see the Selected Reading at the end of this chapter.

his soul. But he proved to be the most dogged of all in search of a principality in the Holy Land and earned a reputation for being miserly. When we turn to Hugh of Vermandois, brother of the king of France, we see some interesting motives at work. As enthusiasm for the crusade grew, King Philip of France convened a meeting of his family, as a result of which he wrote to the pope in July 1096 offering his submission in the matter of his marriage, and announcing that his brother, Hugh of Vermandois, would take the cross. Bohemond of Otranto held rich lands in southern Italy including the city of Bari, but he had been disinherited by his father, Robert Guiscard, in favour of Roger Borsa, his son by his second, Lombard, wife. It is possible that Guiscard had intended to compensate Bohemond with lands in Byzantium which he had attempted to conquer in 1081–85. From the first, Bohemond approached the crusade in an acquisitive and political spirit and his whole career, as will be seen later, suggests that he took the cross in the hope of gain.

What we know about these very prominent men suggests mixed motives. We know very little about lesser men as individuals. The charters left by a few of them, as we have seen, suggest a variety of religious reasons. However, since these were written by clergy they would confine themselves to religious reasons and would not go any further. Moreover, the bulk of this evidence bears upon men who held lands, and many of the knights, we have reason to believe, were landless. Only by an examination of the social and economic position of this group as a whole can we throw more light on their motives. But first it is worth noting that Urban was concerned about possible motives; in Canon 2 of Clermont noted above it was insisted that spiritual rewards were only for those who went 'for devotion alone, and not for the purpose of gaining honours and wealth'. Right intention was vital if a participant was to receive spiritual benefit: the crusader indulgence was not a catch-all which forgave every sin that a person committed on crusade, or permitted actions which might tend to a good end but which were undertaken for reasons of personal gain or satisfaction. This was why the crusaders undertook personal and collective penances on their journey – because they were aware how far their behaviour fell from this standard. The crusader indulgence had a narrow focus and demanded high standards of behaviour from beneficiaries. The roots of this idea were theological, but it had a real political consequence – Urban could not be accused of unleashing cruel and lust-driven mayhem upon the world in the name of God – a charge which had been made against Gregory VII who had never developed a theological justification of violence.

But Urban did nothing practical to prevent those with selfish motives from going, although he was clearly aware that his expedition embodied this kind of appeal. The anonymous author of the *Gesta Francorum* records the watchword the knights passed amongst themselves as encouragement in the crisis of the battle of Dorylaeum, 1 July 1097: 'Stand fast altogether, trusting in Christ and in the victory of the Holy Cross. Today, please God, you will all gain much booty.'[26]

---

26 *Gesta Francorum*, 19–20.

In the popular mind, righteous war would surely bring rightful booty and other benefits. Battle was seen as a kind of trial before God and land and plunder were the tokens of victory. Moreover, at this time when armies could carry only limited amounts of food, plunder was what fed an army. They were out to capture the Holy Sepulchre, and perhaps much else besides, so that acquisition was a natural consequence of Urban's objective, something which would have immediately been apparent to the aristocrats and knights whom he sought to enlist.

It was with good reason that Urban had been at pains to secure the support of the count of Toulouse, one of the great princes of the west. Emulation and competition were undoubtedly influential: 'product endorsement' is a modern phrase for an ancient phenomenon. Princes had enormous influence. It should not be forgotten that when we speak of the 'conversion of Europe' in the Dark Ages what we mean is the conversion of the elite, the leading elements in its society whom others were obliged to follow. Urban was, in a sense, trying to convert people to a new kind of war. Not all princes were susceptible, as we have noted, but few would actually dare oppose him. A rare example of one who apparently did was Abbot William of St Florent de Saumur near Angers who seems to have quarrelled with Urban when the pope refused to concede his case in a land dispute: no crusader is known to have come from the abbey's lands despite the fact that Urban stayed there on his journey. Urban failed to convert Fulk Rechin of Anjou (1060–1109) and William of Aquitaine: when the latter changed his mind and took the cross in 1101 he brought with him a vast force. For this was a world where almost all people lived in patronage groups. Every great man had his *mouvance*, those who lived within his sphere of influence and, in some way, owed him allegiance. That of Godfrey de Bouillon, duke of Lower Lorraine, has been closely studied. He was accompanied on the crusade by some relatives and many others from his immediate *mouvance*. In addition, there were lords and knights from the surrounding areas of the Ardennes. Because he was the most prominent subject of the emperor to take the cross, many from Upper Lorraine and adjacent parts of France took him as their leader. Moreover, he seems to have been friendly with Baldwin of Hainaut who accompanied him; after Baldwin's death in the summer of 1098 his followers seem to have transferred their allegiance to Godfrey. Godfrey was not a prince of the first rank, but this illustrates his influence and in turn casts light on the motivation of those who joined him and other princes. Below the princes were the powerful land-owning aristocrats, and in Aquitaine it was amongst these that Urban scored substantial successes, notably with Raymond of Turenne. These men in turn had their own *mouvances* and from them they drew their retinues who accompanied them on the crusade. Plenty of minor lords and landed knights can be traced whose lords did not go, and we know of some on the crusade who had no special attachment to a prince. But most of those who did go seem to have been in the *mouvances* of the great.

These must have included many landless men who served the great for rations, money and lodging on a precarious basis. We have already noted that the people whom we call knights were a very mixed group indeed, ranging from substantial landowners to men who could barely afford the full fighting equipment of an armoured cavalryman. In Spain there were *caballeros villanos* who were distinguished from the high-born knights, the *caballeros hidalgos*. In Poitou we hear of non-noble knights *milites ignobiles* while in England there are references to 'country-knights', *agrarii milites*. In northern France, Flanders and Germany unfree men, *ministeriales*, served the same function. On the crusade we hear of poor knights, *milites plebei* who seem to have been mounted only when horses were plentiful. For such people the *mouvances* of greater men formed a theatre of ambition where men could rise, by war or by some other form of service. For this was an age of great social fluidity. These were the kind of people who followed the Norman leaders to Italy, and took service with Duke William for pay rather than in anticipation of a landed reward, in his great enterprise of England. In 1101 Henry I concluded the Treaty of Dover with Robert of Flanders who promised, in return for a substantial sum, to raise, if required, 1,000 mounted troops, each with three horses. Ordericus Vitalis complained loudly that local war in Normandy just before the First Crusade attracted men seeking plunder and ransoms and was thus made worse and more protracted. Of all those who joined the crusade and the 'Crusade of 1101' only about 545 names can be identified, some of whom were clergy; in most cases we know only names and nothing else about them. Yet some 6,000 aristocrats and knights went on the First Crusade and probably about the same on the 'Crusade of 1101'.[27] Amongst the vast mass of unknowns must have been many of these rootless, ruthless and ambitious men. As early as the autumn of 1097, Baldwin, younger brother of Eustace of Boulogne and Godfrey of Bouillon was quarrelling with another younger son, Tancred d'Hauteville, for possession of the cities of Cilicia. Moreover, during the crusade many soldiers took over enemy lands and fortifications, and a substantial number remained in the east to hold the newly conquered lands. It is likely that about 2,000 knights and aristocrats survived the First Crusade and that something approaching a half of these initally remained, though some later went home. It is interesting that a substantial number of Flemish knights remained in Jerusalem after the departure of Count Robert. It has to be appreciated also that there was real money to be made in the east even if clerical writers chose to make little of it. In 1096 England, with great difficulty, raised 10,000 silver marks which King William Rufus paid to his brother Robert for possession of the duchy of Normandy while Robert was off on crusade. In January 1099, when the crusade was in a crisis of leadership, Raymond of Toulouse paid at least 31,000 gold *solidi*, each worth 10 per cent more than a mark, to persuade some of the other leaders to follow him to Jerusalem.

Motives amongst the arms-bearers, the princes, lords and knights were, therefore, mixed. Religious feeling touched all; it was the basic driving force of the crusade and at times would grip the army in a storm of enthusiasm. But it subsisted

---

27 See the list given in J. Riley-Smith, *The First Crusaders* (Cambridge: Cambridge University Press, 1997), 197–226.

in most participants alongside greed and hope for plunder and land. The success of the crusade depended on the very people who were driving forward the frontiers of the 'Catholic core' and to suppose they were changed by Urban's appeal would be naïve. When individuals decided whether or not to go on crusade, family and political alliance and interest must have played their part as families balanced the needs of their immediate situation against the appeal of the crusade. The spirit of emulation and rivalry amongst local dynasties was undoubtedly a factor. The early adhesion of Raymond of Toulouse was an enormous triumph for Urban II and stimulated others to go on the journey. But what of the rest of the crusaders, the lesser people, commonly referred to by the chronicler simply as the *pauperi*, the poor? The Greek princess, Anna Comnena, contrasted their simple enthusiasm for the liberation of the Holy Sepulchre with the calculating greed of their leaders. Anna did this because when she wrote, some 40 years after the crusade, she was anxious to vilify Bohemond and the other lords who had supported his seizure of Antioch from the Byzantine empire. Her picture was reinforced by Guibert of Nogent's portrayal of humble men moved by the charismatic preaching of Peter the Hermit, though we should remember that he was concerned to write off the failure of these forces. However, the antithesis of zealous poor and calculating princes has become a cliché of crusading writing. In fact, very large numbers of the 'poor' were probably the servants and retainers of the knights and aristocrats. A knight needed two or three servants to keep him in the field and look after his horses. This alone would account for something like 20,000 of the 'poor'. Greater lords needed hosts of servants, and some of them also had retinues of infantry. These humbler people would have had little choice but to follow their masters, though that is not to say that the spirit of religious enthusiasm was lacking amongst them. In the past expeditions of the great had attracted poorer people anxious to make the dangerous journey to Jerusalem, and this impulse was certainly at work. Evidently wives and children accompanied many of these people, as they accompanied many of their social superiors, and all this would have swelled numbers.

Economic factors were also at work. The years before 1095 had seen a series of poor harvests in northern France and western Germany, and desperation may have driven some peasants, and, indeed, influenced some knights and nobles. But enthusiasm there certainly was and the means of its generation escape us. As early as 1095/6 Warner, count of Grez in Lorraine, was selling land to go on crusade. In the spring of 1096 his kinsman, Godfrey of Lorraine, took the cross. By the end of May 1096 a group of Saxons and others from North Germany led by Folkmar was at Prague. These were men living in the empire well away from Urban's preaching, though the reform papacy had sympathisers amongst the Saxons. This strong German involvement is often connected with the 'People's Crusade'. Peter the Hermit lived in the Berry in France, and probably very soon after Clermont he began preaching the journey to Jerusalem, claiming that after terrible experiences in the east, he had been divinely instructed to raise forces to liberate the Holy Sepulchre. If this did fall upon a public already excited by a religious revival, and perhaps shaken by famine, the highly charged emotions which resulted seem understandable. By early March one of Peter's followers, Walter-the Penniless, a well-known soldier, led a small force towards the Rhineland as the first stage of a journey down the Danube valley, the well-known pilgrim road, to Constantinople.

At the same time the cities of the Rhineland were wracked by a violent persecution of the Jews and in the early spring the Emperor Henry IV ordered the local authorities to protect the Jews. The persecution seems to have started in France where there was an anti-Semitic riot at Rouen. In early April 1096 Peter the Hermit arrived at Trier bearing a letter from the Jews of France advising their co-religionists to give him money. Although Peter's own group seems to have been reasonably disciplined, a wave of attacks on Jews swept across the Rhineland cities and Germany. Prominent amongst the persecutors was a German contingent led by Count Emicho who massacred the Jews of Speyer and Mainz. But there were plenty of others and the climax of their activities was a month-long pogrom at Cologne. This 'first holocaust' reached even Prague where the band led by Folkmar was probably responsible. These terrible events were confined to the early stages of the crusade, and to the French and German groups who chose to follow the route down the Danube to Constantinople. The impulse to persecute has been put down to the special enthusiasm whipped up by Peter the Hermit and the belief that these simple people regarded Muslims and Jews as equal enemies. Interestingly, 30 years before, Pope Alexander II (1061–73) had dealt with a similar outburst of persecution in Spain and had stressed that while Jews and Muslims were both enemies of the true faith, they were to be dealt with differently, and the former were to be protected. It has been suggested that Urban II had introduced the theme of conversion of the infidel into his message, and that as a result conversion may have been the underlying motive, even more important than extortion, in the persecutions.[28] However, this seems rather unlikely because Urban never pressed for the conversion of the conquered Muslim or Jewish populations of Spain and Sicily. Probably the persecution was the result of a spontaneous hatred of all 'infidels', sharpened by other motives like greed. But what needs to be emphasised here is that these earlier expeditions were not very different from the so-called 'official' armies that followed, except in two respects: they lacked really important leaders and they were desperately trying to raise resources in a hurry, while the later armies took their time. It may be that there were tensions in the German cities. The bishops stood in defence of the Jews, but laymen led the persecution. Henry IV acted quickly, but it seems that many had ambivalent attitudes: Godfrey de Bouillon threatened the Jews, but was restrained by the emperor's orders. The Jewish communities at Cologne and

---

28 This was not the first major persecution of Jews in the medieval west. In 1009 a wave of persecution of Jews in France was justified by the story that they had conspired with the Caliph of Cairo to destroy the Holy Sepulchre in that year: Glaber, *Histories*, 132–7.

Mainz felt it wise to pay Godfrey 500 pieces of silver each, though he did nothing to protect them in their hour of need. At Mainz the citizens, in defiance of their bishop, opened the gates of the city to Emicho's crusaders and joined in the assault on the bishop's palace where the Jews had taken refuge. The arrival of French contingents, in the first flush of crusading enthusiasm, seems to have triggered local tensions. But the enthusiasm itself was not confined to the 'People's Crusade'. The massacres are a real indication of the religious zeal that suffused all the people who went on the First Crusade. It was to be the driving force of their army.

Urban saw the great expedition which he launched as a fulfilment of the historic role of the papacy as the guiding force in the whole Christian world. Fulcher of Chartres was a convinced supporter of Urban. He was present at Clermont and joined the crusade. His account of the Council of Clermont portrays Urban II seeking to reform the Church, to end the 'Investiture Contest' and to bring proper order to all Christendom:

> Nor is it a wonder that the whole world was disquieted and disturbed. For if the Church of Rome, the source of correction for all of Christianity, is troubled by any disorder, then immediately the members subject to it derive the malady though the chief nerves and are weakened by suffering along with it. Yet truly this church . . . was rudely smitten by that proud Guibert [Henry IV's antipope, Clement III (1080–1100)]. And when the head is thus struck, the members are hurt immediately. Moreover, when the head was sick in this way, the members were enfeebled with pain because in all parts of Europe peace, virtue and faith were brutally trampled upon by stronger men and lesser, inside the church and out. It was necessary to put an end to all these evils and, in accordance with the plan initiated by Pope Urban, to turn against the pagans the fighting which up to now customarily went on among the Christians.[29]

The expedition, for Fulcher 'the soldiers of Christ', would free the eastern Christians and expedite their return to the authority of the Holy See. The seizure of Jerusalem would contribute to the rolling back of the wicked heresy of the Muslims. Precisely how Urban intended all this to be achieved is more difficult to say. His legate was highly respectful of the Greek Patriarch of Jerusalem whom he met in Cyprus, and the Greek Patriarch of Antioch was restored after the capture of that city in 1098. There may have been some expectation that Alexius himself would lead the expedition, but this is only mentioned by Raymond of Aguilers, a chronicler who was very hostile to Alexius. It is very difficult to believe that the Byzantine emperor would have committed himself to such a journey in his

---

29 Fulcher of Chartres, *A History of the Expedition to Jerusalem*, ed. F. R. Ryan and H. S. Fink (Knoxville, TN: University of Tennessee Press, 1969), 67, 70–1.

contacts with Urban, though he did try to profit from the crusade. We have, in short, very little sense of a detailed plan for the expedition: rather Urban laid down its general objectives and bestowed upon it a legate who knew his mind and would see to the achievement of his objectives. But Urban's real achievement was to enlist many of the aristocracy in this cause by linking its achievement to their sense of piety and desire for salvation. The crusade was a religious exercise with a very intense, though far from universal appeal. It chimed with the spirituality of the aristocracy and knights by offering them salvation through slaughter and meshed with a contemporary mood of confident expansionism. It gave meaning and significance and *post facto* legitimisation to a whole series of expansionist adventures. It offered the prospect of conquest of the riches of the east. In an age when the spiritual was envisaged in a very concrete way and temporal ends could be sought by spiritual sanctions, when the sacred and profane were intimately mixed, this was a potent mixture. The crusade did not offer something for everybody, but it did offer something for large numbers of people. Mention of the name of Jerusalem may occasionally have stirred millennial expectations, because the city figures large in the Apocalypse, while in certain places the appeal may have fallen upon a rural population already excited by religious revival, and perhaps destabilised by famine. What is striking in the sources is that Urban's appeal was regarded by contemporaries as something new, a unique opportunity for salvation.

SELECTED READING

The most important work on the origins of the crusade is C. Erdmann, *The Origin of the Idea of the Crusade*, translated from a German original of 1935 by M. W. Baldwin and W. Goffart (Princeton, NJ: Princeton University Press, 1977). For a critical view of Erdmann, see J. Riley-Smith, 'Erdmann and the historiography of the Crusades, 1095–1995', in L. Garcia-Guijarro Ramos (ed.), *La Primera Cruzada, Novecientos Anos Después. El Concilio de Clermont y los Oríenes del Movimiento Cruzado* (Madrid: Amat Bellés, 1977), 17–32. A stimulating study of the development of Christian ideas about war and a comparison with the Muslim experience is provided by J. Flori, *Guerre sainte, jihad, croisade. Violence et religion dans le christianisme et l'islam* (Paris: Seuil, 2002). Erdmann was impressed by the great reform of the papacy in the later eleventh century and believed that it was only then that the Church began to take a positive view of violence. In his view this developed in the court circles of Gregory VII, and Urban II used it in launching the First Crusade, whose main purpose was to foster Church unity, by establishing a closer relationship with Alexius Comnenus. His emphasis on papal policy led him to believe that at Clermont Urban mentioned Jerusalem only as the goal of the march, while aid to the eastern churches was the real object of the war. H. E. Mayer, *The Crusades*, tr. J. Gillingham of 1965 German original (2nd edition, Oxford: Oxford University Press, 1990) felt that Jerusalem had so powerful an appeal that it would have dominated had the pope mentioned it. Rather, he suggested, popular enthusiasm for the city took over and changed the pope's priorities. H. E. J. Cowdrey, 'Pope Urban II's preaching of the First

Crusade', *History* 55 (1970), 177–88 reviewed all the evidence and his conclusion that Jerusalem was at the forefront of Urban's appeal has been widely accepted. The case for Peter as the originator of the crusade rests on Albert of Aachen who wrote his account of the crusade, the *Historia Hierosolymitana*, RHC Oc.4, by about 1102 and in Book 1. 1–5 says that Peter began the preaching of the crusade to which Pope Urban responded later. It has to be said, however, that Albert was an imperialist who may well have minimised the papal input, on which see S. B. Edgington, 'The First Crusade: reviewing the evidence', in J. Phillips (ed.), *The First Crusade. Origins and Impact* (Manchester: Manchester University Press, 1997), 55–77. Albert's discretion on Urban's role was supported by Anna Comnena whose *Alexiad* suggests that Peter was the originator of the crusade, but Anna wrote long after events, may not have known much about the origins of the crusade, and was in any case anxious to absolve her father from any blame for the crusade, on which see J. France, 'Anna Comnena, the *Alexiad* and the First Crusade', *Reading Medieval Studies* 10 (1984), 21. It has more recently been thought that Peter was merely a preacher whose enthusiasm got out of hand, but E. O. Blake and C. Morris, 'A hermit goes to war. Peter and the origins of the First Crusade', in W. J. Shiels (ed.), *Monks, Hermits and the Ascetic Tradition*: Studies in Church History 22 (Oxford: Blackwell, 1985), 79–107 have suggested that he had an independent role in the conception and raising of the crusade. The only full biography of Urban II is A. Becker, *Papst Urban II (1088–99)*, 2 vols (Stuttgart, 1964–88). On Urban's journey, see J. Riley-Smith, *The First Crusade and the Idea of Crusading* (London: Athlone, 1986), 13–30 and his *Atlas of the Crusades* (London: Times Books, 1991), 28–9.

For the position of the papacy a good general survey is C. Morris, *The Papal Monarchy.The Western Church 1050–1250* (Oxford: Clarendon, 1989), while H. E. J. Cowdrey, *Pope Gregory VII, 1073–85* (Oxford: Clarendon, 1988) is magisterial. S. Runciman, *The Eastern Schism* (Oxford: Clarendon Press, 1955), 28–77 was inclined to minimise the effects of 1054, but F. Dvornik, *Byzantium and the Roman Primacy* (New York: Fordham, 1979), 124–37 stresses the significance of the underlying issue of authority. For a good survey, see D. M. Nicol, 'Byzantium and the Papacy in the Eleventh Century', *Journal of Ecclesiastical History* 13 (1962), 1–20. There is no doubt that Urban saw the crusade as a means of diverting the warlike energies of Christendom against an external enemy and this is stressed by T. Mastnak, *Crusading Peace. Christendom, the Muslim World and Western Political Order* (Berkeley, CA: University of California Press, 2002).

On the expansion of the 'Catholic Core', for a summary, see R. Bartlett, *The Making of Europe. Conquest, Colonization and Cultural Change* (London: Penguin, 1993), 5–23 and for South Italy, see G. Loud, *The Age of Robert Guiscard. Southern Italy and the Norman Conquest* (London: Longman, 2000). On Spain, A. MacKay, *Spain in the Middle Ages. From Frontier to Empire, 1000–1500* (Basingstoke: Macmillan, 1977) is useful while D. Lomax, *The Reconquest of Spain* (London: Longman, 1978) provides an excellent outline of the wars. On Spanish ideas about the sanctity of their war against Islam, see J. Flori, *La Guerre Sainte* (Paris: Aubier, 2001), 227–60 whose work also provides an interesting modern treatment of the nature of 'Holy War'. R. A. Fletcher, 'Reconquest and crusade in Spain, 1050–1150', *Transactions of the Royal Historical Society* 37 (1987), 31–47 is much more sceptical about the influence of such ideas on the reconquest before the later eleventh century. For a view of Christian ideas about war in the Dark Ages which is rather different from that of Flori, see J. France, 'Holy War and Holy Men: Erdmann and the lives of the saints', in M. Bull, P. W. Edbury, N. Housley and J. Phillips (eds), *The Experience of*

Crusading, 2 vols (Cambridge: Cambridge University Press, 2003), 1. 193–208. A good study of the career of 'El Cid' is provided by R. A. Fletcher, *The Quest for El Cid* (London: Hutchinson, 1989). M. Bull, *Knightly Piety and the Lay Response to the First Crusade. The Limousin and Gascony, c.970–c.1130* (Oxford: Clarendon, 1993), 70–114 has also argued that the Spanish wars made little impact upon Europe as a whole, while Flori, *La Guerre Sainte*, 272–84 argues against this. It seems to the present writer that while Flori is right to emphasise the impact of Spain upon papal thinking, especially because Urban II had been at Cluny which was connected to Spain, Fletcher and Bull are right to stress the minimal impact upon laymen across Christendom, at least until the very end of the eleventh century. For the crusading vow, see J. Brundage, *Medieval Canon Law and the Crusader* (Madison, WI: University of Wisconsin Press, 1969). It used to be believed that the 'Peace Movement' of the early eleventh century was a significant precedent for the crusade, but its role seems to have been minimal, on which see Bull, *Knightly Piety and the Lay Response to the First Crusade*, 21–69: Urban proclaimed the Truce of God as a device to protect absent crusaders' properties. For the medieval religious outlook and sense of sin, see B. Hamilton, *Religion in the Medieval West* (London: Arnold, 1986). The best treatment of the sense of sin in early medieval Christianity is G. C. Coulton, *Five Centuries of Religion*, 4 vols (Cambridge: Cambridge University Press, 1929–50), especially 1. 67–99; on Cluny, see B. H. Rosenwein, *To be the Neighbour of St Peter* (Ithaca, NY: Cornell University Press, 1989), 202–7. A good introduction to the cult of saints is provided by B. Abou-al-Haj, *The Medieval Cult of Saints* (Cambridge: Cambridge University Press, 1994) and to pilgrimage by J. Sumption, *Pilgrimage: an Image of Medieval Religion* (London: Faber, 1975), and see D. Birch, *Pilgrimage to Rome in the Middle Ages* (Woodbridge: Boydell, 1998). On the place of Jerusalem in eleventh-century piety, see C. Morris, 'Memorials of the Holy Places and Blessings from the East: devotion to Jerusalem before the Crusades', *Studies in Church History* 36 (2000), 90–109 and Riley-Smith, *First Crusade and the Idea of Crusading*, 21. The subject of numbers on the First Crusade is a vexed one. The figures used here are from J. France, *Victory in the East. A Military History of the First Crusade* (Cambridge: Cambridge University Press, 1994), 122–42. J. Flori, 'Un problème de méthodologie. La valeur des nombres à propos des effectifs de la première croisade', *Le Moyen Age* 94 (1993), 399–422 has pointed to some of the problems presented by our sources on this difficult subject. B. S. Bachrach, 'The siege of Antioch: A study in military demography', *War in History* 6 (1999), 127–46 has argued for an army of 100,000 armed men plus 20,000 non-combatants at the start of the siege of Antioch, which means that much larger numbers gathered at Nicaea. J. Duncalf, 'The Peasants' Crusade', *American Historical Review* 26 (1921), 440–53 was the first to argue that these expeditions were not peasant rabbles, but S. Runciman, *History of the Crusades*, 3 vols (Cambridge: Cambridge University Press, 1951–4), 121–41 strengthened the older view, while N. Cohn, *The Pursuit of the Millennium* (London: Secker and Warburg, 1957) portrayed them as alienated representatives of the masses. On their defeat, see France, *Victory in the East*, 88–95. French writers have tended to emphasise the influence of apocalyptic expectation, especially on the 'People's Crusade', on which, see Flori, *Guerre sainte*, 349–52. For the whole subject of millennial expectation, see T. Head and R. Landes, *The Peace of God. Social Violence and Religious Response in France around the Year 1000* (Ithaca, NY: Cornell University Press, 1992). On motivation there is a good survey of older views in J. A. Brundage, *The Crusade. Motives and Achievements* (Boston, MA: Heath, 1964). Riley-Smith, *First Crusade and the Idea of Crusading* and Bull, *Knightly Piety* argue fiercely for the primacy of spiritual motives, but France, *Victory in the East* sees much more mixed motives. On armies, aristocrats and knights, see J. France, *Western Warfare in the Age of the Crusades 1000–1300* (London: UCL Press, 1999), 39–63, and on Godfrey's forces A. V. Murray, 'The army of Godfrey de Bouillon, 1096–1099: Structure and dynamics of a contingent on the First Crusade', *Revue belge de philologie et d'histoire* 70 (1992), 301–29, 'The origins of the Frankish nobility of the Kingdom of Jerusalem, 1100–18', *Mediterranean Historical Review* 4 (1989), 281–300. On the persecution of the Jews, see Riley-Smith, *First Crusade and the Idea of Crusading*, 49–57.

3

THE FIRST CRUSADE

We speak of the First Crusade, but we need to be clear that this apparent unity disguises the fact that it was made up of several main armies with their own leaders, and many smaller contingents which attached themselves to these, and that the fighting elements were accompanied by large numbers of non-combatants. These diverse groups were welded together by an ideological purpose, the liberation of Jerusalem, but the unity imposed by that aim was more deeply felt at some times than at others, and by some people more than others. The First Crusade was only loosely united, and at times its unity broke down, but never sufficiently to deflect strong forces within it from their goal.

The earliest expeditions to leave were those which were aroused by an inspirational North French preacher, Peter the Hermit. They are commonly referred to as the 'People's Crusade' because it was for long believed that they represented a spontaneous 'popular' movement, somewhat distinct from the 'official' expeditions of the great princes. The first to depart was Walter the Penniless and a force of eight knights and many others who were probably a vanguard for Peter's main force. They attracted more supporters in the Rhineland where they seem to have ignited the persecution of Jews. They were heading for Constantinople via the well-worn pilgrim route down the Danube. They left Cologne on 15 April 1096, travelled peacefully across Hungary and reached imperial territory about 11 June where, after a dispute about arms purchases, the Byzantines refused to permit them a market. However, by mid-July they were at Constantinople. Peter the Hermit's own force left Cologne on 20 April and crossed Hungary peacefully. It was certainly numerous, and military command was vested in four captains, Godfrey Burel in charge of the infantry, Raynald of Broyes, Walter FitzWaleran and Fulcher of Chartres who ended his life in the east as a vassal of the county of Edessa. There were problems over food supplies as they reached Byzantine territory, and in early June they stormed the city of Semlin, with their force led by knights in full armour. Subsequently they were scattered by Byzantine forces at Nish, but regrouped and reached Constantinople on 1 August. Only organised, financed and well-supplied forces could have marched so far down the Danube with such little trouble. Peter is said to have had 40,000 men and 2,000 wagons which stretched about a mile along the road, and though this is probably an exaggeration it suggests organisation and support.

Close behind them came Folkmar and his Saxons. It seems unlikely that a force originating so far away from the Rhineland could have been inspired by Peter the Hermit. They attacked Jews at Prague on 30 May and shortly after were scattered by the Hungarians. Another group led by a Rhineland priest, Gottschalk, pillaged Hungary as they travelled. King Coloman (1095–1114) surrounded them, persuaded them to lay down their arms, and massacred them. They seem to have been well-organised enough to defy the Hungarians in arms. Because of these incidents, in mid-August Coloman refused permission for Count Emicho and his band to cross his frontiers. Emicho was a Rhineland count, though he had had French, German, English and Lorrainers followers. They were clearly well organised because they immediately besieged the frontier fortress of Wieselburg for three weeks, in the course of which they used siege machinery. Only chance enabled the Hungarians to defeat them, and some of their leaders later joined the army of Hugh of Vermandois.

Peter the Hermit was well-received by the Byzantines who advised him not to confront the enemy, but shipped his army across the Bosphorus to Nicomedia (modern Izmit), presumably anxious to avoid trouble in and around Constantinople. There his force was joined by a substantial army of Italians about which we know nothing. Peter was advised to await further forces before attacking the enemy and he was inclined to follow Alexius's advice. However, it is always difficult to persuade an armed force to do nothing, especially as the Seljuk capital of Nicaea was only some 40 kilometres away. Restless elements in the army began to raid its lands, with a large force of Franks enjoying spectacular success. In late September a force of Germans and Italians tried to emulate this success but were trapped and massacred at Xerigordo, close to Nicaea. Peter was at Constantinople asking for a reduction in food prices, so perhaps the need to forage was a factor in inspiring the raids. Walter the Penniless seems to have been left in charge and he faced popular demands for vengeance. Presumably because he recognised the dangers of a confrontation with the forces of the Sultanate of Rūm, Walter resisted and was supported by all the other leaders except Godfrey Burel. In the end the agitation led by Burel was so great that it was agreed to attack Nicaea in retaliation for the losses at Xerigordo. The army was organised into six divisions, each round its own banner. They encountered the Turkish army at the point on the road to Nicaea where woodland gave way to open country. Two divisions of knights led the attack, but were eventually driven back and their foot broke. The Turks then fell upon the main camp on 21 October and a complete massacre was only avoided by the arrival of Byzantine forces.

It is a mistake to see these elements of the crusading movement as being very different from those that followed them. The chroniclers of the twelfth century dismissed them as a mere rabble, partly because they had failed. But in fact they were organised enough to manage a long march and they fought well against the

Turks. They had large numbers of non-combatants in their ranks, but so did the armies of the great princes that followed them. Their make-up was not so very different from the armies which came after, for in their ranks were very substantial people including counts and many knights. Their fatal weakness was command. In an age when authority went with social rank they lacked anybody with sufficient status to command obedience, and no strong personality emerged able to impose himself, while Peter was a cleric and could not lead in battle. In these circumstances tensions over food prices opened fissures within the force, particularly national divisions, and personality clashes as well. These were all problems faced by the main armies when they gathered, but they had men of high rank who, despite frictions and breakdowns, imposed a degree of unity. We should not, however, exaggerate this. At times the armies almost broke apart. Overall, it should be recognised that the term 'People's Crusade' is a misnomer because it suggests a unity which never existed. The enthusiasm for the crusade that swept across the 'Catholic core' produced large numbers of small forces. When the first of these arrived at Constantinople the Byzantines were anxious to ship them across the Bosphorus and thus disparate groups became lumped together and, up to a point, cooperated. There were many other similar groups, but because their arrival at Constantinople coincided with that of the great armies, they were simply assimilated and we hear nothing of them. What is important about these first expeditions is that they reveal the real enthusiasm aroused by the appeal for the crusade, the mixed motives at work amongst participants and the problems of controlling such diverse forces.

The armies of the great princes took much longer to gather. Urban had suggested they meet at Constantinople under the leadership of the papal legate, Adhémar of Le Puy on 15 August 1096. He had almost certainly informed Alexius of their coming and it was perhaps at his suggestion that some of the leaders wrote individually to the emperor announcing their impending arrival. For men of substance, raising money for the journey took time. Sale and mortgage of land were the traditional methods by which Jerusalem pilgrims raised money for a journey which probably cost at least the equivalent of one year's income. It is probable that in 1095/6 prudent men were seeking to raise much more than this because the journey was of uncertain length and they would have to allow for losses of horses and equipment and the upkeep of a retinue. Achard of Montmerle, who would die at the siege of Jerusalem, mortgaged an estate to the abbey of Cluny:

> Because I wish fully armed to join in the magnificent expedition of the Christian people seeking for God to fight their way to Jerusalem. . . . I give in mortgage to these eminent men one of my properties which came to me by right of inheritance from my father, receiving from them the sum of 2,000 *solidi* of Lyons and four mules . . . no person . . . can redeem it except myself. Thus if I die on the pilgrimage to Jerusalem, or if I should decide to stay in those parts, that which is the subject of this mortgage.

... shall become a rightful and hereditary possession of the monastery of Cluny in perpetuity.[1]

Great princes took much longer than this minor Burgundian lord to organise their affairs. Godfrey de Bouillon seems to have mortgaged all his lands, but like Achard, reserved for himself the right to redeem the property if he returned. We do not know much about how the other princes raised money, probably because records have not survived. Raymond of Toulouse was exceptionally rich and controlled territories with a thriving money economy which he could tax. By contrast, Robert of Normandy pawned his duchy to his brother and rival, William Rufus. Bohemond seems not have resorted to selling land to finance himself, but his army was relatively small and he ruled a small but very rich territory in south Italy including the great trading city of Bari. All this took time: the mortgage for Normandy was agreed in the spring of 1096, but payment was received only in early autumn. Robert then had to buy supplies, carts etc. It is hardly surprising that most of their armies departed late.

Hugh Magnus, brother of King Philip I of France (1060–1108), left France in mid-August, travelling into Italy and crossing the Adriatic from Bari to Dyrrachium (modern Durrës), the Byzantine fortress-city at the western end of the *Via Egnetia*, the great road across the Balkans. This was another long-standing pilgrim route. He was shipwrecked, but rescued by the Byzantines. He was cared for 'but he was not granted complete freedom' and reached Constantinople by November 1096 where he was the guest of the emperor.[2] Godfrey de Bouillon left about the same time, made an agreement with King Coloman and passed through Hungary peacefully into the imperial lands where his army received ample supplies of food. Alexius had clearly made careful logistical preparations, and, of course, this was a good time of the year to be travelling with all harvests in. By early December they were approaching Constantinople when problems arose. Godfrey seems to have heard that Hugh of Vermandois and his captains were being held prisoner at Constantinople, and sent envoys demanding their release. When this was refused his army devastated the countryside and arrived at Constantinople on 23 December in a hostile and prickly temper.

The North French, led by Robert of Normandy, Robert of Flanders and Stephen of Blois, arrived in southern Italy as winter began. They were advised not to risk a crossing of the Adriatic so late in the season. Robert of Flanders, however, crossed to Dyrrachium, arriving at Constantinople at an unknown date. Stephen and the Norman duke wintered comfortably in Norman Italy, though many of their poorer dependents, dismayed at this delay, turned back. In late March 1097 they set out again and arrived at Constantinople on 14 May. The count of

---

1 A. Bernard and A. Bruel (eds), *Recueil des Chartes de l'Abbaye de Cluny*, 6 vols (Paris: Imprimerie nationale, 1876–1903), 5. 51.
2 Comnena, *Alexiad*, 313–15.

Toulouse crossed the Lombard plain into the Balkans, then turned south through the mountains of what is now Croatia and Albania towards Dyrrachium. His was by far the biggest army, perhaps constituting between a quarter and a third of the entire crusade. Sheer numbers and the difficulty of finding boats to cross the Adriatic in winter probably explain his unusual choice of route. Despite a treaty with Constantine Bodin king of Zeta (by 1070–after 1101) his army was attacked by the mountain peoples, but fought its way to Dyrrachium by February 1097. The Provencal journey along the *Via Egnetia* was marked by constant skirmishes with the imperial forces that Alexius had sent as escorts. In one of these the Papal Legate, Adhémar of Le Puy, was injured so badly that he was left at Thessalonica. The climax was the sack of Rusa on 12 April. Shortly after, imperial ambassadors, supported by messages from the leaders already in Constantinople, begged the count to hasten ahead of his army, where he arrived on 21 April. In his absence his army suffered a major defeat, much to the anger of Raymond. The difficulties of the Provencal march across the empire arose from their numbers and from the fact that they were travelling in winter as food stocks were being depleted: fighting with their imperial escorts clearly arose from their habit of foraging for food across the countryside. This situation was made worse because they were following other forces, including those of Robert of Flanders and Bohemond, along the *Via Egnetia*.

Bohemond's journey to Constantinople was in some ways the most interesting of all. The journey to Jerusalem was so popular in the eleventh century that most of the important leaders would have had some notion of distances and climates. But for the Normans of the south the difference was that crusade was not so much an adventure into strange and exotic lands as a military expedition which would take place within their normal sphere of political activity. They had conquered Italy and Sicily from the Byzantines and the Muslims. Many had served Byzantium as mercenaries; Guy, Bohemond's brother-in-law was in the Byzantine army at the time of the crusade.[3] Bohemond had participated in his father's attempt to conquer Constantinople in 1081–85. This probably explains why he chose to land his forces at Avlona, well south of Dyrrachium: he wanted to avoid the presence of a strong Byzantine garrison. His was a relatively small but well-disciplined army which had very little trouble with the imperial authorities. They took their time: they left Avlona on or about 1 November 1096 and did not arrive at Constantinople until 26 April 1097, though Bohemond himself had gone ahead and was there by 10 April. This was a journey of 178 days but it took almost six months, at a daily average rate of march of just over 5 kilometres. By contrast, the Provençals, with a very much larger army, left Dyrrachium in February 1097 and arrived at Constantinople just a few days after the Normans, averaging 11 kilometres per day. Bohemond was loitering with intent.

And the nature of that intent is not difficult to understand. The expedition

---

3 *Gesta Francorum*, 63–4.

proclaimed by Urban II was certainly intended to help the Byzantine Empire. Even if most of the participants were focused on Jerusalem, they would have to come to a political arrangement with Alexius Comnenus if they were to cross his empire. At the very simplest level, they needed boats in order to cross the Bosphorus. As Fulcher of Chartres put it succinctly: 'For it was essential that all establish friendship with the emperor since without his aid and counsel we could not easily make the journey.' When Raymond of Toulouse was approaching Constantinople, it is reported that he received a letter from the other leaders urging him to journey ahead of his army to make arrangements with 'Alexius who might take the cross and become leader of God's army.' However, the same source reports that when the count arrived, he expressed himself willing to accept Alexius as his lord only if the emperor would become leader of the army. This does not suggest any real expectation that the emperor would do this.[4] Indeed it is very hard to believe that Alexius would ever have committed himself to such a course of action. The whole expedition was very risky, and the Byzantines had no substantial interest in Jerusalem whose delivery from the Muslims would not necessarily profit the empire. Anna Comnena is very frank on the point: 'Alexius would have liked to share in the expedition, but he feared the enormous numbers of the Kelts' and later again, 'even if his presence was unwise, he realised the necessity of giving as much aid to the Kelts as if he were actually with them'.[5] Alexius clearly had no intention of leading the crusade and it seems unlikely that he would ever have suggested doing so to Urban: in the event he would not even join them in the siege of Nicaea, though he sent help. In the early summer of 1098 Alexius and his armies were in Asia Minor, but clearly they were profiting from the successes of the crusade rather than seriously intending to fight alongside them. Alexius was far from hostile to the crusaders, but his priorities were Byzantine. He needed to control their activities if he was to profit from them.

According to Anna Comnena, Alexius asked Hugh of Vermandois to swear the 'customary oath of the Latins' and it is evident in all the sources that he asked some such oath from all the leaders. He asked it not merely from the princes, but also from all substantial men: Bohemond's nephew, Tancred, evaded the oath at Constantinople, but was made to take it later after the capture of Nicaea, while Anna records that Alexius required it of all sorts of Franks, some so obscure that we cannot identify them. This was a very solemn form of the oath. According to Albert of Aachen: '[Godfrey] gave him [Alexius] his hand and declared that he was his vassal, and all the leading men who were present at the ceremony did the same.' Moreover, this was only one component of the oath. All the leaders also

4 Fulcher, *History of the Expedition to Jerusalem*, 80; Raymond of Aguilers, *Historia Francorum qui ceperunt Iherusalem*, ed. J. H. and L. L. Hill (Philadelphia, PA: American Philosophical Society, 1968), 22–3.
5 Comnena, *Alexiad*, 330–6. Anna, following ancient Greek practice, uses the term Kelts to mean people from the west.

swore to return to the emperor all former Byzantine lands. Many of the sources, including Anna report this, and when possession of Antioch became controversial in the army in the summer and autumn of 1098 the issue was whether Alexius had lived up to the terms of the agreements made at Constantinople. For Alexius had to offer something in return. The Anonymous says that he promised to come to their aid, to give them naval and military support and to send them supplies. Within the limits of practicality, he lived up to these promises, but it is unlikely that he bound himself to come personally to their aid. [6]

The princes were at a grave disadvantage in dealing with Alexius. Their minds were on Jerusalem. They knew little of the politics of the Byzantine Empire. Above all, they were dealing with Alexius as individuals, and those who came later found that others had already taken the oath. Bohemond was familiar with the politics of the area and seems to have tried to construct a united front: about 20 January 1097 he wrote to Godfrey suggesting an alliance against the emperor. When this came to nothing, he decided that the best thing to do was to pose as a loyal friend of the emperor. He took the oath quickly and with minimal fuss and supported Alexius in the quarrel over the oath precipitated by Raymond of Toulouse. He understood that in Byzantine eyes the crusaders were mercenaries of the emperor, and asked to be made 'Grand Domestic of the East' that is to say, military commander in Asia Minor. This would have given him a claim to be commander of the whole crusade. It seems to have been refused, but in equivocal terms which may have allowed him later to pretend that something was promised. The leaders clearly lacked any guidance on how to relate to the emperor. Hugh was in a very weak position. Godfrey was inflamed against the Greeks by rumours about the fate of Hugh and others, so that when he arrived at Constantinople he rejected Alexius' assurances. Alexius withdrew food supplies and when the crusaders started to pillage, skirmishing broke out culminating in a full-scale attack on the city walls close to the Blachernae Palace. In the end Godfrey, isolated and apparently shocked by Bohemond's proposals, made peace. The count of Toulouse arrived at Constantinople on 21 April and immediately refused Alexius' demand for homage, but stated that he would follow the emperor faithfully if he would undertake the journey: Alexius explicitly refused do this. Then Raymond learned that in his absence his army, while ravaging, had been scattered by imperial escorts. He angrily accused Alexius of treachery. The other leaders failed to support him, and Bohemond loudly proclaimed that he was on the side of Alexius. Ultimately a compromise was arranged: Raymond did not do homage but took a form of oath common in his native Provence, by which he promised not to harm the emperor or his lands. [7]

The agreement between the leaders and Alexius was mutually beneficial.

6 Albert of Aachen, *Historia Hierosolymitana*, RHC (Recueil des Historiens des Croisades), 4. 311; *Gesta Francorum*, 5–7.
7 Raymond, *Historia Francorum qui ceperunt Iherusalem*, 23–4; *Gesta Francorum*, 6–7, 11–13.

Alexius had an opportunity to control and profit from the actions of these westerners. They had a promise of support, and the prospect that cities in Asia Minor which they captured would be taken over by imperial forces, thus not depleting the crusade itself. Considering the large forces which had marched into the empire, things had gone remarkably smoothly and fighting had been minimised. Alexius was surprised by the 'People's Crusade', but by the time the other forces arrived he was prepared. The papal legate was not at Constantinople during the crucial period, but he does not seem to have objected to the arrangements. Virtually everybody of any standing had taken the oath: this was important because there were a large number of small contingents in no way connected to the great princes, yet all were now bound to the alliance. The sources stress Count Raymond and Bohemond because of their later importance, but Alexius seems to have gone to some trouble to establish good relations with all the major leaders, and to have enjoyed much success. When the North French finally arrived on 14 May they stayed for about 14 days and Stephen of Blois shortly after wrote to his wife praising 'the pious emperor' who he praised in fulsome terms, 'there has not been a prince so distinguished for general integrity of character'.[8]

The alliance was to be put to the test quickly, for about 6 May the first elements of the crusader army led by Godfrey, Robert of Flanders and Tancred, arrived before Nicaea, the capital of the Sultan, Kilij Arslan I (1092–1107) of Rūm. This important ancient city was formidably well fortified. The walls were about 10 metres high, and their circuit of 4,970 metres was studded with 114 towers, the whole sheltered by a flooded double ditch. On the west the city walls followed the shore of the huge Ascanian Lake, some 40 kilometres long. It was a target of convenience for both elements in the alliance. Alexius wanted to retake Asia Minor from the Turks. Kilij Arslan was the most powerful of their leaders, so the capture of his capital was vital. As for the crusaders, they would have to fight their way through and the capture of the city was an excellent place to begin.

The Turks were formidable militarily. On their native steppe lands they were horse-archers and they had brought this style of war into Asia Minor where there was also steppe grassland. They were, therefore, highly mobile and capable of a ferocious firepower, perhaps a bowshot every 7 seconds, with a range of 60–80 metres or more. They relied on small ponies, and each warrior would have a string of three or more when in action. They were perfectly prepared to close with their enemies because they were equipped with lightweight armour. Lamellar and scale armour consisted of strips or scales of metal fastened to leather or cloth. They employed chain-mail also, sometimes in the form of the *hazagand*, a leather and cloth jerkin in which the mail is under the soft materials. Alexius advised the westerners about Turkish tactics of encircling their enemies, pounding them with arrows to open their formations or drawing them by feigned flights into ambushes. They had obvious weaknesses in close-quarter conflict with the more heavily

8 A. C. Krey, *The First Crusade* (Gloucs, MA: Peter Smith, 1958), 100–1, 107–9.

armoured western knights. However, knightly horses were not especially large: Richard of Aversa is said to have liked a horse so small that his feet almost touched the ground, but generally they were bigger than the Turkish ponies. The Turks lacked infantry which give stability to an army. But the greatest problem of all was that there were not many Turks: it is unlikely that they could raise an army greater than 7,000–10,000, though these would all be mounted. They had been fewer than the Byzantines, but their boldness and ferocity gave them an enormous psychological advantage and enabled them to exploit the divisions of their enemies. The Seljuks of Rūm had developed some specialised forces, for Nicaea was well-garrisoned. But in the crusaders they faced a very large army, and a very determined one.

Nicaea was bigger and stronger than western cities, but siege was a reassuringly familiar activity for the crusaders. Bohemond took up station around the northern wall of the city and Godfrey positioned his army to the east. On 16 May the Provençals arrived, but as they approached the southern gate reserved for them Kilij Arslan launched a savage attack, designed to reinforce the city and to panic the crusaders, vulnerable as they encamped. But the Turkish horsemen had no room for manoeuvre in the narrow plain between the city and the steep hills to the south where Kilij Arslan had chosen to attack, and were drawn into a close-quarter struggle with a numerically superior enemy. Once they were driven off, the army assaulted the city using catapults to cow the garrison and penthouses, armoured roofs, under whose cover soldiers tried to undermine the wall. Casualties were very heavy, and though the Provençals managed to bring down a tower, the results were indecisive. Although the attacks on the city were ferocious, the sources suggest that in this assembly of armies they were poorly coordinated, and hence not particularly effective. About mid-June, however, Alexius sent boats which shut off the lake. This coincided with the arrival of the North French army, and the garrison surrendered secretly to the Byzantines on 19 June. This was perfectly acceptable to the crusaders. Some may have been disappointed that they were deprived of pillage, but Alexius was generous with gifts and food, and in the letters, written soon after by Stephen of Blois and Anselm of Ribemont, there is every indication that relations with the Byzantines were good. The Emperor met the leaders and advised them to send an embassy to Cairo, presumably to play off the Egyptians against the Seljuks of Syria: this was to be a significant factor in crusader success. He also sent a substantial imperial force under Taticius to accompany the crusader army. Taticius was charged with taking over former imperial lands and aiding the crusaders. His forces would also have known Asia Minor very well and been able to advise on routes. On 28 June the army left Nicaea and began the long march, over 1,000 kilometres, to Antioch.

They had a choice of routes, amongst which the most obvious was the old 'Pilgrim Road' due east via Ancyra (modern Ankara) and thence through the Cilician Gates and the Belen Pass to Antioch. Instead, they determined to mount the Anatolian plateau to the south at Dorylaeum (modern Eskisehir). Very soon after their departure from Nicaea on 26 June the army became divided. This was evidently an accident. The crusade consisted of separate armies under their own commanders, each with different proportions of cavalry and infantry and different-sized followings of non-combatants. Maintaining a uniform rate of march would have been difficult. The result was a gap of about 5 kilometres between the vanguard, consisting of the armies of Bohemond, Robert of Normandy and Stephen of Blois about 20,000 strong, and the main force of about 30,000.[9] They were aware that Kilij Arslan was about: he had returned to the fray after his defeat at Nicaea, with an army of 6,000–7,000 mounted men, including his new allies, the Danishmend Turks. Early in the morning of 1 July, at the junction of two valleys just north of the modern town of Bozüyük the Turks fell upon the crusader vanguard. At first sight they must seem to us too few, but simple numbers obscure realities. The crusader vanguard could not have had as many as 3,000 knights, and if they could be drawn into battle and defeated their flight would probably carry away the cavalry of the main crusader force. Bohemond was the only one of the leaders who had ever commanded a large army, and the occasion brought him to the fore. He ordered the unarmed and the infantry to make camp, while the knights moved southwards to shield them from the Turkish attack. The Turks outflanked the western cavalry-line which panicked, and had to be rallied by Bohemond and Robert of Normandy. They fell back on the camp where, supported by the infantry in the tangle of carts, pack-horses, guys and tents, they held the enemy off for 5 hours. The battle ended when the cavalry of the main force came into action and hurled themselves at the Turkish flank. There had been losses amongst the knights and in the camp, but most of the casualties had been suffered by the elements of the crusader force strung out between the vanguard and the main force.

Dorylaeum had been a nasty surprise for the crusaders. Fulcher of Chartres noted the novelty of the enemy's methods: 'All were mounted. On the other hand we had footmen and bowmen. . . . We were stunned. Nor is this remarkable because to all of us such warfare was unknown' he spoke vividly of the moral effect of such tactics, reporting how the non-combatants were 'huddled together like sheep in a fold, trembling and frightened, surrounded on all sides by enemies so that we could not turn in any direction'. The Anonymous was a knight, deeply impressed by 'the skill and prowess and courage of the Turks' and their tactic of surrounding their enemy, showering him with arrows and blanketing him with strange sounds, whooping and drumbeats.[10] Kilij Arslan had come within an ace of success, because his men had actually penetrated the crusader camp and some of the women had dressed up in their best clothes to impress their captors, when

---

9 All the sources agree that there was a division, but while some offer no explanation others offer explanations. This was evidently a matter of debate for long afterwards because Ralph of Caen wrote his life of Tancred after 1113, and he was moved to explain that while some thought the division deliberate, it was actually an accident: Ralph of Caen, *Gesta Tancredi*, RHC Oc.3., 620–1.

10 Fulcher, *History of the Expedition to Jerusalem*, 84–5; *Gesta Francorum*, 21.

the second part of the army came up. As at Nicaea, the Turks had been drawn into a close-quarter battle against a numerically superior enemy. It says much for the crusaders that they were able to hold on in the face of a ferocious attack. But the whole episode revealed the fatal weakness of the crusader army – their lack of a unified command, for the attack was made possible by the separation of their forces. This was a problem that would dog the crusading movement throughout its existence.

But for the moment the Turks of Asia Minor were not minded to challenge the army and there was no serious resistance to their march across Asia Minor. The crusaders travelled south via modern Afyon to Antioch in Pisidia (modern Yalvaç). This was not the most direct route, but it brought them into the well-watered lands of Pisidia south of the Sultan Daglari mountains. This was an important imperial centre and the following spring two Byzantine armies, one following their route, the other coming up from the western coast of Asia Minor, would rendezvous nearby. Thus it seems likely that a conjunction of Byzantine and crusader interests had brought the crusade to this area, after which it proceeded to Iconium (modern Konya) and Heraclea (modern Eregli). There was only sporadic Turkish resistance, partly because the Christian inhabitants of the cities welcomed them. However, this was an appalling time to be crossing the Anatolian plateau, with soaring temperatures, and the crusader forces suffered terribly: 500 are recorded as dying in a single day. But the most important loss was that of horses, for by the time they reached Antioch about 20 October the army had no more than 1,000 animals, many not of the best quality.

As they moved beyond Heraclea the army faced a choice of route. The most direct way to Antioch was to turn south and mount the pass that led to the famous 'Cilician Gates' into the Cilician plain, from which they could pass to Antioch via the Belen Pass, a journey of about 350 kilometres. The alternative was much longer, some 650 kilometres, turning north to Caesarea-in-Cappadocia (modern Kaiseri) and then dipping south in a great arc through Coxon (modern Göksun) and Marash (modern Kahramanmaras). It is extraordinary that they took the longer route. In terms of terrain this offered a terrible passage through very high mountains, with passes just as narrow, and significantly higher, than the 25 metres of the Cilician Gates. Moreover, they did not leave Heraclea until about 14 September, so that the long journey over the mountains was a calculated risk under the threat of early autumn snows. What made the route preferable was the fact it lay through lands heavily settled by Armenian Christians. The liberation of such peoples was one of the ideological goals of the crusade, but it would also create a friendly zone near Antioch and encourage the support of the Armenians of Syria. In the event the main army was highly successful in liberating Armenian lands and enlisting their support, at the same time passing important places over to the emperor. But the march was grim, especially on the precipitous descent below Coxon, that 'damnable mountain' on which so many horses were lost.[11]

11 *Gesta Francorum*, 27.

After Heraclea detachments of the army led by Tancred, nephew of Bohemond, and Baldwin, younger brother of Godfrey, passed through the Cilician Gates into Cilicia. This has generally been presented as a private enterprise affair by these two young men, but they had substantial forces with them which suggests that they were dispatched by the leaders. They were probably despatched to do much the same thing as the main army – to liberate the native Christians, and we know that they were well-received by the Armenians. However, it seems to have been the rule of the army that whoever liberated a place could fly his banner over it in token of possession and this is probably why they quarrelled over possession of Tarsus and came to blows over possession of Mamistra. Baldwin apparently had the bigger force, but eventually he left Cilicia to Tancred because he was persuaded by Bagrat, an Armenian who had travelled with the army since Nicaea, to strike east into the Armenian territories beyond Tell-Bashir. He made such a reputation that Thoros, Armenian ruler of Edessa asked him to go to help protect that city. He arrived there in February 1098, and by early March 1098 had made himself ruler of the city. The Armenian strategy of the First Crusade probably owed much to Alexius, and it was a stunning success, for by 20 October, when the crusaders forced passage of the Iron Bridge across the Orontes, to arrive before Antioch the next day, they had established a powerful circle of Armenian alliances which would help to sustain them in their hour of need in a siege which would last almost nine months.

They were also sustained by sea-power. Urban had written to the port of Genoa to enlist their support, and they certainly sent 13 ships which left on 15 July 1097 and arrived at Antioch on 17 November. But we know that St Symeon, the port of Antioch, and Laodicea (modern Lattakia) were in crusader hands before the army arrived there, and there seems every reason to believe that this was the work of an English fleet of at least 30 ships. This was certainly reinforced by another English fleet which arrived in March 1098, and there are indications that a Flemish fleet was also present early in the siege in these waters. Pisan and Venetian ships are also mentioned as supporting the crusade. The overall importance of naval support is underlined by three simple conjunctions of events: on 17 November the Genoese fleet put into St Symeon and on 23 November the army began to build the tower of Malregard in Bohemond's sector of the siege, and at about the same time constructed a bridge of boats across the Orontes: on 4 March 1098 an English fleet arrived at St Symeon and the next day the leaders resolved to build a tower outside the Bridge-Gate of the city: on 17 June 1099 a fleet put into Jaffa and the supplies they brought and the skills of the sailors enabled the army to build machines with which to assault Jerusalem. But for the siege of Antioch, at least, the most important naval support came from Alexius Comnenus. He controlled Cyprus which seems to have acted as a supply-base and it was to and from this island that shipping plied to support the crusaders. This Greek support, and the Armenian strategy pursued by the army created a logistical base without which the siege of Antioch could never have been brought to a successful conclusion. Problems of logistics and supply would dominate the whole course of the crusade, and in particular of the siege of Antioch.

As the crusaders arrived at Antioch a dispute over military strategy broke out amongst the leaders. It was suggested that the army should mount a distant blockade of the city because they were tired, and many of their forces had been dispersed to protect liberated towns and villages. They could thus sit out the winter and await reinforcements from the emperor and late-arriving crusaders. Nobody is named as putting forward this plan, but in February 1098 it was revived by the Byzantine general Taticius, and it seems likely that it was his plan. He probably knew that this was how the Byzantines had captured the city in 969. The count of Toulouse successfully pressed for an immediate close siege. The reason for this debate is pretty clear: the sheer strength of Antioch. The city is situated on the southern flank of the deep valley where the Orontes flows between the Jebel al-Ansariye to the south and the Amanus mountains to the north. The fortified area is egg-shaped with its points aligned roughly north–south: it is 3 kilometres long and 2 kilometres wide. But only a fraction of the width was occupied by the city. Its western wall touched the river Orontes at the Bridge Gate, but half a kilometre to the east Mount Silpius, on the edge of the Jebel al-Ansariye, rises steeply to just over 500 metres. The walls of the city climb this massif and on their northern circuit was the citadel. It is an extraordinary topography which conferred great advantages on the defenders. The bulk of the walls face barren, waterless broken ground where no besieger could easily accommodate his forces. Moreover, it was easy for the garrison to maintain contact with the outside world across this waste. The strong walls were studded with about 60 towers, the smaller of which were grouped around 12 to 14 very large keep-like towers. In the plain the towers seem to have been much closer together than elsewhere, and the long north wall in this area was reinforced by an outer wall.

The decision to mount a close siege was probably taken because the leaders felt the need to keep their army together. However, it raised further problems. They were clearly not strong enough to assault the city. Nor were they numerous enough to surround even that part of the city which lay in the plain. They had approached from the north and set up camps outside the three gates on the northern wall with Bohemond at the foot of Mount Silpius, Robert of Normandy to his west, and the armies of the count of Toulouse and Godfrey in the angle between the Orontes and the city walls. This left the Bridge Gate open: it commanded the road down to St Symeon, the port of Antioch, and therefore threatened crusader supplies, while the St George Gate on the southern wall was left open. If the crusaders had tried to cover these gates their forces would have been overextended and exposed to defeat in detail by the strong garrison. In the first phase of the siege all went well. The garrison were cowed by the size of the crusader army, there was plenty of food and with the aid of a Genoese fleet they were able to build a bridge of boats across the Orontes behind Godfrey's camp to facilitate communications with St Symeon. They also constructed a siege-castle,

Malregard, in Bohemond's camp. This was primarily intended to fend off raids from the fortress of Harem higher up the Orontes valley. Bohemond led an expedition against this place in mid-November, and though he inflicted casualties, was not able to take it. Between the Bridge of Boats and the Bridge Gate there was constant fighting as the garrison tried to close off their access to the sea. But as winter closed in a second phase in the development of the siege became apparent, food became desperately short and the army entered a period of desperate crisis. The crusaders had eaten out their immediate vicinity, while the mountain snows would have restricted supplies from the Armenian lands.

Authority in the crusader army was exercised by a council of leaders. This was much wider than merely the great princes. It certainly embraced the bishops and the Papal Legate probably presided, but there were many others present and on occasion it may have had the character of a general meeting. It was in this assembly that at the start of the siege the leaders took oath to see the matter through to the end. This was a pretty cumbersome decision-making machinery, but given the make-up of the crusader army it was probably the only one which could be envisaged. Shortly before Christmas 1097 this assembly resolved to send out a foraging expedition under the command of Bohemond and Robert of Flanders, while the rest of the army remained before Antioch. On 28 December this detachment set off south-west across the Jebel al-Ansariye to Ruj in the Orontes valley, where the count of Toulouse had a base, and then ravaged in the Syrian plain. In the vicinity of Albara, on 31 December 1097, they bumped into a large army sent to the relief of Antioch by Duqaq of Damascus. Our descriptions of the battle are pretty vague and its precise location is unknown. What is significant is that while Count Robert attacked the enemy, Bohemond stood as a rearguard to protect the army from envelopment by the enemy. This was a significant adaptation to eastern warfare and the whole event enhanced even further Bohemond's reputation as a leader. But on one thing all the sources are clear – the enemy might have been defeated but evidently not destroyed, for the army could not ravage and returned to Antioch empty handed. There a sally by the garrison had inflicted a severe defeat upon the besiegers. The army was now in deep crisis. They were desperately short of food. Horses were dying, to such an extent that the knights were refusing to cover foraging expeditions for fear of risking their mounts. This forced the leaders to promise to compensate any who lost their horses on such expeditions. Morale was low to the point that the clergy began a series of religious celebrations and fasts to invoke God's aid. It was in these circumstances that Taticius revived the idea of a distant blockade. When this was rejected, he decided to return to Constantinople to urge the emperor to expedite supplies and reinforcements.

Shortly after, the crisis deepened even further when it became known that a major relief force led by Ridwan of Aleppo was approaching. Yaghi-Siyan, governor of Antioch, had taken a very independent line with his master who had been reluctant to send aid, thereby exposing him to attack by Duqaq. The defeat of Duqaq's forces at Albara forced Yaghi-Siyan to turn to Ridwan. Aleppo was only 100 kilometres away, a mere two days journey. On 8 February the crusader leaders met to consider the situation. The upshot was a daring plan. Bohemond was given command and he took all the cavalry they could raise – a mere 700 – and mounted an ambush on the Aleppan army as it approached the city on the old Roman road. The infantry stayed in their camp to fight off sallies by the besieged. The cavalry departed by night to avoid enemy observation, and on the morning of 9 February gathered in the lee of a large *Tell*, now called Tainat Höyügü, just north of the road. This mound is 102 metres high and 622 metres long aligned north-east from the road. Ridwan was probably expecting the crusaders to defend the crossing of the Orontes at the Iron Bridge, 2 kilometres to the rear, so his forces were surprised by the sudden onslaught of five divisions of cavalry which charged into their vanguard. The fighting was fierce, but when Bohemond committed his rearguard, the enemy's forward forces were pushed in confusion into the main force which was not properly deployed, and the whole mass fled before him. This victory, known as the Lake Battle because it took place near to the lake of Antioch, further enhanced Bohemond's reputation as a military leader: this was the first occasion on which a single leader had been placed in command.

On its own this victory might not have been enough to deliver the army from its crisis, though morale improved, especially as an agreement with the Egyptians, whose ambassadors were in the camp during February, was reached and this may have raised the possibility that Jerusalem would be delivered over to them. On 4 March 1098 an English fleet arrived at St Symeon and this ushered in the third phase of the siege. The supplies and expertise it brought enabled the crusaders to build a fort, called the Mahommeries Tower, to block the Bridge Gate. The garrison of Antioch reacted furiously to what it recognised would be a fateful extension of the siege. The supply convoy coming up from Port St Symeon was ambushed on 6 March and suffered heavy losses, but the crusaders drove the enemy back decisively and the new tower was built. This enabled the leaders on 5 April to commission Tancred to command another fortification outside the St George Gate. This same period brought the good news that Baldwin of Boulogne had become ruler of Edessa on 9 March 1098. The consolidation of a Frankish principality on the Euphrates was an enormous help to the main crusading force which now had a new source of food and supplies, though many ambitious knights were drawn off into the service of a prince who had lands and incomes to give.

We know very little about the period between April and the fall of Antioch on the night of June 2/3 1098. Our sources give us hints, but there is no real outline of events. After the Lake Battle Yaghi-Siyan had asked for aid from the Atabeg of Mosul, Kerbogah, who was the representative of the Sultan of Baghdad. Armed with his authority Kerbogah began to raise a great army. In the meantime it seems as if the citizens of Antioch came to some kind of arrangement with the crusaders perhaps to surrender if relief did not arrive within a specified time. This may explain why the crusaders took no military countermeasures against Kerbogah's approach until immediately before his arrival, although they must have known about his army for some time because at the request of local Muslim princes, Kerbogah besieged Edessa unsuccessfully from 4–25 May. Expectation that Antioch might surrender would explain the curious inactivity of the leaders in this period, but with the benefit of hindsight the chroniclers may have decided to bury this episode of collusion with the enemy. Perhaps also the leaders thought Kerbogah was simply attacking Edessa: he ultimately gathered a very large army but it would have taken time to concentrate at Edessa, and in this way his intentions might have been masked. On 25 May Bohemond approached the other leaders. The commander of three towers, a man called Firuz, 'struck up a great friendship' with Bohemond and offered to surrender the towers to him. Bohemond concealed this from the other leaders, and suggested that they all enter into a competition to find a way into the city, the prize for the winner being rule over it. They rejected the notion as inequitable: 'we will all share alike as we have had equal toil', and in any case contrary to the oath to Alexius. By May 29 the crusaders knew that Kerbogah was marching on Antioch and they were forced to reconsider. Even so they were willing to make Bohemond only a conditional promise of the city: he could have it if Alexius did not come to take it. Even in this extreme position, therefore, the crusaders stood by their oath to Alexius. This must make us realise not only how seriously they took their oath, but also how much they owed to Byzantine help, and the extent to which they expected that to continue. Once they had secured Antioch they immediately despatched Hugh of Vermandois to ask Alexius to receive the city, and allowed him plenty of time to mobilise an army.[12]

Events now moved very quickly. On 2 June Bohemond gathered his forces and marched away from the city, as though he was planning to ambush the approaching army as he had done in February. By night his troops returned and secretly gathered in the darkness outside Firuz's towers high on Mount Silpius. Sixty knights climbed into the city before the ladder lowered by Firuz broke. Those in the city opened a postern-gate and Bohemond was able to seize ten towers along the east wall of the city, though Godfrey's attempt to seize the citadel failed. As 3 June dawned the army saw the banner of Bohemond waving on a tower close to the citadel, and as the inhabitants panicked they broke in and sacked Antioch. On 5 June Kerbogah's enormous army approached Antioch. The fall of the city seemed to the crusader chroniclers, writing after the event, as a great delivery, and indeed it was because without the betrayal they would surely have been trapped by Kerbogah.

But their situation was now almost as desperate. Their army was much reduced in size: certainly not as numerous as 30,000, while even the Muslim chroniclers stress that Kerbogah had much larger forces. After the long siege, Antioch was short of supplies, especially as much was wasted in the sack. The citadel remained

---

12 The quotations are from the *Gesta Francorum*, 44–8, whose story of the betrayal has been generally accepted by historians. For Hugh's mission, see *Gesta Francorum*, 72.

in enemy hands and could admit Kerbogah's troops into the city. Kerbogah established his main camp about 5 kilometres north of Antioch. In the first phase of his attack he drove in crusader outposts like that at the Mahommeries Tower, which the defenders abandoned and burned, by 8 June. The crusaders, now clearly trapped, were terrified. There were substantial desertions. Stephen of Blois had withdrawn from the army due to illness some time before, but on seeing Kerbogah's army he turned and fled westwards. This was a heavy blow because at Easter he had been appointed as commander of the whole army. On 12 June Bohemond set fire to parts of the city to drive out elements of the army who were cowering in the houses. By this time Kerbogah had opened the second phase of his attack, sending a very substantial force to set a camp close to the citadel. From there some of his troops attacked the city wall while others entered the citadel and sallied out into the city. On 10 June a crusader sally against this camp was defeated with heavy loss outside the walls. However, the citadel at Antioch is in a very isolated position and the only route down into the city immediately below it is at one point rather less than 30 metres wide. It was here that the crusaders made their stand and ultimately built a wall about 12 June. By this time we are told, the enemy 'moved their camp and set siege to all the gates of the city'. The sheer difficulty of maintaining large forces in the rough ground in the mountains, and the determined resistance of the crusaders, had driven Kerbogah into a third phase of attack – a close siege of all the gates.

Famine and terror raged in the city, but the army had survived and this must have been a factor in reviving its morale. Another was the rise of visionaries. On 10 June a poor Provençal reported that the Holy Lance was buried in the cathedral of Antioch and that it should be dug up on 14 June. The following day a priest, Stephen of Valence, in a vision which seemed to confirm this, reported a vision promising divine aid. Emboldened by these visions, Adhémar demanded that all the leaders take oath not to abandon the army. Both visionaries urged the army to repent and gain the Lord's favour and invoked the notion of the army as the chosen of God. On the 14 June a lance-head was duly recovered and hailed as the Holy Lance which pierced Christ's side, now delivered to the army as a symbol of God's favour. More visions followed, and, in a sign that the leaders were prepared for an inevitable confrontation, on 20 June Bohemond was appointed to command the army. On 28 June the crusader army prepared to break out of the city.

Their force was ordered in five divisions: the North French under Hugh of Vermandois, Robert of Flanders, the Normans under Robert of Normandy, the Lorrainers under Godfrey, the Provençals under Adhemar (because Count Raymond, was left to watch the citadel) and a rearguard under Bohemond. Preceded by a bombardment of arrows which drove back the Turks, they marched out and thrust into the enemy, pushing most of the force outside the Bridge Gate northwards. The North French turned sharp right, resting their flank on the river and the units behind them followed suit. The Provençals behind them marched deep into the plain to outflank enemy detachments, while Bohemond stood in reserve. As the crusader divisions thrust into the enemy, sizeable elements of Kerbogah's army were cut off in their rear, and to counter them a sixth division was formed. Kerbogah had stretched his army, especially his infantry, by blockading all the gates of the city, and these forces were drawn into the conflict piecemeal as they rushed up to help their comrades who were being driven from before the Bridge Gate. As the battle developed along the west bank of the Orontes, Kerbogah's main force, almost entirely cavalry, came rushing down from their camp 5 kilometres to the north, only to recoil in flight as they saw the elements near the city being destroyed. This was an astonishing victory, and in order to explain it much attention has been paid to the divisions in the Muslims' ranks. The Muslim sources emphasise these divisions, caused especially by Kerbogah's attempts during the siege to draw in Ridwan of Aleppo, to the intense annoyance of the Damascenes. These divisions certainly existed, but on the day it is hard to see how they had much influence. There is a much more obvious explanation. Kerbogah had dispersed his army and it was defeated in detail. First the troops outside the Bridge Gate were driven back and overwhelmed, then as groups from the other locations joined they too were caught up in the rout. His main force, largely cavalry, unwisely posted well away from the city, arrived too late to influence events. Kerbogah's army was dispersed and never able to bring its superior power to bear upon the crusaders – in short, it was defeated in detail. This was precisely the risk that had led the crusader leaders to proceed so slowly and so systematically during the long months of their siege.

But the crusader victory was the more remarkable because it was won by an almost entirely infantry army. We have very good reason to believe that by 28 June the crusader army had only about 200 horses left because a substantial number of our sources report the fact. This meant that in each of the divisions of the crusader army there could only have been a handful of cavalry, though presumably they were not evenly distributed. It is remarkable that two great princes, Godfrey of Bouillon and Robert of Flanders, had to beg horses from Raymond of Toulouse on the eve of the battle. As a contemporary chronicler remarked: 'They knew that our knights had been reduced to weak and helpless footmen.' This is why most of the casualties in Kerbogah's army were confined to the infantry, while the cavalry got clean away. Only Tancred's small force pursued the defeated enemy beyond his camp 5 kilometres north of Antioch. It was the suddenness of the crusader strike and the speed and vigour with which the crusaders flung themselves into the battle which enabled them to defeat the enemy in detail before his massive forces could be gathered and brought to bear. This aggressiveness was the hallmark of Bohemond, and it was he who gained enormous prestige from this victory.[13]

With the forces of Duqaq, Ridwan and Kerbogah all defeated, the crusaders had destroyed effective Seljuk resistance to their journey and confirmed possession of

13 Fulcher, *History of the Expedition to Jerusalem*, 103.

Antioch. But their moment of triumph was soured by the outbreak of disputes amongst the leaders. As Kerbogah's army fled the commander of the citadel prepared to hand it over to Raymond of Toulouse, but Norman knights persuaded him to surrender it to Bohemond. Shortly after the leaders met and: 'sent the high-born knight Hugh the Great to the emperor at Constantinople, asking him to come and fulfil the obligations which he had undertaken towards them. Hugh went, but he never came back.' At the same time the Greek Patriarch of Antioch, who had spent some of the siege hung in an iron cage from the front of his cathedral, was restored to his full and proper dignity. This shows how seriously the leaders took the Byzantine alliance and their obligations. But this action was necessary because Bohemond was demanding possession of the city. Shortly after, on 3 July, they met again and resolved to delay their journey until 1 November. It can be no coincidence that this period of four months was precisely the time it had taken the crusader army to march from Nicaea to Antioch in the previous year.

The question of Antioch was already causing divisions in the crusader ranks. Bohemond was determined to seize the city, while Raymond of Toulouse, who held the Bridge Gate and the Governor's Palace, had emerged as his chief adversary. On 14 July Bohemond, acting as though he was already ruler of the city, granted a charter giving trading privileges to the Genoese who in return promised him military support against any enemy attack: 'But they will not fight against the count of St Gilles; if he wishes to withdraw we will give him council, if not we will remain neutral.' In short, all out fighting between the two was seen as a distinct possibility.[14] There were other reasons for delay. Bohemond left the city to consolidate his hold on Cilicia to which Tancred had staked the Norman-Italian claim the year before. This had been confirmed by Taticius just as he left the army in February 1098. Godfrey and Robert of Flanders seem to have had interests in the Afrin valley where they cooperated with Baldwin of Edessa. Raymond of Toulouse held Ruj and in the course of the summer extended it by capturing Albara. Encouraged by prosperity, small forces, like that led by Raymond Pilet, a Limousin, led raids into enemy territory: his came to grief near Marra in mid-August. Moreover, the leaders may have believed that they might have come to the end of their fighting. They enjoyed good relations with the Egyptians. On 26 August the Egyptians, taking advantage of the Seljuk defeats, seized Jerusalem, introducing the possibility of liberating Jerusalem peacefully. Finally the leaders must have been very worried about manpower. Their losses had been enormous, and they were aware that many were being drawn off to Edessa. For the moment the political divisions were subdued and Antioch emptied, leaving it in charge of the papal legate, who, we can safely assume, was a force for concord. It was not to last.

On 1 August Adhemar, the papal legate, died of the plague. As legate of the pope and leader of a substantial army, he was the nearest thing to an overall

---

14 Quotations are from *Gesta Francorum*, 72 and Hagenmeyer, *Kreuzzugsbriefe*, 155–6, tr. J. France.

leader, and nobody could take his place. His death was followed by a series of visions from Peter Bartholemew, who had discovered the Holy Lance. This relic carried by the Provençals in the great battle, was seen as a token of victory. Raymond of Toulouse gained great prestige from the fact that it had been delivered over into his care. But another note appears in the vision of Peter: anger and impatience at the delay in going on to Jerusalem, and this clearly expressed the feelings of many in the army. But the most decisive event was that knowledge spread of an event which had occurred in June during the siege of Antioch. Stephen of Blois, the designated commander of the crusader army, had fled from Antioch at the very moment of Kerbogah's arrival. About 20 June he encountered Alexius and the Byzantine army at Philomelium (modern Aksehir) close to Antioch-in-Pisidia. During the winter of 1097–98 Byzantine forces had cleared the western coast of Asia Minor of Turkish garrisons and pursued them inland as far as the general vicinity of Philomelium. There they were joined by Alexius who appears to have come from the north via Dorylaeum. According to his daughter Anna, who wrote a biography of her father, Alexius was 'ready to march to the aid of the Kelts [Franks] in the Antioch region'. We may take leave to doubt this. Alexius was clearly seeking to profit from crusader successes and his campaign bid fare to consolidate Christian possession of the cities, like Iconium, which they had precariously liberated. But his earlier refusal to join the siege of Nicaea suggests that he was not prepared to risk fighting alongside these western barbarians. Byzantine policy was, broadly, to profit from western successes, while risking the absolute minimum. It is hardly surprising that when Stephen told him about Kerbogah's attack, he broke off his expedition and returned to Constantinople.[15]

Whatever Alexius had intended to do, when news of these events broke in the crusader army, probably in August, they caused an enormous reaction. Bohemond could now reasonably argue that Alexius had failed to meet his obligations, and that, therefore, the city should be his. The count of Toulouse was wedded to the Byzantine alliance. Discontent was rife in the army. On 11 September the leaders wrote asking Urban to come and be their leader. This was a useful delaying tactic as they considered what to do. But in this letter they urged him to come: 'For we have driven out the Turks and pagans; the heretics, however, Greeks and Armenians, Syrians and Jacobites, we cannot expel.' It is extraordinary that the Greeks, whose Patriarch they had restored to full authority only two months before, should now be characterised as heretics. There had been nothing like this hostility to the Greeks in any of the letters written by the crusaders. Philomelium had put the future of the Byzantine alliance in doubt.[16]

---

15 Comnena, *Alexiad*, 345–50.
16 Letter of the Princes to Urban II, 11 September 1098 in Hagenmeyer, *Kreuzzugsbriefe*, 155–6, tr. Krey, *First Crusade*, 195. The problems posed by this letter are noted in Selected Reading at the end of this chapter.

On 1 November the whole army gathered at Antioch for the march to Jerusalem, and a council of the leaders was convened. There was a brutal confrontation between Bohemond who claimed the city and Count Raymond who stood by the Byzantine alliance. The other princes probably rather sympathised with Bohemond, but they were unwilling to say so openly because that might open a permanent breach with Count Raymond whose army was by far the biggest on the crusade. At the same time there was open discontent in the army and real anger at the continuing delay. In these circumstances Bohemond and Raymond patched up what one chronicler called a 'discordant peace', by which Antioch would remain divided between them and both would continue with the crusade. So the Normans and the Provençals fortified their positions in Antioch, but prepared to march on to Jerusalem at the same time. This was hardly a stable settlement. In fact the army went no further than Marra, a little beyond Albara. It is hard to believe that this expedition was any more than a gesture to relieve popular pressure, because only Raymond, Robert of Flanders and Bohemond participated in the siege. Marra, which had already trounced Raymond Pilet, resisted stoutly from 28 November to 12 December, and fell only after a great siege-tower had been deployed. Bohemond claimed a share of the city and tried to trade it off for the count's holdings in Antioch, and this destroyed the 'discordant peace'. There was enormous discontent in the army, the more so in that it was starving because that part of Syria had been pillaged in the past. Some in the army, desperate for food, resorted to eating the bodies of their fallen enemies. The prevarications of the leaders were the subject of widespread anger, and the visions of Peter Bartholemew demanding that the army press on to Jerusalem fanned the flames.[17]

About 4 January Raymond of Toulouse attempted to resolve the impasse in a meeting of the leaders held at Ruj. Bohemond was not present. Raymond offered 10,000 gold *solidi* to Godfrey and Robert of Normandy, 6,000 to Robert of Flanders and 5,000 to Tancred. These were enormous sums: a total of 31,000 gold *solidi* is mentioned, and additional though unspecified sums were offered to unnamed minor leaders. In 1096 the English king had strained to collect 10,000 silver marks: marks, each of which was worth about 10 per cent less than the gold *solidus*. Either Count Raymond had done very well out of the crusade, or he was in receipt of a large subsidy from Alexius whose interests he was championing, or both. These were money fiefs, probably based on the number of knights each controlled. In the case of Tancred we know that he promised to serve Raymond all the way to Jerusalem and he had enlisted 40 knights. From this we can guess that Robert of Flanders had 50–60, and Godfrey and Robert of Normandy about 100 knights. Raymond of Aguilers explicitly tells us that Raymond's own army had at this time 300 knights. In the event only Robert of Normandy and Tancred

---

17 The phrase *discordem pacem* is from Raymond of Aguilers, Hills, *Liber*, 94, tr. Krey, *First Crusade*, 209.

accepted the money, and on 13 January, barefoot, the count marched out of Marra. It is unlikely that with such a small army he intended to go to Jerusalem. This was another extended raid into Syria, made possible by the region's political and military weakness. Cities like Shaizar were happy to offer tribute, food and safe passage to the army, which ambled at a remarkably low speed across the Syrian plain. It took them 32 days to march the 160 kilometres from Marra to Arqa, including 20 rest-days, a crude average daily rate of only 5 kilometres. If we exclude rest-days they were making at best 13 kilometres per day over very easy terrain. Though harassing attacks occurred, there was no significant opposition to their march, which reached Arqa close to Tripoli, on 14 February 1099.

Arqa belonged to the Emir of Tripoli. Its significance for the crusaders was that Tripoli marked the northernmost extent of the influence of the Fatimids with whom the crusaders were still negotiating. We are told that the count wanted to besiege Arqa in order to extort money from Tripoli. The Fatimids were unlikely to be disturbed by such predatory raids on their troublesome vassal at Tripoli, but any further penetration of their sphere of influence would stir up grave military consequences and the leaders still seem to have had hopes of a deal over Jerusalem. In any case the army was not strong enough to challenge the Fatimids. For the count, Arqa, if captured, would give him a base in the important Syrian gap, the route between the inland plains and the coast, passing between the Jebel al-Ansariye to the north and the Lebanese mountains to the south. This would help to round out his lands in Syria. Even if it was not captured, tribute from Tripoli was welcome and the seizure, early in the siege, of the nearby ports of Maraclea and Tortosa (modern Tartus) was a useful bonus.

At Antioch the departure of Raymond had given Bohemond the opportunity to seize the city completely. Godfrey and Robert of Flanders remained within the city and seem to have made no protest at this violent action, perhaps because they felt thoroughly alienated from Count Raymond – we can only guess why, but personal rivalries and dislikes must have played a part. Their position was, however, anomalous, and in the face of rising discontent within their armies, on 2 February they agreed to gather their forces at Byzantine Laodicea in preparation for the march south. In the event they did not get far because they could not bring themselves to join Count Raymond at the siege of Arqa and instead attacked Jabala from 1–11 March. However, early in March Raymond received news of an enemy army marching against him, and so informed the forces at Jabala. Godfrey and Count Robert responded to this appeal to crusader solidarity and reached Arqa on 14 March, only to find that the news was false. There was much tension as a result and they had to be pacified with rich gifts. Tancred apparently stirred the hostility and defected to Godfrey. In these circumstances the siege of Arqa, which has a very strong position and formidable defences, did not flourish. Discontent arose within the army because most of the rank-and-file wanted to press on to Jerusalem. Matters came to a head in early April when an imperial embassy arrived. Alexius complained of Bohemond's seizure of Antioch, but promised troops and money if the army would wait for him to arrive on 24 June, the feast of St John. Count Raymond pointed to the advantages this would bring in terms of military strength and added that to abandon the siege of Arqa would be a defeat. Others, amongst whom Godfrey was pre-eminent, bluntly distrusted Alexius and urged the army on to Jerusalem. As this dispute simmered, it was given another dimension by a further vision of Peter Bartholemew on the night of 6–7 April. In this Count Raymond and the Provençals were clearly proclaimed as the chosen of the Lord and those in other armies as backsliders, even enemies of God. This was totally at odds with sentiment in the army which wanted to press on to Jerusalem, and those who doubted the Lance now came into the open. Peter unwisely offered to undergo the ordeal by fire on Good Friday 8 April, and although the result was ambiguous (some said he was burned, others that he was mobbed by joyous supporters as he emerged from the flames) he soon died. This was a severe blow to the prestige of Count Raymond who was finding it increasingly difficult to hold the army at Arqa. Successful raids on Tripoli and the Syrian gap paved the way for a move south.

Then in early May a Fatimid Embassy arrived, escorting the crusaders own legates back to their army. The Fatimids must have felt they had all the cards. They held Jerusalem. They probably knew of the breach between Alexius and the westerners because after the battle of Ascalon letters from Alexius disowning his western allies were found in the Egyptian camp. They may well have known of the divisions amongst the crusaders. The Egyptians told the crusaders that they would permit groups of not more than 300 to visit Jerusalem. This was scorned, and on 13 May the army as a whole marched south towards Jerusalem. They were now working against the clock because they knew that the Egyptians would mobilise rapidly and that they must seize Jerusalem as quickly as possible. In contrast to the dilatory march from Marra to Arqa, they covered the 360 kilometres from Tripoli to Jerusalem in only 23 days, including only eight rest-days. The crude average daily rate of march was 15 kilometres. However, they actually averaged 24 kilometres per day when they were marching and between Tripoli and Beirut seem to have made 40 kilometres per day for two days. The Fatimid alliance, which they were now breaking, continued to serve them well. There were no substantial forces in the area to oppose them, and Jaffa, the port of Jerusalem, was slighted and abandoned because it could not be defended. Only at the last minute was an elite force of 400 cavalry sent to reinforce the garrison of Jerusalem before which the crusader army arrived on 7 June 1099.

The city was formidable. The valley of Josaphat between the city and the Mount of Olives, made its eastern flank unassailable. The land falls away very sharply from the southern wall of the city, except for a level area about 160 metres wide outside Zion Gate. The approach to the western wall is prohibitively steep, and to the north where the slope was less marked stood the citadel, the Tower of David, and a double wall with a ditch outside which went right along the northern face of the city. It was here in the north that Jerusalem was most vulnerable. At the western end of the north wall the land rises so sharply from the line of the walls that the defences incorporated a very strong bastion, later known as

'Tancred's Tower'. Elsewhere the walls mount every possible rocky outcrop, but their aspect is markedly less than intimidating because the line of the defences is so far below the brow of the hill. This was by no means the sum of the difficulties faced by the crusaders. Their army was by now quite small – probably about 1,500 cavalry in a total force of 12,000–14,000. They were 500 kilometres from the nearest friendly outpost – Laodicea. The whole area around the city had been devastated, and particular care had been taken to destroy timber needed for ladders and siege-engines. The wells had been poisoned and water had to be brought from afar. Some of it contained leeches which choked men when they stuck in their throats. Only 80 kilometres to the south-west was the fortified Egyptian city of Ascalon whose garrison could easily cut their road to the sea, and raiders could find safe shelter in many nearer Muslim communities. And all the while enemy forces were gathering.

The army quickly deployed in two parts for an early attack on the city on 13 June. Outside Zion Gate stood the Provençals, while the rest of the army threatened the north wall. This division may have owed much to the bitter disputes within the army as a whole. The assault was poorly prepared: the only ladder they could make was made from wood which Tancred discovered when driven by dysentery into a cave. As a result it failed and a more systematic approach was adopted. On 17 June a Genoese fleet put into Jaffa and an armed expedition was sent to convoy its goods to Jerusalem. This precipitated heavy fighting near Ramla which the crusaders had captured en route to Jerusalem. So great was their success here, however, that raids on the crusader army ceased to be a major problem. The Genoese were surprised by a Fatimid fleet and beached their ships, except one which got away. But timber for construction, sailors with their building skills, and food in quantity were escorted back to Jerusalem. William Ricau, a Genoese engineer, was employed by Count Raymond to build his great siege-tower outside Zion Gate. To the north-west of the city the North French, under the supervision of Gaston V of Béarn who was something of a specialist in such matters, began to build another siege-tower, and a great ram to break through the outer wall. These siege-towers had to be 15–17 metres high, roughly the equivalent of a modern four-storey house. The kind of structural timber ships could provide was vital, and so were the skills of the mariners themselves. So far had enemy raids abated that more timber was brought from afar and supplies of water regularised. In this way the crusaders were able to build catapults, probably the lever-action stone-throwers called *perriers* and some *ballistae*, great crossbows which were essentially anti-personnel weapons, as well as to manufacture wooden mantles to protect attackers and ladders for the escalade.

The defenders were not idle during these preparations. Opposite the North French they built up the wall with wooden platforms and brought up supplies of rope and timer. They had 14 *perriers* and an unknown number of *balistae*. But they were worried by the proximity of Raymond's attack to the citadel and no less than nine of their *perriers* were deployed against him. Then on the night of 9/10 July the North French suddenly moved their tower and ram from the west to the east end of the north wall, a distance of almost a kilometre. This had obviously been carefully prepared and it completely wrong-footed the defenders who had to improvise defences quickly. It was vital that the ditches outside the walls be filled in because the massive weight of a siege-tower could only move on flat ground. On the north wall the ditch seems to have been filled in very quickly, but Raymond was still completing this process when the assault began on 13 July. In the north the ram was dragged up to the outer wall and broke through on 14 July, despite a vigorous defence which attempted to set fire to it. Once the outer wall was broken the crusaders needed to get rid of the ram because it obstructed the tower, so they set fire to it, while the enemy tried to save it by throwing water. The northern tower suffered badly in this process and it leaned heavily as a result of enemy catapult attack. The southern tower was much stronger, but there had been no room for the Provençals to switch their line of attack and they were subject to a terrible battering and by midday the tower was on fire and retreat was being seriously considered. This was only prevented when news came through of a break-through in the north. There the North French machine had been man-oeuvred right up to the wall. Now the purpose of the towers was to dominate the wall by firepower and so enable others to attack with ladders and mining. However, on this occasion two brothers, Ludolf and Englebert improvised a bridge from the tower directly onto the wall by hacking off some of the wooden structure of the tower. Under cover of a hail of missiles they got onto the wall, and soon the army was penetrating the city. In the south where the count of Toulouse's attack had been stalled, the garrison of the citadel surrendered to save their lives. Many of the citizens got away – we know that they founded a suburb of Damascus and managed to save their sacred books. But many perished including those Jews who took refuge in the Synagogue, although here again we know that many Jews were ransomed because records survived in the Cairo Synagogue. Later Muslim writers grossly exaggerated the massacre at Jerusalem in order to stir up support for holy war, *jihad* in the Islamic world. In fact, the garrison and inhabitants of any city which held out to the last was at mercy, and it would have been impractical to try to restrain troops who broke into a city in the heat of battle. What was far more appalling was that although Tancred offered ransom to many, who took refuge on the roof of the Dome of the Rock, the next day other crusaders killed them, women, children and all, to Tancred's great annoyance. Three days later the crusader leaders decreed that all Muslims remaining in the city should be killed regardless of sex or age. This was undoubtedly in anticipation of the coming of an Egyptian army. These were the horrors of war in a brutal age, made worse by religious zeal and self-righteousness.

On 22 July the leaders met to consider the future of the city. Some of the clergy had already expressed the view that Jerusalem should belong to the Church, and this is perhaps why when the kingship was offered to him Raymond of Toulouse 'confessed that he shuddered at the name of king in Jerusalem'. As a result Godfrey de Bouillon was chosen to rule Jerusalem. Raymond of Aguilers says that he was accorded the title of 'Advocate' and others use the term 'Protector' of the

Holy Sepulchre, and it is possible that this represented a compromise with the clerical view. However, the title of king is used in other sources. Godfrey's reign was so short that the matter is obscure. What is clear is that Raymond was intensely annoyed, and agreed to hand the Tower of David over to Godfrey only under immense pressure. He then went down to the Jordan, which was the tradition for departing pilgrims, and in the meantime Arnulf of Choques, chaplain of Robert of Normandy and chief of those who had doubted the Holy Lance, was chosen as Patriarch. It is impossible not to see in this a rebuff to the count of Toulouse; despite his immense contribution to the success of the crusade he seems to have been a man who others disliked. But, although he was obviously resentful, Count Raymond made no effort to leave: all the leaders must have been aware that the Fatimids would respond and that all were needed for this final crisis.

Egypt had a complex military administration resembling that of the Baghdad Caliphate organised around a ministry of military administration, the Diwan al-Jayish. At Cairo there were huge military storehouses for weapons and supplies, and up to 10,000 regular troops were housed close to the Caliphal palace, with about the same numbers scattered elsewhere. Armenians were especially notable because this was the nationality of the ruling Vizier, al-Afdal, but there were also Berbers, North Africans, Bedouins and others, and the crusaders would note the high quality of black Sudanese infantry. All were organised in ethnic units. Not all the regular forces would have been available to gather at Ascalon, but the fact that al-Afdal himself was to join this expedition suggests that a major effort was made. The result was probably a core of regulars, augmented by volunteers and hired irregulars amounting to 15,000–20,000 troops in all. Since it is clear that Palestine had been stripped of troops at the time the crusaders entered in early May, their mobilisation seems to have taken time. By late July the crusaders were aware that this force was preparing for action. On 9 August Godfrey, Robert of Flanders, Tancred and Eustace of Boulogne marched to Ramla, and on confirming the enemy's presence sent for Count Raymond and Robert of Normandy who marched out on 10 August. On 11 August the army marched south towards Ascalon, a distance of some 40 kilometres. They marched in a lozenge formation of nine squadrons so that if they were ambushed in the rolling plain they could turn to face their enemies from whatever quarter. This is a revelation of how disciplined the army had become. That evening they captured many animals from the huge herds assembled to feed the Egyptians army, and camped at Ibelin, 25 kilometres north of Ascalon.

Next morning, 12 August, the crusader army advanced for battle. They seem to have suffered 25 per cent casualties in the attack on Jerusalem for they could muster no more than 9,000 troops, of whom 1,200 were cavalry. The Fatimids probably thought their depredations of the day before were executed by a mere raiding party and were totally surprised in their camp north of the city. The crusaders deployed in three divisions, with Count Raymond on their right against the coast, the two Roberts and Tancred forming the centre and Godfrey on the left. Al-Afdal was taken by surprise, but his Ethiopian infantry, supported on the flanks by light cavalry, charged out and gave a good account of themselves with their war-flails. But the bulk of al-Afdal's army never seems to have deployed properly and was overwhelmed in a victory which consolidated for the moment the crusader hold upon Jerusalem.

The victory of the First Crusade was a very qualified one. It had established what were no more than bridgeheads in the Holy Lands and in conditions that in some respects rendered their consolidation difficult. Antioch was reasonably securely held, but both Byzantium and the Islamic powers were determined to regain the city. Edessa was a precarious outpost on the Euphrates whose Armenian population was becoming disillusioned with their new masters. At Jerusalem Godfrey held the city with about 3,000 men. These were the principalities of what came to be called *Outremer*, the 'Lands beyond the Sea' held by the Latins. Most of the army, its pilgrimage completed, returned home via Laodicea. By the following year Godfrey's forces were reduced to 200 knights and 1,000 foot and the Patriarch was writing to Germany begging for money so that he could retain troops for the protection of the Holy Sepulchre. Godrey's greatest vassal was Tancred, who held the Galilee, but had only 24 knights in his service. Godfrey fortified Jaffa, the port of Jerusalem whose fortifications had been destroyed by the Egyptians, but this was the only territory he held apart from Jerusalem. The First Crusade had enjoyed enormous good fortune and had succeeded despite very deep divisions. These came to the fore in the immediate aftermath of Ascalon. The citizens were prepared to surrender the city to the count of Toulouse, but Godfrey opposed this and the offer was withdrawn. A little later Raymond had arranged the surrender on terms of Arsuf until Godfrey blocked it.

It is unlikely that there were more than about 5,000 crusaders in all the principalities and little enclaves which they held, and many of those must have been non-combatants. But the crusaders remained highly aggressive. Despite his tiny force, Godfrey attacked Arsuf, and though forced to lift the siege in December 1099, by the following August he was receiving tribute from the city. In May 1100 he and Tancred ravaged the environs of Damascus and forced Duqaq to a peace. Time after time tiny numbers of crusaders engaged large enemy forces. They were capitalising upon the ascendancy the First Crusade had established. In the late summer of 1099 a Pisan fleet under the command of the new papal legate to the east, Archbishop Daimbert of Pisa, arrived in the east, after various clashes with the Byzantines, to aid the crusade. Bohemond, harried by the Byzantines, persuaded Daimbert to attack their base at Laodicea at the very moment when the forces of Count Raymond and the two Roberts arrived on their way home. They were scandalised by this open attack on the Greeks. Count Raymond was a firm Byzantine ally and the two Roberts doubtless wanted to make sure of their journey home to the west. The siege was abandoned and Raymond spent the winter at Laodicea before going on to Constantinople the following year.

However, Daimbert, supported by the Pisan fleet, stayed in the east. At

Christmas 1099 Bohemond travelled with Baldwin of Edessa and Daimbert to Jerusalem in fulfilment of his vows. At Jerusalem Daimbert, apparently with the backing of Bohemond, demanded the deposition of Arnulf of Choques, whose election may have been provisional, and himself became Patriarch. It seems as if he knew of sentiment in the army at the time of the capture of Jerusalem that Jerusalem should belong to the Church, and he demanded that both Bohemond and Godfrey recognise him as overlord. This was probably welcome to Bohemond. His title to Antioch was open to challenge on the grounds that he had usurped it. Such high ecclesiastical recognition gave him legitimacy while at the same time, because of distance, posing no practical threat to his position in his principality. For Godfrey this was most certainly unwelcome, for he now had a master in his own city. Further, at Candlemas 1100 Godfrey conceded a quarter of Jaffa and the whole of Jerusalem to Daimbert, though on condition that he would hold the incomes of Jerusalem until such time as he had made suitable conquests for himself. It was, of course, the strength of the Pisan fleet and Godfrey's need for military support that made him agree to all this. In June he aided Tancred in the north, but shortly after fell ill. The arrival of a Venetian fleet enabled Godfrey to envisage an attack upon Acre which was to be led by Tancred and the Patriarch, but on 18 July he died. This precipitated a crisis.

Tancred and Daimbert, for reasons which are unclear, decided to use the Venetian fleet to attack Haifa which fell on 20 August. In the meantime Godrey's *familia* had secured the tower of David and Jerusalem, and sent for Baldwin of Edessa to succeed his brother at Jerusalem. Alarmed by the blatant disregard for what he conceived as his rights, Daimbert wrote to Bohemond to ask for his support. But his messenger was detained at Laodicea by the Provençals, and in any case Bohemond had already left Antioch to assist the Armenian lord of Melitene against the aggression of the Danishmend Turks. On 15 August Bohemond was ambushed and captured by the Danishmends who held him until May 1103. Baldwin appointed his cousin, Baldwin of le Bourcq to rule Edessa and made his way to Jerusalem where Tancred sulked and refused homage. Daimbert was finally persuaded to crown Baldwin but at Bethlehem. Daimbert's position weakened, especially after Tancred became regent of Antioch early in 1101. Shortly after he was driven from Jerusalem and in 1102 replaced by Evremar of Choques. Baldwin, we are told, had barely 300 knights and about the same number of foot to hold Jerusalem, Ramla, Jaffa and Haifa and his situation was precarious in the extreme. In 1101 he drove off an Egyptian army at the battle of Ramla, but he must have looked forward to reinforcements promised from the west.

Urban II seems always to have recognised the need for conquest in the east. He had urged the crusader cause at the Roman Synod of April 1099 and written to Anselm, Archbishop of Milan, suggesting that he use the forces he was raising to attack Egypt. After his death on 29 July 1099 (it seems unlikely he ever knew of the capture of Jerusalem) his successor, Paschal II (1099–1118) was just as enthusiastic, writing to France directing the clergy to raise new armies, and most

particularly to pressurise those who had failed to make good on earlier commit-
ments, for the support of the precarious new settlements in the Holy Land. The
Pisan and Venetian fleets seem to have been part of this continuing crusade, and
the very large army of Lombards under Archbishop Anselm left for Constantinople on 13 August.

The so-called 'Crusade of 1101' was in fact a continuation of Urban's
expedition of 1095, although it is likely that recruitment was enormously
encouraged by news of the capture of Jerusalem. On 18 November a great council
at Poitiers was addressed by papal legates and a large army enlisted under William
IX, duke of Aquitaine. A very big Burgundian force was led by Odo, duke of
Burgundy and Stephen, count of Burgundy. Another distinct and large group
gathered under the leadership of William II, count of Nevers, Auxerre and
Tonnerre. In northern France the deserters, Hugh of Vermandois and Stephen of
Blois headed a smaller contingent which never functioned as a separate army. In
South Germany Welf IV, duke of Bavaria emerged as the leader of a very large
army, most of whose leading members were intimately associated with the reform
papacy in the long wars of the 'Investiture Contest'. Overall, these were men of at
least equivalent rank to those who had led the First Crusade, and it is unlikely that
the numbers involved were any less. However, Paschal II never seems to have put
any thought into organisation, perhaps overconfident after the capture of
Jerusalem. In fact, all the armies seem to have regarded themselves as free to do
what they wanted, and there was no junction of forces as there had been in spring
1097 at Constantinople. But across the Bosphorus the Lombards were joined in
their camp at Nicomedia by the North French under Stephen of Blois, the
Burgundian contingent and a group of Germans led by Conrad, the Constable of
Henry IV. The Lombards got to hear about the captivity of Bohemond and they
were determined to rescue him even though this meant venturing into wild and
unknown territory. Alexius was not anxious to help Bohemond and the north
French, led by the experienced Stephen of Blois, wanted to go on to Jerusalem.
Also at Constantinople was Raymond of Toulouse who had stayed for most of
the preceding year at Laodicea, and he was appointed by Alexius to lead the
expedition. They set off for Jerusalem in late June, but almost immediately the
Lombards showed their determination to attempt to free Bohemond and
the other leaders had to concur because they were so numerous.

A coalition of Muslim powers had been formed by Ridwan of Aleppo. They
disposed of a large army and, as a result of their confrontations with the First
Crusade, did not rush into battle. After the crusaders seized Ankara, the Turks
began a campaign of harassment made the easier because the crusaders did not
know the country and quickly began to run out of food in north-eastern Anatolia.
Only when the westerners were exhausted and in danger of starvation did the
Turks bring them to battle near Merzifon in mid-August. A total breakdown of
discipline in the crusader camp and a terrible panic enabled the Turks to destroy
them, though most of the leaders got away. The army of the Count of Nevers

arrived at Constantinople after the Lombards had left and tried to follow them, but despairing of this turned south from Ankara to Iconium and Heraclea, only to be destroyed by the victors of Merzifon about 26 August. The Aquitanians under William IX had joined in a formidable army with the Bavarians and arrived at Constantinople. Their army met the victors of Merzifon and was destroyed near Heraclea about 20 August. The survivors seem to have blamed Alexius for these disasters. Many held Alexius' close ally, the count of Toulouse to blame, and Tancred imprisoned him when he arrived at Antioch. Despite these disasters, most of the leaders survived, though Hugh of Vermandois died. Probably at least 4,000 troops arrived in the Latin Kingdom in late 1101. Some of these joined with a Genoese fleet to capture Tortosa early in 1102. As a result, when, in May 1102 Baldwin confronted another Egyptian attack he was supremely confident. On 17 May he charged the Egyptian army, but was repulsed. He fled to Arsuf, then summoned all the troops of the kingdom and a few days later defeated the Egyptians who had failed to follow-up their advantage. In 1105 the Egyptians allied with Damascus and challenged Baldwin again at Ramla, and this time were defeated by skilful hard fighting. In 1104 Bohemond, now free, Baldwin of Edessa and all the princes of the north were defeated at the battle of Harran, of which almost nothing is known, ending hopes of expansion towards the Euphrates.

The tide of conquest unleashed by Urban II in 1095 was clearly now spent. The First Crusade had succeeded because it caught Islam divided and vulnerable, at a time when its spirit of *jihad* had all but vanished. The crusade had immense spirit, was led by able princes and enjoyed remarkable luck. The leaders adapted their fighting methods to the conditions of the east and never allowed their divisions to interfere with their primary objective – Jerusalem. The great expeditions of 1101 were poorly coordinated and lacked real unity. They came up against an enemy no longer quite so divided, and animated again by a spirit of *jihad*. Once the impetus of conquest was gone, the tiny principalities would have to expand slowly, and by traditional means.

Moreover, tensions between Byzantium and the westerners were high in the wake of the quarrel over Antioch and the defeats in 1101–02 and clearly Asia Minor was not going to be reconquered. Therefore, there was no 'land-bridge' from the 'Catholic core' to the Latin states of the east. In these circumstances everything depended upon sea-power, and this meant the willingness of the Italian city-states to support the crusaders in the east. The situation was complicated because the First Crusade was only one of a number of expansions into the Mediterranean which impacted upon Byzantium. The rise of the Norman power in Italy-Sicily was another, as was the growth of the trading cities of Venice, Genoa and Pisa. Crusading was an ideological movement, yet it could never be distinct from the practical politics created by these expansionisms. Byzantium had long been distinct from western Europe, and was itself the core of a civilisation which dominated the Balkans and eastern Europe. The First Crusade essentially proposed a merger with the 'Catholic Core'. But the new world inaugurated by the First Crusade created complex conditions which reacted upon that ideal.

SELECTED READING

There are a number of general histories of the crusades and crusading. A very fine and avowedly popular introduction is to be found in M. Billings, *The Cross and the Crescent. A History of the Crusades* (London: BBC Publications, 1987) which has a good study of the First Crusade, 15–77. T. F. Madden, *A Concise History of the Crusades* (Lanham, MD: Rowman and Littlefield, 1999) serves much the same purpose. J. Riley-Smith, *The Crusades. A Short History* (London: Athlone, 1987) is perhaps the most useful. H. E. Mayer, *The Crusades*, tr. J. Gillingham (Oxford: Oxford University Press, 1972), presents an older view of crusading focused on Jerusalem and has a useful chapter on the First Crusade, 38–57 as has J. Richard, *The Crusades c.1071–c.1291*, tr. J. Birrell of a French original of 1996 (Cambridge: Cambridge University Press, 1999), 19–76. On the history of the First Crusade this chapter draws heavily upon J. Riley-Smith, *The First Crusade and the Idea of Crusading* (London: Athlone, 1986) and for military affairs J. France, *Victory in the East. A Military History of the First Crusade* (Cambridge: Cambridge University Press, 1994). Also useful is T. Asbridge, *The First Crusade* (London: Free Press, 2004). For an understanding of how money was raised by crusaders, see H. E. J. Cowdrey, 'Pope Urban II's preaching of the First Crusade', *History* 55 (1970), 177–88, Riley-Smith, *First Crusade and the Idea of Crusading* and his *The First Crusaders 1095–1131* (Cambridge: Cambridge University Press, 1997) which provides an excellent list of likely crusaders. Little has been written on the vital question of logistics, though this is touched upon in France, *Victory in the East*. On the journey itself, see J. W. Nesbitt, 'Rate of march of crusading armies in Europe. A study in computation', *Traditio* 19 (1963), 167–82, and M. Bennett, 'Travel and transport of the crusades', *Medieval History* 4 (1994), 91–101. On the technical aspects of war, see J. France, 'Technology and the success of the First Crusade', in Y. Lev (ed.), *War and Society in the Eastern Mediterranean, 7th–15th centuries* (Leiden: Brill, 1997), 163–76. There are a number of biographies of crusader leaders: J. C. Andressohn, *Ancestry and Life of Godfrey de Bouillon* (Bloomington, IN: University of Indiana Press, 1947); J. Brundage, 'Adhemar of Le Puy: the bishop and his critics', *Speculum* 34 (1959), 201–12; J. Brundage, 'An errant crusader: Stephen of Blois', *Traditio* 16 (1960), 380–95; C. W. David, *Robert Curthose, Duke of Normandy* (Cambridge, MA: Harvard University Press, 1920); J. H. and L. L. Hill, *Raymond IV of Toulouse* (Syracuse: Syracuse University Press, 1962); M. M. Knappen, 'Robert of Flanders on the First Crusade', in L. J. Paetow (ed.), *The Crusades and other Essays presented to D. C. Munro* (2nd edition, New York: Books for Libraries, 1968), 79–100; R. L. Nicholson, *Tancred. A Study of his Career and Work in their Relation to the First Crusade and the Establishment of the Latin States in Syria and Palestine* (Chicago, IL: Chicago University Press, 1940); R. Yewdale, *Bohemond I Prince of Antioch* (Princeton, NJ: Princeton University Press, 1917). On relations between Alexius and the crusaders the most important general works are those of R. J. Lilie, *Byzantium and the Crusader States, 1096–1204*, tr. J. C. Morris and E. Ridings of a German original of 1981 (Oxford: Clarendon Press, 1994) and J. H. Pryor, 'The oath of the leaders of the First Crusade to the Emperor Alexius: fealty, homage', *Parergon* 2 (1984), 111–41, but there is useful information in the biographies of crusader leaders and see also J. Shepard, 'Cross purposes: Alexius Comnenus and the First Crusade', in J. Phillips (ed.), *The First Crusade. Origins and Impact* (Manchester: Manchester University Press, 1997), 107–29 and G. Loud, 'Anna Komnena and her sources for the Normans of South Italy', in G. Loud and I. N. Wood (eds), *Church and Chronicle in the Middle Ages: Essays presented to J. Taylor* (London: Hambledon, 1991), 41–57; J. France, 'The crisis of the First Crusade: from the defeat of Kerbogah to the departure from Arqa', *Byzantion* 40 (1970), 276–308. The best introduction to the politics of the Middle East at the time of the crusade is P. M. Holt, *The Age of the Crusades* (London: Longman, 1986) and to the origins of the Turkish domination in Asia Minor Cahen, *Pre-Ottoman Turkey*. On the key figure of Ridwan of Aleppo, see R. W. Crawford, 'Ridwan the Maligned', in J. Kritzeck and R. Bagley-Winder (eds), *The World of Islam. Studies in Honour of P. K. Hitti* (London: Macmillan, 1960), 135–9. For Turkish fighting methods the best introduction is to be found in various parts of D. Nicolle, *The Medieval Warfare Source-Book*, vol. 2 (London: Brockhampton, 1996), which is useful for Middle Eastern warfare generally, and there are specialist studies in V. G. Parry and M. E. Yapp (eds), *War, Technology and Society in the Middle East* (London: Oxford University Press, 1975) and an interesting reflection on the Turkish horse-archer by C. R. Bowlus, 'Tactical and strategic weaknesses of horse archers on the eve of the First Crusade', in M. Balard (ed.), *Autour de la Première Croisade* (Paris: Publications de la Sorbonne, 1996), 159–66. On the geography and roads of Asia Minor the work of D. French is indispensable, notably his 'A study of Roman roads in Anatolia', *Anatolian Studies* 24 (1974), 143–9. On the Armenian strategy and its purposes, see France, *Victory in the East*, 190–6, and on Baldwin's takeover in Edessa, A. A. Beaumont, 'Albert of Aix and the county of Edessa', in L. J. Paetow (ed.), *The Crusades and other Essays presented to D. C. Munro* (2nd edition, New York: Books for Libraries, 1968), 101–38. The whole question of sea-power and the Crusade, which is of immense importance, has received far too little attention. A major contribution has been made by J. Pryor, *Geography, Technology and War. Studies in the Maritime History of the Mediterranean 649–1571* (Cambridge: Cambridge University Press, 1987). For the First Crusade, see J. France, 'The First Crusade as a naval enterprise', *Mariner's Mirror* 83 (1997), 389–97 and *Victory in the East*, 209–20. For a discussion of the visions and the person of Peter Bartholemew, see France, 'The crisis of the First Crusade' and C. Morris, 'Policy and visions. The case of the Holy Lance at Antioch', in J. Gillingham and J. C. Holt (eds), *War and Government in the Middle Ages. Essays in Honour of J. O. Prestwich* (Woodbridge: Boydell, 1984), 33–45. On the Fatimids and their army, see Y. Lev, *State and Society in Fatimid Egypt* (Leiden: Brill, 1991) and on their navy W. Hamblin, 'The Fatimid navy during the early crusades', *American Neptune* 46 (1986), 77–83. On Jerusalem at the time of the crusader siege, see J. Prawer, 'The Jerusalem the crusaders captured: contribution to the medieval topography of the city', in P. Edbury (ed.), *Crusade and Settlement* (Cardiff: University College Cardiff Press, 1985), 1–16. S. D. Goitein, 'Contemporary letters on the capture of Jerusalem by the Crusaders', *Journal of Jewish Studies* 3 (1952), 162–77 discusses the survival of Jews after the sack of Jerusalem. There is considerable controversy over the title of Godfrey de Bouillon. J. France, 'The election and title of Godfrey de Bouillon', *Canadian Journal of History* 18 (1983), 321–9 argues that he was only an advocate, but J. Riley-Smith, 'The title of Godfrey de Bouillon', *Bulletin of the Institute of Historical Research* 52 (1979), 83–6 leans towards *princeps* while A. V. Murray, 'The title of Godfrey of Bouillon as ruler of Jerusalem', *Collegium Medievale: Interdisciplinary Journal of Medieval Research* 3 (1990), 163–78 is convinced that he was a king. It was long disputed that Daimbert of Pisa was a Legate but this has been accepted since the discussion by B. Hamilton, *The Latin Church in the Crusader States. The Secular Church* (London: Variorum, 1980), 14. On the expeditions of 1101 the work of J. L. Cate, 'The Crusade of 1101', in K. Setton and M. W. Baldwin (eds), *A History of the Crusades*, 6 vols (Madison, WI: University of Wisconsin Press, 1969–88), 1. 343–67 has been substantially updated by A. Mulinder, *The Crusading Expeditions of 1101–2* (Unpublished Ph.D. thesis, University of Wales Swansea, 1996) on which I have relied, which emphasises the very close relationship between Count Raymond of Toulouse and the Emperor Alexius.

4

CRUSADE AND EXPANSION IN THE EARLY TWELFTH CENTURY

The First Crusade seemed to contemporaries a wondrous event by which God bestowed the Holy Land on His faithful. The novelty of the event and the staggering scale of its achievement astonished contemporaries. The monastic chroniclers of the first quarter of the twelfth century sought to find a place for this phenomenon in the Christian revelation. They elaborated the notion, found in its simplest form in the eyewitness accounts, that the crusade was the army of God chosen by Him to do His work. In this view the crusaders enjoyed victory not merely because they fought well, but because by their spiritual exercises, and above all by their penance, they pleased God who favoured them with triumph. The crusade was a religious exercise, not merely a war. This feeling was reinforced by the failures of the expeditions of 1101–02 which underlined the success of 1095–99 and were attributed to God's vengeance on the pride and luxury of the leaders. It is important to understand this view of events because the First Crusade became the model for all others. When Eugenius III (1145–53) issued his Bull for the Second Crusade he was consciously modelling it on the appeal of 1095. All subsequent appeals embodied this view of the events of 1095–99. But this 'Idea of the Crusade', important as it was, needs to be separated from the realities which the course of the campaign itself revealed.

Nobody who reads the story of the First Crusade can fail to be impressed by the burning religious fervour which at times inspired the army. Without a real belief that they were set on the path to salvation, it is difficult to see how anybody could ever have set out, let alone endured such terrible hardship. But ruthless self-interest and opportunism were also powerful influences. The First Crusade had no clear structure of command, and this was in the nature of an expedition which was drawn from many peoples amongst whom rank was the determinant of authority. This would be a problem for almost all crusades. By the summer of 1098 the expedition was breaking up as differences over attitudes to the Byzantines, personal ambitions and personal feuds amongst the leaders came to the fore, and these were still evident on the morrow of the victory at Ascalon as the story of how this city avoided surrender reveals. Even during the siege of Antioch there were frequent complaints of lesser crusaders pursuing their own ends by taking over towns and fortresses away from the combat zone. The seizure of Edessa seems to have made this problem more acute, and defections by men seeking land there certainly depleted the army as it moved south to Jerusalem. The veneer of ideological unity was broken and the kinds of individual expectations which underlay almost all aspects of the expansion of the 'Catholic core' came to the fore. Once the new states in the Holy Land were founded their princes behaved much as marcher lords in Wales or Saxony had – with little regard for ideological factors and every regard for self-interest, even to the extent of alliance with the enemy. Of course this could not be revealed too openly because the settlers were aware that a façade of ideological unity was essential to impress the peoples of the west. However, as in Spain, though the main line of division was between Islam and Christianity, for as William of Tyre observed:

> War is waged differently and less vigorously between men who hold the same law and faith. For even if no other cause for hatred exists, the fact that the combatants do not share the same articles of faith is sufficient reason for constant quarrelling and enmity.[1]

But bitter conflicts were waged amongst Christians and amongst Muslims also. Moreover, the First Crusade was the victory of an alliance. Byzantine and Armenian support were vital factors in its success. This was something that the 'Crusade Idea' disguised, though the papacy always recognised. Finally, it was a grim and close-fought military campaign in which military skills, determination and much plain good luck played a major part. This kind of analysis was not emphasised by the clerical writers who were the main publicists of later crusades. The image of crusading, of ideological commitment, was somewhat at odds with the reality of the business itself as all who went to the east would discover. But the image of crusading, compelling as it was, served another essential purpose which was to clothe its originating institution in an aura of glory.

The chief beneficiary of the whole astonishing sequence of events was the papacy. The crusade had made real its longstanding pretension to the leadership of the world and now it stood as a giant over the secular powers because the whole immense event was unequivocally its brainchild. The confidence which this generated is evident in the much sharper and far-reaching claims for papal authority characteristic of this period. The greatest spiritual figure of the age was St Bernard of Clairvaux who wrote a tract, De Consideratione, which was in effect a long letter of advice to Pope Eugenius III, a fellow-Cistercian monk. In it Bernard proclaimed the extent of papal power in uncompromising terms: 'Glorify your hand and your right arm and deal out vengeance on the nations and punishment on the peoples; bind their kings in chains and their nobles in fetters of iron.'

---

1 William of Tyre, Chronicon, ed. R. B. C. Huygens, 2 vols, Corpus Christianorum Continuatio Medievalis 63–63A (Turnhout: Brepols, 1986), 13.16, tr. E. A. Babcock and A. C. Krey, A History of Deeds done beyond the Sea by William of Tyre, 2 vols (New York: Columbia University Press, 1943), 2.25.

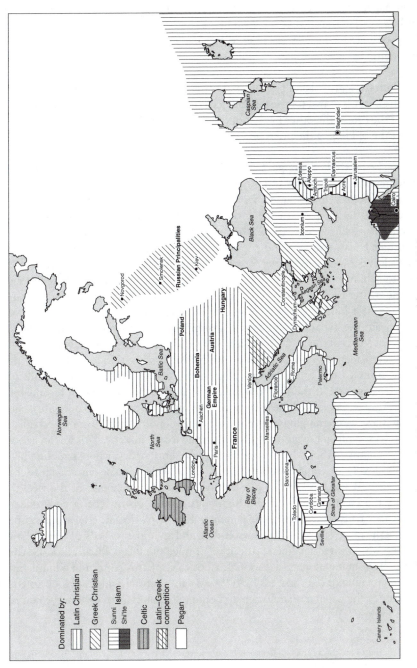

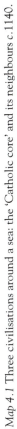

Map 4.1 Three civilisations around a sea: the 'Catholic core' and its neighbours c.1140.

Bernard was aware of the dangers of the situation in which such power is vested in the papal office because 'you are the successor not of Peter, but of Constantine' but he regarded this as rightful. And, most particularly, he defended the right of the papacy to make war, as long as neither pope nor priest drew the sword personally:

> Both the spiritual and the material swords . . . belong to the Church, but the latter is drawn for the Church and the former by it. One by the hand of the priest, the other by that of the soldier; but the latter surely is used at the bidding of the priest and by the order of the emperor.[2]

Long before 1095 the popes had to a degree sanctified war when it was in their own interests. The prestige and the glory of this new instrument, derived from the capture of Jerusalem, provided them with a novel means of exerting influence. Before and during the crusade Urban had offered its characteristic spiritual benefit, the indulgence, to those who fought in Spain. Crusading was particularly important because it gave the papacy initiative in secular affairs which it had always lacked; we should never forget that one of Urban's purposes in 1095 had been to enhance papal standing in Christendom. The prominence of the papacy was the greater because much of the 'Catholic core' was in the hands of aristocrats who were not kings. After the Investiture Contest the German monarchy was never again the dynamic force for expansion in eastern Germany which it once had been. Many of the leaders of the First Crusade had been French, but the royal house of Capet was not especially prominent amongst them. The growing contribution to the Spanish wars from north of the Pyrenees owed little to Capetian support. In the Mediterranean the Italian city-states were formidable and aggressive, but lacked the pretensions of kings. In Scandinavia new Christian monarchies were emerging and needed papal support if they were to establish themselves. Only in England was there a formidable monarchy. This was an age of princes, amongst whom the papacy was a giant. The papacy, whose structure had been radically reformed under Urban II, developed the most advanced governmental machine in the whole of the west. In the course of the twelfth century the papal court became a highly articulated instrument of governance which can truly be called a papal monarchy. In particular, the papal courts became the most developed in Christendom and an immense body of Canon Law grew up which directly affected the lives of huge numbers of Catholics. By the mid-century many monarchies were anxious to copy this pattern of administrative improvement. The success of 1099 was an essential building block in the structure of the papal monarchy which became so dominant a force in the course of the twelfth century.

2 The footnotes are from *De Consideratione*, cited and translated by E. T. Kennan, 'Antithesis and argument in the *De Consideratione*', in M. B. Pennington (ed.), *Bernard of Clairvaux. Studies presented to Dom Jean Leclerq* (Washington, DC: Cistercian Publications, 1973), 95, 100,102.

The strength of the papacy and the glory of 1099 enabled it to stand as the ultimate authority in what was increasingly called 'Christendom'. This was a word with an ancient pedigree and a great future. In its most simple sense it encompassed all of the peoples who accepted the religion of Christ. But the word also had a political connotation because under Constantine the Great 'Christendom' was to all intents and purposes, coterminous with the Roman Empire and the Carolingians inherited much the same idea, seeing the emperor as the guarantor of the unity of the Church. From the eleventh century the word is used to include all the peoples of the 'Catholic core' and the 'Catholic fringe' and soon others who were recruited into it. Diplomatically, it could be used to include all other Christians, but its implication was always that these were the peoples of the true faith under Rome. In effect Christendom was the most commonly used collective for the lands and peoples who accepted Rome's authority. The Roman pontiff, now increasingly referred to as the 'Vicar of Christ', was in some undefined way supreme over all Christendom and the army of God was his to direct. The pretensions in this direction, so evident in earlier papal history, were given a reality by the success of 1099.

The growth of the Church as a highly centralised papal monarchy is reflected in the elaboration of the law of the Church. This culminated in the early 1140s in the production of Gratian's *Decretum*, the authoritative collection of canon law. It is interesting that this document attempted no definition of papal power or of its great instrument which we call crusade. Gratian set war in the traditional circumscriptions of Augustine. The dramatic deliverance offered by Urban II and his successors was not really encompassed by canonical definitions until the thirteenth century. From the perspective of the mid-twelfth century papacy and crusade were linked and apparently boundless institutions. This is why we are left in doubt as to what a crusade was. Contemporaries did not use the term, and usually referred to those who went to the east to fight as *peregrini*, pilgrims. This word is used indifferently of those on a merely pious journey, on an organised expedition or on an individual but armed journey to Jerusalem. This is hardly surprising, especially as pilgrims to the Holy Land were expected to rally to the military support of the kingdom if needed. In May 1102 the unexpected arrival of men from a pilgrim fleet saved Baldwin I after his defeat at Ramla, while in 1153 pilgrims were virtually conscripted into the army of Jerusalem besieging Ascalon: 'the Christians despatched messengers from the army forbidding all sailors and pilgrims, by the king's command, to return home. All, under promise of pay, were invited to take part in the siege, a labour so acceptable to God.'[3] The elements of crusading existed: papal initiative and authorisation, the indulgence or remission of sin, pilgrimage, the vow and the taking of the cross, but not until the time of Innocent III were they brought together in formal definition. There were crusades

---

3 William of Tyre, Book 17, Chapter 24.

long before crusading: events and experience defined what became a movement. And a movement there had to be, because by 1105 it was clear that easy conquest had ceased and that a grim struggle was ensuing in the east. This was made the more difficult because in one respect the crusade had not succeeded. Bohemond's seizure of Antioch, meant that relations with Byzantium remained difficult. The Turks of Asia Minor had not been crushed and the 'Crusade of 1101' showed that there was no secure 'land-bridge' to the Middle East. As a consequence, the naval power of the Italian maritime states became essential to the establishment of the Latin enclaves in the Middle East.

And it must be emphasised that the crusade was not simply a matter of freeing the Holy Land. It was an instrument of papal power to be used as the pope thought fit – though of course he would have to persuade others that it was appropriate. The underlying ideas of a penitential reward for participation in war inspired by the papacy had first been elaborated in Spain before 1095. In 1114 a crusade was proclaimed against the Muslims of the Balearic Islands and eastern Spain. In 1118 Gelasius II (1118–19) promoted a crusading expedition which, with French help, captured Zaragoza. In 1120, after the heavy defeat of the principality of Antioch at the battle of the 'Field of Blood', Calixtus II (1119–24) sent out letters proclaiming crusades to Spain and to the Holy Land and threatened sanctions against those who, having taken the cross, had not departed by Easter 1124. This appeal gave rise to the large Venetian fleet which helped to capture Tyre on 7 July 1124. A further crusade was proclaimed to Spain in 1125 and to the Holy Land for an attack on Damascus in 1128. The crusade, however ill-formed, was never solely associated with Jerusalem. Even before his appeal at Clermont in 1095 Urban had asked Robert of Flanders to help the bishop of Arras regain lands lost to Henry IV 'for the remission of your sins', and Paschal II in 1103 wrote to the same potentate urging him to attack the imperialists at Liège in a war whose merits he equated with the First Crusade. In 1105, after his release from captivity and the defeat at Harran, Bohemond found his lands under heavy military pressure from the Byzantines. He travelled to the west where he received a hero's welcome and married Constance, of the royal house of Capet. Bohemond persuaded Paschal II to proclaim a new crusade which raised large numbers of troops especially from France. Bohemond led these forces against Byzantium in a bid to seize Constantinople in 1107, but was defeated. It has been suggested that Bohemond tricked Paschal into declaring a crusade which Bohemond diverted without his consent against Byzantium, but it is at least as likely that Paschal had clear intimations of Boemond's purpose and was not averse to the notion of a more sympathetic ruler being imposed at Constantinople. In 1127 Honorius II (1124–30) urged a crusade against the Normans of South Italy and in 1132 Innocent II (1130–43) was calling for a crusade against his rival for the Holy See, Anacletus II (1130–38). His appeal was systematised by the Council of Pisa in 1135 which offered the same remission as had been decreed by Urban II. Now it is true that we cannot, in all these cases, find all the elements of a crusade, but since this was a time when definition had not proceeded far, that is hardly surprising. This is a remarkable record of adaptation, especially when we consider that until 1122 the popes were deeply preoccupied by the Investiture Contest.

The early twelfth century saw an astonishing expansion and diversification of Christendom. Peasant populations attacked the wastelands and overcame the problems of topography and climate to expand the area of cultivation. Cities and trade grew apace. In eastern England Herbert Losinga (1091–1119) bought the bishopric of Thetford from the crown in 1091 for at least £1,000. He transferred it to Norwich, a much bigger place, in 1094. He was an entrepreneur and developer on a remarkable scale, to whom many of the cities and small towns of the area owed their prosperity and growth. By the end of the twelfth century a great cycle of trade fairs in Champagne stimulated city-growth in the area and served as a vital connection between the northern economy and that of the Mediterranean. The eleventh century had seen an efflorescence of new religious orders. The most successful of these experiments became the Cistercians. They sought solitude and settled in empty lands and frontier zones, but these were often the very areas which benefited from the economic development of the age. In northern England the great Cistercian abbeys of Fountains, Jervaux and Riveaux fostered sheep-ranching on the wild moors and so profited immensely because wool was an important commodity in international trade. In Flanders the Cistercian house at Les Dûnes flourished on the proceeds of wool production to such a degree that it even owned its own merchant ships. The Augustinian Canons ministered to the new commercial and industrial classes who lived within city walls and flourished as these groups became richer and more important.

But the richest of all trades remained that across the Mediterranean, principally in the spices and the other luxury goods of the east. Italy was the vital funnel by which Mediterranean trade flowed northwards, and its cities were the biggest in Catholic Christendom. Milan had defied the Emperor Henry IV throughout the Investiture Contest and it was followed along the road to independence by a whole network of others, such as Cremona, Como, Brescia and Verona. But the most extraordinary consequence of the economic development of Italy was the rise of its maritime cities. Venice, throughout the early Middle Ages, had been a Byzantine outpost and held a privileged trading position in the empire which it continued to enjoy despite throwing off imperial domination. Indeed, in the late eleventh century its position was enhanced by the decline of Amalfi and the South Italian cities as the Normans penetrated the area. However, as the Norman regime consolidated, South Italy became a booming maritime rival. Participation in Byzantine trade was an enormous boon to Venice because Byzantium shared richly in the economic revival of the later tenth and eleventh centuries. Far Eastern goods, especially spices, were imported across the Indian Ocean and found their way to Constantinople via Basra and Baghdad. An alternative route along the 'Silk Road' from China terminated on the Black Sea, equally to the benefit of the Byzantines. However, much of the Indian Ocean trade entered Egypt via the Red Sea, and as a result Alexandria became an increasingly important port of call for western merchants. Trade with the Byzantine and

Islamic lands seems to have increased enormously. In the western basin of the Mediterranean Genoa and Pisa looked enviously on Venetian wealth as they attempted to increase their share of Mediterranean trade.

For maritime powers such as these, trade was only part of the equation of wealth and power. Merchantmen were also naval assets which could serve for the projection of power. Predatory naval raids were part of the pattern of life in the Mediterranean and the ports of its western basin, amongst which the Italian city-states of Pisa, Genoa and Venice were pre-eminent, kept specialised vessels, war-galleys, which were vitally important in a sea where the winds were all too often light. Piracy and warfare between Christian fleets was endemic. There was no real distinction between pirates, traders and navies, and this would continue to be true throughout the period of the crusades. Pisa and Genoa were willing participants in naval adventures, especially against the Muslim bases on Corsica and Sardinia. In 1087 the Genoese led a great expedition that seized the island of Pantelleria and ravaged the Tunisian coast. In part this was a response to Tunisian raids upon their shipping encouraged by the Zirid ruler Tamin (1062–1108). The rise of Norman power in South Italy seemed to threaten Venetian control of the Adriatic, prompting the Genoese to support the Hautevilles. When the Normans invaded Byzantium in 1081 Venice allied with Alexius I Comnenus, receiving substantial privileges by the 'Golden Bull' of May 1082, which entrenched their position in the Byzantine and Black Sea trade. These privileges included a quarter for their merchants at Galata with legal jurisdiction over their own people there, and freedom from most trade imposts. The link between trade and military power was all too clearly understood by these cities. In 1111 Alexius Comnenus bought off the Pisans, who had been raiding Byzantine shipping, by extending to them some of the privileges already granted to the Venetians, including a quarter in Constantinople. The First Crusade received substantial support from the Genoese, probably because they recognised the opportunity to establish secure bases outside the Byzantine/Venetian sphere which would enable them to tap into eastern trade. Genoese ships put into St Symeon, the port of Antioch, bringing essential supplies during the long siege of 1097–98 and later brought supplies to Jaffa during the siege of Jerusalem. One of their leaders, William Embriaco, supervised the construction of siege-machinery for the count of Toulouse and went on to found a dynasty which was for long influential in the affairs of the Holy Land. As a record of their contribution to the success of the First Crusade, the Genoese built a memorial in Jerusalem. A great Pisan fleet reached the Holy Land, as we have noted, just after the capture of Jerusalem and helped to fortify Jaffa which then became a raiding centre for Christian ships who disrupted the trade of the Muslim cities of the littoral. The Venetian victory over the Fatimids in 1123 was the indispensable prelude to the capture of Tyre in the following year. Throughout the twelfth century the sea-power of the Italian cities was the primary means of communication between *Outremer* and its western homelands. The Fatimid fleet offered only a passing challenge. An Egyptian fleet bottled up the Genoese in Jaffa during the First Crusade, obliging the ships to unload their cargoes and scuttle. They mounted infrequent raids, such as that against Beirut in 1126, when the ships ran out of water. Not until the Saladin was there a real effort by the Muslims to mount a real maritime challenge, and that was short-lived.

This remarkable western dominance is very hard to explain, because in earlier times Arab fleets had been formidable. We need to remember that the sources for Muslim shipping have been little explored. However, westerners had always had an appetite for the luxuries of the east and the enormous profits which they generated, and this provided a powerful incentive for westerners to invest in sea-borne trade. There were plenty of Muslim merchants, but their most profitable sphere of activity was across the ocean to India and the Far East. Once the position of Muslim traders in the Mediterranean was challenged, they were found to be at a grave disadvantage. The ships of the day all handled badly. The round ships with single masts which were the staple merchantmen for the Christians and their enemies were clumsy, while the specialised warship, the oared galley, was long and thin which made it difficult to handle except under oars: it also lacked carrying capacity and therefore range. In these conditions ships preferred to cling to the coast, and the wind-pattern of the Mediterranean favoured the routes along its northern shores. The key landfalls for east–west trade were Sicily, Crete, Rhodes and Cyprus. These areas were all under Christian control and, therefore, much more amenable to Christian than to Muslim shipping and the crusader capture of the Palestinian littoral increased this advantage. Further, in the Islamic lands bordering the great sea timber was in short supply. In the thirteenth century the Mamluks of Egypt bought timber from Anatolia for their fleet and in the fourteenth and fifteenth centuries the Ottomans used these rich forests to create their navy. However, the Seljuk Turks of twelfth-century Anatolia were land-locked, while the great Seljuks of Baghdad taxed the trade of the Indian Ocean. Lebanon had been an important source of timber supply for Egypt, but this was lost after 1099. Christian galleys carried their water in timber casks which were lighter and more capacious than the ceramic pots used by the Egyptians, but this should not have limited them badly as at first Egypt controlled most of the ports of the Palestinian littoral.

In the end it seems to have come down to a matter of will. The Italian city-states competed ferociously with one another and were ready to seize any opportunity. Supporting the crusade was highly speculative, but it brought rich rewards because pilgrims needed to travel to Jerusalem by sea, and paid for their passages in cash. The great convoys that crossed the sea to Acre and other ports twice a year could then use those profits to buy luxury goods to sell on in the west. This was rich pickings for which the Italians were ready to fight, even each other when necessary. Islamic traders could do well from the trade across the Indian Ocean to Basra and the Red Sea, then sell on via Alexandria to westerners and North Africans who in turn traded with Spain. As long as the Christians did not interfere with the routes along the North African coast there was little need to change, and Egyptian government became weaker and weaker as the twelfth century wore on. The Italian dominance of the Mediterranean which made possible the crusading movement was a consequence of the remarkable economic expansion of the eleventh and twelfth centuries. The rivalries and tensions between Venice, Genoa, Pisa, Marseilles, Montpellier and Barcelona, like the rivalries and tensions between western kingdoms, principalities and dynasties, fuelled expansion.

Competition between the various elements of a divided Christendom continued to be a major driving force of expansion, but there was a countervailing trend of great importance for the future. The increasing wealth and complexity of society turned men and women to central authority to provide a framework of law and stability. Change meant a need to adopt institutions and ideas. It was to the monarchies and to the papacy that people looked in these new circumstances. Churches profited enormously and churchmen looked to monarchy to protect them. In northern France, Suger, abbot of St Dennis, initiated a massive expansion of the cultivated area on the enormous waste-lands of his abbey. He was only one of many churchmen who enjoyed the profits of this colonisation, but their riches brought them into conflict with powerful lay lords. This is why Suger, abbot of St Denis, when he wrote his biography of Louis VI (1108–37), portrayed him as a kind of internal crusader fighting troublesome barons in the cause of peace. Frederick Barbarossa sought to revive Roman Law as a basis for his imperial authority, and it is no accident that it was in his lands that the university of Bologna emerged as a centre of legal education. In England a system of judicial and financial administration was developed under Henry I (1100–35) of whom it was said: 'He ennobled others of base stock who had served him well, raised them, so to say, from the dust, and heaping all kinds of favours on them, stationed them above earls and famous castellans.'[4]

Under Henry II of England (1154–89) bureaucracy became so elaborate that in the late 1170s, one of its senior members wrote a handbook for new administrators, *The Dialogue of the Exchequer*.[5] In 1188, after the collapse of the Kingdom of Jerusalem, the papacy proclaimed a new tax, on moveable wealth all over Christendom, which kings were quick to imitate. At a quite different level systems of accountancy and control were needed to govern the estates of monarchs, churches and aristocrats. Trade required regulations of weights and measures and security. The result was a marked trend towards a new regularity and system in the government of Church and monarchy. This in turn generated a boom in education and intellectual development that has been called the 'Renaissance of the Twelfth Century'. The effects of this should not be exaggerated. Monarchy remained highly personal and monarchs had to establish

---

4 Ordericus Vitalis, *Historia Aecclesiastica*, ed. M. Chibnall, 6 vols (Oxford: Clarendon, 1969–79), 6.16–17.

5 Richard Fitznigel (or Fitzneale), *Dialogus de Scaccario*, ed. C. Johnson, revised by F. E. L. Carter and D. E. Greenway (Oxford: Clarendon, 1983) provides an excellent translation.

good relations with great aristocrats who continued, everywhere, to control local government and to be their chief advisors. Monarchical ascendancy was precarious and depended heavily on the personal qualities of individual kings, for as yet there was no bureaucratic machine capable of ruling and commanding respect. Monarchs had to be managers of their aristocracies and they did not always succeed. The English monarchy under Henry I became somewhat bureaucratic, but when he died and was succeeded by a lesser man, England dissolved into civil war and Normandy was conquered by the counts of Anjou. There was nothing inevitable about the triumph of monarchical power, and indeed some states failed. Even the papacy, for all its high claims, was fragile. Popes were the 'Vicars of Christ', but they too depended on active collaboration from the bishops and abbots, who were overwhelmingly aristocratic and tied into royal and dynastic interests, to exercise practical power. The enormous internal expansion of the monarchies of Christendom would be of great importance for the future, but as yet it was limited and they remained in the shadow of Rome.

The confident and prosperous society emerging within Christendom quite evidently stimulated emulation to an even greater degree. In Scandinavia in 1100 only in Denmark was Christianity totally dominant. By the mid-century the Danish kings closely resembled their fellows in the rest of Christendom. Elsewhere in the north progress was slower, but the Christian missionary drive and the emulatory desire of the local elites drove it on. In Sweden the pagan sacrificial cycle performed every 8 or 9 years by the king powerfully mobilised opinion against christianising rulers, and may have led to their deaths into the twelfth century. Monks in the north was never missionaries. The leaders of the Scandinavian churches needed monasticism to accommodate the range of spiritual experience offered by the new religion and they attempted to bring the spiritual experience of their peoples into tune with that of the 'Catholic core' which they followed in new developments and new ideas. Because this was an essentially twelfth-century development, the new order of the Cistercians was pre-eminent in Scandinavia. Further east, Bohemia, Hungary and Poland became fully assimilated. Poland and Hungary contained strong Orthodox enclaves and, therefore, felt Byzantine influence. Moreover, they bordered the steppe and the need for light cavalry to guard against raiders meant that their military and social development was somewhat different from that of the more westerly parts of Christendom who they shielded from this particular threat. The need for light cavalry to counter steppe-raiders fostered the growth of a numerous class of petty nobles in Poland, Hungary and elsewhere.

Success inspired emulation. Conquest remained slow and difficult, and for very good reasons. Although society was becoming richer, kings still could not afford to maintain standing armies. Forces were raised for short periods, usually in the months after the harvest, and kept together for the minimum of time because of cost. It mattered little whether soldiers were raised from the lands of a ruler or paid as mercenaries, costs were high. In 1184 the lands of Baldwin V of Hainaut (1171–95) were invaded by the count of Flanders, the archbishop of Cologne and the duke of Brabant. Gilbert of Mons, Baldwin's Chancellor, commented on the huge costs incurred in raising troops to avert this threat:

> During this war the count of Hainaut had the services of about 300 paid knights (*stipendiarios milites*) together with 3,000 sergeants some on foot some mounted. In addition he enjoyed the services of about 300 knights, many of them from France and Lorraine, whose expenses he paid although they received no pay. At that time the Lord Count Baldwin drew into his service a handsome, brave and gallant knight, Baldwin Carun, son of Roger de Rume, who had broken with the count of Flanders over some difference; he gave to Carun a fief in liege homage valued at some £600 secured against the renders of the village of Querenaing close to Valenciennes. In the same way he secured the services of a poor knight, Hugh d'Antoing, brother of Gosselin and William d'Antoing, by giving him the renders of the village of Artrain in Brabant which he had received from his ancestors as valued at £400 per annum. Baldwin de Neuville, brother of Eustace, and Robert de Beaurain, a knight of proven valour and great renown were both retained in much the same way; the former received a fief of £300 with the assignment of £20 on the *winage* of Maubeuge, the latter land at Forest with £200 per annum. Walter de Wargnies, a gallant knight adept in war and all necessary skills, received in liege homage the sum of £700 guaranteed against the incomes of the village of Bellaing near Valenciennes. Richard d'Orcq received £200 for a similar fief. In addition the count conferred *fiefs rentes* on some brave and renowned knights of France, Robert de Condé, Gérard de Géri and William de Pierrepont: to the first £20 in deniers, to the second £20 and to the third 20 marks.

Unsurprisingly, as soon as the fighting, though not the war, was over, the count dismissed all his mercenaries:

> The count of Hainaut paid those who had supported him for their costs and their losses, thanking them and cordially permitting them to take their leave. All the men who he had hired, knights, vassals, horsemen, foot-soldiers and crossbowmen were honourably and generously paid.[6]

The high costs of war, the short-term retention of armies, and the problems of maintaining garrisons in conquered lands explain why conquest was so difficult. In general, central authorities entrusted it to frontier peoples with a vested

---

6 Gislebertus Hanoniensis, *Chronicon*, ed. L. Vanderkindere (Brussels: Kiessling, 1904), 174. Translated as Gilbert of Mons, *Chronicle of Hainaut* tr. L. Napran (Woodbridge: Boydell, 2005).

interest, and intervened fitfully. Within the 'Catholic core' the imposition of a new domination usually involved winning over the elites to the new regime: when Geoffrey Martel seized Tours from the count of Blois in 1044 he left undisturbed those vassals who were prepared to accept the new regime and expelled only those intimately connected with the Blésois, and even some of these were ultimately permitted to return. William the Conqueror extended a similar indulgence to many Anglo-Saxon notables in 1066, but a series of piecemeal revolts, combined with the very heavy losses sustained in the battles of 1066 by the Anglo-Saxon nobility, enabled him to establish an almost entirely Norman ruling class by 1086. Where elites resisted fiercely conquest was very problematic.

Wales is an interesting case-study. It was a small, thinly populated, relatively poor and deeply divided land, in close proximity to powerful and rich neighbouring England, yet over two centuries were to elapse after 1066 before it was finally conquered. The complex geography of Wales had long encouraged the development of very localised political units. They were obviously vulnerable to attack because they were small, but geography also served as a powerful protector. The Conqueror established powerful earldoms at Chester, Shrewsbury and Hereford to guard his border, but they and their men quickly took up the challenge of conquest. Norman power advanced quickly into south-eastern Wales by the 1080s, while Montgomery and its locality were annexed to the earldom of Shewsbury, and by 1090 seemed to offer the prospect of a rapid advance. In 1081 William the Conqueror mounted a great progress in Wales to follow-up the victories of his vassals. The Normans were so dominant in North Wales that in 1092 one of their own was appointed to the see of Bangor. In 1093 Normans killed Rhys ap Tewdr, ruler of Deheubarth, at Brecon and, encouraged by William II who mounted a royal expedition in 1097, their power surged into West Wales with the conquest of Cardigan and Pembroke, and the advance in the south into Glamorgan. However, this surge was partially driven back by the early twelfth century because Welsh resistance stiffened and many of the great earls and lords of the March, deeply involved in Anglo-Norman politics, fell victim to conflicts at the royal court. This tendency of the important magnates to be preoccupied with English affairs left advance in the hands of lesser people, fragmenting the offensive effort, particularly when they quarrelled amongst themselves. Henry I backed expansion in Wales, but the outbreak of civil war in England under Stephen (1135–54) saw notable setbacks as the Lords of the March became deeply involved in the fighting. Moreover, the Welsh adapted skilfully to the limited technical advantages which the intruders enjoyed. As early as 1094 Pembroke castle was subjected to a systematic siege, while many of the Norman castles of the north were captured by Gruffudd ap Cynan of Gwynedd (1081–1137). Norman cavalry may have come as a surprise at first but their limitations in hilly Wales soon became apparent, and at the battle of Crug Mawr in 1136 a Welsh army with 2,000 cavalry defeated a substantial Marcher force. But the decisive advantage of the attackers was command of the sea. This was particularly important in the south where a line of castles on the major rivers anchored the Norman dominion. But even here in the south, where the power of the invaders was most manifest, they faced grave difficulties in cowing the native Welsh, and had to resort to importing foreigners to provide a strong and loyal economic base. In Gower and in Pembrokeshire plantations of reliable subjects were established. Prominent amongst such people were Flemings. In 1109 Wizo, acting for Henry I, established a Flemish settlement at Wiston which, with its motte-and-bailey castle, would for long stand as an outmost bastion on the frontier of secure control in West Wales. To the north lay the Preselli mountains which for long formed a buffer-zone between the Anglo-Normans and the native Welsh. But importing dependable populations and securing their settlement was complex and expensive. By the mid-twelfth century the Anglo-Norman March extended deep into South Wales, while substantial gains had been made in the 'Middle March' west of Shewsbury, but the North Wales largely reverted to Welsh control. The further progress of conquest was uncertain, but most of the native princes were prepared to recognise the supremacy of the English monarchy and were starting to emulate the institutions of their enemies by building castles, reorganising their lands and copying their methods of war.

The papacy had taken a very active interest in events in Spain since the later eleventh century but this had very little impact on Spanish expansion. The great leap forward in Spain, the capture of Toledo in 1085, had been achieved by Alfonso VI of Léon-Castile without any external aid. But he had difficulties with his own nobles and was deeply suspicious of Rodrigo Diaz de Vivar, 'El Cid', who he exiled for undertaking a raid on Toledo in 1081. The Cid then served in the army of Muslim Zaragoza, though he always refused to fight Alfonso. Alfonso, troubled by independent-minded nobles, was deeply suspicious of other Christian rulers and checked the growth of the little kingdom of Aragon growing by supporting its enemy, Muslim Zaragoza. The strength of the Almoravids made expansion difficult for Léon-Castile, and it was weakened when Alfonso's son, Sancho, was killed at the battle of Uclés in 1108. As a result, when Alfonso died in the following year he was succeeded by his daughter Urraca who was quickly plunged into civil war with her second husband, Alfonso I of Aragon (1104–34). It was to the Ebro valley and Aragon that the great French expedition of 1087 had marched, and in the early twelfth century crusading continued to focus on this area of north-eastern Spain. This was not only a matter of contiguity. The small kingdom of Aragon was struggling to emerge from the shadow of Léon-Castile and was very ready to welcome such supporters. In 1095 Huesca fell, but the great step forward came under Alfonso I the Battler (1104–34) who welcomed foreign crusaders and established close ties with the world beyond the Pyrenees. By 1118, with the aid of French and Normans nobles, he was threatening Zaragoza. In that year Gelasius II held a great council at Toulouse and launched a crusade which Alfonso led to the siege of Zaragoza. Amongst its leaders was Gaston V of Béarn, who now used his expertise with siege engines, so notable at the siege of Jerusalem in 1099, to bring this city to surrender. The Ebro valley fell quickly and in 1125

Alfonso led a great expedition to Granada, the very heart of Muslim power: he failed to capture it, but this was a propaganda coup. His reign clearly established Aragon as a major force. Léon-Castile recovered somewhat under Alfonso VII (1126–57) whose efforts strengthened Toledo. However, the Christians signally failed to take advantage of the decline of the Almoravids, which was very evident by the 1130s. From the Christian point of view this was the more unfortunate because general opinion in Muslim Spain welcomed the Almohads, who had replaced them in North Africa. Their rise coincided with Christian divisions. Under Afonso I (1128–85) Portugal increasingly went its own way. The death of Alfonso the Battler without heir ultimately led to a union of Aragon and Barcelona under Raymond Berengar IV (1131–62) of Barcelona, but much land was lost to Léon-Castile and in the Pyrenees Navarre remerged as a kingdom. In 1157 on the death of Alfonso VII his lands were divided between Sancho III (1157–58) of Castile, and Fernando II (1157–88) of Léon and Galicia.

There were few battles during the long wars in Spain. Sieges were not uncommon, but for the most part the war was a grinding affair of raids and counter-raids. The occasional leaps forward, as in 1085, 1094 and 1118, were the results of political fragmentation combined with the effects of this 'wearing-down war'. The Almoravid revival ended any hope of a rapid *reconquista*. For much of the eleventh century the struggles of the small Christian kingdoms had had little ideological resonance, and they had fought almost as much amongst themselves, often in alliance with Muslim rulers, as against Islam. The papacy, for reasons of its own, had tried to shape the conflict into a holy war, and towards the end of the century this enjoyed a degree of success. The concomitant of Alfonso the Battler's encouragement of foreign crusaders was the increasing number of 'French' clergy in the Church of Aragon, and to a limited extent this spilled over into Castile. As a result, the wars in Spain more and more took on the complexion of crusades. Spanish chroniclers of the twelfth century evinced little interest in events in Christendom, but they were deeply interested in what happened in Jerusalem. Under Alfonso the Battler the new military monastic Orders of the Temple and the Hospital, which had emerged in the Holy Land, were invited into Spain and when he died childless he bequeathed his kingdom to them. Though this arrangement did not stand, the Orders became a mighty force in Aragon and were soon copied in Castile. But overall the Spanish reconquest was remarkably self-contained and its progress in the first half of the twelfth century was subject to much the same limitations as that of the Anglo-Normans in Wales. Interestingly, all the kingdoms suffered from the independence of powerful nobles and cities whose military power enabled them to defy Muslim attacks and royal authority. Marches were difficult areas for monarchs to rule.

And so it was in Germany. The expansion along the Baltic coast, which had been checked so sharply in 983, resumed only tentatively in the eleventh century. The German Christian frontier rested on the river Elbe, and between its valley and that of the Oder lived a loose federation of tribes, the Wagrians, Abotrites, Polabians, Rugians and Liutizians, who were collectively known as Wends. They were settled agricultural peoples with aristocratic elites of their own, and it is quite obvious that the civilisation of the Germans attracted at least some of these. The major tribal group of the Abodrites was ruled by the Nakonids, a dynasty who were sometimes prepared to espouse Christianity and to pursue a policy of coexistence with their German and the Danish neighbours. This encouraged a major missionary effort sponsored by Adalbert, archbishop of Hamburg-Bremen. The Nakonid, King Gottschalk, patronised this mission, but many of his nobles were emphatically pagan and in 1066 he was deposed and German influence suffered a major check. The turmoil of the Investiture Contest meant that the major forces of Germany were preoccupied, and the affairs of the Baltic coast were left to local powers. Amongst these were the border people of northern Saxony, Nordalbingia, where a violent frontier society emerged, living by raids on their Slavonic neighbours. Gottschalk had gone rather too far in his pursuit of western ways, but his career showed the attractiveness of German civilisation. His son, Henry, in alliance with the East Saxons, achieved a great victory in 1093 which enabled him to become prince of the Abotrites and to impose Christianity, though this was only skin-deep. The situation once more became fluid after the last of his sons died in 1129. The Nakonids had married into the Danish royal house, and this involved the Wends in the Danish civil wars which in 1134 resulted in the accession of Eric II (1134–37). There was, in fact, a marked period of confusion on the Wendish frontier in the first quarter of the twelfth century because there was no obvious dominant power in the area. Indeed it was the Polish ruler, Boleslaw III (1102–38) who forced the Pomeranians of the Baltic shore east of the Oder to accept Christianity, though he had to rely on Bishop Otto of Bamberg to implant the new religion. Duke Wartislaw of Pomerania, however, soon felt the need for a rapprochement with the Germans, and Bishop Otto's mission came under their patronage as the duke became a vassal of the empire.

Lothar of Supplinburg, duke of Saxony and emperor (1125–37) faced bitter hostility from his Hohenstaufen rival to the German throne. As a result he was never able to focus on the eastern frontier despite his obvious interest in the area. He established the outpost of Segeberg in 1131 during his intervention in the Danish wars, but this place was soon destroyed and both he and his successor as Emperor, Conrad III (1138–52), had other preoccupations. The great see of Hamburg had long inspired missionary activity and was deeply interested in converting the Slavs, but it was reliant on the military power of others to defend it against Slav attack. Adolf of Schauenburg, count of Holstein (1110–26), and his son Adolph II (1126–64), were formidable and ambitious princes who aspired to a powerful position in the area. However, they had a rival, Henry of Badwide, who enjoyed good relations with the Saxon dukes. When the Emperor Lothar died in 1137 Saxony was plunged into civil war between Albrecht the Bear and Henry the Proud over succession to the duchy, freeing the Slavs to raid the Germans in their traditional way. In response to this, Adolf II and Henry of Badewide ruthlessly advanced into the Slav lands destroying many of the native leaders and establishing themselves in Wagria and Polabia respectively. The establishment of fortifications manned by well-armed men was a key factor in this sudden advance, but the real novelty was the settlement of western peasants as a loyal populace. In 1143 Adolf founded Lübeck, which rapidly became a very important Baltic trading city. Adolf's success was really the culmination of decades of German pressure, but his pre-eminence was to be short-lived. In May 1142 the Saxon succession dispute was settled in favour of Henry the Lion, whose rival, Albrecht the Bear, was confirmed only in his control of the North Mark (Brandenburg). The missionary, Vizelin, long active in the area, was created bishop of Oldenburg, providing a veneer of Christian respectability.

The lands of the pagan Slavs formed a great temptation to the German elite on the Saxon frontier, and they were able to justify their ambitions because they saw the Slavs as inferior pagans who, moreover, had at various times in the past paid tribute to Germans and tithes to the Church. The process of conquest was slow because the normal high costs and problems of war were complicated by the prolonged political fragmentation in Denmark and Germany. The Investiture Contest was a major cause, but so were the rivalries of various Christian powers, such as Denmark and the German rulers, and succession disputes with the consequent needs for allies played their part. The spirit of this northern expansion was aggressively secular. Lords saw land and power, while merchants wanted to secure a share of the rich trade in furs, amber and northern produce which came through the Slav lands. The religious divide and the stubborn paganism of the Slav elites gave an ideological colour to the conflict. The see of Hamburg had a traditional interest in conversion, which interested Christian lords because of its potential to pacify newly conquered subjects. In 1108 there was an appeal for a 'crusade' from the Magdeburg diocese, calling Christians to come to seize the lands of the Wends. Thereafter there was an increase in the tempo of missionary activity. But religion was merely a veneer. Adolf II did not thrust Christianity upon his new Slav subjects. His hold on his new territories was far from secure, and he reached an accommodation with Nyklot, the pagan Abodrite chieftan, under which both cooperated in developing the frontier zones. But these circumstances in the north were all about to be modified by two factors: the rise of Henry the Lion as duke of Saxony, and the impact of the crusading spirit which had such prestige as a result of its successes in the eastern Mediterranean.

Quite commonly conditions for the settlers in the Holy Land are portrayed as being radically different from those they were used to in their homelands. This was not altogether true. The climate was different from that of the more northerly parts like England, France and Germany, but not so novel to Italians and Provençals who formed a substantial element of the population. These Latins were a tiny minority in the Middle East dominated by their own upper class. But rule by tiny elites who had only limited contact with the mass of the population was the common everywhere. This was most clearly the case in England where Normans were so distinct from the bulk of the population. The great gap which yawned between the conquerors and the native populations in the Middle East was religion, but even that should not be exaggerated. Many Muslims fled before the western advance: those who remained often accustomed themselves to their rule. Ibn Jubair, a Muslim traveller passed through the Kingdom of Jerusalem in 1181, remarking that his coreligionists:

> live in great prosperity under the Frank . . . the Muslims are masters of their habitations and rule themselves as they see fit. . . . One of the troubles which afflict the Muslims is that under their own government they must always complain about the injustice of their chiefs, whereas they cannot but praise the behaviour of the enemy, on whose justice they can rely.[7]

Now this cannot be taken to imply that all the Muslim inhabitants of Jerusalem, let alone the other crusader states, were all contented. Nor is it evidence that they accepted crusader rule with anything less than deep hostility. But the crusaders had driven off their traditional elites and the remaining Muslims had adapted to a new one: the mass of any population was always in this position. Moreover, the Turks who ruled the adjacent Muslim lands were almost as alien to the native population as the crusaders. In any case, as Ibn Jubair says, the crusaders left the Muslim communities to rule themselves, in return for obedience and renders. The crusaders inherited from their predecessors a well-established tradition of confessional administration which was necessary in an area where there were numerous religions and sects. On the eve of the crusader conquest Christians formed a very substantial section of the population of the Middle East, and the Muslim authorities, in any case pledged to tolerance under Koranic injunction, were disinclined to alienate so many people. All such groups were left to regulate their own affairs, as long as they respected the government and paid their taxes. The effect of the coming of the crusaders was to change the pecking order amongst the religions. The Muslims, hitherto totally dominant, were now reduced to the lowest level. The Orthodox, who had always enjoyed Byzantine support and therefore enjoyed a pre-eminence amongst the Christian sects, were demoted and treated much like the other eastern Christians, and much of their land was seized by Latin clergy.

Urban II had called the crusade in part to liberate the eastern Christians. In Antioch and Edessa there was a large population of Armenian Christians who had at first welcomed the crusaders. Many later regretted this, and the emergence of an independent Armenian kingdom in Cilicia in the later twelfth century would give them an alternative focus of loyalty. However, even after that they remained closely aligned to the crusader cause. The Maronites of Lebanon were consistently friendly to the crusaders and in 1181 they formally united under Rome, but this

---

7 Ibn Jubair, *Voyages*, RHC Or. 3.448, translated by J. Prawer, *The World of the Crusaders* (London: Weidenfeld and Nicolson, 1972), 55.

was unusual. For the most part the evidence suggests that the other Christians of the area, Syrians and Jacobites, enjoyed fairly good relations with the Catholic settlers, despite the fact that their churches were always subordinate to the Latin hierarchy whose officials did not always treat them well. Recent research suggests that there was substantial western settlement in the Kingdom of Jerusalem, almost always in association with native Christians. It is probable, therefore, that relations between the communities were generally good and that native Christians were at times a significant element in the army of Jerusalem. The real enemy for the crusader bridgeheads was not the native population of Palestine, but the Islamic elites in the surrounding areas – the Fatimids of Egypt and the Turkish rulers of Aleppo, Homs, Damascus and other significant places, like the Emirates to the north-east of Antioch. By the time of the First Crusade these powers had totally lost the sense of struggle against the infidel, *jihad*. They had treated the crusaders as yet another of the numerous forces which swept in and out of the Middle East, and some at first may have thought that they were a Byzantine expedition whose presence would be brief. The cities of the Palestine coast, although they were subject to Egyptian sovereignty, provided safe passage to the crusade on its way to Jerusalem, seeing it as no business of theirs to offer opposition. Gradually the local elites began to suspect that the newcomers wanted to roll back Islam and to establish a Christian empire of Asia. But their response sprang from the needs of their localities and this particularism always conditioned the Islamic response. However, from almost the first moments of the confrontation precipitated by the First Crusade there was some evidence of a spirit of *jihad*. In the accounts of the fighting against the First Crusade the Islamic sources make frequent references to *ghazi*, religious volunteers inspired by the sense of *jihad*, to fight against these representatives of an alien religion: many of those who died in Kerbogah's failed attempt to relieve Antioch were 'volunteers'. *Jihad*, essentially an appeal to all Islam, was never absent from the riposte to western aggression, but it was always informed by local interests and personal ambitions.

But of course the settlers in the Holy Lands themselves were not united any more than were those of the Welsh March or northern Germany. Given the nature of the western aristocracy this was the natural order of things. Even during the First Crusade ideological unity had been strained by severe conflicts over policy and personality. Once the crusade had ended, the western settlements tended to go their own way. Jerusalem was the only kingdom, but its ruler had no direct authority over Antioch or Edessa, both of which had been founded before it. Tripoli was only taken in 1109 with help from Jerusalem, and was less independent. In general the rulers of these precarious bridgeheads were prepared, though sometimes only in dire emergency, to help one another. However, at various moments they quarrelled, even allying with Muslim powers against fellow-Christians. Tancred, Regent of Antioch after 1104, made his cousin, Richard of Salerno, ruler of Edessa, because its count, Baldwin II, had been captured at Harran. Richard was not a strong ruler and under him the principality weakened. In 1108 Baldwin was freed, only to be refused possession of Edessa, probably because he was not willing to hold it as a vassal of Tancred. In the end Edessa was restored to him, but in 1108 there was war between an alliance of Chavli of Mosul and Baldwin against Tancred and Ridwan of Aleppo which robbed the settlers of a chance to profit from Chavli's rebellion against Baghdad. In 1102 Tancred arrested Raymond of Toulouse when he arrived at Antioch with the remnants of the 'Crusade of 1101'. After Baldwin I of Jerusalem's defeat at Ramla in 1102 Tancred rallied to his aid, but only on condition that Baldwin restored Daimbert to the Patriarchate. In his momentary weakness, the king agreed, but soon deposed Daimbert again. Such bitter personal feuds were characteristic of the settlements of *Outremer* throughout its existence. In 1187 Raynald of Châtillon refuses to obey King Guy of Jerusalem's order to make restitution to Saladin for his raid on a Muslim caravan near Kerak. Raynald replied to the king's demand that 'he would not do so, for he was lord of his land, just as Guy was lord of his'.[8]

Personal conflicts were reinforced by different strategic opportunities and problems. At first the position of Antioch seemed to be the most favourable. Much of its population was Christian, and its north-eastern frontier was guarded by the principality of Edessa. The nearest Muslim power, Aleppo, was relatively weak and isolated and its rulers were far from loyal to the Sultan at Baghdad. The patchwork of emirates to the north-east were similarly independent-minded. Bohemond, enjoyed great prestige and a powerful internal position which was inherited by his immediate successors. However, he faced hostility from the Turkish powers of Asia Minor and from the Byzantines who had never reconciled themselves to his seizure of Antioch. To the east the politics of the minor Turkish principalities could certainly offer opportunities, but equally could produce threats. It was the Byzantine threat, and the failure at Harran, which had persuaded Bohemond to go to the west in 1105. In time of difficulty Antioch could appeal for aid to the king of Jerusalem, but this in no way implied that he was regarded as overlord of the principality. After Bohemond's departure, Antioch passed under the regency of Tancred. He fought off Byzantine encroachments and regained control of Cilica. Much that had been lost in Syria was also regained by 1108 and Byzantine Lattakia firmly brought within the rule of Antioch. The crucial area for expansion lay to the east. Antioch stood in a gap where the Orontes penetrated between the Ammanus mountains to the north and the Jebel al-Ansariye to the south. Due east, only about 100 kilometres away, lay Aleppo in the open plain of north Syria. Roughly equidistant between the two cities is the crucial geographic feature, the Jebel Talat, across whose low stony hills the traveller must pass for about 20 kilometres. This was, in a sense, a natural boundary. To the west it was guarded by Artah, while to the east the villages of

---

8 P. Edbury (ed.), 'The Old French Continuation of William of Tyre 1184–97', in *The Conquest of Jerusalem and the Third Crusade* (Aldershot: Scolar, 1996), 29.

al-Atharib, Zardana and Sarmada stood across the road to Aleppo. The Jebel Talat forms a northern extension of the great limestone mass of the Jebel as-Summaq which forms the eastern bank of the Orontes and extends southwards beyond Marra and Apamea towards Hama. Key parts of this upland zone, Marra and Albara, had been conquered by the First Crusade and absorbed into the principality of Antioch along with the upper Orontes valley which the crusaders called Ruj. Antioch ruled most of the northern reaches of the Jebel Ansariye and the Mediterranean littoral as far south as Marqab. It was these settlements to the east of the Orontes which Tancred recovered after their loss in 1104, and it was here that the decisive struggle for expansion was to take place.

Tancred died in 1112. He had ruled Antioch for much longer than Bohemond I and he seems to have been universally regarded as truly prince of Antioch rather than merely regent for his absentee uncle. Bohemond himself had died in Italy in 1111, and his son Bohemond II was still a child. In these circumstances Antioch accepted the claim of a cousin, Roger of Salerno. It is difficult to say how the claims of Bohemond II were regarded at this stage, but, pragmatically, a land in a constant state of war needed an adult male to lead it and Roger certainly belonged to Bohemond's kin. Antioch was the dominant power in north Syria. The principality controlled the road to Aleppo as far as al-Atharib and extorted tribute from that city and Shaizar to the south. Aleppo was further weakened by the accession of a child on Ridwan's death in 1113. Even before then the spirit of *jihad* had been revived by Maudud of Mosul who had striven to erect coalitions amongst the Muslim powers of the north and this was now continued under Bursuq of Hamadan who enjoyed the support of Baghdad. But this was not welcome to his Islamic rivals and when Bursuq raised a great army to attack Antioch in 1115 two leading Muslim rulers, Il-Ghazi ibn-Artuk of Mardin and Tughtegin of Damascus, allied with Roger and together they confronted Bursuq at Apamea. Moreover the Antiochenes were expecting aid from Jerusalem under Baldwin I. Confronted by this formidable alliance, Bursuq retreated and the allies split up, supposing the emergency to be over. But Bursuq appeared once more, threatening Antiochene possessions in the Jebel as-Summaq. Roger, however, surprised Busuq's army in a great victory at Tell Danith on 14 September. Antioch extended southwards down the coast to Marqab, and consolidated control of the Jebel al-Ansariye by seizing Saone. At the same time heavy tribute was laid upon Aleppo and the ring of villages under Antiochene control advanced almost to the city itself. With Aleppo in such danger, in 1119 Il-Ghazi ibn-Artuk and the Aleppans raised a great army and attacked al-Atharib and Zardana. Roger of Antioch had appealed to Baldwin II for support, but it seems that many of his chief magnates were anxious to prevent loss of territory and unwilling to wait for Baldwin. Roger had to enlist their support to fulfil his ambitions; thus Robert the Leprous, lord of the fortress of Saone, was made lord of the threatened town of Sardana. Perhaps such men were overconfident after Tell Danith. The Antiochene army advanced to relieve the besieged towns, but was cut off from Antioch by enemy patrols and confronted by the main Muslim army. Roger chose to try and break out of the trap by battle and was killed in a great slaughter of the Antiochene aristocracy later called the 'Field of Blood' on 28 June 1119. The principality lost everything east of the Jebel Talat. However, Baldwin II of Jerusalem then took control of Antioch and, in alliance with Edessa, by 1123 had virtually restored the 1119 boundaries. The concerted campaign in the north was interrupted by the capture of Jocelin of Edessa in 1122 and Baldwin II himself in 1124. In October 1125 Baldwin laid siege to Aleppo, but it was relieved by Aksungur of Mosul. In 1126 Baldwin relinquished his control of Antioch to the now adult Bohemond II (1126–30), but his death during an attempt to secure control of Cilicia enabled Aleppo to reconquer al-Atharib and led to a prolonged succession crisis in the principality.

The kingdom of Jerusalem faced quite different strategic opportunities and threats. The first priority was to seize the cities of the coast and so to guarantee communication with the west. This inevitably involved cooperation with the Italian cities whose expertise in such operations was enormous and who alone could bring reinforcements for large-scale sieges. Haifa fell with the aid of a Pisan fleet in 1100. In 1101 the arrival of a Genoese squadron enabled Baldwin I to seize Arsuf, which surrendered on terms and Caesarea which resisted to the end and suffered a dreadful massacre. In the following year Tortosa was sacked by Raymond of Toulouse, with equally fatal results for its inhabitants. In 1104 Baldwin I of Jerusalem captured Acre with the support of Genoese and Pisan fleets. Genoese and Pisan ships were available to seize Beirut in 1110. Sidon was besieged in the same year with the help of a Norwegian fleet under King Sigurd who had come on pilgrimage, but an Egyptian fleet arrived and was only put to flight by the fortunate arrival of a Venetian fleet, and Sidon capitulated. Tyre was the greatest of the sieges of the coastal cities. It had resisted successfully in 1112 but Baldwin II appealed to Rome for a crusade and this stimulated the Venetians to send a fleet to the east in May 1123. This emboldened the crusaders to try again. The siege lasted five months and was marked by bitter fighting against the garrison and relief attempts from Damascus. On 7 July it surrendered on terms, with those who wished leaving with their goods, and others being permitted to stay. Tripoli, which fell in 1109, was a particular case. Raymond of Toulouse had been implacably opposed to Bohemond's capture of Antioch, which he regarded as an imperial territory. This is why Tancred arrested him when he returned to the city with the remnant of the 'Crusade of 1101'. Raymond seized Tortosa in 1102, and in1104 attacked Tripoli, establishing 'Pilgrim's Castle' as a base. He died in 1105 and his cousin William Jordan continued the siege, but in 1109 his position was threatened by the arrival of St Gilles' son, Bertram, in the east. William Jordan then allied with Tancred against the interloper, but Bertram appealed to Baldwin I. Baldwin, supported by most of the lords of the east, took the opportunity for a general settlement of a number of disputes amongst the settlers, and Bertram emerged as count of Tripoli, held of the king of Jerusalem, when it surrendered in 1109, though he also acknowledged the Emperor Alexius as overlord. The new county was the last of the principalities to emerge, and because of the way in which it had been acquired it was the most closely associated with Jerusalem.

The establishment of the kingdom had depended heavily on conquering the cities of the coast, for which the aid of the Italian city-states had proved essential. There was a price to pay for this naval support. The Italian city-states received quarters in the cities, tax privileges and the right to try their own people under their own law. These were substantial privileges, but not excessive considering the assistance which they brought to the Latins. These settlements were valuable in another way: pilgrims in large numbers paid the Italians for passage to the Holy Land. From these friendly bases the Italians could tap into trade from China and the Indies, especially that in spices, which since time immemorial had been the staple of Mediterranean trade. This in turn developed the cash-flow through the cities which the kings of Jerusalem could tax. In fact royal control of Tyre and Acre, together with Jerusalem where all pilgrims went, was probably very important to the monarchy. In effect the benefits of this great trade were partitioned between the monarchy and the cities. The Italian city-states are usually portrayed as money-grubbing and ruthless pursuers of self-interest, but this is perhaps unfair. If trade had been their sole concern they could easily have come to agreements with Muslim powers. The Muslims had nothing against trade with the infidel and throughout the period and far beyond offered generous terms in places like Alexandria. The truth seems to be that the city-states, like individual crusaders, were moved by religious as well as by material interests. The First Crusade revealed to them the possibilities in the east and they certainly took every advantage, but they preferred to conduct their business in the congenial surroundings of the Latin states where they felt at home.

If we know a great deal about the capture of the Palestinian littoral, it has to be said that we are very badly informed about the inland expansion of the kingdom. During the First Crusade, Tancred seized Bethlehem, and shortly after captured Nablus and later Baisan and Tiberias in the Galilee, while Godfrey granted Hebron to Gerald of Avesnes. By the 1130s the records reveal a pattern of lordships across the kingdom, but never show evidence of the kind of royal administrative command systems which were emerging in the west. This may well be because the kings saw no real need for them. This was a small kingdom with a narrow ruling class. The monarchs exercised real control over the lordships which were manipulated skilfully. No major unit was allowed to develop on the sensitive Damascus border where there was for long a real possibility of expansion: the adjacent lordships of Galilee and Toron, for example, were separated shortly after the death of their lord, Hugh of St Omer, under Baldwin I. Most of the lords seem in origin to have been relatively petty people, immigrants from Christendom who were trying to make their way. There were relatively few of them, and this can be connected to the fact that their lordships were far from rich. They could raise only 600–800 knights from their lands, and many of them seem to have been in grave economic difficulties almost from the moment they emerge in the 1130s. High morality rates due to disease and constant fighting tended to undermine dynastic stability. The boundaries of the kingdom seem to have been reached largely by the chances of piecemeal conquest. Some time before 1115 Roman of Le Puy had established the fief of *Oultrejourdain* in the area of Petra, centred on the fortress of Montreal (modern Shawbak). This outpost enabled the kingdom to levy a toll on caravans plying between Egypt and Syria and stood as an outwork of defence for the kingdom. It was strengthened at royal initiative by the building of Kerak in the 1130s. This castle was so important that it was amongst those enormously strengthened in a new style in the 1160s.

The Latin settlements were always in close touch with Catholic Christendom and the Church helped to maintain awareness of their difficulties amongst the elites of the west. Towards the end of his reign Baldwin II persuaded Fulk of Anjou to be his successor. Raymond of Poitiers became prince of Antioch, 1136–49. Reynald of Chatillon was a knight-adventurer who went to the east and married the heiress of Antioch, so becoming its regent 1153–60, until he was captured by the Muslims. After a long captivity he went on to become Lord of Kerak in the Kingdom. Gerard of Ridefort, Master of the Temple (1185–89), originally came to the east as a sword for hire. The brothers, Aimery and Guy of Lusignan fled the west after difficulties with their overlord, the duke of Aquitaine: they both later became kings of Jerusalem and Cyprus and founded a family which would in time also rule Armenian Cilicia. We know that men came to the east to fight for short periods, *milites ad terminum*. In addition there are references in the sources to the employment of mercenaries. Many of these were probably drawn from native populations, but others were evidently westerners. As part of his penance for the murder of Becket Henry II of England promised to maintain 200 knights in Jerusalem; since Henry provided the money, it seems to have been assumed that such men were readily available. Presumably they were of the same sort as Reynald and Gerard, but never reached such lofty heights. The ruling elite in the crusader states could count on a steady if limited stream of reinforcements from the homelands but many of these may have come only for short terms. The Latin settlements shared in the money-economy of the Middle East and it is possible that young men of good family were attracted by the prospects of cash. Many knights in the east received landed fiefs, but very commonly they were retained by money-fiefs, *fiefs en besant*. These were worth 400–500 besants a year. As the besant was worth about 7 shillings and 6 pence this was a major incentive because Henry II was paying his knights only about 2 shillings a day.

It has been suggested that in the Latin states: 'The desperate shortage of manpower encouraged every device by which stones might do the work of men.'[9] Early historians of the Latin East were so deeply impressed by the more spectacular castles like Marqab and Crac des Chevaliers that, not realising that these were products of the thirteenth century, they supposed that the Latins had copied the art of stone fortification from Byzantium and perhaps even Islam, because these

9 R. Fedden and J. Thomson, *Crusader Castles* (London: Murray, 1957), 18.

structures seemed so much more advanced than anything contemporary Europe had to offer. In fact, the settlers used stone because numerous ruins provided ample supplies of cut stone and because wood, which was commonly used in the west for fortifications, was scarce. Crusader castles have commanded attention quite disproportionate to their real military importance. Castles were numerous because they were the consequence of the seigneural structure of the society which the Franks brought with them, and they were much more than mere military centres. They were part of a general pattern of settlement, as they were in the west, and in military terms few were especially formidable or advanced. They served as centres of estate administration and local government, tax-collecting points and storage places for the products of the countryside. The 'Red Tower' (al-Burj al-Ahmar) in the plain of Sharon was a two-story tower rising to some 13 metres, surrounded by an enclosure about 60-metres square. Modest fortifications of this kind are quite common: Belmont, near Jerusalem later became quite a formidable fortress, but in its early years was essentially a secure store and administrative centre. These structures were quite enough to overawe local resistance and to secure the settler population when there were raids. But they could hardly offer real resistance to a major attack. Where there was a greater threat, something stronger was built: Bethgibelin was quite formidable and was raised to check raids from Egyptian Ascalon in the 1130s, while Kerak, in what is now Jordan, was a strong fortress situated where it could tax caravans between Syria and Egypt. In a small land the numerous castles formed a network of communications and offered support to the field army of the kingdom in times of campaign. Saffuriyah was comparable in size to the 'Red Tower', but its copious springs meant that Latin armies operating in the Galilee often used it as a base. It must be said that in the second half of the twelfth century some castles became much more formidable, but it was essentially control of the cities which anchored the Latin states just as they anchored the Islamic states.

Of immense importance to the holding of the Holy Lands were two entirely new institutions which arose to defend them and which provided constant reinforcements. These were the military monastic orders of the Temple and the Hospital. Their roots are fundamentally ideological. Very soon after the capture of Jerusalem in 1099 men came to the east to serve for a time for the good of their souls. Amongst them was a minor lord of Champagne, Hugh of Payns. He founded a confraternity of like-minded pious men who swore an oath to defend the dangerous pilgrim routes from the coast. They enjoyed a modest success and were given quarters in the 'Temple of the Lord', the Mosque al-Aqsa, on the Temple Mount by Baldwin II. They seem to have attracted considerable admiration amongst pilgrims. Fulk V of Anjou, later king of Jerusalem, associated closely with them during his pilgrimage in 1120 and Hugh count of Champagne actually joined them in 1125. In 1128 Hugh of Payns was at the Council of Troyes and here the Order attracted the attention of the greatest spiritual figure of the age, St Bernard of Clairvaux, under whose influence a new and more formal rule was drawn up for the organisation. After 1128 the Order attracted much more attention, many more recruits and enormous gifts all over Christendom. So extensive were its lands that a system of provinces was devised, each ruled by a retired brother. The Provinces of France and Provence were the earliest, but others soon followed. In this way the order directed the idealism of pious young men into the service of the Holy Land. If there were losses, they could be compensated for by new recruitment, and the economic resources in the west could be used to sustain them. The knights were the central figures, but lesser men, sergeants, could also join and be subordinate members of the order. Around this core of brothers and sergeants the Order could, in time of need, recruit *milites ad terminum*, mercenaries and the eastern light horse known as *Turcopoles*, to produce a formidable military power. The Hospital was originally founded in Jerusalem to care for pilgrims. Its Master at the time of the First Crusade is said to have been imprisoned and, when forced to throw stones at the attacking crusaders threw loaves of bread. As pilgrimage grew, so did the fame of the Hospitallers who soon became an independent order with Hospitals all along the pilgrim routes to the Holy Land – notably at Marseilles which was a major point of departure for pilgrims. As their fame grew, so did their wealth. Shortly after 1135 King Fulk of Jerusalem gave to the Order the new fortress of Bethgibelin which was one of a series of castles built to enclose Egyptian Ascalon, and from this time on the militarisation of the order proceeded quickly and they became very important guardians of castles. However, they retained their function of caring for pilgrims and the sick. The enormous popularity of the Orders is a revelation of the enthusiasm in Catholic Christendom for the new conquests in the east, and of its ideological roots. All over Christendom the two Orders skimmed the wealth of a continent whose economic development was proceeding apace and creamed off many of its most pious young men, and applied these resources to the defence of the Holy Land. It is hardly surprising that the most striking tribute to their importance came in Spain. In 1134 Alfonso the Battler died without heir, and he willed his kingdom to the Orders of the Temple and the Hospital. This extraordinary bequest was quickly overturned by the nobility, but the Orders were very willing to come to a compromise and became great landowners in Spain.

The Jerusalemite monarchy always recognised great strategic possibilities in its situation. When the First Crusade arrived at Ramla it was suggested that to attack Fatimid Egypt which held Jerusalem, was the surer way to proceed. This was dismissed, and indeed it was far beyond the strength of the crusade. But it was strategically perceptive, for in the first 20 years of its existence Egypt was the major threat to the kingdom. Al-Afdal did not accept the verdict of the battle of Ascalon, and down to 1107 he sent annual expeditions, facilitated by the continuing control of Ascalon which was not captured by the crusaders until 1153. Thereafter savage raids were mounted, in 1115 almost capturing Jaffa. But all these attacks failed, except the wasted victory of 1102, as did a major expedition launched by al-Afdal's successor in 1121. In 1118, as al-Afdal's regime weakened, Baldwin I launched an attack on Egypt during which he died. After 1121 internal tensions meant that Egypt ceased to be a threat, while the

Jerusalemite kings had interests elsewhere. Damascus was relatively isolated and quite close to the kingdom. In 1127–28 King Baldwin II appealed for a crusade to seize the city and a series of embassies to the west arranged the marriage of his daughter, Melisende to Fulk of Anjou who was thus his designated successor, and raised men and money for a great expedition. It is not certain that a crusade was ever formally preached by the pope, but in the autumn of 1129 a large Christian army menaced Damascus which had no obvious military saviour. However, ill-fortune and the ill-advised division of their army to allow for a raid into the Hauran, enabled the Muslims to force the attackers to retreat. Thereafter the isolation of Damascus and its anxiety to maintain its independence from the powers of north Syria, led to an alliance with Jerusalem, although the possibility of conquest remained for a long time. It was the particularism of the Muslim powers, and especially the Fatimid schism, which was the most essential condition for the survival of the Latin states. In 1105 an alliance between Damascus and Egypt was defeated only after very savage fighting, while in 1126 Bursuq coordinated his attack on Antioch with an Egyptian naval assault on Beirut. What is surprising, in view of the possibilities of its own situation, is how much time the kings of Jerusalem devoted to the north. In part this was because both Baldwin I and Baldwin II had been counts of Edessa, and knew how weak and exposed this county was. Moreover, Antioch was exposed to many threats, especially after the 'Field of Blood' in 1119. Probably just as decisive was the need of the Jerusalemite kings for recognition. The successions of Baldwin I and II were all subject to dispute, and acting as champions of the Christians and settling the quarrels of their great neighbours was a clear demonstration of their royalty and prestige. And, of course, they could then call for aid for their own ambitions – in 1129 there were contingents from the north in the army which failed before Damascus. Fulk I (1131–43) continued this interest in the north, but in a different form for Antioch was rent by a succession dispute while his own claim to the throne of Jerusalem was cast into doubt.

The heir of Bohemond II was his daughter Constance for whom a suitable marriage was, therefore, a priority. But her mother, Alice tried to retain power and even to exclude her child from the succession. There was a party amongst the nobility of Antioch which supported her and she could count on some help from her elder sister, Melisende, Queen of Jerusalem. At the time of his marriage Fulk was promised the kingship absolutely, but Baldwin II seems to have repented of this and before he died to have insisted that the monarchy should be shared between Fulk, Melisende and their child, the future Baldwin III (1143–63). Moreover, Pons of Tripoli, who held much land within Antioch, supported Alice, perhaps because he saw this as a way of weakening Jerusalemite hegemony over his county. There was nothing unusual about this kind of situation because hereditary claims and the spirit of aristocratic independence were major factors in the politics of Christendom. Matters were complicated at Antioch because Roger II of Sicily (1130–54) had some claim to the succession. Fear of Sicilian expansionism inevitably stimulated the Byzantine Emperor John Comnenus

(1118–43) to revive his claims derived from the oaths made at Constantinople by the leaders of the First Crusade to his father, Alexius, in the spring of 1097 and from the oath of Bertram to regard Tripoli as held of the empire. At the same time a new force had arisen in Islam. In 1128 Zengi became governor of Mosul and ruler of Aleppo, and while he had many preoccupations in Iraq, he was a highly effective soldier. In 1135 he hammered at the Franks of Antioch, driving back their frontier. The impact of these attacks forced the Antiochene barons to agree with Fulk on the marriage of Constance to the vigorous Raymond of Poitiers, younger son of the duke of Aquitaine. The arrival of John Comnenus in 1137 with a formidable army forced Raymond to do a homage which he never intended to observe, and he was freed from the consequences of this in 1143 when John arrived again and prepared to invest the city, only to die suddenly.

The death of John Comnenus ended the risk that the crusader states might have to submit to a Greek overlord, and doubtless many were relieved by that, notably Raymond of Antioch. But the principal beneficiary was Zengi. He held Mosul and Aleppo and his great aim was to seize Damascus. The acquisition of Homs in 1138 was a step in that direction, but Damascus responded by alliance with Jerusalem. Zengi's involvement in the affairs of Iraq was a major diversion. In 1144 the Artukid lord of Diarbekir died, and his son Kara-Arslan allied with Jocelin II of Courtenay, count of Edessa (1131–59) who lead an army to aid him. Zengi took advantage of his absence to lay siege to the city. Raymond of Antioch refused all aid because of quarrels with Count Joscelin dating from the period of the succession struggle, the city fell and all the Franks within were killed, though the native Christians were spared. The capture of Edessa has elevated Zengi in the eyes of posterity to the role of champion of Islam. There is no doubt that he had at various times appealed to religious feeling, as others like Bursuq had done before him. He certainly avoided open collaboration with the Latins. His career set a precedent for his son, Nur al-Din, who posed much more consciously as an Islamic warrior, but for the moment he was deeply preoccupied with establishing himself. The fall of Edessa led directly to the Second Crusade whose summoning reveals how far the western presence in the Middle East was the product of ideological considerations.

In the first half of the twelfth century the expansion of Christendom continued. The papal institution of crusading made a substantial contribution to the growth of Aragon, especially with the capture of Zaragoza, though Castile never seems to have looked with favour upon any intervention from north of the Pyrenees. Thus the crusading movement helped to drive back Islam and to shift the balance of power amongst the Christian kingdoms of the Iberian peninsula. Moreover, the intense interest of the papacy meant that the war in Spain took on a more clearly sanctified aspect than it had ever had before. However, the rhythm of conquest still depended on strong monarchs who could cooperate and control their ambitious subjects. Crusading helped to give a religious unity to the diversity of purpose between kings and aristocrats, but their ambitions remained the fundamental driving force of the *Reconquista*. This was very evidently the case also on Germany's Wendish frontier where raiding, conversion and emulation were the dynamics of the Catholic expansion. However, even here a new spirit was emerging. In 1108 there was an appeal, couched in crusading terms, from the Magdeburg diocese for westerners to come to fight the Wends. The settlers in the Latin East behaved much like the aristocrats who drove Catholic domination into the margins of the Europe land-mass. This is hardly surprising because they were just the same kind of people. Nor were they in a radically different position as has sometimes been supposed.

All the elites of Catholic Christendom, wherever they expanded, needed dependable subjects. There was a substantial humble settlement in the Holy Land and we find there people originating from all over the west. In fact, this phenomenon, the readiness of sizeable numbers of people of all ranks to wander and seek their fortune in obscure and difficult places, is one of the most important factors that underlay the expansion of Christendom. We know far too little about settlement in the Holy Land, but where we have names of settlers they point to diverse origins. The Canons of the Holy Sepulchre established the village of Magna Mahomeria about 1120; by the 1150s it probably had 450 inhabitants and by 1187 some 700. We know the names of relatively few of those who lived there, and some of those we do know suggest that they had come to the village from other places in the Holy Land. But of the remainder that can be identified, 80 per cent were from central France, though none from north of Paris, while there were others from Catalonia and Italy. A very much shorter list of settlers from Bethgibelin, however, shows a preponderance of settlers from southern France and northern Spain, with an element from Italy. When Adolph II of Holstein wanted to establish his new city of Lübeck in 1143 he needed dependable subjects and he recruited them from what is now Westphalia, Holland and Flanders, offering them rich lands and freedom in the east. However, he gave the most secure territories to people from his own frontier zones, and left the Slavs in possession in the most exposed and remote. The great Norman expansion in Wales after 1093 was short-lived and very largely rolled back because it had no firm underpinning. As a result, Henry I encouraged immigration on a large scale. Gower and Pembrokeshire, strongholds of the English domination, were settled by English and Flemings and, as we have noted, Wiston in Pembrokeshire stands on the very edge of the English Pale in West Wales. In Spain the kings anchored their frontier by establishing cities. The inhabitants were highly privileged and largely self-governing, and in return provided determined militias which protected against Muslim attack. Even after Alfonso VI had been defeated by the Almoravids at Badajoz in 1086, the line of Christian cities which he had established barely faltered. The Almoravids were not able to capitalise on their victory and their Spanish Muslim allies lacked the will. These cities were populated by Spaniards from the north and refugees from Islam, but also by settlers from all over Christendom. Tortosa was captured by Aragón after a seven-month siege in 1148, and a 'cemetery of the English' was established for those of that nationality who had fallen in the fighting. But some of the survivors stayed

on, Englishmen like Gilbert Anglicus and Osbert Anglicus who became substantial citizens.

In Spain, it has been said that there emerged a 'society organised for war'. This
was not unique to that area. In Wales an alien subject-group imposed itself and
strengthened the March. These were not gentle beings. St Caradoc (died 1124)
was a Welsh monk who was persecuted by the Flemish castellan Richard Tankard.
But then such settlers had a lot to fear. Decapitation of enemies remained a
common practice amongst the Welsh who were very effective raiders of the
frontiers of the March, and, indeed, of England beyond. The Saxons living on the
north-eastern frontier, close to the Wends, the Nordalbinagians, were notorious
for their rapaciousness and brutality. In the Holy Land a small settler population
was able to produce at least 5,000 foot-soldiers, a remarkable 20 per cent of the
estimated active male non-noble western population.[10] It is hardly surprising that
the story of expansionism in the twelfth century has focused on the magnates and
the knights, because they are the focus of the sources. But they could never have
succeeded on their own and the willingness of thousands of very ordinary people
to uproot themselves in search of a better life, even at great risk was the secret
weapon of the expansion of Christendom.

The papacy had enormous influence and there can be no doubt of its power to
move the west, especially for the Latin East in whose cause the popes were tireless.
But there were considerable limits to their power. In 1124 papal preaching stirred
the Venetians whose support brought about the seizure of Tyre, but the crusade as
such never got off the ground. Other crusades were successful to the extent that
they enlisted forces already predisposed to particular lines of action, like the
monarchy and nobles of Aragon who had long wanted to seize Zaragoza. Some
papal initiatives, like the crusade against Anacletus, barely raised a ripple of
interest. Despite its commanding presence in the Europe of the early twelfth
century and despite the prestige gained by the liberation of Jerusalem proclaiming
a crusade was quite different from raising effective support and strong armies. But
the Magdeburg appeal showed that wherever Catholic Christendom fought
pagans the notion of crusading was starting to take root.

SELECTED READING

The seminal discussion of the way in which the twelfth century viewed the First Crusade is
that of E. O. Blake, 'The formation of the "Crusade Idea"', *Journal of Ecclesiastical History*
21 (1970), 11–31. This has been enormously developed by J. Riley-Smith, *The First*

---

10 For the Nordalbinagians, see Helmold of Bosau, *The Chronicle of the Slavs by Helmold Priest of
Bosau*, ed. F. J. Tschan (New York: Columbia University Press, 1935 and New York: Octagon
Books, 1966), Chapter 47; for Caradoc, see S. Baring-Gould and J. Fisher, *Lives of the British
Saints*, 4 vols (London: Honourable Society of Cymmrodorion,1908), 2.3–33.

Crusade and the Idea of Crusading (London: Athlone, 1986). The very conservative attitude of Canon Lawyers is discussed by J. T. Gilchrist, 'The Erdmann Thesis and the Canon Law, 1083–1104', in P. Edbury (ed.), *Crusade and Settlement* (Cardiff: University College Cardiff Press, 1985), 37–45. In fact historians have found it very difficult to understand precisely the nature of the Crusade, because before the thirteenth century contemporaries made little distinction between what we recognise as great expeditions (the First and Second Crusades), personal journeys to Jerusalem that might involve fighting and expeditions elsewhere which enjoyed great public enthusiasm. J. Riley-Smith, *What were the Crusades?* (3rd edition, Basingstoke: Palgrave, 2002) articulated the notion that a crusade was defined by papal authorisation. In this view expeditions for any purpose, and at any time right through to the modern period, were crusades provided that the papacy had so pronounced them. This, the 'pluralist' view has found wide favour and extensive support, notably in N. Housley, *The Later Crusades. From Lyons to Alcazar* (Oxford: Oxford University Press, 1992). By contrast, Mayer, *The Crusades* argued that Jerusalem was central to any concept of crusading, and in later editions of his work vigorously contested the ideas of Riley-Smith. The state of the controversy is outlined by C. Tyerman, *The Invention of the Crusades* (Basingstoke: Macmillan, 1998). The present writer takes the view that the Crusade was an instrument of papal policy, but that after 1099 political opinion always saw its special goal as Jerusalem. This does not mean that political opinion in Europe believed that the Crusade was limited to expeditions to Jerusalem. It does mean that the papacy had to consider carefully before using this weapon in order to make it acceptable to the leaders of European society.

On the 'Investiture Contest', see U. R. Blumenthal, *The Investiture Controversy. Church and Monarchy from the Ninth to the Twelfth Century* (Philadelphia, PA: University of Pennsylvania Press, 1988) and on the development of the papal monarchy, Morris, *Papal Monarchy*. For the crusades of the early twelfth century, J. Riley-Smith, *The First Crusaders* (Cambridge: Cambridge University Press, 1997). N. J. G. Pounds, *An Economic History of Medieval Europe* (London: Longman, 1974) is a fine account of the growing wealth of this period, while M. Barber, *The Two Cities. Medieval Europe 1050–1320* (London: Routledge, 1992) and J. H. Mundy, *Europe in the High Middle Ages 1150–1309* (London: Longman, 1973) provide substantial pictures of the internal growth of Western Europe. For the economic expansion of Byzantium, see A. Harvey, *The Economic Expansion of the Byzantine Empire, 900–1200* (Cambridge: Cambridge University Press, 1989). The date of Alexius I's *Chrysobull* is contentious, but T. Madden, 'The *Chrysobull* of Alexius I Comnenus to the Venetians: the date and the debate', *Journal of Medieval History* 28 (2002), 23–41 reaffirms 1082. A fine illustration of the process of state-building in France was provided by Suger, abbot of St Denis, *Deeds of Louis the Fat*, tr. R. Cusimano and J. Moorhead (Washington, DC: Catholic University of America, 1992) while the elaboration of the English state-machine is very evident in Richard FitzNigel (or FitzNeale), *Dialogus de Scaccario*, ed. C. Johnson, revised by F. E. L. Carter and D. E. Greenway (Oxford: Clarendon, 1983). The extraordinary range of learning which developed in the twelfth century was first explored by C. H. Haskins, *The Renaissance of the Twelfth Century* (Cambridge, MA: Harvard University Press, 1928), but a more systematic study is that of J. W. Baldwin, *The Scholastic Culture of the Middle Ages 1000–1300* (Lexington, KY: Heath, 1971). For a study of its greatest figure, see M. T. Clanchy, *Abelard. A Medieval Life* (Oxford: Blackwell, 1997). On the general problems of war and conquest, see France, *Western Warfare*, but for Anjou, see Bachrach, *Fulk Nerra* and for England R. A. Brown, *The Normans and the Norman Conquest* (London: Constable, 1969).

R. R. Davies, *The Age of Conquest. Wales 1063–1415* (Oxford: Oxford University Press, 1987) is by far the best overall account of the conquest of Wales, though J. E. Morris, *The Welsh Wars of Edward I* (Oxford: Oxford University Press, 1901; 2nd edition Stroud: Sutton, 1996) is still very useful, while for Edward's castle-building the best authority is A. J. Taylor, *The King's Works in Wales 1277–1330* (London: HMSO, 1974).

The Spanish reconquest is covered by many works, notably D. Lomax, *The Reconquest of Spain* (London: Longman, 1978), J. F. O'Callaghan, *History of Medieval Spain* (Ithaca, NY: Cornell University Press, 1975) and B. F. Reilly, *The Kingdom of Léon-Castilla under Alfonso VII (1126–57)* (Philadelphia, PA: University of Pennsylvania Press, 1998). On the German expansion in the early twelfth century, Bartlett, *Making of Europe* has much to contribute and there is an excellent study covering much of the eleventh and twelfth centuries by F. Lotter, 'The crusading idea and the conquest of the region east of the Elbe', in R. Bartlett and A. MacKay, *Medieval Frontier Societies* (Oxford: Oxford University Press, 1989), 267–306. For a specialist study of the whole topic, see E. Christiansen, *The Northern Crusades. The Baltic and the Catholic Frontier 1100–1525* (London: Macmillan, 1980). For a general study of Eastern Europe, see F. Dvornik, *The Slavs in European History and Civilization* (New Brunswick, NJ: Rutgers University Press, 1962). On frontier societies, see R. Bartlett and A. MacKay, *Medieval frontier Societies* (Oxford: Oxford University Press, 1989). On the various populations of the European states in the Holy Lands, see J. Prawer, *Crusader Institutions* (Oxford: Clarendon, 1980) and the same author's more popular *The World of the Crusaders* (London: Weidenfeld and Nicolson, 1972). For the latest ideas about European settlement in the Latin Kingdom of Jerusalem, see R. Ellenblum, *Frankish Rural Settlement in the Latin Kingdom of Jerusalem* (Cambridge: Cambridge University Press, 1998). There is no comparable study for any other crusader state, except for a significant work on the early history of Antioch, T. Asbridge, *The Creation of the Principality of Antioch 1098–1130* (Woodbridge: Boydell, 2000). The most useful accounts of the early history of the crusader settlements are provided by H. S. Fink, 'The Foundation of the Latin States, 1099–1118' and R. L. Nicholson, 'The growth of the Latin states, 1118–44', in Setton, *Crusades* 1, 369–409, 410–48. For the strategic consequences of this, see France, *Western Warfare*, 204–29. There are biographies of most of the leaders of the First Crusade, and amongst these that of Yewdale, *Bohemond I* is perhaps the most useful for the present subject. On Zengi and the rise of the Muslim *jihad* there is an excellent short study by C. Hillenbrand, '"Abominable Acts": the career of Zengi', in J. P. Phillips and M. Hoch (eds), *The Second Crusade. Scope and Consequences* (Manchester: Manchester University Press, 2001). On the Byzantine interest in the area there is a detailed study by R. J. Lilie, *Byzantium and the Crusader States 1096–1204*, tr. J. C. Morris and J. E. Ridings (Oxford: Oxford University Press, 1994) and the wider diplomatic context of the crusader settlements the key study if that of J. P. Phillips, *Defenders of the Holy Land. Relations between Latin East and the West 1119–87* (Oxford: Oxford University Press, 1996). Study of the ruling elite of the European settlements, and especially the Kingdom of Jerusalem, has generated a long-running controversy on the question of whether the lords dominated the crown or were dominated by it. Currently, opinion leans to the view that the monarchy was actually very strong. A very useful study of the European elite is provided by S. Tibble, *Monarchy and Lordships in the Latin Kingdom of Jerusalem 1099–1291* (Oxford: Clarendon, 1989). The best introduction to the study of their castles is that of H. Kennedy, *Crusader Castles* (Cambridge: Cambridge University Press, 1994), but the key modern study is that of D. Pringle, *The Red Tower* (London: British School of Archaeology in Jerusalem, 1986). The Military Religious Orders have attracted an enormous amount of attention. A. Forey, *The Military Orders. From the Twelfth to the early Fourteenth Centuries* (Basingstoke: Macmillan, 1992) provides an excellent introduction while H. Nicholson, *Templars, Hospitallers and Teutonic Knights. Images of the Military Orders 1128–1291* (Leicester: Leicester University Press, 1993) is a perceptive study of how they were seen in their own age. For the individual orders, see M. Barber, *The New Knighthood. A History of the Order of the Temple* (Cambridge: Cambridge University Press, 1994) and J. Riley-Smith, *The Knights of St John in Jerusalem and Cyprus, c.1050–1310* (London: Athlone, 1967). For their activities in Spain, A. Forey, *The Templars in the Corona de Aragón* (London: Oxford University Press, 1973). There is an excellent chapter on peasant mobility in Bartlett, *Making of Europe*, 106–32. On the population of the Spanish cities and their military role, see J. F. Powers, *A Society organised for War. The Iberian Municipal Militias in the Central Middle Ages* (Berkeley, CA: University of California Press, 1988) and the same author's 'Life on the cutting edge: the Luso-Hispanic frontier in the twelfth century', in I. A. Corfis and M. Wolfe (eds), *The Medieval City under Siege* (Woodbridge: Boydell, 1995). For a study of the capture of Tortosa, N. Jaspert, 'Capta est Dertosa, clavis Christianorum', in J. P. Phillips and M. Hoch (eds), *The Second Crusade. Scope and Consequences* (Manchester: Manchester University Press, 2001). There is a study of Wizo's settlement by K. Murphy, 'The Castle and Borough of Wiston, Pembrokeshire', *Archaeologia Cambrensis* 114 (1995), 71–102.

5

CRUSADE, EXPANSION AND CHECK, 1144–92

The First Crusade had brought the 'Catholic Core' into intimate contact with two other centres of expansion, Byzantium and the Turks of North Syria whose weakness was the immediate cause of the crusade. The Turkish expansionism which had dominated the Middle East in the eleventh century remained vigorous, despite divisions amongst its leaders. In December 1144 the Muslim ruler of Aleppo, Zengi, recaptured Edessa for Islam. News of this disaster filtered through to the west rather slowly. Bishop Hugh of Jabala arrived in Rome on an ecclesiastical mission in late 1145 and seems to have discussed the matter with the pope, but it is far from certain that he was carrying any appeal from the leaders of the settlers in the Holy Land. Pope Eugenius III was facing considerable difficulties in Rome, where a commune led by Arnold of Brescia was defying him, but despite this on 1 December he issued *Quantum Praedecessores*, an appeal for a crusade chiefly directed to Louis VII and the French. Quite independently, Louis VII of France (1137–80) seems to have conceived of leading an expedition to the Holy Land, but at his Christmas Court of 1145 his barons proved unwilling. This was not surprising: no ruling monarch had taken the cross and such an event posed great risks for a kingdom in an age of personal monarchy. However, it was agreed to consider the matter again at Easter 1146, and Louis consulted the greatest preacher of the age, St Bernard of Clairvaux. Eugenius approved of Louis' plans, reissued *Quantum Praedecessores*, and commissioned St Bernard to preach. At the Easter Court at Vézelay his rhetoric inspired the barons. News of Bernard's preaching and his message of salvation through participation in the great expedition spread abroad and in northern France a Cistercian preacher, Radulf, enjoyed great success. However, his vicious anti-Semitism forced Bernard to come north to silence him and prevent a repetition of the horrific pogroms of Jews which had characterised the First Crusade. His reception in northern France and Flanders seems to have inspired Bernard to widen his appeal and to send letters to Italy and England. Radulf moved on to Germany, forcing Bernard to follow in October. There he encountered Conrad III (1138–52) who permitted him to recruit in the imperial lands. After further preaching Bernard again confronted Conrad at Speier at the Christmas Court, and on 27 December persuaded him to take the cross.

130

At some time after Vézelay Eugenius had been approached by Alfonso VII (1126–57) of Castile, and early in 1146 extended crusading privileges to his proposed expedition in eastern Spain supported by the Genoese which ultimately captured Almería. Louis VII met with St Bernard and German representatives at Châlons-sur-Marne on 2 February to discuss the journey to Jerusalem, and on 16 February he and his own nobles dealt with the matter at Étampes. But at the Frankfurt Court on 13 March some of the German nobles, mainly Saxons, proposed that they should be allowed to take the cross against their traditional enemies, the pagan Wends on the Baltic coast. This expedition was sanctioned by the papacy on 13 April 1147 by the Bull, *Divina Dispensatione*. Then in April 1147 came another expedition: Flemings and Germans left by sea and joined a large English fleet at Dartmouth on 19 May. It is likely that the initial impetus for this sea-borne expedition came from St Bernard's preaching in Flanders and the Rhineland. The participants seem to have been people of merchant and even more modest status, though they chose nobles as leaders. This fleet would later attack Lisbon in alliance with Afonso I of Portugal (1128–85), but there is no indication of the pope sanctioning this attack.

Bernard and Eugenius spoke of all these as opportunities for salvation on a par with the expeditions to Jerusalem, although we have no certain knowledge of their attitude to the attack on Lisbon, and saw them as a great single effort against unbelievers. This accorded with Urban II's ambitious attempt to roll back the tide of Islam and the attempts of the popes to inspire crusading since the time of the First Crusade. Some chroniclers took up the same theme, notably Helmold of Bosau: 'The initiators of the expedition, however, deemed it advisable to design one part of the army for the eastern regions, another for Spain and a third against the Slavs who live hard by us.'[1]

However, while it is undoubted that the pope and St Bernard saw these expeditions as aspects of a great thrust against non-believers, it does not mean that in any sense they planned for it. *Quantum Praedecessores* was concerned with the Holy Land and addressed to the French only. Eugenius III may have hoped to use Conrad III to put down the Roman revolt and he seems to have been unenthusiastic about the German's participation. He spent more time at the court of Louis VII than any pope of the twelfth century spent with any other monarch. Eugenius seems to have felt a responsibility for keeping the peace of the two lands whose kings had joined the crusade and stayed north of the Alps for some 14 months. But he refused Conrad's invitation to meet him at Strasbourg on 18 April 1147, ventured into imperial territory only long after he had left, and then only for four months, significantly less than his sojourn in France. Spanish initiatives against Islam seem always to have been regarded as crusades, but it is evident that the attack on Almería was at the initiative of Alfonso of Castile, whose Genoese allies had their own ambitions in the Western Mediterranean. The Saxon nobles

---

1 Helmold of Bosau, *The Chronicle of the Slavs by Helmold Priest of Bosau* ed. F. J. Tschan (Columbia: Columbia University Press, 1935 and New York: Octagon Books, 1966), 172.

who wanted to fulfil their vows by a Wendish crusade were, for the most part, old enemies of Conrad III, while the Danes who joined them were their bitter rivals for influence in the Baltic. It was certainly not the case that the pagans were on the offensive. Count Adolf of Holstein had come to an excellent working relationship with the chief Wendish leader, Niklot Prince of the Obotrites. Indeed it may be that some of the leaders were motivated by a desire to undo the position he built up. Helmold, writing some 20 years later, exposed the political shenanigans of these Saxon and Danish 'crusaders' of 1147.

In effect the unitarian view of the crusade is no more than a rationalisation for the fact that Bernard and Eugenius were making the best of all the offers they received. This crusade was planned only in the most limited sense, and certainly not as a broad assault on all non-Christians. The expedition to Jerusalem was always to the front of Eugenius' mind, but planning was minimal. The pope wrote to notify Manuel Comnenus, but never seems to have followed up the Emperor's demand that he guarantee the behaviour of crusaders in the Byzantine Empire. Eugenius appointed Henry of Olmütz to negotiate with Manuel on relations between the Latin and Greek Churches, but when this cleric joined the Wendish crusade, he does not seem to have appointed a replacement. The rest of the legates whom he appointed for the various armies seem to have been allowed to make their own ways to Jerusalem and their other destinations and they had little impact on events. Louis VII and Conrad certainly coordinated their movements down the Danube valley, with the French following the Germans and using the bridges they had built. But there is no evidence that there was any plan to continue cooperation beyond this. Odo of Deuil, the chronicler who travelled with Louis VII, tells us that as Louis approached Constantinople he appealed to Conrad to wait for him on the eastern side of the Bosphoros, suggesting that both armies 'should use a common plan of action', which is a way of saying that one did not already exist.[2] Odo was generally critical of the conduct of the Germans, but does not reproach them for ignoring this appeal. There is certainly no indication that Eugenius or St Bernard tried to coordinate the movements of this eastern expedition with those of other expeditions beyond setting departure dates.

June 29 was set as the date for the 'Wendish Crusade' to leave Magdeburg. Nyklot appealed to Adolf to stand by their pact and, when the latter reluctantly refused, destroyed Lübeck and devastated the area around, sparing native villages but destroying those of the Flemings and other colonists implanted by the Germans. He also struck sharp blows against the Danes who were preparing to join the crusaders. In the event only a part of the crusading force had gathered by mid-July, led by Henry the Lion of Saxony. They joined with the remnants of the Danish forces and the allied army besieged Nyklot's stronghold of Dobin. However, there was tension amongst the Danes who had broken off a civil war to

2 Odo of Deuil, *The Journey of Louis VII to the East*, ed. V. G. Berry (New York: Columbia University Press, 1948), 50–1.

join the expedition, and also between Germans and Danes, so the siege went badly. Some of the crusaders wanted to devastate the land, but others, especially Saxons, saw things differently: 'Is not the land we are devastating our land, and the people we are fighting our people?' It was a nice revelation of the reasons why they were fighting – in hope of loot and perhaps domination, so it was better not to kill the only geese who could lay golden eggs. In August they made a peace which in no way changed the balance of power on the frontier. Bernard had written that pagan peoples should be converted or destroyed – but so little attention was paid to this that the pact between Adolf and Nyklot was resumed: 'Our count now repaired the broken friendships and made peace with Nyklot and with the other eastern Slavs.' In August the major German force, led by the papal legate, Anselm of Havelberg arrived, but it failed before Demmin. Part of the army threatened to attack Christian Stettin, before being dissuaded by the citizens. By late September it was all over. It had achieved all that could be expected from a major frontier raid: loot and promises of obedience. However, the balance on the frontier remained, dependent on an interplay between emulation and armed might. Interestingly, when Nyklot's Slavs attacked a large Flemish settlement and offered surrender on terms, the local priest, Gerlav, rallied the Flemings against it, not because it involved surrender to pagans but simply on the pragmatic grounds that the Slavs, because they hated the Flemings deeply, were not to be trusted.[3]

The successful attack on Almería on 17 October 1147 was made possible by the breakdown of Almoravid power in North Africa. However their successors, the Almohads, were determined to assert power in Spain and had captured Seville by spring 1147. They recovered Almería in 1154. There is little sign that the fleet which gathered at Dartmouth on 19 May intended to support the French and German expeditions, as the fleets of the First Crusade had supported the land armies and even less that it sought or received any kind of official sanction from the leadership for the attack on Lisbon. Afonso of Portugal knew the crusader fleet was coming to Portugal. According to the our main source, *The Conquest of Lisbon*, when they put into Oporto the local bishop told them that the king had written to tell him that if a crusading fleet should arrive at Oporto he was to receive them well and urge them to make an agreement with Afonso for an assault on Lisbon. But there is no need to account for this by assuming arrangements had been made via St Bernard. Indeed the fact that the bishop of Oporto had been informed by a letter from the king only a few days before the arrival of the fleet argues against it: he would have known of a major diplomatic initiative to the pope or St Bernard. Moreover, the author of the *Conquest of Lisbon* explains that they themselves had informed the king of their coming by means of a group of five ships sent ahead of the main fleet.[4] In fact the circumstances suggest that the siege

3 Helmold, *Chronicle of the Slavs*, 178–9, 180–1.
4 C. W. David (ed.), *The Conquest of Lisbon* (New York: University of Columbia Press, 1936 and 2001), 68–9, 98–9.

was arranged at short notice. The key event was Afonso's capture of the fortress of Santarém by a surprise attack on 15 March 1147 which opened real prospects for an attack on Lisbon. This capture was only made possible by complex political and military factors which depended on the decisions of the Almohad forces that had seized Seville in the spring; until virtually the last moment the king could have found himself on the defensive. It must have taken a little time for the possibilities of the new situation to sink in, which would barely have left time for a diplomatic mission to be mounted. On the other hand, Afonso had attacked Lisbon some five years before with the support of an Anglo-Norman fleet, so he would have known where to address the appeal for help.[5]

The message born by the five ships sent ahead by the fleet at Dartmouth may have been no more than a request for port facilities for the fleet. It could hardly have been a full commitment to aid Afonso in view of the great reluctance of many of the crusaders to participate in an attack on Lisbon. Once Afonso had formally offered terms for aid in an attack on Lisbon there was a lively debate amongst those in the fleet about whether to accept it. Hervey de Glanville, commander of a section of the Anglo-Norman fleet, emerged as a great ally of Afonso, so it may well have been he who was behind the message sent on the five ships. The leaders had to work very hard to persuade the ordinary rank and file of the fleet to join in the attack on Lisbon. One of the most vigorous objectors was William Veil. He had participated in an earlier attack on Lisbon in c.1142 which he felt Afonso had betrayed. But he also cast light on the fleets intentions when he argued that to delay would compromise their chances of making a good passage. He made it clear that he did not expect to sail directly to the Holy Land, because once in the inland sea he wanted to attack Muslim shipping for plunder, so that he was probably reckoning on an arrival in September 1147. This would still have been within the summer sailing season. However, any substantial delay, and the earlier attack on the city c.1142 had proved that Lisbon was capable of strong resistance, would mean missing the sailing season and awaiting the new one in early spring of 1148. Ultimately, we know that some of the crusaders went on from Lisbon on 1 February 1148. They attacked Faro and made it to the Holy Land later in the year in time to join in the abortive Damascus expedition of July 1148. It is unlikely that anybody in early 1147 expected that the great armies of the kings would take so long to reach the Holy Land. Given the problems of wind and weather and the fact that these were quite obviously crusaders, though with their own agendas, it seems unlikely that there could have been any thought of their supporting the march of the French and German armies. The siege of Lisbon was ultimately a great success for the city fell on 24 October. Yet the author of the *Conquest of Lisbon* is at great pains to justify the whole expedition, and in particular absolve it from the charge that it was merely undertaken for booty. This was not without reason. Booty figured large in the terms offered by Afonso, and

5 H. Livermore, *A New History of Portugal* (Cambridge: Cambridge University Press, 1967), 56.

the siege was marked by sharp differences between the contingents on its division. The author reveals that at least some of the crusaders felt the need to renew their vows, as if they had doubts about what they were doing. In all this self-justification there is not the slightest hint of papal approval – surely the trump card in any defence. These were crusaders to the Holy Land, but they had chosen this diversion of their own free will. These men had chosen to go to the Holy Land by sea. They had chosen their own leaders and would have seen themselves as being free agents who might or might not join others as conscience and interest decided.

The German and French expeditions set off in May/June 1147 in the eye of a diplomatic storm. When Louis VII took the cross he seems to have been prepared to take any route and wrote to the rulers of Hungary and Sicily. Roger II of Sicily sent a delegation to Louis VII offering to send his son on the crusade, together with a fleet and full logistical support. It is not entirely clear what this offer amounted to. If the idea was to take the whole French force all the way to Jerusalem this would have been a remarkably novel and generous offer. It may be that the offer was to take only Louis VII's own troops, who actually formed the core of the whole French force. It is even possible that all that was implied was free transport and supplies across the Adriatic if Louis decided to follow the route of the North French on the First Crusade, including his great-uncle, Hugh of Vermandois, who went through southern Italy in 1096. Roger faced an alliance of his enemies, Conrad III and Manuel, and he may have felt that supporting the crusade would reduce the likelihood of an attack. From this perspective Conrad III's decision to take the cross might have seemed to presage an even closer relationship with Manuel. Louis refused the offer, perhaps because he did not wish to be caught in the tensions between Roger and Manuel, and took the Danube route. Both armies made good progress to Constantinople, but they arrived just as Roger launched a fierce raid on the Byzantine Empire. The indiscipline of the Germans caused such problems that Conrad and his ally Manuel never met. An element in Louis' army was fiercely hostile to the Byzantines and difficulties over supplies confirmed their suspicions. At Regensburg Byzantine delegates had demanded that Louis take oath to Manuel, and though he was not unwilling to come to an arrangement, the precise form was inevitably controversial, especially as it had to be confirmed by the nobles as a whole. Manuel's suspicions were enhanced by news of Roger's great raid, while the crusaders heard that the Emperor had made a treaty with the Turks of Anatolia – something they saw as betrayal of the Christian cause. In the event, like Conrad, Louis promised to respect the lands of the Emperor and to return any conquests, in return for supplies and guides.

The crusade was a disaster. The German army was very indisciplined, and had barely landed in Asia Minor when at Nicomedia the infantry and the non-combatants broke away under Otto of Friesing to travel down the western coast of Anatolia. This was the route suggested by Manuel because it passed through Byzantine territory. Conard and the cavalry pressed along the route of the First Crusade, only to be destroyed in a Turkish attack at Dorylaeum on 25 October

1147. Conrad joined the French for a short time, then fell ill and resumed his journey by sea. Louis's force followed the same route as Otto of Friesing whose men had been wiped out. Although the French fought bravely, they suffered badly in a Turkish ambush on Mount Cadmus made possible by their vanguard failing to maintain contact with the man force. The badly mauled army arrived at the port of Attalia in early February. The possibility of going to Antioch by sea then arose, but there were not enough ships for the whole expedition. Louis wanted to press on by land, but his barons rebelled, pointing to the heavy losses of horses. In the event the king and his barons took the ships, arriving at Antioch on 19 March 1148, and abandoned the infantry, very few of whom got to the Holy Land. Because most of the attacks on them had occurred in Byzantine territory many of the French were convinced that Manuel had conspired with the Turks to destroy them. In reality Manuel had only the loosest control over these border lands, but he was probably quite happy to see the crusade founder: any great success it might achieve could only strengthen Antioch which he regarded as part of the empire.

The incoherence of the crusader force should not surprise because this was in the nature of medieval armies and especially crusading armies. Germany and France were not nations and their rulers had little direct authority outside their own lands. Divergent interests within the vast area of Germany were so strong that since the outbreak of the 'Investiture Contest' it had proved relatively easy to stir up rebellion against its rulers. In France the great princes dominated the land with little reference to their nominal king. In this context the indiscipline of the Germans becomes understandable. The French were little better. Louis took responsibility for supplying only his own division and left the others to forage for themselves, and one group simply left him in the Balkans and made their own way to Constantinople. Strong elements broke away at Worms and proceeded through Italy, arriving late at Constantinople. At Metz, where Louis gathered his army in mid-June 1147, he proclaimed the 'Laws of the Camp' to which all the leaders swore obedience. 'But because they did not observe them well, I have not preserved them either', comments Odo of Deuil. At Worms in late June the army paused and rioted against the merchants who brought food by river. 'Here' says Odo, 'we first perceived the foolish arrogance of our people.' The reputation of the army in the Balkans was so bad that the cities on their route were terrorised and so provided only poor supply, increasing the need for pillaging. At Constantinople Odo admits that Manuel made good arrangements for the provisioning of the army, but the French still plundered and looted. Ultimately the French were betrayed by the indiscipline of their own vanguard at Mount Cadmus. Louis turned to the Templars who set an example of discipline and reorganised the army for the rest of its journey to Attalia.[6] The situation was made worse because, as crusaders, each person was an equal in the quest for salvation. In practise, humbler men would follow greater ones, but major leaders were under no obligation to

6 Odo, *The Journey of Louis VII to the East*, 21, 23, 25, 41–3, 45.

obey others. Conrad and Louis were equal and could only be coordinated to the extent that they agreed. As it happened, neither was a dominant personality, and so neither achieved a personal ascendancy. The glow of success achieved by the First Crusade disguised the precariousness of its unity and the fact that its army ultimately broke up over personal disputes amongst the leaders. There is, in this respect, no contrast between the First and Second Crusades. Both were also accompanied by large numbers of non-combatants who were left to die when they became burdensome.

If the crusaders were divided, so were the magnates of *Outremer*. Eugenius III never seems to have consulted them about the launching of a crusade and they all had different hopes from the new expedition. Joscelin of Edessa had almost recovered Edessa in late 1146 but the only result of his failure was its complete destruction which weakened his case when he begged Louis VII to march to its recovery. Raymond of Antioch begged Louis to help him attack Aleppo, the heart of the power of Zengi's son, Nur ad-Din, but Louis hesitated, perhaps because this was so far removed from traditional crusading objective of Jerusalem. Raymond of Tripoli begged his support for the recovery of Montferrand; then Alfonso-Jordan, count of Toulouse arrived by sea with a Provençal force. He had a claim to Tripoli and his sudden death aroused suspicions that he had been poisoned by Raymond, causing the count of Tripoli to hold aloof from the crusade. But the root cause of this aimlessness was the situation in Jerusalem. Baldwin II of Jerusalem (1118–31) had provided for the succession to the kingdom by marrying his daughter, Melisende, to Fulk of Anjou. Fulk (1131–43) who had supposed that he would be king in his own right, but Baldwin changed his will and decided that Melisende and her son Baldwin III should have a share. This rather unlikely situation hampered Fulk. On his death Melisende became regent: she was an able woman, but no soldier and was quite unable to impose herself on the princes of the east or to compose their differences. The feud between Joscelin of Edessa and Raymond of Antioch worsened and was a major factor in enabling Zengi to take Edessa in 1144. In 1147 a rebellious vassal of Unur, ruler of Damascus, offered to surrender the Hauran, an important area between the city and the borders of the kingdom of Jerusalem. The barons were divided because Unur was an ally against Nur ad-Din, but after much hesitation the enthusiasm of the army panicked Melisende and King Baldwin into agreeing to an expedition which failed in late 1147, redounding to the credit of Nur ad-Din. Even worse, the young Baldwin III performed well in the expedition and now chafed at the direction of his mother.

On 24 June 1148 Conrad, Louis VII and Baldwin and their chief barons met in council at Acre. The Princes of the northern states stayed away and no heed at all seems to have been taken of their wishes. The final decision was for an attack on Damascus. This was a sensible idea. Damascus was close and the crusaders could rally an army of perhaps 50,000 which would have a real chance of seizing it. Unur of Damascus was an ally against Nur ad-Din, but his state was still a barrier to Jerusalemite expansion and his isolation made him vulnerable. It was still a chancy business and some seem to have advised against it, but Baldwin III's anxiety to make his name and avenge the defeat of the previous year was probably decisive. In the event the siege was botched and Nur ad-Din was able to relieve the city. The crusade broke up in recriminations. Some westerners felt the native barons had betrayed them, and some in the kingdom felt that relations with the great lords of Christendom had been compromised. Many of the French, though not Louis VII, blamed Manuel and the Byzantines, overlooking their own divisions and incompetence. As the fiasco ended some returning crusaders joined Raymond Berengar IV of Barcelona in a successful attack on Tortosa with Genoese help. Such small successes were poor compensation for the humiliations in the Holy Land.

The crusade to the Holy Land was a dismal failure, and for a time at least, the papacy was very cautious about calling for new expeditions to the east. However, this was only very temporary. The popes could hardly have failed to be impressed with what was achieved in arousing enthusiasm across Christendom. From their perspective it reinforced the view that crusading could have something to offer very large numbers of people and promised to extend papal influence. In the second half of the twelfth century the papacy focused its crusading concerns on the Middle East. That very little was achieved in this period was mainly due to circumstance. The bitter conflict which erupted between papacy and empire in Italy, in which imperial anti-popes were again created, raged from the late 1150s until the late 1170s and drew in the Sicilian-Norman Kingdom. France, to which Eugenius III had looked with such hope before the Second Crusade, was tied up in the conflict with the Angevins, which itself was further complicated by the 'martyrdom' of Thomas Becket, archbishop of Canterbury (1162–70). In these circumstances it is difficult to see who might have led a major expedition to the Holy Land. Moreover, *Outremer*, despite the disaster of the Second Crusade and the defeat and death of Raymond of Antioch at the battle of 'Inab in 1149 at the hands of Nur ad-Din, must have seemed fairly secure, for the most part. We are inclined to be mesmerised by the disaster at Hattin in 1187, but the settlers in the east remained as aggressive as ever. The young Baldwin III (1143–63) was an able ruler who rallied Antioch and triumphed over his mother's attempts to dominate the kingdom. In 1153 he captured the Egyptian city of Ascalon, the last Muslim stronghold on the Palestinian littoral. The rise of Nur ad-Din, and in particular his seizure of Damascus in 1154, were threatening. However, a promising campaign in which Thierry, count of Flanders (1128–68), participated, almost captured Shaizar in 1157, while Nur ad-Din failed before Banyas a year later. Moreover, Baldwin III was prepared to look to Byzantium as an ally, even though this meant recognising Byzantine overlordship of Antioch and giving the Greek Church there a degree of freedom. Manuel had much to gain from the alliance because he wanted to isolate the Seljuks of Asia Minor and to secure his hold on the coastal plains of Asia Minor. In 1158 Baldwin III married Manuel's niece, Theodora and in 1159 a large Greek army arrived in Syria to receive the homage of Antioch. These links with Byzantium were reinforced in 1163 when

Manuel married Bohemond III's sister, Maria of Antioch. The settlers may have been disappointed that Manuel was not prepared to make a major attack on Nur ad-Din's power in Syria, but the Byzantine protectorate in the north certainly prevented the Muslims from making progress. It also formed the context for the Jerusalemite alliance with Byzantium and the expeditions against Egypt in the 1160s.

With the accession of Amalric (1163–74) expansionism continued. The Fatimid regime in Egypt was decaying and this invited outside intervention. Amalric found support there, but so did Nur ad-Din and his agent, Shirkuh. In 1167 Amalric invaded and subjected Egypt to a Frankish protectorate, but two years later Shirkuh was triumphant. This provoked a huge Byzantine/Jerusalemite attack in 1169 which Saladin, Shirkuh's successor, managed to fight off. His position was far from secure, even after the abolition of the Fatimid Caliphate in 1171, especially because Nur ad-Din was deeply suspicious of his ambitions, and in 1174 he faced the prospect of a joint attack mounted by Jerusalem and the Sicilian Norman kingdom. But this came to nothing because Amalric died, plunging the Kingdom of Jerusalem into a succession problem at the very moment when the death of Nur ad-Din enabled Saladin to unite Egypt and Syria. Amalric's son, Baldwin IV (1174–85) was a leper whose health would often oblige him to hand over power to a *baillie* (regent). Moreover, since the king could never sire a child, the succession would rest with his sisters Sibyl and Isabel whose marriages, therefore, assumed great importance. To add to the problems of the settlers in the Holy Land Manuel Comnenus's attempt to seize Iconium, the seat of the Seljuk Suntanate of Rūm, ended in disaster at the battle of Myriokephalon in 1176 and his death in 1180 plunged the empire into a series of succession squabbles which weakened it.

In the society of Catholic Christendom power and wealth were distributed by inheritance because this seemed to offer the best guarantees of stability. The uncertainties raised by the succession of Baldwin IV were therefore very important and inevitably influenced the ability of the kingdom to respond to the challenge of Saladin. The first effort to remedy the situation merely made things worse. In 1176 Sybil married William Longsword of Montferrat, but he died suddenly and Sybil gave birth to the future Baldwin V (1185–86), thus offering the prospect of a continuing regency. By and large the baronage of Jerusalem responded well to this difficult situation until the marriage of a newcomer to the east, Guy of Lusignan, to Sybil, raised very serious questions about the succession. Bitter personal feuds came to the fore and when the child king, Baldwin V died in 1186, a coup by his friends enabled Guy to claim the throne. The bitterness of feeling thus engendered almost brought the kingdom to a state of civil war, particularly as Raymond III of Tripoli seems to have believed that he should have had the succession. In these circumstances the kingdom's ability to respond to the power of Saladin was limited. Although his attack in 1177 was defeated by Baldwin IV at Montgisard, he was able to destroy the new castle of Jacob's Ford on the Damascus frontier in 1179 and by 1183 had united all of Syria by his seizure of

Aleppo. Saladin skilfully portrayed himself as the champion of Islam against the unbelievers. He had much trouble in uniting the Turkish powers, most particularly as he was a Kurd whose family had been taken into the service of the Zengids who were now his chief rivals. His successes were limited against the settlers because the kingdom was anchored by fortified cities, especially Jerusalem and Acre, and it was impossible to besiege them as long as the settlers had a formidable field-army. In 1183 Guy of Lusignan, as *bailli* sensibly refused to engage Saladin's large army as it invaded, but his close presence prevented it achieving anything.

Seen from Saladin's perspective, his considerable strategic problem was compounded by tactical problems. The settlers had adapted their fighting methods to the demands of the Middle East. As a society which was constantly threatened and totally outnumbered, the crusaders had learned to mobilise their manpower. They were able to raise at least 5,000 settler foot to support a levy of 600 knights. The forces of the Military Orders probably contributed another 600 knights, and they and the kings also hired paid men. In addition the settlers recognised the need for light cavalry, called *Turcopoles*, who were raised from both the native Christian and settler population. Native Christians could also be paid to serve as footsoldiers, so that in 1187 an army approaching 20,000 could be raised, whose core was 1,200–1,500 knights. Because key elements of this force were used to working together, cavalry and infantry were coordinated carefully. In battle the disciplined knights developed the tactic, barely known in the west, of the mass charge. In the armies of Islam light horse predominated, and amongst them the most effective were the Turkish horse-archers: infantry were very vulnerable in open, waterless country and speed of manoeuvre could be vital. But the core of Saladin's armies was his heavily armoured *ghulams* whose equipment was comparable to that of the settler knights. Because of the diversity and mobility of their forces, Islamic commanders had the option of manoeuvre on approach to battle, but they had every reason to fear the settler knights who were protected by the bows, crossbows and pikes of their infantry. Moreover, Saladin suffered from another problem – his armies took time to raise and would melt away in time and while his settler enemies had the same problems, his were made worse by the fact that he had to fight in enemy territory studded with castles which could harass his men. But he had one enormous advantage: sheer numbers. The crusaders seem, for a long time, to have enjoyed a qualitative advantage over the Muslims. It is difficult otherwise to account for their victories over superior numbers. It is even more difficult to identify precisely in what this consisted. At first it was partly motivation: the crusaders were convinced of the righteousness of their cause, but gradually as the spirit of *jihad* grew this was countered by the Muslims. In part it was equipment. Turkish horse-archers and other troops were very useful, but at close quarters the well-protected knight on his heavy horse was formidable. However, Saladin in particular seems to have increased the equipment of his *ghulams* to counter this. He inspired his fellow-Kurds to form a fighting elite amongst his regular troops. By the 1180s the settlers still had a reputation for being ferocious fighters, but their air of invulnerability was long gone. They retained their aggression, and though careful about engaging in battle were ever-ready to do so. On 1 May 1187 a group of 150 knights with perhaps 400 foot attacked a large Muslim raiding party perhaps 7,000 strong – only to be destroyed at the Springs of Cresson.

By that time Saladin was in need of a victory, for his enemies charged that he had made a truce with the settlers and waged war more upon fellow-Muslims than upon them. In early June a force of about 30,000 entered the kingdom and in early July attacked Tiberias, held for the Christians by the Countess Eschiva, wife of Raymond III of Tripoli who had only recently been reconciled with King Guy. The aim of the siege was transparently to draw the crusader army into an area without water and there to defeat it. This was Saladin's response to the strategic problem that he could hardly challenge a major city with a hostile field army at his back. In 1183 Saladin had invaded in much the same area and Guy had adopted Fabian tactics, standing off from battle but shadowing Saladin's army. Guy's enemies had accused him of cowardice and soon after he had been deprived of authority by Baldwin IV. Now he needed victory to establish himself firmly as king, and on Friday 3 July he led his army out on a 26 kilometres march towards Tiberias. This was not so irrational as it is sometimes suggested. The settler hold on Galilee had been weakened by Saladin's frequent incursions and if Tiberias was allowed to fall it might mark a real erosion of territory. We do not know in any detail what happened in the two-day battle which followed, but at Hattin Saladin was triumphant and destroyed the army of Jerusalem capturing King Guy. He then went on to seize all the cities except Tyre. The expansive impulse of the Catholic Christendom had suffered its first major setback since the Slav uprising of 983.

St Bernard had hoped that the triumph of Christian arms amongst the pagan Wends would lead to mass conversion. To the bishop of Stettin, who persuaded the crusaders to end their attack on his city, this seemed a nonsense: 'If they had come to strengthen the Christian faith . . . they should do so by preaching, not by arms.'[7] Evangelisation had enjoyed considerable success on the frontier because it responded to the spirit of emulation amongst the pagan elites. It accompanied, but was not coordinated, with the familiar regime of border raids and tribute-taking. But a new spirit was coming to the frontier. The conquest led by Adolf of Holstein and Henry of Badewide in 1140–43 had used foreign settlers to ensure control of new conquests by breaking up Slav society. The ideology of crusade was growing in strength and reviving the notion of forced conversion amongst the German clergy. This process was speeded up because the fashionable Cistercian Order spread along the frontier where its monks were a powerful force for economic development and the pacification of native populations. Henry the Lion of Saxony at first cooperated happily with Nyklot and perhaps shared in the profits of the pagan ruler's raids on Denmark. However, the Danes improved their

---

7 Vincent of Prague, MGH SS 17.663, quoted by E. Christiansen, *The Northern Crusades* (Harmondsworth: Penguin, 1997), 58.

defences and when they began to strike successfully against the pagans, with Waldemar I's (1154–82) raid on Rügen in 1159, Henry cooperated with them and together they killed Nyklot in 1160, and repeated their alliance against his son Pribislav in 1164. The Danes capitalised on their possession of superior ships to develop a technique of raiding and destruction along the coast which destroyed the naval power of the pagans. In 1168 Waldemar conquered Rügen and went on to dominate Pomerania. Henry and Waldemar were as much rivals as allies. Waldemar presented his war as a holy crusade and deliberately encouraged the Cistercians and crusading institutions in his lands, securing his new dynasty by creating a 'Crusading State'. In 1169 he announced his triumph to Alexander III (1159–81) who canonised his 'martyred' ancestor, St Canute. Actually this was skilful manipulation of the crusading ideal. No spiritual rewards had been granted for fighting in the north since the Second Crusade, and *realpolitik* ruled in the politics of the Christian powers. Both Waldemar and Henry recognised the limitations of military power. Henry the Lion re-established Niklot's son, Pribislav as a vassal ruler of his father's principality, while a native ruler of Rügen was left in power as long as he obeyed the Danes. Such accommodations are a testimony to the balance between military power and emulation. But they were acceptable because they permitted implantations of dependable colonists and made it possible for the Church, and especially the Cistercians, to expand their missionary effort. As Helmold remarked, after the foundation of Plön with its city and market-place: 'The Slavs who lived in the villages round about withdrew and Saxons came and dwelt there: and the Slavs, little by little failed in the land.'[8]

It was a sign of the assimilation of the new territories that in 1171 or 1172 Alexander III issued *Non parum animus noster* which offered all the rewards of crusading to Jerusalem for war against the pagans of the north – by which was meant the Estonians, Finns and other peoples of the Baltic. In this the papacy was undoubtedly animated by the hope of intensifying its influence and by fear of a rival evangelisation, that of the Russians who adhered to Greek Christianity.

The convergence of interest between the Church and the magnates of the German frontier was always imperfect. Henry the Lion resisted a reorganisation of the churches in his new lands because it might have limited his power. The Danish kings manipulated the spirit of crusade for dynastic security. Both these and others brutalised the native population without regard to the stipulations of Christianity. However, there was a real convergence of interest, and there is no doubt that this gave the papacy and its agents and allies greater influence. The popes had held aloof from the crudities of conquest, but successes like Rügen were interpreted as convincing manifestations of God's will and encouraged a more active participation for the future, as *Non parum animus noster* demonstrates. Elsewhere the expansion of the 'Catholic core' and the assimilation of lands to Catholic Christendom continued apace, but in a more peaceful way. Sweden was

8 Helmold, *Chronicle of the Slavs*, 225.

the most stubbornly pagan of the Scandinavian lands, but it was largely assimilated by the 1180s, while Poland, Bohemia and Hungary were all recognisably western entities which looked to Rome, not Constantinople, though their borders contained much religious diversity. In Wales Henry II at first favoured a forward policy. In 1157 the Welsh used their knowledge of the difficult terrain to maul his large army at Coleshill on the North Wales coast, and he achieved little when he came again in 1165. In 1171–72 he came to an agreement with the Lord Rhys of Deheubarth and the Prince of Gwynedd which stabilised the March. These rulers acknowledged his supremacy in return for being left alone: it was much the same kind of settlement the rulers of Denmark and Saxony had come to in the Slav lands. It had rather similar results. Although Welsh culture and life remained intact, the upper class reorganised their lands along feudal lines and assimilated largely through emulation. The first native stone castle was Cardigan built in 1171, and others followed. By 1200 Wales was transformed and intermarriage between noble Welsh and Anglo-Norman families was accepted. Hostility remained: warfare was a matter of cruel raiding by both sides, and relations were at best ambivalent. In 1214 Giles de Braose, bishop of Hereford excused himself from attending a church council because he was escorting a papal legate amongst 'the barbarous Welsh nations', although his sister was married to Gruffudd ap Rhys of Deheubarth.[9]

Scotland, like Wales, was a Celtic and largely tribal country on the fringe of Anglo-Norman England, but its relations with the new power to the south were radically different. In 1066 the Scottish monarchy was struggling to impose itself upon the western lands of what is now Scotland, especially the Lord of the Isles whose independence was not entirely extinguished until the thirteenth century. But the Scottish royal house was clearly emerging as a powerful force with whom other rulers enjoyed diplomatic relations. Malcolm III Canmore (1058–93), married St Margaret of the Saxon royal house, had close relations with the new Norman nobility of England and encouraged immigration from the south. There was a reaction under Donald Bane (1094–97) but he was overthrown by an army led by St Margaret's brother, Edgar Aetheling, who imposed his nephew, Edgar (1097–1107) who has been called a 'Scoto-Norman King'. Under Alexander III (1107–24) and David I (1124–53) Norman families like the Brus, the Balliols and the Comyns became firmly established and the Scottish Church was reorganised along lines familiar to its southern neighbour. This new Anglo-Norman nobility was regarded with great hostility by the clans of the north, but they nevertheless dominated Scottish affairs. This willing emulation of the society of the 'Catholic Core' distinguished Scotland sharply from Wales. Moreover, Scotland was less attractive to the Normans, being distant from the centres of Norman power. The

9 J. Barrow, *English Episcopal Acta VII: Hereford 1079–1234* (Oxford: Oxford University Press, 1993), Letter to Stephen Langton of 1214, No. 248, 185. I owe this reference to my colleague, I. W. Rowlands.

two kingdoms were separated only by a specific problem, the allegiance of what is now northern England. The Norman kings and their successors saw the line of the Solway-Tweed as being the frontier, but the Scottish kings claimed Cumbria and Northumbria. This was the cause of frequent wars, notably in 1138 when David I tried to take advantage of the civil wars attendant upon the reign of Stephen to seize the north. He was defeated at the Battle of the Standard on 22 August 1138 after a campaign in which his tribal levies are said to have launched a campaign of terror in northern England. However, he was able to establish a hegemony over the disputed zone until his death and the accession of Henry II in England restored the balance of power. Despite this, by and large England and Scotland enjoyed good relations. Scottish kings were granted major fiefdoms, like Hertfordshire or the northern counties, which tied them to the rulers and aristocracy of England. These relations were to improve in the thirteenth century, by which time their societies closely resembled each other.

There could be no question of a crusade or holy war against the Celts of mainland Britain, but something rather like one was sent against Ireland. In 1155 Henry II of England (1154–89) had entertained ideas of conquering Ireland, and had gone so far as to obtain from Pope Hadrian IV (1154–59) the Bull *Laudabiliter* sanctioning his plan of conquest. Ireland was a land in confusion, divided between numerous kings who vied with one another for supremacy as High King or merely fought in pursuit of the profits of raiding or feud. This situation was complicated by the existence of the Ostman towns like Dublin, places originally developed by Viking settlers which enjoyed virtual independence. Indeed even towards the end of the eleventh century they seemed to lie within the sphere of Scandinavian influence. It was this constant conflict which drew in Henry II. Diarmait Mac Murchada of Leinster and Tigernán Ua Ruairic of Bréifne were rivals for control of Meath, and a new dimension was added to their rivalry because the former had abducted and raped the latter's wife. By 1166 Tigernán Ua Ruairic, in alliance with Ruaidrí Ua Conchobair, High King of all Ireland, was clearly dominant. Diarmait sought out Henry II in France and offered to become his vassal and liege-man for his kingdom of Leinster: the parallels with events slightly later in Wales are very obvious and reinforced because of the close relations that prevailed between Ireland and South Wales. Henry was too busy to intervene himself but he permitted Diarmait to recruit mercenaries and supporters especially in South Wales. Foremost amongst these was Richard FitzGilbert de Clare, earl of Pembroke and Strigoil, known as Strongbow. With his support and the horsemen, crossbowmen and archers in his train, Diarmait defeated his native Irish enemies and captured Dublin, despite the intervention of Ruadrí Ua Conchobair. Strongbow had married Diarmait's daughter Aoife, and on her father's death it became known that the dead king had designated him as his successor to Leinster, in despite of Irish succession laws and the claims of his own sons. A king whose lands straddled the Irish Sea was not acceptable to Henry II. Moreover, he knew that the pope was deeply concerned about the political confusion in Ireland which had severe repercussions for the Irish Church, and so obtained a reissue of *Laudabiliter* from Alexander III. Henry came with a great army to Ireland in 1171. The leading Irish churchmen saw this as an opportunity for stability and welcomed him, while the other kings of Ireland were happy to transfer their allegiance from the discredited Ruaidrí Ua Conchobair, at least for the moment.

Henry II took Dublin, Wexford and Waterford, while Strongbow was established in Leinster and Hugh de Lacy in Meath. The power of these men aroused Irish hostility and they took advantage of the rebellion of Henry II's sons in 1173 to attack, led by Ruadrí Ua Conchobair. In 1175 Henry came to terms with the High King on the basis of the *status quo* but the greed of the Anglo-Norman lords and their followers undermined this compromise, as petty noble settlers hacked out lands for themselves and planted castles. After Strongbow's death in 1176 Hugh de Lacy seems to have had pretensions to an Irish crown through his marriage to a daughter of Ruadrí Ua Conchobair. To counter this Henry appointed his youngest son, John, as Justiciar of Ireland and established a more regular administration based on Dublin. John's hard rule alienated many of his Anglo-Norman vassals as well as the native Irish, but he came again in 1210, put down the rebels and came to terms with the Irish kings outside the English Pale in the south around Dublin and the old cities of the Ostmen. The conquest of Ireland was never really planned by the English crown – it was rather a result of the interaction between peripheral lords and Irish political weakness combined with the desire amongst the native elites to emulate the booming 'Catholic Core'. This intervention was given a respectable gloss by papal approval. Both Henry II and John were anxious to come to terms with the native powers, as long as their supremacy was unquestioned, for fear of frontier lords who might challenge their power. The result of these competing forces was an island in which the main division was now between native kings and Anglo-Norman lords, and the Church was similarly divided between these two peoples. But by the end of the twelfth century Ireland was firmly assimilated to Catholic Christendom.

It was in Spain that the notion of crusade was strongest. Spanish chronicles pay little attention to what happened outside the peninsula, except for the Holy Land. One of the notable features of Spanish history in this period was the emergence of Military Orders as a real force. The military confraternities of Belchite and Monreal, founded in 1122 and 1128 by Alfonso I, were essentially responses to the same kinds of conditions which produced the Temple and the Hospital in the Holy Land. Such fighting confraternities were not uncommon in the cities of Spain, but Alfonso was acutely aware of the need to forge links with Christendom as a whole. In the foundation charter of Monreal Alfonso I famously spoke of defeating the Muslims of Spain and opening a new route to Jerusalem along the North African coast. On his death Alfonso willed the kingdom to the Orders of the Temple and Hospital. This was too much for the nobles to bear, but an amicable settlement was reached by which the two Orders became major landholders in the kingdom, although they minimised their commitment there, preferring to send resources to the east. Calatrava was an important fortress conquered in Alfonso VII's expansion in the wake of the second Crusade. It was given to the Temple in 1147, but, in line with their policy of husbanding their resources for the Holy Land, they renounced it as Islamic counterattacks grew. Raimundo, Cistercian abbot of Fitero, formed a group of volunteers and the Archbishop of Toledo promised remission of their sins to all who defended Calatrava. By 1164 the Order of Calatrava was a recognised fighting element of the Cisterican Order and under the protection of the pope. Fernando II of Léon (1157–88) supported the Order of Santiago which came into existence in 1170 while the Order of Alcántara came into existence before 1176. It is no accident that all these were Castilian. In Aragon the Temple and the Hospital dominated. This contrast reflected the isolationism of Castile compared to Aragon's openness to outside influences.

But it has to be said that the Spanish kingdoms missed the boat at the time of the Second Crusade. The collapse of the Almoravid Empire offered golden opportunities for expansion. The Aragonese advance to the Ebro, like the capture of Lisbon, was a solid achievement, but the expansion of Castile proved ephemeral. In 1148 Alfonso VII's crusade against Jaén failed. Almería fell to the Muslims in 1157 and most of Alfonso VII's conquests in Andalucia perished, inaugurating a half-century when the reconquest stalled. One reason for this was the break-up of Spanish unity. The kings of Léon-Castile had always been recognised as enjoying a paramount position in Spain, and indeed Alfonso VII had styled himself 'Emperor'. But the conquests of the period of the Second Crusade had consolidated both Aragon and Portugal, while in the wake of the failed will of Alfonso the Battler, Navarre had regained its independence. Alfonso VII divided his lands between his two sons: Sancho III (1157–58) took Castile and Fernando II (1157–88) took Léon. Sancho's early death ushered in the regency of the child, Alfonso VIII (1158–1214) which coincided with that of Alfonso II of Aragon (1162–96): both precipitated noble rebellion. These political circumstances enabled the new North African power of the Almohads to establish itself in Spain.

The Spanish Muslim states did not all welcome the Almohads, and Almoravid strong-points resisted. A Spanish Muslim, Lobo, created a powerful kingdom in south-central Spain which resisted the Almohads, but his power was eroded by minor Christian attacks. On his death in 1172 he ceded his lands to the Almohads. Feuds amongst the Christian powers, such as that which led to an alliance of Léon and the Almohads against Portugal and Geraldo the Fearless, a Christian adventurer and vassal of Alfonso I of Portugal, who had besieged Muslim Badajoz in 1169, helped the Almohads to drive back the frontier to the Tagus. Christian powers could often count on the naval support of the Almoravid Kingdom of Majorca against the Almohads. Muslim aggression provoked Christian militancy: in 1183 Castile and Léon agreed an alliance, opening a period of savage fighting. In 1189 an English fleet on its way to the Third Crusade helped them seize Silves. Persistent quarrels amongst the Christian kingdoms had undermined their ability to drive back the Almohads, and although these were composed a legacy of distrust remained. In June 1195 the Caliph Ya'qub (1184–99), provoked by the building of Alarcos north of the strategic Despeñaperros Pass, attacked with a great army. Alfonso VIII refused to await his allies Alfonso IX of Léon (1188–1230) and Sancho VII of Navarre (1194–1234) and flung himself into a disastrous defeat at Alarcos in 1195, all the worse in that Christendom was still reeling from the news of Hattin. It was a famous victory, but like many such had indifferent consequences. Christian territorial losses were minor, though the fall of Calatrava was a moral blow. The Christian kings continued to quarrel and perforce stood on the defensive, prepared to make treaties with the enemy, to the disgust of the pope and his legates who were desperately trying to forge alliances. A period of Almohad dominance would last for some 20 years.

The war in Spain was seen by contemporaries as a crusade, but in reality it only occasionally had the character of holy war. It was not merely that few expeditions received papal endorsement. More importantly, the Christian forces along the frontier waged war as a series of raids and attacks, and were prepared to ally with Muslims against Christians. The ultimate direction and location of the conflict was ideologically determined, but the actual course of most phases of conflict was governed by considerations of local advantage. Moreover, outside involvement was becoming less and less welcome. This was partly a matter of strength and confidence. The struggling Christian kingdoms of the early eleventh century had now been transformed. More importantly, as they grew stronger they became involved in external quarrels. Aragon had always been the most open of the kingdoms, but by the 1170s its ruling house was involved in a long and bitter struggle in Languedoc and Provence. Castile had never been very encouraging to any foreign intervention. Moreover, all the kingdoms contained large Muslim populations which they had to watch carefully. Common practice was to encourage ordinary Muslims and even gentry to surrender on terms rather than to wage a war of annihilation: nobody wanted to wage war for a desert in Spain or Eastern Saxony or Wales. The First Crusade had terrorised many of the Muslims of the Holy Land into flight and subsequently much effort had to be spent to bring them back. A complex of factors, in fact, governed the rhythms of progress on the Spanish frontier, and the papal crusade could only interact with these. The Spanish kingdoms suffered from the normal instabilities of contemporary political structures, especially failure of hereditary succession. Like all contemporary kingdoms they lacked articulated administrations and kings had to rely on great magnates. In Spain the need for garrisons in the cities which held the frontier meant that the cities enjoyed extensive *fueros*, liberties, and they were not always amenable to royal control. Moreover, as the frontier advanced, once exposed cities clung to their privileges and allied with the nobility against the king when it suited them. In these circumstances it is hardly surprising that the first representative institutions appeared in Spain. In 1188, 1202 and 1208 Alfonso IX of Léon (1188–1230) summoned representatives of all groups, including the cities, to his *Cortes*. These assemblies of churchmen, nobles, gentry and bourgeois commanded real power and any king had to listen to them. Alfonso had a difficult succession, but it is significant that he was not merely seeking political recognition from the nobles but also acknowledging the economic power of the cities.

Barcelona was a major trading port of the Mediterranean by the end of the twelfth century. But smaller towns, like Sahagún, had a merchant community whose members demanded and received privileges from the abbot of the great monastery there. On the frontier the offer of privileges and land which tempted people from safe areas and from abroad presented opportunities for social mobility. On the other hand the violence of life there often impoverished peasant-cultivators. The *Mozarabs* in the newly liberated areas of Léon-Castile often suffered, and their lands were bought by great churches, military orders or wealthy aristocratic families. Very frequently these great landholders went over to cattle and sheep ranching which suited the frontier better than arable farming. Thus the pattern of lordship came to dominate the frontier and was accepted by kings because it was militarily efficient. The new lordships needed soldiers, so it was by military service that men rose, and the cities took on a militaristic caste with their councils dominated by petty knights. Because of their military service such men paid no taxes, shifting the burden onto the increasingly tied peasants. This was a society organised for war. In that it was not unique, for the same could be said of the Anglo-Norman settlements in South Wales or any of the dangerous frontiers of Christendom. In these areas, as in Spain, fighting and plunder were paths to preferment and military values were supreme. Corraquín Sancho was a *caballero* of Avila who once rescued 20 shepherds from Muslim captivity and was commemorated in the Avila chronicle:

> People sing of Roland and Oliver
> But not of Corraquín who was a fine *caballero*
> They sing of Oliver and Roland,
> But not of Corraquín who was a fine young man.[10]

The popes took a keen interest in Spain. Adrian IV (1154–59), hearing that Louis VII and Henry II were considering an expedition to Spain, wrote urging them to consult the rulers of Spain pointing out that this had not been done by those who led the Second Crusade. But they had to be wary of the sensitivities of the Spanish monarchs and the complex factors which bore upon the progress of the reconquest. Gregory VII's claims to be overlord of the Spanish kingdoms had been much resented. Even in the reign of Alfonso VII (1126–57) the 'Roman papacy was an alien presence' and it took time before the Church of Léon and Castile became less isolated.[11] It was only after the defeat of Alarcos that papal

---

10 *Crónica de la población de Avila*, translated and quoted by A. McKay, *Spain in the Middle Ages. From frontier to Empire, 1000–1500* (London: Macmillan, 1977), 55.

11 B. F. Reilly, *The Kingdom of Léon-Castilla under Alfonso VII (1126–57)* (Philadelphia, PA: University of Pennsylvania Press, 1998), 263.

intervention became really active, because from a papal perspective the quarrels of the Spanish kings were putting the whole Christian cause at peril.

The papacy was deeply committed to assisting the Holy Land despite the failures of the Second Crusade. There was an endless diplomacy, much of it directed to the Byzantine Empire. In 1157 Adrian IV called for a crusade. Alexander III (1159–81) did the same in 1165 in response to appeals for help from the Holy Land. This was amplified very vigorously in 1166 when the pope mentioned various disasters which had befallen the east, notably the loss of Banyas in 1164, and there is some evidence of a limited response to the calls. In 1167 Eustace Cholet, a lord from Ponthieu, and a Sicilian, Hugh of Creona, were killed fighting in Egypt, and William of Nevers took the cross in 1167, but died in 1168 as he arrived at Jerusalem, leaving his knights leaderless. In 1169, after Saladin seized power in Egypt, an important delegation from Jerusalem led by Frederick, archbishop of Tyre, arrived in the west, and Pope Alexander used the occasion to issue his third crusading bull, *Inter Omnia*. This mission had been carefully prepared and targeted people with known crusading sympathies, above all Louis VII, and family connections with the east, as in the case of Henry II. But Louis VII and Henry II, although they professed support, distrusted one another too much and the bitterness of Henry's dispute with Becket also made his departure difficult. In 1171 Henry II promised to go to Jerusalem, in remorse for the murder of Becket, and this formed part of the Avranches settlement by which the king was reconciled to the Church. However, the outbreak of the great revolt of 1173 which raised substantial sections of their nobility against the Angevins, meant that this never materialised, though in accordance with Avranches, Henry sent 2,000 silver marks a year to the Holy Land. Further diplomatic pressure from Jerusalem, supported by the papacy, produced a positive result. William II of Sicily (1166–89) had only just emerged from a long minority, but he agreed to mount a major naval expedition in a joint attack on Egypt with Amalric. This came to nothing because Amalric died and no crusading army came to support the Sicilian fleet which failed before Alexandria in 1174. In 1177 Philip of Flanders arrived in the east, but his expedition came to nothing. The contrast between these meagre results, despite much diplomatic activity and papal backing, and the Second Crusade is enormous. The major difference lies in the activity of the popes concerned. Eugenius III had recruited Bernard and flung himself into arousing enthusiasm. Alexander, locked in a struggle with the Emperor Frederick Barbarossa (1152–90) until 1177, was in no position to indulge in such activity, while the conflict of Capetian and Plantagenet soured relations north of the Alps.

Alexander III must have reflected that while the pope could propose, the fate of crusades lay in other hands. After his victory over Barbarossa in 1177, Alexander called together the Third Lateran Council. Its key function was to present the pope as the propagator of proper order and peace in the world. A wide scheme of reform was proposed for the Church as a whole, but beyond this an effort was made to bring unity and peace into Christian society, notably by the banning of tournaments. But most interesting of all, Alexander offered remission of sins to all who would fight against the heretics and mercenaries (*routiers*) who were disturbing the peace of the Church in southern France. This was an area scarified by two great wars – that between Capetian and Plantagenet, and the much less-known conflict between the Kings of Aragon and their enemies in Provence, notably the counts of Toulouse. The Angevins and Capetians became entangled in this long-running conflict which created a demand for mercenaries. Like all contemporary warfare it was episodic and some of the nobility of the Auvergne were willing to create safe-havens for discharged mercenaries who were waiting employment. There is no real evidence that anybody ever received such a crusading reward, but the papal offer may have helped to arouse the enthusiasm of ordinary peasants. There arose in this area the movement of the 'Capuchins', hooded peasant warriors, whose armies put pressure on those nobles who had sheltered the mercenaries and ultimately helped to annihilate them. However, it was essentially other nobles who achieved this, and they went on to destroy the 'Capuchins' who they saw as a threat to the social order as least as grave as that of the mercenaries. This propagandist stance by Alexander was clearly intended to underline his supremacy over the squabbling kings of Christendom with their mercenary armies. It also represented another attempt to enlist crusading enthusiasm against internal enemies and paved the way for the later crusades within Christendom.

When Pope Urban III (1185–87) was told of Hattin and the fall of Jerusalem, it is said that he died of grief. His successor, Gregory VIII (1187) sent out an appeal for a fresh crusade, but died soon after, so the task of organisation fell to Clement III (1187–91). The tax which he declared should be levied on all Christendom to support the expedition, the 'Saladin Tithe' was not entirely novel for Henry II had agreed to a levy to help the Holy Land in 1166. But the scale of the new tax, levied on moveables, was the real novelty. In January 1188 Josias, archbishop of Tyre, the only remaining city in the kingdom of Jerusalem, approached Henry II and Philip of France (1180–1223) at Gisors where both kings and many of their nobles promised to take the cross. Philip of Flanders soon after again took the cross. On 27 March 1188 Frederick Barbarossa also took the cross. With the best will in the world it would take such armies time to get to the Levant. Frederick collected a great German army but it was May 1189 before it set off from its concentration point at Regensburg. King Philip and Henry II fell to quarrelling, then the latter died on 6 July 1189 at Chinon and his successor, Richard I (1189–99) inevitably needed time to settle his lands. It was not until 4 July 1190 that Richard and Philip met with their armies at Vézelay, ready to set out. It was three years since Hattin.

In the panic in the kingdom after Hattin Acre surrendered on 10 July and most of the cities of the coast soon followed. Totally isolated, Jerusalem surrendered on terms on 2 October. But one city had not surrendered. Numerous refugees had found haven in Tyre, and on 14 July Conrad of Montferrat, an experienced soldier who had been serving in Byzantium, arrived and organised its defence. Saladin returned to the city in November, but it was even better organised. He pushed on northwards into the principality of Antioch taking Bourzey, Tortosa, Lattakieh and Saône in 1188. But this excursion merely tired his army and left time for the settler elements to rally. William II of Sicily sent a fleet to the east led by his admiral, Margarit, and this and other forces now arriving were able to foil Saladin's forces. These small survivals were important because they formed bases for the crusading armies. Moreover they were very valuable as bases for the fleets which were vital to any reconquest.

In July 1188 Saladin released King Guy on condition that he return to the west and trouble Muslims no more. Unsurprisingly a priest released him from these conditions imposed under duress when he returned to Tripoli which was now held by Bohemond III of Antioch. There a court formed around him, but Conrad of Montferrat was regarded as the man who had saved Tyre and led the resistance, and he claimed to be holding the city in trust for the Christian kings who were on their way. Conrad wanted to wait for them, but the crusader contingents arriving in the east, notably the fleet of 52 Pisan ships, wanted to do something other than await events. Guy adroitly turned the tables on Conrad by leading these forces to besiege Acre on 28 August 1189. All this was made possible because Saladin had partially demobilised his army and was playing a passive role. Acre was formidable, but more and more contingents joined Guy, and Conrad felt obliged to come also. Saladin now woke up to the danger and encamped close to the city around which the crusaders had established field-fortifications. There was a major battle on 4 October, but he was quite unable to defeat them on land. Saladin had revived the Egyptian navy which achieved a maritime supremacy during much of the winter of 1189–90. Because of this he was able to reinforce and resupply Acre by sea, and the city held off a serious assault on 5 May 1190. On 19 May Saladin attacked in an eight-day assault on the crusader camp. On 25 July the sergeants and foot of the army insisted on mounting a surprise attack on Saladin's camp, contrary to the wishes of their leaders. Saladin massacred them and one chronicler commented, 'Thus did our Lord allow the haughtiness of the sergeants towards the knights to be avenged', a revelation of social divisions harboured in all the Christian armies.[12] A deadlock now ensued which both sides recognised could only be broken by the arrival of armies from the west.

The Emperor Frederick Barbarossa had been on the Second Crusade, and had certainly learned its lessons. His army was very large: a contemporary estimate of 100,000 is almost certainly an exaggeration, but it was certainly big and very highly disciplined. However, as it entered Byzantine territory it confronted difficult problems, not dissimilar from those confronted by the Second Crusade. The First Crusade had been designed to bring aid to Byzantium and to bridge the gap between the two sectors of Christendom. Bohemond's seizure of Antioch created an inheritance of mistrust so evident during the Second Crusade. More

---

12 P. Edbury (ed.), 'The Old French Continuation of William of Tyre', in *The Conquest of Jerusalem and the Third Crusade* (Aldershot: Scolar, 1996), 95.

importantly, the ideologically inspired crusades coincided with other aspects of expansionism in the Mediterranean which vitiated relations between Constantinople and the west. The perennial hatred between Normans and Byzantines had soured the atmosphere at the time of the Second Crusade. Manuel Comnenus invaded South Italy unsuccessfully in 1155. This attack profoundly annoyed Frederick Barbarossa who had claims in this area. In 1185 the Normans took advantage of a disputed succession in the Byzantine Empire to invade, and seized its second city, Thessalonika. They pretended to act in the name of Manuel's son, Alexius II (1180–83), who had been supplanted and probably killed by Andronicus II (1182–85). When Andronicus panicked, Isaac II Angelus (1185–95) overthrew him and expelled the Normans, but in the following years faced a series of pretenders, notably Isaac Comnenus who installed himself as emperor in Cyprus, as well as Slav and Bulgarian revolts. The Norman kingdom of Italy dissolved into a profound succession crisis on the death of William II without heir in 1189, but Isaac was too weak to profit from this, and in any case he had other western enemies. The privileged trading position of Venice arising from the Golden Bull was bound to create tensions with Byzantium. Manuel Comnenus had abrogated the arrangements and played off Pisa and Genoa against the Venetians. In 1172 the Venetians were expelled from Constantinople. However, the empire still needed naval support and their place was taken by Pisans and Genoese. In Constantinople there was bitter hatred of these privileged foreigners and in 1182 Andronicus allowed this to climax in a terrible massacre of westerners. Although westerners were readmitted and some restoration was made, all distrusted the weak successors of Manuel and Venice wanted the restoration of its former dominant position at Constantinople. Isaac II Angelus was suspicious of any western incursion, and this fear was deepened by news of the coming of the Third Crusade. Isaac may well have agreed to an alliance with Saladin against the crusaders. In the event he faced the huge crusading army of Frederick I which marched down the Danube valley. Frederick did not want to attack Constantinople but he was faced with the consequences of the fragmentation of the Byzantine empire. Because of this he came to arrangements with the rebels in the Balkans and this further alienated Isaac. The large German army inevitably pillaged imperial territory. Matters were made worse by the emperor's own envoys who tried to involve Frederick in attempts to overthrow Isaac. In the end, after some limited fighting, the two emperors agreed arrangements that allowed the German army to cross into Asia Minor. But time had passed: the Germans entered the empire on 23 June 1189, but it was only in March 1190 that they crossed into Asia Minor.

No crusading army since the First Crusade had successfully fought its way through Asia Minor. Frederick had attempted to negotiate passage with the Sultan of Iconium, but this failed. The Germans defeated the army of Iconium and seized the city itself on 17 May. These were considerable achievements and can be contrasted with Manuel's failure on the same route in 1176. A well-found and well-led western army was very formidable, so it is little wonder that Saladin saw it as divinely willed when news came that Frederick had died crossing the River Calycadnus (Gök-Su) in Cilicia. Quite why Frederick died we shall never know. But loyalty in the Middle Ages was personal rather than ideological; this was a fundamental problem of all medieval political structures. Its effect was immediate: the German army fell apart and most returned home. A sizeable force under Leopold of Austria arrived at Acre, but without Frederick it had no driving force. This was a catastrophe in another way. Frederick's age, eminence and status gave him an undisputed hegemony amongst all the leaders – now there was nobody else who could stake such a claim to leadership. A contemporary Muslim writer, Ibn al-Athir reported that 'When we had news that the King of Germany had come we were convinced that we would no longer be able to hold Syria', so Saladin was mightily relieved by news of his death: 'Thus God liberated us from the evil of such a man.'[13] However, this was not the end of his troubles.

Saladin could not end the stalemate at Acre where the western army, even after the death of Frederick, was encouraged by the expectation of mighty reinforcement. In 1187 Richard, heir-apparent to the Angevin Empire, had taken the cross. His father, Henry II, and Philip of France rather reluctantly followed his lead. Their espousal of the crusader cause promised much, but it brought in its train enormous complications. Henry was not fond of Richard who had to wage war for his father's recognition as heir in 1189. Philip II of France (1180–1223) profited greatly as their overlord. The articulation of monarchical states was one of the great processes of western history. Philip was seeking to impose himself upon the great dynasties over whose lands he held overlordship. Flanders was notable amongst these, but the Angevins were the most powerful. Once his father was dead Richard I had first to busy himself with diplomatic arrangements to counter French pressure. So deep was their mutual distrust that neither Richard nor Philip would leave without the other. In the end they agreed to divide any spoil they might capture equally between them at Vézélay, and on 4 July 1190, three years to the day from the battle of Hattin, they set off together. Their journey would be a long one because kings had great diplomatic entanglements.

Richard has been much blamed for his neglect of England in favour of foreign expedition. Undoubtedly he had a taste for war and adventure, but he was king of England, not an English king. He was as French as his great rival, Philip II, and much of his reign was spent in his lands in France. Piety and adventurousness may have inclined him to go on crusade, but he was also head of he house of Anjou, a branch of which ruled Jerusalem. King Guy, now besieging Acre, was a member of a vassal family from Poitou. Philip II was the son of the first crusader king, Louis VII, and the settlements in Outremer which had just been destroyed, were heavily French in make-up. The very existence of Outremer created not just an ideological obligation amongst western people but also family and other connections

13 Ibn al-Athir, *The Collection of Histories*, translated in F. Gabrieli (ed.), *Arab Historians of the Crusades* (London: Routledge, 1969), 210, 212.

which enormously reinforced it. So the two kings, in taking the cross, would have been seen as fulfilling a whole set of very proper obligations. But as kings they were also entangled in much else. King Philip wanted to control the Angevin, who ruled such vast lands in France. He was painfully aware that Richard had a larger army and could easily outshine him. Richard was determined to escape from his engagement to Philip's sister, Alice, in order to marry Berengaria of Navarre whose father was a good ally. To this end he blackened the lady's reputation, forcing Philip to agree to annul the engagement. In the end he married Berengaria in Cyprus. In late September Richard and Philip and their fleets gathered at Messina. William II of Sicily had died the previous year and rule had fallen to an Hauteville bastard, Tancred of Lecce. His dominion over the Hauteville lands was uncertain and he feared the rival claim of Henry of Germany, son of Barbarossa. Moreover, he had kept the dowry of Joanne, widow of William II and sister of Richard, and refused to implement that part of William's Will which provided money for Henry II's crusade to the Holy Land that Richard believed should go to him. These political problems exacerbated the natural tensions between the crusader armies and their unwilling hosts, and on 4 October Richard seized Messina. By the time all these complications had been settled it was winter and too late to sail, so that it was not until 10 April 1191 that Richard left Sicily.

But there was further delay. Richard, like Barbarossa before him, encountered the consequences of the decay of Byzantine power. Isaac Comnenus had set himself up as 'Emperor' in Cyprus. Some of Richard's ships were wrecked on the island the the passengers poorly treated, and his fiancéé, Berengaria, was trapped on her ship in Limassol harbour. Richard arrived in Cyprus on 6 May 1191. By 1 June, after a brilliant campaign the whole island was in his possession. It is possible that Richard had always contemplated such an assault, but equally he may have simply improvised when provocation was offered. This was yet another blow to the Byzantine Empire, and another extension to Catholic Christendom in the Mediterranean. In the short run Richard had a rich base for his attempt to liberate Jerusalem. Richard's arrival at Acre on 8 June galvanised the besieging army. However, tension amongst the crusaders remained high. Richard supported Guy in his claim to be the king of Jerusalem, while the surviving barons of the kingdom and Philip favoured Conrad of Montferrat. The decision was that Guy should rule till his death when he would be succeeded by Conrad. This was less a settlement than a delaying tactic to prevent open war. Moreover Richard was arrogant and tactless to many of the leaders. Despite this, on 12 June Acre surrendered. By the end of the month Philip had returned to France and Richard marched south, defeating Saladin at Arsuf on 7 September and taking Jaffa on 10 September. Richard probably wanted to secure Ascalon as a priority, but the bulk of his army wished to press on to Jerusalem. Saladin still had an army and the weather was appalling, forcing Richard to turn back and to refortify Ascalon. By this time events in the west were pressing upon him and the endless factional struggles in the army were undermining all that had been achieved. The native barons demanded the election of Conrad and Richard acquiesced and compensated Guy by making him ruler of Cyprus. When Conrad was assassinated Henry of Champagne succeeded as king and in the spring of 1192 the army once more attacked Jerusalem. But the risks of a siege when Saladin had a large army in the field were too great and they fell back. On 27 July 1192 Saladin tried to recapture Jaffa, but was driven back. Both sides were exhausted and on 2 September a truce was agreed by which the Christians would hold the coast as far south as Jaffa, though Ascalon had to be surrendered. For all its triumphs the Third Crusade had only preserved a rump of Jerusalem.

Hattin had been the first major set-back to western expansionism. Significantly, the Holy Land was at the very end of its reach and threatened by Islam which was the most powerful of the centres of influence which it faced. Elesewhere, in Wales and the Baltic, the assimilation of new peoples to the civilisation of Christendom proceeded. But the coincidence of defeat in Spain gave Islam a more terrifying aspect and seemed to some to presage a general threat to Christendom. The difficulties of the experience of the Third Crusade made western people think more rationally about strategy and the means to overcome their enemies. Richard had wanted the crusaders to attack Egypt using the dominant western naval power. The failure of the two attacks on Jerusalem doomed the old concept of a pell-mell attack on Jerusalem. Islam was now stronger and held the cities and fortresses which had been the strength of the old kingdom. A new line of attack was needed and this was clearly signalled by Richard. To accompany this a new ideological rekindling was also needed, to mobilise the resources of Christendom for the task in the east. This was the task of the papacy and the Church. For although the record of the second half of the twelfth century may appear mixed, to say the least, from the point of view of the papacy it was in some ways highly positive. The crusade was unequivocally a papal institution and through it the popes had gained influence over almost all aspects of the European expansion. Catholic Christendom continued to look to Rome for a lead in the affairs of the Holy Land and its role as a mobiliser of opinion and resources was being felt on the Baltic and in Spain. The next half-century would see the zenith of the crusading movement. But if Christendom was anxious to recover Jerusalem and looked to the papacy for leadership, the Third Crusade pointed to the future in another way. On the Second Crusade Conrad III and Louis VII played only a limited role, but on the Third Richard and Philip enjoyed much greater prestige and influence. This binding in of the princes, counts and great lords to the structure of the monarchical states was as yet very limited, but it had very far-reaching implications for the crusade and for the whole dynamic of the expansion of Catholic Christendom.

SELECTED READING

For the career and importance of Zengi, see the study by C. Hillenbrand, '"Abominable Acts": the career of Zengi', in J. Phillips and M. Hoch (eds), *The Second Crusade. Scope and*

Consequences (Manchester: Manchester University Press, 2001), 111–32. The indispensable guide to the context of the Second Crusade is J. P. Phillips, *Defenders of the Holy Land. Relations between Latin East and the West 1119–87* (Oxford: Oxford University Press, 1996). The best outline of the events of the Second Crusade is V. G. Berry, 'The Second Crusade', in Setton, *Crusades*, 1. 463–512. However, historians' thinking about the crusade has been dominated by G. Constable, 'The Second Crusade as seen by Contemporaries', *Traditio* 9 (1953), 213–79 who propagated the idea that it was planned as a grand offensive against Islam everywhere and against the pagan enemies of Christianity. Although this view was formulated many years ago it continues to hold sway and none of the contributors to two recent collections of essays on the subject have contested it: M. Gervers (ed.), *The Second Crusade and the Cistercians* (New York: St Martin's Press, 1992) and J. Phillips and M. Hoch (eds), *The Second Crusade. Scope and Consequences* (Manchester: Manchester University Press, 2001).

However, doubt has been cast on this whole unitary notion of the Second Crusade by A. Forey, 'The Second Crusade: scope and objectives', *Durham University Journal* 86 (1994), 165–75 whose article deserves to be better known. The present writer sympathises with this attitude. For Eugenius III's contribution to the crusade and in particular his preference for the French, see the essay by R. Hiestand, 'The Papacy and the Second Crusade', in Phillips and Hoch (eds), *The Second Crusade*, 32–53. For the Will of Baldwin II, see H. E. Mayer, 'Studies in the history of Queen Melisende of Jerusalem', *Dumbarton Oaks Papers* 26 (1972), 93–182. Historians have traditionally been very critical of the decision to attack Damascus, but the case for this line of action has been ably argued by A. Forey, 'The failure of the siege of Damascus in 1148', *Journal of Medieval History* 10 (1984), 13–25 and M. Hoch, 'The choice of Damascus as the objective of the Second Crusade: a re-evaluation', in M. Balard (ed.), *Autour de la première croisade* (Paris: Publications de la Sorbonne, 1996), 359–70. On the sources for the attack on Lisbon articles by S. Edgington, 'The Lisbon letter of the Second Crusade', *Historical Research* 69 (1996), 328–39 and 'Albert of Aachen, St Bernard and the Second Crusade', in Phillips and Hoch (eds), *The Second Crusade*, 54–70 are invaluable. On the Wendish Crusade and its continuations, see A. V. Murray (ed.), *Crusade and Conversion on the Baltic Frontier, 1150–1500* (Aldershot: Ashgate, 2001), especially the essay by W. Urban, 'The Frontier Thesis and the Baltic Crusade' and K. V. Jensen, 'Denmark and the Second Crusade: the formation of a crusader state?', in Phillips and Hoch (eds), *The Second Crusade*, 54–74, 164–79. On the Second Crusade in Spain, see Lomax, *Reconquest of Spain* and more specifically N. Jaspert, '*Capta est Dertosa, clavis Christianorum*', in Phillips and Hoch (eds), *The Second Crusade*, 90–110. For Byzantine attitudes to the Second Crusade, see especially P. Magdalino, *The Empire of Manuel I Komnenos, 1143–80* (Cambridge: Cambridge University Press, 1993). On the history of the crusader states after the Second Crusade, see H. A. R. Gibb, 'The career of Nur ad-Din' and M. W. Baldwin, 'The Latin states under Baldwin III and Amalric I, 1143–1174', in Setton, *Crusades*, 1, 513–62. On the struggle in Northern Europe and Eastern Germany, Christiansen, *The Northern Crusades* remains the most convenient account. For a brilliant analysis of English relations with the Celtic lands, see R. R. Davies, *The First English Empire 1093–1343* (Oxford: Oxford University Prerss, 2000) whose *Age of Conquest* provides a very useful history of Wales. R. Bartlett, *Gerald of Wales* (Oxford: Clarendon, 1982) is a study of a key source for Welsh history in the twelfth century. On the history of Scotland, see R. L. G. Ritchie, *The Normans in Scotland* (Edinburgh: Edinburgh University Press, 1954) and G. W. S. Barrow, *Robert Bruce and the Community of the Realm of Scotland* (London: Eyre and

Spottiswood, 1965) and his *Kingship and Unity. Scotland 1000–1306* (Edinburgh: Arnold, 1981). For the conquest of Ireland, see A. J. Otway-Ruthven, *A History of Medieval Ireland* (London: E. Benn, 1968) and S. Duffy, *Ireland in the Middle Ages* (London: Macmillan, 1997). A. McKay, *Spain in the Middle Ages. From frontier to Empire, 1000–1500* (London: Macmillan, 1977), provides a good account of Spanish history, but for a brilliant insight into the militarised nature of its society, see two works by J. F. Powers, *A Society organised for War. The Iberian Municipal Militias in the Central Middle Ages, 1000–1284* (Berkeley, CA: University of California Press, 1988) and his 'Life on the cutting edge: the Luso-Hispanic frontier in the Twelfth Century', in I. A. Corfis and M. Wolfe (eds), *The Medieval City under Siege* (Woodbridge: Boydell, 1995), 17–34. The war in southern France and its intimate connection with the Capetian-Angevin has not been much studied by R. Benjamin, 'The Forty Years War: Toulouse and the Plantagenets, 1156–96', *Historical Research* 61 (1988), 270–85, while M. Bull, *The Miracles of Our Lady of Rocamadour. Analysis and Translation* (Woodbridge: Boydell, 1999) is a modern work which provides some insights into the problem. There is a good narrative account of the last phase of the history of the Kingdom of Jerusalem by M. W. Baldwin, 'The decline and fall of Jerusalem, 1174–1189', in Setton, *Crusades*, 1, 590–621. A more modern view of this period is provided by B. Hamilton, *The Leper King and his Heirs. Baldwin IV and the Crusader Kingdom of Jerusalem* (Cambridge: Cambridge University Press, 2000), while P. Edbury has produced a brilliant analysis of the divisions in the kingdom on the eve of Hattin in his 'Propaganda and faction in the Kingdom of Jerusalem: the background to Hattin', in M. Shatzmiller (ed.), *Crusaders and Muslims in Twelfth-Century Syria* (Leiden: Brill, 1993), 173–89. The consequent problems of Guy of Lusignan as king are examined by R. C. Smail, 'The predicaments of Guy of Lusignan, 1183–87', in B. Z. Kedar (ed.), *The Horns of Hattin* (London: Variorum, 1992), 190–207. On the rise of Saladin the best study is that of M. C. Lyons and D. E. P. Jackson, *Saladin. The Politics of Holy War* (Cambridge: Cambridge University Press, 1982). Our understanding of the battle of Hattin is extremely limited because of the weaknesses of the sources, but an exceptionally fine study showing familiarity both with the sources and the ground across which it was fought is that of B. Z. Kedar, 'The Battle of Hattin revisited', in B. Z. Kedar, (ed.), *The Horns of Hattin* (London: Variorum, 1992), 190–207. For the story of the Third Crusade, see S. Painter, 'The Third Crusade: Richard the Lionheart and Philip Augustus', and E. N. Johnson, 'The crusades of Frederick Barbarossa and Henry VI', in Setton, *Crusades*, 2, 45–122. The German crusade is also discussed in P. Munz, *Frederick Barbarossa. A Study in Medieval Politics* (London: Eyre and Spottiswoode, 1969). Richard of England was the dominant influence on events and his role is well explored by J. Gillingham, *Richard the Lionheart* (London: Weidenfeld and Nicolson, 1978). For the role of Philip of France, see J. W. Baldwin, *The Government of Philip Augustus. Foundations of French Royal Power in the Middle Ages* (Berkeley, CA: University of California Press, 1986). For Richard's seizure of Cyprus and its subsequent history there is a good survey by P. Edbury, *The Kingdom of Cyprus and the Crusades 1191–1374* (Cambridge: Cambridge University Press, 1991).

6

THE ZENITH OF THE
CRUSADING MOVEMENT,
1192–1254

The failure of the Second Crusade had induced a deep mood of pessimism about crusading and its prospects. It did not last long, but it produced bitter criticism of St Bernard. Gerhoh of Reichersberg went as far as to suggest that Antichrist was at liberty in the world, seducing men whose greed vitiated the gallantry of the crusaders. The failure of the Third Crusade was not absolute and its achievements gave promise of recovery in the future. The emotional force of the defeat at Hattin served as a real impulse for the crescendo of crusades which followed: the Third Crusade, 1187–92, the Fourth Crusade in 1202–04, the Fifth Crusade 1217–21, the Crusades of Theobald of Champagne and Richard of Cornwall in 1239–41 and the Crusades of St Louis, 1249–50 and 1270. There were also minor expeditions and such popular manifestations of the desire to liberate Jerusalem as the 'Children's Crusade' of 1212. There were far more crusades in the thirteenth century than ever before and they went, far more often, to different places. The special regard for Jerusalem continued and crusades there were very frequent despite all the disasters and failures.

The explanation for this is complex. Certainly people could no longer assume Christian control of Jerusalem as they had between 1099 and 1187. Hattin was a terrible shock to all Christian people and a special challenge to the elite of Catholic Christendom. The increasing wealth of the west in the twelfth century produced substantial threats to their pre-eminence. Kings, in England and France, came to rely increasingly on skilled, literate and above all obedient administrators, men 'raised from the dust', who could administer their realms for them. In the new cities mercantile wealth demanded privileges and political influence. In reaction to these changes, the aristocratic elite increasingly emphasised their exclusiveness, their special role as the advisers of kings and their military status. Society was actually becoming more peaceful and settled and many nobles were no longer necessarily soldiers, but as a whole they emphasised their military function. In a society conventionally divided into those who fight, those who labour and those who pray, their military function was the moral underpinning of their social and political ascendancy. One tangible result was the building and rebuilding of stone castles which were essentially palaces: their military structure emphasised the monopoly of war which their owners claimed.

As a result, despite the emergence of professional warriors, rank continued to determine command in war and these men were confined to subordinate or advisory roles. At the end of the century Edward I of England described Earl Warenne his commander in Scotland, as a 'turd', but he remained commander until he lost disastrously to William Wallace at the battle of Stirling Bridge in 1297. Shortly before this Edward had wanted to replace Warenne with the able Brian FitzAlan, but he declined because he had not the resources to serve the king on such a scale. It was a nice illustration of the way in which the traditional elite maintained their hold on military matters. The upper echelons of society had always adhered to a crude 'Warrior Ethic', a delight in war and its virtues of bravery and companionship. But wealth and stability encouraged its elaboration into a code of aristocratic life embracing displays not only of prowess but also of piety and attraction to women. Its most characteristic institution was the ritualised combat of the tournament. Tournaments had become a great fashion in the early twelfth century, but they were condemned as early as 1130 at the Council of Clermont and this ban was only revoked by John XXII (1316–34) in 1316, by which time it was apparent that it was simply ineffectual. Originally they were an important means of providing young men with practice for war, but increasingly they offered an opportunity for ostentatious display. Magnates paid professional swords for hire, like William Marshal, to fight for them and the whole affair tended to become a social occasion with a role, albeit limited, for women, as well as a training ground for war. The Church tried by many other methods to modify the behaviour of the aristocratic elite. The process of investing a young man as a knight became a religious one involving an overnight vigil in a church before the ceremony. Such ceremonial emphasised the duty of the Christian knight to protect the weak and the Church against evil. Sword-blessings and other rituals pointed in the same direction.

But despite this, the nobility could hardly be ignorant of the clash between their life-style and the demands of the Church. The real piety of the upper class sat uneasily with delight in war, wenching and graceful social attributes like reciting and even composing poetry, as the more zealous clergy often pointed out. Crusade, sacred war, offered a ready justification for their role. Urban II had directed his appeal for the First Crusade to the knights and the nobility. He certainly hoped that it would form a useful channel for their warlike energies. According to Fulcher of Chartres, who may have been present and certainly went on the First Crusade, Urban proclaimed:

> Let those who are accustomed to wantonly wage private war against the faithful march upon the infidels in a war which should be begun now and be finished in victory. Let those who have been robbers now be soldiers of Christ.[1]

---

1 Fulcher, *History of the Expedition to Jerusalem*, 66–7.

Crusading, therefore, became an annexe of the aristocratic life-style and an intimate part of the moral justification of their privileges. It is upon this elite that the accounts of crusades centre and they seem to have seen it as an especially aristocratic undertaking, linked to their status in society. The *Chansons de Geste* were poems written for the upper class telling exciting tales of valour in war. The most famous of them, the *Song of Roland*, is based on the destruction of part of Charlemagne's rearguard by the Basques in the pass of Roncevalles as they returned from a campaign in Spain in alliance with the Baghdad Caliphate and its friends in Spain. But the poem transforms Charlemagne's expedition into a crusade and portrays Roland dying in battle against the Muslims. Another group of poems were the cycle of four concerned with William of Orange, which were recast to portray him as a champion of Christendom against the Saracens. This suggests the special appeal of the crusade to the leaders of western society. It has to be said that crusading was always a minority activity even amongst the elite. There were 'Crusading families' whose members expressed their piety by participation, and as long as the kingdom lasted other families may well have been happy to leave crusading in their hands. However, the elite clearly had a susceptibility to the appeal of crusading and this was enormously enhanced by the loss of Jerusalem in 1187. Moreover, this susceptibility was skilfully exploited in what was a reinvention of crusading, at the end of the twelfth and start of the thirteenth centuries, carried out under the aegis of Innocent III (1198–1216).

Innocent set in train a major reform of the Church that culminated in the Fourth Lateran Council of November 1215. For Innocent the proper order of Christian society demanded that the Church be reformed and that Jerusalem be recovered. He intensified the papal attempt to achieve unity in Catholic Christendom, to rally it behind the standard of crusade. Innocent pursued the old claims of the papacy with a new vigour. He did not claim to rule all the lands of Christendom, but to be the judge of rulers, determining the worthiness of their rule. This papal project, now reinvigorated, would play a major role in the politics of the thirteenth century as his work would be continued by his successors. It was very far from an empty idea. In 1213 King John of England (1199–1216) resigned the kingdoms of England and Ireland to Innocent III and received them back as papal fiefs. Both Afonso II (1211–23) and Sancho II (1223–48) were forced to refrain from their attempts to limit the wealth of the Church in Portugal and to accept papal overlordship of the kingdom. Of course all these and other submissions had complex causes, but they were deeply impressive achievements.

Innocent III's energy and drive in the cause of the crusade were remarkable. He sponsored two major expeditions to the Holy Land: the Fourth and the Fifth Crusades. This last was inaugurated at the Lateran Council by the decree *Ad Liberandum* of 30 November 1215, though Innocent died before the muster-date of 1 June 1217. In addition, he widened the scope of crusading by launching the enormous enterprise of the Albigensian Crusade against the heretics of southern France in 1204 and by bestowing crusading privileges on the German expansion in the Baltic. This remarkable work in inspiring particular crusades was accompanied by a structuralist approach to crusading. Canon 71 of Fourth Lateran proclaimed with particular force the old notion that the peace of Christendom was essential for the liberation of Jerusalem, but it now laid down a four-year peace with severe punishments for those who offended. Tournaments were prohibited for the same reason, on pain of excommunication. Such measures were to be part of papal diplomacy in preparing the way for crusades throughout the thirteenth century. The need for peace was to be constantly rehearsed in Church services before the laity who would thus be reminded of the perils of the Holy Land. In effect, it was laid down that Christian rulers must consider benefit to the Holy Land in all aspects of their political decision-making. Under his aegis Fourth Lateran explicitly offered a full remission of sin to crusaders, a much fuller and more flexible concession than the remission of enjoined penance granted hitherto. Naturally it was also much more popular. He regularised in Canon Law a custom, almost as old as crusading itself, of allowing people who had taken the cross to commute and redeem their vows if new circumstances prevented their departure, and he granted partial indulgences for material contributions to crusading. This was not cynical fund-raising, though that charge was made in later reigns and with some justification and acted as the ultimate provocation to Martin Luther. For Innocent it was a method of increasing participation in crusading – of mobilising Christendom for the liberation of Jerusalem. It was with much the same objective that Innocent developed liturgical celebration and intercession for crusading. On 16 May 1212 he organised lavish solemnities at Rome in support of the Spanish Crusade of that year. Such occasions were an expression of his conviction that all Christians should be involved in the crusade, even those who could not possibly participate in person, and that support for such events purified Christian society and made it more pleasing in the eyes of God. At the same time Innocent controlled and directly commissioned preachers to spread the word systematically under papal control: the missions of men like Fulk of Neuilly and Robert of Courson were the fruits of this. Such centralised control of propaganda was not essentially new: Urban II had commissioned preachers, but it was now made the rule. Nor was the protection extended to crusaders, their lands and their families, during their absence in any way new. But again, Innocent clarified and defined the law and practice of the Church.

But the most important and controversial step that Innocent took was to impose taxation upon the Church for the support of crusaders and the Holy Land. Again, this was not entirely new. Louis VI appears to have levied a tax on his realm to support his participation in the Second Crusade and in 1166 he and Henry II imposed a levy on the laity and clergy of their kingdoms in aid of the Holy Sepulchre which was, in effect, an income-tax. In 1188 Clement III (1187–91) proclaimed the Saladin Tithe, a tenth of the incomes of the laity and clergy of all Christendom, which was to be collected by royal governments. These imposts were not popular. Churches and laymen demanded that the tax on moveable wealth of 1166 should not be regarded as a precedent. Philip II was obliged to drop his attempt to collect the Saladin Tithe by the reaction against it from the French

Church, though it was collected in England. This may, in part, explain why Richard was so much richer than Philip on the Third Crusade. Despite this, Innocent was determined to mobilise the wealth of Christendom, and in 1199 imposed a fortieth on clerical incomes for the Fourth Crusade, though he promised it would not form a precedent. In 1209 a tenth was levied on the French Church to support the Albigensian Crusade. The next general levy imposed upon the Church was the triennial twentieth decreed by the Lateran Council in 1215 for the support of the projected Fifth Crusade. With the weight of the Council behind him Innocent obviously hoped that resistance would be overcome and declined to make any promise that this would not form a precedent. This scale of taxation evoked ferocious opposition. The Cistercians refused to pay the Saladin Tithe of 1188 and Innocent was obliged to excuse them from the levy of 1199. They and some other orders subsequently obtained exemptions from that of 1215. Payment was often badly in arrears. In England the protracted quarrel with King John over the Canterbury election meant that sums were still outstanding from the 1199 impost as late as 1217, while the twentieth of 1215 encountered much opposition and some contributions were still outstanding after 1220. The Spanish Church took the view that all its resources should be directed to the *Reconquista* and effectively frustrated collection of the tax of 1215.

Innocent's determination and the very evident value of such levies ensured that taxation for the crusade became an established part of papal policy. Honorius III (1216–27) imposed a triennial tenth on the French Church to support the Albigensian Crusade in 1221. In 1228 Gregory IX (1227–41) demanded a tenth across Christendom to support his campaign against Frederick II and a thirtieth in 1238 for the aid of the western Emperor of Constantinople. In 1244 Innocent IV (1243–54) demanded a tax for his war against the Hohenstaufen and in 1245 the Council of Lyon levied a triennial twentieth for the crusade to the Holy Land. Innocent IV agreed a tenth on the incomes of the French Church for the crusade of St Louis, but this was extended in 1251 and it has been calculated that the total proceeds amounted to £950,000, two thirds of the total cost of the expedition. There was much criticism of this impost, and even more of the triennial tenth granted by Innocent IV in anticipation of Henry III (1216–72) going on crusade in 1256. Discontent in the English Church at this pressure from pope and king was a factor in the rebellion against Henry III which broke out in 1258.

One reason for these frequent taxes, as will be evident from the summary above, was the growing diversity of crusading. This had been evident almost from the very beginning of crusading, as we have noted. However, Innocent III took a highly positive view of crusades. If the enemy in the east remained normative, Innocent inherited all the old papal enthusiasm for the war in Spain. Inhabitants of Iberia seem to have been regarded as *de facto* crusaders in their wars against Islam there. In 1211 Innocent issued an appeal to all the faithful to join the war against the Moors and this was followed up by the liturgy of 16 May 1212. The pope regarded himself as the master of the war against the enemies of Christendom who determined its priorities. In 1213 Innocent revoked the crusading indulgence for non-Spaniards going to fight in Spain. This in part underlay Spanish resistance to the taxes intended to support the Fifth and other crusades to the east. The first half of the thirteenth century was a period of very rapid expansion as James I of Aragon (1213–76) and Fernando III of Castile (1217–52) destroyed the Almohad dominance and all but expelled Islam from Spain. The Christian victory at Las Navas de Tolosa in 1212 was a great blow to Almohad prestige but produced few major advances for the Christian kingdoms, not least because both Aragon and Castile soon underwent periods of minority rule. Yusuf II (1213–24) failed to take advantage of this circumstance. On his death civil war broke out amongst the Almohads, releasing all the tensions within the regime. Tunisia broke away, but, worst of all, tensions exploded between the Berbers and their Almohad rulers. The consequence in Spain was a plethora of small Muslim states which quickly fell victim to Christian reconquest. In 1229–30 James I conquered the Balearics and Ibiza fell in 1235. In 1236 James began the siege of Valencia which surrendered on 28 September 1238, and subsequently drove south towards Murcia. Portugal was able to annexe the Algarve, but the greatest triumphs fell to Fernando III of Castile. Intense fighting, including a notable victory in battle at Jerez in 1231, opened the way to conquest of the south-west. In the ensuing chaos a group of marauding Christians managed to break into Cordoba in January 1236. They were not strong enough to seize the city, but they sent to Fernando who improvised an army which consolidated the breach and forced the surrender of the city on 29 June. In token of his victory Fernando sent back to Santiago the bells of the great church which al-Mansur had looted in 997. By 1243 Fernando held Murcia and in 1244 Jaén fell. But the greatest prize of all was Seville. Operations against it began in 1246 and it finally capitulated on 23 November 1248. Of all al-Andalus only Granada remained and it was a vassal state of Castile.

This process was watched with enormous admiration by all of Christendom. Fernando III was particularly admired. 'That king alone has done more for the honour and profit of Christ's Church than the pope and all his crusaders ... and all the Templars and Hospitallers', said a contemporary.[2] The glory of these victories was indeed a striking contrast with the disasters in the Eastern Mediterranean. They can be directly attributed to the breakdown of the Almohad empire at a time when two able kings, Fernando III and James I, were able to exploit any weakness. Moreover, they avoided quarrels with one another and with Portugal, so that relentless pressure was brought to bear upon al-Andalus. And it must be said that crusade, as such, had played little part in the great events. A substantial number of French crusaders joined the army of Peter II (1196–1213) and Alfonso VIII (1158–1214) as it gathered for the campaign of Las Navas de Tolosa, but most of them deserted before battle was joined. In 1217 200 shiploads of Dutch and German crusaders on their way to the Fifth Crusade helped the Portugese to

---

2 The English chronicler, Matthew Paris, quoted in Lomax, *Reconquest of Spain*, 156.

seize Alcácer do Sal. However, when they asked for permission to discharge their vows by staying in Spain the pope refused permission and urged them to go to Egypt.

But the papacy, and particularly Innocent III, actually deserves much credit for the triumphs in Spain. In the wake of the Almohad victory at Alarcos in 1195 the kings of Navarre and Léon saw the opportunity to pursue their long-running dispute with Castile and allied with the victorious Almohad, Yaq'ub (1184–99) against the defeated Alfonso VIII. Celestine III (1191–98), much concerned about these tensions, tried to arrange a truce amongst the Christian kings as early as 1191. In 1196, scandalised by events in Spain, he excommunicated Alfonso IX (1188–1230) of Léon and this was repeated in 1198 by Innocent III. In 1204 Peter II of Aragon asked Innocent for a papal legate to organise an offensive, but the pope refused because of the bitterness of the disputes between the Spanish Christian kings. Only the Orders of Calatrava and Santiago were anxious to renew the war and they enjoyed papal support. Innocent confirmed their rules and privileges. In 1210 he ordered Rodrigo, archbishop of Toledo, to press Alfonso

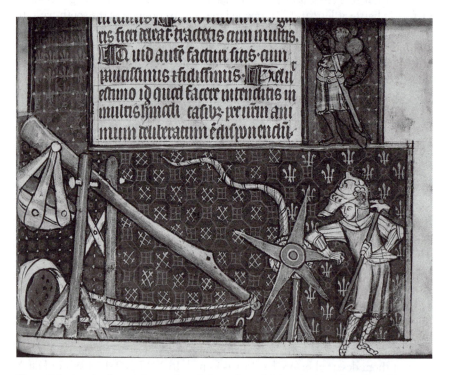

Figure 6.1 A trebuchet with winch and sling. A useful, but far from decisive addition to the armoury of siege warfare. These machines appear at about the same time, the late twelfth century, in both Islam and Catholic Christendom.

Source: Christ Church, Oxford, Milemete MS 92, f. 67.

VIII to attack the Muslims and threatened any Christian who attacked him with excommunication. In the course of the fighting which followed the Order of Calatrava lost its precarious outpost of Salvatierra. As news of this disaster spread Innocent III wrote to France urging a crusade for the aid of Spain. The main French effort came from the south and was led by the archbishops of Bordeaux and Narbonne. Although many of the French withdrew from the expedition after quarrelling with the Spaniards, some remained. Innocent was not able to persuade Léon and Portugal to end their war, but Alfonso VIII of Castile and Peter II of Aragon raised a large army and were supported by half the income of the Castilian Church. The victory of Peter and Alfonso at Las Navas de Tolosa on 16 July 1212 which was such a terrible blow to the prestige of the Almohads owed much to the efforts of Innocent and his predecessors. Innocent subsequently deprived foreigners (but not Spaniards) of crusading privileges in the interests of the Fifth Crusade, but Honorius appointed Archbishop Rodrigo as Papal Legate charged with raising a new crusade in Spain. This had little success even when Alfonso IX of Léon joined. Fernando III's campaigns were crusades in the full sense of the word strongly supported by the papacy which confirmed the full indulgence in 1225 and 1231 and the pope intervened to keep the peace between Castile and Navarre in 1234. There was constant papal support for the Orders. The papacy always saw the crusade to the east as the highest priority, but Spanish resistance to taxation for this purpose gradually made its point and the papacy acquiesced in resources being used for this purpose, with some clerical taxation being directly levied by the kings. The papacy played a crucial role in rallying Christian Spain in the wake of Alarcos and injected a certain backbone into an undignified scramble to please the Almohads. As the century proceeded, however, the papacy played less and less of a role in Spain as the Spanish kingdoms became stronger and more successful.

The papacy, and Innocent in particular, encouraged the crusade in the north. The Second Crusade had shown the way and continuing German expansionism on the eastern frontier and along the Baltic coast had been given papal encouragement. The dynamic for Christian advance in the Baltic was not purely religious. The Danes had seized Rügen and looked to Estonia for further expansion, though here they came into conflict with Sweden. German princes like Henry the Lion tried to expand their frontiers. The Poles were also deeply interested in expansion at the expense of the pagan peoples of the Baltic. In these circumstances convergent pressures gradually brought about the conversion of the Wendish peoples to the east of the Jutland peninsula. But beyond them lay the many pagan tribes who lived in the remote and inaccessible lands of Prussia, Lithuania, Livonia and Estonia. Moreover, they were formidable warriors well-adapted to the rough country and harsh climate in which they lived. The traditional pattern of expansion was for border lords in Christian lands to take the lead, but that would have been a slow process. The Wends had been subject to heavy German and Polish pressure for over a century before they were absorbed.

Plenty of people were interested in the Baltic lands. German merchants wanted to control the Baltic trade in furs, wax and other profitable goods of the north. The Poles saw Prussia as their natural way to the sea, while the Russian princes were in the habit of taking tribute from the northern tribes. After 1181 the Emperor, Frederick Barbarossa, and the German princes turned against Henry the Lion and broke up his vast lands. This blunted German advance, but a new champion appeared in the form of Hartwig II archbishop of Bremen (1185–1207) who was anxious to reassert the old claims of his see to dominate the northern world. This injected an ideological drive into the situation in the Baltic. He appointed a missionary, Meinhard, as bishop of Livonia (1186–96). When he made little progress in the face of stubborn pagan resistance the pope recommended forced conversion. His successor as bishop of Livonia, Berthold (1196–98), was at first equally unsuccessful. In 1195 Celestine III, at the urging of Hartwig, offered crusading privileges for all who would fight in support of the mission and Berthold returned to Livonia in 1198 with a Saxon army. They were victorious but in the battle he was killed, providing a martyr for the northern mission. But the real agent of success was Hartwig's nephew, Bishop Albert of Buxtehude (1199–1229). The new bishop moved the site of his see to Riga and began a systematic conquest. He drew on the support of his own extensive kin who became key landowners in Livonia, and he could count on regular reinforcements because the disturbed state of Germany produced plenty of restless knights and aristocrats. Innocent III created an important precedent when, in 1199, he offered an indulgence equal to that for a pilgrimage to Rome for those who fought in Livonia. Albert kept on good terms with Frederick II of Hohenstaufen (1212–50) when he emerged as emperor, with the other princes of Germany and with Innocent III and his successors. This network of contacts enabled him to raise money and troops and this was facilitated by papal grants of crusading privileges. As a result Livonia enjoyed the benefits of a continuing crusade with fresh waves of crusaders arriving in Livonia almost on an annual basis.

Albert brought systematic administration to these wild border-lands and a careful application of a tried and tested strategy. The short summer and long bitter winter imposed particular conditions on the crusade in the north. The summer season was long enough for pagan villages to be taken, but once they had satisfied their religious aspirations and greed for booty crusaders tended to vanish. Thus, in 1195 Earl Birger of Sweden harried the Estonians for three days, but terminated his crusade when they offered tribute. To consolidate gains Albert established fortified block-houses, and in this way his power was pushed down the river valleys, appointing magistrates in the conquered villages. In winter the frozen rivers of the area became great highways, offering to both sides the opportunity for raiding. As the nucleus of settlers remained very small, in imitation of the Temple and the Hospital, Albert formed some of them into the 'Order of Sword-Brothers' dedicated to the expansion of Livonia and the conversion of its inhabitants. Their task was to lead the incoming crusaders, to establish and defend block-houses and to take up the burden of leading winter raids and countering those of the enemy. Bishop Christian (1215–44), a Cistercian appointed to press forward the mission in Prussia, was similarly isolated amongst hordes of pagans who were unlikely to capitulate to mere persuasion. He too appealed for crusaders, and formed a body of settlers into the 'Knights of Dobrzyn' to provide the core of an army for the conquest of the Prussians. Innocent III recognised and championed both these 'Orders' but ecclesiastical approval did not last long. By an agreement in 1204 with Bishop Albert, the 'Sword-Brothers' were permitted to keep a third of all conquests, but their greed and exploitation caused revolts amongst the subject peoples, notably in 1222. They even breached the 1222 agreement by which Estonia was largely delivered over to the Danes and they constantly defied the bishops of Riga. They were rough frontiersmen whose manner of life only approximated to that of the disciplined monastic orders of the Temple and Hospital. In 1237 the 'Sword-Brothers' led an attack on the Lithuanians and were almost totally destroyed.

This emergency was an opportunity for all their many enemies, and a new force was brought into the area. The Teutonic Order was founded at the siege of Acre in 1190 as a hospital order to care for the German sick as the Order of the Hospital of St Mary of the Germans in Jerusalem. The Germans who went on the crusade of Henry VI in 1197 enriched the Order and transformed it into a military force and by 1220 its headquarters was the castle of Montfort, also called Starkenberg. But it was the election as Grand Master of Hermann von Salza (1210-39) which made the Order a political force. He gained great influence as a close associate of Frederick II. It was through Hermann's agency that Andrew II of Hungary (1205-35) established the Order in Hungary. The Cumans were a pagan people of the western steppe who often raided Hungary through the passes of Transylvania. The Hungarian nobles had little interest in establishing themselves in this dangerous and thinly populated area. But the Teutonic Knights were accustomed to hazardous frontiers, and they built castles and brought in German peasants whose fortified settlements kept out the Cumans, and created a new prosperity in the area. All this aroused the envy of the Hungarian nobles who, led by the heir-apparent, prince Bela, forced Andrew to expel them. The enemies of the Order were greatly served by the vague terms upon which Transylvania had been conferred.

As agitation grew in Hungary, Hermann of Salza found another opportunity. Poland was a divided land at this time, but all its rulers regarded Prussia as the natural route to the Baltic. However, the pagan Prussians were a formidable enemy who confined the Poles to a precarious footing in Kulmerland. The attention of the papacy was drawn to the area by Bishop Christian of Prussia who was supported by the Poles in his missionary activity. As a result, Honorius III (1216-27) proclaimed a German/Polish crusade. Its total failure led one of the Polish dukes, Conrad of Mazovia, to offer his border outposts in Kulmerland to the Teutonic Order. Hermann gave a firm basis for the Order's intervention by obtaining from Frederick II the Golden Bull of Rimini in 1226: in 1234 Gregory IX accepted Prussia as a fief held by the Order. From Kulmerland the Order drove up the valley of the Vistula towards the Baltic. Quite apart from the Prussians, they faced many Christian rivals: the 'Knights of Dobrzyn' claimed sections of the land, as did the Poles while the Danes and the merchants of Lübeck had strong interests. The advance of the Order alarmed Duke Swantopelk of Danzig (modern Gdansk) who felt that they threatened his control of the Frische Haff and in 1242 he launched a war which would last ten years. However, in 1254 Ottokar of Bohemia (1253–78) joined the crusade and paid for the new fort of Königsberg while Russian pressure on the pagan Lithuanians meant they were unable to resist the construction of the vital fort at Memel. The sheer difficulties of fighting the pagans meant that the Order, as in Livonia, relied heavily on attracting fighting men to take part in regular *Reisen*, fighting journeys against the pagans. It was mainly to Germany that the Order made appeal, and in 1245 they were given the exceptional privilege of enlisting crusaders in Germany and endowing them with that status without reference to the papacy. This was popularised so skilfully by the Order that participation in *Reisen* became a notable aspect of German chivalry. The obvious skills of the Teutonic Order led to their implantation in Livonia after the demise of the 'Sword-Brothers' in 1237, though it took them twenty years to win back the Christian position there. But until well after the fall of Acre in 1291 the main effort of the order remained in the Holy Land.

The German expansion in the Baltic was a remarkable example of conquest at a distance in which the Teutonic Order undertook the same role as local nobilities in such areas as Wales and the Wendish frontier – by establishing a permanent presence with a vested interest in growth. Like the Temple and the Hospital on which it was modelled, the Teutonic Order had vast endowments – mainly in Germany – which they could mobilise when they suffered local defeat. Moreover, the interest and concern of the papacy reinforced their efforts by regular crusades which brought much needed manpower to this remote area. Some crusaders stayed either in the Order or as local settlers. Once they had established a strong presence the Germans could exploit the bewildering divisions amongst the native peoples. Curonians, Samogitians, Lithuanians, Selonians, Semigallians, Lettigalli, Livs and Estonians warred with one another and with Poland and Russia, as much as they warred with the German newcomers and their Scandinavian rivals. The advantages of heavy cavalry, armour and crossbows were fairly marginal in the broken and wooded lands around the Baltic. The German mastery of stonework was important because stone had to be imported into an area in which it was lacking, and it was very difficult for the tribes to construct siege-machinery like catapults and siege-towers to overwhelm stone castles. Undoubtedly the sheer volume of iron weapons possessed by the Germans was an important advantage and crossbows were very useful in defence of fortifications. But the key to the German expansion in the Baltic was sea-power. Crusaders, weapons, stone, all were conveyed to the missionary lands by the great ships, the cogs, of the merchants of Lübeck and the other developing Hanseatic ports. Merchants had always been important benefactors of the Teutonic Order and supporting them was an outlet for their piety. The pagan peoples lacked any counter to this naval domination which in summer could be deployed down the great rivers of the area. Merchants were important because they provided the key technological advantage, ships, which delivered the means of support to the new settlements. But they were not missionaries or dedicated settlers: they were primarily interested in trade and anxious to establish privileged precincts from which to tap trade. It is difficult to see how the Baltic could have been absorbed into the Germano-Christian orbit if it had not been for the interest of the papacy. The 'Continual Crusade' in the Baltic lands became a respected institution throughout Christendom and especially in Germany.

At the root of this lay the papacy which, from the time of Innocent III, poured money and organising skills into the far north. This was partly sheer belief in missionary effort which embraced coercive conversion. It was partly fear of Russian influence, for Russia lay within the Byzantine sphere of influence and its Church looked not to Rome but to Constantinople for leadership. The popes had once looked at eastern Christianity as misled and wayward – the crusades had been designed to impress the easterners with a sense of Christian fraternity and so to bring them back into the fold. When that failed, Orthodoxy was increasingly seen as a rival centre of influence, to be resisted at all costs. The Swedish interest in Finland confronted the Russian principality of Novgorod in an area where it had traditionally exercised great influence and was actively sending out missionaries. Pope Gregory IX appointed an Englishman, Thomas, as bishop of Finland. When his mission failed a crusade was proclaimed against the schismatics in 1237. The Swedes, Finns and Teutonic knights invaded Novgorod but were defeated at the battle of Lake Peipus in 1242 by Alexander Nevsky. The expedition had badly stretched the Teutonic knights who were just establishing themselves in Livonia and Prussia and from now on they avoided attacks on Russian territory. But it was by no means a crushing victory. In 1249 King Eric XI (1222–29 and 1234–50) sent his fleet and a strong army under the command of his brother Birger Jarl, though it is not clear if this was ever formally a crusade in papal eyes. Gradually the Swedes established themselves in Finland, but it was not until after a third 'crusade' in 1292 that they achieved an uneasy domination of the Gulf of Finland, which was a vital link in the northern trade.

But in some ways Innocent was at his most innovative in launching crusades within Christendom itself. In November 1199 he proclaimed a crusade against Markward of Anweiler, an adventurer who tried to seize Sicily in the uncertainty after the death of the Emperor Henry VI (1189–99). From 1201–03 Walter of Brienne and a crusading army fought there for the pope. This was not a total innovation because, as we have seen, Innocent II in 1135 had proclaimed a crusade against the antipope Anacletus. There was no opposition to Innocent's declaration of a crusade to this end. After he had completed negotiations with the Venetians in connection with the Fourth Crusade, Geoffrey de Villehardouin encountered Walter and his men in the Alps. In his memoirs, written some time later, he regretted that they had not been able to join his crusade, but clearly admired these 'very good and valiant men' for their courage and conviction.[3] When Innocent became embroiled in an ecclesiastical dispute with King John of England (1199–1216) over the Canterbury election, Innocent's threat to sanction a projected French invasion as a crusade was a powerful factor in bringing about a resolution of the conflict and persuading John to accept that England was a vassal state of the Holy See. Gregory IX (1227–41) followed this precedent and offered a lesser indulgence for all who joined his war against the excommunicate Emperor Frederick II in 1229. In 1239, however, Gregory proclaimed a full crusade against the same emperor. At the Council of Lyon in 1245 Innocent IV followed this precedent, and in 1250, after the death of Frederick II, offered the same rewards for all who would fight against the Hohenstaufen heir, Conrad. Contemporary opinion did not make the modern distinction between 'political' and other crusades, and criticism, at least until the mid-century, was more directed at timing than the direction of such expeditions. Much contemporary criticism of these 'Crusades against Christians' has survived, but it came, for the most part, from interested parties like the friends of Frederick II and it did not reflect Catholic opinion as a whole. A storm of criticism arose from another initiative of Innocent III, the crusade against the Albigensian heretics of the Languedoc which he launched in 1205, but once again it was largely self-interested. Once more Innocent was not innovating. In 1179 Third Lateran had offered a limited indulgence to all who would fight for the extirpation of the heresy which had become firmly established in Languedoc and in 1181 a small expedition seized Lavaur. But by the end of the century heresy had grown to an alarming extent. Between 1174 and 1177 the heretics staged a great council at St Felix-de-Caraman and subsequently appointed a hierarchy of bishops in rivalry to the orthodox at Albi, Toulouse, Carcassonne and Agen. It was all too evident that the heretics were impervious to orthodox preaching and so Innocent determined to resort to force: characteristically, he did so systematically.

Philip of France had declined to take action against the heretics because he was afraid that John of England would attempt to recover the lands of his house in France which he had lost in 1204. Innocent's problem was, therefore, to create a military movement and find a leader. The murder of the papal legate, Peter of Castelnau was widely blamed upon Raymond VI of Toulouse and the heretics he was believed to be sheltering. Philip of France permitted his barons to rally to the papal call for a crusade, and they had every reason to do so, for the lands of heretics were promised to them as well as crusading privileges and the possibilities of loot. Amongst the minor baronage of northern France was a soldier of genius, Simon de Montfort, upon whom Fourth Lateran bestowed the lands of the deposed count of Toulouse. He became the real driving force of the crusade, and at Muret in 1213 won a tremendous victory over a large Spanish and Provençal

---

3 Geoffrey de Villehardouin, 'The conquest of Constantinople', in M. R. B. Shaw (ed.), *Chronicles of the Crusades* (Harmondsworth: Penguin, 1970), 36.

army, in the process killing Peter II of Aragon, one of the victors of Las Navas de Tolosa. The northern French barons imposed themselves upon the south in a welter of blood, in the process destroying the distinctive culture of the area. The crusaders were brutal and pretty careless of Innocent III's concern for the faithful and his anxiety to coax souls back to God. According to Caesarius of Heisterbach, the papal legate cared little for the fate of orthodox Christians within Béziers, and as the crusaders broke in, he urged them 'Kill, kill. God will know his own.'[4] Innocent did his best to moderate such excesses and to limit confiscation of lands to those of actual heretics. At Fourth Lateran it was at the insistence of the Council, and not Innocent, that the lands of Raymond VII were conferred upon Simon de Montfort. But in the end he was in the hands of the men on the spot whose persecution of the heretics in the years 1209–11 paid little attention to judicial process. Simon de Montfort was killed at the siege of Toulouse in 1218 and the grip of the northern barons was greatly relaxed with the heretics regaining freedom of worship. Louis VIII of France (1223–26) saw real possibilities for the monarchy in the weakened state of the south and he bullied the papacy into sanctioning his attack as a crusade. The progress of the French was barely delayed by the death of Louis and the accession of the child, Louis IX (1226–70). There is no doubt that the French monarchy gained the real benefit from the Albigensian Crusade, and under its aegis the Inquisition systematically extirpated the heretics over the course of a century.

Nevertheless, the Albigensian Crusade was one of Innocent's triumphs. The Albigensian heresy was highly dangerous and the crusade was a major contribution to its destruction. In the circumstances of the very early thirteenth century, with a vacancy in the Empire and the French and English monarchies locked in conflict it is hard to see what else Innocent could have done. In Italy he was much more circumspect in dealing with the same heresy which had established itself in the cities there. The autonomy of the Italian city-states, and their peculiar hierarchies of power required a different approach. The notion of Christ as a poor man suffering in poverty was highly dynamic. It elevated the notion of poverty as an example to churchmen and laity alike and enabled the urban and rural poor to identify with the Church. Unfortunately there was an enormous gap between this ideal and the way many churchmen lived, and the preachers of the Cathar Church, the *perfecti*, of whose austerity there can be no doubt, exploited it. To counter this Innocent used the new Orders of preachers, the Franciscans and Dominicans, who exemplified orthodox austerity of life and brought to bear sophisticated preaching and propaganda. The situation in southern France was very different and preaching had clearly failed there just as it was useless against the Baltic pagans and the heretics enjoyed the sympathy and support of many of the local elite. The Albigensian Crusade was enormously

---

4 Caesarius, quoted in J. Sayers, *Innocent III Leader of Europe 1198–1216* (London: Longman, 1994), 160.

popular in Christendom where toleration of dissent was simply not considered possible. In another and wider sense Innocent was successful, in that he had widened the use of crusading in the sense of it being an instrument of papal influence. Innocent had reorganised the infrastructure of crusading and particularly of crusading finance. No pope had ever sanctioned so many crusades and thus so firmly and unequivocally placed the papacy in a commanding position in the movement. However, that position of command was to prove more notional than real when it came to events.

Innocent and his successors were clerics and what they could not do was to create a strategy for crusading in the eastern Mediterranean. Between 1095 and the end of the Third Crusade the movement was dominated by the events of the First Crusade. This had succeeded because in the circumstances of 1096–99 the brute onslaught of a large army was sufficient to achieve the aim of liberating Jerusalem. The splendour of this achievement masked the disasters of 1101. Moreover, clerical thinking about the crusade exalted its example and emphasised the role of the divine will, effectively discouraging other ways of thinking about it. Subsequently what happened was the successful expansion of the bridgeheads into viable principalities. They were supported by Italian sea-power which brought pilgrims who could fight for a season, augmented by a flow of emigrants and mercenaries and spasmodic larger expeditions. Failure tended to be explained in religious rather than military or political terms. Very notably the disaster of the Second Crusade was seen as a result of the pride of the crusaders or the venality of the settlers, though some blamed the Byzantines. The military and political circumstances in the Holy Land changed, but the only institution in Christendom whose head really tried to consider and adapt to those changes was the papacy which made valiant and substantial efforts. But the popes were not soldiers, so it is hardly surprising that they never evolved a military strategy. Nobody else did either. This was partly because western kings had preoccupations of their own and partly because this was not an age when strategies were drawn up in a vacuum. In the Jerusalemite kingdom there was a keen perception of the need to change strategies and that shows in the assault on Egypt under Amalric I and in the construction of new kinds of fortresses, begun in 1168 with Belvoir, the first genuinely concentric fortress built by westerners. But these were strategies for the kingdom, not for crusading as a movement.

In fact it was Richard I who invented a crusading strategy. He saw clearly that conquering Jerusalem would not solve the problem of the Holy Land. If it had been liberated in isolation it would soon have been swallowed up by the Muslim powers when the crusade went home. Instead, he urged his fellow crusaders to think of an attack on Egypt. This had been the goal of Amalric I and it was a thoroughly reasonable one. Egypt was rich and its population was traditionally passive, accustomed to foreign rule, and contained a substantial Christian minority, the Copts. If Saladin's army could be broken Christian rule there was perfectly possible, and Palestine was traditionally an outwork of defence for the country. Richard was a brilliant soldier but he was high-handed, aggressive and clumsy in his dealings with other contingents on the crusade. Because of this the other leaders rejected his idea of attacking Egypt, reacting to his bloody-mindedness by championing the traditional aim of the crusade, Jerusalem, and successfully insisting upon it. The attractions of Richard's strategy were enormously enhanced by events after the death of Saladin on 4 March 1193. His descendants, the Ayyubids, divided the empire between them, and most normally Egypt was separated from Syria, with the rulers of these lands vying for pre-eminence. All the crusades of the period 1192–1250 attempted to exploit this division.

But though Richard gave crusading in the eastern Mediterranean an enduring strategy, he could not remedy its other military defects. All the crusades had been dogged by problems of command. Substantial forces had defected from the First Crusade in North Syria. The Crusade of 1101 had been characterised by splintered and diverse expeditions that sought different objectives and never united, and much the same could be said of the Second Crusade. On the Third Crusade bickering between Richard and Philip of France was a major problem and after Philip's departure tensions amongst the crusaders almost reached the pitch of civil war. So bitter was Leopold of Austria that when Richard was shipwrecked on his return from the Holy Land and fell into his hands, Leopold imprisoned him and demanded an enormous ransom. This kind of division was not an accident but inherent in the nature of crusading. Great nobles might defer to greater ones and to kings, but in essence a crusade simply combined a number of retinues gathered around important men and these leaders were bound to be suspicious of others, especially if they were strangers. This was especially the case between declared enemies like Richard and Philip, but on the Second Crusade Louis VII and Conrad III had very little to do with one another, although they had little cause for actual hostility. On the First Crusade there were great tensions between the leaders, and almost all the rest seem to have conceived a personal dislike of Raymond of Toulouse. Catholic Christendom was exporting its internal tensions along with its leading soldiers to the Holy Land and there was little the pope could do about it. Urban II had not tried to impose a leader on the First Crusade: leaders had emerged. This seems to have been what was expected because there is no reason to believe that a papally-imposed commander would have been accepted by other leaders. The pope could inspire, organise, supply, even fund, a crusade, but despite all the glory of Innocent III, his ability to control events was very limited. These fatal weaknesses were all demonstrated by the events of the Fourth Crusade.

From the first, crusades to the Holy Land were enmeshed in Mediterranean diplomacy. Crusading had in part been brought into being by Alexius I's desire to exploit the divisions of the Seljuks, and the crusaders had exploited their quarrel with the Fatimids of Egypt. Bohemond's seizure of Antioch created a bone of contention between the Byzantines and the crusaders, made worse by the disasters of 1101 and Bohemond's crusade against Byzantium. John and Manuel both attempted to impose overlordship on Antioch and in the 1150s this was accepted by the kings of Jerusalem. However, there was always tension in the relationship between Byzantium and the Latin states. Appeals to the west for military support sometimes referred to the Greeks as a threat and the leaders of Antioch were unwilling to see the establishment of a Greek Patriarchate in their city. As far as westerners in general were concerned, they seem to have been indifferent rather than hostile. There were moments of bitterness. In the wake of the Second Crusade Odo of Deuil emphasised the treachery of the Greeks, endorsed the view that 'Constantinople is Christian only in name' and denounced Manuel as 'the idol of the Greeks'.[5] But this kind of visceral religious hatred was quite exceptional. Western chroniclers rarely comment on religious differences, and though they were convinced of the softness of the Greeks who they regarded as poor soldiers who relied on mercenaries, there was little real hatred. As the empire stabilised and strengthened in the twelfth century under the dynasty of the Comneni, so it was seen more and more as a rival centre of power. As for the papacy, Alexander II cultivated good relations with Manuel because of his struggles with the anti-popes of Frederick I and did not press the issue of the supremacy, especially as he recognised the need of the Latin States for a Byzantine alliance. Manuel himself was impressed by the vigour of the Latins. He had married his daughter, Maria, born of his own marriage to Maria of Antioch, to Renier of Montferrat. The emperor himself participated in western tournaments and kept about him a strong guard of Latins who were his most effective soldiers. However, many of the ordinary people of Constantinople were suspicious of such western ways and convinced that the papacy was trying to extinguish the Greek Church. They were not without organisation and leaders, and could find support in the factional struggles of the court aristocracy who dominated Byzantine politics. When Manuel died, Byzantine politics became unstable and the empire was no longer able to act as the ally of the crusader states, unleashing further instability into eastern Mediterranean politics.

But the crusading movement was only one aspect of western expansion into the Mediterranean. On the Second Crusade Roger of Sicily's attack on the Empire embittered relations between Manuel and the crusaders. Manuel tried to take advantage of problems in Norman Italy to attack through Ancona in 1159. His thrust was defeated but it angered Frederick Barbarossa who regarded Manuel as merely 'King of the Greeks' and himself as the true heir of Rome. Relations were embittered when Manuel supported the pope in his long conflict with Barbarossa. German experiences on the Third Crusade did nothing to improve relations with Byzantium. In 1185 William II of Sicily attempted to take advantage of the succession disputes that had broken out on the death of Manuel Comnenus by sending an army against Constantinople. The Norman attack captured Thessalonika, proof that the long feud between the house of Hauteville and the Byzantines had lost none of its vigour. In the event determined Byzantine resistance and the indiscipline of the Norman army brought this expedition to

5 Odo, *The Journey of Louis VII to the East*, 69, 76, 91.

nothing. William II of Sicily died in 1189, but by 1195 power in the kingdom had passed into the hands of an even more threatening force, Henry VI of Hohenstaufen (1190–97) who had inherited all his father's contempt for the 'King of the Greeks' and their 'empire'. He too was interested in crusading, partly at least to enhance the prestige of his house, and partly because the feuds in the Ayyubid house were reaching new levels, dividing Egypt and Syria. By 1197 a substantial German crusade was in the east attacking Beirut when news came of their emperor's death. As Germany and Sicily dissolved in civil war none could have been more pleased than the Emperor Alexius III (1195–1203) who had been forced to extract the 'Alamanikon', a tax in aid of the German crusade forced on him by Henry VI. Henry's dream of a Mediterranean empire was, for the moment, no more. But all too evidently Byzantium was increasingly isolated. The papacy and the western empire were major players in Mediterranean politics and both viewed Byzantium with a degree of discontent. Moreover the Hohenstaufen claimant to the Empire, Philip of Swabia, was married to Irene, the daughter of Isaac Comnenus (1185–95) who Alexius III had deposed. And there were other western powers with an interest in the Mediterranean.

Venice, Pisa and Genoa had all offered naval aid to the crusader states and profited by establishing themselves in the ports of the Palestinian littoral. Their interests were primarily commercial, though this was not distinct from the need for prestige and a desire for power and influence of a more general kind. Venice, probably because of its strong interests in Byzantium, only really became established in the Holy Land with the capture of Tyre in 1124. The Venetian settlement in Constantinople flourished as a base for trade across the whole eastern Mediterranean, bringing benefit to its merchants and to Byzantium. They were not alone. After 1111 the Pisans also had a settlement there and the Genoese followed. But the special status of the Venetians was a problem, for by the various *Chrysobulls* they were virtually exempt from the control of Byzantine officials, and intermarriage with Greeks was creating problems, especially as they spread to virtually all the cities of the empire. Greek writers make much of the arrogance of the westerners and speak of their vast numbers. It is hard to evaluate this, but certainly natives viewed their prominence with suspicion. In 1162 the Pisans sacked the new quarter of the Genoese and both sides were expelled, leaving Venice in a monopoly position. But in 1167 Byzantium re-established its power in Dalmatia and Croatia and the Venetians reacted angrily to this incursion into their sphere of influence on the Adriatic. In 1170 Manuel readmitted the Genoese whose quarter the Venetians promptly attacked. Manuel demanded that Venice pay for the damage but the Doge refused and threatened a naval raid against the empire. On 12 March 1171 all Venetians within the empire were arrested and intermittent war broke out. By 1179 Manuel readmitted Venetians, having found the Genoese and Pisans at least as troublesome.

Manuel left a child of twelve, Alexius II, as his successor. The regent was a westerner, Manuel's second wife, Maria of Antioch, and she ruled at a court notable for the presence of many westerners. It seemed as if the whole empire was being taken over by the westerners. In 1182 a coup by Andronicus Comnenus unleashed the fury of the mob of Constantinople who slaughtered all the westerners they could find, including the Papal Legate John, while others were captured and sold as slaves to the Turks. Andronicus carried out a bloody purge of the nobility of the capital, and one of his victims was Renier of Montferrat. But Andronicus II (1183–85) needed naval support and very soon turned to the Venetians, who had suffered very little in 1182, but before an agreement could be made Andronicus was overthrown. His craven response to the Sicilian attack of 1185 and to the fall of Thessalonika aroused the mob against him and a coup installed Isaac II Angelos. He too needed Venice and reaffirmed her quarter and rights in the capital, but relations continued to be damaged by evasiveness on the subject of compensation for the Venetian losses of 1171. Isaac permitted an enlargement of the Venetian settlement and made lavish promises of compensation which were not fulfilled by the time of his overthrow in 1195 by Alexius III Angelus (1195–1203). The new emperor demanded taxes from the Venetians and granted privileges to Pisa and Genoa. But in the end Alexius III too found it prudent to come to terms with the Venetians and his *Chrysobull* of 1198 was the most extensive and carefully worded definition of Venetian privileges throughout the Byzantine world. This *Chrysobull* maintained the fiction of the special relationship between Venice and Byzantium. The Venetians are praised as 'allies, friends and supporters' while the Doge continued to enjoy the title of *protosebastos* and was called 'most loyal to the emperor'.[6] But the truth was that Venice was a mighty and independent force in the affairs of the Mediterranean. It had a great fleet which could inflict heavy punishment on its enemies and vast financial resources to back it up. Byzantium could not afford to defy such a force. Manuel had taken a firm line in 1171, but he had to climb down in the end. Every emperor since then had been in a much weaker position and showed anxiety to play to the hatred of westerners so evident in the mob of Constantinople, but they had all been forced to terms. The fine detail of the *Chrysobull* of 1198 is a revelation of the deep distrust between Venice and its former patrons, the Byzantine emperors.

On becoming pope, Innocent III proclaimed a new crusade but no army had gathered by the appointed time in March 1199. Innocent, however, levied a tax upon the Church and sent preachers to France, notably the Cardinal-Legate Peter Capuano and the charismatic Fulk of Neuilly. He imposed a blockade on trade with the infidel, though later, under pressure, he agreed to permit the Venetians to carry non-strategic goods. His original appeal had made no mention of kings, probably because there was little hope of any participating. England and France were locked in war, while the sudden death of Henry VI had precipitated a civil war in Germany between Philip of Swabia and the papal candidate, Otto of

---

6 Quoted in D. M. Nicol, *Byzantium and Venice. A Study in Diplomatic and Cultural Relations* (Cambridge: Cambridge University Press, 1988), 123.

Brunswick. Sicily, as we have seen, was in a state of civil strife. The only king to respond was Bela III of Hungary (1172–96). The breakthrough which made a crusade possible came at a tournament at Ecry-sur-Aisne on 28 November 1199. On this occasion two great magnates from a house with a crusading tradition, Count Thibaut of Champagne and his cousin, Count Louis of Blois, took the cross. On 23 February 1200 at Bruges, Count Baldwin of Flanders followed suit; again he was from a house with a crusading tradition and had married Thibaut of Champagne's sister. Amongst other prominent figures who joined were Geoffrey and Stephen of Perche and Renaud of Montmirail, cousins of Thibaut. Geoffrey de Villehardouin, one of the most prominent of the crusaders who later told their story, was Marshal of Champagne. Count Hugh of St Pol came of a famous crusading family from Picardy.

In his account of the crusade Geoffrey de Villehardouin lists some 90 barons who took the cross at this time, and it has been estimated that they and their followers would have constituted an army of 8,000–10,000 strong.[7] Although Thibaut was seen as the most prominent of the leaders it is not at all clear that he was ever formally elected to a position of authority. After an abortive meeting of leaders early in 1200 at Soissons, there was a further conference at Compiègne in March. There was disagreement on almost everything. While the big three, the counts of Flanders, Champagne and Blois, might command respect, there was no dominating figure. This was the old problem of command which had dogged every crusade. It was to have a pervasive influence on the events which followed. The assembly seem to have agreed to go by sea and each of the big three appointed two plenipotentiaries to make arrangements for a sea passage, leaving them to decide with whom and at what price. One of those chosen by Count Thibaut was his trusted councillor, Geoffrey de Villehardouin. This was a device, in the absence of agreement, to take things forward. In the event Pisa and Genoa were at war, so there was little option but to go to Venice.

The Treaty with the Venetians, concluded by the plenipotentiaries in April 1201, is often blamed for all the problems which subsequently arose. In return for 85,000 marks of Cologne, Venice undertook to raise a fleet sufficient to transport 4,500 knights with 4,500 horses, 9,000 squires and 20,000 foot, and to feed them all for one year. In addition they provided a fleet of 50 war-galleys on condition that the Republic would receive half of all conquests. This was not a bad deal. The transport costs were not extortionate at contemporary prices. It was not unreasonable for the Venetians to demand half the conquests. They were virtually suspending all other activities for a year against the promise of future benefits. A shipbuilding programme of enormous proportions was involved and the fleet

---

7 Geoffrey de Villehardouin, 'The conquest of Constantinople', in B. Radice and R. Baldick (eds), *Joinville and Villehardouin: Chroniclers of the Crusades* (Harmondsworth: Penguin, 1963), 29–31; E. H. McNeal, 'The Fourth Crusade', in K. Setton and M. W. Baldwin (eds), *A History of the Crusades*, 6 vols (Madison, WI: University of Wisconsin Press, 1969–88), 2. 160.

would require 27,000 sailors who had to be recruited from the city and beyond. This was a prodigious risk, and the question arises as to why the Republic was willing to take it because the Venetians did not have a strong track-record of supporting crusades.

Their greatest effort in 1124 led to the capture of Tyre, and on that occasion their fleet plundered Byzantine territory. This precedent probably explains why, although he approved their participation, Innocent III from the first demanded that the Venetians undertake not to attack Christian states. He knew that the Venetians had lost control of some of the Dalmatian ports, notably Zara, and would be tempted to use a great fleet and army to recover them. This was a matter of real concern to Venice because they feared an alliance between Hungary and Pisa at a time when their position in Constantinople was far from secure. So the crusade was an opportunity to secure its trade supremacy by controlling new ports in the east – Alexandria if all went well. If this suggests less than pure motives for crusading, it has to be said that there was nothing exceptional in that.

As for the crusaders, their envoys have been much blamed for their over-estimate of the army, because no more than 11,000 eventually turned up at Venice. This is not altogether fair. As we have noted, the three major barons had raised about 8,000 troops, while the assumption seems to have been that the crusaders marching against Markward of Anweiler would join them. In addition, we know that at least 3,000 chose to go to the east via other ports. The figure for which they agreed transport was probably a known overestimate: after all, the worst possible scenario was that willing crusaders would be left on the dock. In the event, with great effort, the army paid just over 50,000 so if something like 20,000 had joined them the debt would have been discharged. As the army gathered and they waited on the Lido for the situation to be resolved, many in the army felt they had paid their passage and that was an end to their obligations. They were quite right: crusaders were self-financing and those not directly connected with the leaders had no obligation beyond their own fares. Many went home disgusted. Others never even came to Venice, for they saw no obligation to do so and made their own way to the Holy Lands, many via Marseilles. Even Louis of Blois, hearing of the difficulties at Venice, had to be dissuaded from this course of action. The whole event is a revelation of the fundamental weakness of the crusade as an ideological force. Men could be stirred, but not organised and equipped for war. Leaders had real authority only over their immediate dependents and, in this case, had no way of ensuring that others obeyed them. The pre-sealed charters created obligations for those who gave them without conferring any real authority over the gathering army. The situation was made worse by the lack of any really striking and experienced figure amongst the leaders whose charisma would enable him to galvanise the gathering army. Of course, such a figure could have emerged in the course of events, as did Bohemond on the First Crusade or Simon de Montfort during the 'Albigensian Crusade'. It so happened that none did. And the Venetians had to be paid for they had more than fulfilled their obligations and faced ruin if the expedition dispersed.

The leadership issue was soon raised again in a more acute form. In May 1201, shortly after the return of the envoys from Venice, Thibaut of Champagne died. Villehardouin suggested his replacement should be Boniface, marquis of Montferrat through whose lands he had passed returning from Venice. This choice was supported by Philip of France who was personally hostile to the obvious choice, Baldwin of Flanders. Boniface had a fine crusading pedigree, but the crusade was now headed by someone unknown to its largely French partici-pants and his preparations took so long that he did not arrive at Venice until August 1202. As the army slowly gathered on the Lido at Venice in the summer of 1202, they were joined by the papal Legate, Peter Capuano, but the Venetians refused to recognise his legatine authority and he seems to have had little influence on events. So the crusade was beyond Innocent's control. Indeed it was outside anybody's control.

The Venetians are often portrayed as the villains of the piece who manipulated events in their own interests. But Doge Dandolo and the crusader leaders must have been equally desperate as they conferred in the summer of 1202. For the Doge political and perhaps personal survival was at stake. In 1172, after an unsuccessful attack on the Byzantine empire, the popular assembly had assassinated Doge Vitale Michiel. Dandolo had been one of his advisors and had played a leading role in the failed expedition. If payment was not forthcoming it would be an unprecedented disaster for Venice whose citizens would certainly turn on the leaders who had committed them to it. Spurred by this, he drove a hard bargain in suggesting that the interest on the debt be remitted if the army would help Venice to reconquer the Adriatic port of Zara from the Hungarians. The conquest of the city was quickly achieved, but it caused great division in the army as many deplored this attack on Christians. And the seizure of Zara did not pay the debt owed to the Venetians so the future of the crusade was still in doubt. At this point another factor intervened. At Christmas 1201 Phillip of Swabia, Hohenstaufen claimant to the German throne, had entertained Boniface of Montferrat. Also present was his relative, Prince Alexius, the son of the deposed and blinded Isaac Angelus, who had escaped to the west. The young prince had written to the crusader leaders at Venice suggesting that they should aid in his restoration in return for Byzantine support for the crusade and the leaders sent a delegation to Philip of Swabia. In early 1203 this returned with proposals to restore Alexius in return for lavish promises of support. Innocent III had refused to entertain any support for Alexius, but he had also failed to act over the capture of Zara, fearing, as everybody did, the dissolution of the crusade. With much hesitation, amidst sharp divisions and with many reservations, the leaders of the crusade agreed, by the Treaty of Zara of spring 1203, to support Alexius's bid for power, chiefly as a means of keeping the crusade going. Not all agreed. Simon de Montfort had played an energetic role in the crusade, but he had been against the attack on Zara and now left the crusade, along with many others, to make his own way to Jerusalem.

The crusader fleet inspired great terror when it arrived at Constantinople.

There was no welcome for Prince Alexius, but little enthusiasm for their ruler, Alexius III. Factional divisions made it difficult to mount a determined resistance and when the crusaders attacked with much success, penetrating the Golden Horn all too easily, Alexius III fled and Isaac and the young Alexius IV were restored. Their promises to the crusader army were lavish, but probably unrealisable and provoked bitter resistance amongst the population of Constantinople and many of the nobles of the court. The failure of the high nobility to unite behind a single emperor or a single line to pursue in the face of Latin demands was one of the crucial factors in exasperating the crusaders. In January 1204 the leader of the anti-foreign faction in Constantinople, Mourtzouphlus, seized power. The crusader army, angered by what they saw as Greek treachery, prepared for a major attack on the city. On 12 April they captured the city, Mourtzouphlus fled, and a three-day sack ensued. Innocent III was appalled by the attack on Constantinople, but he had been ignored and ultimately had to accept the new 'Latin Empire' and the long desired Union of the Churches made possible by the election of Baldwin of Flanders as Emperor. The Byzantine Empire was parcelled up amongst the leaders of the crusade. Boniface had hoped to be emperor, but the Venetians feared a strong ruler and stage-managed the choice of Baldwin. However, in right of Renier he claimed the 'kingdom of Thessalonica' and Crete and these were conceded to him, though he sold his claim to Crete to the Venetians. At a lower level Geoffrey de Ville-hardouin became Marshal of the Empire and a great magnate. Aristocratic ambition had always been a driving force of the expansion of Catholic Christendom and it was here displayed at its most ruthless. Little was given to the rank-and-file who felt betrayed by the course of events. In Catholic Christendom there had never been any great hatred for the Greeks, but the capture of Constantinople could be easily justified as bringing schism to an end. Moreover, a new western and truly Catholic bastion in the east would surely only strengthen the crusade and the chances of restoring Jerusalem to Christian hands.

Historians have played a 'blame-game' with the Fourth Crusade. 'Whose fault was it?' has dominated all considerations. The key personality in the controversy was Doge Dandolo. With his very survival at stake, he had a powerful incentive to find a way out of the various impasses into which the expedition fell. He was clearly the dominant personality and he could play upon the divisions and uncertainties of the others. Zara was a worthy prize to fling before Venetian opinion. In Alexius he undoubtedly perceived the prospect of a new regime at Constantinople friendly to Venice. And because Pisa and Genoa were at war they would not be able to contest events. In the crusader army at Constantinople his influence increased because he was consistently the best war-leader. It seems unlikely that Dandolo or anybody else sought from the first to divert the crusade and all the evidence suggests that he and the Venetians shared the enthusiasm for the renewal of the war on Islam. A series of decisions had to be made to retrieve the difficulties into which the crusade fell, and there is no doubt that Dandolo was the dominant influence, and he had to be seen to be working in the interests of

Venice. He was certainly aided and abetted by the simple fact that none of the other major crusading leaders seems to have had much force of personality. They too were faced with bankruptcy if the crusade failed and this seems to have inclined them more and more to a course which served their self-interest: this became all too apparent after the fall of Constantinople when they took every opportunity for profit, even at the expense of their followers. But they were not merely catspaws of the Venetians. Boniface of Montferrat had considerable claims on Byzantine territory and these must have influenced his attitude to the long negotiations with the young Alexius which began even before the siege of Zara. What all this reveals is the weakness of crusade as an instrument of policy. Innocent III, by common agreement, was the greatest of medieval popes, yet he exerted virtually no control over events. Into the vacuum of power on the crusade stepped Dandolo. That was in the nature of crusading. Its ideological bond constrained, but could not control the feuding war-lords of the First Crusade. The disasters of the Second and the lost opportunities of the Third clearly led Innocent to reform crusading, but this did not prevent the attack on Constantinople which he had never envisaged. The limitations of crusading became even more evident with Innocent's Fifth Crusade, the more so because the event was so carefully prepared.

In planning this further expedition Innocent could exploit a considerable sentiment in favour of liberating Jerusalem. In the spring of 1212 there occurred the so-called 'Children's Crusade'. This was a great agitation in western Germany and northern France in which great masses of poorer people, certainly not those traditionally associated with crusading, demanded the liberation of Jerusalem and prepared to march there. It undoubtedly owed much to the preaching of the Albigensian Crusade and to the expectation of a new call to liberate Jerusalem. The leader of this agitation was one Nicholas, who bore a badge in the shape of a Tau-Cross, and he seems to have led a mass of followers, perhaps as great as 7,000, into Italy seeking ships for the Holy Land. Ultimately the whole thing fizzled out and a few stragglers returned. These were not 'children' as has so often been suggested, but poor from the margins of a dynamic and changing society who were imbued with one of the central ideas of contemporary piety, the apostolic poverty of Christ. It was their conviction that they, the poor, had been chosen by God because the great and the rich had failed miserably in the divine task of liberating Jerusalem. A contemporary writer, Renier of St Jacques of Liège (1157–1230) commented: 'They wanted to cross the sea and to do what kings and mighty men had not succeeded in doing, to liberate the Sepulchre of the Lord.'[8] Crusading enthusiasm had always extended far beyond the chivalric classes of Christendom. Huge numbers of poor non-combatants had hampered the First and Second Crusades. Many of those in the expedition which captured Lisbon were merchants and seamen. Frederick Barbarossa had learned much from the failure of

---

8 *Annales Reineri Sancti Iacobi Leodiensis*, ann.1212 in MGH SS 16, 665, author's own translation.

the Second Crusade and prohibited the poor from joining his expedition on the Third Crusade; but the need to prohibit is evidence of such enthusiasm. The later failure of St Louis' crusade provoked the popular agitation known as the 'Shepherds' Crusade' in 1251. All this is evidence that by the thirteenth century crusading had bitten deep into the consciousness of Catholics of all classes. Such movements cast light on Innocent III's anxiety to open up crusading to a wider public.

When Innocent III announced the calling of the Lateran Council in 1213 he appointed Procurators who were to prepare the way for the crusade in every province of Christendom. It was not a propitious time to be recruiting because England and France were at war in alliance with the rival pretenders to the German throne, Otto of Brunswick and Frederick of Hohenstaufen whose conflicting influences were also felt amongst the cities of Italy. This great conflict by no means ended with Philip II's victory at Bouvines on 14 July 1214 which established Frederick II on the German throne, because England dissolved into civil war, Otto IV continued to contest Frederick's power in Germany, and the shapeless and constant conflict between the cities of Italy continued; indeed Innocent died at Perugia on 16 July 1216 on his way to compose their quarrels. It is a tribute to Innocent's organising drive that in these circumstances so many took the cross. It is sometimes asserted that the pope avoided recruiting kings and preferred the more controllable lords, but there is no evidence of this. King Andrew of Hungary actually participated, while in 1215 Frederick of Germany took the cross. The proclamation of the crusade at Fourth Lateran provided a springboard for Innocent's appeal for a new crusade. However, the absence of kings meant that the problem of command emerged very quickly because this was a crusade of many contingents. There was a substantial force from France, but Italy, various parts of Germany and even England contributed forces. Things went wrong from the very start. Innocent wanted the armies to gather at Brindisi and Messina in the spring of 1217, and probably thought that the assembled leaders would there elect a leader. He was dead by then but his successor, Honorius III (1216–27) was equally keen and energetic. However, relatively few of the western leaders were ready to depart by the appointed time, so the Hungarians under King Andrew and the Austrians under Duke Leopold VI were the first to arrive in the Holy Land. Andrew did not stay long and returned in early 1218. In these early months the expedition had to await more substantial forces. They made a demonstration towards Damascus, refortified Caesarea and built the castle of Athlit, but this was enough to cause considerable nervousness in the Islamic world.

With the arrival of a large force of crusaders from Germany in April 1218 a decision was taken to attack Damietta in the delta of the Nile as a preliminary to an assault of Egypt. This had been made the object of the crusade by Fourth Lateran, to take advantage of the divisions between the Ayyubid rulers of Syria and Egypt. King John of Jerusalem was chosen as military leader of the crusade. Damietta was well-fortified and the Sultan of Cairo was able to mobilise a strong army which encamped in the vicinity of the siege. Moreover, in the autumn of 1218 many of the Germans left and were replaced by newcomers, some of them French. It was at this time that the papal legate, Pelagius, joined the army. His task was to maintain the peace in the army, many of whose elements had been fighting one another at home, and to act as the voice of the Church. He was able and energetic and during the long winter played a major role in maintaining the morale of the army, while John and the lay leaders pressed forward the siege as best they could. Then, in May of 1218, Leopold of Austria, who had fought so boldly, left. There seems to have been a general feeling that a year's service discharged crusader vows, but as the siege and later operations in Egypt dragged on this resulted in a turnover. Moreover, it is clear that the newcomers reinforced the belief that Frederick of Hohenstaufen's arrival was imminent. But few new crusaders arrived in the summer of 1219 and there were so many departures in the autumn that the crusader siege was barely viable. In August the Sultan, al-Kamil, offered to restore the kingdom of Jerusalem to Christian hands if the army would leave Damietta. King John and most of the army favoured the offer, but Pelagius supported by the Hospital and the Temple, successfully opposed it, apparently on the grounds that many key fortresses were not included. This opened a rift in the leadership. Damietta fell suddenly in November of 1219 and further quarrels broke out between Pelagius, who claimed the city for the Church as per his instructions from the pope, and King John, to whom it was provisionally entrusted, while there was bad feeling against Pelagius over the distribution of the rich spoils.

The fall of Damietta was clearly a great success but the army was too weak to attack Egypt, while it is uncertain what strategy they wished to pursue: did they really intend to conquer Egypt, or should they seek to exchange it for Jerusalem? The constant coming and going of forces tended to favour the power of the Legate whose power was supported by the Imperial Mission in the camp which tried to safeguard the emperor's position pending the arrival of Frederick. The power of Pelagius was increased also because the army depended more and more on Church money from the west. In early 1220 King John left the army to pursue a claim to the kingdom of Armenia and did not return until July 1221. This created a vacuum of leadership amongst the lay magnates into which Pelagius stepped. By the time of John's return the Legate, very much acting under papal guidance, had rejected another offer of Jerusalem in return for Damietta. The army was reasonably strong by this time and fretting at inactivity and Pelagius, apparently intent on conquering Egypt, persuaded the reluctant John to lead it to attack Cairo on 17 July. By this time Syrian aid for the Egyptian Sultan had arrived so the enemy army was greatly strengthened, and with the Nile floods due the army became isolated in the Nile delta and was forced to purchase its own retreat by the surrender of Damietta.

It was a terrible defeat, yet it had almost succeeded – Cairo had been evacuated amidst scenes of panic and the fighting strength of the army might well have overcome the Muslim forces but for their ignorance of the Nile and its delta. Pelagius has been much blamed by historians, but there were good reasons for refusing the peace terms, and Honorius III, expecting the participation of Frederick II, seems to have been unwilling to accept any peace. The constant turnover of contingents meant that strategy and tactics had to be debated again and again, while for long periods the army was so weak that its survival was in doubt. It should be born in mind that many of the contingents came from states which had been fighting each other in the west, and that this must have complicated the problems of command. As in all medieval politics the accidents of personality were crucial. King John of Jerusalem, the selected leader, was quite able, but he was less strong a personality than the Legate and chose to absent himself leaving Pelagius to take charge of military functions which were clearly beyond his competence but which nobody else who was consistently present was fitted to discharge. Moreover, Pelagius had to bear in mind instructions from the papacy and the expected arrival of Frederick II. Innocent and Honorius had prepared the way for the crusade as well as possible, but in the end they were dependent on others for the success of their schemes. In this case the crucial failure was the time it took for all the elements of the crusade to rally. Thus overwhelming force was never brought to bear on Egypt. Pelagius set off in July 1221 at a time very close to the Nile flood. He probably felt that the army would fall apart if there was any further delay. Really, he had to gamble, and he lost.

The next venture in the Mediterranean would emphasise the fragility of the crusade as an instrument of papal control. Frederick II had taken the cross after his coronation in 1215. He seems to have taken this step in the excited atmosphere created by the preaching of the Fifth Crusade as an act of thanks to God for his elevation to the Empire, in order, as he wrote afterwards, 'to repay God for the many gifts bestowed on us'.[9] But if the decision to take the cross was largely a spontaneous one which Innocent III both promoted and endorsed, Frederick's eventual espousal of the crusading cause was a much more complex affair. In the first place he knew that he was widely blamed for the failure of 1221 because he had not gone to Egypt as all had anticipated. Of course there were good reasons for this but it was a deficit to his prestige that had to be addressed. The popes were deeply suspicious of Frederick because they feared that he intended to make permanent the union of Sicily and was evidently ambitious to dominate the quarrelling cities of Lombardy. A united Italy was a papal nightmare, and as the quarrel developed Frederick needed to safeguard himself against the charge of apostasy by fulfilling his vow. His made the papacy particularly sensitive. An imperial crusade which liberated Jerusalem, might serve to overwhelm the papacy and its objections to Frederick's imperialism. It is even possible that he was seeking to espouse an imperial crusade in opposition to the papal project to which Rome was dedicated. At the very least crusading would serve his imperial diplomacy. Moreover, there seems to have been a wider dimension to his crusading policy. His grandfather, Barbarossa, had spoken with scorn of the Byzantine

---

9 Quoted in D. Abulafia, *Frederick II. A Medieval Emperor* (London: Penguin, 1988), 212.

emperors as 'kings of the Greeks' and his father, Henry VI, had made them impose a tax to pay for the evils they had inflicted upon Barbarossa's army as it passed through the imperial lands. Henry VI had died before he could go to the Holy Land, but he had made plain his ambitions on Byzantine territory. Frederick II was heir to the Hohenstaufen pride, but he had also been brought up in Sicily whose Norman kings had dreamed of a Mediterranean Empire. Frederick may well have seen hopes of realising these dreams in the enfeebled state of the Eastern Mediterranean.

The capture of Constantinople in 1204 had given birth to a series of quarrelling successor-states. The dominant force amongst the conquerors of Constantinople was Venice, and it was their manoeuvring which secured the election of Baldwin of Flanders as emperor. But Baldwin was only given five-eighths of the capital and a quarter of the empire. The rest was to be allocated by a mixed commission of crusader leaders and Venetians. The lion's share went to Venice, which received three-eighths of Constantinople and of the territory of the empire including all the islands, as much as had been allocated to the western barons as a whole. Moreover, Baldwin had to concede to Boniface the kingdom of Thessalonica which he claimed by family right. Boniface sold his claim to Crete to the Venetians who eventually made of it a great base. The position of the emperor has often been seen as hopeless from the first. He had powerful rivals, was obliged to rule with rather than over the Venetians and the greater barons, and faced many enemies. But medieval rule was about personality rather than anything else. Baldwin's resources were substantial. He might not be the grantor of lands, but many of the territories given to Latin lords were still actually in Greek control, so a ruler who could possess men of their rightful property would be in a strong position. The Latins had many enemies and a leader who could unite them against these forces in a successful programme of conquest would be respected. Moreover, these external enemies were formidable, but divided because the old Byzantine Empire had now fragmented amongst a series of successor-states.

Byzantine power over the Balkans had all but evaporated in the later years of the twelfth century, and in its stead two new powers had emerged. The Bulgars were a people who had settled on the lower Danube, pre-eminently to the south of the river and into Thrace, though Wallachia and Transylvania to the north of the river had substantial Bulgar settlement. The 'First Bulgarian Empire' had been destroyed and incorporated into the Byzantine Empire by Basil II 'the Bulgar-Killer' (976–1025), but as Byzantium weakened after the death of Manuel Comnenus, Ioannitsa (1197–1207) was able to establish himself as Tsar with a capital at Tarnovo. Innocent III skilfully exploited his need for recognition: in 1207 a papal legate consecrated a primate for the Bulgarian Church and crowned Ioannitsa. This attempt to lure Bulgaria into the Catholic sphere of influence was ruined by the arrogance of Baldwin I of Constantinople who inherited the pretensions of Byzantium to govern Bulgaria, only to be defeated and captured by Ioannitsa at the battle of Adrianople in 1205. The southern Slavs settled in the Balkans accepted Orthodox Christianity during the ninth century. Byzantium claimed the whole area, but its authority was weak, while the Dalmatian coast and cities like Ragusa looked to Venice and Italy. In the course of the twelfth century the Serbs came under the domination of two important *Zupans*, those of Zeta and Rashka, but it was only with the ascendancy of Stefan of the Rashka house of Nemanya that a degree of unity was imposed. The *Zupan* Nemanja abdicated in 1196, and though he had designated his younger son, Stefan 'the First Crowned' (1196–1227), the elder son, Vukan contested his authority. It is a sign of how Byzantine power in the area had deteriorated that in 1200 or 1201 Stefan disowned his wife, Eudocia, daughter of Isaac II. Stefan was able to build a formidable state, but he faced constant intervention from Hungary, which meant that both these powers were preoccupied. These disputes and the fact that the Dalmatian coast was largely Catholic in allegiance, meant that the papacy sought to establish its power in return for recognition. Moreover, both Serbia and Bulgaria were very fragile and succession problems brought out the local particularism of their nobilities. Thus in Bulgaria the death of Iohannitsa ushered in a violent period before John Asen (1218–41) established himself as a formidable successor.

But the key successor-states of the old empire were Greek. Byzantine court life had long been dominated by factions grouped around the great families, and when the capital fell they established themselves as rulers in areas where they had traditional dominance, and aspired to regain the empire. Epirus was a Greek state on the Adriatic coast ruled by the old imperial line of the Angeli. Theodore Lascaris, who had been offered the imperial crown on the eve of the sack of Constantinople, created the 'Empire' of Nicaea, while a branch of the Comnenan dynasty established themselves at Trebizond. More remotely, the Hungarians saw opportunities for expansion in the Balkans, while the Seljuk dynasty of Rūm, centred on Iconium, had close relations with both Trebizond and Nicaea.

That there was enormous potential is evident from the reign of Henry of Flanders (1206–16). He played upon the divisions of his internal rivals, and pursued a skilful diplomacy against external enemies. He profited enormously from the civil war within Bulgaria after the death of Ioannitsa. At one stage it seemed as if Bulgaria would become Catholic when in 1213 Boril espoused the Roman cause, but he was ultimately overthrown by John Asen and the Orthodox triumphed. The difficulties of Stefan of Serbia were also helpful, and so Henry was abler to expand the lands in Latin control. One most important factor in his success was that Henry conciliated his Greek subjects, particularly by recognising their religious sensitivities. In the old provinces of the Byzantine empire there were plenty of local nobles who were quite prepared to come to some accommodation with the Latins. The old Byzantine court had been very remote from them and they shared nothing of the bitter hatred of Catholicism so characteristic of the mob at Constantinople. The key to coming to terms with them was religion and Henry recognised this by his tolerant policies. But he was hampered by the attitudes of the Latin hierarchy. In the wake of the conquest the Venetians had seized control of the Patriarchate and the chapter of St Sophia, with their vast lands. The pope resented this, as did the other Latin clergy. It was thus virtually impossible to pursue a consistent policy towards the native religion and this was made the more difficult by succession problems. However, many of the Latin lords of Greece were very pragmatic in their religious attitudes and at a local level managed to reconcile native gentry to their rule.

Henry's successor was his nephew, Peter of Courtenay (1217–18), but he never reached Constantinople because he was captured *en route* by Theodore of Epirus. His successor, Robert of Courtenay (1221–28) was quite unable to cope with his enemies, and in 1224 Theodore of Epirus (1214–30) seized Thessalonika while in 1225 John Vatatzes (1222–54) of Nicaea captured Adrianople. It was only the competing ambitions of these powers and John Asen of Bulgaria (1218–41) that enabled the empire to survive. Robert made an unsuitable marriage and fled before the rage of his knights to the west, dying in 1228, leaving a son of 11, Baldwin II whose age necessitated a regency. In the event John of Brienne, former King of Jerusalem, was invited to become emperor (1229–37), with the proviso that Baldwin II would succeed him. Though he was able to fight off a Nicaean–Bulgarian attack on Constantinople, the empire remained terribly weak at his death in 1237. The capture of Constantinople had been justified by the belief that it would help the crusader states of the Holy Land. This proved to be an illusion: some knights left the Palestine to seek fiefs in Greece. Far more significantly, the settlement in Greece was so weak that it needed crusades for its support. In 1223 a crusade was preached to defend Thessalonika, threatened by Theodore of Epirus. It was led by the Montferrats and others with particular claims in Thessalonika, and was a total failure. Despite the urgings of the papacy northern crusaders like Richard of Cornwall preferred Palestine: Matthew Paris records that the crusaders who took the oath for this crusade at Northampton on 12 November 1239 displayed a disdain for the settlements in the Aegean. Baldwin II (1237–61) was so impoverished that he depended heavily on Gregory IX (1227–41) and spent much time in France petitioning Louis IX for help which came only at a price. In 1238 Baldwin mortgaged his county of Namur to Louis for 50,000 *livres*, enabling him to hire 30,000 troops, but such was his poverty that the effort could not be sustained and he was soon back begging for help. Matthew Paris recorded: 'Also at this time some hungry foreign nobles arrived in England with empty stomachs and open mouths gaping for the king's money, namely Baldwin, emperor of Constantinople, with some of his supporters.'[10] St Louis' decision to go on crusade to Egypt, arriving in the east in 1249, was, therefore, unhelpful to his cause, while by 1254 Innocent IV (1243–54) was thinking of coming to terms with Nicaea. Michael VIII Palaeologus (1258–61) was in a strong position by 1261 and in order to seize Constantinople he concluded an alliance with Genoa. While he waited the coming of a Genoese fleet Michael VIII despatched two armies, against

---

10 Matthew Paris, *The Illustrated Chronicles of Matthew Paris*, ed. R. Vaughan (Cambridge: Sutton, 1993), 27.

Bulgaria and Epirus. The commander of the latter force discovered that almost all the Latin garrison of Constantinople had gone to attack Daphnusia, and he was able to get into Constantinople by treachery and restore it to Byzantine control.

At no stage in its existence was the Latin domination of Constantinople secure. The Emperor Henry had shown the way, but his successors had grave problems and regencies were unhelpful. Most fundamentally the empire failed to attract settlers or support. Henry I, for all his success, complained: 'nothing is lacking for the achievement of complete victory, except an abundance of Latins'.[11] For the Catholic elite crusading to Constantinople lacked the cachet of Jerusalem or the convenience of crusading in the Baltic. In any case Constantinople had to compete for manpower with the Albigensian Crusade, the campaigns in Spain which culminated in Las Navas de Tolosa in 1212 and the new crusade to the east which Innocent began to prepare almost immediately after the events of 1204. In addition, the churches of Christendom objected to taxation to support Constantinople. The Latin barons of Greece had their powerbase in the Peloponnese where their fiefs attracted relatives and family friends from home. The Venetians, by far the dominant western power, did little until 1260 when they proposed to subsidise a regular garrison for Constantinople drawn from the barons of southern Greece, and by then it was too late. It was its numerous enemies and their rivalries that enabled western-dominated Constantinople to survive for as long as it did. It was largely a matter of chance and personality that determined that Nicaea was ultimately successful. An important influence was the rise of a new power on the Eurasian steppe, the Mongols. Hungary was deeply preoccupied by the Mongol threat, and in 1241 its army was virtually destroyed by them. They menaced Bulgaria, whose power in any case waned after John Asen's death in 1241, and in 1243 reduced the Seljuks of Rūm to vassal status. This opened the way for Michael VIII's vigorous and successful attack in 1261.

In these circumstances it is possible to see why Frederick II was so sanguine of success in his crusading effort. With England and France caught in regencies, he was the sole hope for the recovery of Jerusalem. And he knew that the Ayyubids of Syria and Egypt were bitterly divided. Moreover, the situation in the Kingdom of Jerusalem favoured his ambitions. After Richard I's treaty of 1192 with Saladin, Henry of Champagne (1192–97) succeeded as king by right of his marriage to Isabel, daughter of Amalric of Jerusalem, while Guy of Lusignan was compensated with Cyprus. Henry fell out of a window in 1197, leaving no son, and the succession went to Amalric II of Lusignan, who had succeeded his brother Guy as king of Cyprus (1192–94). When Amalric died in 1205 the kingdom reverted to Isabel, on whose death it passed to her daughter Mary. The barons of Jerusalem, led by

---

11 Quoted by M. Barber, 'Western attitudes to Frankish Greece in the Thirteenth Century', in B. Arbel, B. Hamilton and D. Jacoby, *Latins and Greeks in the Eastern Mediterranean after 1204* (London: Cass, 1989), 111–28.

John of Ibelin, arranged for Mary to marry John of Brienne, an experienced soldier nominated by Philip of France, who now became king. His position was weakened by his wife's death in 1212. This was one reason he was so eager to intervene in the affairs of Armenia during the Fifth Crusade. In 1222 he went to the west to seek a husband for his daughter and heiress, Isabel and in 1225 agreed her marriage to Frederick II, probably on the assumption that he would be allowed to rule for at least a while. John was infuriated when Frederick immediately claimed the kingdom with the support of the nobles and the Military Orders who saw in him real military power.

Frederick had much to gain by a crusade, but he had delayed for a very long time when, in 1225 he came to terms with Pope Gregory IX (1227–41) at San Germano by which he promised to depart with an army by 15 August 1227. In the event his army went, but Frederick was stricken with plague. Gregory IX denounced him in extreme terms and excommunicated him, revealing clearly that it was political differences over Frederick's ambitions in Italy which were at stake. In the event, Frederick sailed for the Holy Land in 1228 and the following year concluded a ten-year truce with the Sultan of Egypt under which Jerusalem and much of the old kingdom was returned. During his absence Gregory launched an attack on Sicily, while news of his excommunication caused bitter divisions in the Holy Land where many were shocked by his friendly diplomacy with Egypt. Moreover, Frederick demanded that the barons of Jerusalem submit fully to his royal authority. But they had enjoyed a long period of ineffective royal government during which kings were, at best, first among equals, and were disinclined to accept such masterful views. A faction, led by the Ibelin dynasty, rebelled, precipitating a bitter civil war within the kingdom which lasted for nearly 20 years. Frederick, with other concerns in his own lands, was never able to settle the matter in his favour. Gregory IX was forced to come to terms with the emperor, shining with his prestige of liberating Jerusalem, by 1230, but ultimately the papacy was to wage war on Frederick till his death in 1250.

In effect Frederick had done what kings had earlier threatened to do, used the crusade as an instrument of prestige for political ends. Richard's crusade was almost inseparable from his own political interests, while John of England (1199–1216) took the cross to pacify Innocent III. Crusading depended upon men and women identifying all kinds of interests with the ideological ends proclaimed by the papacy, and this quite naturally brought the risk of the tail wagging the dog, of private and political interest submerging the ideological. We do not have to believe that Enrico Dandolo was a caricature of self-interest to perceive that forces other than the ideological influenced him. Those who went on the Fifth Crusade seem to have had a keen sense of the limitations of their commitment – one year was quite enough. Baltic crusaders were pre-eminently Germans for whom the voyage was much shorter than to the Holy Land where few of them had kin. Frederick II, whatever his later calculations, may have taken the cross in a fit of enthusiasm. The papacy was dedicated to the reconquest of Jerusalem, but crusading enthusiasm came in waves whose power was unpredictable and whose success depended on factors beyond its control and individual popes at times faced conflicting priorities. The crusades of Theobald of Champagne and Richard of Cornwall 1239–41 illustrate some of these themes very nicely.

Frederick II's truce of 1229 was to endure for only ten years. By 1235 the papacy was issuing calls for a new crusade. These were made all the more urgent because of the situation in the kingdom. In July 1228 Frederick landed in Cyprus over which he claimed suzerainty. Amalric, brother of Guy of Lusignan, had legitimised his possession of the island and its separation from Jerusalem by performing homage as king to the Emperor Henry VI at the time that he was preparing for a crusade which was aborted by his death. Now Frederick was in a position to do something about it and the moment was favourable. Henry I of Cyprus (1218–53) was a child and the regent was his mother, Alice of Champagne. However, effective power was held, though rather dubiously, by John of Ibelin and his family who were amongst the most powerful lords of Cyprus and *Outremer*. Frederick demanded wardship of the child-king and control of the incomes of Cyprus and deposed John of Ibelin. Frederick went on to liberate Jerusalem, but his view of kingship was so dominating that he made many enemies and they had a perfect excuse for resisting him when they heard of his excommunication. Civil war broke out in Cyprus and in Syria between the imperial representatives and the Ibelin party. Cyprus fairly quickly fell to the Ibelins, but civil war raged in Jerusalem with the native barons claiming to act in the name of Frederick's child son, Conrad who they regarded as their true monarch after the death of Isabel. To justify their position the barons of *Outremer* rewrote the history of the Latin Kingdom of Jerusalem to make it appear that the kings had never been more than first amongst equals. A series of legal tracts and law codes, like that of Philip of Novara, were key instruments in their propaganda. In these circumstances little had been done to consolidate the tenuous hold on Jerusalem gained by Frederick II's diplomacy. In 1239 Egyptian forces seized the city of Jerusalem, though the Tower of David remained in Christian hands. But if the situation in the east was full of threat, by the time crusader armies arrived in Jerusalem it also offered promise. The death of al-Kamil in 1238 initiated a power struggle in the Ayyubid house whose chief protagonists were al-Salih Ismail of Damascus (1239–45) and the ambitious al-Salih Ayyub (1240–49) who seized Egypt during the crusade.

The crusaders were delayed because although the settlers urged them on, they faced considerable complications. Gregory IX had called for a crusade to the Holy Land, but by 1236 he was also appealing for aid for Latin Constantinople in its parlous state and trying to persuade at least some of those taking up arms to go there. He made considerable efforts to raise money for Constantinople and the Emperor Baldwin II raised money from Louis of France that enabled him to collect 30,000 troops who he led to Constantinople in 1239: how far they weakened the effort in the Holy Land must remain a matter for speculation. At the same time Frederick II was unwilling to allow crusaders to cross his lands in Germany and Italy before the truce of 1229 had expired. As a result, it was not until 1239 that the French barons gathered at Lyon in July 1239 under the leadership of

Theobald IV of Champagne and they did not reach Acre until September. The lack of leadership in the kingdom immediately began to influence events. The Templars pursued a policy friendly to Damascus, while the Hospitallers favoured an Egyptian alliance. The barons seem to have been divided. In the event the army decided to menace the Egyptian frontier by rebuilding the castle at Ascalon, prior to an attack on Damascus. This was a most unhappy compromise. In the event as the army moved south Peter of Dreux led a successful ambush of an enemy food convoy. This inspired some of the other leaders to attempt to raid the Egyptian forces at Gaza. Theobald was sensible enough to oppose this but as Peter of Dreux had not forewarned him of his expedition, so the proposers of the raid on Gaza defied him. However, they were ambushed with heavy losses at Beit-Hanun north-east of Gaza. The main army then retired to Acre and contemplated the final surrender of the Tower of David in Jerusalem without doing anything.

However, they remained an army in being and as such a threat to the Muslim powers whose quarrels were becoming very complex indeed. At first Theobald allied with al-Salih Ismail of Damascus who ceded Galilee and promised much else, and the joint army confronted the Egyptians at Gaza. However, zealots, led by the holy men of Damascus, objected to the alliance with infidels, and so great was their influence that the Damascene army melted away. So Theobald held what had been ceded and obtained the rest of the old kingdom from al-Salih Ayyub of Egypt. This was a substantial achievement, even if it had been reached by inglorious means. Theobald, perhaps exasperated by the quarrels of the local lords and the Orders, returned home before Richard of Cornwall arrived at Acre on 8 October 1240. He found the Hospitallers in favour of the agreement and the Templars against, still hoping for an accord with Damascus. Richard confirmed the agreement with the Egyptians over the protests of the Temple, rebuilt the castle at Ascalon and returned to England in May 1241, leaving behind the bitter and legalistic quarrels of the settlers.

These two crusades, undertaken in the teeth of obstacles, reveal the substantial force of crusading ideology to move at least some of the great men of the west, and this was to be quickly reaffirmed. By 1243 Frederick II's attempt to rule in the east was over. The nominal ruler was Conrad, son of Frederick II who reached his majority in 1243. But he was far away in Germany and the regent, Henry I of Cyprus (1218–53) had other preoccupations. Balian of Ibelin, who was Henry's *bailie* at the time of his death in 1247, was the leading figure in the High Court of Jerusalem and his the leading family in the kingdom. Effectively there was nobody in charge. The Orders had different landholdings in the kingdom and, therefore, different interests, which goes far to explaining their quarrels over policy towards Egypt and Damascus. The Hospitallers had latterly come to favour Frederick II in the civil war because he had threatened their extensive lands in the empire and this sharpened the differences between the two Orders. The Italian cities owned self-governing colonies in the cities of the Holy Land, and their constant quarrels meant that they tended to side with the factions in the kingdom. The end of the Hohenstaufen intervention in 1243 found the Templars as the strongest single force in the kingdom. Therefore, when war broke out between Damascus and Egypt the kingdom favoured Damascus with whom the kingdom formed an alliance. However, al-Salih Ayyub of Egypt found a useful ally in the Khorezmian horde. The Khorezm-Shahs had dominated Transoxiana, but as Mongol pressure destroyed all the powers of the southern steppe around them they attempted to expand and employed a vast army of Turks whose depredations pressed heavily upon the native population. Under Muhammad (1200–20) they seemed to be a rising power, reaching into Iran and Iraq, but they incurred the hostility of the Mongols who destroyed their empire in 1219–20. The army survived under the command of Muhammad's son, Jalal-ad-Din, who tried to establish a new domination, profiting from the quarrels of the area, but he died miserably in 1231. The remnants of his horde were therefore happy to take Egyptian pay and to attack Damascus and its Christian allies. As these gathered their forces the Khorezmians swept into Palestine and sacked Jerusalem on 11 July 1244 before riding on to join the Egyptian army at Gaza. The army of the kingdom, consisted of about 1,200–1,500 horse in a total of 5,000. Their allies, the Damascus army, contributed about 4,000 horsemen. The Ayyubid force had about 3,000–5,000 Egyptian foot and 20,000 Khorezmian cavalry, encamped at Harbiyah (La Forbie) north of Gaza, and it was here that the battle took place on 17 October 1244. The leaders of the Damascus army advised that the allies should stand on the defensive in a fortified camp: the Khorezmians would not attack a defended position and would then become restless. However, the Latins were impatient. Probably they were made overconfident by the weakness of the Ayyubid regime in Egypt. The crusaders launched an attack, but the Khorezmians broke through the army of Damascus on the left and surrounded the Franks who were assaulting the Egyptian infantry. The result was a massacre. Al-Salih Ayyub went on to conquer Damascus and most of the kingdom, confining the Latins to Acre and a small coastal strip from Acre to Arsuf.

News of these disasters provoked a new expedition, revealing the persistence and force of crusading. This was doubly impressive because the Mongols, whose emergence we have already noted, were threatening Christendom. The steppe of central Asia had always been dominated by nomad tribes whose way of life depended on pastoral farming and hunting. This way of life in a harsh environment made them excellent soldiers and ferocious raiders of their settled neighbours on the edges of the great plains. From time to time federations arose which made a much greater impression. The Roman Empire was attacked by the Huns in the fifth century, while the Avars in the sixth and the Hungarians in the tenth also threatened the west. In general the 'Catholic core' was shielded from the raiders by the peoples to the east, in particular Hungary and Poland. The need for light cavalry to combat such raids is one reason why these regions developed very numerous petty aristocracies. However, this shield faltered before the new threat arising in the steppe lands. Amongst the tribes to the north of China there was born about 1162 a leader of genius, Temüjin (died 1227), who welded the peoples of the steppe into a great political power. By 1206, as Chingis Khan

('Universal Ruler'), he dominated all of Mongolia, establishing his capital at Qaraqorum. He unleashed an astonishing expansion, attacking China, where a Mongol dynasty established itself by the 1260s. Persia was devastated in 1220, Kievan Russian destroyed in 1240 and Baghdad sacked in 1258. The Khans imposed upon their lands a sophisticated governmental system, derived from the Chinese and the other peoples whom they conquered. This sustained the army whose organisation skilfully disciplined the natural martial skills of the Mongols.

The major fighting unit of a Mongol army was the *tümen*, of 10,000 mounted men, subdivided into elements of 1,000, 100 and 10. Iron discipline reinforced the natural habits of cooperative hunting and herding. This was the secret of their military success. The Khans incorporated conquered peoples into this structure, notably the Turks who often were a major element in their cavalry, and Chinese and others who provided infantry and engineers. Mongol cavalry were poorly armed and mounted on ponies, but each soldier had a whole string of animals, so that they could move quickly across the steppe, or sustain concentrated combat over long periods by changing mounts. Individually, Mongol horsemen were inferior to almost all their enemies in the settled lands. To compensate, Mongol generals tried to marshal superior numbers whose discipline enabled them to operate in a concerted manner and to accept heavy casualties. However, in preparing campaigns they employed careful reconnaissance. They also recognised the value of terror and deliberately unleashed destruction on enemy lands to frighten their foes. So dreadful was their reputation that westerners called them Tartars, denizens of Tartarus or Hell. The primary weapon of attack was the bow. The best archer in a Mongol group used special arrows incorporating whistles as a guide to the rest. Waves of mounted archers would break up the formations of their enemies before engaging at close quarters. A favourite tactic was to lure the enemy into ambushes by feigned retreat in the certain knowledge that encircling them would undermine morale: this was directly derived from the great encircling movements by which Mongol tribes rounded up game over vast areas to slaughter them for the winter. Their horse-archers were very poorly armoured, but increasingly Mongol armies incorporated better protected elements of heavy cavalry, sometimes raised from subject peoples, for the close-quarter battle.

Under Khan Ögödei (1227–41) a deliberate decision was made to move westwards and the great general, Sübedei, was chosen to command the assault on Rus which brought Christendom into the Mongol view. The southern and eastern principalities of Rus fell to Mongol domination by 1240. Some of the Cuman tribes who had contested their advance now took refuge on the eastern plains of Hungary whose monarch, Bela IV (1235–70) viewed them as a useful support against both his internal enemies and the threat from the steppe. It may be that the primary purpose of the attack in 1241 was to punish him rather than to make new conquests before Rus had been digested. Good intelligence would have told the Mongols that no great power would fight them because of the bitter conflict between the Emperor Frederick II and the papacy. However, the intention of the Mongols to move west was well-known by 1240 and this brought together Bela

IV, Duke Wenceslas I of Bohemia (1230–53), the warring rulers of the four principalities into which Poland had dissolved and other minor powers. Such a coalition could have successfully resisted the Mongols. Sübedei had an army of about 150,000, but he was well aware of the fighting power of western infantry and knights. He therefore sent a diversionary force of 30,000 under Baidar and Kadan into Poland in the hope of distracting the allies, while his main force prepared to assault Hungary. Henry II of Silesia, the most important of the Polish princes, rallied an army 20,000 strong, consisting of the levies on foot and horse of the other Polish princes, volunteers like the Bavarian gold-miners of Silesia, some French members of the Temple and the Hospital and a formidable force provided by the Order of the Teutonic Knights who saw the Mongols as a grave threat to their position in the Baltic lands. They gathered near Liegnitz and awaited support from Wenceslas.

Sübedei's diversion had been very successful. It divided into two groups with Baidar thrusting into Poland burning as he went. His men lured out and massacred the garrison of Cracow, which was sacked, then advanced towards Breslau where he joined Kadan. Henry of Silesia was awaiting the army of 50,000 Bohemians, but as the Mongols approached he chose to give battle on 9 April 1241, not realising that Wenceslas was only a day's march away. Accounts of the battle are confused but Duke Henry was killed and his army destroyed. The thrust into Poland had prevented any junction of the allies with Hungary and produced a major victory on a quite unexpected scale. On 11 April Sübedei's main army destroyed the Hungarian army at Mohi. Then, unaccountably, Mongols went home. Ultimately this was due to the death of the Khan Ögödei (1227–41) which precipitated a struggle for succession at Qaraqorum. However they did not then give up control of Rus. It is likely, therefore, that their retreat was due to heavy casualties in the two battles, difficulties in feeding their vast numbers of horses, and to a sense that they had achieved their real purpose, the punishment of Bela. Although they remained a threat to Poland and Hungary the Mongols became more and more preoccupied with the conquest of China and the assault on the Muslim Middle East.

But when Louis IX of France took the cross in December 1244 it was with the purpose of freeing Jerusalem. Louis was deeply respected and his charismatic personality was matched by considerable organising ability. For once a crusade would be entirely homogenous, have united leadership and a strong command structure, though this was largely an accident of the politics of Christendom. Louis wanted to lead the whole Catholic west to the rescue of Jerusalem. But, despite his efforts, the conflict between Innocent IV (1243–54) and Frederick II over Italy became more savage when, at the Council of Lyon in July 1245, Innocent declared Frederick deposed. To Louis' indignation Innocent then extended crusader privileges to those who fought for him in the Italian war and diverted much preaching to this end. Henry III of England (1216–72) still hoped to regain Angevin lands in France, though a small English contingent, including William Longespée earl of Salisbury, served under the king's half-brother, Guy of

Lusignan. Haakon IV of Norway (1217–63) had taken the cross in 1237, but he preferred to discharge it by an expedition to Estonia in 1240. Spain was at the crest of a great wave of conquest in which Cordoba, Valencia and Seville all fell to the Christians. Poland and Hungary had been devastated in 1240–41 by the Mongols. Effectively, Louis could find no allies.

On the other hand Louis enjoyed the support of the papacy, and the French church was to raise nearly a million of the estimated million and a half *livres* cost of the crusade. With the financial backing of the French crown Louis was able to raise a great fleet which gathered at the newly built port of Aigues-Mortes. He paid great attention to logistics and created vast stockpiles in Cyprus which was his chosen base. Inspired by their king, the nobility of France made a supreme effort and an army 15,000 strong gathered, with perhaps 2,500 knights as its core. Louis sailed for the east on 25 August 1248 and arrived there on 17 September. However, it took time for his army to gather in Cyprus and for forces from Jerusalem to join them. This delay has been blamed for many problems. Many crusaders died of disease in Cyprus and others found the long delay expensive and ran out of money. More importantly, al-Salih Ayyub, Sultan of Egypt, had a rival in the person of an-Nasir of Aleppo, against whom he led an expedition in the winter of 1248–49. His own illness and the obvious threat from Cyprus forced him to a compromise and he returned to Egypt in April 1249. Louis was unable to profit from this disarray in the Ayyubid family. In fact it is unlikely that any sea borne assault could have been mounted before spring 1249. Louis arrived at the end of the summer sailing season and few would have wanted to embark a great army on a grand enterprise at such a time of the year. That many of the barons arrived late was unsurprising: coordinating medieval armies was difficult and subject to every kind of delay. Some of the ships carrying his followers wintered at Acre which was a better port than any on Cyprus. In the spring of 1249 a bitter quarrel between Genoese and Pisan sailors erupted there and was not settled until 19 March. Moreover, Louis seems not to have entirely settled upon his strategy until he arrived in Cyprus.

The Mongol devastation of Hungary and Poland had terrified all Christendom, but Innocent IV recognised that these people might be useful allies. The papacy knew that the Mongols were pagan shamanists who had Christians in their ranks. If they could be won for Christianity they would be useful allies against Islam, which is why he sent an embassy to the Great Khan. St Louis too contacted them, although he must have realised that any response from the great Khan would arrive too late to effect his operations. However, serious consideration was given to an expedition to Asia Minor where the Seljuks of Rūm had recently been defeated by a Mongol army. Some French sergeants, perhaps moved by the costs of staying on Cyprus actually went there. However, the Sultan of Egypt controlled Jerusalem, so he had to be defeated if it was to be liberated. In any case Louis used the delay well, acquiring flat-bottomed boats which could be used to assault the beaches of Egypt. The crusaders did not sail from Cyprus until 13 May, and even then they had to regroup after a storm and only on 4 June appeared before

195

Damietta. The Sultan kept his main army back from the coast and dispatched elite units to repel the attack, but Louis' knights stormed ashore covered by crossbow fire. Then the French had a remarkable stroke of luck – the garrison of Damietta, where the Fifth Crusade had delayed so long, panicked and fled the town which by 6 June was securely in Louis' hands. Further advance had to wait, partly because Louis was still awaiting more troops and partly because of the rising of the Nile which made movement through the delta impossible.

When reinforcements arrived in October there was disagreement over what to do next. The idea of an attack on Alexandria was mooted – the crusaders commanded the sea and its fall would fatally weaken Egypt. However, Robert of Artois, the king's brother, successfully urged an attack on Cairo following the precedent of the Fifth Crusade. In this debate Louis seems to have been rather passive, allowing others to make the running, and this perhaps reflects his limitations as a general which were soon to be more cruelly exposed. On 20 November the army set out towards the fortress of Mansourah, making painfully slow progress as they had to keep filling in canals and countering enemy attacks. By the time they got there and began a difficult siege al-Salih Ayyub was dead and his heir, Turan-Shah, was far away. However, Fakhr-ad-Din, supported by the dead Sultan's wife, rallied the troops and averted a crisis. On 7 February 1250, guided by a renegade, elements of the crusader army were able to cross the Bahr as-Saghir which separated them from Mansourah. But Robert of Artois charged into the enemy camp before Louis's main force was deployed, then rushed into the town where it was cut to pieces in the narrow streets. The Egyptians then counter-attacked, but Louis kept his nerve and fought them off.

However, although he won a victory, it was at terrible cost and Mansourah, supported by a formidable army, stood between him and Cairo. Louis remained, but his army was weakened by disease and by enemy attacks which became worse when the Moslems used their ships to cut the river link with Damietta. Only on 5 April did Louis order a retreat, but by then he was outnumbered and his helpless army surrendered. Louis, refusing to abandon them, also fell into captivity. A huge ransom was asked for the king and the army, and the surrender of Damietta was demanded. In the event half, 400,000 bezants, was paid very rapidly, Louis was released and went to Acre. But by this time Turan-Shah had been assassinated and war broke out between the Egyptians and Syrians, enabling Louis to free more of his army and to cancel the remainder of the ransom. He tried to take advantage of the fighting between Syria and Egypt and he fortified Acre, Caesarea, Jaffa and Sidon. His room for manoeuvre was limited when Syria and Egypt came to a peace in 1253. Louis returned to France in 1254 leaving a permanent force of 100 knights under Geoffrey of Sargines at Acre. He had come very near to success but had been defeated by the hydrology of the Nile delta and by his own limitations as a general. He was a good organiser and a brave leader. Many of his misfortunes were typical of those of medieval western armies, notably the indiscipline of Robert of Artois. But unlike Richard on the Third Crusade

Louis did not have much sense of the limitations of his power. Richard called off the advance to Jerusalem – Louis could not bear to abandon Mansourah.

The period from 1192 to 1254 saw significant changes in crusading. It became a more directed and organised activity, supported by a piety focused on Jerusalem and an elaborate ritual all of its own. It also became even more obviously centred on the papacy. Innocent III gave new impetus to the papal project to unify Catholic Christendom around the papacy and the crusade, to give a political and military expression to Catholic Christendom, the cultural and religious unity of the peoples who accepted papal authority. The liberation of Jerusalem was to be the goal of the whole of Catholic Christendom. Remarkably, his successors maintained this impetus. In this period all major kings were to justify their policies by reference to the crusade to one degree or another. Reform, peace and the proper order of Christian society, the liberation of Jerusalem, were the goals of the papacy. None dared dissent openly and kings found it politic to adopt this purpose as their own. In 1246 Louis IX justified his seizure of Provence for his brother, Charles, in terms of preparing and settling matters to make possible a crusade. In 1254 Alfonso X of Castile and Henry III of England presented the settlement of their dispute over Gascony as the preliminary to a crusade against the Muslims of North Africa. The papal project was not entirely uncontested. Frederick II may have had an alternative vision of imperial leadership, but ultimately his belief that emperor and pope should cooperate for the good of Christendom overshadowed this. He was adept at turning papal propaganda against the papacy and claiming to act for the peace of Christendom, but his successes were transient. The fact was that papal leadership was clearly recognised and there was no coherent body of critics prepared to contest it. The vision of the papacy and of Christendom as a whole focused on Jerusalem. This does not mean that other objectives were seen as wrong or demeaning of a noble ideal. But in the minds of western Christians Jerusalem had come to enjoy a special place and the popes were its special advocate.

St Louis exemplified the qualities of an ideal monarch and the conventional pieties of his age. It is no accident that his crusade aimed to liberate Jerusalem, though by the means of conquering Egypt. Crusades to other places were more successful, but they enjoyed nothing like the attention of prestige of the attack on Jerusalem. The period covered by this chapter was the zenith of the crusading movement, but it enjoyed greatest success where it enlisted other forces: the greed of Baltic merchants and German nobles, the ambitions of Spanish kings. These forces were paralleled elsewhere – in the Welsh March, in the English Pale in Ireland, in the obscure extirpation of Central European paganism. The papacy could, in certain circumstances, endow such drives with real force and moral appeal. But there were limits, as the failure of support for the western domination of Constantinople shows. The crusade to Jerusalem was the ultimate ideological appeal, and it was fostered by all possible means. But ideology in itself had a limited appeal and visibly far too few people had a direct stake in what happened in Jerusalem. In this crescendo of papal crusading it is easy to chart the popularity of the movement, not least in the 'Children's Crusade', but it is easy to forget that passive resistance limited the extent to which the popes could mobilise power. Criticism of crusading was relatively rare, but so was crusading. Its ideological drive drew upon the notion of Christendom with its sense of community and identity, but that was limited in a fissured and particularist continent.

Moreover, the crusade of St Louis pointed to another factor, the rise of the monarchical state. In France and England monarchs were increasingly able to command the loyalty of their barons. In the empire and the kingdom of Sicily Frederick II proclaimed a vision of monarchical power based on Roman law. His skilful use of the crusade as a diplomatic instrument was a grave warning to the papacy. The popes were no longer the giants of Christendom, towering over petty princes. They had always had to negotiate with kings, but the balance of power was visibly shifting. St Louis was the very model of a Christian king, but he was far from being the creature of the pope and the crusade to Damietta was his project, not that of Rome. However, the trend towards monarchical centralisation was as yet limited, but the case of Frederick II showed that it could pose a threat to the vision of a Christendom united against infidel and heterodox alike under the banner of the papacy.

SELECTED READING

The history of the Crusader States in this period is outlined by M. N. Hardwicke, 'The Crusader states, 1192–1243' and S. Runciman, 'The Crusader states, 1243–91', in Setton, *Crusades 2*. 522–98. This same volume also contains chapters on individual expeditions: E. H. McNeal and R. L. Wolff, 'The Fourth Crusade', 153–86; T. C. Van Cleve, 'The Fifth Crusade', 429–62; S. Painter, 'The crusade of Theobald of Champagne and Richard of Cornwall, 1239–41; J. R. Strayer, 'The crusades of Louis IX', 487–521. However, there are more modern treatments of some of these. D. E. Queller and T. F. Madden, *The Fourth Crusade. The Conquest of Constantinople 1201–4* (2nd edition, Philadelphia, PA: University of Pennsylvania Press, 1997) remains the most authoritative work. His collection of articles, *Medieval Diplomacy and the Fourth Crusade* (Aldershot: Variorum, 1980) is also very valuable. There is an absolutely magisterial treatment of the Fifth Crusade by J. M. Powell, *Anatomy of a Crusade 1213–21* (Philadelphia, PA: University of Pennsylvania Press, 1986). For the crusades of St Louis the work of J. Richard, *Saint Louis, Crusader King of France* (Cambridge: Cambridge University Press, 1992) is very valuable. The best work on criticism of the crusade, including that of Gerhoh of Reichersberg, is E. Siberry, *Criticism of Crusading 1095–1274* (Oxford: Clarendon Press, 1985) which provides a sharp modern analysis but one which treats with respect older ideas on this subject. A good understanding of the evolution of chivalry is provided by R. W. Kaeuper, *Chivalry and Violence in Medieval Europe* (Oxford: Oxford University Press, 1999), who stresses its violent nature. Bouchard, *Strong of Body, Brave and Noble* analyses the nobility and the literature created around them, as does J. Flori, notably his *L'Essor de chevalerie* (Geneva: Droz, 1986). J. Riley-Smith has done much to establish the concept of crusading families, notably in his *The First Crusaders* and 'Family traditions and participation in the Second

Crusade', in M. Gervers (ed.), *The Second Crusade and the Cistercians* (New York: St Martin's Press, 1992). For Innocent III and his reign in general, see J. Sayers, *Innocent III Leader of Europe 1198–1216* (London: Longman, 1994). For particular aspects of the reign B. Bolton, *Innocent III. Studies in Papal Authority and Pastoral Care* (Aldershot: Variorum, 1995) is very useful. J. C. Moore (ed.), *Pope Innocent III and his World* (Aldershot: Ashgate, 1999) provides many new insights, notably the article by C. T. Maier, 'The Mass, the Eucharist and the Cross: Innocent III and the relocation of the Crusade', 351–60. On the weight of Innocent's influence on papal crusading policy in the thirteenth century M. Purcell, *Papal Crusading Policy 1244–91* (Leiden: Brill, 1975) is indispensable while there is a very useful article by B. Weiler, 'The *Negotium Terrae Sanctae* in the political discourse of the thirteenth century, 1215–1311', *The International History Review* 25 (2003), 1–36. For Spain, see Lomax, *The Reconquest of Spain* McKay, *Spain in the Middle Ages* and J. F. O'Callaghan, *Reconquest and Crusade in Medieval Spain* (Philadelphia, PA: University of Pennsylvania Press, 2003). James I of Aragon left us his fascinating memoirs which have been translated in *The Chronicle of James I King of Aragon*, ed. J. Forster (Farnborough: Gregg, 1968). On the crusade in the Baltic the standard authorities in English are: Christiansen, *The Northern Crusades* and W. L. Urban, *The Baltic Crusade* (Dekalb, IL: Northern Illinois University Press, 1975), *The Livonian Crusade* (Washington, DC: University Press of America, 1988) and *The Teutonic Knights. A Military History* (London: Greenhill, 2003). Especially good on frontier societies and their peoples is R. Bartlett and A. Mackay (eds), *Medieval Frontier Societies* (Oxford: Clarendon, 1996). J. R. Strayer, 'The political crusades of the thirteenth century', in Setton, *Crusades 2.* 343–77 provides a useful outline of this subject, but it should be remembered that this categorisation is modern and that criticism of crusading was actually very muted, on which see Siberry, *Criticism of Crusading.* J. Sumption, *The Albigensian Crusade* (London: Faber, 1978) provides a good introduction to this remarkable event and takes the view that the crusade itself was a failure; the opposite view is taken by J. R. Strayer, *The Albigensian Crusades* (New York: Dial, 1971). An important source for the Albigensian Crusade available in English is William of Tudela, *The Song of the Cathar Wars. A History of the Albigensian Crusade*, ed. J. Shirley (Aldershot: Ashgate, 1996). There is an excellent introduction to the Medieval Inquisition in B. Hamilton, *The Medieval Inquisition* (London: Arnold, 1981) who thinks that it was set up to 'moderate popular zeal against heretics' (98). J. B. Given, *The Inquisition and Medieval Society* (Ithaca, NY: Cornell University Press, 1997), however, suggests that the Inquisition was 'draconian' and able to 'make concrete the ideas, fears and fantasies that resided only in their own minds' (213). For the whole context of the Inquisition, see R. I. Moore, *The Formation of a Persecuting Society. Power and Deviance in Western Europe 950–1250* (Oxford: Blackwell, 1987). Richard and his Egyptian strategy are discussed in the preceding chapter and its suggestions for further reading. There is a good survey of Byzantine history and its relations with the west in M. Angold, *The Byzantine Empire 1025–1204* (London: Longman, 1984). For the expanding state of the Byzantine economy with indications of the positive role of western merchants, see Harvey, *Economic Expansion of the Byzantine Empire.* D. M. Nicol, *Byzantium and Venice. A Study in Diplomatic and Cultural Relations* (Cambridge: Cambridge University Press, 1988) surveys Byzantine–Latin relations from a Byzantine viewpoint. A rather different perspective, with a more modern view of crusading, is offered by T. Madden, *Enrico Dandolo and the Rise of Venice* (Baltimore, MD: Johns Hopkins University Press, 2003). For an excellent modern study that considers how the two Christian communities viewed one another, see M. Angold,

The Fourth Crusade (London: Longman, 2003). Geoffrey de Villehardouin, Marshal of Champagne, who wrote *The Conquest of Constantinople*, in B. Radice and R. Baldick (eds), *Joinville and Villehardouin. Chroniclers of the Crusades* (Harmondsworth: Penguin, 1963) was one of the envoys chosen by the crusader leaders. He was deeply involved in all the major events of the crusade and later became Marshal to Baldwin of Flanders who was made emperor after the crusaders seized Constantinople. He presents the progress of the crusade as the result of a series of decisions forced upon the leadership by circumstances beyond their control. This is the view taken by Queller, *Fourth Crusade* who argues forcefully against the older notion that from the first there was a conspiracy to pervert the crusade and to seize Constantinople. He surveyed the literature on this controversy in *The Latin Conquest of Constantinople* (New York: Wiley, 1971). Queller's view is now very widely accepted by modern writers. There is a revealing study of the actual Venetian fleet, the sailors needed to man it and the full scale of the Venetian effort by J. H. Pryor, 'The Venetian fleet for the Fourth Crusade and the diversion of the Crusade to Constantinople', in M. Bull, P. Edbury, N. Housley and J. Phillips (eds), *The Experience of Crusading*, 2 vols (Cambridge: Cambridge University Press, 2003) 1. 103–126. In fact, every view of the Fourth Crusade rests on interpretations of Villehardouin's work because he was so involved in events, but the idea that he was basically honest, while persuasive, is still open to question, because there are crucial gaps in the narrative, especially regarding the activities in Germany of Alexius IV (1203–04), and the silence on the attitudes and actions of Innocent III. Papal records present the pope as suspicious from the first of the Venetians and anxious to prevent an attack on Christians, but Queller, *Fourth Crusade*, 7–8 dismisses this as *post facto* justification of Innocent's stance. The whole subject has been surveyed by T. Madden, 'Venice, the Papacy and the Crusades before 1204', in S. J. Ridyard (ed.), *Crusades and Crusading in Medieval Life* (Sewanee, TN: University of the South Press, 2003). Robert of Clari, *Conquest of Constantinople*, ed. E. H. McNeal, (New York: Columbia University Press, 1936, 2nd edition, New York: Norton, 1969) was a humble knight who wrote in Old French. His account is lively, not least because of his complaints about the greed of the leaders, but he was an outsider who knew little about the key decisions. Niketas Choniates, *O City of Byzantium*, ed. H. J. Magoulias (Detroit, MI: Wayne State University Press, 1984) presents a Greek standpoint but is ignorant of the inner dynamics of the crusade. Many of the other sources bearing upon the crusade, including key documents of Innocent III, have been gathered together and translated by A. J. Andrea, *Contemporary Sources for the Fourth Crusade* (Brill: Leiden, 2000). Amongst them is the *Devastatio Constantinopolitano* which, like Robert of Clari, criticises the leadership for misleading the rank-and-file, but goes further and doubts the validity of the whole enterprise. On those who did not join in the attack on Constantinople and made their own way to the Holy Lands, see D. E. Queller, T. K. Compton, D. A. Campbell, 'The Fourth Crusade: the neglected majority', *Speculum* 49 (1974), 441–65. There is a penetrating review of the literature and sources in T. Madden, 'Outside and inside the Fourth Crusade', *International History Review* 17 (1995), 724–43. P. Lock, *The Franks in the Aegean 1204–1400* (London: Longman, 1995) provides an excellent study of the western settlement in Greece, while M. Barber, 'Western attitudes to Frankish Greece in the thirteenth century', in B. Arbel, B. Hamilton and D. Jacoby (eds), *Latins and Greeks in the Eastern Mediterranean after 1204* (London: Cass, 1989), 111–28, explains a great deal about the weakness of the Latin Emperors. On the nature of the 'Children's Crusade' and its protest against earlier failure to liberate Jerusalem, see P. Raedts, 'The Children's Crusade of 1212', *Journal of Medieval History* 3 (1977), 279–333. The myth of the

'Peasants' Crusade' was admirably exploded by Duncalf's 'The Peasants' Crusade' but has proved remarkably persistent. On accusations of cannibalism, see L. A. M. Sumberg, 'The "Tafurs" and the First Crusade', *Medieval Studies* 21 (1959), 224–46, and for modern overviews of the role of the poor on the First Crusade, see France, 'The crisis of the First Crusade' and C. Morris, 'Policy and visions'. Two valuable works on Frederick II are those of T. C. van Cleve, *Frederick II of Hohenstaufen, immutator mundi* (Oxford: Clarendon, 1972) and D. Abulafia, *Frederick II. A Medieval Emperor* (London: Penguin, 1988). P. W. Edbury, *The Kingdom of Cyprus and the Crusades, 1191–1374* (Cambridge: Cambridge University Press, 1991) is the authority on crusader Cyprus and provides a useful analysis of Frederick II's dealings there and their later consequences. A very good study of the divisions in the Ayyubid house is that of R. S. Humphreys, *From Saladin to the Mongols. The Ayyubids of Damascus 1193–1260* (New York: State University of New York, 1977). There is a vast literature on the Mongols. J. Chambers, *The Devil's Horsemen. The Mongol Invasion of Europe* (London: Phoenix Press, 2001) and Robert Marshall, *Storm from the East. From Ghengis Khan to Khubilai Khan* (London: BBC Books, 1993) present popular accounts, the latter based on a BBC Television series. D. Morgan, *The Mongols* (Oxford: Blackwell, 1986) covers the subject very well, while J. M. Smith, 'Mongol society and military in the Middle East: antecedents and adaptations', in Y. Lev (ed.), *War and Society in the Eastern Mediterranean, 7th–15th Centuries* (Leiden: Brill, 1997), 249–66 reveals a great deal about their military capacity.

For the crusade of St Louis the primary source is Jean de Joinville, *Life of St Louis*, ed. B. Radice and R. Baldick (Harmondsworth: Penguin, 1963), while a different perspective is offered by Matthew Paris, *The Illustrated Chronicles of Matthew Paris*, ed. R. Vaughan (Stroud: Sutton, 1993). Muslim sources in English translation are to be found in F. Gabrieli (ed.), *Arab Historians of the Crusades* (London: Routledge, 1969) and U. Lyons, M. C. Lyons and J. Riley-Smith, *Ayyubids, Mamlukes and Crusaders*, 2 vols (Cambridge: Cambridge University Press, 1971). W. C. Jordan, *Louis IX and the Challenge of the Crusade. A Study in Rulership* (Princeton, NJ: Princeton University Press, 1979) provides very valuable information about St Louis' government and his preparations for the crusade.

7

PROGRESS AND
MISCALCULATION, 1254–1337

In the second half of the thirteenth century Catholic Christendom remained deeply concerned with the Holy Land though there was undoubtedly some feeling of discouragement. Conditions in the eastern Mediterranean were very difficult for the Latin settlers, especially in the face of the growing strength of Egypt and her empire. But they could count on a network of support which included Christian Cyprus. When Acre fell in 1291, however, it came as a sudden and rude shock to Christendom. The papacy remained as committed as ever before to the recovery of Jerusalem, and made great efforts to support the crusade in the Baltic, although the Spanish wars became more and more self-contained. But the decisive factor in the history of the crusades to the east was the involvement of the papacy in an alliance with the Angevin rulers of Naples which dragged it into a bitter war in Italy. The result was a failure to support the settlements in the Holy Land and the complete wreck of crusading policy in the east. This came just as conditions turned radically against western intervention. In the words of a contemporary:

> The Church of Rome doth fall
> Into the mire, and striving to combine
> Two powers in one, fouls self and load and all.[1]

By the 1250s Catholic Christendom and the Mediterranean lands were enjoying a sustained economic expansion. Population probably doubled in the period 1000–1340. Mediterranean commerce expanded to such an extent that all of what we call Europe was drawn into a single trading area. The whole structure of society was sustained by peasant farmers who brought more and more wastelands into cultivation in a long process which we are only beginning to understand. Sometimes development was more spectacular. Lambert of Ardres described West Flanders as 'waste and desolate' at the start of the eleventh

---

1 Dante Alighieri, *Purgatorio* ed. D. L. Sayers (Harmondsworth: Penguin, 1955), Canto XVI, Ll. 127–9, 191.

century, but by its end the Count was making grants of land 'which had been recovered from the marsh' or even 'has grown through the surge of the tide', so that a church was built to serve an area hitherto 'watery and uninhabitable.'[2] On the frontiers of Germany *locatores*, land-agents, were luring productive German peasants into empty areas like Silesia which would have a large German population until 1945. Such development led to more efficient farming methods, particularly rotation of crops and generated a demand for improved technology: iron tools, better ploughs, efficient carts, efficient mills and presses. Ratios of grain to seed were very low – of the order of 4:1 at best, so expansion of agricultural production was only possible by bringing in new land: intensification was risky because it threatened to destroy the soil. Peasants who owned land or managed to acquire it could often exploit buoyant demand for food. However, the fluctuating demand for labour across the agricultural cycle anchored to the land a huge labour-force which for much of the year lived in a state of chronic under-employment and therefore on the edge of subsistence. As the area of arable cultivation expanded forests and wastelands shrank. Lords tried to protect them as hunting reserves, but only enjoyed a limited success. In England the crown sold the right to *assart*, to bring royal forest into cultivation, in effect a tax on new agricultural production. In mountainous areas pastoral farming flourished. Huge areas like the Pennines of Yorkshire, the Massif Centrale of France and the *Mesta* of Castile, were dominated by sheep runs. Wherever possible, however, grain was grown. On the moors of northern England the remains of thirteenth-century ploughlands can be seen to this day. Much of the surplus which the peasants produced went to the landlords, kings, lords, churches and monasteries, and as it increased so did their purchasing power. The consequences of this can be seen today in the remains of the stone castles, monasteries, cathedrals and churches which they built. But it was inconvenient for lords to receive rents in kind, and there was a general tendency for them to be commuted, in whole or in part, for cash. This was available because the demand of agriculture for metal and a modest level of luxury goods generated small trading centres, towns and occasionally cities.

The armies of the First Crusade were amazed by the huge cities they encountered in the Middle East. By the end of the thirteenth century such urban communities were commoner in the west, though the biggest were in the south. In Italy, Florence, Milan, Venice and Genoa all had populations of 50,000–100,000 while in Spain, Cordoba and Grenada were of this order. In northern Europe only Paris was certainly of this size while Gent and Bruges may have approached 50,000. Cities in the range 25,000–50,000 included Padua, Bologna, Verona, Pavia, Lucca, Rome, Naples and Palermo in Italy, Barcelona and Valencia in Spain, Toulouse in Provence and only Bordeaux, Lyon, Rouen, London and

---

2 Quoted by N. J. G. Pounds, *An Economic History of Medieval Europe* (London: Longman, 1974), 170–1.

Cologne further north. In the 10,000–25,000 range Italy had Cremona, Mantua, Modena, Parma, Pavia, Rimini, Forli, Faenza, Ravenna, Cesena, Orvieto, Perugia, Sienna, Pistoia, Pisa while Spain had Zaragosa; northern Europe could count Abbeville, Amiens, Arras, Lille, Ypres, Douai, Valenciennes, Mons, Louvain, Liège, Beauvais, Chartres, Troyes, Augsburg, Metz and Dijon. For the rest the cities we hear of probably numbered between 2,000–10,000. Rather less than 5 per cent of the population lived in these cities by 1300. The pre-eminence of southern Europe owes much to the Mediterranean fondness for city life and to rich lands, as in the plain of the Po, which could support comparatively intensive agriculture. Royal courts and administration stimulated London and Paris which became capitals. Cologne, some of the cities of the Low Countries, and to a degree the cities of al-Andalus, throve because of their metallurgical industries. But many cities on this list are associated with the development of industry and trade in wool, notably Florence, Bruges, Ghent, Ypres and Toulouse. However, the greatest cities were those that traded with the Middle East. The luxury trade in spices, silks and other precious goods of India and China made its way across the Indian Ocean to Basra and Baghdad, from whence it might pass to Acre or through Anatolia to Constantinople. Alternatively these commodities came along the great 'Silk Road' across Central Asia or were landed in Egypt and passed on to the Mediterranean world via Alexandria. This trade, funnelled into Christendom via Italy, fuelled the growth of the major cities. Genoa and Venice were the greatest trading centres and Milan an important staging post to the lands beyond the Alps. Florence was a major manufacturer of woollen cloth, the commodity which was the heart of the trade. Other commodities for which there was a demand in the Islamic world were metal goods, lumber especially for shipping and ships stores like wax and rope. But food travelled across the Mediterranean also: grain from the *Maghreb* and Sicily fed Italy and northern Spain. On the coast near Acre a plantation economy developed to feed the European taste for sugar.

Almost all this trade was carried by Italian trading cities, especially Genoa and Venice. They even occasionally intruded into the carrying trade along the North African coast between Egypt and Spain. Because almost all ships could be used for fighting, the western maritime ascendancy was also a naval ascendancy. Islam was not averse to naval endeavour. Saladin tried to rebuild the Egyptian fleet. The fleets of the *Maghreb* attacked Christian Spain and for long dominated the islands of the Western Mediterranean. In 1207 the Seljuk Sultanate of Rūm broke through to the Mediterranean coast of Anatolia at Attalia and promptly began to build a fleet which could have threatened the Christian supremacy. However, in 1243 the Mongols destroyed their power which was replaced by minor Turkish *ghazi* principalities. These could build only small fleets that could harass the Christians but not alter the balance of naval power. It should be stressed, however, that ships were not yet sufficiently developed to create the kind of naval supremacy familiar to us from the eighteenth century. Their capacity for manoeuvre, especially against the wind, was limited and they could not stay at sea long enough to impose blockades. Only a limited and episodic supremacy could be achieved.

The general growth in trade owed much to the prosperity of the 'Silk Road' from China made possible by the peace imposed on Central Asia by Mongol Great Khans. Venetian merchants met this trade at Tana on the Black Sea coast, while the Genoese controlled Kaffa in the Crimea. A branch of this trade turned south from Bukhara into Iran and thence to Trebizond, Antioch and Ayas, the port of Cilicia, where it was met by western merchants based in Cyprus. Some of this trade went further south still to Acre which also received the luxuries imported from across the Indian Ocean via Basra. Acre was so rich that it became notorious for its loose-living and godless luxury. All around the Mediterranean gold circulated freely in the form of Byzantine *nomisma* and Islamic *dinars*, except in the west where silver was the norm. However, in 1252 Florence issued gold Florins and Genoa immediately followed suit. In 1284 Venice adopted the gold Ducat. By the end of the thirteenth century France had the gold Écu, while in the fourteenth century England would produce the gold Noble. This was symptomatic of the way in which all of Catholic Christendom was drawn into the trading system centred on the Mediterranean.

The economic heart of the north was Flanders. Bruges, Gent, Ypres and others were important wool-processing cities. Their merchants imported wool from England, a trade which became vital to the prosperity of their industry. The Flemings had an obvious trade route down the Rhine corridor to cities like Cologne which served as the centre of an international trade in iron. At the same time Flanders was the natural point of entry for trade with the north from which came lumber, fish, wax, ivory, amber and, above all, furs. Increasingly this trade was carried by German cities like Lübeck, which would later band together in the Hanse whose interests were so bound up with the progress of the crusade in the Baltic. As all wealthy people wanted the spices and silks of the east this rich trading zone was always to some extent connected with the Mediterranean. During the twelfth century this interchange had become focused on the great cycle of fairs in Champagne. Here the goods of the north were exchanged for the Mediterranean commodities on a regular basis, and the cycle of fairs served as settlement times for large-scale credit generated by merchant transactions. Some of this trade was carried up the Rhône–Saône corridor, but it also stimulated the improvement of the Alpine passes from Italy to France and Germany, promoting the growth of Augsburg which tapped into the trade of the Danube valley. The fairs of Champagne declined, however, as new routes opened between Italy and the north. By the end of the thirteenth century ships had improved greatly. In the lands around the Baltic and the Atlantic a relatively efficient ship-type, the cog, had developed, and by the end of the century this was adopted widely in the Mediterranean. This made it possible to pass the Straits of Gibraltar from east to west: tides and winds made this much more difficult than the west–east passage. This new trade route was also made easier because of the progress of the Spanish *reconquista* which meant that ports close to the straits were available to Christian ships. They were needed because ships often had to lay up close enough to the Straits to take advantage of favourable conditions. However, it would have been

Figure 7.1 Cog with a stern rudder from the *Luttrell Psalter, c.*1335–40. This kind of ship marked an important stage in the development of maritime technology which was to have such an impact on Catholic Christendom's relations with its neighbours.

Source: BL Add 42130, f. 161v. By permission of the British Library.

much easier had the ports of Granada and North Africa been in Christian hands, and this focused the attention of Christendom upon them. Italian ships now entered the ports of England, France and Flanders. With Italian merchants came Italian bankers, the Lombards who would be so influential in royal finance in the fourteenth century.

The Christian naval ascendancy in the Mediterranean was highly fragmented. The two major powers were Venice and Genoa. The need of ships to cling to land generated demand for watering points, while in particular places the growing scale of their trade required the development of wharves and factories. In the race to develop this kind of infrastructure Venice was in a very strong position. The conquest of Constantinople in 1204 gave her a virtual monopoly there and created a sea-borne empire including Crete. Venice held key islands of the Cyclades directly, and from 1207 the rest of the archipelago was vested in the possession of one of their nobles, Marco Sanudo as Duke of the Archipelago (1207–27): his family held them into the fourteenth century. However, while the Venetians had only a settlement under Mongol authority in the Black Sea port of Tana, the terminus of the 'Silk Road', the Genoese held nearby Kaffa. The Genoese were excluded from Crete, but they had helped to establish the Lusignan government in Cyprus and had held great privileges there since 1232. However, there was great friction between them and the royal government which increasingly began to favour Venice. Each city preyed upon the other's shipping whenever the opportunity presented itself. But major war broke out as a result of events at Acre where each city had a quarter. The Genoese tried to profit from the prevailing factional struggles in the kingdom to eject Venice in what is known as the 'War of St Sabbas', because the seizure of that small monastery between the Genoese and Venetian quarters in 1256 by the Genoese opened the struggle. This became a full-blown naval war culminating in a Venetian naval victory off Acre in June 1258. The bitterness between Pisa and Genoa was made worse by Michael VIII Palaeologus' seizure of Constantinople in 1261, as a result of which Genoa took over the special position hitherto held by Venice. By 1268 Michael VIII readmitted the Venetians to Constantinople where they scowled over the waters of the Golden Horn at the Genoese suburb of Pera. In 1270 the two cities came to an uncertain peace. Venice and Genoa were the leading cities in Mediterranean trade but there were also networks centred on lesser cities. Pisa had seemed set for greatness in the twelfth century, but it was rent by factional struggles: in 1254 the Commune was overthrown by the *Popolo*, and it persistently picked quarrels with its powerful neighbours, Genoa and Florence. In part this was due to Pisa's adherence to the imperialist cause in the conflicts amongst the Italian cities. However, Pisan shipping remained important, though secondary. Barcelona, Montpellier and Marseilles had long been lesser cities, but they traded across the inland sea and in 1190 received privileges in the kingdom of Jerusalem. Ragusa (Dubrovnik) was subject to Venice, but had its own network of trade stretching as far as Alexandria and was particularly important as an outlet for the Balkans. Sicily was an important trading partner especially because it was a great producer of silk and grain. But the most significant development of the second half of the thirteenth century was the emergence of a new trading power.

The expansion of Aragon under James I was a great stimulus to the trade of Catalonia and dependent Montpellier. The seizure of Majorca established the kingdom across major Mediterranean trade routes, inspiring the kings to foster trade. Barcelona was an important city trading across the whole Mediterranean area, while Majorca developed into a great Mediterranean emporium. James I established Majorca as an appendage for his younger son James II (1276–1311) and it retained this status till 1349. In this time Palma de Majorca linked Italy, France, Spain and North Africa. Catalan trading connections reached into Africa, Greece, the Levant, and even to Atlantic Morocco, England, France and Flanders. The heavy traffic through the Straits of Gibraltar created an interest in the geographic knowledge of the ancient world, for Greece and Rome had known that there were islands in the eastern Atlantic. Moreover, it was inevitable that ships were driven off-course by contrary winds and storms, and this probably led to knowledge of the Canary Islands. This is probably why there was a Majorcan expedition to the Canaries in 1342. Catalonia enjoyed an especially intense relationship with Sicily from which it imported grain. This was, however, a fateful connection. The rise of Aragon to Mediterranean eminence was not entirely welcome to the papacy, because Peter III (1276–85) had married Constance of

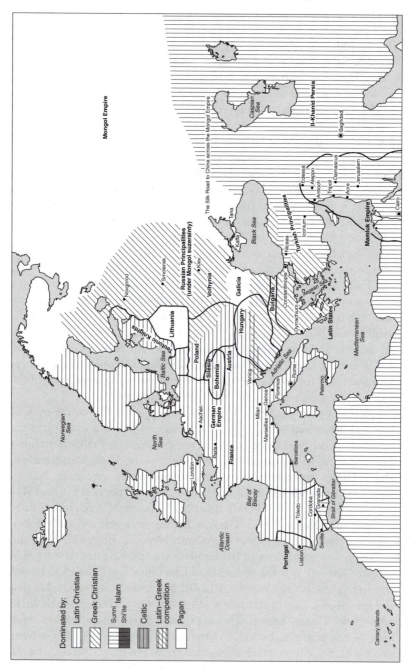

Dominated by:

Latin Christian

Greek Christian

Sunni Islam

Shi'ite

Celtic

Latin–Greek competition

Pagan

Mongol Empire

Il-Khanid Persia

Baghdad

The Silk Road to China across the Mongol Empire

Caspian Sea

Edessa
Aleppo
Antioch
Damascus
Tripoli
Acre
Jerusalem
Mamluk Empire

Cairo

Russian Principalities (under Mongol suzerainty)

Smolensk

Kiev

Novgorod

Volhynia

Galicia

Tana

Caffa

Black Sea

Bulgaria

Nicaea
Constantinople
Iconium
Turkish Principalities

Aegean Sea

Latin States

Dyrrachium

Teutonic Knights

Lithuania

Poland

Silesia

Bohemia

Austria

Hungary

Adriatic Sea

Venice

Rome

Florence

Mediterranean Sea

Palermo

Baltic Sea

Aachen

German Empire

Milan

Genoa

Marseilles

France

Paris

London

Barcelona

Norwegian Sea

North Sea

Bay of Biscay

Atlantic Ocean

Toledo

Cordoba

Granada

Seville

Strait of Gibraltar

Portugal

Lisbon

Canary Islands

Map 7.1 Three civilisations around a sea: the 'Catholic core' and its neighbours c.1300.

Hohenstaufen, daughter of Manfred of Sicily, and therefore could make claims on the inheritance of that most hated of all royal houses.

'Let the heavens rejoice' proclaimed Innocent IV, when he heard of the death of Frederick II of Hohenstaufen in 1250.[3] Frederick's offence had been to unite the Empire and the Kingdom of Sicily which threatened papal independence. His success in freeing Jerusalem in 1229 while excommunicated and the subject of a holy war waged by the papacy in Italy seems only to have added to the bitterness. The suspicion that Frederick was deliberately championing the empire as the secular leader of Christendom made things worse. For Frederick did not simply fight: he issued letters and proclamations and posed a literate challenge to the claims of the papacy. He must have seemed a real threat to the whole papal project as it had evolved under Innocent III. His struggle to make real his power over the cities of Central Italy and Lombardy inspired Gregory IX to preach a crusade against him in Lombardy and Germany, while in 1245 at the Council of Lyon Innocent IV offered precisely the same indulgence to those who joined it as to those who went with St Louis to Egypt. This development was coldly regarded by Louis IX of France who could only have regarded the affair as a distraction when it came at the same time as his attack on Egypt. Frederick's death was, therefore, a cause for papal rejoicing and support was given to all the enemies of the Hohenstaufen in Germany, Lombardy, Tuscany and Sicily. Frederick's son, Conrad IV (1250–54), therefore, faced grave difficulties. In Sicily he relied on his bastard half-brother Manfred who was a more than competent viceroy. However, when Conrad died the whole Hohenstaufen position seemed to be undermined, for his son, Conradin, was a mere child. Innocent IV was in a strong position. He was overlord in Sicily with a perfect right to decide on the rule of the old Norman kingdom. Conrad's death encouraged all those in Lombardy and Tuscany who were hostile to the imperial cause, the Guelfs, and weakened the imperialists, the Ghibellines. In Germany William of Holland was the papal pretender to the imperial throne. After his death in 1256, both Alfonso X of Castile (1252–84) and Richard Duke of Cornwall, brother of Henry III of England, were elected as kings of Germany, each by a rather different electorate. The crown had been so long in the hands of the Hohenstaufen that it was not clear who were the electors, and nobody was in a position to clarify the matter. But Manfred was enthusiastically accepted as king in Sicily and the northern Ghibellines rallied to him. He was clearly in the ascendant when, in 1260, Sienna defeated Guelf Florence at the battle of Monte Aperto. The papacy badly needed a champion to take on this formidable figure and was prepared to proclaim a crusade to achieve its ends. This could be and was justified to Christendom as a whole as freeing the papacy for further crusades.

As the candidate would need substantial resources and should preferably be of royal blood the choice was limited. Henry III of England (1216–72) was willing to put forward his son, Edmund, but the English baronage baulked at the costs

3 Quoted by S. Runciman, *The Sicilian Vespers* (Harmondsworth: Penguin, 1961), 30.

involved and the country dissolved into civil war. In the meantime the whole crusading position in the Mediterranean was deteriorating. In 1260 the Mamluks of Egypt defeated the Mongols at Ain Jalut, thus freeing themselves to destroy the settlers in Palestine, while in 1261 Constantinople fell to the Greeks of Nicaea. Louis IX was anxious to promote another crusade, but he was persuaded to agree that his brother, Charles of Anjou, Count of Provence, should be the papal champion. Charles' expedition to claim the throne of Sicily and South Italy was blessed by the pope and given the status of a crusade. In 1265 Charles gathered a mixed force of crusaders which included some very notable French barons, and a mass of mercenaries who cannot easily be distinguished from crusaders. Contemporaries alleged the whole army numbered 6,000 cavalry, 600 mounted bowmen and 20,000 foot half of whom were crossbowmen. However, when it came to battle at Benevento on 26 February 1266 they had to struggle to defeat Manfred whose cavalry did not exceed 4,000 so probably we can reduce these numbers considerably. If we suppose that the accretion of allies and losses were somewhat in balance this would seem to have been a very large and well-equipped army of about 4,000 cavalry and 10,000–12,000 infantry. The crusade proclaimed by Urban IV (1261–64) must be given some of the credit for raising such a force. By contrast Manfred's forces suffered some defections, and many of the barons of South Italy anyway probably leaned to Conradin. In 1268 Conradin came with a great army to claim his inheritance. It was Charles' turn to suffer defections and open rebellion in Sicily and elsewhere, but he defeated Conradin at Tagliacozzo on 23 August 1268. The most important elements in the armies of Charles of Anjou were French, and they clearly equated their service to him with that to St Louis on his crusade to Egypt.

But the papacy was under great pressure to restore the situation in the eastern Mediterranean, not least from Baldwin, the western pretender to Byzantium, and St Louis of France who was anxious once more to go to the liberation of Jerusalem. The papal response was that a settlement in Italy was a necessary preliminary to crusading against Greeks and Muslims. And there was a certain truth in this because as early as 1267 Michael VIII of Byzantium, terrified that Charles intended to attack Constantinople, made approaches to the pope with proposals for the Union of the Churches and participation in the crusade. After 1268 Charles was able to solidify his position by patronising the Guelfs in the Lombard and Tuscan cities. Because he provided them with men and money their ascendancy was also his. He allied with the Emperor Baldwin and the Latin settlers in southern Greece, all in preparation for an attack on Constantinople. This was initially thwarted by Louis IX's determination to go on crusade. Charles could not dissuade his great brother who would never have consented to an attack on Constantinople. However, he managed to persuade him to attack Tunis whose ruler had refused the traditional tribute to the Sicilian king and was harbouring fugitives from Charles' regime. Louis IX died at Tunis, as did his ally Theobald of Navarre, and though Charles gained a great tribute his fleet was damaged by a storm as it returned and his plans to attack Constantinople were crippled.

A further blow to his ambitions was a change in papal policy. The readiness to negotiate of Michael VIII, fearful of Angevin attack, inspired Gregory X (1271–76) to pursue a negotiated Union with Byzantium which would be a preamble to a unified attack on Jerusalem. At the Council of Lyon in 1274 a Union of the Churches of east and west was, indeed, agreed and it was seen as a preliminary to a crusade to liberate the Holy Land. Gregory's successor, Nicholas III (1277–80) was set on the same course of conciliating the Byzantines as a first step to launching a new crusade for the recovery of Jerusalem. Real as the concern for Jerusalem of both these popes was, they were also afraid of Charles' growing strength in Italy which could only be made stronger if he captured the Byzantine Empire. In effect Charles' grasp on the north and south of the Italian peninsula replicated the stance of Frederick II of Hohenstaufen. However, no crusade materialised, while the 'Union of Lyon' was increasingly seen as a sham, so hated by the Greeks that it could not be implemented. As this became obvious, in 1281 Charles got his own pope, a Frenchman who took the name of Martin IV (1281–85). With firm papal backing Charles pressed ahead with preparations, supported by Venice whose rulers were exasperated by Genoa's good fortunes in the empire of Michael VIII. To a remarkable degree Charles underwrote papal policy, for since his purchase of the kingdom of Jerusalem from its heiress in 1277 he had offered support and real hope for its survival. He had no rival in South Italy, while he supported the Guelfs in the cities of Lombardy and Tuscany. He had established Angevin claims to Albania and Achaea and cultivated the western barons in southern Greece, providing him with a firm base. With the prospect of more lands in Greece and a restored Latin empire at Constantinople, fully confident of much French support, Charles and Martin could hold before Christendom the vision of a restoration of Jerusalem to Christian hands.

The vision was destroyed in 1282 by the 'Sicilian Vespers'. Charles of Anjou had always viewed Sicily as suspect, and preferred to reside at Naples. He had crushed the Sicilian rebellion of 1268 in favour of Conradin ruthlessly and ruled the island through a clique of Amalfitan administrators with limited local involvement, backed up by a small French garrison. His predecessors had held their courts at Palermo and the withdrawal of this source of patronage and influence was a blow to the local nobility, few of whom were admitted to the councils of the king. At Vespers on 30 March 1282 some French soldiers insulted a local woman, a brawl became a riot which in turn became an insurrection that spread to Messina which fell to the rebels on 28 April. The Vespers was probably spontaneous, but discontent in Sicily may have been fanned by Michael VIII and certainly some rebels had taken refuge in Aragon where Constance of Hohenstaufen claimed to be the true ruler of the island. It is not certain that the rebellion was fostered by Peter III of Aragon because the rebels were clearly uncertain what to do, and in April 1282, even as they held off Charles' onslaught on Messina, appealed to the pope for his protection. Martin IV not merely refused, but excommunicated the rebels. By this time Peter had landed in North Africa on a crusade, he claimed, to fight the Moors. Martin IV offered no encouragement, and could hardly have been surprised when Peter was received as king of Sicily in August 1282. Peter set out to claim the whole Hohenstaufen inheritance, but he was not able to conquer South Italy. The papacy strained every nerve to defend the Angevin kingdom, even when Charles' son was captured in 1284. As the overlord of Aragon, Pope Martin declared it forfeit and in 1285 proclaimed a crusade, led by Philip III of France (1270–85) to place Philip of Valois on its throne. But the crusade against Aragon was a disastrous failure and King Philip died at Perpignan in October 1285. In fact that was a year of deaths, for Charles had died in January, to be replaced by Charles II (1285–1309) and Martin IV in March. This might have offered an opportunity for peace, but the war dragged on until 1302 by which time James II (1291–1327) was king of Aragon and his brother, Frederick III, King of Sicily (1291–1337). Thereafter there was permanent tension between the Catalans and their Angevin rivals.

It was no coincidence that during this bitter conflict Acre fell. After the defeat at La Forbie it was evident that Jerusalem was no more than a rump, dependent for its survival on outside forces. The barons recognised Frederick II's heir, Conrad II (1250–54) and his son Conrad III (1254–68), perhaps because they were absentees and they had grown used to living without a king. The *baillies* of these absentee kings were the kings of Cyprus, but when Henry I (1218–53) died his son was a minor. As a result power fragmented between the Orders, the factional nobility and the settlements of the city states. Conflict between Genoa, Pisa and Venice exploded into the 'War of St Sabbas' in 1256 which drew in all the factions and did terrible damage to both Tyre and Acre. This drift and division occurred at a time when a new threat was looming all around them. The Mamluks were soldier-slaves drawn from the Turks of the steppe. They had been an element in Islamic armies since the ninth century, but had come to greater prominence with the mobilisation of Islam against the crusaders begun under Zengi and Nur al-Din. The Ayyubids had been great employers of Mamluks who were vital for their struggle against the crusaders and for the wars they waged against one another. This was why they were in a position to overthrow Turan Shah in 1250. They created a highly centralised regime in which all the key positions were allocated to soldiers, and made to serve what amounted to a regular army built around a brilliant cavalry force. The militarisation of government in Egypt was necessary, first to preserve the regime from Ayyubid revenge and later to protect it against the Mongols. For this was the real reason for the survival of Jerusalem. In 1258 a Mongol army under Hulagu captured Baghdad and swept into Syria, sacking Damascus in 1259.

The Mongols had offered both a threat and a promise to Christendom. Their victories in 1241 inspired terror. Matthew Paris accused them of cannibalism:

> For touching upon the cruelty and cunning of these people, there can be no infamy great enough; and, in briefly informing you of their wicked habits, I will recount nothing of which I hold either a doubt or mere opinion, but what I have with certainty proved and what I know. . . . The

Tartar chief, with his dinner guests and other cannibals, fed upon their carcasses [of their enemies] as if they were bread and left nothing but the bones for the vultures.[4]

At the same time the presence of Nestorian Christians in their ranks and the fact that they were not Muslims seemed to offer the possibility of alliance and conversion. Innocent IV and St Louis had both explored this possibility. The same choices now presented themselves to the settlers in the Holy Land.

The northern principality of Antioch/Tripoli was at this time under the influence of the Armenians of neighbouring Cilicia, a roughly triangular area at the north-eastern angle of the Mediterranean where Anatolia meets Syria. At the time of the First Crusade its population was largely Armenian, though the Turks ruled the cities of the plain, Tarsus and Adana, while Armenian nobles held out in the castles of the mountains. During the First Crusade the Armenians welcomed the crusaders and the cities of Cilicia submitted to Antioch, though the nobles maintained effective independence in their castles. By playing off Antioch, the Seljuks of Rūm and the Byzantines the Armenian lords enjoyed a precarious independence, and sometimes disputed Greek or western control of the cities of the plain. The weakening of Byzantium after 1176 and the problems of the Latins opened the way for Armenian expansion, but this was made difficult by the fissiparous nature of Armenian noble society, and most especially the feud between the two families who were rivals for the throne, the Rupenids and the Hetumids. However, Levon II the Magnificent (1187–1219) gained an ascendancy over the Hetumids. He was able to expand in the chaos after 1187 at the expense of the Seljuks and Antiochenes and to establish a precarious domination over the cities of the Cilician plain where Ayas was a vital port for trade. In 1199 the Armenian Church submitted to Rome while Levon did homage to the western emperor, Henry VI, when he was about to go on crusade, and was recognised as king. He attempted to create a union of Cilicia and Antioch by marrying into the house of Bohemond, but this failed because of Latin opposition. The nobilities of Cilicia and Antioch had much in common, not least a taste for living in castles, but the Latin settlers remained suspicious of all orientals and disliked the Armenian Church which did not recognise Roman supremacy. Hetum I (1226–69) married his daughter to Bohemond VI (1252–75) and thereby exercised substantial influence over Antioch. The Mongol destruction of the Seljuks in 1243 inspired Hetum and the Antiochenes to support the Mongols as they swept into Syria in 1259 and threatened Egypt. The leading figures at Jerusalem were as divided in their attitude to the Mongols as in virtually everything else, and so decided to stand aloof as the Mongols and Mamluks clashed. The Egyptian victory at Ain Jalut in 1260 opened the way for the

4 Matthew Paris, *Chronica Majora*, ed. H. R. Luard, 7 vols (London: Longman, 1972), 4.76–7. There is a reproduction of Matthew's sketch of Tartars eating human flesh in Matthew Paris, *Illustrated Chronicles*, 14.

reconquest of Syria which quickly became a dependency of Egypt. Hulagu settled in Iran and founded the empire of the Il-Khans which became Islamic in 1295, though it remained hostile to the Mamluks.

In 1263 Baybars, the Mamluk ruler, attacked the kingdom of Jerusalem, but in 1265 he came again, capturing Caesarea and Arsuf and destroying Haifa. In 1266 he captured Safed, Toron and Chastel Neuf and plundered Antioch/Cilicia. Hugh III of Cyprus (1267–84) claimed to be the *baillie* of Jerusalem for Conradin and the barons were prepared to recognise him because the proximity of Cyprus offered the possibility of support, and disregarded the claims of Maria of Antioch. On Conradin's death in 1268 he was recognised as king. But Jerusalem had not had a real resident king since the departure of Frederick II in 1229, the royal demesne had vanished and barons, Orders and Italian cities all pursued selfish policies. In 1268 Baybars captured Antioch with a terrible massacre. The imminence of another crusade by Louis IX moderated his attacks, but after the fiasco at Tunis little immediate help could be expected from the west. In 1271 Baybars seized the castles of Safita, Crac des Chevaliers and 'Akkar, then concluded a truce with the remnant of the crusader state in 1272. In that year Hugh III's vassals in Cyprus objected to service in Jerusalem – the Cypriot baronage were now clearly distinct from that of Jerusalem, and by 1276 Hugh had ended his attempt to rule in Jerusalem. In 1277 Maria of Antioch sold her claim to the kingdom of Jerusalem to Charles of Anjou who sent Roger of San Severino to Acre as his *baillie*. The Angevin position was disputed by Hugh III of Cyprus who was recognised in Tyre and Beirut, and after the Vespers it deteriorated so that Henry II of Cyprus (1285–1324) once more united his realm and Jerusalem. In 1285 the new Mamluk ruler, Kalavun, seized the great castle of Marqab. In 1287 Laodicaea fell and in 1289 Tripoli. Kalavun's death in 1290 aborted an attack on Tyre but on 6 April 1291 al-Ashraf-Khalil appeared before Acre with a huge army equipped with 100 siege engines. On 18 May the city fell with a great massacre. Tyre and Sidon capitulated immediately and by the end of August all the western possessions on the coast were evacuated.

This loss was bitterly regretted, but it was not accepted as final and certainly did not banish Jerusalem from the hearts and minds of Christendom. Almost as soon as Acre fell plans began to be drawn up for new expeditions encouraged by Pope Boniface VIII (1294–1303). The Mamluk regime was not stable: the murder of al-Ashraf Khalil in 1293 ushered in a turbulent period which only ended when al-Nasir Muhammad reached his majority in 1310. The Mamluk army was formidable, but not invulnerable. In 1299 Il Khan Ghazan defeated them in battle, causing celebrations in Christendom. But nothing was done to seek an alliance with Il Khan and the opportunity passed as the Mamluks consolidated their hold on Syria. A major reason why nothing could be done was that the papacy had established itself as the initiator of crusading, and it was locked into the Vespers war which was partly the result of its determination to unite the catholic world behind the banner of papal supremacy. This was to be implemented by a strategy of absorbing Byzantium, but that clearly was not going to happen for some time. The French monarch was the natural alternative leader for a crusade. A cadet, Hugh of Vermandois, had participated in the First Crusade, Louis VII was the leader of the Second, Philip II fought on the Third and St Louis had led two crusades. But the crusade against Aragon was only ended by the treaty of Tarascon of 1291. Three years later Philip IV (1285–1314) was at war with Edward I of England (1272–1307) who was himself embroiled in expensive wars in Wales and Scotland. In 1296 Philip became involved in a war in Flanders which would drag on for the rest of his reign. For the moment there was simply no possibility of capitalising on the sense of shock provoked by the fall of Acre, as there has been a century before when Jerusalem was captured.

Moreover, it had long been recognised that a real strategy was needed. At the Council of Lyon Gregory X and the fathers had debated the virtues of a *passagium generale*, a crusade in the ordinary sense of the word whose way would perhaps be prepared by a *parvum passagium*, as distinct from a *passagium particulare*, a small force sent with a particular task. There was sense in all this, but it took the edge off affront and anger, and such debates were a substitute for action. Nor could resources easily be made available. At Lyon Gregory X had imposed massive taxes upon the Church for his projected crusade, but the money had been spent on the Italian wars. Some of those who came to the Council of 1274 brought with them memoirs, as Gregory had asked, and it is evident from these that recent failures had caused confusion and despair, while many people were critical of the buying of crusader privileges, a system which was reformed. There was considerable criticism of the papacy for its failure to support the crusade of St Louis. It is hard to know how far such feelings went or how Catholics saw all these factors after 1291. Edward I of England continued to be an enthusiast for the crusade, Philip III of France had supported the east with money and crusading ideas were debated at the court of his successor, Philip IV, and there were plenty of nobles and clergy who devoted their lives to the ideal. Moreover, popular enthusiasm for the crusade surfaced from time to time, and, as Housley has pointed out, crusading continued to influence western politics and indeed crusades continued to be launched. Yet in a real sense the second half of the thirteenth century marks a watershed: crusading tended to become in a sense a niche activity supported by those with special interests.

It must be stressed that in the history of western expansionism the liberation of Jerusalem stands out as the ideological goal. Crusading was conceived of as a religious exercise with universal appeal. It always retained something of this character, but from the first there were other reasons for participating. The success of the crusade and the establishment of settlements in the Holy Land created vested interests, the settlers themselves who had relatives in the west, the Orders and the Italian cities. While the crusade to Jerusalem retained its popularity in the fourteenth century its most frequent practitioners came to be those with, self-evidently, other reasons for participating. In terms of the interest of the peoples of Christendom, crusading was shrinking in favour of other activities. There were now other forms of religious devotion. The magnificent 'Books of

Hours' which have survived in large quantities from the later Middle Ages are evidence of that. There were other ways of gaining indulgences and their equivalents. Moreover, it became a much more fragmented activity. Some people specialised in the northern, others in the Mediterranean crusade, very much according to their interests and origins. There were times when consciousness of crusading was much wider spread and there were outbursts of popular enthusiasm for the liberation of Jerusalem, but they were very exceptional and the main focus of development was elsewhere. Crusading was acknowledged as a papal prerogative and criticism of its uses was relatively subdued, but enthusiasm for it limited. Moreover, the structure of power in medieval Christendom was changing in ways that did not favour an international movement led by the papacy.

The expansion of the frontiers of Christendom was accompanied by a growth in governmental strength and competence, especially in France and England where bureaucratic structures collected taxes with a new efficiency. As a result the nobility were increasingly caught up in the structures of these new states and exploited them to satisfy their ambitions. This process should not be exaggerated because aristocratic adventurism continued and royal control was rarely very strong. But rising prosperity and the growing importance of administration drew into royal service many who might otherwise have sought their fortunes elsewhere. The papal taxation of the thirteenth century was usually collected by kings who took a share. Kings relied on literate professional servants and councillors for advice and to impose their wills on subjects great and small. In England under Henry II this process had gone so far that in the 1170s an important functionary produced the *Book of the Exchequer*, a handbook for young functionaries. When the modern study of history began amongst English-speaking peoples in the nineteenth century they were deeply interested in the origins of 'English liberties' and the extensive records left behind by this growth fascinated them and led to an elaborate development of English Constitutional history and to a deep interest in administrative methods. Governmental strength tended to be measured by the growth of centralised machinery. This still stamps our approach to history, because modern government is based on systems and structures. Seen in this light the thirteenth century is dominated by a straightforward development of monarchical governmental structures which bind subjects ever closely to their kings. Therefore, when, at the end of the century, the papacy of Boniface VIII quarrelled with Philip IV, over taxes and clerical privileges it seemed to be the doomed struggle of an international institution confronted with the growth of 'modern' and even 'national' bureaucratic government. This was not how it appeared at the time.

The death of Frederick II in 1250 opened a period of great confusion in German affairs. This was not immediately apparent because, as we have noted, Frederick left a son, but his death and that of Conradin in 1268 created an interregnum in Germany and the empire. By the early fourteenth century it was evident that the German monarchy had been fatally weakened. After Conradin no candidate for the kingship enjoyed wide support and the more powerful princes, lay and ecclesiastical, asserted their right to be 'Electors' and were able to seize royal demesne and rights. The imperial *ministeriales* were absorbed into the power of their aristocratic neighbours. At the same time quarrels between the overlapping rights and ambitions of the nobility enabled centrifugal forces to emerge, splintering their authority. The greater cities asserted their privileges, and those in the north tended to ally in the Hanseatic League centred on Lübeck. All this consolidated the sense of noble autonomy not unnatural in such a huge area as Germany with its absentee monarchs. Thus what was said of later medieval Germany: 'Every nobleman, however modest his standing, is king in his own territory; every city exercises royal power within its own walls' was already becoming true in the second half of the thirteenth century.[5] The death in 1273 of one of the most important candidates for the empire, Richard of Cornwall, offered an opportunity to end the interregnum, especially as Gregory X was not averse to an imperial restoration to counterbalance Charles of Anjou. Rudolf I of Hapsburg (1273–98) used his new eminence to build his family lands and attempted a restoration of imperial rights. This frightened the electors who chose Adolf of Nassau (1292–1298) but he was killed by Albert I of Austria (1298–1308), who was in turn assassinated, and succeeded by Henry VII (1308–13). In 1303, to gain support for his own position as emperor, Albert had agreed that the papacy had a right to veto the Electors' choice of candidate and could extort an oath of obedience from the chosen king. Philip III and Philip IV of France were both interested in the imperial elections, and in 1308 the latter unsuccessfully put forward his brother, Charles of Valois. The sheer size and diversity of Germany made it difficult to rule centrally, and the long interregnum weakened it. In addition it was not a nation, but part of the 'Empire' which included Italy and Slav lands like Bohemia. German expansionism into the east and north continued, partly because in the absence of a strong monarchy the nobility felt free to travel and participate in the northern crusades, though this was not true in periods of civil war. More importantly, the decay of the German Empire meant that there was a vacuum in what we call Central Europe. This allowed for the development of other monarchies and native cultures in the area, but it also meant that this was a zone of political fragmentation.

The papacy claimed to be the overlord of the Spanish kingdoms which gave it a legal basis for intervention in their affairs. In Spain the need for the support of the nobility in the *reconquista* meant that they enjoyed a high degree of independence, while substantial privileges had been conceded to attract people to the cities that anchored the frontier against Islam. Neither of these groups was willing to surrender these privileges as the kingdoms became more secure and settled. A powerful Church was always a factor in the affairs of the Spanish kingdoms, though it was not always amenable to papal control. In 1188 the kings

---

5 Quoted by B. Arnold, *Princes and Territories in Medieval Germany* (Cambridge: Cambridge University Press, 1991), 284.

of Leon summoned the nobles and representatives of the cities and the Church to a meeting of his council and this rapidly developed into the *Cortes* of Castile, assemblies of nobles, churchmen and cities which were insistent on their privileges and watchful of royal power. In Aragon the royal position was even more difficult. Not only were the Aragonese kings vassals of the Holy See: they were only counts of Barcelona and the two areas had rather different interests. Moreover, like the kings of Castile, they had to deal with assemblies, *Cortes*: in Aragon there were three, for Catalonia, Aragon and Valencia. Even the formidable Peter III had to concede the *Privilegio General* in 1283 to the *Cortes* to retain their support against the pope and the Angevins, while keeping a close eye on the cadet branch holding Majorca. His successor Alfonso III (1285–91) was much weaker and was driven to issue an even more far-reaching set of concessions by the *Privilegio de la Unión* as he attempted to make peace with the pope and France by the Treaty of Canfranc in 1288. In 1213 King John of England had acknowledged the overlordship of the Holy See, and this realm with an apparently developed administration dissolved into civil war when Henry III (1216–72) demanded heavy taxes: out of such difficulties arose the parliaments which were summoned so often in the reign of his son, Edward I (1272–1307). France was the strongest of the Christian powers, yet the regency of Louis IX witnessed civil war, while Gascony was ruled by the English king and the Flemings were unhappy at their absorption into the French realm.

In medieval Christendom allegiance was directed to the king rather than to any impersonal concept of the 'state'. Loyalty was highly contingent. While the transcendent power of kingship was everywhere acknowledged, loyalty was most obviously influenced by the personality of the king. Great nobles enjoyed an intermediary position between the crown and its humbler subjects and this had to be respected, the more so in that distance and poor communications were a constraint on the king's ability to act. Many of these nobles owed loyalty to more than a single monarch: Flanders was uneasily suspended between the Empire and France. There were real conflicting interests within these kingdoms. In Germany the north looked to the Baltic, while the south was deeply interested in the Danube valley and the affairs of Italy. Inland Aragon had little interest in the struggle in the Mediterranean from which mercantile Catalonia had much to gain. Many of the lands ruled by the French monarchy had been recently acquired. Flanders was in open revolt by 1300 and in the south the harsh rule of Philip III and Philip IV was by no means welcome. French churchmen were loyal to the king, but very conscious of their duty to the pope. The monarchies of Christendom were, therefore, quite fragile and very open to 'outside' influence.

When Boniface VIII quarrelled with Philip IV of France, therefore, he had every reason to believe that he could win. The problem began as a result of war between Edward I of England and Philip over Gascony. Philip needed money for the war and demanded taxes from the Church. Taxation of this kind was relatively new and it came on top of the papacy's own demands for money to finance the crusades in Italy. In 1296 Boniface issued *Clericis Laicos* outlawing lay taxation of the Church, and, more interestingly, *Ineffabilis*, which restated the old papal claim so strongly championed by Innocent III to supervise kings 'by reason of sin'. By raising issues of principle Boniface ranged against himself Philip's enemy, Edward of England, who also wanted to tax the Church. Edward announced that clergy who refused to obey him would be outlawed while Philip of France forbade the export of all money from the kingdom of France to Italy. Since Boniface anticipated tax collection by borrowing from Italian bankers Philip was threatening to bring down the whole international credit system. In the end Boniface gave way, largely because he became involved in a bitter struggle within Rome against the Colonna family. This was partly the kind of feud which was endemic between the noble families of Rome arising from Boniface's gifts to his own Caetani clan. But it was also partly a result of the Vespers war in that the Colonna Cardinals were favouring a peace with Sicily. Finally the Colonna began to rehearse their doubts about the legitimacy of Boniface's own position because he had succeeded the saintly Celestine V (1294) whose resignation from the papacy could be viewed as invalid. Boniface proclaimed a crusade against the Colonna and defeated them decisively, but he was forced to admit the right of kings to tax their clergy.

Problems arose again in 1301 in Languedoc. Bernard Saisset, bishop of Pamiers, shared the hostility of many southerners to royal power in an area which felt alien from France. He grumbled rather more indiscreetly than others, and although his offences were minor Philip arrested him and seized his lands. This was an affront to the judicial immunity of the clergy, the principle for which Thomas Becket had died, probably prompted by the need to make an example to head off rebellion in the south. Boniface was concerned about events in Languedoc. The cities resented the Inquisition and the royal authorities were increasingly showing hostility to the inquisitors. He must have been disturbed that many of the Colonna had taken refuge there. So he responded to Philip's provocation in extreme terms by the Bull *Salvator Mundi* and his letter to Philip, *Ausculta Filii*, which declared that the king was subject to the Holy See. Then he summoned the bishops of France to a council in Rome to consider reform in France. The French monarchy responded with propaganda alleging that Boniface wanted to subordinate France to papal rule and calling the first assembly of townspeople, clergy and nobles, the Estates General, in April 1302. This was an opportunity to present French opinion as being behind the king. Boniface's response was the Bull, *Unam Sanctam*, of November 1302, the most far-reaching proclamation of papal supremacy with its stirring conclusion: 'Indeed we declare, announce and define that it is altogether necessary for salvation for every human creature to be subject to the Roman Pontiff.'[6] The French monarchy was in some difficulty by this time because in July 1302 their army had been destroyed by the rebellious Flemings at Courtrai in the 'Battle of the Golden Spurs' in which

6 M. M. McLaughlin, *The Portable Medieval Reader* (Harmondsworth: Penguin, 1977), 236.

Philip's great advisor, Pierre Flote was slain. A compromise must have seemed likely, but Guillaume de Nogaret replaced the dead man as the king's chief adviser. He went to Italy and, with the support of the Colonna and their allies, kidnapped Boniface at Anagni on 7 September 1303. He failed to hold the pope but Boniface died on 11 October on his way to Rome. This spectacular set of events has generally been seen as marking the triumph of the monarchical, even the 'national' state, over the international monarchy of the papacy and its pretensions to guide the catholic world.

It certainly was a significant pointer to the growing strength of monarchical states, but the papacy continued to be highly interventionist whenever its interests so demanded, and this was especially true in Germany and Italy. The ultimate cause of Boniface's humiliation was papal policy as it had evolved in the late thirteenth century. Strong monarchies were not an entirely new phenomenon. Innocent III had played them off against one another. But since the death of Frederick II the papacy had ruthlessly weakened Germany and after the election of Martin IV had focused its crusading efforts upon the alliance with the French monarchy and its Angevin offshoot. In the 'War of the Vespers' the Aragonese rulers of Sicily attacked the Angevin domination in Italy and, by extension, this whole strategy so the popes supported the Angevins against their Aragonese enemies: the victory of this coalition would prepare the way for the liberation of Jerusalem. But this was persisted in to the point where the Italian wars created chaos in Italy. It triggered struggles between cities and factional struggles within them, so that the war took on a momentum of its own and persisted far beyond the peace between Naples and Sicily made at Caltabellotta in 1302. The papacy, therefore, had no useful allies against Philip, for Edward of England was heavily involved in Scotland. Even so the Flemish victory at Courtrai ought to have helped Boniface. Fatally, the Italian chaos meant that the papacy had no secure power-base and it was this that made the coup of Anagni possible. The ascendancy of France could have been circumvented by a shrewder policy, but the state of affairs in Italy was much harder to tackle. This is why Anagni had such immense consequences.

The new pope, Benedict XI (1303–04) was totally unnerved and promised immediate foregiveness for the outrage at Anagni, but his death in July 1304 produced a bitter debate amongst the cardinals on the issue of relations with Philip IV. They met at Perugia in July 1304, but not until June 1305 did they choose the archbishop of Bordeaux, Clement V (1305–14), who had great experience of the papal court but as a Frenchman was acceptable to Philip. At his coronation in Lyon he proclaimed his anxiety to bring about peace between England and France in order to facilitate the crusade to Jerusalem. His first priority, however, was to settle relations with Philip IV who pressed for a formal condemnation of Boniface VIII. The pope was forced to agree to a trial. A condemnation was avoided, but Clement had to annul all Boniface's acts and to restore the Colonna. The process dragged on through the Council of Vienne 1311–12 and this probably explains why Clement stayed in France, first in the

Comtat-Venaissin which was a papal territory, and then in Avignon in both of which he was protected by the count of Provence who was also, of course, king of Naples. In 1309 he required all the cardinals to join him, presumably in order to secure their advice and support. The papal presence at Avignon was the occasion of much criticism, but it was not unreasonable. In the wake of the Sicilian Vespers the domination of the Guelfs in Italy was destroyed and the conflicts this collapse engendered had engulfed the Papal States. In the papal absence the principality of Rome descended even further into disorder and the longer the pope was away the worse became the situation. In order to prepare the way for a papal return the chaos in Italy needed to be curbed and vigorous efforts were made to that end. In 1309 Venice seized papal Ferrara, and Clement proclaimed a crusade which was successful in restoring it. In 1319 John XXII (1316-34) launched a major military effort lasting the rest of his pontificate to restore papal authority in Italy, but with little success despite the incentive of crusading privileges. All this tended to anchor the papacy in Avignon. Clement was further distracted when, on 13 October 1307 Philip IV ordered the arrest of all the Templars in France on charges of heresy. They were treated with terrible brutality: torture was used to extract confessions and many were burned when they retracted them. Philip may have believed the charges, perhaps because after the death of his wife Joan in 1305 he became deeply religious, but almost nobody else did. The scepticism widespread in Christendom clearly emerged at the Council of Vienne in 1311-12. Clement was aware of the sympathy for the Templars in the Council, but he had to conciliate Philip IV and so he dissolved the Order on his own authority and acquiesced in the execution of the leading 'offenders'. But he managed to transfer most of the Order's lands and assets to the Hospital.

Despite all these distractions the crusade to the Holy Land preoccupied Clement and absorbed much energy in Christendom. In 1306 Clement conferred with the Grand Masters of the Temple and the Hospital about the prospects and the notion of a *passagium generale* was floated. All the kings of Christendom agreed in principle to support this. Philip IV's emphatic piety after 1305 led to a new interest at his court. A Norman lawyer, Pierre Dubois, who had served on the Estates General and was familiar with the royal court produced his tract, 'On the Recovery of the Holy Land' about 1306. Part One dealt with the crusade to the east, here envisaged as French-led, but Part Two, for Philip's eyes only, set this in the context of a hegemony for France. Guillaume de Nogaret, about 1310, argued in a memorandum that if the king was to take the cross the Church as a whole should place its incomes at his disposal and advocated the suppression of the Temple as a means of raising money. Louis of Durand, bishop of Mende was an active advocate of the crusade while Louis of Clermont was an influential leader who dedicated his life to its furtherance. One of the most detailed and practical considerations of the problems of crusading was produced by Marino Torsello Sanudo, a Venetian who belonged to the family of the Dukes of the Archipelago. His *Book of the Secrets of the Faithful of the Cross* brought to bear his considerable experience of the eastern Mediterranean and was widely circulated. He suggested an economic embargo on trade with Mamluk Egypt as a prelude to a military assault. Much of the business of the Council of Vienne was concerned with the crusade, notably the raising of a clerical sixth. Every effort was made to prohibit trade between the west and Egypt. Although governments consented to this there were grave difficulties of enforcement. It was not in the interests of traders and trading cities. Lusignan Cyprus and Hospitaller Rhodes liked the embargo because their lands would become the obvious termini for trade, but they were not strong enough to enforce it. In 1311 the Hospitallers seized a Genoese galley making for Alexandria, and in retaliation Genoa paid Turkish pirates to attack the knights. Ultimately, by the 1320s the papacy discovered in the granting of licences to trade a profitable source of income. Little happened to bring about the liberation of Jerusalem. In 1310 papal diplomacy created an alliance between Cyprus, Genoa and the Hospital which was able to complete the Order's conquest of Rhodes. This was the first of many naval leagues sponsored by the popes, a limited kind of response to Muslim attack. The capture of Rhodes was a valuable outcome, a stimulus to crusading effort and a check to the piratical activities of the minor Turkish principalities. But it contributed little to the liberation of Jerusalem.

For that the papacy looked to the French monarchy. In 1313 at a grand occasion in Paris Philip IV took the cross, promising to lead a crusade in 1319; he was joined by Edward II of England (1307–27). But Clement V and Philip died in 1314. The papacy became deeply enmeshed in Italian affairs. Louis X (1314–16) was deeply preoccupied by internal problems. The financial exactions of the French crown caused by its extensive ambitions had precipitated the revolt of the *Pastoureaux*, bitterly discontented peasants, in 1309 and these recurred in 1320. This was essentially a violent explosion of rural discontent, but, perhaps inspired by contemporary plans and publicity, the rebels called for the liberation of Jerusalem and criticised the lords for their failures in this respect. Far more dangerous were the noble leagues demanding concession from the monarchy. Louis' death in 1316 and that of his baby son led to the election of his brother, Philip V the Tall (1316–22), though he had to contend with those, including some of the Leagues, who championed the cause of Louis' daughter, Joanna. He in turn was succeeded by his brother Charles IV (1322–28) whose death without male heir brought to an end the Capetian line which had ruled France since 987, precipitating a major succession crisis and the election of Philip VI (1328–50), the first of the Valois kings. Philip V and Charles IV had been enthusiasts for the crusade, the latter projecting a crusade to help Armenia in 1323. But the intensive planning of this period revealed just how costly a crusade was likely to be. The projected *passagium particulare* was costed at 1,600,000 *livres*. Nevertheless, Philip VI was very interested in crusading. For the king of a new line, the first elected ruler since 987, support for the crusade provided an opportunity to seek legitimacy and a place amongst the monarchs of Christendom – particularly as his claim was contested by Edward III of England. He persuaded the papacy to levy a tenth for six years on the clergy across Christendom and established a royal committee to organise the crusade to Jerusalem, but he faced grim opposition from the French towns. The outbreak of war with England in 1337 ended the whole thing, and the only tangible outcome was French financial aid for a naval league in the Aegean in 1334.

Concern for the crusade to Jerusalem did not lead the papacy to abandon the Latin lordships in Greece which were the last remnant of the conquest of Byzantium in 1204. The threat to them from the restored Byzantine Empire after 1261 led to proclamations of crusades in 1262 and 1267, but these had no effect. The Latin presence in Greece was quickly reduced to the duchy of Athens ruled by the de la Roche clan and the Principality of Achaia (or the Morea) in the Peloponnenes under the Villehardouins who were the leading power. They survived because the Greeks were divided, and in particular they could play off the Despot of Epirus against the restored Byzantine Empire, while Bulgaria and Serbia also offered possible allies. The Greeks could rarely defeat the settlers in battle, but they could ravage their lands, nibbling away at the loyalty of Greek notables on whose allegiance they were partially founded and seizing weakly garrisoned places. The great problem the Latins faced was lack of men, and this process of reconquest took away land which would have been an incentive for people to come and settle. The war was increasingly waged by mercenaries who were prepared to serve any master. By 1267 the Latin lordships seemed on the point of extinction before the tide of Greek reconquest. Clement IV (1265–68) called together the leaders of Frankish Greece in May of that year and under his auspices the lords of the western settlements agreed to accept Charles of Anjou as their ruler, and William of Villehardouin, Prince of Achaia, promised that his lands would pass to Charles. By the terms of the Treaty of Viterbo the lordships found a defender and could look forward to a restoration of western power at Constantinople under the terms of an agreement between Charles and Baldwin II (1261–73), the pretender to the empire. The Angevin dominance gave the settlers a valuable breathing space. They were fortunate that the outbreak of the Vespers war coincided with the weakening of Byzantium after the death of Michael VIII which allowed them to cultivate the Greek powers resistant to dominance from Constantinople, notably the despots of Epirus. In the early fourteenth century Angevin interference in Greece became more and more episodic, though they retained a nominal suzerainty exercised through local lords. Even at this very late date Clement V was concerned to encourage the scheme of Charles of Valois to reconquer Constantinople in pursuit of the claim through his wife, heiress to Baldwin II 'Emperor' of Constantinople, but her death in 1308 deprived him of his title. Their daughter, Catherine of Valois, married Philip of Taranto of the Angevin house of Naples who had lands in Greece, but by 1320 the conquest of Constantinople was ceasing to be important. It is interesting, however, that the papacy only dropped it at such a late date. The papacy had always regarded reclaiming Byzantium for Christendom as an essential step to the liberation of Jerusalem, but its evident weakness undermined this aspect of the papal strategy and papal concern soon switched to shoring it up.

The Angevin dominance in Greece was brought to an end, albeit indirectly and accidentally, by their enemies, the Catalans. Warfare had been endemic in Italy in the thirteenth century and this had resulted in the creation of mercenary companies which often had long lives. After the end of the Vespers war in 1302 a large group of Catalan mercenaries gathered around a German and former Templar, Roger de Flor, were looking for employment. Andronicus III (1282–1328) was becoming anxious at the growth of one of the myriad *ghazi* principalities of Asia Minor, that of the Ottomans, whose forces had reached the Black Sea and the Sea of Marmara by 1302. The Catalan army which arrived at Constantinople was a battle-hardened force of 1,500 cavalry, 4,000 *Almogavers*, the highly effective light infantry of the Catalonian reconquest, and 1,000 other foot. This efficient and disciplined army, known as the Grand Catalan Company, was effective in checking the Turks but Andronicus could not afford to pay them. They might have been satisfied with a principality in Asia Minor, but in April 1305 Roger was assassinated at the court of Michael IX (1295–1320) and the Catalans turned to ravaging Byzantine territory and entered the service of Charles of Valois, the pretender to the throne of Constantinople, but by 1310 they were in the service of Gautier de Brienne, Duke of Athens. On 15 March 1311, after Gautier had tried to discharge and break up the Grand Catalan Company, his army of 700 knights was defeated and he was killed at the battle of Halmyros. The Catalans then became the rulers of Athens until 1388. To create a focus of loyalty they recognised Frederick III of Sicily as their overlord, but they were little interested in wider Catalan interests or trade.

By 1337 the Aegean was in chaos. The Byzantine Empire had been driven out of Asia Minor and replaced by competing Turkish principalities amongst whom the Ottomans, after their conquest of Bursa in 1326, were assuming considerable importance. In the Byzantine Empire Andronicus III (1328–41) emerged as emperor after the civil war which began in 1320. He was strong enough to seize much of Thessaly and Epirus when their independent rulers died and advanced to the borders of Athens. The western principalities were prepared to offer him submission, so there was some possibility of stability. However, Byzantium had no interest in crusading and in any case was soon overcome by civil war which enabled Serbia to advance southwards. The duchy of Athens under Catalan hegemony was not very stable and was permanently at odds with the principality of Achaea dominated by their Angevin enemies but often divided. The Latins were also threatened by Byzantine enclaves like Mistra and increasingly subjected to Ottoman attack. The Knights of St John controlled Rhodes and their resources in the west and on Cyprus generated the means to support a small fleet and substantial military forces, but they were not strong enough to dominate the area. Venice controlled Crete, Negroponte and most of the Aegean islands, but after 1346 Genoa secured Chios and Lesbos. Venice and Genoa remained bitter rivals. In 1294 a Venetian fleet escorting a trade convoy to Cilicia attacked Genoese territories in Cyprus. The war culminated in a Genoese victory in the Adriatic, but it was costly and factional strife in Genoa ended the war in 1299. From 1324

Venice sought the friendship of Byzantium, strengthening its hold on the Aegean islands. Genoa had profited from the Byzantine collapse in Anatolia by seizing islands and ports, though Chios was wrested back from them. Though western sea-power was dominant its effect was severely limited by the rivalry of these two cities. The Hospitaller fleet was really too small to be decisive and Lusignan Cyprus was dangerously exposed in an area where the Mamluks were building up their navy. In any case what was needed if there was to be any success in liberating Jerusalem was a land army and none seemed likely to appear. Moreover, there was grave discontent in Christendom. Since the failure of St Louis' crusade to Tunis the papacy had taxed the Church in one way or another many times. The money had vanished into the wars in Italy with no apparent result. The nepotism of Clement V and the extravagance of some of his Avignon successors brought the papacy into disrepute. Their apparent subservience to France annoyed people outside that land. The idea of crusade remained, but papal crusading policy lay in ruins.

However, outside the eastern Mediterranean, the crusade continued to enjoy successes. In Spain the great expansion of Aragon largely came to a halt with the death of James I because with the Castilian domination of Murcia the kingdom ceased to have an active frontier with Muslim Spain and the Catalans turned to the Mediterranean. Castile remained on the offensive, but its expansion slowed. In 1262 Alfonso X (1252–84) seized the tributary kingdom of Niebla and seemed about to do the same to Murcia and Granada. But in North Africa another great dynasty had arisen, the Marinids. In 1264 Granada allied with them and raised a great revolt of Muslims living under Christian rule. Alfonso, without awaiting papal confirmation, preached the crusade and put down the revolt savagely, while James I conquered Murcia which he then handed back to Castile. The revolt exposed one of the key weaknesses of the Spanish kingdoms. The conquests had involved leaving large numbers of the Muslim inhabitants, *Mudejars*, on the land which, without inhabitants, would revert to waste. In general the strategy was to import Christian settlers to hold the cities and then spread out across the countryside: this was the policy of *convivencia* which extended a highly restricted religious toleration to Muslims and allowed them to live by their communal law. But colonisation of this kind was by no means easy. James I of Aragon claimed that he needed 100,000 Christian families to hold Valencia securely, yet only 30,000 had come. After the revolt of 1264 many *Mudejars* were expelled, and Catalans were imported to colonise some of Murcia, yet economic necessity compelled the continuity of *convivencia*. Further, as the kingdoms solidified and expansion slowed, Christian populations began to demand that toleration of such alien elements as Muslims and Jews should be limited or even ended.

This kind of demand was harder to resist in Aragon because of the extra-ordinarily high development of the *Cortes* which severely limited the freedom of action of the kings. In Castile the *Cortes* never developed this kind of collective cohesion because they were overshadowed by the higher nobility who represented a problem in themselves for the monarchy. However, there was enormous local diversity, for Castile was truly an agglomeration of kingdoms, each with their own law and custom. Alfonso X's famous *Siete partidas* was an attempt to systematise the laws. But the greatest problem of the Castilian crown was the privileges and wealth of the *ricos hombres*, the high nobility. In the course of the reconquest they had received vast land-grants which they extended by buying land from smallholders. Expulsion of Muslim peasants who could not always be replaced by Christians encouraged the development of pastoral rather than arable farming. In this way vast areas of Castile were given over to ranching, transforming the newly conquered areas to the advantage of the *ricos hombres*. These were not men the crown could order around. As a further complication there were great tensions between them and the lesser nobility and city-dwellers. Such tensions could explode at moments of royal weakness, particularly disputed successions, of which there were many in the kingdom of Castile.

Alfonso X's son died in 1275 and a bitter internal struggle began between his grandsons and his younger son who eventually succeeded him as Sancho IV (1284–95). The conflict in the Mediterranean also divided Spain, as Sancho was inveigled into a French alliance against Aragon. Ferdinand IV (1295–1312) also had to struggle to maintain his succession to the throne of Castile, but he recognised that it was vital to establish control over the Straits to prevent Marinid attacks, and he was anxious to attack the last Islamic realm. Granada was small, but well protected by mountain ranges which its Nasrid dynasty strengthened by modern fortifications. Its position on the straits of Gibraltar made it a centre of rich trade. Although in general content to pay tribute to Castile, its rulers could appeal to the Marinids, who were now the leading power in North Africa, and proved skilful in playing them off against the Christian powers. In 1308 Aragon and Castile agreed the Treaty of Alcalá de Henares by which the two powers resolved to attack and partition between them North Africa and Granada. The campaign of 1309–10 was a fiasco which ended Aragonese interest in the conquest of Granada, while Castile was plunged into the long minority of Alfonso XI (1312–50). Alfonso recognised the real threat posed by the Marinids and he obtained crusading privileges for his attack on Teba in 1329–30 where the siege was joined by a few foreigners. Then in 1340 the Marinids raised a very large army which, in alliance with that of Granada, attacked Tarifa. The threat was so grave that Peter IV of Aragon (1336–87) sent a fleet while Pope Benedict XII (1334–42) preached a crusade and allowed crusading taxes. Alfonso was supported by Afonso IV of Portugal (1325–57) in his effort to relieve Tarifa which culminated in a victory over the Marinids at Salado on 30 October 1340. This broke the Marinid threat to Christian Spain, but Granada survived. But what is notable is the decreasing role of foreign crusaders in events in Spain after the early thirteenth century. Castile had never favoured their incursions and as it became the focus of the expansion so they vanished. The consolidation of the kingdom and the growth of the nobles as rich landowners within it discouraged adventurers who were seen increasingly as interlopers.

In the Baltic the crusade was similarly alive and well. Sweden had seized most of Finland and established the important port of Viborg on the eastern end of the

Gulf of Finland. Their rivals here for the rich trade in furs, blubber and fish coming from the north were the Russians of Novgorod. These goods were passed on to the cities of the German Hanse whose great ships and developed systems of credit served to bring them into the heartlands of trade and ultimately to the Mediterranean. The papacy supported Sweden and Norway because any extension of Russian power in the North would also be to the advantage of the Orthodox Church. Therefore the popes were content to allow a proportion of the crusading taxes raised in this period to go to the crown for the support of the wars. The main focus of fighting was Lake Ladoga, but the Swedes were never quite strong enough to control it and this was a purely domestic crusade involving few others. At the start of this period the Teutonic Order was establishing itself in Prussia (in what later became East Prussia) and Livonia. However elements within the order were deeply attached to the Holy Land. It is indicative of this sentiment that on the eve of the siege of Acre in 1291, Grand Master Burchard joined the Hospitallers. The Grand Masters then settled at Venice and a heated debate about the future ensued. Indeed, all the Orders faced grave problems at this time. The Templars took refuge in Cyprus, then tried to establish themselves on the isle of Ruad off the old crusader port of Tortosa, but it was captured in 1302 by the Mamluks. They seem to have had few ideas about how to adapt to the new circumstances, even though their presence in Cyprus was discomforting for King Henry II (1285–1324) who disliked such a concentration of power which was unamenable to his authority. The Hospitallers were equally insecure in Cyprus, but they began to build up a fleet and in 1306 started the conquest of Rhodes which was completed by 1310. The Teutonic Order ultimately transferred the centre of its activities to Prussia and Livonia.

Prussian resistance to the advance of the Order had been strong. In 1260 the Prussians rebelled. They were well-organised and equipped with siege-engines and crossbows which they had learned to use from their enemies. The Order was saved because Urban IV (1261–64) permitted those taking the cross to go to discharge their vows by going north and major German expeditions were mounted, notably those of 1265, 1266 and 1272. The Germans ravaged the territory of the Prussian rebels, relieved besieged forts and built new ones so the war petered out. By the 1280s the Prussian Order was firmly in control of East Prussia and the most important castles, notably Memel, Königsberger, Marien-werder and Marienburg, were rebuilt in brick. The Order had a strong presence in Livonia but there it faced the hostility of a powerful bishop and the merchant communities. In 1298 quarrels became so bitter that the citizens of Riga called in the pagan Lithuanians who defeated the Order. The quarrel became so severe and claims on both sides so wild that the papacy was called in to settle the matter. At this very time the Templar Trials from 1307 onwards were a nasty reminder of what could happen to the irrelevant or incompetent. In 1308 there occurred an event whose consequences were to haunt the Order for the rest of its existence. Vladislav Lobietek of Poland asked the Order to relieve the siege of Danzig (modern Gdansk) which was being attacked by Brandenburg. When Vladislav

Figure 7.2 Part of the castle at Marienburg, Germany. This mighty fortress served as the capital of the *Ordenstaat* founded on the hard fighting of the Teutonic Knights and the shrewd economic development of their conquests.

Lobietek refused to pay the Order for their trouble, the knights seized Danzig and the surrounding territory of Pomerelia, the general area later called West Prussia. The effect of this was to round out the 'Order-State' by establishing a direct connection with the German lands, and this was so valuable that in order to retain it the knights were willing to fight the Poles. In 1309 the Grand Master, Siegfried of Feuchtwangen, established himself at Marienburg, the great brick-built fortress which would become the Order's 'capital'. The Teutonic Order had conquered Prussia by sheer persistence and organisation. Their government was structured around the Grand Master and his chief officers. They showed real genius in expanding the economy of these lands and implanting peasant settlers. They were supported by rich lands in Germany, especially in the south, and intimate connections with the German aristocracy who provided a useful recruiting ground. The Order's domination of Prussia, it could claim, was threatened now only by the stubborn pagans of Lithuania and their occasional schismatic allies, the Russian princes, and by taking up arms against them the Teutonic Knights could demonstrate a clear purpose and crusading zeal, which had the advantage of extending their rule.

Lithuania under Mindaugas (d. 1263) had become a centralised monarchy very much on the model of its Christian neighbours, though it was obliged to accept the autonomy of Samogitia. A remarkable series of able rulers strengthened Lithuania by an expansionist policy to the south and east where fear of the Mongols had weakened the Russian princes. Much of Black and White Russia fell to them under Viten (1293–1315) while Gedymin (1315–41) became lord of Kiev. They were adept manipulators of their neighbours, as shown by their interventions in the quarrels between the Order and the people of Riga in Livonia which lasted until 1330. In 1326 Viten exploited Polish resentment of the Order's seizure of Pomerelia by allying with Vladislav Lobietek of Poland across whose lands his troops marched to attack the crusader duke of Brandeburg. In every way Lithuania was a very modern kingdom, at least as advanced as its neighbours. But it was pagan and its paganism suffused the Lithuanian state. Mindaugas had claimed to be a Christian and it was part of the sophisticated diplomacy of his line that rulers were not averse to pretending to lean to the new religion when external circumstances pressed. So the Order was taking on a well-organised state whose heartlands were remarkably inaccessible. The value of the Order's position in Livonia was that it enabled them to tap trade into the interior and served as a base for attacks on fiercely pagan Samogitia on the northern flank of Lithuania.

The Order's position was made more difficult by the growing strength and unity of Poland. Boleslaw III died in 1138, and by the terms of his will power remained within his Piast dynasty but the realm was divided amongst his sons, with the provision that the eldest was always to enjoy a hegemony and to enjoy the prestige of ruling from the throne of Cracow, the system of the *Seniorate*. The result of this was that Poland fragmented: the main divisions were Silesia, Great Poland, Lesser Poland, Mazovia and Kujawy. However, as each Piast line tried to make provision for its children, there was a tendency to greater fragmentation and external powers were able to take advantage of this. In particular, Denmark replaced the Polish ascendancy in Pomerania, while Brandenburg pushed ever more aggressively into Polish territory and Silesia, heavily settled by German immigrants, tended to drift away. The Piast rulers of Masovia always claimed that the Teutonic Order were their vassals, but they were not strong enough on their own to assert their authority over the Grand Masters. This division of the old kingdom was, of course, a key reason for the weakness in the face of the Mongol attack in 1241. The Polish Church and much sentiment amongst the nobility believed in unity and in Vladislav Lobietek (1320–33) they found a champion whose coronation was approved by the pope. However, Masovia held aloof, while the rich and Germanised area of Silesia drifted into the sphere of the kings of Bohemia. Vladislav Lobietek was deeply hostile to the Order because Danzig was Poland's only possible port to the Baltic, but he had to watch Bohemia whose king, Wenceslas II of Bohemia, had exploited family claims to make himself king of Poland 1300–05. Though his line died out in 1308 with Wenceslas III (1305–08), his successor, John of Luxembourg (1310–46), inherited all of its claims. As so often in the Mediterranean, crusading could not be disentangled from diplomacy and dynastic relationships. The close connection between the Order and the Bohemian kings was founded on mutual hostility to Poland.

Poland had conceded Kulmerland to the Order as a base for its conquest of the Prussians. Once the quarrel over Danzig had begun Poland demanded recognition that it and other territories were held of the Polish crown and even demanded their return. The Order seems to have underestimated Polish determination to recover Danzig, but when Vladislav Lobietek allied with Gediminas of Lithuania the Order attacked Lithuania from Livonia and called in John of Bohemia as a crusader who came to Prussia in 1228–29 with a large army. The papacy pressed the Order for payments of Peter's Pence from their lands, and when they refused, inclined to support Poland. The war culminated in the battle of Plowce on 27 September 1331 where the Order routed Vladislav Lobietek but at a high cost. Casimir III of Poland (1333–70) wanted peace in order to exploit the possibilities on the western steppe opened up by the decline of the 'Golden Horde': in 1335 he surrendered Silesia to John of Bohemia and in 1343 made a peace with the Order accepting their possession of Danzig. The Order had made little progress against the Lithuanians, but had settled the quarrel with the merchants and others in Livonia in its own interests. From there it was able to launch heavy attacks on Samogitia. In 1336 the crusade, Louis of Wittelsbach, and his crusading army were appalled when the garrison of a small fort in Samogitia killed their families and themselves, setting fire to the place, rather than surrender. In 1337 John of Bohemia and Henry of Bavaria built Bayerburg which defied a siege by Gediminas and served as a forward base for raids, but gradually the intense fighting petered out.

By the early fourteenth century papal crusading policy in the Mediterranean was in ruins. The whole thrust of policy since Urban II had been to unite the religious and cultural entity of Christendom behind the banner of the crusade. In the first half of the thirteenth century that leadership had attained a degree of reality, though actual papal control was inevitably limited. The papacy had worked with monarchies, in the case of St Louis, and with others like the count of Champagne, to achieve a number of near-misses and some limited successes. The record in the second half of the century was far worse. In 1099 Urban had hoped the reestablishment of the true religion in the Holy Lands would persuade the Greek Church to unity. After 1261 the reunification of the Orthodox, by persuasion or force, was to be the means by which Jerusalem was to be liberated. This was largely because a substantial vested interest had developed in dominating Greece amongst western Mediterranean powers and that had to be accepted if the Italian cities, France and Sicily were to be enlisted in the papal army of liberation. But no liberation happened, or came near to happening as the whole structure of crusading policy fell apart. The western powers interested in the Mediterranean had competing concerns and these destroyed the papal drive to unity. Furthermore, by the early fourteenth century the attempt to eliminate Constantinople as a rival centre of influence was a disastrous failure.

Not only did Orthodoxy remain, it flourished, buttressed by a series of monarchies whose religious and cultural focus was Constantinople. Eastern Europe and the Balkans was a mosaic of peoples whose settlements did not usually correspond to any obvious border. The fluidity of the monarchies which emerged reflects this. In Russia spaces were vast, but the changing pattern of principalities which emerged all bore the stamp of Byzantium. These states inherited from Byzantium not merely a Church, but also the idea of Empire – and many would call themselves empires at one time or another. This was not merely a cultural inheritance, it was also an expression of the reality of the power of their ruling houses over complex groupings of peoples. Like Catholic Christendom, the 'Byzantine Commonwealth' had a cultural but not a political unity, and it lacked the papacy as a focus. The greatest triumph of the eastern Church was the conversion of Russia in the tenth century, hence the problems of the papacy with Orthodox Novgorod in the far north. The Russian Slavs occupied a vast area, from Finland in the north to Kiev in the south. Though this area was divided into a number of principalities, the pre-eminent power was Kiev. The foundation of this Kievan Russia was vigorous trade between Scandinavia and Constantinople. However, as western powers expanded in the Mediterranean this route to Constantinople and the Caliphate became less and less important, and with it declined the trading cities like Smolensk and Kiev, though Novgorod and Pskov, because connected to Germany and France via the Baltic area, continued to be rich. Real authority increasingly passed to rural-based principalities where a class of nobles, the *boyars*, ruled over peasants from fortified centres. In 1240 Kiev was destroyed by the Mongols and virtually the whole of the Russian lands, save Novgorod, which paid tribute, were subject to their rule. The Mongols ruled through the *boyars* and their leaders, the princes, and interfered little in their internal affairs providing obedience and tribute were forthcoming. The princely dynasties, like those of Tver and Moscow, were responsible to the 'Golden Horde' as the Western Mongols came to be called, and to stabilise their positions needed to please the Khan. In this situation the Orthodox Church solidified its position amongst the Russian people. The attempt of the pope to press his jurisdiction by conferring a kingship upon the princes of Volhynia-Galich in 1253 were thus very marginal to Russian development. The Golden Horde, centred on the lower Volga, found it increasingly difficult to impose its will on the Russians as a whole, and the expansion of pagan Lithuania to embrace Smolensk, Kiev and the principalities of the Dneiper basin under Gediminas in the early fourteenth century was possible because these areas preferred his pagan rule to that of the Mongols or the Catholic Poles. In effect Orthodox Russia was able to balance Lithuania and the Golden Horde to achieve a degree of autonomy.

One consequence of the fall of Constantinople was the rise of strong powers in the Balkans. The Bulgarian Empire reached new heights under Ivan Assen II (1218–41). He pushed the frontiers of his dominion deep into the Balkans and by 1230 was threatening Latin Constantinople. This provoked an attack by Theodore, Despot of Epirus, who was defeated and killed at the battle of Klokotnitsa in 1230. In 1235 Ivan established the autonomous patriarchate of Tarnovo, this time with Greek recognition. He also established a new coinage and patronised foreign merchants, notably those of Ragusa. But the Bulgarian dynasty suffered from divisions over inheritance which found support amongst the factious *boyars*. This enabled another power to intervene: the Hungarians set up a puppet ruler at Vidin in the west. In addition, the Bogomil heresy presented a challenge to Orthodox authority which was difficult to meet because its adherent enjoyed widespread sympathy. In 1277 a peasant revolt placed Ivailo the Swineherd on the throne, but Byzantine intervention and a *boyar* uprising put paid to him. George Terter (1280–92) sought to throw off Byzantine dominance by alliance with Charles of Anjou, but after 1282 the Byzantines overthrew him in alliance with the Mongols who set up a puppet ruler, while the Shishman clan seized Vidin and ruled in the west. Theodore Svetoslav (1298–1322) was a vigorous ruler who was able to take advantage of the decline of Byzantium and when his son died the *boyars* elected Michael Shishman (1323–30), reuniting Vidin and Tarnovo. However, his elevation was unwelcome to another successor-state to Byzantium, Serbia, which claimed lordship over western Bulgaria, and Michael died in battle against them in 1330.

In the wake of the Latin conquest of Constantinople Stephen of Serbia, 'the First Crowned', sought to strengthen his position against his many internal enemies and asked the pope for recognition of his kingship. In 1217 Honorius III sent a legate who crowned him. But Stephen wanted ecclesiastical independence and in 1219 turned to Nicaea, with whose agreement an archbishop was appointed, the king's own brother, who crowned him by Greek rites. Factional struggles amongst the nobles and the chronic tendency of the royal family to become involved in them weakened the Serbian kingdom, especially as both Hungary and Bulgaria were rivals. However, under Stephen Urosh II (1282–1321) trade through independent Ragusa developed and with the wealth this generated mercenaries were hired. Urosh was able to take Skopje from the Greeks and to seize some of the Bulgar fortresses. In his later years the Hungarians fomented rebellion and seized Belgrade, though he was eventually victorious. Stephen Urosh III (1322–31) made his son Stephen Dushan under-king of Zeta and in the confusion of his early reign he abandoned much of the Dalmatian coast. However, on 8 July 1330 he decisively defeated the Bulgarians and killed Tsar Michael (1323–30). The chief architect of the victory, Stephen Dushan (1331–55), overthrew his father in the next year and ushered in a brief period of Serbian glory.

By the early fourteenth century, therefore, a belt of Orthodox monarchies contained the expansionism of Catholic Christendom. They were deeply interested in the imperial inheritance of Constantinople to which they were pretenders. However, the Empire was fragile and so were Serbia and Bulgaria whose monarchs had no established rule of succession and had to contend with troublesome and powerful nobilities. Further west, in what we call Central Europe, there was plenty of evidence of papal success. Poland was firmly Catholic, and the revival of its monarchy in the early fourteenth century offered the possibility of expansion at the expense of Orthodoxy by penetrating in the Ukraine and Russia, though the alliance with pagan Lithuania was profoundly disturbing. Bohemia was a monarchy in all but name. Its conversion to Catholicism is associated with St Wenceslas, martyred in 935, and had largely been achieved from Germany. As a result its Premyslid dukes held their lands of the western empire. They had often aspired to independence but tensions with Poland meant that they found it wiser to accept a rather distant vassalage to the German Emperor. The Dukes enjoyed very great power. However, there was no rule of inheritance, so that civil war within the ruling house was common. German influence was extremely powerful and dominant in the cities. The aristocracy prided themselves on their Slav ancestry, but married into German noble families and imbibed their culture and outlook. During the civil war which broke out on the death of the Emperor Henry VI, Ottokar I (1198–1230) secured the title of king and in 1212 a Golden Bull limited the kingdom's obligations to the emperor, though it remained a vassal state. Ottokar II (1253–78) was regarded as one of the German electors and in 1269 he absorbed the lands of his Babenberg relatives in Austria and Styria when their line was extinguished. However, his attempt to become emperor was unsuccessful because Rudolf I of Hapsburg (1273–91) was elected. When he resisted, he was stripped of all his new lands and then killed at the battle of Marchfeld. Wenceslas II (1283–1305) acquired the duchy of Silesia and, briefly, the crown of Poland, but his attempt to place his son on the Hungarian throne met with fierce resistance and when Wenceslas III died in 1306 the Premyslid line was extinguished. There followed a protracted succession struggle, the outcome of which emphasised the integration of Bohemia into Christendom. The nobles settled upon John of Luxemburg, son of the Emperor Henry VII (1308–13), on condition that he marry the daughter of Wenceslas II. He was a vassal of the Empire but one with intimate French connections. Charles IV (1322–28) and John II (1350–64) of France, and Richard II of England married respectively his sister, daughter and granddaughter, while his second wife was a French princess. The succession crisis stirred up sharp tensions between Germans and Slavs, and many of the barons resented the new king's foreign advisers. In 1318 John had to agree to a settlement which effectively left the barons to rule Bohemia, while he remained as king and his foreign adventures, especially crusades to Lithuania, were richly funded. Curiously, his skilful diplomacy made substantial gains for Bohemia, notably in Silesia which was effectively annexed during his reign. He became blind in 1341, and died fighting on the field of Crécy in 1346, leaving the throne to his son Charles IV (1346–78).

Hungary also had been a vassal state of the western empire, but it was much further away from the centres of German power. After the German victory over the Hungarians at the Lech in 955 the ruling Arpad dynasty pursued a cautious policy to Germany and was prepared to accept Catholic Christianity and missionaries. However, there was already an Orthodox mission, while the movements of steppe people into the Hungarian plain implanted Islamic settlements and growing stability brought Germans and Jews into the towns. St Stephen (1000–38) adopted Roman Christianity, probably out of fear of German intervention, but he supported the Byzantine Emperor Basil II against the Bulgars and the Greek influence remained strong, while there was evident paganism at least until the 1060s. His rule rested on the vast estates of the monarchy and the support of the *ispan* or counts who ruled their districts from castles. The Church was brought firmly under royal control in a series of Law Codes throughout the next century. Succession problems dogged the Arpad dynasty, and when Geza I (1074–77) succeeded Pope Gregory VII demanded recognition of papal overlordship. As a result Geza sought a crown from Michael VII of Byzantium (1071–78). It is symbolic of the position of Hungary at the end of the eleventh century that the 'Crown of St Stephen', without which no monarch could claim legitimacy, was made of two crowns fitted together, one Greek and the other Latin. Louis I (1077–95) returned to Roman allegiance. He strengthened the monarchy and developed the cult of St Stephen. He also annexed Croatia and Sclavonia, providing his kingdom with an outlet to the sea. However, Hungary remained suspended between east and west. Geza II (1141–62) was faced with the hostility between Frederick I of Germany and Manuel of Byzantium. A party favouring a Byzantine alignment tried to overthrow him in 1157 and there followed a period of intense Byzantine pressure and civil war until the reign of Bela III (1172–96) who proved to be a good son of the Roman Church. As Byzantium weakened after the death of Manuel, Bela recovered Dalmatia and attempted to annexe Galicia for his son Andrew. The weakening of Byzantine power was the opportunity for Hungary to parade its loyalty to the Holy See to find papal approval for its ambitions.

With the accession of Emeric (1196–1204) Hungary clearly emerges as part of the polity of Catholic Christendom and as a staunch prop of papal policy. The Hungarians seized Bosnia with papal support because it had a reputation for being a nest of heretics, and undoubtedly much of the rage of Innocent III at the

Venetian seizure of Zara in 1203 was because of this friendship. Hungarian ambitions in Russian Galicia were endorsed by the popes, although attempts to conquer Orthodox Serbia failed. Andrew II (1205–35) signalled his devotion to the Holy See by accepting Fourth Lateran's demands for action against the Orthodox and Muslims in Hungary, by joining in the Fifth Crusade and by settling the Teutonic Order in Transylvania with disastrous results. The establishment of the Friars quickly brought an end to Hungarian tolerance of Orthodox and Muslims and Church organisation was vigorously modernised. Andrew attempted to reorganise his realm by building up a group of eminent noble supporters to whom he made great grants, but this and his foreign marriage produced difficulties from the conservative Hungarian nobility who, in 1213, murdered his German wife, then forced him to concede great privileges by the Golden Bull of 1222. His son Bela IV (1235–70) had championed the reaction against the Teutonic Order in Transylvania and upset the nobles who had benefited from his father's grants by resuming the land. The Cumans were a Turkic steppe people who had unsuccessfully fought the Mongols. Bela saw in their desperation an opportunity to strengthen the monarchy by allowing them to settle in Hungary. This provoked the wrath of the nobles who regarded them as interlopers and angered the Mongols to whom they were an enemy. Quarrels between the king, his barons and the Cumans were a potent cause of the destruction of the Hungarian army at Mohi in 1241, after which 'The kingdom of Hungary, which had existed for 350 years, was destroyed by the army of the Tartars.'[7] There was terrible depopulation, especially in the Hungarian plain, while trade with Kiev virtually ceased. The weakness of royal power because of the short reign of Stephen V (1270–72) and the long minority of his son, Ladislas IV (1272–90) revealed the diversity of the realm. Because of depopulation in the wake of the Mongol occupation the Hungarian plain developed into a pastoral area quite distinct from western areas, and this distinction was reinforced by settlements of the Cumans, brought in by Bela IV to provide soldiers.

After Mohi Bela IV renewed his father's policy of land grants in order to facilitate the building of stone castles and the creation of a knightly army, strengthening the high nobility. But the sequence of short reigns and regencies amongst the later Arpads favoured the emergence of the 'Oligarchs', great noble families who seized power over vast tracts of land and ruled in their own interests. Without a strong monarch noble factions dissolved into civil war and fought the hated Cumans. In Transylvania the consequence of the Teutonic Order's government there was a large settlement of 'Saxons', Germans who developed their autonomy: the Szekely were a Turkic tribe who enjoyed autonomy under a Hungarian Count, while there was a large Romanian population in eastern Transylvania. Out of these circumstances arose meetings of the 'Estates' of the

---

7 Hermannus Altahensis, *Annales*, MGH SS 17.394, quoted in translation in P. Engel, *A History of Medieval Hungary, 895–1526* (London: I. B. Tauris, 2001), 100.

realm, inspired by the Church which was desperate to restore order. From these the nobility emerged with great privileges. Andrew III (1290–1301) was unable to restore the monarchy whose lands in Dalmatia submitted to the Angevins of Naples. With his death the Arpad dynasty came to an end. Three major claimants to the throne emerged: Wenceslas of Bohemia, Otto of Bavaria and Charles of Naples whose claim was through Maria, last wife of Ladislas IV. With the nobility divided, the support of the Church and papacy for the Angevin Charles-Robert I (1301–40) was decisive. He was not formally crowned until 1310 but then had to wage war to recover the royal position, and this was not complete till 1322. Charles had to acquiesce in the loss of Dalmatia where the cities accepted Venetian hegemony rather than that of the petty mountain lords who had emerged during Hungary's time of troubles. His ambitions to dominate Serbia were frustrated by the growing strength of that kingdom in the 1330s, but overall the Hungarian monarchy was much stronger by 1340 than it had been for over a century.

Except on the Baltic frontier where the Teutonic Knights confronted Lithuania the Catholic frontier with Orthodoxy had ceased to advance by the 1330s. This was not to say that it had stabilised. The successor states of the old Byzantine Empire, Bulgaria and Serbia, had a tradition of fragmentation, and all of them contained many peoples and troublesome nobilities. As against this Charles seemed to have imposed a degree of unity on Hungary, and of course he enjoyed the support of the papacy and Naples, while Venice and Genoa were great powers in the Aegean. Byzantium, torn by internal strife and uncertainties over succession, might well be prepared to negotiate over Church Union. Spectacular as this rise and fall of empires and kingdoms might be, we should recognise also that there were other kinds of expansion at work to transform the lands of middle, eastern and northern Europe and to forge its connections with the west. The lands of middle Europe had small populations and so were happy to invite in settlers who often received their land on generous terms. By 1250 most of the lands between Elbe and Oder had German colonies. Poland, it has been calculated, received about 250,000 German settlers into a native population of 1.5 million in the course of the thirteenth and fourteenth centuries. Little Poland developed a substantial German minority while Silesia was virtually transformed into a German territory. We have already noted large German settlements in western Bohemia, the later Sudetenland, and Transylvania, quite apart from the Baltic lands. For the most part this was not a political process. No German authority directed a colonial movement into these lands and those who went were not carrying out the 'civilising mission' of Nazi myth.

The empty lands of middle Europe were the 'Wild West' of medieval Christendom, offering plenty of land on advantageous terms. These immigrants brought to the east their ideas about crop-rotation, the heavy plough and the whole development of western agricultural technology which helped to develop the eastern lands. But German penetration was not limited to peasants. The establishment of monarchies and the development of western tastes linked Catholic Central Europe into the trading system of the west. The nodes of this system were Flanders in the north and Italy in the south. The great rivers flowing into the Baltic carried trade into Poland and Russia, primarily through the German cities which gathered together in the Hanseatic League. The Rhine valley was a vital trade-link from which goods reached the Danube through the important south German cities of Nuremberg and Augsburg. These cities had direct connections with Italy and especially with Venice where settlements of *Tedeschi* were a feature of the city. They also traded down the Danube. More and more cities were established in Germany. The pattern of urban foundations in Westphalia has been calculated as follows:

Before 1180: 6
1180 and 1240: 36
1240–90: 39
1290–1350: 57[8]

These cities were increasingly constructed on a grid pattern which was reproduced further east. At Cracow the fortress and the Polish settlement around it were known as the 'Polish Law', but beyond them was the grid of the German town, established in 1257. Similar areas are found in Poznan, Breslau and Prague, while official documents at Sopron and Pressburg, and even the law code of Buda, were drawn up in German. It was their access to banks and credit which made German merchants so important, and although Italians were also active in the Danube cities they were never as important. Thus the political and family connections of the Central European aristocracies were complemented by the economic links of the great German trading centres. With these economic links came cultural ones. The later Premyslids invited German *Minnesinger* to their court and like their contemporaries to north and east developed the code of 'Chivalry'. The Gothic style, originating in France, travelled eastwards along the trade routes. The German settlements, especially those in the larger towns, generated tensions. The murder of Andrew II's German wife by Hungarian aristocrats in 1213 was an extreme case. In Bohemia Czech poets adopted the models of the German singers, but grafted on a sharply anti-German current from the later thirteenth century. But despite such tensions, for the most part western ideas and culture reached Central Europe through Germany. By the end of the thirteenth century the fringe of German settlement coincided with the fringe of Catholicism in the east. German trading, cultural and familial connections bound these monarchies firmly to those further west and served to differentiate them from the lands of the 'Byzantine Commonwealth'.

The Mongols had terrified what we call Central and Eastern Europe, and certainly had a profound effect on the development of Russia. Hungary and

---

8 C. Haase, *Die Entstehung der westfälischen Städte* ((Münster, 1965), quoted in N. J. G. Pounds, *An Economic History of Medieval Europe* (London: Longman, 1974), 251.

Poland suffered from raiding by the Golden Horde, though as it weakened Lithuania profited from the weakness and instability on the western steppe. These areas acted as a buffer against the Mongols for the heartlands of the Christendom whose elites learned much and profited greatly because the Mongols extended knowledge of a wider world. About the year 1000 the 'Catholic Core' had only a limited and vague perception of the world beyond Islam. India was known through the legends of St Thomas and occasionally visited by pilgrims in the twelfth century, but beyond that there was little but rumour and wondrous stories. In the thirteenth century, under the aegis of the Great Khan, a degree of security was established in Central Asia and this stimulated trade, though it would be something of an exaggeration to speak of a free trade zone. This had a dramatic effect on the Italian city-states and their trading patterns. The settlements on the Black Sea gave access to the 'Silk Road' along which high value commodities like eastern spice and Chinese silk flowed from east to west. In 1340 the Florentine merchant and banker, Francesco Balducci Pegolotti, exaggerated when he wrote that the route from Tana to Peking was safe by day and night, but it was certainly passable. The reward for getting there, of course, was ready access to the luxuries of the Far East. The most famous of all these travellers was Marco Polo who left Acre in 1271 and entered the service of the Great Khan in China. He remained there, travelling widely, until 1292 when he left Fukien, returning to Venice in 1295. The tombstone of a Venetian lady, Caterina Vilioni, who died at Yangchow in 1342, suggests the existence of a Venetian community in China. The Genoese were established in the lands of the Il Khan in Iran by the end of the thirteenth century. In 1290 the Il Khan Arghun enlisted Genoese sailors to build galleys to be used against Mamluk trade in the Indian Ocean, but they fell to quarrelling amongst themselves and nothing came of it. Il Khanid Iran was a useful staging post for penetration of India by Venetian and other merchants. This opened the minds of the peoples of Christendom to wider perspectives on the world. These trading links were, however, very exposed, and with the break-up of the Mongol dominion decline set in. At the same time maritime technology was improving under the stimulus of ever-growing trade. *Portolani* were notebooks of sailing instructions, but the development of the compass and the sand-glass enabled mariners to develop them into charts. The new knowledge of the world developed these into real maps. In the early fourteenth century the famous *Catalan Atlas*, a fine example of a new genre, used Marco Polo's account of his adventures in the east in an attempt to incorporate the new geographical knowledge into a representation of the world. This represented a real advance on the theologically based *mappa mundi* such as the splendid late thirteenth century example in Hereford cathedral.

Almost as soon as the Mongols appeared Innocent IV grasped their potential value to crusading in the Mediterranean. At the Council of Lyon in 1245 he despatched the Franciscan John of Carpini as leader of an Embassy to Qaraqorum where they arrived in time for the enthronement of Kuyuk as Great Khan on 24 August 1246. Louis IX sent a mission in 1253 led by another Franciscan, William of Rubruck. Neither embassy was successful in securing an alliance against Islam. However, both leaders wrote accounts of their missions, and the *Historia Mongolorum* of Carpini circulated very widely and excited great interest, though that of William, which is much more discursive, seems not to have been well-known. The salient point upon which many seized was the presence of substantial numbers of Christians in Central Asia, especially Nestorians, and their prominence at the Mongol Court.[9] John of Carpini seems to have misunderstood the tolerance of religious diversity at the court of the Khan and exaggerated the influence of the Nestorians who may have encouraged him in this optimism. William of Rubruck was deeply sceptical of the Nestorians, but his views were less known. As a result there were constant rumours of the imminent conversion of the Mongols, as well as hopes for their conversion and an alliance. After the Mongol defeat at Ain Jalut in 1260 hopes for an alliance focused on the Il Khan established in Iran where conversion to Islam in 1295 did not reduce interest in an alliance against the Mamluks. As a result the papacy embarked on extraordinary diplomatic and missionary activity. Embassies were sent to the Il Khan in 1264, 1278 and 1288. No strategic alliance resulted, but Dominican and Franciscan missionaries became established in the empire of Il Khan. In Asia the Franciscan, John of Monte Corvino, reached Peking in 1293 or 1294 and enjoyed such success that in 1307 Clement V appointed the first archbishop of Peking.

This extensive missionary activity focused the attention of the intelligentsia of Christendom on matters geographic and forced them to embody empiric knowledge into their world view. It also raised the question of languages which Raymond Lull had already encountered in his attempts to convert Islamic North Africa. As a result the Council of Vienne in 1311 decreed the establishment of Chairs of Hebrew, Arabic, Greek and Syriac in the universities. A vast missionary activity opened up as a result of which the Franciscans were given responsibility for activity in the Mongol lands and China, while Iran, Central Asia and India were allocated to the Dominicans. Far flung provinces were established, notably the archbishopric of Sultaniyeh which served the Il Khanid empire and had a network of dioceses. But these missionaries were operating far beyond effective support. In the fourteenth century the Mongol empire tended to break up and in 1368 the Mongols were expelled from China. In Asia Islam was resurgent. Gradually the whole eastern mission petered out. It is interesting as a genuine mission, unsupported by the political pressures and military threats which had brought Christianity to Germany, then to Scandinavia, northern and Central

---

9 Nestorians were the followers of Nestorius, Patriarch of Constantinople (428–31) who was sceptical of the official doctrine of the perfect union of the two natures of Christ, and refused to accept that Mary could be described as 'Mother of God', preferring to call her 'Mother of Christ'. He was condemned by the Council of Ephesus in 431 and his followers were expelled from the Roman Empire in 489. They formed an Iranian Church whose missionaries reached into India, Central Asia, Tibet and China. Tamerlane's persecution in 1380 devastated their Church, but they are established to this day in Iran, Iraq, Syria and the USA.

Europe. Out of it arose a new strategy for the liberation of Jerusalem. Early in the period of Mongol contact great hope had been vested in 'Prester John', a fabulous Christian king of the east. Interest in him was stimulated when, in 1310 an embassy from the resurgent Christian kingdom of Ethiopia reached Christendom with suggestions for a joint attack on Egypt. Nothing came of this but desultory contact continued and would play a part in stimulating Portuguese and Castilian expansion in the fifteenth century.

The expansion of Christendom had never been a matter of simple military subjugation, and advance by conquest was rather obviously faltering by the early fourteenth century. The Vespers war and its complex ramifications preoccupied the papacy and the Christian powers of the Mediterranean. Although Christian cities had the most effective navies in the Mediterranean, sea-power there was heavily dependent on friendly coasts. As a result their position was challenged by the Turkish powers of Asia Minor and the Mamluks. On land westerners were meeting their match. The Mamluks developed a military organisation far in advance of anything in the west, and sustained a regular army with its own complex drill. This was why they could both destroy the crusader settlements and hold off the Mongols. The Mongol threat to Christendom abated, but not because it was repelled. The twin disasters of Leignitz and Mohi were the triumphs of a superior military machine which could sustain armies far from home in a hostile environment. In Lithuania an organised pagan kingdom was a formidable power. Of course the waging of war was changing also in the west. Most of the fighting in the Balkans in the late thirteenth and early fourteenth centuries was the work of professional mercenaries and the triumph of the Grand Catalan Company over the forces of Latin Greece was a symptom of the changes in the style of war. Another was the victory of the Flemings over an army of French cavalry – the famous 'Battle of the Golden Spurs' at Courtrai in 1302. These changes are sometimes represented as the triumph of infantry over cavalry, but that is a highly simplified view. Expansionism by conquest was still very evident in the Baltic, and also in the British Isles where changes in military development were very evident.

The notion that the British Isles had once been united was well-remembered amongst the Welsh who throughout our period called themselves Britons and their language the British speech. The Scottish kings had a mythology which would eventually derive their line from a 'King of Athens'. The Irish were deeply divided, but they had a 'High King'. In Anglo-Saxon England the most powerful king at a given moment had been *Bretwalda*, 'King of Britain' and this claim to supremacy was inherited by the Anglo-Norman kings. Geoffrey of Monmouth's *History of the Kings of Britain*, written about 1135, evoked the realm of Arthur whose people, the Britons, would one day rise up and regain the whole island. Geoffrey's work was important because it appeared to fill in huge gaps in historical knowledge, connecting a world of unity and peace in the post-Roman age under Arthur with the troubled and divided islands of the 1130s. The rulers of England generally regarded this inheritance as their own and disdained the 'barbarians' of

Wales, Scotland and Ireland. However, the Normans and Angevins were usually too preoccupied with events in their French lands to do much about them. English interventions tended to be spasmodic though, as a matter of fact, the kings of Scotland and the princes of Wales had all, at various times, accepted English kings as their overlords and the same was true of the Irish after Henry II's intervention there. Moreover, English power and wealth had changed the Celtic lands very substantially. England was the focus of the trade of all the Celtic lands, and their cities were English cities, just as most of the cities of Central Europe were German. Scotland was dominated by an Anglo-Norman aristocracy intimately linked to their relatives in England.

In Wales the English crown had only limited lands and had generally been content to leave expansion there to the Lords of the March. Long and intimate contact with these people had led the princes of Welsh Wales, the centre and the north, to emulate their Marcher neighbours and to become lords on the English model. Amongst these the leading power was Llywelyn ap Iorwerth, prince of Gwynedd (c.1195–1240) who consolidated his territories around the great heartland of Snowdon and firmly annexed the island of Anglesey. From there he reached out to contest the homage of the lesser Welsh lords to the south against the Marchers and the crown. After his death succession disputes in the Gwynedd family enabled Henry III to be able to extract homage from many of the lesser princes of Wales to push forward the power of the crown. However Llywelyn ap Gruffudd (1246–82) took advantage of the troubles of Henry III after 1258 to push back the Marchers and to consolidate his control over all the lords of Welsh Wales. Ultimately he was able to extract from the English king the title 'Prince of Wales' by the Treaty of Montgomery of 1267. But this grew out of something greater than a mere expanding feudal lordship. Llywelyn capitalised on a strong sense of the identity of people, language and country evident in the words *Cymru* = Wales, *Cymry* = the Welsh and *Cymraeg* = Welsh language. These were powerful buttresses for his authority in Wales at a time when royal government outside the March and Welsh Wales was looking ever more stringent and threatening and, above all, alien.

In Edward I (1272–1307) England had a masterful king and one who was not unduly concerned with continental affairs until late in his reign. Edward, moreover, was a great legalist, and in his eyes the homage that a prince like Llywelyn owed was something closely defined, to the advantage of the overlord. Homage and subjection were very much the same thing: the vague submissions of the past were to be interpreted by the mind of a thirteenth century lawyer whose centralising and controlling tendencies were self-evident. And his political animosity against Llywelyn could, to English minds at least, be easily justified in terms of taming savages and making war on barbarians. And there were plenty of causes of tension. The barons of the March wanted to recover their losses. Gilbert Clare, earl of Gloucester began the castle of Caerphilly which Llywelyn destroyed in 1270, but by 1272 a mighty fortress had been erected there which was a decisive check to the power of the Prince of Wales. Humphrey Bohun, heir to the earldom of Hereford nibbled away around Caerleon. In some areas, like Brecon, local Welsh lords were reluctant to concede to the demands of the new 'Prince of Wales', while even further north others were reluctant followers of Llywelyn. Their long tradition of local independence chafed at central control, English or Welsh. And uncertainties over the succession provided a focus for such tensions. The prince's brother, Dafydd, plotted with Gruffudd whose lordship was in Powys, against Llywelyn's life and fled to England in 1274. There he joined Llywelyn's enemy, the bishop of St Asaph, with whom he had quarrelled over the rights of the Church. The tacit support of the English court for these Marcher and Welsh enemies and their raids against his lands, alarmed Llywelyn. It was a bad time to be annoying the English king by building Dolforwyn castle as a challenge to royal Montgomery. Then in the winter of 1275–76 Eleanor of Montfort arrived in England on her way to marry Llywelyn. This alliance with the daughter of Simon de Montfort, the arch-rebel against Henry III, was, to say the least, unwelcome to Edward, more especially because Guy de Montfort had killed Henry of Almain in 1271 in revenge for Simon's death. But Eleanor's arrest heightened tensions. It was probably because of all these factors that Llywelyn failed to do homage to the new king when summoned in January 1273 and absented himself from the Coronation in August 1274. He then failed to respond to a series of summonses to perform homage, notably in 1275 when Edward travelled to Chester. On 12 November 1276 Llywelyn was proclaimed a rebel. He had not refused homage or denied his status as a vassal, while Edward had shown restraint, but the decision was now for war.

Although English propagandists were not slow to portray the Welsh as barbarians, the truth was that Wales, while retaining its own culture, was firmly assimilated to the political system of Christendom. The outcome of the wars which followed the conquest of Wales, confirmed that. But the difficulties which Edward faced are interesting because we can see a military system changing, and revealing its strengths and its limitations. Edward encouraged the Marcher Lords to attack, but this was to be a campaign firmly under royal authority. Commands were established at Chester, Montgomery and Carmarthen and the pressure they exerted was such that by July 1277, when Edward reached his base at Chester, Llywelyn was confined to his core land of Gwynedd. Edward then marched slowly and carefully along the North Wales coast and simultaneously launched a sea-borne assault which seized Anglesey, the grain-basket of Llywelyn's principality. There was nothing very new about the assault along the northern coast of Wales which was precisely the method used by John in 1211 and Henry III in 1241 and 1245. It was the scale of mobilisation of resources which was striking. The commanders in southern and central Wales unpeeled the onion of Llywelyn's power by attacking his castles and coercing native princes to do homage. Edward's main force at Chester gathered huge numbers of footsoldiers, some 15,600 men who opened the way for the army by cutting down woods and improving roads. An important fleet was gathered for the attack on Anglesey. A huge logistical effort channelled the resources of the kingdom into supporting the army. Skilled men like carpenters and masons were recruited from all over the kingdom while crossbowmen came from Gascony and war-horses were imported from France. Italian money-lenders, notably the Riccardi of Lucca, provided the credit to sustain this.

The fruit of this effort was the Treaty of Aberconwy of 1277. On the face of it Edward was moderation itself. Llywelyn was permitted to retain his title of Prince of Wales, Edward paid for and attended his marriage to Eleanor of Montfort at Worcester in 1278, and promised 'that he would be benevolent to Llywelyn in all things'.[10] But the reality was rather different. Llywelyn was confined to Gwynedd, shorn of Anglesey and substantial lands bordering England, and forced to make provision for his brothers, Owain, Rhodri and Dafydd from the rump. The Marchers regained what they had lost in the years before 1267. But the real gainer was the crown which hitherto had enjoyed only modest land-holdings in Wales. Edward seized a great demesne and an ascendancy over the Welsh lords between the March and Gwynedd on whom he imposed English administrators and law. The king's position was strengthened by the building of royal castles at Flint, Rhuddlan, Aberystwyth and Builth. All were strong but Rhuddlan is notable because Edward connected it to the sea by a deep-water canal nearly three miles long, an expensive acknowledgement of the importance of sea-power. In all some £30,000, more than the costs of the war of 1276–77, was spent. The harshness of Edwardian rule provoked a strong reaction: the Welsh lords who had backed Edward against the despotism of Llywelyn now began to waiver. In 1278 Llywelyn claimed possession of Arwystli, a strategic area in central Wales, and was forced to treat as a supplicant before the king's justices. Edward's high vision of kingship certainly tolerated, even welcomed, the vassalage of a Prince. But the legalism of the thirteenth century, the emphasis on sovereign power, would not tolerate special privileges and local autonomies. Across Wales there was resentment at English administrators imposing an English law. This resentment exploded in March 1282 with coordinated attacks by Dafydd, the rebel brother, on Hawarden, a major raid on Oswestry and successful assaults on important castles such as Aberystwyth.

This was not a 'national revolt' in the simple sense of the word: South-East and South-West Wales held aloof and some important families, like the Tudors, stood for the king. Edward's domination had failed to conciliate enough of the Welsh elite: military conquest needed to inspire emulation and at least a degree of assimilation, and to do that a tolerance of difference and identity was needed which was lacking in Edward's government. Again Edward set up three commands for north, central and south Wales and again he prepared the way by attacking the lesser rebels before assaulting Snowdonia, but this time a savage guerrilla war

---

10 J. G. Edwards (ed.), *Calendar of Ancient Correspondence concerning Wales* (Cardiff: University of Wales Press, 1935), 163, cited in R. R. Davies, *Conquest, Coexistence and Change. Wales 1063–1415* (Oxford: Clarendon, 1987), 340.

delayed him until late August before he could move his main armies and use his fleet to seize Anglesey. In this war to the knife Edward prepared his men for a winter campaign, while Llywelyn tried to seize the initiative by attacking in the Wye valley. He was killed on 11 December 1282 near Brecon and though Dafydd held out for a while, the revolt was quickly extinguished. The house of Gwynedd was extinguished and most of the native princely lines deprived of their lands. By the Statute of Wales of 1284 Edward imposed the English pattern of shires on all of Wales outside the March, and even in that sensitive area a beginning was made in the royal lands of Carmarthen and Cardigan. English administrators moved in and English taxes were exacted. Welsh law was respected to a degree unless it offended English tastes or important elements of royal law: thus primogeniture replaced the Welsh custom of division. This was assimilation with little patience for the more gradual process of emulation. To hold down the land a great ring of castles was constructed around Gwynedd: Hope, Flint, Rhuddlan, Conway, Caernarfon, Cricieth, Harlech, Aberystwyth, and, after the revolt of 1294 Beaumaris on Anglesey. Conway, Caernarfon, Harlech rank amongst the greatest castles ever built while Beaumaris, constructed in great haste in 1295–96, is the perfect concentric castle. The guiding hand was Edward's, but his instrument was the Savoyard architect, Master James of St George. By 1301 Edward had spent nearly £100,000 and to meet the needs of this immense building effort resources were mobilised from all over his possessions. Around his castles towns were built, with a view to exploiting the country and providing loyal English settlers as a bulwark against revolt. In 1287 Rhys ap Maredudd, a former ally of the English crown, was goaded into revolt by heavy-handed English administrators but this isolated revolt in the south-west was soon crushed and an English town founded by his castle of Dryslwyn. But discontent was fanned by taxation and as Edward prepared for a campaign in Gascony in 1294 serious revolt exploded all over Wales and important castles like Caernafon, Denbigh and Ruthin fell. Its leader, Madog ap Llywelyn, was from a branch of the line of Gwynedd and he assumed the title 'Prince of Wales'. In the winter of 1294–95 Welsh guerrilla attacks captured the royal supply train, pinning Edward with his hungry army in Conway, and they dared to confront an English relief army, albeit unsuccessfully, at Maes Moydog on 5 March 1295. But Edward mobilised huge resources – 35,000 infantry in all – and by the summer it was all over and Wales was pacified for a century.

Edward justified his conquest of Wales by reference to his civilising mission. It was little more than a fig-leaf for the principality was effectively assimilated to the civilisation of Christendom. In the case of Scotland no such justification was really possible. Because of a long history of good relations it was natural that when the dynasty of Scottish kings ended with the deaths of Alexander III (1249–86) and his daughter Margaret (1286–90) the Scottish nobility, Anglo-Norman in origin and enjoying close relations with the English court and nobility, should prefer to seek Edward's adjudication rather than risk civil war. Edward adjudicated in favour of John Balliol (1292–96) but he proceeded to treat him as just another English vassal in accordance with thirteenth century ideas of royal sovereignty. His rebellion was crushed in 1296 when Edward took his great army, supported by a powerful fleet, as far north as Elgin. Edward's broad strategy seems to have been to bring the great nobility of Scotland, who were so intimately connected to the English court, to terms, but their feuds and factions which had so favoured his incursion into the northern kingdom now made it difficult for him to build a party and those minded to resist could always find shelter in the inaccessible north of the country. Moreover, Edward's overbearing ways alienated wider Scottish opinion which exploded in the rebellion of a minor knight, William Wallace, and his defeat of the English army at Stirling Bridge in 1296. But Wallace was crushed at Falkirk on 22 July 1298 and by 1304 most of the nobility of Scotland had made submission to Edward. Edward made a moderate settlement by the Ordinance of September 1305, but his earlier overbearing ways and the horrors of a war that had been increasingly brutal after 1297 increased distrust and after his death the weakness of Edward II opened the way for further resistance.

Edward I's assaults on Wales and Scotland show the remarkable administrative expertise of the thirteenth-century English monarchy. The rapid implementation of the Statute of Wales and the Ordinance of 1305 for Scotland show competence of an advanced kind. But the insensitivity of the governmental machine is also very clear. England showed itself able to organise for war remarkably well. The logistic achievement of sustaining very big armies, especially big armies in winter, is remarkable, and the regular creation of fleets to support them is impressive. This was, of course, the outcome of administrative development, as was the pattern of recruitment. Edward recognised that he needed large numbers of infantry. They could mass against their enemies in hills and slopes unsuited to cavalry and were available to press sieges, clear roads and cut down woods. Amongst those infantry he recruited many bowmen and out of this arose the idea of concentrated fire. In March 1295 the Welsh rebels isolated Edward in Conway and the earl of Warwick marched to his relief. On 5 March Warwick with a force of cavalry and archers caught Madog ap Llywelyn's army in the open. Because his entire infantry force could not retreat in the face of the English cavalry, the Welsh commander concentrated his men into a dense circular formation to hold them off. Warwick used his archers *en masse* to weaken the Welsh and then charged home. Edward would use the same formation at Falkirk in 1298 to destroy the army of William Wallace.

The essential recruiting device which created these huge infantry forces was the Assize of Arms. The law required all free men to have arms according to their means, and to practice with them. These local bands were paraded by royal officials and persuaded, perhaps by payment, to join the army in the service of a trusted captain. We know that they deserted in droves but enough remained to overwhelm Edward's enemies. These universal obligations were quite commonly established in the monarchies of Christendom by this time and served much the same purpose. In France the great lords and the cities were obliged to raise units of foot, 'constabularies' of between 50 and 150 men. In the cities of Flanders and

Italy all citizens were obliged to carry arms and to rally to the host. However, in Italy war was almost continuous in the thirteenth century. The Italian cities controlled only small hinterlands and, therefore had limited manpower, and so relied on the employment of mercenaries to augment their citizen armies. They tended to rely on subcontractors, captains, who retained willing soldiers and mobilised them on need, and as a result soldiers became used to serving together, accepted more readily and so became militarily more effective. The 'Grand Catalan Company' was simply the most spectacular outcome of this process. Edward continued to raise the feudal host, but for heavy cavalry he relied primarily on tough and experienced professionals, paid 'men-at-arms', commanded by his military household. The French king also levied the host and in a country which was rich in open land suitable for horse-riding, relied heavily upon them rather than the infantry. The richer classes of the cities of Italy were expected to serve on horseback and in full armour, but their limited numbers meant that increasingly they had to call upon mercenary cavalry. They had always called upon the broad mass of their citizens to serve as infantry, but they too became increasingly professionalised in the fourteenth century. In Flanders rich citizens also had to serve as cavalry and the masses were enlisted as infantry and served with enthusiasm in defence of their cities.

In much of Christendom armies were growing bigger and the professional elements within them were growing in importance. They were also generating specialised commanders like the French 'Masters of the Crossbowmen' and the military governors on the disputed frontier with English Gascony. Tactics were improving and the 'all arms' approach so evident at Maes Madog and Falkirk was showing its value. Cavalry remained important, but increasingly they needed to operate in conjunction with infantry and bowmen. However, kings still had to appoint men of rank as commanders at the highest level, though professionalisation grew apace below that level. Only exceptionally, as in the long Italian wars, were armies kept in being for any period of time and there was nothing to rival the expertise of the Mamluks or the Mongols. And much still depended on personality. At Bannockburn in 1314 Edward II had a huge army with ample cavalry, archers and foot, but he was no soldier and failed to control it. The Scots baulked his cavalry by forming *schiltroms*, dense formations of archers and spearmen, like the Welsh at Maes Madog, and succeeded. In fact, Scottish tactics at Bannockburn were precisely those used by Wallace at Falkirk, and were successful primarily because the English army was badly handled. The professionalism of government had spilled over only to a limited extent into the conduct of war because aristocratic domination of war continued. The coincidence of Courtrai in 1302, Halmyros in 1311 and Bannockburn in 1314 has led historians to speak of the new supremacy of infantry in this period, but the reality was that properly handled cavalry continued to be very important and leaders were learning how to integrate its operations with improved and more numerous infantry. But all western medieval armies suffered from the lack of an infrastructure of war in terms of training, barracks and intellectual analysis. Commanders had to learn their task on the job and to rely on the support of an upper class amongst whom the cult of chivalry in a sense perpetuated the cult of personal bravery. Grave problems of logistics hampered their operations at all times. When we reflect on how close to his bases Edward was in Wales and even Scotland, and consider how difficult he found the process of conquest, we can begin to understand the limitations of the expansion of Christendom.

Crusading remained a living force in Christendom at the start of the fourteenth century and nobody could mistake the continued enthusiasm of the papacy as the vigour with which it promoted the 'Mongol Mission' shows. But the papal project was faltering. The rise of powerful monarchies meant that the dominating position in Christendom which the popes had once enjoyed was now being eroded. It also meant that those to whom it naturally looked, the aristocracy, were being drawn to a greater degree than ever before into service and loyalty to monarchs. The reliance of the papacy on the French monarchy was in part the natural outcome of this process, but it was also prompted by the need for diplomatic and military support in Italy. This dependence, allied to changing circumstances in Christendom and in the eastern Mediterranean, had severely damaged the prestige of the popes and hopes of recovering Jerusalem. At the root of the crusading disasters of this period was the papacy's visceral hatred of the Hohenstaufen and their espousal of the Angevin cause. Gregory X and Nicholas III had attempted to revert to the traditional papal policy of balancing the powers in the interests of papal authority, but when this was abandoned, papal fortunes were tied into those of the Angevins of Naples. The 'War of the Vespers' was far more than a mere distraction, and the chaos which it caused in Italy was one of the fundamental causes of the papacy's failure in the quarrel with Philip of France. At the same time the expansionism of Christendom was visibly slowing, partly because Islamic centres were stronger, while the 'Byzantine Commonwealth' demonstrated a stubborn sense of its own identity. Perhaps more surprisingly, Lithuania was demonstrating the adaptability and modernity of paganism and showed a remarkable ability to exploit changing conditions. None of these conditions were irreversible. Stability in Italy was possible. Chaos in the Aegean could turn to the advantage of western forces, especially as western sea-power remained dominant here and in the eastern Mediterranean. The Mamluks had internal problems and faced a rival in Il-Khanid Iran. The situation in the north remained fluid and quite evidently the political disintegration of the German monarchy and the weakness of its successor states meant that nobles and knights were willing and able to join the crusade in Prussia and Livonia. Poland and Hungary offered possibilities of expansion into their spheres of interest and were interested in enjoying crusading support. But crusading was correspondingly narrowing: Germans went to the north because it was of special interest to them, while Genoa, Venice and Cyprus were those most interested in crusading in the eastern Mediterranean, though this fluctuated according to how they saw their interests. The Angevin connection served to draw some Frenchmen to the support of their kin in Greece. Crusading was a hallmark of chivalry while the widespread disturbances in France in the 1320s reveal that crusading could still arouse enthusiasm across the social spectrum. Nothing ruled out radical change which could add dynamism to the impulse for expansion in Catholic Christendom and revitalise crusading. We know what happened next in the story of the development of Catholic Christendom – the people of the time did not and this is the perspective which we need to understand.

SELECTED READING

The most authoritative general account of European history in this period is that of the *New Cambridge Medieval History* vol. V for the period down to 1300 edited by D. Abulafia. For the general context of economic development Pounds, *Economic History of Medieval Europe* remains authoritative, and there are interesting insights into particular aspects of economic change in Bartlett, *Making of Europe* and Bartlett and MacKay, *Medieval Frontier Societies*. There are excellent maps relating to Mediterranean trade in Riley-Smith, *Atlas of the Crusades*. A. McKay and D. Ditchburn, *Atlas of Medieval Europe* (London: Routledge, 1997) has a wider focus and contains a great deal of very useful and authoritative commentary. On the general history of war and trade in the Mediterranean the finest study remains Pryor, *Geography, Technology and War*, though G. Hutchinson, *Medieval Ships and Shipping* (Leicester: Leicester University Press, 1994) adds much, while S. Rose, *Medieval Naval Warfare 1000–1500* (London: Routledge, 2002) concentrates on the military aspects. For the history of the Mediterranean trading cities, see S. A. Epstein, *Genoa and the Genoese 958–1528* (Chapel Hill, NC: University of North Carolina Press, 1996) which is much more modern than R. W. Carden, *The City of Genoa* (London: Methuen, 1908). F. W. Carter, *Dubrovnik (Ragusa). A Classic City-State* London: Seminar, 1972), F. C. Lane, *Venice. A Maritime Republic* (Baltimore, MD: Johns Hopkins University Press, 1973) and J. Ross, *The Story of Pisa* (London: Dent, 1909) are all useful. There is an excellent account of the emergence of Majorca as a great trading centre in D. Abulafia, *A Medieval Emporium. The Catalan Kingdom of Majorca* (Cambridge: Cambridge University Press, 1994). For the rise of Catalonia as a major power a recent study is that of T. N. Bisson, *The Medieval Crown of Aragon* (Oxford: Clarendon, 1986). On the rivalries in the Mediterranean and the Vespers two fine studies are those of L. V. Mott, *Sea Power in the Medieval Mediterranean* (Gainesville, FL: Florida University Press, 2003) and D. Abulafia, *The Western Mediterranean Kingdoms 1200–1500* (London: Longman, 1997). An older, though very readable account of this rivalry is to be found in S. Runciman, *The Sicilian Vespers* (Harmondsworth: Penguin, 1961). There is a very good biography by J. Dunbabin, *Charles of Anjou: Power, Kingship and Statemaking in Thirteenth Century Europe* (London: Longman, 1998). The best account of Charles's campaigns in Italy and the wars that followed is that of N. Housley, *The Italian Crusades. The Papal–Angevin Alliance and the Crusades against Christian Lay Powers 1254–1343* (Oxford: Clarendon Press, 1986). For the general history of the crusader states of the Levant see the reading suggested for the previous chapter. The key books on crusading in this and later period are K. M. Setton, *The Papacy and the Levant 1204–1571*, 4 vols (Philadelphia, PA: American Philosophical Society, 1976–84) and N. Housley, *The Later Crusades. From Lyons to the Alcazar 1274–1580* (Oxford: Oxford University Press, 1992) and I must acknowledge an enormous debt to these works. Housley argues that the expulsion of the settlers from the Holy Land in

1291 did not mark the effective end of the crusading movement which henceforth became marginal and that crusading continued to play an important role in European politics for another three centuries. S. Schein, *Fideles Crucis. The Papacy, the West and the Recovery of the Holy Land 1274–1314* (Oxford: Clarendon, 1991) argues that Clement V's reign marks the start of serious efforts to regain the Holy Land. On Armenia the essays in T. S. R. Boase (ed.), *The Cilician Kingdom of Armenia* (Edinburgh: Scottish Academic Press, 1978) are very useful, but R. W. Edwards, *The Fortifications of Armenian Cilicia* (Washington, DC: Dumbarton Oaks, 1987) is magisterial on its subject and generally highly useful on the history of the area. For the Mongols see the reading suggested for the previous chapter. The authority on the Il Khan regime in Iran is R. Amitai-Preiss, *Mongols and Mamluk. The Mamluk–Ilkhanid War 1260–81* (Cambridge: Cambridge University Press, 1995). B. Arnold, in his *Medieval Germany 500–1300* (London: Macmillan, 1997) and *Princes and Territories in Medieval Germany* (Cambridge: Cambridge University Press, 1991) offers a brilliant analysis of the problems of the German monarchy, while J. Leuschner, *Germany in the Later Middle Ages* (Amsterdam: North Holland, 1980) and F. R. H. du Boulay, *Germany in the Later Middle Ages* (London: Athlone, 1983) provide excellent guides to events and analysis. The best introduction to the development of representative institutions is A. R. Myers, *Parliaments and Estates in Europe to 1789* (London: Thames and Hudson, 1975). On the quarrel between Boniface VIII and Philip the Fair the study of J. R. Strayer, *The Reign of Philip the Fair* (Princeton, NJ: Princeton University Press, 1980) is important, though it has a bias in favour of 'state-building'. An interesting insight into the quarrel is offered by R. W. Dyson (ed.), *Three Royalist Tracts* (Bristol: Thoemmes, 1999) while the text of *Unam Sanctam* is translated in J. B. Ross and M. M. McLaughlin, *The Portable Medieval Reader* (Harmondsworth: Penguin, 1977), 233–6. On the Flemish revolt, see J. F. Verbruggen, *The Battle of the Golden Spurs. Courtai, 11 July 1302*, ed. K. Devries, tr. D. R. Ferguson (Woodbridge: Boydell, 2002). The revolts of the *Pastoureaux* have been neglected by writers in English, but M. Barber, 'The *Pastoureaux* of 1320', *Journal of Ecclesiastical History* 32 (1981), 143–66 provides an excellent study stressing their origins in the desperate economic condition of the French monarchy. S. Menache, *Clement V* (Cambridge: Cambridge University Press, 1998) takes a positive view of Clement and stresses his commitment to the crusade. The authority on the trial of the Templars is M. Barber, *The Trial of the Templars* (Cambridge: Cambridge University Press, 1978). Pierre Dubois' famous tract is available as *The Recovery of the Holy Land*, ed. W. I. Brandt (New York: Columbia University Press, 1956). There is no good translation of Sanudo but there is a useful study by C. J. Tyerman, 'Marino Sanudo Torsello and the Lost Crusade: lobbying in the fourteenth century', *Transactions of the Royal Historical Society* 32 (1982), 57–73. For the European presence in Greece, see Lock, *Franks in the Aegean*. For Spain, see Lomax, *Reconquest of Spain*, McKay, *Spain in the Middle Ages* and O'Callaghan, *Reconquest and Crusade in Medieval Spain*. For the crusade in the north, see E. Christiansen, *The Northern Crusades* (Harmondsworth: Penguin, 1997), though it should be noted that he has little to say about Poland, and Urban, *Baltic Crusade, Livonian Crusade* (Dekalb, IL: Northern Illinois University Press, 1975) and *Teutonic Knights* (London: Greenhill, 2003). For the history of Poland N. Davies, *God's Playground. A History of Poland*, 2 vols (Oxford: Clarendon, 1981) and J. Topolski, *An Outline History of Poland* (Warsaw: Interpress, 1986) are very useful. The key study of Lithuania is S. C. Rowell, *Lithuania Ascending. A Pagan Empire within East-Central Europe 1295–1345* (Cambridge: Cambridge University Press, 1994). On Russia, see J. D. Clarkson, *A History of Russia from the Ninth Century* (London: Longman, 1961) and for the period of the

'Golden Horde' L. de Hartog, *Russia and the Mongol Yoke* (London: Tauris, 2000). For the general history of the Balkans the best introduction is that of J. V. A. Fine Jr, *The Early Medieval Balkan. A Critical Survey from the Sixth to the Late Twelfth Century* (Ann Arbor, MI: University of Michigan Press, 1983) and *The Late Medieval Balkan. A Critical Survey from the Late Twelfth Century to the Ottoman Conquest* (Ann Arbor, MI: University of Michigan Press, 1987). On particular Balkan countries, see D. M. Lang, *The Bulgarians from Pagan Times to the Ottoman Conquest* (London: Thames and Hudson, 1976) and H. W. V. Temperley, *History of Serbia* (London: Bell & Sons, 1919). For the history of Bohemia a good introduction is M. Teich, *Bohemia in History* (Cambridge: Cambridge University Press, 1998) and for Hungary, see P. Engel, *A History of Medieval Hungary, 895–1526* (London: I. B. Tauris, 2001). On German settlement, see Pounds, *Economic History of Medieval Europe*, P. Knoll, 'Economic and political institutions on the Polish–German frontier in the Middle Ages', in R. Bartlett and A. MacKay, *Medieval Frontier Societies* (Oxford: Oxford University Press, 1989), 151–76 and A. Thomas, 'Czech–German relations in Old Czech Literature', in Bartlett and MacKay, *Medieval Frontier Societies*, 199–216. The accounts of the Mongols by John of Carpini and William of Rubruck, and much other relevant source-material, are available in C. Dawson, *The Mongol Mission* (London: Sheed & Ward, 1955) which has been reprinted under the title *The Mission to Asia* by the Medieval Academy of America (Toronto: University of Toronto Press, 1980 and 1986). On the conquest of Wales there is an excellent account in R. R. Davies, *Conquest, Coexistence and Change. Wales 1063–1415* (Oxford: Clarendon, 1987) and in the same author's *Age of Conquest. Wales 1063–1415*, while J. E. Morris, *The Welsh Wars of Edward I* (Oxford: Oxford University Press, 1901, revised edition Stroud: Sutton, 1996) is still very useful. On the building of the Edwardian castles in Wales A. J. Taylor, *The King's Works in Wales* (London: HMSO, 1974) is indispensable. For the history of Scotland the books cited in earlier chapters remain useful, but A. D. M. Barrell, *Medieval Scotland* (Cambridge: Cambridge University Press, 2000) is a clear modern textbook. On European warfare, see France, *Western Warfare in the Age of the Crusades*, and on the development of mercenaries M. Mallett, *Mercenaries and their Masters. Warfare in Renaissance Italy* (London: Bodley Head, 1974).

8

FAILURE AND
FRAGMENTATION,
1337–1444

The history of Catholic Christendom in the fourteenth century is often seen as a catalogue of disasters. Undoubtedly the best known event of the period was the 'Black Death' of 1348 which wiped out about a third of the European population. It owed much of its impact to the series of famines which had broken out in Christendom after 1315. These are thought to have been the consequence of food supply failing to match the expanding population which was, thereby, weakened when the plague appeared. In Central and Eastern Europe, where the countryside was emptier and food resources greater, the population seems to have suffered less. There can be no doubt of the debilitating effect of the 'Black Death' in the west: the large armies raised by England and France at the very beginning of the 'Hundred Years War' in the 1340s were rarely equalled again. But horrific as the impact of the plague was, it was by no means the only disaster to afflict Europe. The papacy under Clement V (1305–14) was moved to Avignon and, partly as a result, the principality of Rome fragmented and this helped to worsen the general political chaos in Italy with warring city-states in the north and a decaying Neapolitan monarchy in the south still locked in a war to regain Aragonese Sicily. When the papacy tried to return to Rome in 1378 this only precipitated a great schism between the Roman and Avignonese popes. Germany was a divided land, a geographical expression rather than an entity, where the empty title of 'Emperor' was disputed by rival families each hoping to use it as a bargaining-counter in their conflicts. England and France were locked into the 'Hundred Years War' which became more and more destructive and sucked in more and more of the powers of Christendom. Scotland was usually in alliance with France and this spread the zone of devastation to both sides of the frontier with England. Where cities flourished there were tensions with the countryside around, particularly its nobility. Social unrest within the great cities of Italy and Flanders threatened the urban patricians, while there were peasant revolts, some of unprecedented savagery, in the countrysides of England and France. In 1357–58 the horrors of war, political hatred and class tension in Paris exploded in a revolution, albeit one which was short-lived. This is a rather one-sided picture and it must not be assumed that the people of Catholic Christendom, faced with this gloomy political and social landscape, became inward-looking and preoccupied. Rather, the ruling elites were aware that the political environment within which Catholic Christendom subsisted was becoming more and more unfavourable to expansion at a time when they were more and more deeply preoccupied by the growing authority of monarchical states. In these circumstances crusading enthusiasm was episodic and largely confined to particular groups and areas. The rise of the Ottoman Turks whose advance threatened to engulf the 'Byzantine Commonwealth' and even to overwhelm Catholic Christendom itself transformed the crusade into a mechanism for the defence of Christendom. In effect the papal project of Urban II and Innocent III had been wrecked by a series of factors. The rise of the Mamluks created a great power dominating the Middle East. The outbreak of the 'War of the Vespers' wrecked the strategy of a grand alliance embracing Byzantium which would sweep away the Mamluk power. Underlying this, the rise of strong monarchies, and particularly the French power, eroded the fundamental assumptions of the whole papal project. The Roman pontiff was no longer a giant dominating petty rulers, but a power alongside powers. And these powers mediated papal authority over the aristocracy whose energies and ambitions were increasingly absorbed by the structure and manipulations of the monarchical state. The dream of Jerusalem's liberation remained and it continued to have an enormous emotional appeal, but the practice of crusading became rarer and its objectives more defensive.

In Spain Alfonso XI's victory at Salado on 30 October 1340 did not open the way for any further major Christian advance. If Muslim Granada was to be destroyed it was vital to seize the ports of the littoral, but it was not until 1342 that Algeciras was besieged. The two-year siege which ensued was bitterly fought and strained Castile's resources. Alfonso received strong financial support from the papacy and the whole enterprise assumed something of the character of a pan-Hispanic enterprise. The Portuguese continued to provide the military assistance so vital at Salado, while naval support came from Aragon and King Philip of Navarre (1328–43) died supporting the siege. There was even a scattering of foreign crusaders, notably the earls of Salisbury and Derby, but in a sense this was a portent of the troubles to come, for they were primarily interested in seeking allies against the French in the struggle which we now know as the 'Hundred Years War'. After the siege of Gibraltar failed in 1350 the advance stalled. This was partly because Granada was strong. The mountain ranges of southern Spain were barriers to conquest and the Nasrid rulers of Granada were at pains to strengthen them with modern fortifications. The population of Granada was largely made up of families who had been expelled from the Christian kingdoms and was, therefore, very determined. In addition the Nasrids, while anxious to maintain independence, could call upon North African powers for help. Moreover, Granada was a great trading centre and, as a consequence, very rich. The kingdom was particularly important to the Genoese because it was there that they tapped into the lucrative spice trade from Alexandria. Because of their bitter rivalry with Catalonia over control of Sardinia and influence in the western basin of the Mediterranean, the Genoese were strong supporters of the independence of

Muslim Granada. The wealthy Nasrids could choose to pay tribute or to subvert the nobles of Castile, as circumstances permitted. Thus a number of Christian forces developed a vested interest in the continued existence of Granada.

The kings of Castile faced considerable financial difficulties. It was hard to find enough settlers for some of the less fertile upland areas so that enormous grants of land were made to the nobles and the Military Orders. In general the crown could control the Orders by appointing their Grand Masters, but the nobility and their great landed estates became virtually autonomous. All over the *Mesta*, the high plateau, the nobility created vast ranching enterprises centred on the raising of sheep. Export of wool linked Castile into the woollen industries and trade of England and Flanders, though not that of Catalonia. The wealthy great nobles were, therefore, in a position to pressure smallholders and even the senior clergy and privileged royal cities. So powerful were these great families that the estates or *Cortes* of Castile did not flourish because the nobles had no need of such defensive associations. Ferdinand V of Castile complained that:

> They act as they do so as to keep kings under pressure and take what is their own from them. They look for ways in which they can disinherit and dishonour them . . . they want always to have a foot [in Granada], as well as one here.[1]

In these circumstances lesser nobles, cities and bishops were often prepared to gather together in *Hermandades*, brotherhoods for their own defence against the great. Ultimately they were not very successful because the nobility came to dominate the cities and thus to control trade and commerce. In the countryside smallholders were absorbed into the great estates and reduced to something like serfdom. In these circumstances it was very difficult for the crown of Castile to tap the wealth of the country through taxation because the obvious tax-payers were those well placed to resist. One of his own nobles remarked to Henry IV of Castile (1454–74) 'You should not, lord, press me so hard, for you know that I could give the castles I hold to the Moors and be a vassal of the king of Granada and live as a Christian there as others do.'[2]

Aragon was also a divided land. Catalonia, and especially Barcelona, was deeply involved in Mediterranean trade which brought in great wealth. Its mercantile class developed their own banking and adapted to developments in maritime technology, replacing older ships with new ones like caravels. They were strongly interested in North Africa, both as a source of trade and as a possible theatre of expansion. But the noble elite of the city were highly privileged and

1 Quoted in N. Housley, *The Later Crusades. From Lyons to the Alcazar 1274–1580* (Oxford: Oxford University Press, 1992), 271.
2 Quoted in J. N. Hillgarth, *The Spanish Kingdoms 1250–1516*, 2 vols (Oxford: Clarendon, 1976), 2.126.

ruled in their own interests. After 1359 Barcelona was empowered to levy its own taxes. As a result, especially in Barcelona, there was considerable social strife with an urban bourgeoisie and the more important guilds, the *Busca*, contesting the supremacy of the *Biga*, the nobility. The crown sometimes tried to exploit these conflicts to reassert its power. There were also tensions between the urban elites and the rural nobility, but both had a common interest after the Black Death in tying the peasantry, the *remensas*, to the soil and this created a running sore of rural unrest. The need of the Spanish kingdoms for labour had led to a general policy of *convivencia*, toleration of conquered Muslims and Jews. The *Mudejars*, Muslims living under Christian rule existed everywhere, though they were most numerous around Valencia in the crown of Aragon. In general they were allowed to live in their own communities under their own laws and leaders of their community often enjoyed important positions in the courts and cities because of their valuable skills. This general tolerance was also extended to Jews who were notable as doctors and as skilled artisans. More dangerously, Jews were involved in finance and often in collecting taxes and making loans. But as the kingdoms became more confident and less fearful of enemy attack, *conviviencia*, which was always a grudging and limited tolerance, came under pressure. In 1391 a great wave of persecution of Jews swept across the kingdoms of Spain with massacres and forced conversions. In Seville, in the heart of an area of heavy Jewish settlement, Archdeacon Martinez whipped up the mobs while in Valencia the patron of the anti-Semitic storm was the Dominican friar Vicent Ferrer who staged a series of disputations between Christians and Jews in 1413–14 which encouraged hatred of the Jews. The effect of all this was that it was increasingly difficult for kings to employ Jews and Muslims in high positions, and many important Jews became *conversos*, but even they quickly came under suspicion.

Alfonso XI of Castile (1312–50) had dominated his nobles and to a degree united them in war against Granada. His son, Peter I (1350–69), tried to rule in much the same tradition. He was a centralist surrounded by men raised from the dust and efficient Jewish tax-collectors, quite ready to use Muslim troops from Granada in his armies. He recognised that Aragon was significantly weaker than Castile and turned his aggression against Peter IV (1336–87) in an attempt to conquer the whole Peninsula. Peter failed because the nobles of Castile were restive and found natural leaders in his half-brothers, notably Henry of Trastamara. In addition, Aragon and Castile were drawn into the Hundred Years War with English and French mercenary companies employed by both. In 1367 the Black Prince and his Anglo-Gascon army won a great victory for Castile over Aragon and its French allies at Najera. Ultimately, however, Peter was assassinated and the French, with the support of Aragon backed Henry of Trastamara who became Henry II of Castile (1369–79). In Aragon the war saw a decisive transition of power from the crown to the numerous *Cortes*. In Castile Henry of Trastamara was never secure and he and his son Juan I (1379–90) faced English support for Portuguese intervention. Internally they were obliged to base their rule upon the nobles to whom they made lavish grants, but this ultimately enfeebled the crown. In 1383 Juan I tried to seize Portugal in the name of his wife, the daughter of its dead king, Fernando (1367–83). But many of the Portuguese nobility resisted and with English support they inflicted a decisive defeat on the Castillians and their French allies at Aljubarrota in 1385, clearing the way for the rule of Joao I (1383–1433). When Henry III (1390–1406) died, power in Castile was assumed by his brother, Ferdinand, in the name of the dead king's infant son, Juan II (1406–54). The house of Trastamara had trumpeted its crusading intentions but this had not amounted to very much. However, Ferdinand was anxious to consolidate his power and a series of Muslim raids after 1397 created conditions which permitted this. In 1410, after managing to get substantial support, he captured the important city of Antequera. The foundation of this success was the development of a more professional army, begun in the 1390s. The operations of a fleet were coordinated with the siege and cannon were employed. There were even a few foreigners in the army, but pre-eminently this was a victory for the updated Trastamara army and Ferdinand's temporary ascendancy over the fractious nobility. The capture of Antequera was the first major expansion of Christian Spain since the 1340s and so impressed the childless Martin I (1396–1410) of Aragon that when he died childless he bequeathed his kingdom to Ferdinand who became monarch in 1412. Thereafter the Trastamara kings of Aragon possessed considerable landholdings in Castile and their faction amongst the Castilian nobility became a major problem for Juan II throughout his long reign. Joao of Portugal inherited a tradition of centralised monarchy which his striking victory at Aljubarrota preserved and perpetuated. He was an able king, playing off nobles and cities in the *Cortes* and pursuing an expansionist policy. In 1415 the Portuguese seized Ceuta in Morocco in an expedition which received crusading privileges, though they were not announced beforehand for fear of revealing the objective to the enemy. It was quite natural for the Hispanic powers to be interested in controlling such North African ports because their possession was important for trade through the Straits of Gibraltar. However, Ceuta was a black hole for treasure and men, but in his will Joao insisted that it and other such outposts be retained, so it seems that crusading enthusiasm, combined with the need of the new dynasty for legitimacy, was dominant at the court. Joao's younger son was Henry 'the Navigator' who patronised a series of adventurers who reached Madeira (1419–21) and the Azores (1427–32) and helped to establish footholds along the Saharan littoral of Africa. This momentum continued into the reign of Duarte (1433–38) who, however, failed to take Tangier. His son, Afonso V (1438–81) was a child but under the strong regency of his uncle, Peter, the expansion into the Atlantic was pushed forward.

In many ways what was happening in Spain exemplified the new forces of expansionism in Catholic Christendom. The internationalist ideology of crusading was visibly declining. That it was not dead is evident from a few great expeditions elsewhere and occasional enlistments in Spain. But in late medieval Spain foreign intervention was not primarily about crusading, but about alliances in the 'Hundred Years War'. The accidents of succession and civil war had much to do with the course of events in the peninsula, but underlying the stasis was the factionalism of the nobility. This was, of course, nothing new. However, like nobilities across Christendom, they were enmeshed in the fabric of states and profiting from their workings. The wars in Spain had never been a simple matter of Christians against Muslims, although since the 1080s that had usually been the most important division; in these years other quarrels became dominant and as a result expansionism, which in Spain had always been inseparably connected with crusading, languished. The expansionist impulse in Christendom, which had made the crusade real, sprang from the attitudes and perceived needs of the nobility. By this time those interests had changed decisively. In Spain there was always hope of a revival of a new spirit of crusade to sweep away Granada, but it could only be in connection with the consolidation of Christian regimes. Since the mid-thirteenth century crusading in general had largely centred on enlisting monarchical support, and this lesson was reinforced by the experience of Spain. For the monarchies of Christendom crusading still retained considerable utility. It gave new regimes legitimacy in the sight of Christendom as a whole, enabled monarchies to tap the wealth of the Church and legitimised certain kinds of taxation. In a sense, what we see emerging very clearly is niche crusading – the adoption of the institution to existing interests to the extent that they needed it. This is a pattern which will be seen repeated across Europe. Crusading has its higher points in this period, but essentially it had become the servant of greater forces, because the old driving force of European expansionism, noble ambition, could gain only marginally from it.

In the absence of an accepted dynasty after the destruction of the Hohenstaufen, German elections in the later thirteenth and early fourteenth centuries had tended to dissolve into civil war. North Germany was fairly indifferent to the ensuing struggles in which the dominant forces were the dynasties of southern Germany. Moreover, the papacy had a strong interest in the succession because of the Emperor's claims to rule Italy which formed its vital power-base, and advanced the idea that, as overlord of the Empire, the papacy could control the choice of sovereign. Candidates engaged in civil war, like Albert I of Hapsburg, were prepared to recognise this in their own short-term interests. The situation was further confused because there was no clear definition of who was entitled to elect an Emperor. Moreover, the notion of primogeniture was not yet established in Germany and the noble houses routinely divided their lands amongst the male heirs: the Wittelsbach family became so numerous and so divided that it lost influence. As a result, it was difficult to say who, in a given family, was an elector. Moreover, divided inheritance produced a considerable fragmentation of landowning and associated rights which made communications and the exercise of authority very difficult. In addition, many Imperial cities were anxious to preserve their status and worried by the tendency of competing 'Emperors' to deliver them over to noble control in return for support. To protect their interests, they formed themselves into leagues. Charles IV (1347–78) waged an unsuccessful war against the Swabian League, and as a result was forced to guarantee their privileges.

Equally intractable were the 'Knights of the Empire', lesser lords and petty landowners who claimed subordination to the emperor alone as a means of excusing themselves from all controls. These were especially numerous in South-West Germany where they were little more than robber-barons. In general, cities and countryside were rivals, but in the area we now call Switzerland an alliance between rural cantons and cities emerged, and was able to throw off its Hapsburg masters. This independence rested partly on military methods adapted to the mountainous terrain. The Swiss were hardy mountaineers and they had learned how to work together in coherent formations using long pikes to hold off cavalry. They were victorious in battles at Mortgarten in 1315 and Sempach in 1386, and they were able to manipulate the quarrels of the German dynasties, as in 1368 when Charles IV supported them against Rudolf IV of Hapsburg. The 'Empire' was a shell, but its prestige and residual claims to power, such as the right to tax imperial towns, could still be useful, so great families competed bitterly for the honour. But essentially they were using imperial claims to further dynastic ambitions.

Many in Germany were deeply affronted by the claim of the papacy to control the imperial election, but there was no clear rule about who was and was not an elector. Any definition was difficult because inevitably this would exclude as well as include. Moreover, the interventions by Henry VII (1308–13) and Louis IV (1314–47) in Italy increased the determination of the papacy to interfere in German affairs. The emergence of three competing great families, Luxembourg, Wittelsbach and Hapsburg, meant that it was difficult for any incumbent emperor to offend anyone with a claim to be an elector. Louis IV of Bavaria was a Wittelsbach, but his succession was contested by the Hapsburgs who he defeated in a civil war at Gammelsdorf in 1313 and Mühldorf in 1322 before he was secure. Pope John XXII (1316–34) claimed that as the papacy had been vacant at the time the election was invalid, and in this he enjoyed the support of the French king. By 1337 papal intransigence was such that all the Electors gathered at Rense declared that they were empowered to elect without papal confirmation. But this was a dead letter without a definition of the body of electors. The Luxembourg ruler and king of Bohemia, Charles IV (1347–78), saw when he became emperor that there was no basis of imperial power in Italy and focused on increasing his power and lands in Germany. His 'Golden Bull' of 1356 defined the Electors by attaching the title to specific lands and insisting on primogeniture for its transmission. This was essentially possible because of a tacit understanding – that the emperor would not disturb Italy and in return the pope would leave elections to the German Empire to the Electors. The 'Golden Bull' established a superior range of princes, and popularised the notion of primogeniture, but did little to repair the fragmentation which had already occurred.

German expansionism in the north and east had always to a degree rested on peaceful penetration. Bohemia was an integral part of that empire, and indeed its Luxembourg kings, like Charles IV, were themselves elected to the title. Yet it was a Slav state, albeit one with a substantial German minority. Because it was

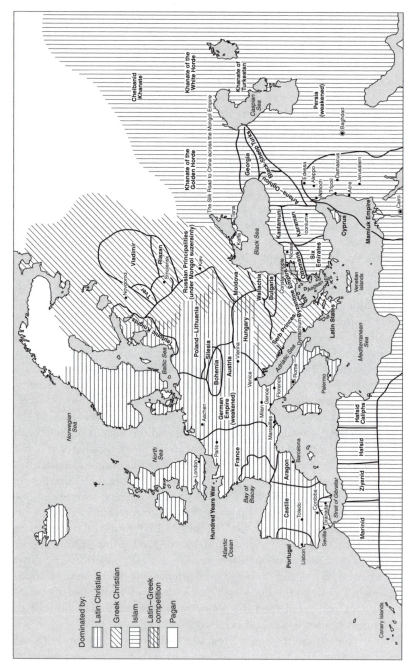

Map 8.1 Three civilisations around a sea: the 'Catholic core' and its neighbours c.1377.

adjacent to Germany it was very powerfully influenced by German trade and culture, and was ruled by a dynasty which was German though with strong French connections. The South German cities were vitally important and their merchants dominated the trade of Central Europe and reached even further east, carrying with them German culture which was becoming more developed and self-conscious at this time. German peasants were prepared to travel to distant places in search of land, and they were generally very welcome because they were disciplined and productive. As a result there were pockets of Germanic settlement across all the lands east of what we regard as Germany. Silesia became a German duchy within Poland attached to the crown of Bohemia, Transylvania had Saxon communities and in time they would even spread across what is now European Russia. German traders and bankers were to be found in all the cities of Central and Eastern Europe. In North Germany Lübeck formed the focus of a league of cities, the *Hanse*, which extended far outside the boundaries of Germany. In one sense these cities weakened the power of the emperor by accepting the sovereignty of their league, but that league was totally dominated by German interests. In fact, at this time '*Deutschland*' was not a common usage, but the plural *deutsche lande* might often be found.[3] There were, indeed, many Germanies, whose attitude to the crown varied. Nuremberg, in royalist Swabia, had close connections with the monarchs and undoubtedly these helped to accelerate its growth as a financial centre, but the connection was between individual citizens and particular monarchs. Charles IV was often there, but his son, Wenzel (1378–1419) more rarely. Lübeck was first and foremost the centre of the *Hanse* and its influence extended far into the northern lands. The Welf family dominated twelfth-century Saxony, but it suffered badly from partible succession, and as a result Hanseatic cities like Brunswick took over much of their leading role. In general North Germany was little interested in the Empire. Germany was enormous, perhaps too big for any single political authority to control, and the fact that its kings were also rulers of Italy and Burgundy meant that they had always lacked focus. The long interregnum and the rise of new families like the Hapsburgs all resulted from the chaos caused by this circumstance. Under Charles IV disinterest in Italy meant a closer focus on German affairs, but although all the royal rights had not vanished many had, so that Charles, like his immediate predecessors, used his imperial authority to build up dynastic power. This was no more than a reasonable policy – if the empire was to be meaningful its holder needed power and authority. The problem was that any particular ruler made enemies and the electoral principle permitted them to take a posthumous revenge, or simply the opportunity to build up the power of their house.

German economic and cultural influence in Central and Northern Europe, however, should not be seen as entirely independent from German political strength. It was the failure of Germany as a political force which permitted native

3 F. R. H. du Boulay, *Germany in the Later Middle Ages* (London: Athlone, 1983), 19.

cultures to become more developed and conscious of their individuality. They were able to assert this individuality and identity because in the absence of any strong outside power there was no political penalty to pay for this independence. Without a German ascendancy, Central and Northern Europe tended to fragment, though some German powers like the Hapsburgs of Austria were very influential. The other obvious centre of influence, the Byzantine Empire, was in long-term decline and the Orthodox lands around it, the 'Byzantine Common-wealth' was also splintered. Rus had been fragmented by the Mongols. The 'Golden Horde' remained powerful, but they asserted their influence westwards only fitfully. After the destruction of Kiev, Russia broke up under a series of princely houses. Those in the north and north-east were somewhat remote from the horde which was generally content to rule through obedient local leaders who competed for primacy as Grand Princes. These princes were all descendants of a common dynasty, but their positions and influence rested on recognition by the Khans, and the Christian rulers became very active in the politics of the horde. Novgorod, with its access to the Baltic Sea was effectively a merchant republic and other cities like Smolensk emerged as very important centres. The other major princes were those of Vladimir, Muscovy, Tver, Rostov, Suzdal, Iaroslav, Mologa, Riazan and Galich. The independence of Russian principalities was favoured by the division after 1359 of the Golden Horde into the Blue Horde and the White Horde of west and east respectively. By 1382 they reunited to crush the restless princes of Rus. However, they were never able to dominate the whole area and at the end of the fourteenth century the Horde was conquered by a new Mongol leader, Tamerlane, and tended to break-up into distinct parts. By the early fifteenth century the competing dynasts of north-eastern Russia were engaged in a struggle for supremacy which would result in the rise of Muscovy. By the end of the fourteenth century a new great power, the Ottomans, had emerged within the area of the 'Byzantine Commonwealth', but at the start of this period they controlled only a small principality amongst many others in Asia Minor.

In the meantime there was a host of native powers, all with their own ambitions. In the north the Teutonic Order controlled Prussia and bent its efforts to conquer pagan Lithuania, but was frequently embroiled in conflict with Poland. Lithuania was a highly successful state which expanded substantially into the fragmented zones of Russia, playing off enemies, Orthodox and Catholic. Bohemia had annexed Silesia and was also interested in the vacuum of power in Rus and the western steppe. Hungary, under the rule of a branch of the Angevin dynasty of Naples was aggressive, while Bulgaria and Serbia belonged to the Byzantine sphere of influence, though the empire itself was in steep decline. Muscovy, at least before the reimposition of Mongol rule in 1382, was attempting to become the pre-eminent power in Rus. But these were only the major powers. There was a host of petty princelings of uncertain loyalty and equally uncertain borders. Novgorod was a city-state whose rich trade gave it influence. Mazovia's independence was a thorn in the side of the Poles while the lords of Volyn and Podolia could play off their numerous neighbours. This was a rich theatre of ambition for the bigger powers. In effect, there was a huge vacuum of power in the area between the Mamluk dominion in Syria and the eastern border of the French monarchy. This was not an entirely new situation in that Central and Eastern Europe and the Balkans had always been fragmented. However, German influence was no longer ascendant, Byzantium was weak and the Seljuk ascendancy in Asia Minor, replaced by the Mongols, had vanished. Broadly, three spheres of influence, the Islamic, the Byzantine and the Catholic, were leaderless because of the decline or disappearance of key powers. It was not at all obvious how they would be replaced or how these spheres would fare in the competition.

The Teutonic Order in Prussia was a token of the continuing crusade. In many ways this period represented the apogee of the Order and its state. They had created what was later known as East Prussia and seized West Prussia, and they ran these territories as an *Ordenstaat*, 'Order-State'. The brothers were relatively few, though they recruited Polish and German knights to settle the land and form centres of loyalty. In the cities which the Order fostered around its fortresses, traders settled and were protected and patronised by the monks. Western peasants were brought to form loyal farming centres which stimulated the economy. Town and village militias were important military reinforcements and were supported by mercenaries in time of need. At the same time native nobles and communities who were willing to submit were welcomed and allowed to maintain their own law and customs. In the sixty years after 1283 the Order issued about 500 grants of land or privileges in Prussia, bringing in peoples from the west – the area name *Preussisch Holland* is suggestive – and even Poles and other more local settlers. In their attempt to hold on to Pomerelia the Order set out to germanise it. By c.1400 Danzig was a largely German city of 20,000, while 508 settlement privileges were issued for the area around. Prussia was governed by the Grand Master, supported by the key officers, Commander, Marshal, Master Draper, Master Hospitaller and Treasurer, but he had to take counsel on all important matters with the Chapter General. The mighty fortress of Marienburg served as the seat of the Master and, in effect, capital of the whole *Ordenstaat*. The unit of local administration was the Commandery. The Livonian province was organised in much the same way. The economic success of this 'Order State' was remarkable and gave rise to 'Pledge Treaties' by which the Order bought up territories from hard-up rulers. The most spectacular example was the purchase of Estonia from Denmark for 10,000 marks in 1346. The creation of this new state was a remarkable achievement of the crusading movement, most particularly because in the fourteenth century the Order enjoyed little support from the papacy. In effect the Teutonic Order had established a state which enjoyed widespread approbation, but only limited support, in Europe as a whole.

The source of this approbation was, of course, the constant war against the pagan Lithuanians. The staple of fighting were the *Reisen*, which might vary from minor raids to great campaigns. There is no doubt that in the late thirteenth and early fourteenth centuries the military vigour of the Order diminished. The absence of an emperor meant that lords and prelates preferred to stay at home to deal with unpredictable political events. The Prussian branch, because of its superior resources, was the dominant force, though there continued to be a German Master. The Livonian branch of the Order remained distinct, developing a recruiting base in the Rhineland. It cooperated with Prussia but, as we have noted, was preoccupied by a long dispute with the Bishop and merchants of Riga. The papacy was annoyed by the failure of the Order to pay 'Peter's Pence' and concerned to support Catholic Poland which it conceived of as in the front line against the Orthodox and the Mongols, even though its rulers sometimes allied with the pagan Lithuanians. The war with Poland dragged on until the Peace of Kalish in 1343, by which Casimir the Great (1333–70) renounced Danzig and Pomerelia in order to take advantage of the weakness of the Golden Horde in the south. The leaders of the Order became adept at appealing to the chivalrous exclusivism of the European aristocracy. Their *Reisen* were seen as opportunities for aristocrats to live the chivalric ideal, and for young nobles to train in the arts of war. Overwhelmingly it was Germans who came. At particular times and in particular areas German nobles were caught up in civil war but they were much less drawn into the machinations of monarchical states than those elsewhere. However, there was strong support from elsewhere in Europe. The famous Marshal Boucicaut came to Prussia in 1384 and 1385. He came once more in 1390–91 when another distinguished crusader was Henry, Earl of Derby, later Henry IV of England (1399–1413). There was also skilful exploitation of atrocities committed by Lithuanians upon Christian communities (which were well-publicised, unlike those of the Order against Lithuanians). The sheer commitment of the Order to the struggle gained them European-wide respect and support. This fighting in the north served to keep alive the spirit of crusading amongst the European upper classes. It was not, however, especially effective in defeating the pagan Lithuanians.

The chief reason for the slow progress of the Lithuanian crusade was the strength of pagan Lithuania. In the late thirteenth century the dynasty of the Jagiellonians established themselves as Grand Dukes, and they were able to maintain a remarkable unity. They seem to have directed the pagan cult which gave Lithuanians a powerful sense of unity. This was based on worship of a pantheon of gods very like those which had been at the centre of the cults of other Indo-European peoples before their conversion to Christianity. Amongst them Perkunas, the Thunder God, was pre-eminent. This was a dynamic religion, adapting features of their rivals. At Vilnius a Christian cathedral had been established by Mindaugas who converted to Christianity in 1251, only to apostatise in 1263. His pagan successors replaced it with a stone temple. The Lithuanians had always been skilful soldiers, but under the Jagiellonians their armies became well organised and ruthless, while the dynasty proved skilful at exploiting the political fragmentation all around them. Under Gediminas (1315–41) Lithuania expanded into Black and White Russia, but although this rested upon ferocious military attacks upon declared enemies it was supported by a careful diplomacy. The Grand Dukes forged alliances, often by marriage, with the neighbouring powers. They also exploited economic policy – their control of trade routes was important in persuading Smolensk to accept their overlordship and even Kiev in 1323. By such methods Lithuania built up friendships with a host of lesser lords and cities who feared Poles and Muscovites. They had supported the bishop of Riga against the Teutonic Order and allied with Poland in her quarrel over Pomerelia. A key factor which facilitated their advance into the lands of Rus was the willingness of minor Orthodox lords to accept tolerant pagan domination in preference to rule by Catholic Poles or the Teutonic Order. Indeed the Grand Dukes spent much effort in persuading Constantinople to set up a Metropolitan in their lands removed from the power of Muscovy. Algirdas (1345–77) continued this advance which by the fifteenth century created an empire embracing Poland and extending from the Baltic to the Black Sea.

In many ways the *Ordenstaat* and Lithuania were parallel beings. They both began (in the case of the Order one should add in this area) at about the same time. They were ruled by single-minded men. In the case of the Order ideological conviction imposed its pattern; the Jagiellonians formed a united family. The Lithuanian elite had observed the extinction of their fellow-pagans and were prepared to accept this leadership. Both powers enjoyed substantial wealth outside their core-zones – the Order had properties in Germany while the Jagiellonians conquered lands in Rus whose tribute enabled them to fight the Order. Neither was in any very precise sense 'national' for the Jagiellonians enlisted many tribes, such as the semi-independent and fiercely pagan Samogitians and even Orthodox Christians, while the Order was prepared to recruit Christians of any origin and was sometimes tolerant of the observances of native subjects. The great difference was that the Order was single-minded because to step outside its crusading remit would alienate support, while the Jagiellonians had a catholic taste for conquest and power. Dynasticism and Religious Order were different principles of organisation by which men sought to mould the present and the future and to give stability to their lives. In this sense, as we shall see, the contest between Lithuania and the Order was a draw. However, the Order was inevitably drawn into diplomacy and generally maintained a friendly relationship with Luxembourg Bohemia, based on shared dislike of Poland.

Casimir III was the real builder of Poland. He codified law and systematised a taxation system which gave the monarchy a more regular income. The privileges of the Germans in the towns were curbed in favour of natives, and the foundation of the University of Cracow in 1364 provided a centre for native culture and learning to rival the University of Prague founded in 1348. The provinces of Kuavia and Mazovia were largely incorporated, though by 1348 all parties accepted that germanised Silesia was part of the Bohemian crown. He established 'General Assemblies' of the estates of the realm which helped to strengthen Polish solidarity. Casimir accepted the loss of Danzig in order to free himself to campaign in the east where, by 1360 he had enormously extended the frontiers of Poland into Podolia. In these campaigns he went to some trouble to portray himself as Catholicism's champion against the Orthodox and his rivals, the Lithuanians, and for this reason often enjoyed papal support against the Order, but he was never able to make much ground against them. Casimir had no children and by 1339 he seems to have envisaged that his heir would be his sister's husband, Charles-Robert king of Hungary (1310–42). In the event Charles-Robert's son, Louis (1342–82) became king of Poland when Casimir died, though Casimir's grandson, Casimir of Slupsk, was given a great appendage in the north of the kingdom. Louis was able to continue the relatively centralised monarchy of his predecessor. But he had no son and had to persuade the Polish nobles, by means of considerable privileges, to accept the accession of his younger daughter Jadwiga. His eldest daughter was married to Sigismund of Luxembourg who Poles regarded as German and unacceptable and in any case a member of a royal family which had always been favourable to the Teutonic Order. Jadwiga's succession, when Louis died in 1382, coincided with events in Lithuania.

Algirdas's heir in Lithuania was Jogaila (1382–1401). In 1381, after an attempted coup, his cousin Vytautas fled to Marienburg and procured the support of the Grand Master by accepting Christianity, though eventually he was reconciled with the king. A strong section of the Polish nobility favoured a union with Lithuania and in February 1386 the marriage negotiations culminated in the Union of Krevo. Jogaila converted to Christianity and promised to baptise his people, married Jadwiga and was crowned as king at Cracow. He then began the process of converting the Lithuanians. The conversion marked the final assimilation of Lithuania to Catholic Christendom, but it threatened the very *raison d'être* of the Teutonic Order and created a mighty empire stretching from the Baltic to the Black Sea which could dominate the *Ordenstaat*. However, the leaders of the Order were well aware of certain weaknesses in the new union. There was tension between pagan Lithuanians and Catholic Poles. In both Lithuania and Poland the aristocracy formed a highly privileged body whose attachment to the monarchy might not survive the ordeal of battle. In the event, the leaders of the Order underestimated Polish hatred of them, principally arising from their seizure of Danzig, which overrode the Polish aristocracy's doubts about their allies.

The Teutonic Order denounced the union and gathered its strength and foreign support for a series of attacks on Lithuania. It was helped because Vytautas turned to them for support for his ambitions. The campaign culminated in a major victory for the Order in 1399, leading to substantial territorial gains in Samogitia. After the death of his wife in 1399 Jogaila obtained recognition of his kingship from the Poles, while retaining his hold on Lithuania at the price of recognising Vytautas as vassal Grand Duke of Lithuania. A precarious peace between the Order and Jogaila broke down in the face of revolt in Samogitia which probably had covert support from Lithuania and Poland. Arrogant demands by the Order brought Jogaila and Vytautas together, and both sides marshalled their forces. The Grand Master, Ulrich von Jungingen, mustered perhaps 20,000 against Jogaila's 30,000, but both forces included unreliable and poorly armed elements, notably Vytautas's Mongol allies. The Livonian Order held aloof. When the two armies confronted one another on 15 July 1410 at Tannenberg it is likely that both were much reduced in size. Faulty generalship by Ulrich von Jungingen is probably the primary reason why the Order lost the battle. Losses on both sides were massive and as a result Jogaila was in no position to follow up his victory, while Heinrich von Plauen, commanding the Order's forces left in West Prussia, defended shrewdly. However, the Order was never again able to take the offensive against its neighbours and in any case the conversion of Lithuania deprived the Order of its appeal: few were prepared to 'crusade' for an *Ordenstaat* which had lost its *raison d'être*. Recruitment to the Order slowed markedly and its army came to depend more and more heavily upon mercenaries. The costs of these troops and the nagging wars with Poland, which ended indecisively in 1435, bore heavily upon the cities, merchants and knightly settlers in Prussia, with the result that the Grand Master found ever more resistance to his central and despotic control.

Tannenberg set the seal on the changing balance of power, and by Jogaila's death in 1434 the succession to Poland-Lithuania was firmly in the hands of his dynasty. But although many claimed that in the long run the Order could never have dominated Poland-Lithuania, it has to be recognised that defeat at Tannenberg might have blown the two lands apart, and in this sense the victory was decisive. A mighty empire had now arisen in Northern and Eastern Europe. It was a Catholic empire which carried Catholic norms and ideas out into the steppe against Orthodox, Muslim and Mongol alike. Without the crusade it does not seem likely that would have been the case. The case of Lithuania proves the viability of pagan organisational potential and the Grand Duke's patronage of Orthodoxy could easily, as the Order often proclaimed, have led to a different kind of supremacy. The Teutonic Order provided a single-minded and well-resourced pressure upon Lithuania, and its influence was very evident in the circumstances of Jogaila's succession struggle. The Order was hindered by the collapse of German unity after 1250 which threw it back upon its own resources. However, it adapted well, and tapped into the ideological convictions of the European upper class founded on Catholic devotion and chivalry. But there is no doubt that the Poles and Lithuanians deeply resented German influence. All over Central and Eastern Europe there was a reaction against German cultural and economic penetration made possible by German political weakness. This should not be exaggerated: German economic and cultural influence remained considerable. This was because, despite the Black Death, the German economy was much more developed than those of the lands to the east. Its banking and merchant houses provided the essential sinews of trade and formed the channels by which the Danube basin and the Baltic came into contact with the Mediterranean economy which remained the dynamo of economic development. Ultimately German culture was only one of many forms of Catholic civilisation which was in the ascendancy in Central Europe, and the fragmentation of the Orthodox sphere offered great possibilities there.

But without a strong western power these possibilities could not really be realised, and Germany, though resented and reacted against, was weakened. Charles IV (1346–78) of Bohemia as emperor ruthlessly pursued the interests of his Luxembourg dynasty. By adroit diplomacy, marriage alliances and careful use of force Charles acquired the Upper Palatinate and Brandeburg which, together with earlier gains like Silesia were incorporated into the 'Crown of Bohemia'. Charles had to deal with a very powerful upper nobility. He had considerable lands and castles, but it was they who monopolised positions of power and were strong enough to force him to withdraw the law-code, the *Maiestas Carolina*, which he issued in 1355, because they interpreted it as against their interests. He was able to tax other sections of society and to cultivate the burghers of the developing cities, but he owed his independence to the burgeoning silver-mines of Bohemia, and when they began to dry up his regime weakened. But the most interesting development of his reign was that the aristocracy became more fixedly native. They shared the chivalrous culture of the European upper class with whom they established close links. Charles' own family became intimately connected with the royal houses of France and England. Even amongst the burghers Bohemians rather than German predominated. In 1348 Charles founded the first university in Central Europe at Prague, and this proved to be an enormous stimulus to native culture. On the one hand all of this was a sign of the development of native culture, on the other of the fragmentation of power in Central Europe.

To the south of Bohemia lay the lands of the Hapsburgs. Their family lands lay in the Rhineland, Swabia and Switzerland, but Rudolf I (1273–91) had used his tenure of the empire to acquire for his family the huge Danube territories of Austria and Styria. This was consolidated by his son, the Emperor Albert I (1298–1308). From now on the Hapsburg lands formed a virtually independent principality in Central Europe whose marriage alliances at various times gave them claims to the thrones of Bohemia and Hungary. While the Swiss revolt weakened their position in their Swabian homeland, the acquisition of Carinthia and Carniola, to which was added Tyrol in 1356 and Trieste in 1382, created a great principality with access to the Adriatic. The Golden Bull of 1356 deprived them of ever being Electors, and in turn they limited their obligations to the empire, though they remained part of it. But this collection of lands was not a great power in the fourteenth century because of divisible inheritance within the family and the consequent rise of noble estates in their lands.

To the east lay Hungary. There Charles-Robert (1310–42) had crushed the 'Oligarchs' and re-established a strong monarchy. Charles ignored the Estates and created new men as great magnates and advisors. A class of literate laymen were encouraged and they strengthened the royal administration. His triumph in the civil wars allowed Charles to acquire nearly a third of territory of the kingdom in direct lordship. The crown enforced a monopoly of the newly-discovered goldmines and controlled the coinage, while salt taxes and levies on trade raised enormous sums. The Angevins fostered the new towns as a source of income. Louis I (1342–82) was, therefore, rich and powerful, but he dissipated his energies in many directions. After the death of Robert of Naples (1309–43) Louis despatched major expeditions to Italy to make good his claim to the throne of Naples, until in 1352 he was forced to accept failure. From 1345 to the peace of Zadar in 1357 he was engaged in a war in which he eventually wrested control of Dalmatia, Croatia and Bosnia from Venice. This was partly the result of alliance with Genoa in its long conflict with Venice. He remained on generally good terms with the Luxembourgs of Bohemia and the Hapsburgs, but his succession to Poland in 1370 was a tremendous accession to his prestige. Although he was primarily king of Hungary he maintained the strength of the Polish crown, at least until his attempts to secure the succession for his daughter led to a policy of concession. The break-up of Serbia after the death of Stephen Dusan in 1355 offered prospects of expansion but Louis had few successes there, while his interventions in Wallachia brought little reward. In all these ventures into the Orthodox sphere Louis's narrow Catholicism and insistence on regarding the population as schismatics contributed to his failure. Louis' death brought the union with Poland to an end, while the succession in Hungary of his eleven-year-old daughter, Mary, ushered in a period of crisis. She was betrothed to Sigismund, brother of Wenceslas IV of Bohemia (1378–1419), but a strong element of the nobility objected to descent in the female line and urged the cause of Charles of Durazzo who became king of Naples in 1384. He was murdered in 1386 but Sigismund (1410–1437) faced a long struggle to crush the Angevins, and he had to acquiesce in the formation of a noble league whose members robbed the Hungarian crown of land, wealth and castles. In these circumstances Poland-Lithuania was able to dominate Wallachia, while Hungarian influence in Bosnia and Serbia shrank. Gradually Sigismund got the upper hand, but by this time Hungary faced a new and dangerous neighbour, the Ottoman Turks. Sigismund was a Luxembourger, more French than German and, of course, the brother of the king of Bohemia, and this may well have led him to appeal to the European powers for a crusade to rid himself once and for all of the Ottoman threat. When this came to disaster at Nicopolis in 1396, he sought to take advantage of the Ottoman threat to push aside the noble league, but he was distracted by the need to visit Bohemia to vindicate his claim to succeed his childless brother, Wenceslas IV (1361–1419) and this enabled his enemies to revive the Neapolitan. Sigismund was victorious, but not secure until 1404.

The history of Northern and Central Europe in this period is paradoxical. On the one hand a series of unions of crowns suggests that local 'national' feelings were unimportant, and the ethnic and linguistic mix of many of the states of the area appears to support this. On the other hand there were bitter hatreds. Bohemians feared German domination and Polish revanchism, while the Teutonic Order was an object of hatred to Lithuanians and Poles. The Hapsburg 'state' was essentially German, but was deeply involved in the politics of its non-German neighbours. Hungary had a Bohemian king, but a rebellious squire is said to have described him as a 'Czech swine' and its kings had long broken away from subordination to the German Empire.[4] Perhaps the most important factor was the nature of the nobilities of the area. Almost all the states had a very numerous class of petty nobles who enjoyed great privileges. Like the nobilities of the west they were factious, but unlike them they were rooted in ties of kin and locality to a degree that made them indifferent and even hostile to the states which embraced them. They were unable to use their energies as the Normans had done earlier by freebooting, except in limited ways, because their environment was hostile, and they were drawn into the fabric of new states for which they had little taste. As a result they were prepared to hazard the very fabric of those states in a way that the nobilities of France and England were not. The League of Nobles which was so powerful in late fourteenth-century Hungary was quite different from the 'Community of the Realm' which Henry III had faced in mid-thirteenth century England.

The decline of Byzantium in the fourteenth century was very important. Andronicus III seemed to be on the verge of absorbing Frankish Greece and thereby restoring Byzantine power when he died in 1341. Byzantium had barely recovered from the civil war that raised him to power when the regency of his nine-year-old son John V (1341–91) loomed. The Grand Domestic, John Cantacuzenus, claimed the regency, but a coterie of nobles led by the Empress Anna held Constantinople as a council of Regency. In the ensuing civil war Cantacuzenus declared himself co-ruler as John VI, and after six years managed to seize Constantinople. In the course of the war Serbia under Stephen Dushan seized Macedonia while the Bulgarians gained Philippopolis. In order to resist these attacks Cantacuzenus asked the Ottoman Sultan for military assistance and this enabled the Turks to establish a base on the western side of Gallipoli. The Black Death then did further damage to the empire. In 1353 civil war broke out again as a party formed around John V, who resented his tutelage under Cantacuzenus. This enabled the Ottomans to consolidate their precarious hold on Gallipoli and establish a permanent presence in Europe. By 1369 they had seized Adrianople and confined the empire to a small area around Constantinople. Cantacuzenus abdicated in 1355, but John V lacked resources or determination. He reclaimed some territory from Bulgaria during a succession crisis and in 1369 went to Europe to appeal fruitlessly for help. By 1373 he was performing homage to the Ottoman Sultan who was intervening and manipulating Byzantine quarrels so that by the death of John V Constantinople was effectively an Ottoman client state.

The other two main Balkan powers were Bulgaria and Serbia, though Epirus continued for a while to be independent and the Kotromanic dynasty built up a state in Bosnia. On the fringes of these powers were semi-independent princes taking advantage of circumstances to enjoy power. The greatest of these powers was Serbia under Stephen Dusan (1331–55). He came to power as the champion

---

4 P. Engel, *The Realm of St Stephen. A History of Medieval Hungary 895–1526*, tr. T. Palosfalvi (London: I. B. Tauris, 2001), 202.

of a party amongst the nobles who favoured an aggressive attitude towards Byzantium, and in particular wanted to conquer Macedonia. He certainly bent all his efforts in that direction, permitting much independence to the port of Dubrovnik and only attacking Bosnia briefly in 1350. The Byzantine civil wars enabled him to achieve a great deal of success, for he was able to seize Thessaly, Macedonia and Epirus. At Easter 1346 Dusan gathered a great assembly at Skopje which raised the head of the Serbian Church to the status of Patriarch, and shortly after was crowned 'Tsar of the Serbs and Romans': he had hitherto called himself King of Serbia, Albania and the coast. Tradition would later assert that Dusan wanted to seize Constantinople, and certainly he did open negotiations with the Venetians. However, they did not relish a strong power at Constantinople and Dusan was soon distracted by his Bosnian campaign. Serbia in 1355 seemed a powerful empire destined to replace or dominate Constantinople. However, Dusan's supremacy was personal and largely based on the rewards of successful conquest which he was able to offer to his noble followers. He placed governors and mercenary garrisons in some cities as a pressure on the local nobles, but the Serb 'Empire' lacked any articulated control over the nobles. His son Uros (1356–71) was probably simple-minded, and kept in a semblance of power by the nobility who feared a more masterful ruler. The 'Empire' fell apart with Epirus overrun by the Albanians and Thessaly becoming a fiefdom of the family of the Angeli, nominally held of Constantinople. In the west rulers like George Balsic took power, and Dubrovnik drifted into independence. In Bosnia Tvrtko I (1353–91) strengthened and enlarged the state and interfered in the affairs of his Serbian neighbours. In Bulgaria Ivan Alexander (1330–71) ruled at Trnovo and might have been expected to profit by the decline of Serbia. However, he divided the realm by a second marriage and the disinheriting of his son John Stracimir who, with Hungarian support, established a separate state based on Vidin, and this opened the way for Andronicus to intervene. Overall, therefore, in the mid-fourteenth century the 'Byzantine Commonwealth' was in a state of acute political fragmentation.

In southern Greece and the Peloponnese there was a matching fragmentation. The dominant force was the Duchy of Athens ruled by the Grand Catalan Company. Their very existence was an affront to the accepted norms of aristocratic Europe where position and power largely depended on blood, even if professional administrators were recognised as necessary. The Catalans were mercenaries ruled by a hierarchy of senior leaders under a Captain-General. After 1312 they recognised the overlordship of the Aragonese royal house, but this was fairly remote and the Company never seems to have forwarded Catalan trading interests in the Aegean. There were constant bitter complaints about the savagery of the Catalans and their employment of Turkish mercenaries, but they were not the only rulers of this area who employed infidels and practised military brutality, and at bottom the hatred they inspired seems to have been social. To the south were the petty Frankish lords of the Peloponnese. They had been under Angevin protection since the late thirteenth century, but the decline of Naples in the fourteenth century made them restless and fearful. They hated the Catalans and faced hostility from Byzantine outposts like Mistra, and were increasingly open to Turkish raids. Yet it was from here that the Catalan dominion was eventually ended. In 1325 the Angevins mounted a great attack on Mistra, and when it failed they paid off the Acciaioli, a family of Florentine money-lenders, with substantial fiefs near Andravida. The family flourished and became major lords of Frankish Greece, but it was by exploiting divisions amongst the Catalan rulers that, in 1388, Nerio Acciaioli destroyed the Catalan domination and made himself Duke of Athens, a title which the family held until 1460 when Francesco I was murdered by the Ottoman Sultan. The Franks of Greece represented a crusading effort which few were prepared to support, and they were far too weak and divided to influence the course of events. It was the interests of Angevin Naples which sustained them, but they had little appeal beyond their sphere of influence and the connections of their families.

Crusading and Jerusalem continued to be important to western Europeans, and of the deepest concern to the papacy whose prestige was committed to the whole project of uniting Christendom and crushing Islam. But the entire political and military environment of the Eastern Mediterranean was changing. Byzantium was clearly no longer a base and potential ally for the liberation of Jerusalem. Its weakness was such that its rulers were prepared to appeal to the papacy for help, though its people were resolutely hostile to Union with the Latins. Potential assets in the area were very limited. The Knights of St John held Rhodes, but they were far too few to affect the balance of power. Lusignan Cyprus faced decline as its economic base shrank. The Franks in the Peloponnese were clearly on the defensive and in any case hostile to Catalan Athens. Worst of all, the European maritime supremacy in the eastern Mediterranean waters was imperilled by the deep hostility of Venice and Genoa who snapped away at each other's shipping even when there was no open war. The situation in Europe was equally difficult. From 1337 England and France were locked into the 'Hundred Years War' which absorbed all their efforts and finance. The pauses in the conflict, after the Treaty of Bretigny in 1360 and the accession of Richard II (1377–99) in England, both provided occasions for an upsurge in crusading.

In 1341, when Hugh IV of Cyprus (1324–59) and the Hospitallers appealed to Clement VI (1342–52) for aid against the increasingly aggressive Turkish principalities of Asia Minor, the pope approached Venice to form a new naval league. The Republic was willing because the Turks were becoming a menace to her shipping and she was not, for the moment, at war with Genoa. The papacy provided substantial funding, while Cyprus, the Hospitallers and Venice created a league to last for three years. On 13 May 1344 they defeated a Turkish fleet and on 28 October seized Smyrna (modern Izmir) which the crusaders managed to hold till 1402. These successes were gained with a modest force of 30 galleys. It is worth noting that the Genoese victory at the battle of Curzola in 1298 during the second Veneto-Genoese war involved 90 Venetian and 80 Genoese galleys. The news of the fall of Smyrna created a wave of enthusiasm and a follow-up expedition led by

Humbert of Vienne was despatched, but he proved incapable and the Venetians soon made peace. The problem was that these limited successes could not be followed up because resources were so limited. The civil wars in Byzantium enabled the Ottoman Turks to cross the straits into Europe. In 1359 the papal legate, Peter Thomas, persuaded the Byzantines to support a Venetian and Hospitaller attack on Lampsakos on the Asian side of the straits opposite Gallipoli. The success of this expedition showed the real possibilities, if appropriate resources could be mobilised. But in the absence of a powerful input from the west, the weakness of Byzantium was critical, and its whole position was complicated by the papal demand for union which really could not be imposed upon the Greeks.

Moreover, the primary instrument of western power, naval supremacy, was threatened by the wars of Genoa and Venice. In 1350 a quarrel over rights to trade at Tana on the Black Sea escalated into a large-scale war between Venice and Genoa, in which Catalonia became involved on the Venetian side because of her dispute with Genoa over control of Sardinia. A series of immensely bloody battles gave Genoa the advantage, but the war precipitated bitter internal disputes within the city and as a result ended indecisively in 1354 in an imperfect peace. In 1378 Venice and Genoa again quarrelled over possession of the small island of Tenedos at the mouth of the Gallipoli strait. The Genoese allied with the Hungarians and, in the climax of the war, seized Chioggia in the Venetian lagoon on 16 August 1379. The Genoese were only driven out after an epic struggle which ended in June 1380, but both parties were exhausted and Venice agreed not to fortify Tenedos and had to concede Dalmatia to the Hungarians. Genoa dissolved into factional struggle with 12 Doges appointed between 1383 and 1394. As a result a faction in the city asked Charles VI of France to appoint a ruler and in 1401 his choice fell upon the famous Marshal Boucicaut. He set out on a series of crusading raids, but, most decisively, fought off attempts by the kings of Cyprus to seize Famagusta.

Genoa and Venice had rather different but overlapping trading patterns. Genoa had three key ports: Kaffa on the Black Sea, Pera on the Golden Horn opposite Constantinople and the island of Chios in the Aegean. Though much high-value low-bulk trade passed through Kaffa, the Genoese depended heavily on bulk commodities like grain, sugar etc. and traded much less with Alexandria. By contrast, this Egyptian port seems to have become more and more important for Venice which used galleys to transport the high-value low-bulk spices and eastern luxuries. Both had an extensive network of ports, but Venetian dominance of Crete and its strong position in the Aegean and southern Greece and the Adriatic gave it huge advantages. Venice was also interested in Cyprus, and this may be why Genoa was so aggressive towards the Lusignans. But the great difference between the two cities was internal. Genoa was racked by faction and dominated by personality. In a sense it was a 'failed state': political turbulence was acute and continuity of policy impossible. Even in the establishment of its 'empire' family and personal initiative were the rule. Thus the Grimaldi seized

Monaco and the capture of Chios in 1346 was a result of the initiative of Simone Vignoso. Pera, the great Genoese colony at Constantinople, was ruled by a coalition of families to which Genoa was a party rather than a governing force. Venice, by contrast, established a homogenous elite which dominated a strong constitution for deciding state policy and ruled all its citizens. The political instability of Genoa invited intervention from its neighbours, with Milan, Aragon and France vying for influence. Moreover, by the early fifteenth century Venice was discovering new sources of power and income by dominating parts of the neighbouring plain of the Po, an option simply not open to Genoa. But while it is possible to draw contrasts between Venice and Genoa, with regard to the crusade they were very similar – they were prepared to fight but only when their trade was threatened, and for the most part preferred to come to terms with Ottomans and Mamluks.

Other Christian assets in the eastern Mediterranean also had very different interests. Peter I of Cyprus (1359–69) suddenly revived the whole idea of a crusade to liberate Jerusalem. He founded the Order of the Sword to attract foreign knights to the east, and in 1362 went to the west to drum up support. It was a good moment because the Treaty of Bretigny had brought what was hoped would be an end to the Anglo-French war. John II (1350–64) of France supported the new expedition, perhaps to recover his prestige after a long imprisonment in England following his capture at the battle of Poitiers in 1356, but his death really ended serious French involvement. A revolt against Venetian rule in Crete and Peter's own dispute with the Genoese delayed matters, but in August 1365 Peter gathered a fleet of 165 ships with 10,000 men, including 1,400 cavalry, off Rhodes. There is great uncertainty about Peter's intentions. It seems unlikely that he seriously thought he could recover Jerusalem with such a force. Urban V (1362–70) was highly confused about the expedition which he referred to as directed against both the Turks and the Mamluks of Egypt. In the event Peter attacked Alexandria, but this seems to have been a last-minute decision because it surprised the Venetians who provided much of the fleet. Seizing Egypt, or a part of it, as the key to regaining Jerusalem, was the strategy of the thirteenth century, but much larger armies had been employed and failed. Perhaps Peter counted on enemy resistance being weakened by factional struggles at the Mamluk court, at least to the point where he could exchange the city for Jerusalem. It has been suggested that Peter's real motive was to threaten Egyptian trade in order to gain trading privileges over both Islamic and western merchants. This would help to reverse the economic decline of Cyprus which was no longer an intermediary in the east–west trade because Venice, Genoa and the other cities were increasingly dealing direct with Egypt. On 9 October Peter's fleet appeared before Alexandria which they seized and sacked the next day. But by 16 October the Mamluks were back in control.

This was not the last of Peter's raids on Mamluk ports, but it was by far the most spectacular, and ultimately it was ineffective. Alexandria recovered and was soon trading vigorously with the west. In 1369 Peter was assassinated; his internal enemies alleged that he had acted arbitrarily in making war without their agreement, had favoured foreigners and had levied heavy taxation. He was perhaps influenced by his Chancellor, Philip of Mézières, a great enthusiast for the crusades who was soon driven out of the island. It is likely that Peter's vigorous effort to revive interest in crusading was the best hope of a realm in difficulty. The western trading cities like Venice preferred to trade direct with Alexandria, depriving Cyprus of income, while Turkish and Mamluk sea-power was becoming a threat. The more limited policy of his predecessors in raiding southern Asia Minor and establishing dominance over local ports had not really halted the economic decline and something else was needed. His attempt to revive crusading was by no means ill-judged because the Anglo-French war had apparently ended and, in the event, he raised a substantial army. But there was not enough interest in the west and his policies foundered on the particularism of his nobles. The regency government set up for the child Peter II (1369–82) was sharply divided. In 1372 Peter II was crowned but at his coronation a quarrel between Venetians and Genoese escalated into a full-scale attack on the latter who were expelled. Peter II refused Genoese demands for compensation, and in 1373–74 a major Genoese fleet ravaged the island. Ultimately the royal government came to terms, but Genoa continued to hold Famagusta and extorted reparations and a heavy tribute, crippling the kingdom. King Janus (1398–1432) tried vainly to regain Famagusta from the Genoese, but in 1425 the Mamluks launched a devastating raid which even captured Janus who was obliged to ransom himself and the island became a vassal-state of Egypt. This turbulence hastened the impoverishment of Cyprus where the rule of John II (1432–58) saw the island adopt a passive role.

The weakening of potential Christian assets in the eastern Mediterranean came at a time when the Islamic enemy was far from secure. The Kalavunid dynasty had established itself in Mamluk Egypt at the end of the thirteenth century and Nasser Muhammad (1293–1341) was a formidable autocrat, but his successors were young and short-lived, and dominated by the great officers of state. Sultan Al-Nasir Hasan (1354–61) tried to assert himself and was put to death by his minister, Yalbogah, ushering in a volatile period out of which there emerged the Circassian, Barkuk who usurped the Sultanate in 1382 and ruled until 1399, though he failed to found a dynasty. Underlying the palace coups were changes in the Mamluk world. The Black Death sharply reduced the renders of the Egyptian land-tax so that the government pressed much harder upon Syria, and this caused great tensions. A remarkable feature of Mamluk society was the constant renewal of its personnel from steppe Turks, so that generation by generation it was newcomers who held great offices and high command. From the mid-fourteenth century the rise of the Ottomans in Anatolia siphoned off these recruits and within Egypt noble dynasties became more important. Moreover, within the ruling class other groups, like the Circassians, aspired to power. The Mamluks remained militarily formidable during this period, but relative decline was manifest.

But as far as the papacy and the west were concerned, the major problem which they faced was the rise of a new power, the Ottomans. The Seljuks of Rūm had survived the attacks of the First Crusade and gone on to create a powerful inland Sultanate based on Iconium (modern Konya) and Caesaria-in-Cappadocia (modern Kayseri) which defeated Manuel Comnenus at the battle of Myriokephalon in 1176 and also held off aggression from the Ayyubids of Syria. But in 1243 the Sultanate was conquered by the Mongols. The Sultans survived for a while as satraps of Il Khanid Iran, but as Mongol power ebbed the old Sultanate broke up into warring minor Turkish states. Amongst these principalities or *beyliks* was Menteshe in the south-west, whose pirates infested the Aegean, while further north was Aydin around Smyrna which was also a maritime power. To the east, hard up against Byzantine territories, was the Ottoman *beylik* which took its name from its founder, Osman Gazi. Originally the Ottoman *beylik* was not especially formidable. It was a small principality around Sögut and was hemmed in to the east by other petty powers and more substantial ones like Karaman, based on Iconium, which ruled a great belt of land extending from the Black Sea to the Mediterranean. All these *beyliks* attracted Nomad tribes and unstable elements from the steppe, the *ghazi*, attracted by war against unbelievers, many of whom might otherwise have joined the Mamluks. The lands of Osman (1281-1321) attracted more than most because they were immediately adjacent to Byzantine territory which was somewhat neglected because of the emperors' preoccupation with their lands on the European side of the Bosphorus. Osman was an able soldier whose Turkish horsemen came to dominate a vast area of western Asia Minor. He needed to lead his armies to success otherwise the tribal leaders would not follow him, but without trained infantry and engineers he found attacking cities difficult. It was only in the first year of the reign of Orhan (1326-62) that Bursa fell. The possession of a city gave the dynasty prestige and became their capital. In 1331 Nicaea fell and soon after Orhan had driven his frontier to the Straits of Gallipoli and south towards the Mediterranean. The Byzantine civil war under John Cantacuzenus provided the opportunity to expand further. In 1345 Umur, prince of Aydin, who had often provided the emperor with troops, was preoccupied by the crusader occupation of Smyrna. Cantacuzenus, therefore, asked Orhan for troops and was forced to grant to them the fort of Jinbi in Gallipoli, which formed a Turkish base west of the straits. The pace of Turkish conquest now became remarkable. Taking advantage of the chaotic fragmentation all about them, they had seized Philippopolis by 1363. The isolation of Constantinople shocked Urban V who made great efforts to raise another crusade, while John V begged Louis of Hungary for aid in 1365-66. The only outcome of all this effort was the crusade of Amadeo VI of Savoy who sailed with 3,000 men from Venice in June 1363, almost certainly in the expectation of meeting a Hungarian army. When none appeared he joined with the Greeks in a successful assault on Gallipoli. The fact was that the empire of Murad I (1362-89) was really based on savage and successful raiding, and his army of Turkish light cavalry was not yet equipped for major siege-warfare. His 'Empire' was vulnerable, but there was nobody to follow up the success of Amadeo. John V professed himself ready to accept Union with Rome and visited the west in 1369, but with war between England and France resuming, Hungary indifferent and tension still evident between Genoa and Venice there was nobody to provide military support when, in that same year, Adrianople fell to Murad who promptly made it his capital.

The Ottomans clearly posed a major threat to the Christian powers of the Balkans and the Lower Danube and this caused something of a rapprochement between Rome and Constantinople, but effective resistance was left to the local powers. The papacy had great hopes of Louis of Hungary, but he was preoccupied elsewhere and his son, Sigismund, had great difficulties in establishing himself in the kingdom. In 1371 two Serbian princes gathered a strong army and marched on Adrianople, but they were surprised by the Turks at Crnomen on the river Maritza and crushed. By 1386 Murad had captured Sofia and Nish and forced John Sisman, the Bulgarian Tsar and the Emperor John V to accept his suzerainty. Murad was distracted in 1387 by major resistance to his advance in Asia Minor from the principality of Karaman and this enabled a Serbian prince, Lazar, to create a coalition of powers including John Sisman who renounced his homage to Murad. But Murad defeated Karaman and then crushed the coalition at Kosovo on 15 June 1389. This was all the more remarkable because Murad was killed during the battle. However, his son, Bayezid (1389–1403) took over and the battle was won. Bulgaria was firmly annexed to the Ottoman Empire and by 1391 the Turks had reached Skopje in the western Balkans. Although the *beyliks* of Asia Minor continued to exist the Ottomans annexed much of western Asia Minor and their power reached towards that of the Mamluks and the newly resurgent power of the Central Asian Mongols under Tamerlane.

The papacy had been a fairly helpless witness to these events because from 1378 it was in a state of schism with rival popes at Avignon and Rome competing for the loyalty of Christendom. Pope Gregory XI (1370–78) had returned to Italy in 1377, but after his death the legitimacy of the election of Urban VI (1378–89) was challenged by the French cardinals whose choice of pope, Clement VII (1378–94), took up residence at Avignon. Both could make some claim to legitimacy and it was just bad luck that both had relatively long reigns. In a Europe sharply divided by the 'Hundred Years War' neither could gain a decisive weight of support because France and its allies supported the Avignon line while England and its friends preferred the Roman pontiff. In this new situation the war between France and England took on something of the character of a holy war. In 1383 Henry Despenser, bishop of Norwich, led an English crusade to assist a rebellion in Flanders against French domination, and, therefore, the Avignon papacy. After some limited success this turned into a fiasco. In 1382 Clement VII granted a crusade indulgence to Frenchmen prepared to help Louis of Hungary to overthrow King Charles X of Anjou who adhered to the Roman pope. The English and French exported their conflict into Spain with the support of the rival popes. However, it soon became apparent that Richard II of England was not anxious to continue the war with France and that both powers were increasingly disillusioned with the schism. The truce concluded in 1384 and reaffirmed in 1389 produced an atmosphere of reconciliation. This was fostered by Philip of Mézières, the tutor of Charles VI of France (1380–1422), who had been Chancellor to Peter of Lusignan. In 1390 a French expedition led by Louis of Bourbon, uncle of Charles VI, attacked Mahdiya in Tunisia, being granted crusading indulgences by both popes. By 1395 the idea of a joint crusade by the English and French kings was being floated. In this atmosphere the appeals for aid from Sigismund of Hungary, whose realm was now in direct confrontation with the Ottomans, aroused sympathy. In 1393 a small Anglo-French force was sent to aid him. Preparations were quite well advanced by 1395 with John of Gaunt, duke of Lancaster and Philip the Bold of Burgundy playing leading roles and the enterprise enjoyed the support of both the contending popes. The whole expedition was clearly intended to be a symbol of the new Anglo-French amity but difficulties arose over Richard II's proposed marriage and there was a revolt in Gascony. As a result, John of Gaunt withdrew while Philip the Bold entrusted the leadership of his army to his son, John of Nevers. As a consequence the bulk of the troops who left for Hungary in April 1396 were Burgundian and French, though a few English accompanied them.

The size of the army was probably quite limited, and to make matters worse it had a plethora of prominent leaders including John Boucicaut, Philip of Artois and John of Vienne, respectively the Marshal, Constable and Admiral of France, Henry of Bar and James of Bourbon. They arrived in Hungary and were joined by a number of smaller contingents, notably that of Enguerrand of Coucy. The Burgundians were the single largest group amongst the crusaders, but John of Nevers was not an experienced leader and none of the others emerged as a dominating personality. Almost all crusades had faced this problem of leadership, and it was made worse because the French distrusted the Hungarian king, perhaps despising also his Wallachian and Transylvanian allies. Tensions between the Burgundians and Sigismund seem to have been increased when the king suggested that the army should stand on the defensive in order to make Bayezid come to them. However, as the Sultan was besieging Constantinople there were good grounds for rejecting this and advancing to make him come to battle. The army seized some castles and then invested Nicopolis, forcing the Turks to battle on 25 September 1396. The result was a crushing defeat for the crusaders. The primary cause of this seems to have been the insistence of the French cavalry that they should be the vanguard of the attack. Chivalric pride may have influenced this decision, but distrust of their allies was probably the dominant factor. The French cavalry overwhelmed the Turkish light screening forces and infantry, but by this time the momentum of their attack was lost and they were slaughtered by the enemy's heavy horse, the *sipahis*. Stephen Lazarevic, a Serbian vassal of the Sultan, crushed the Hungarians while many of their allies deserted. Curiously, the survivors of this disaster, notably John of Nevers, were feted on their return from captivity and the whole affair raised consciousness of crusading, particularly at the court of the wealthy dukes of Burgundy whose increasing independence from the kingdom of France was such a feature of contemporary politics. The French monarchy despatched a substantial force under Boucicaut to garrison Constantinople, and this encouraged Manuel II Palaeologus (1391–1425) to undertake a fruitless visit to Western Europe in search of aid.

Nicopolis was a tremendous triumph for Bayezid and it raises the question of why this new centre of power and influence was rising and to such an extent. The Ottoman *beylik* probably owed much of its success to the genius and aggressiveness of its rulers, particularly Murad I. It was very important that Murad lived so long, because the Ottomans had no established rule of succession and the death of a Sultan precipitated bitter conflict which could have led to the dissolution of the nascent state. The fact that they were adjacent to Byzantine territory enabled them to attract *ghazi* eager for plunder at the expense of infidels. They were able to expand because in the first instance the Byzantine emperors were much concerned with events in Greece. Then a series of civil wars within Byzantium meant that they were invited in, most notably in 1345 when Cantacuzenus conceded bases on the western side of the Gallipoli Strait, opening the way for enormous conquests in the Balkans. Such growth was not welcome to the other *beyliks*, but the rapid accretion of power enabled Murad to swallow up many of them, and no Christian power seems to have thought to seek alliance with them. The dissolution of the Byzantine Empire exposed the fragmentation of the wider 'Byzantine Commonwealth'. Both Bulgaria and Serbia were deeply fissured states whose nobilities largely capitulated after the initial defeats. The Turkish onslaught came at a time when determined leadership had failed in both lands. This freed the petty princelings on their peripheries and independent nobles in former Byzantine territories, to pursue their own interests, while religious tensions with Catholic Hungary made an alliance difficult. Essentially the Turks were expanding into a vacuum and the precarious nature of their position was revealed clearly by the success of Amadeo of Savoy's expedition. But for the next 30 years resistance was piecemeal. Fragmented Serbia went down to defeat at Crnomen in 1371 and again at Kosovo in 1386, after which its nobility came to their own arrangements with the Sultan, while Hungary was happy to profit in the west. However, the rise of the Ottomans was something more than the happy good fortune of capable war-leaders, because the Sultans were forging 'state-building' policies which gave a permanence to their growth which might otherwise have been dissolved by the struggles for succession.

From the first the Ottomans had found it politic to pursue a policy of religious toleration. Christian peasants and petty landowners in Asia Minor had been driven to accept Ottoman rule, alienated by crushing taxation on behalf of an emperor at Constantinople who could not protect them. Moreover, in the early stages of their dominance in the Balkans, although there was some movement of Turkish settlement into critical parts of the area, Murad found it politic to continue this policy. He was prepared to accept vassalage from Christian princes, nobles and communities as long as they were faithful and provided tribute. On the frontiers Ottoman rulers made arrangements with both Christian and Muslim potentates who would act in alliance with them. Indeed Christian soldiers and allies provided reliable military support when he and Bayezid fought their Turkish enemies in Asia Minor and overawed their restless subjects who might easily have allied with them. For Murad, and even more, Bayezid, were determined to transform the Ottoman domination. They understood the dangers of remaining leaders of fighting tribes and sought instead to create a centralised tax-collecting bureaucratic state comparable to that of the Mamluks. In pursuit of this they recruited administrators from the former Seljuk lands, from Egypt and from Iran, and even recruited Christians knowledgeable about Byzantine administration, and divided their lands into provinces or *sancaks* whose administration collected taxes. In this way the Byzantine and Middle Eastern traditions of centralised government fused and were given a clearly Islamic character because authority, on the model of the Caliphates, was both spiritual and temporal. In effect a totally autocratic system was constructed in which rank and power were controlled by the Sultan. Although an aristocracy would ultimately emerge, western writers of the sixteenth century were struck by the meritocratic structure of Ottoman society and contrasted it with their own experience where inheritance was the determinant of rank and power.

But it was in the military sphere that change was most radical, for the Sultans could not afford to continue their reliance on forces of Turkish nomads whose leaders, quite accurately, viewed the entire process of centralisation as inimical to their whole position. This seems to have happened piecemeal and pragmatically, but it was soon developed systematically. From the time of Orhan salaried infantry and cavalry had been employed by the Sultan. As more territory was conquered the cavalrymen were given *timar*, somewhat like western fiefs, which were grouped to form the ruling elites of the unit of local government, the *sancak*. From these groups came the heavy cavalry, the *sipahis*, so important at Nicopolis. Gradually this group came to form a special elite, later virtually an aristocracy, within the Ottoman dominion. But the most remarkable feature of military organisation was the distinctive development of the slave-soldier (Mamluk) system so common in the Islamic world. This was the levying of young Christian children who were formed into the *yeni ceri* or janissary corps who were profoundly loyal to the Sultan. This reorganisation of the Turkish military was accompanied by a readiness to embrace technical development. In 1387–88 Murad employed firearms in his campaign against Karaman and the Turks continued to keep abreast of developments in this direction. A standing army, loyal to the Sultan, thus emerged. Murad was killed at Nicopolis, but command passed to his son Bayezid who went on to win the battle.

The strength of this new empire was soon tested. From 1381 the Mongols in Central Asia were energised and unified by the emergence of a brilliant new leader, Tamerlane. In 1400 the Turkish princes of eastern Asia Minor asked for his aid against the rising threat posed by Bayezid. Tamerlane seized this opportunity to reassert Mongol dominion in this area and in 1402 destroyed the

Ottoman army at the battle of Ankara, capturing Bayezid who died soon after in captivity. The Ottoman lands in Asia Minor were divided and Tamerlane went on to recover Smyrna from the Christians, perhaps to demonstrate that he was truly a Muslim at heart. But Tamerlane's power did not extend west of the straits and it was this region which was the power-base of the Ottoman dynasty. The great Mongol leader died in 1405 and Mongol unity dissolved. This opened a period of bitter conflict in the Ottoman family which continued to dog the able Mehmed I (1413–21). But the administrators and soldiers raised by the Ottomans had a strong vested interest in the continuation of the structure they served. This was truly a remarkable entity combining Byzantine and Islamic elements, and forming a new centre of influence to stand against that of the Catholic west and the forces of the Orient.

None of the western enemies of the Ottomans was able to profit from their defeat in 1402 and subsequent divisions. Venice was beginning its domination of the western plain of the Po, while Genoa was distracted by internal conflict. The deposition of Richard II of England in 1399 renewed tension between England and France, while the all the major powers were preoccupied by intensive efforts to end the papal schism. In essence the political fragmentation that had characterised the whole zone from the Mamluk frontier in Syria to the frontiers of France, and even beyond, was worsening. The Serbian prince, Stephen Lazarevic, had emerged in the wake of the defeat at Kosovo when he became a vassal of Bayezid, for whom he fought bravely at Ankara. After the battle he was granted the title of Despot by the Byzantine Emperor. But he had many internal enemies, and quickly came to terms with Sigismund of Hungary whose vassal he remained until his death in 1427. He fought for Sigismund against the Venetians in their wars over control of the Dalmatian coast which dragged on until 1433. Ultimately Venice dominated the Dalmatic coast. To the south the Venetians disputed control of Albania whose nobility were torn between them, the Serbians and the Ottomans. By the 1430s the Ottomans had overrun the area, though they often maintained local princes. Zeta (modern Montenegro) was an Orthodox principality owing some allegiance to the ruler of Serbia, but enjoying Venetian support. Stephen Lazarevic exploited the Ottoman civil wars, but once they ended he felt it necessary to mend his fences with the Sultans. His successor, George Brankowic, tried to balance Ottoman and Hungarian influence, but by 1440 Serbia was largely ruled by the Ottomans, with a rump under Hungarian influence. The nobilities of Croatia and Bosnia also felt the influence of Hungary, but Sigismund was too distracted by other matters to absorb them and Ottoman influence there was increased when they and their local allies defeated the Hungarians at Doboj in 1415. However, Tvrtko II (1421–43) of Bosnia sought Sigismund's support against his enemies and this re-established Hungarian influence there. Wallachia had always resisted Hungarian domination and called in Polish support when Sigismund was threatening. After the death of its ruler, Mircea, in 1418, however, its nobility fragmented between supporting Hungary or the Ottomans who defeated Sigismund in 1428 and dominated the whole area.

Hungary clearly was a possible source of stability in the morass of minor powers and it certainly stood firm against the Ottomans. Sigismund was, in many ways, a remarkable and attractive man, but he was never able to focus on Hungary, and most of his distractions ultimately sprang from the fragmentation of the German Empire. The Emperor Charles IV engineered the election of his son Wenceslas IV, his successor in Bohemia (1378–1419), to the empire (1378–1400) with papal approval before his death. Wenceslas faced the problem that the diversity of interests in Germany was now so great that nobody could satisfy them all. North and south, princes, cities, knights and lesser nobles, all represented different interests and Wenceslas was incapable of backing any of them to the point where they would form useful allies. Further, although Germany was strongly inclined to the Romanist party in the Schism, there were marked cross-currents and the emperor himself was suspected of having leanings to the Avignon papacy. Moreover, his failure to produce an heir weakened his position in Bohemia, opening the way for the ambitions of Sigismund who showed little gratitude for his elder half-brother's support in the struggle for the Hungarian succession. In 1400 Wenceslas was deposed in favour of the Elector Palatine, Rupert, prompting a civil war in Germany until his death in 1410, when, after many hesitations, the German electors plumped for Sigismund as Emperor (1410–37). That Sigismund was chiefly known for his being impecunious is hardly surprising when we consider the extent of his responsibilities. But his great business was to end the 'Schism of the West' where recent attempts had only increased the number of papal pretenders to three. With France weakened, Sigismund charmed Henry V (1413–22) of England and so laid the basis for the summoning of the Council of Constance 1414–18. By the time the Council met Sigismund needed its support for another of his entanglements.

Under Wenceslas IV Bohemia had become increasingly Czech and there was a strong reaction against German power and influence, especially in Prague. So sharp was this that after a dispute in 1409 the German professors seceded from the University of Prague and set up a new University at Leipzig. The national divide was sharpened by religious differences. All over Europe there was a powerful demand for reform of the Church, but amongst the Czechs this took a vigorous anti-German tinge because Germans were seen as the corrupt establishment. Moreover, amongst Czechs there was strong sentiment in favour of Utraquism, the taking of communion in bread and wine by all the faithful which was regarded as quite wrong by Catholic Germans. Jan Hus was a Czech reformer who was strongly influenced by the English heretic, John Wycliffe, and his radical ideas for reform found a substantial following. Agitation for reform and dislike of Germans meant that the demand for religious change spread far beyond the noble elite, and an important role was taken by the gentry and lesser nobility, some of whom were drawn to the radicalism of Hus. These gentry had gained much experience of politics in the long agitation to pressurise Wenceslas to respect their rights. As a result he was cautiously protective of the Czechs, but he did not wish to be accused of heresy. In 1414 Hus went to the Council of Constance under the protection of Sigismund as emperor, but he was imprisoned and executed as a heretic. This sparked an upheaval in Prague where the radicals gained the upper hand and the sympathy of many of the great nobles. Broadly the opposition group formed a spectrum from the Taborites, mostly drawn from the broad spectrum of the population though dominated by the gentry, who effectively denied papal authority, to moderate Utraquists who just wanted to enjoy communion in both kinds. They were united only by the martyrdom of Hus and fear of the succession of Sigismund when Wenceslas IV died in 1419. Sigismund called for a crusade against the heretics in order to make himself effective ruler of Bohemia, but a series of campaigns failed disastrously as the Czechs showed themselves to be hardy and efficient soldiers, inspired by fine leaders and a deep hatred of German intervention. Under Jan Zizka the Czechs made up for their lack of cavalry by using laagers of wagons – *wagenburgen* – which held off the chivalry of Germany and were even used offensively to attack their enemies. Extensive use was made of firearms to strengthen these. The Hussites did not stand on the defensive – they ravaged the lands of German supporters of Sigismund and provided military support to Poland in its struggle with the Teutonic Order. These tactics spread to Hungary and were even adopted by the Ottomans who noted their effectiveness. Under the strain of war the moderate Utraquists quarrelled with the Taborites and destroyed them at the battle of Lipan in 1434, opening the way for reconciliation with Sigismund in 1436, who, however, died in the following year. In the light of his numerous distractions he had done well by Hungary, maintaining a position in the Balkans, but the Ottomans were now dangerous neighbours.

But they were neighbours with their own problems. Murad II (1421–51) faced a number of rebellions and a protracted succession struggle in which the Byzantines supported his brother, and as a result he unsuccessfully attacked Constantinople in 1422. Thessalonica had accepted Venetian supremacy in return for support and it was not until 1430 that Murad was able to conquer the city. He was then encouraged to attack Serbia and threaten Hungary by the evident weaknesses which followed the death of Sigismund. Sigismund had wanted to be succeeded in all his lands by Albert of Hapsburg, the husband of his daughter, Elizabeth. Albert was duly elected as Emperor (1438–39). In Bohemia his succession was contested by Casimir of Poland who enjoyed the support of some of the nobility, but he was quickly victorious, and on his death in 1439 was succeeded by his son Ladislas Posthumus (1440–57). In the subsequent struggle over the Regency the divisions between Catholics, identified with Germans, and Utraquists, reappeared, plunging government into major problems. In Hungary many of the nobles were unwilling to accept the succession of Elizabeth, but were willing to support Albert (1438–39) who they knew as one who had fought alongside them against the Turks. However, in return for their support the great nobles demanded land grants which impoverished the crown and recognition of the rights of their class to share in the direction of the realm. Albert's attempts to renege on his promises simply resulted in deadlock. As a result when Murad extinguished Serbia in 1439 the Hungarian army gathered, but failed to intervene. However, dysentery broke out in the camp killing King Albert. The centralists, who objected to any weakening of the crown, gathered around Elizabeth who, on the death of Albert, championed the claim of Ladislas Posthumus. But many of the nobles offered the crown to Ladislas III of Poland (1434–44), and the result was the outbreak of civil war in 1440 in which the country was fairly evenly divided, with neither party in the ascendant. In 1440 Murad attacked Belgrade, only to be fought off by local forces. During the civil war there emerged the remarkable figure of John Hunyadi. He was a minor noble who emerged as a military leader in the party of Ladislas III who gave him extraordinary authority in the eastern frontier zones. In 1441–42 he took over command in Belgrade and smashed two Ottoman armies, thus emerging as the champion of Hungarian Christianity. His victories owed much to careful exploitation of the methods of the Hussites. His infantry, many of them Bohemian mercenaries, anchored their positions with carts and canon, and used handguns to fight off cavalry attack. The Ottomans quickly adapted this pattern and their Jannissary corps soon became heavily armed with the new gunpowder weapons. The Ottoman war machine was certainly as flexible as that of any western state.

The victories of Hunyadi aroused great interest and enthusiasm across Europe and even encouraged Slav revolt against the Ottomans and resistance by Karaman in Asia Minor. At the same time John VIII (1391–1425) went to the Council of Florence in 1438/9 to appeal for support for beleaguered Constantinople. He encountered a difficult situation because although the Council of Constance had brought the schism to an end the manner in which it had been done raised the gravest questions about where ultimate authority in the Church lay. A new conference had convened at Basle in 1431 where popes and council became locked into a bitter conflict and it eventually reconvened at Florence in 1438. Eugenius IV (1431–47) was at the height of this quarrel with the Council and threw himself into the organisation of a new crusade which would promote his standing in Europe. A Union with the Orthodox was agreed and preparations were made for the crusade. Eugenius' legate, Julian Cesarini, persuaded the warring parties in Hungary to suspend hostilities. Relatively few westerners went east, but the pope raised large sums of money and a great army gathered in Hungary under the command of John Hunyadi. The pope's idea was that the Hungarians should strike into Ottoman territory while a fleet protected Constantinople and made Ottoman communications in the straits difficult. The Venetians were lukewarm, but the Hungarians inflicted a series of devastating defeats upon the Ottomans in late 1443 in the 'Long Campaign', September 1443 to January 1444. In the following year a repeat of this campaign was projected, and this time the Venetians agreed to join with a strong fleet. Murad was deeply demoralised by the Hungarian successes, and he offered generous terms by the Treaty of Oradea, including the restoration of Serbia. The Hungarians appear to have accepted this offer, despite the best efforts of Cardinal Cesarini, and then changed their minds. On 22 September the Hungarians attacked, but their forces were smaller than in the previous year – perhaps less than 20,000. Murad had raised a huge army in Asia Minor and crushed the crusaders on 10 November 1444 at Varna, killing Cesarini and Ladislas III. Once again the effectiveness of the Ottoman war-machine had been demonstrated. So had the divisions of their enemies. The Poles saw little reason to support the Hungarians, despite having the same king, while the Serbs accepted the Treaty of Oradea. Many Hungarian nobles, preoccupied by their internal crisis had stayed at home. The Venetians were half-hearted and their fleet did not interfere when Murad's army crossed the Straits. There were virtually no western crusaders to support the Hungarians.

It has often been remarked that the nobilities of Poland/Lithuania, Hungary and Bohemia were selfish and mutually hostile. All over Central Europe highly privileged estates of nobles had emerged, usually by taking advantage of failures of succession and of personality in their ruling dynasties. This particularism and selfishness was hardly new, and it was certainly not confined to the nobilities of Central and Eastern Europe. Under the stress of war France was all but dismembered after the victories of Edward III and Henry V of England and the emergence of the Burgundian state is clear evidence that the west too could suffer from the same ambitions which further east were so destructive of resistance to the Ottomans. But whereas in the eleventh and twelfth centuries, and to a degree in the thirteenth, some members of the western nobilities had been willing to seek their fortune by emigration and this had been one of the motors of expansionism, this ceased to be the case in the later Middle Ages. The fabric of the state had grown considerably and the game of aristocratic power had changed. Their aim now was to seek to profit from the operations of the state, while at the same time safeguarding their privileges and rights. In the process some nobilities became, to a degree, servants of their states. In England this process was probably the most developed, probably because the English crown had for so long been able to offer lucrative employment in the wars in France. Sir Edward Dalyngrygge was able to build himself a luxurious home at Bodiam Castle on the proceeds of the profits of war, and real prospects of such gain kept a war party alive amongst the English nobility long after the crown had become immersed in debts. In Central and Eastern Europe this coherence was much less marked. On the other hand their nobles were much too preoccupied for adventure and deeply suspicious of alien groups. By contrast, the circumstances of the *ghazi* state enabled the highly intelligent Ottoman Sultans to create a nobility of merit, essentially by distributing the profits of expansion. The Ottoman Beys were much like the nobility of Carolingian Europe. The great difference was that the Ottomans also created a strong state-structure and even at its most vulnerable it was strong enough to hold off the forces around and within it.

The efflorescence in Catholic Christendom of late medieval chivalry with its elaborate and profligate rituals and grand Orders proclaimed the distinctiveness of the noble class and their dominance and was profoundly important because they felt under threat. The centralised court and the professional administrators were challenges which they could fight off by reference to their transcending moral justification – the conduct of war. Hence the paradox that a nobility and knighthood which was actually becoming more and more preoccupied with administration and more 'civil' in its preoccupations, was exalting the warrior virtues which had been so much more obvious and necessary in earlier generations. The Teutonic Order had successfully tapped into this chivalric ethos to promote its northern crusades, and succeeded precisely because they offered an appropriate outlet for martial urges, but one which did not distract individuals from what mattered most – the power-struggle to dominate and profit from the monarchical state. All over Europe the elites recognised the limitations imposed by the changing political context of Catholic Christendom, and adventure abroad of the traditional kind looked less attractive. In the face of growing Islamic strength the prospects of new expansion looked poor, while the Orthodox societies of the 'Byzantine Commonwealth' showed little interest in emulation. Even in Spain where expansion and crusade had always been intimately intertwined, other considerations took precedence over war with Islam. At the same time the papacy, while it never lost its commitment to crusade, was increasingly caught up in more localised struggles and found its pre-eminence compromised by the Schism and its aftermath. Religious men and women were deeply concerned by the issue of Church reform, and perhaps less moved by the need to liberate Jerusalem. Crusading enjoyed occasional upsurges in popularity and its rituals continued to be celebrated across Catholic Christendom but the Christian position in the eastern Mediterranean was deteriorating and nobody was sufficiently interested to do anything about it. The spring of expansionism in Catholic Christendom was running dry, but although this was not readily apparent, new forces which would work in the same direction were coming into play.

SELECTED READING

The *New Cambridge Medieval History* vol. VII for 1300–1415 edited by Michael Jones provides the most authoritative general account of European development in this period. The popular general account of the period by B. W. Tuchman, *A Distant Mirror. The Calamitous Fourteenth Century* (Harmondsworth: Penguin, 1979) emphasises its gloomier aspects. D. Hay, *Europe in the Fourteenth and Fifteenth Centuries* (2nd edition, London: Longman, 1989) is an excellent textbook. There is a brilliantly written account of the nature and ravages of the Black Death by P. Ziegler, *The Black Death* (London: Collins, 1969), but more recently it has been suggested by O. J. Benedictow, *The Black Death, 1346–53. The Complete History 1346–53* (Woodbridge: Boydell, 2004) that the death-toll may have been even higher than a third of the European population. For an analysis of its consequences, see E. Huppert, *After the Black Death. A Social History of Early Modern Europe* (Bloomington, IN: University of Indiana Press, 1998). On the revolution in Paris and its context, see J. Sumption, *The Hundred Years War Volume 2. Trial by Fire 1347–69* (London: Faber, 1999), 294–50. On the continuity of crusading, see Housley, *Later Crusades*. The studies of J. Leuschner and du Boulay, *Germany in the later Middle Ages* remain useful as does Urban's *Teutonic Knights*. Marshal Boucicaut's remarkable career is discussed by N. Housley, 'One man and his wars: the depiction of warfare by Marshal

Boucicaut's biographer', *Journal of Medieval History* 29 (2003), 27–40. There is a list of books on Byzantium, Frankish Greece and the kingdoms of Central and Eastern Europe and the Balkans in the previous chapter, but for the Hapsburgs, see J. Bérenger, *A History of the Hapsburg Empire 1273–1700*, tr. C. A. Simpson of a French original of 1990 (London: Longman, 1994). Amongst the evidence of the continuing interest in crusade was the development of Jerusalem-centred liturgies, often inspired directly by the papacy. This subject has been brilliantly surveyed by A. Linder, *Raising Arms. Liturgy in the Struggle to Liberate Jerusalem in the Late Middle Ages* (Turnhout: Brepols, 2003). The idea that Peter of Cyprus had economic motives for his crusading zeal is suggested by Edbury, *Kingdom of Cyprus*. An essential aid for the study of the Ottoman expansion is D. E. Pitcher, *An Historical Geography of the Ottoman Empire* (Leiden: Brill, 1972). On the Ottomans H. Inalcik, *The Ottoman Empire. The Classical Age 1300–1600*, tr. N. Itzkowitz and M. Imber (London: Weidenfeld and Nicolson, 1973) and the earlier chapters of J. McCarthy, *The Ottoman Turks* (London: Longman, 1997) are extremely useful. A number of works on the history of Spain have been cited in earlier chapters, but here much use has been made of J. N. Hillgarth, *The Spanish Kingdoms 1250–1516*, 2 vols (Oxford: Clarendon, 1976).

9

TOWARDS A NEW WORLD, 1444–1714

The 'Voyages of Discovery' and the European expansion of the sixteenth century are often regarded as continuations of the expansionism of Catholic Christendom which began about 1000, just as that in turn is seen to be based on the growth of Carolingian Europe. But while there were elements of continuity, especially in the case of Portugal and Spain, the scale and range of expansion was infinitely greater and this reflected its very different origins and causes. In the eleventh century an ideological current, the crusade, was married to the buccaneering spirit of the raw aristocracy of the 'Catholic Core'. Their aggressiveness was mostly expressed in internecine warfare which the poorly articulated monarchies of the age could not prevent, and short-distance predatory assaults on less developed neighbours. But this spirit also gave rise to an adventurism which carried Catholic culture into far places. This kind of individualistic and dynastic imperialism was possible because the 'Catholic Core' was then surrounded by much weaker and economically undeveloped political entities. Even where this was most marked, in Northern and Eastern Europe, the process of expansion, with some exceptions, was very slow and, as Lithuania shows, far from inevitable. Beyond these undeveloped areas were two great centres of influence, Byzantium and the Caliphate, both of which were in a state of fragmentation. The crusades were an attempt by the papacy to rally the 'Catholic Core' together with the areas it had come to dominate, into a single Catholic Christendom wedded to a policy of religious expansionism at the expense of these two religious power-blocks. This move to create solidarity out of the diverse elements of Catholic Christendom did not really succeed, because the basic impulse to expansion was too divided and rooted in aristocratic patterns of life. As time passed the world around Christendom changed remarkably, making individualistic and dynastic adventurism ever more difficult. Moreover, the acquisitiveness of the aristocracy found new outlets in the exploitation of the state, though buccaneering adventurism was never entirely dead. By the fifteenth century Catholic Christendom was clearly penned in to the east by formidable enemies. Certain royal dynasties, while they did not dismiss war against their Christian neighbours as a means of enrichment, perceived new possibilities of growth in distant and hitherto unknown areas. This expansionism involved huge investment which was beyond

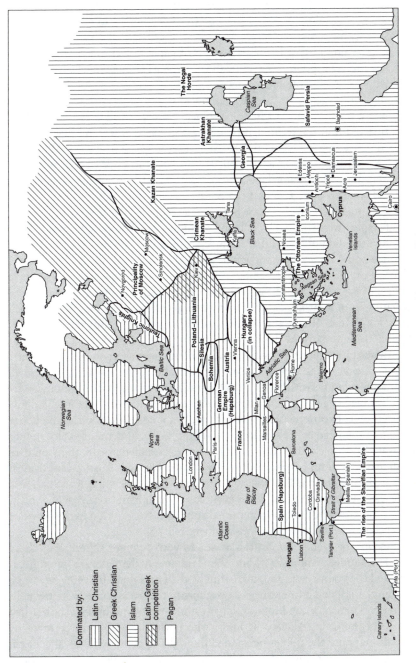

Map 9.1 Three civilisations around a sea: the 'Catholic core' and its neighbours c.1526.

the means of adventurers and only the newly articulated states of the period could sustain it. Though the impulse to explore and seize territory and bases owed something to crusading ideas and the traditions of the past in execution it was fundamentally different.

Since crusading in part began as a result of papal reflections on the wars in Spain, it seems appropriate to examine the process of later medieval development there. Ferdinand of Antequera's accession to the crown of Aragon and his retention of the regency in Castile guaranteed peace between these two states, which was a great benefit to his new subjects. He pursued a cautious policy, attempting to foster trade through treaties with North Africa and Egypt and to restore the position of Catalonia in the western Mediterranean. Alfonso V (1416–58) continued the peaceful policy of his father towards Castile, where he and his brothers were major landowners, reaffirmed the Aragonese position in Sicily and tried to drive Genoa from Sardinia. But from 1430 onwards he was seeking the succession in Naples where he faced opposition from the Angevin, Rêné of Naples, who enjoyed French and papal support. The complex war in Italy which resulted did not end with Alfonso's seizure of Naples in 1444 because his position remained precarious, though he succeeded in setting his son, Ferdinand I (1458–90) on the throne of Naples. Alfonso sought to improve Catalan trade with Egypt by a treaty of 1430 with the Mamluks. He was fond of great gestures, negotiating for a joint attack on Egypt with the ruler of Abyssinia, the alleged 'Prester John', in 1450. He sometimes spoke of a crusade against the Ottomans, but did nothing to prevent the fall of Constantinople in 1453. As a result of his Italian ambitions Alfonso was frequently absent from Aragon and constantly demanded heavy taxes. Yet of all his Spanish lands only Valencia, which had close trading relations with Sicily, really profited from the war. The various *Cortes* took advantage of his preoccupations to demand privileges, while in Catalonia the bitterness between the *Biga* and *Busca* could not be resolved in the absence of the king. In the reign of his brother, Juan II (1458–79), discontent exploded into civil war. In this conflict the strong centralist tendencies of the house of Trastarama came into head-on collision with the contractualist (*pactista*) ideas of the high aristocracy. The war in Catalonia drew in French, Castilian and Portuguese intervention. Juan II was eventually triumphant over his many rivals, but the prosperity of Catalonia was ruined and the entire position of the crown of Aragon compromised by concessions to the nobility and cities.

The course of events in Castile was not so very different. There, a circle of about 15 families, amongst whom the Trastamara family were prominent, dominated the countryside and, increasingly, the cities. Juan II (1406–54) was a minor until 1419 and during this period grants to the great nobles were frequent and lavish. Thereafter the king was largely a nonentity and by 1430 power had fallen to his minister, Alavaro de Luna, who pursued a consistent centralising policy. In response the nobles demanded the right to control the royal council, creating a sort of corporatist state built around the major dynasties. There ensued a series of civil wars in which the crown was never strong enough and the nobles never united enough to dominate, though in 1453 a conspiracy killed Luna. Prominent amongst the rebels was the house of Trastamara, including Juan II of Aragon who remained a great landowner in Castile. In his periods of ascendancy Luna tried to exploit divisions in Granada and so to unite the realm behind the king, but his substantial gains at Granadan expense were soon lost as Castile dissolved into civil wars. Henry IV (1454–74) was a man of gentle disposition and dominated by his favourites, Villena and Beltrán, the latter vulgarly alleged to be the true father of Henry's daughter and heir, Joanna. In these circumstances many of the nobles rallied around the king's half-sister, Isabella, who, in 1469, married Ferdinand, son and heir of Juan II of Aragon. Henry IV had arranged that Afonso V of Portugal (1438–81) should be the protector of Joanna, but Afonso failed to secure support in Castile and by 1479 was forced to bow out of the arena opening the way for the rule of Isabella (1479–1504) and Ferdinand (1479–1516) and the union of the realms of Castile and Aragon.

The rule of Ferdinand and Isabella is commonly seen as marking a new start in the history of a unified Spain and even the point at which 'the history of medieval Spain comes to an end'.[1] This is hindsight: the marriage produced one of those personal unions so characteristic of late medieval Europe, and it might, like many others, not have endured. Its key achievement, the seizure of Granada was clearly the continuation of the crusading tradition. Throughout the fifteenth century the papacy offered considerable incentives for the crusade in Spain. There was much preaching and control of the Orders of Santiago and Calatrava was granted to Juan II and Henry IV. After the fall of Constantinople the pope extended to Spain all the privileges of the anti-Ottoman crusade. This seems to have helped to create a strong mood in favour of attacks on Granada and to have strengthened feeling against *convivencia*. The rebel nobles found it expedient to criticise Henry IV for failing to attack Granada, though this was blatantly unfair, because in 1462 the king had captured Archidona and Gibraltar in a highly successful campaign. In these circumstances Isabella and Ferdinand's decision to attack Granada can be seen as a politic attempt to consolidate their fragile rule and to unleash the Inquisition upon the *conversos* whose loyalty to Christianity was placed in doubt by the new mood. Moreover, although it generally paid tribute, Granada did not hesitate to take the offensive when the opportunity presented itself and in 1481 seized the city of Zahara. This seemed all the more dangerous in that in 1480 the Ottomans had captured and held Otranto and there was genuine fear that they could use Granada for a similar incursion, all the more keenly felt in that Ferdinand, as king of Aragon, ruled Sicily. The royal offensive against Granada began after an unexpectedly successful raid there by the count of Cádiz in 1481. At first progress was slow. However, in 1483 a succession dispute in the ruling Nasrid family of Granada created favourable circumstances, though resistance was ferocious because Islamic fervour responded to Christian aggression. Castile

1 W. T. Waugh, *A History of Europe 1378–1494* (London: Methuen, 1932), 395.

had to mobilise enormous resources to maintain a war which turned on a series of large-scale sieges of cities and fortresses with modern fortifications. An army of 50,000 was needed for the siege of Baza in 1489, costing an estimated 50,000 *marvedis*. This exhausting effort was strongly supported by crusading taxes on the Church imposed in conjunction with the papacy which also aggressively sold crusade indulgences. Even so, it was not until 1492 that Granada finally surrendered on terms. This triumph was followed by decrees in 1492 which expelled all Jews from Castile and Aragon and stepped up pressure on the Moors to convert, provoking a series of rebellions. In 1501 and 1502 the Moors of Castile were offered a choice of expulsion or conversion, though those of Aragon maintained their rights until 1525. Suspicion of the *conversos* resulted in the Inquisition being unleashed upon their communities until, in 1609–14 all *Moriscos* were expelled from the Iberian peninsula.

It is doubtful whether Castile-Aragon would have been able to destroy Granada had not leading ecclesiastics mobilised opinion in favour of the war. The enormous sums raised by the Church and papacy were absolutely vital to the success of the conquest. Significantly, there was no substantial foreign participation in the fighting, though small numbers of North Europeans were occasionally present. This was the crusade harnessed by the monarchy for the business of state-building. In the process the kings usurped through custom the right to tax the Church. Ultimately the victory was made possible by conditions in the Islamic world. Divisions in the ruling Nasrid dynasty enabled the Spaniards to back one candidate for the succession against the other. Granada had traditionally guarded its independence by playing off Castile against the Marinids. However, their rule in North Africa had effectively ended by 1420. The Wattasids and others were vying for control of the region, but they were badly distracted by Portuguese naval assaults on the Mauretanian coast. Spain was as yet beyond the reach of the Ottomans who, in any case, were deeply involved in war against the Mamluk regime in Egypt. However, Granada was formidable and would not have been overcome, even with all these advantages if the whole enterprise had not been skilfully organised by Ferdinand and Isabella. They raised troops from the nobles, the Church, cities and Military Orders in the traditional way, but the creation and support of such big armies over 10 years of constant warfare was a triumph of organisation, validating and strengthening the apparatus of central government which was being created. The monarchy also established a mighty artillery and units of foot equipped with handguns. This was the new face of war which was emerging all over Europe and the 'Catholic Kings' were clearly in touch with the latest military technology. Above all, they nurtured a sense of purpose and discipline amongst their subjects which sustained an enormous effort. The crusading impulse was a vital factor in this, but it was firmly harnessed to the chariot of the monarchical state.

But this was not a simple matter of cold calculation of state interest. The capture of Granada seems to have engendered a mood of immense spiritual exaltation in Spain. Indeed, Columbus, though himself Genoese, seems to have been infected by a spirit of millennial expectation which informed his projected voyage westwards to what he supposed would be the 'Indies'. Ferdinand and Isabella launched a great campaign to seize the North African coast in which they spoke of the prospect of liberating Jerusalem. Their attacks were presented as crusades and enjoyed the support of the papacy which facilitated taxation of the Church. By 1525 a series of major cities had been captured along the North African littoral, notably Mers-el-Kebir in 1505 and Tripoli in 1510, and Algiers had become a vassal city. These assaults on North Africa were clearly a continuation of the *reconquista* and satisfied the crusading fervour aroused in Castile by the victory over Granada. Indeed, they replicated earlier assaults and were useful to Castile's security. The crown of Aragon ruled Sicily, and as a result their nobles and merchants also had a strong interest in the subjugation of North Africa because this would protect the rich trade of the western Mediterranean. Clearly, the North African crusade helped to consolidate the monarchy. A similar process was already under way in Portugal. The crusade which captured Ceuta in 1415 helped legitimise Joao's seizure of the throne and reinforced an active diplomacy which established him as a respected ruling figure and true Christian king. It was, therefore, worth the enormous financial effort of retaining this foothold. One beneficial effect of these conquests was to hamper any Islamic revival, especially one stimulated by the Ottomans. More prosaically, possession of these ports was useful to trade through the Gibraltar Straits and offered access to the trans-Saharan trade in slaves and gold which was carried by Muslim merchants. Genoa, with its trading communities in Spain and Portugal, was anxious to profit from this expansion into North Africa.

Much the same combination of interests motivated Portuguese and Castilian promotion of Atlantic exploration. The Straits of Gibraltar had become a great highway of trade between Northern and Southern Europe and this increased knowledge of Africa. In the eleventh century the Almohads had destroyed the 'Empire of Ghana' in West Africa and facilitated the growth of Muslim Empires, like Mali, in the area. It was, therefore, Muslim merchants who controlled the gold and slave trade of West Africa across the Sahara, and knowledge of this area was spread through their constant contacts with western traders. In the 'Catalan Atlas' of 1375 sub-Saharan Africa is dominated by the figure of Mansa Musa (c.1312–37) ruler of Mali. His spectacular pilgrimage to Mecca in 1324 so impressed Muslims that fabulous stories about him reached Europe. In the late thirteenth century Islam had been driven back into Granada and this opened the way for Mediterranean merchants, especially the Genoese, to trade regularly with Northern Europe. This in turn brought new knowledge of the eastern Atlantic and its islands. At the same time the Mongol dominion in Central Asia spread information about the Far East. It was probably as a result of this new information about the world that in 1291 the Genoese Vivaldi brothers set off down the coast of West Africa to reach the 'Indies', though they were never heard of again.

More importantly, sailors came to know about the Atlantic archipelagos, partly from the geographic knowledge of ancient times and partly from ships driven out into the Atlantic as they clawed their way to Northern Europe or down the Saharan coast. It is in this sense that French historians have spoken of the 'Mediterranean Atlantic' because knowledge of it was a by-product of intense trading patterns around the Gibraltar Strait. In 1342 a Majorcan expedition sent out to seize the Canaries failed. In 1344–45 Pope Clement VI sponsored an expedition with full crusading privileges to these same islands by a Castilian, Luis de Cerda, but nothing came of it. However, merchants and fisherman from Spain, Genoa and even Northern European powers, continued to explore the archipelago and churchmen were anxious to convert the native population. By the 1370s Portuguese and Castilian traders were disputing control of the islands, but the decisive step was the expedition to the Canaries of 1402, led by two Frenchmen, Jean de Bethencourt and Gadifer de la Salle. Both these men had served in Louis de Bourbon's 1390 expedition to Mahdiya and this may have given them knowledge of the 'River of Gold' and the profitable West African slave-trade. The expedition was in contact with Seville merchants, and the difficulties of support from France probably led to the decision to accept Castilian overlordship, though this was bitterly contested by the Portuguese. It was only in 1479 after a long three-cornered struggle involving the native population, which held the larger islands, that the two monarchies resolved their quarrel. This enabled Castile to take over the whole archipelago with Grand Canary falling in 1483, Palma in 1491 and Tenerife in 1495. The earlier explorations which had revealed the existence of islands in the Atlantic triggered a scramble for the Atlantic. For Spain and Portugal it was a continuation of the *Reconquista*, and just as competitive as that process had been. Henry the Navigator, a prince of the royal house of Portugal, failed to seize the Canaries, but he certainly helped to establish Portuguese control elsewhere in the Atlantic. Madeira and the Azores had been known in the fourteenth century, but Portugal took the former about 1420 and the latter from 1432. Madeira would become a very important source of sugar, a business financed by Genoese traders in Portugal. The Cape Verde Isles, first seen in 1444 were gradually controlled after 1460.

But important as the archipelagos were, the main thrust of Portuguese exploration was along the African coast. Henry the Navigator is often regarded as its driving force but his connection with the men who actually sailed the ships is often uncertain and his brother Pedro seems to have had just as much influence. Henry maintained a circle of intellectuals at his court in the modern 'Renaissance' style and enjoyed their flattery. One of them, Azurara, burnished his memory with a sycophantic biography which created his image as 'the Navigator'. But Henry stands in a much older tradition. He may well have hoped, like many younger sons of royalty, to create for himself a new kingdom, perhaps in the Canaries or even in some far-off and hoped for archipelago. He was also a conventional prince of his age, obsessed with the desire to cut a chivalric figure and anxious to support crusades against Islam, for which reason he strongly supported Portugal's North African ambitions. A series of Papal Bulls praised prince Henry and granted Portugal sole rights to trade in Africa and the 'Indies' and referred specifically to the hope of alliance against Islam with 'Prester John' whose realm was now believed to be in a vaguely perceived zone below Egypt. So Henry had a rather typically aristocratic mix of chivalric and religious reasons for interest in exploration. He was also desperately short of money and may well have been, for this reason, attracted by tales of the 'River of Gold'. But just how much impact he had on others beyond his circle is doubtful. After his death in 1460 Portugal came to terms over the Canaries and the tempo of exploration down the African coast picked up enormously. In that year the Portuguese had reached Sierra Leone. In 1470–75 they explored the Gulf of Guinea, and in 1483 Diogo Cão reached the Congo river. Joao II (1481–95) pressed on the process of discovery, encouraged by the flow of gold and the slaves from the trading posts and forts established on the West African littoral. At the same time his orders to his captains made clear his desire to tap into the spice-trade by circumnavigating Africa. But the king was also particularly anxious to find the land of 'Prester John' and this formed part of his instruction to Bartholemew Diaz who in 1488 rounded the Cape of Good Hope, opening the way for the celebrated journey of Vasco da Gama, who, in 1497–99, rounded the Cape, reached Calcutta and returned to Portugal. This remarkable progress towards the 'Indies' probably explains why in 1484 Columbus finally felt that he had no chance of persuading the Portuguese court to support his project to reach the 'Indies' by a westward route.

Expansionism and the growth of trade stimulated the development of shipping and knowledge of navigation. In the thirteenth century *portolani*, collections of sailing directions, began to be written down. The sand-glass for measuring time made possible traverse-tables which provided estimates of time for travelling between set points. Because box-compass were available compass-roses indicating the bearings of one destination from another began to be recorded on charts. The astrolabe enabled navigators to take accurate bearings on the sun and stars and by the end of the fifteenth century they were producing tables of declination. In Northern Europe dangerous currents and tides were a much greater issue than in the Mediterranean and led to detailed records of sailing conditions. We should not exaggerate the impact of these innovations. They had grave limitations, not least because the distinction between magnetic and true north was not yet recognised. Latitude could only be approximately calculated and there was no method of working out longitude until the eighteenth century. Most sailors still relied on dead-reckoning, experience and luck to find their way but the new methods were making an impact. Academic and practical knowledge of the world at large were starting to come together. The *mappa mundi* were productions of the clerical elite of the twelfth and thirteenth centuries, attempts to depict the world based on biblical and classical knowledge. For most of the Middle Ages the finest source of classical geographical knowledge, Ptolemy's *Geography*, was not known and its rediscovery in the early fifteenth century was a great stimulus. However, Ptolemy believed that what would later be called the Indian Ocean was landlocked, and therefore inaccessible by way of Africa. This notion ceased to have great authority as progress was made down the African coast. Pragmatic knowledge gained by seafarers and merchants was growing rapidly and making a substantial impact on intellectuals and their ways of looking at the world. In the fourteenth century the intelligentsia of Christendom began to incorporate detail learned from the actual experience of mariners. The crusading enthusiast, Marino Sanudo produced a remarkable series of charts to support his ideas for new crusades in his *Book of the Secrets of the Faithful of the Cross*, while Majorca and Genoa, both localities with a strong interest in the 'Mediterranean Atlantic', began to produce splendid maps. The 'Catalan Atlas' of 1375 incorporated much of the new knowledge of the world, though it was really a splendid *mappa mundi*. What it portrays is the uneasy subsistence of traditional conceptions of the world based on classical and biblical knowledge with the growing knowledge of new worlds. But in such paradoxes lay a world in flux, with rumours of riches and possible alliances against the infidel tempting bold spirits to ever-greater risks.

Exploration on this scale was only possible because new types of ships were available. The Vivaldi brothers set off down the African coast at the end of the thirteenth century in galleys. These ships, with their oars and lateen sails, were well adapted to Mediterranean conditions. The Venetians relied heavily upon them, despite their limited carrying capacity, because they traded almost entirely across the inland sea and specialised in high-value low-bulk commodities like spices. But Genoa and Catalonia preferred to use large round ships with square sails because they were increasingly carrying bulk commodities: alum for the wool industries of England and Flanders, and Moroccan grain on which Barcelona depended. Moreover, an increasing amount of their trade went through the Gibraltar Strait into the Atlantic where superior sailing qualities were important. The result was that they relied upon the *coche*, a development of the northern 'cog' which was often called the carrack. These ships became more and more complex. By the fifteenth century a three-masted type with sophisticated rigging was in general usage. In the Mediterranean there was a preference for carvel-building in which the planking of the hull was laid onto frames, and this gradually replaced the traditional clinker-building or 'shell-first' method used in the north under which the planks were connected one to another before a frame was inserted. The differences between these two methods were not immense because frames could be inserted at various stages in clinker construction. The Mediterranean method became dominant because it was more suited to the construction of large ships and its triumph is witness to the integration of the economies of Northern and Southern Europe. The countries of the Atlantic coast became especially familiar with southern methods because during the 'Hundred Years War' the French hired Catalan ships whose effectiveness was noted and copied by the English and others. Bigger ships needed proper decks, accommodation, and anchors, while the cog, with its vertical stern, lent itself to the development of the rudder. Many types of ship emerged from this pattern of development, amongst which the carrack was the biggest. But of special interest were the smaller and very seaworthy caravels (or carvels), which was usually in England associated with Spain and Portugal. The caravel was very seaworthy and manoeuvrable. It was the staple vessel which the Portuguese used in their journeys around Africa, and two of Columbus' three ships were caravels. Without this product of the interaction between Mediterranean and Atlantic maritime traditions, the age of discovery would hardly have been possible. The single European economy, created largely by the ambitions of merchants, brought together the mapping techniques and maritime technologies of Northern Europe and the Mediterranean. In this sense the drive into the Atlantic was the logical outcome of the growth of a single economy in the thirteenth century. But this knowledge and technology was at the service of powerful states who could exploit it.

Columbus was able to press his ideas on the Castilian Court because he was tapping into the enthusiasm for Atlantic exploration which gripped Europeans as more and more islands and archipelagos came to light. He was as deeply moved as any of his notable contemporaries by the heady prospect of a reconquest of the Islamic lands and by the hope of taking them in the rear by enlisting supposed oriental Christians. But his conviction that this could best be done by sailing westwards owed a great deal to the new geographic speculations and to the excitement engendered by Castilian and Portuguese discoveries in the Atlantic. It is possible that he and others had some knowledge of the Viking expansion into the North Atlantic or the voyages of Irish monks like St Brendan because contemporary maps occasionally appear to show islands in this general area, though these often reflected classical ideas and speculations. In 1496 a Bristol-based Italian, John Cabot, sailed to Newfoundland. It is likely that he was following in the steps of English and other fishermen who had been fishing the Grand Banks off that island and passing via Iceland despite the prohibitions of the Danish crown. However, there is nothing to suggest that Columbus was inspired by the discovery of Vinland and, indeed, it was a long time before anyone recognised that a New World had been discovered. In his attempts to persuade both the Portuguese and the Castilians Columbus emphasised not only the strategic possibilities for the war against Islam but also the prospects for exploiting the riches of the Orient; he was undoubtedly helped in this by knowledge of the profits the Portuguese were making from their outposts in Africa. He could count on considerable help from the important Genoese trading community in Seville who helped to finance his journey. But in the end it was the monarchs of Castile and Aragon who gave him their support. His first journey in 1492 was followed by another in 1493, and two more before his death in obscurity in 1506. Columbus' expeditions brought few benefits, but Spain claimed the islands he seized and very quickly sought to recoup its investment. The speed with which things then happened was amazing. In 1499 Venezuela was reached and the Amazon, assumed to be the Ganges, was discovered. The first permanent settlement in South America was established in 1505 and in 1513 occurred the first sighting of the Pacific Ocean and discovery of Florida. Three years later Juan Diaz de Solis reached the River Plate and in 1519–22 a Portuguese expedition supported by the Spanish King and Emperor Charles V (1516–56) under Magellan made the first circumnavigation of the globe. But it was with Cortes' overthrow of the Aztec Empire in 1519 that the Spanish investment really began to pay off. Cortes was subsequently Captain-General of New Spain in 1522, only to die in obscurity. In 1539 new sources of wealth opened up as Pizzaro attacked the Incas of Peru. The enormous wealth garnered from the New World made Spain, a relatively poor country, the greatest power in Europe. The explorers and conquistadors were certainly inspired by deep religious conviction and the repeated papal assurances that they were doing God's will by bringing Christianity to benighted and inferior pagan peoples. The continuing the tradition of the *reconquista* lived in them and, indeed, the next generation who set out determinedly to convert the native peoples. In the words of the Franciscan Geronimo de Mendieta (1525–1604):

> As Ferdinand and Isabella were granted the mission of beginning to extirpate those three diabolical squadrons, perfidious Judaism, false Mohammedanism and blind idolatry, along with the fourth squadron of the heretics whose remedy and medicine is the Holy Inquisition, in like manner the business of completing this task has been reserved for their royal successors; so that as Ferdinand and Isabella cleansed Spain of these wicked sects, in like manner their royal descendants will accomplish the universal destruction of these sects throughout the whole world and the final conversion of all the people of the earth to the bosom of the church.[2]

At first sight the conquistadors look much like earlier adventurers, such as Robert Guisard in South Italy, but the significant difference was that they attained their fame and fortune by service to a monarchical state which often repaid them poorly. Moreover, it is easy to exaggerate the continuity between the Catholic fervour of the Middle Ages and that of Mendieta. He was inspired by a new and instructed Catholicism, the product of the Tridentine reform and saw the past through this prism. Even the Inquisition, to which he referred with such enthusiasm, was not the institution established in the thirteenth century, but a new and more efficient version which was effectively an arm of the Spanish state.

With the benefit of hindsight it is all too easy to scorn the Portuguese for dismissing Columbus and his ideas in 1484, but in fact their expansion was just as fast as that of their Hispanic neighbours and pregnant with economic importance. The Portuguese were very determined to break the Arab and Indian Muslim monopoly of the rich trade in spices and other luxury goods of the Orient which passed from India and the 'Spice Islands' (the Indonesian archipelago) to Iraq via the Straits of Hormuz, and to Egypt via the Red Sea. They were able to do this, and to do it very quickly, because they were entering a vast area in which there was no

---

2 P.po-Chia Hsia, *The World of Catholic Renewal* (Cambridge: Cambridge University Press, 1998), 165; I owe this reference to my colleague John Spurr.

paramount power. The East African coast was dominated by Muslim cities whose internecine quarrels enabled the Portuguese to get a foothold. Mamluk Egypt was becoming internally unstable and distracted by its violent confrontation with the Ottomans. In Persia the Safavid dynasty was emerging, also in conflict with the Ottomans. India was divided between Muslim principalities and a number of Hindu States amongst which the empire of Vijayanagar in the south was the most important. Indo-China was a mass of contending states and peoples amongst whom the Vietnamese were emerging as dominant, while Malaya and Indonesia were divided amongst small states. Everywhere the richest trade was in the hands of Muslims. China, under the Ming dynasty, was little concerned with events to its west.

The Portuguese, like the Spanish, were fortified by papal assurances about the righteousness of rule over pagans and inspired by the spirit of crusade against the infidel, as well as by a strong feeling that great wealth was there to be taken. Their ships were certainly equipped with canon and other gunpowder weapons, but so were those of their Islamic enemies. However, their carracks were bigger and heavier than anything in the Indian Ocean. They could carry more guns and men than the ships of their enemies and this enabled them to sustain combat much more effectively. In 1509 an Islamic fleet was destroyed off Diu in Gujarat and this opened the way for the remarkable Afonso de Albuquerque who captured Goa in 1510, then sealed the Persian Gulf by seizing Ormuz in 1515. The taking of Malacca in 1519 established an important naval base in the 'Spice Islands' and enabled the Portuguese to dominate this vital trade. Their control was limited. They could not blockade such a vast area and they failed to close the Red Sea so that Egypt continued to be an important centre for the spice trade. To the east the Portuguese were decisively defeated by Chinese fleets in 1520 and 1521, though by 1557 they had established Macao as an important trading centre with China. Portugal was a small and poor country with a population approaching 1.5 million. Sustaining this huge empire was an enormous strain, though the monarchy and the great merchants profited enormously. There was a constant shortage of manpower, and Portuguese carracks were commonly crewed by Indian and other Asiatic sailors with Portuguese officers, gunners and specialists. A vast trade grew up around the outposts of this empire: the gold of Guinea and other parts of Africa and of Sumatra; African slaves; spices and above all pepper from Indonesia; cotton textiles from India; gold, silk and porcelain from Macao, the Portuguese base in South China. There were grave threats. They needed to conciliate Safavid Persia and, therefore, to open the straits of Hormuz to its traders because the Ottomans were a menace. Because they had not closed the Red Sea Venice continued to be the chief supplier of spices to Europe via Alexandria. In 1571 an alliance between the Muslims of North India and Egypt threatened the very existence of their empire. But the Portuguese were very determined and hung on to almost all their outposts.

Moreover, Portugal was not excluded from the New World. The Portuguese crown had contested Spanish possession of the lands discovered by Columbus on the grounds that they were part of the Azores. As so often in disputes between Iberian powers the matter was put before the pope and Alexander VI (1492–1503) confirmed everything west of the Azores to the Spanish crown. However, by the Treaty of Tordesillas of 1494 Spain agreed to the line being drawn far to the west. As a result, when in 1500 Pedro Alvarez Cabral's fleet en route for the Indies claimed Brazil for the crown of Portugal there was a vast territorial accession which Spain reluctantly endorsed only in 1529 by the Treaty of Zaragoza, which also confirmed the Portuguese monopoly of the spice trade. Brazil became important when it was discovered that sugar would grow there. This stimulated the Portuguese to use Africa, and especially Angola, as a source of slaves to work the new plantations. The empire was a great strain upon tiny Portugal, many of whose people emigrated to Brazil or perished in the unhealthy climates of the Orient. The wealth of the empire was dissipated by the costs of holding it, while its profits fell into the hands of only a few. So short was the country of labour that slaves had to be imported to prop up the economy. King Sebastian (1557–78) was obsessed with the idea of a great crusade to conquer North Africa and fearful of Ottoman domination in the area. He was killed at the battle of Alcazar-Kebir in Morocco in 1578, opening the way for Philip II of Spain (1556–98) to absorb Portugal. Sebastian's fate in a highly unpopular attempt to conquer Morocco is a reminder that the spirit of crusade was not dead in sixteenth-century Europe.

There is no doubt that the enormous European expansion of the 'Age of the Discoveries' was rooted in the medieval experience. The very motives of the discoverers reflected not just universal factors like greed and opportunism, but quite specifically medieval ideas of expanding the Christendom and crusading against heretics and Muslims. The sixteenth century falls within the crusading age, as the example of Sebastian of Portugal shows. However, the expansionism also represented something new. Medieval expansionism was rooted in aristocratic ambition, both personal and dynastic, and it happened because the 'Catholic Core' was surrounded by weaker and less developed peoples, some of whose elites were happy to emulate their more successful neighbours. Even the rival centres of power like Byzantium and Islam were fragmented and vulnerable at particular moments. These circumstances changed radically. Islam was taken over by the Turks who strengthened it, while the 'Byzantine Commonwealth', despite its political weaknesses, resisted the power of Rome. In this changing political context the individualistic aristocratic expansionism which had carried members of the house of Boulogne to rule over the Mesopotamian principality of Edessa and the kingdom of Jerusalem, was no longer practical. The great effort by the popes to capitalise upon this expansionism by creating a Catholic army of God which would give a political dimension to the religious and cultural unity over which they presided ultimately failed. Crusading was annexed to the newly emerging monarchical states. There was no single point at which the change was apparent but as early as the reign of St Louis crusading had become entangled with the interests of the French monarchy and by the reign of the Emperor Charles V (1519–56) it was very evidently a force at the service of the state.

The expansionism of late medieval Europe was fundamentally different from that which had gone before. It was no longer individualistic, but dominated by state organisations. Da Gama, Columbus, Cortes and the rest were swashbucklers as individuals, but they acted in the service of the state and profited from its operations. Their fortunes as individuals were caught up with those of the wider political community. And this for very good reason. It is very evident that the new expansion was not driven by simple mercantile ambition. Venice and Genoa were not at the spearhead of the drive across the Atlantic nor the ruthless destruction of Arab sea-power in the Indian Ocean. The new enterprises required enormous resources and sustained application of power which Genoa certainly could not afford – while Venice was deeply enmeshed in wars in the inland sea. Only the new states of Europe could support this kind of effort – and then only with great difficulty, for we must not exaggerate the competence of the early modern state. Gunpowder weapons gave Europeans some advantages over the peoples whom they encountered. Spain faced only primitive peoples in the New World for whom guns, armour and even horses were a novelty. But the Portuguese faced enemies with more or less equal firepower. The technology which gave the Portuguese their edge was the quality and size of their ships. Only the Chinese Junks could rival them, but China was largely uninterested in the westerners. This maritime technology enabled Europeans to take advantage of the preoccupations of Islam, divided between three competing forces, Ottomans, Mamluks and Safavids, but although they had fulfilled the dream of outflanking their enemy, the effort was so great for the Portuguese that it made little difference to the intensifying struggle in the Mediterranean and the Danube valley. In the face of huge costs the spirit of crusade was abandoned in favour of profit. By contrast, the Spanish adventures in the New World yielded a great booty which was partly expended in religious wars in the Mediterranean and elsewhere. But if Spain and Portugal were exploring actual New Worlds, the process of change elsewhere in Europe was creating novelties of a different kind.

It was ironic that Murad II should have won such a great victory over the 'Crusade of Varna' because he was not a warmonger, and his leading Vizier, Halil Djandarli, enjoyed the derisory nickname, 'Companion of the Infidel'. The reorganisation of the Ottoman Sultanate was designed to transform it into a settled Islamic state, and the revival of the economy encouraged by the order and stability which it imposed. However, the *sipahis* had an endless thirst for *timars* and this was encouraged by the *ghazi* spirit and the existence of political fragmentation on the western frontier. The death of Ladislas III created a succession crisis in Hungary, Bohemia and Poland-Lithuania. Ladislas V Postmumous (1440/44–57) was a child for whom the barons of Hungary appointed John Hunyadi as regent. When Ladislas died the choice of the Hungarian nobles fell upon John Hunyadi's son Matthias Corvinus (1458–90) as king. In Bohemia the minority of Ladislas V was the catalyst for another round of religious disputes which had a national dimension because the Germans were strictly orthodox while the native aristocracy remained devoted to utraquism. As a result, after Ladislas' death George of Podiebrand, Regent since 1451, was elected king (1458–71). His election was far from unanimous and he was forced to recognise Wladislaw II (1471–1516), son of Casimir IV of Poland (1446–92), as his successor, though this was contested by Matthias Corvinus who had to be bought off in 1478 by substantial territorial concessions. In Poland the nobles chose Ladislas III's brother, Casimir IV who managed the delicate task of keeping Poles and Lithuanians, and even many Orthodox Russians, within his government, and to win a great victory over the Teutonic knights. In 1440 the Hapsburg duke of Styria was elected King of the Romans and, became emperor in 1452 as Frederick III (1440–86). He united the Hapsburg lands and established a family claim to the thrones of both Hungary and Bohemia, but for the most part he was ineffectual as ruler of Germany. His support for Poland and Bohemia against Matthias Corvinus led ultimately to a Hungarian invasion of Austria which captured Vienna and reduced the Emperor to beggary. Further west France expelled the English from her soil after the battle of Castillon in 1453, bringing the 'Hundred Years War' to an end. But Charles VII (1422–61) and Louis XI (1461–83) were soon absorbed in a struggle with the restless duchy of Burgundy. England, weakened by losses in France, soon dissolved into the conflicts known as the 'Wars of the Roses'.

In these circumstances it is hardly surprising that the new Sultan, Mehmed II (1451–81), turned against Constantinople. The city had survived partly by manipulating forces within the Ottoman court, and at the time of Mehmed's accession was sheltering Orhan, his rival for the throne. Its other resources were the various interested foreign powers, notably the papacy, the Knights of St John, the Venetians and the Genoese. But the popes always demanded that the Greek Church accept their authority and this notion of union had proved unacceptable across the crusading period despite the obvious political need of the empire for the support which it could, potentially, bring. In 1439 the Byzantine Emperor John VIII (1425–48) agreed an act of union at Florence but this merely precipitated such bitter disputes in the Greek Church that the emperor found it hard to find a Patriarch who would subscribe to it. By the time the first uniate mass was celebrated in the Church of the Holy Wisdom at Constantinople on 12 December 1452 it was only too clear that Mehmed II was taking advantage of favourable circumstances to attack the city. Despite all the best efforts of the pope, little help reached the city. The Venetians, preoccupied by war in Italy, sent some galleys and individual Venetian captains stayed in the city and fought bravely, while a Genoese, Giovanni Longo, brought a strong company and took command of the walls. However, for the most part the Genoese stayed in their suburb of Pera on the northern bank of the Golden Horn and asserted an uneasy neutrality. These forces, together with some Catalans, a few volunteers, and the western ships anchored in the Golden Horn, constituted a small enough force against the enormous army and fleet which the Ottomans now raised. The siege was a great undertaking for the Sultan and necessitated careful logistic and political preparations. By August 1452 a new castle had been built and equipped with canon to cut the Bosphorus at Boghaz-kesen. The army was perhaps 80,000 strong, and its supply-lines reached across the Ottoman lands. It was supported by well over 100 ships. In addition, the army had the latest gunpowder weapons, notably huge canons which were specially cast, apparently by a Hungarian engineer. It is difficult to estimate the number of defenders, but 8,000 is the usually accepted figure. The Golden Horn was sealed with a great chain, so that the city could not be attacked from that direction, while the outer western walls were formidable. The success of the siege could not, therefore, be guaranteed and undertaking it was a risk for Mehmed. Failure could be a signal to the restless Turkish princes of Asia Minor to rebel, while the pretender, Orhan, might well be able to tap into a mood of disillusion after the failure of such an immense effort. Early assaults failed, but on 21 April the Turks carried elements of their fleet across the land to the north down to the Golden Horn. The failure of the Venetians and the Genoese to agree delayed a plan to fire these ships and when it did get underway they were well protected by Turkish guns. The siege, begun on 2 April 1453, ended in a terrible sack of the city after the Turks broke through in the early morning of 29 May.

The capture of Constantinople enormously strengthened Mehemed's position and reinforced his devotion to expansionism, although he was careful to pursue a generally tolerant policy towards non-Muslims. The Greeks were organised as a *millet*, a largely autonomous confessional group ruled by the Patriarch of Constantinople, and this was later extended to Jews and Armenians. The Sultan also set in train a systematisation of government and fostered trade, making peace in 1454 with the Venetians. They, and the Genoese, who had played a very equivocal role in the defence of Constantinople, soon agreed to pay taxes to the new master on the Bosphorus. By 1455 Mehmed had absorbed Serbia and checked the aggressions of Skander Bey (Scanderberg), the defiant despot of Albania. In 1456 a great attack was launched on Belgrade which was clearly a prelude to the destruction of Hungary whose king, Ladislas V, fled to Austria. But the papacy recognised the appalling threat which the Ottomans posed and issued appeals for a crusade, pointing out bluntly that the Turks on the Adriatic threatened all Christendom. At the same time the papacy bent itself to raising large sums of money for a strategy which consisted of sending aid to Hungary while raising a fleet to harass the Ottomans in the Aegean and the Straits. Despite the flight of Ladislas V, John Hunyadi was persuaded to offer resistance supported by the remarkable Franciscan friar, John of Capistrano. The Hungarian crusaders were supported by a polyglot force drawn mainly from, the Balkans, and some Austrians and Poles, and they succeeded, against all expectation, in raising Mehmed's siege of Belgrade in July of 1456, though at the cost of the deaths of John of Capistrano and Hunyadi. It was a remarkable success, but the papal fleet accomplished little and the Ottomans were soon able to renew their advance. Greece had long been divided between the Venetians, who held Negroponte and some key ports, the Latin settlers in southern Greece, amongst whom Acciaioli of Athens were pre-eminent, and the Despotate of the Morea held by the Greek noble family of the family of the Palaeologi. Their incessant quarrels and the interventions by Catalan and other mercenaries encouraged to go there as a means of ridding Europe of their depredations, made them easy meat for Mehmed when he turned his attention to the area. In 1460 the Ottomans took Athens and destroyed Thomas Palaeologos' Despotate of the Morea. Only a few Venetian ports held out, Modon and Coron until 1500 and Nauplia and Monemvasia until 1540. In 1461 Mehmed extinguished the old Byzantine 'Empire' of Trebizond in Anatolia.

But the papacy persisted in calling for a crusade against the Ottomans, and Pius II (1458–64) tried to call grand assemblies to unite Europe, or at least Italy, against the common enemy. But England and France were preoccupied, and Frederick III had no intention of joining such a risky enterprise. Milan, Florence and Naples protested that a successful crusade would only encourage the domination of the Venetians in Italy. Pius resolved to lead a crusade himself, but died as he was on his way to embark at Ancona and with him any chance of a pan-European crusade, leaving Venice to fight alone. The Venetians clearly wished to reassert their old domination of the Aegean and the nearby waters and at first the war went well for them, but their enemies in Italy took advantage of every slip in their fortunes. In 1470 Mehmed sent a huge army to attack the key Venetian island of Negroponte. To the shock of the garrison the Ottomans sent 300 ships which they used to create a bridge between the mainland, and Negroponte which fell before a Venetian fleet based on Crete could intervene. The Venetians sought alliance with Uzun Hassan whose rebellion threatened the Ottoman hold on Asia Minor, but by 1474 he was crushed. Casimir IV of Lithuania-Poland, Ivan III of Muscovy, the leaders of the Golden Horde and the Crimean Tartars were all disturbed by the scale of Ottoman ambitions and Matthias Corvinus tried to profit from this situation. But the Crimean Tartars became Ottoman allies and the other powers failed to combine effectively against the Ottomans, although Corvinus gained enough time to develop formidable fortresses on his southern frontier. Further west Skander Bey had died in 1468 and the Ottoman conquest of Albania proceeded apace. This enabled Turkish cavalry to raid across Dalmatia and into Friuli, threatening a land attack on Venice itself. In 1479 Venice sued for peace, conceding all her footholds in the northern Aegean and agreeing to pay 10,000 ducats for her trading privileges in the Ottoman lands. In 1480 Mehmed used his command of the Balkans to launch an attack across the Adriatic which captured Otranto. This was a terrible revelation of the vulnerability of Italy, but the Turks had to withdraw when Mehmed died.

The Ottoman victories were a reminder of the limitations of sea-power. Venice could usually defeat the Turkish fleets in battle, but in the lands around the Mediterranean massive military dominance was decisive and once the Ottomans had established a reasonably strong fleet they could make their power tell. The whole position of the western maritime powers was now under threat. Genoese Chios, Hospitaller Rhodes and the Venetian strongholds of the Aegean Islands and Crete were the nodal points which now faced assault. Trade with Istanbul was possible for western merchants, but at a cost. Trade via Tana with the Silk Road was declining as the Mongol domination in central Asia broke up and was effectively terminated by Turkish control of the Bosphorus. As a result, Venice focused on its Alexandrine trade in spices while Genoese interests shifted markedly to the Western Mediterranean and North Africa. Thus Venice alone had a real interest in the Eastern Mediterranean and this was reinforced by its acquisition of Cyprus. The death of its king, John II, in 1458, precipitated a succession crisis. His daughter, Charlotte, was successfully challenged by her illegitimate half-brother who became king as James II (1458–73), in part because he attracted the support of the island's overlords, the Mamluks who, in 1460, sent a fleet to supported him in the civil war. His death in 1473 was quickly followed by that of his son James III in 1474, and his widow, the Venetian Caterina Cornaro handed the island over to her native city with the consent of the Mamluks. Both Crete and Cyprus were colonised by the Venetians and became prosperous, serving as very useful bases for the trade route to Alexandria. Venice was able to exploit Mamluk anxieties about Ottoman power to strengthen its position in Alexandria.

The contrast between the confident expansionism and crusading enthusiasm of the Hispanic powers and the situation in the eastern Mediterranean and the Danube valley is instructive. The rulers of Castile and Portugal had used the crusade as an instrument of state-building. In the process it was, of course, transformed as its institutions became subordinated to royal interests. In Castile the *cruzada* simply became a tax which continued to be levied down to the twentieth century. These dynastic states could easily have fallen apart, but in the event they did not and were able to sustain their development. Their competence should not be exaggerated – as late as 1588 Philip II of Spain (1556–98) appointed Medina Sidonia as Admiral for the 'Great Armada', largely on the grounds that he was rich enough to fund the whole venture. But their monarchies had developed far beyond those of the Danube. The problems of the states of Central Europe were certainly not economic. They had been less touched by the Black Death, and Poland in particular was a major producer and exporter of grain. Nor was it simply difficult to create a united front because of the quarrels between individual rulers. Indeed, quite often dynastic marriages created unions between states. A major problem was that nobilities, though caught up in the operations of the new state structures, were primarily concerned to defend their own narrow and local interests. All over Central Europe Estates demanded privileges, like the Golden Bull in Hungary, and in this they were no more than taking their cue from the Empire where the parts had overwhelmed the whole. This kind of aristocratic particularism was not confined to Central Europe. The various Spanish *Cortes* were just as self-interested while in France the fluctuations of royal power opened the way to the same phenomenon, most notably in the rise of Burgundy which, in the fifteenth century, bade fair to become a new state in its own right. There is no doubt that England managed to establish a strong sense of solidarity under the monarchy, because rulers waged external war to the profit of nobility. When the weakness of Henry VI unleashed a factional struggle amongst the aristocracy it took the form of a fight for control of the state machine rather than a process of fragmentation, though this might have come to the fore if the struggles had not been resolved fairly quickly. In Central Europe aristocratic particularism was much more profound and states much newer. Everywhere the elites were divided between lesser nobles and great magnates whose interests often did not coincide. But in Central Europe the petty nobles were especially numerous and they were not dominated by the great magnates as they were in most of the west. In England, for example, the House of Lords defined the parameters of a small dominant group of noble families around whom the squierarchy of lesser lights clustered. In general about 5 per cent of the population in Poland-Lithuania, Bohemia and Hungary claimed to be noble and the modest fortunes of the overwhelming majority made them determined to hold privileges which could protect their status against change of any kind. In addition, there were the city people, or burghers, but their political development varied from one part of Central Europe to another. Nobles made common cause with them only when they had to and preferred to subjugate them as they subjugated the peasantry. Finally, the Church was sometimes a political force and sometimes not. All these groups were caught up in the new states but not necessarily integrated in any meaningful way.

In Bohemia the central problem was that tensions between Czechs and Germans were made worse by the leanings of the former to Utraquism. Partly as a result of this, aristocratic and burgher privilege was guaranteed by the Diet dominated by these groups which, in effect, became partners of kings in the 'Monarchy of the Estates'.[3] But the Diet was divided into three classes, with the high aristocracy, the knights and the burghers meeting separately but coming together on matters of mutual concern. Their decisions were inscribed in the 'Land Register' and had the force of law, and they even generated their own executive officers distinct from those of the crown. Individual churchmen enjoyed authority under the crown, but they had no corporate presence in the Diet. Ladislas II was himself strongly Catholic, but at the Diet of Kutna Hora in 1485 he was obliged to ratify an agreement to guarantee religious freedom to both Utraquists and Catholics. This created an unstable situation, further exasperated by the birth of the 'Unity of Brethren', a radical group from whom are derived the modern Moravian Brethren. It was probably because of the need to enlist the mass of the population in the religious wars that the Bohemian nobles never imposed upon their peasants the savage oppression so characteristic of Poland and Hungary.

In Hungary Matthias Corvinus proved an adept king who manipulated the nobility skilfully, so that in the later stages of his reign he was able to ignore the Diet which he called together rarely. But his death precipitated a succession crisis in which all the aristocratic resentment of Matthias's autocracy and his standing

---

3 For this phrase, see M. Teich, *Bohemia in History* (Cambridge: Cambridge University Press, 1998), 98.

army emerged. Their choice fell upon Wladislaw II (1471–1516), but Matthias' designated heir and illegitimate son, John Corvinus, retained substantial estates and real power. Moreover, Ladislas had to fight off other pretenders to his throne – Maximilian of Hapsburg and John Albert of Poland. In these circumstances Matthias' conquests in Bohemia and Austria fell away. The new king had to rule Bohemia whose Estates insisted he reside there, so that power in Hungary fell to the greater nobles in the royal council. However, they had to collaborate with the Diet, consisting of a Lower House of petty nobles, and an Upper one of the greater magnates and prelates. An ideology of irresponsible noble power was elaborated by Stephen Werboczy in his *Tripartite* which provided an intellectual justification for aristocratic power and privilege. The cities and, more particularly, the peasants, were stripped of their rights. In the succession struggle Ladislas had lost great resources and the Diet was unwilling to vote adequate taxes. Indeed, the aristocracy as a whole were allowed to retain much taxation in order to maintain their own armed forces. Although these were legally obliged to come to the aid of the monarchy, in practice this merely sanctified private forces and reduced the efficiency of the royal army. The security of the kingdom rested upon maintenance of the frontier fortresses in the south. These costs could only be supported because the papacy, anxious to support its crusading spearpoint, donated substantial funds, and an alliance with Venice in 1500–01 netted 188,000 ducats.

The consequences of this military enfeeblement were that Bosnia and Croatia were placed at hazard and Ottoman raids into Hungary became frequent. In 1514 a crusade was proclaimed in Hungary, much against the wishes of the nobility. It aroused enormous enthusiasm amongst the peasants who joined in great numbers and enjoyed the support of a few petty landowners who were exasperated by the weakness of the realm and the growing Ottoman threat. But most of the aristocracy were alarmed because, in common with the nobles of Poland-Lithuania, they were in the process of imposing more and more severe burdens upon the peasantry and, indeed, reducing them to serfdom. The spectacle of these despised inferiors gathered in arms for a crusade so alarmed the nobles that they demanded that the army disperse. When it did not a civil war erupted in which the crusaders were put down by the private armies of the nobility, which, therefore, emerged from the crisis as the dominant force in the state. Moreover, a succession crisis was looming because many nobles objected to Ladislas' son, Louis II (1516–26). As a result Ladislas agreed the Treaty of Pressburg with the Hapsburg Emperor Maximilian (1486–1519) on 19 July 1515. In return for Maximilian's support, Louis II married his granddaughter Mary, while Sigismund I of Poland (1506–48) was persuaded to acquiesce by the offer of help against the Teutonic Order. The succession of the child Louis merely signalled the continuation of internal power struggles which were complicated by the accidents of personality and considerable hatred of the new king's German advisers. This was dangerous behaviour for a Christian neighbour of the Ottomans. The Sultan Selim (1512–20) was preoccupied by his struggle with Persia and the Mamluks, and Suleyman I 'The Magnificent'

(1520–66) was prepared to renew his truce of 1519, but although the great barons were willing, the nobility as a whole rejected the offer. Suleyman besieged Belgrade and Louis II could do nothing because the divided aristocracy would not provide sufficient forces. The city fell on 29 August 1521. By 1525, despite much financial support from the papacy, the southern barrier fortress line had been seriously breached and the finances of the kingdom were in ruin. The popes did everything they could to help the Hungarians, but the weakness of Hungary was so evident that it seemed beyond assistance, and the powers were preoccupied elsewhere. Indeed, for some time much papal and other aid had been channelled direct to mercenary and other leaders who were actually fighting the Ottomans, avoiding the increasingly decrepit machinery of the Hungarian state. Moreover, the nobles continued to be angry about the Germans at the royal court and accused them of importing the new German heresies into their land and civil war was only avoided when the court won over the Diet of 1526 which crushed the leading plotters. But it was too late. In the spring of 1526 Suleyman invaded Hungary with an army 80,000 strong. The Hungarian royal army could only muster 25,000 and was destroyed at Mohacs on 29 August in a battle which lasted only two hours. King Louis II was killed. Although Hungary was not immediately extinguished because Suleyman had problems elsewhere, it was shattered as the forefront of resistance to the Ottomans and the Danube valley was opened to their attack. The nobility of Hungary had demonstrated what can only be described as a suicidal self-interest.

In Poland under the Jagiellonian dynasty, the crown was formally elective, though the monarchs had substantial resources. Under Casimir IV (1446–92) there was a strengthening of the machinery of government with the appointment of royal bailiffs across the kingdom of Poland and the Grand Duchy of Lithuania. However, Casimir became involved in a long war with the Teutonic Order, and although ultimately victory and the acquisition of Danzig gave him much prestige, it was at the price of internal concessions. After Tannenberg, war between Poland and the Order dragged on until 1435. The Teutonic Knights in Prussia faced a difficult situation. With Lithuania now Christian the *Ordenstaat* had no obvious reason for existence and its famous *Reisen* no longer appealed to the aristocracy of Europe. The papacy's crusading priorities lay to the east and the war against the Ottomans. Prussia was simply one of a number of Baltic and Central European states. It was useful to the Emperor Sigismund because he needed its support against the Poles but it had no moral purpose and gradually the flow of recruits to the Order dried up. In the direct military sense this was not very important because the primary military function of the knights had long been as captains of mercenaries and their wealth still enabled them to play that role. However, that wealth was threatened. The lands of the Order had been impoverished during the long war with Poland. The Grand Master's autocracy, therefore, needed money from other sources. Income was raised from their landed possessions in Germany and elsewhere but this was not enough so that the castellans and advocates of the Order in Prussia were ordered to collect more dues and taxes. The reduction in supply of such people lowered quality and discipline and there were accusations that the knights were wasting money in luxurious living. This was particularly damaging for a religious order at a time when all over Europe there was a great demand for reform of the clergy. All over Prussia burghers and gentry clearly recognised that although their taxes were vitally important to the *Ordenstaat*, they had no say in its autocratic government which was pressing heavily upon them. In 1440 this resulted in the formation of the Prussian League – in effect a claim by city people, especially those of Danzig, and gentry, to be Estates comparable to those so common across Central Europe. Grand Master Louis von Erlichshausen (1449–67) was determined to crush all resistance and to restore the autocracy, but the Prussian League appealed to Casimir of Poland and the result was the 'Thirteen Years War' which was only concluded by the Treaty of Thorn of 1466. This is why the great crusading order of the Teutonic Knights was conducting a civil war and fighting Poland at the very time that Latin Christendom was shocked by the fall of Constantinople. The Treaty of Thorn handed over West Prussia and Danzig to Poland, fatally weakening the Order whose master became a vassal of the Polish king. In Prussia the cities took over control of local government while the mercenaries who all sides had hired were bought off by settling them on the land. This was the origin of many of the later *Junkers* who would have such a long history in Prussia and later Germany. The Livonian Order had its own problems with the pretentions of Riga, but could not easily intervene in Prussia because its forces had to watch the Lithuanians and to face the aggressions of Moscow. In a sense they found a moral justification in fighting against the growing power of Orthodox Muscovy, but they too suffered from internal decay.

The union of Poland and Lithuania was a purely personal one and both countries had strong traditions and interests of their own. Casimir guaranteed the privileges of Lithuania and its aristocracy. Lithuania had stood aside from the war against the Prussian Order because her nobility was much preoccupied by the rise of the Grand Duke of Muscovy who seized Novgorod in the1470s. Poland was divided into provinces, each of which had a long history, and these enjoyed substantial privileges in provincial Diets. As elsewhere there were Lower and Higher houses, though here the Church had a strong presence. By the Nieszawa Privileges of 1454 Casimir had conceded that the calling of the army and the imposition of new taxes were dependent on the consent of the provincial Diets. At the very end of the fifteenth century a central Diet, the Seym, emerged in Poland with a parallel in Lithuania. Casimir wanted his son John Albert (1492–1501) to succeed him in Poland while his younger son Alexander became Grand Duke of Lithuania (1492–1506), so during John Albert's reign the union of the two lands was abrogated, though it resumed again with the accession of Alexander to Poland. Poland had played little part in the war against the Ottomans, but John Albert was concerned by the Ottoman advance to the Black Sea in 1484 which threatened his control of Moldavia and his alliance with Wallachia. In 1497, supported by the Grand Master as his vassal with 4,000 men, he launched an attack on the Turks. Little came of it and Poland, deeply concerned at Russian expansion, concluded a peace with the Ottomans. As part of the price of his election as king of Poland Alexander was forced to accept a virtual partnership with the estates, and Poland in the sixteenth century entered a phase where it can be described as a 'Democracy of the Gentry'[4] in which the lesser nobles asserted their right to a substantial and active share in the running of the kingdom along with the monarch, the Church and the great magnates.

The rise of Moscow, which so preoccupied Lithuania, was the result of events on the western steppe. At the end of the fourteenth century Tamerlane subjugated the Golden Horde, and after his death it weakened and broke up into a series of Khanates, notably Kazan on the mid-Volga, the Crimean Khanate to the south and the remnants of the Golden Horde, ultimately the Khanate of Astrakhan, on the lower Volga. Stimulated by the relaxation of Mongol power, the rulers of Muscovy and the other Russian principalities competed for supremacy. The ruling Daniilovich dynasty of Muscovy seems to have adopted primogeniture quite early, and was able to rule with the elite, the *boyars*, who were a very variegated group of landowners. Moreover, a series of very able and long-lived rulers, Vasily II (1425–62), Ivan III (1462–1505) and Vasily III (1505–33) served the dynasty well. But an important reason for its success was the weakness of its rivals. As the Golden Horde disintegrated, the Dneiper valley route across Russia became evermore important and a string of trading cities emerged there connecting the Black Sea with the flourishing trading zone of the Baltic. In the early fifteenth century Vytautas, Grand Duke of Lithuania (1382–1430), dominated the western steppe-lands and secured suzerainty over Pskov and Novgorod. The marriage of his daughter, Sophia, to Grand Prince Vasily I (1389–1425) of Muscovy gave him considerable influence there. This was extended when Vasily nominated him as guardian of his young son, Vasily II (1425–62). The death of Vytautas resulted in a bitter succession struggle in Lithuania. Vasily II plunged into a series of dynastic wars in which his own title to rule was at stake, but good fortune and sheer ability enabled him to emerge victorious as undisputed ruler of Moscow and the most important of the Russian princes. The Metropolitan of Moscow had emerged as the chief ecclesiastical authority amongst the Russians, but the Church was shaken when Constantinople, which had appointed him, announced its allegiance to Rome. There happened to be no Metropolitan at the time and as a result, under the authority of Vasily II, the Russian bishops elected one of their own Iona (1448–61) who was firmly against any union with Rome. Constantinople fell in 1453 before its Patriarch could challenge Iona who now emerged as the greatest prelate in the Orthodox world. Alliance with the Church strengthened the dynasty and ultimately gave rise to the myth of the 'Third Rome' – that Moscow was the legitimate centre of imperial and

---

4 The phrase is to be found in J. Topolski, *An Outline History of Poland*, tr. O. Wojtasiewicz (Warsaw: Interpress, 1986), 67.

ecclesiastical power because the 'First Rome' had wandered from Orthodoxy and Constantinople, the 'Second Rome', had fallen under the alien authority of Islam. The merchant republic of Novgorod was nominally subject to the Grand Prince of Muscovy, but it enjoyed its independence and had been at best cool and at worst hostile to Vasily II. The *boyar* elite which dominated the city established good relations with Lithuania, but Vasily captured Novgorod after a series of wars in 1462. A pro-Lithuanian party remained in Novgorod which was only finally subjugated in 1478 by Ivan III. In the ensuing period, Moscow secured control over most of the nearby principalities such as Riazan, Tver and Iaroslav, while towards the end of the century there was a concerted drive to conquer and convert the lands towards the Urals, driven by desire to control this rich source of furs.

Lithuania had grown to encompass substantial areas of what had been Kievan Russia, so that under Vytautas it controlled the watershed between the Volga, Dneiper and West Dvina rivers, enabling it to dominate north–south trade. The Grand Dukes cultivated friendships with all the princes of Rus and attained great influence in Novgorod. Many refugees from the dynastic struggles in Russia took shelter there, and some petty princes in frontier areas chose to acknowledge Lithuanian supremacy. But involvement with Poland hampered Lithuania's attempts to maintain this position, while the internal evolution of the country in the direction of oligarchy did not help to concentrate resources. Casimir II and his successors were greatly angered by Muscovy's seizure of Novgorod, so this event ushered in a series of wars in which each side enlisted allies amongst the Khanates and the numerous independent princes of the area. In general, the war favoured Moscow. The border princes were Orthodox and when Poland-Lithuania insisted upon obedience to Rome, they tended to drift towards Moscow which claimed to be the champion of Orthodoxy. Moreover, many of the local elites were strongly attracted by the dynamism of Moscow; a highly centralised despotism which could win victories was much more attractive than oligarchic Lithuania. In 1514 Vasily III seized Smolensk and this set the seal on a series of Muscovite gains which established it firmly in control of the vital watershed and enabled it to threaten Kiev. An Orthodox centre of influence now dominated the north-western steppe lands and posed a grave threat to Catholic Poland-Lithuania. When Moscow absorbed Novgorod it came into conflict with the Catholic powers of Sweden and Livonia. This was not primarily a territorial conflict but one over control of commerce, hunting and fishing rights, exacerbated by difficulties of establishing who owned what in a difficult wilderness. Further, the merchants of the Hanse wanted to safeguard their virtual monopoly of trade with Novgorod while the Muscovite rulers wanted to open it to Russian merchants. In a series of wars the Princes of Moscow seized little territory. The Livonian Knights were able to enjoy a last crusading glory against the Muscovite schismatics, and under Grand Master Wolter von Plettenberg (1494–1535) they acquitted themselves well. The Swedes resisted Muscovite expansion in Finland even when the Danes joined the war against them. The northern war became caught up in the conflict between Lithuania/Poland and Muscovy, but this fizzled out inconclusively. In the end the

Hanseatic monopoly at Novgorod was broken and Moscow became a major influence on the trade of the Baltic and a centre for commerce with Central Europe. Visibly Muscovy's command of the trade-routes, backed up by her autocratic rulers, gave her a real ascendancy over Lithuania/Poland.

History has usually been written with the underlying assumption that monarchic centralism is good and all other forms of government were bad, but it must not be assumed that the present writer is simply continuing that old polemic. The fact was that the Ottoman Empire represented a massive mobilisation of power and resources which could only be countered by similar concentrations of power. But the Christian states adjacent to it were, by the end of the fifteenth century, far inferior, in part, at least, because of the diffusion of power within them. The major political forces in Germany and Central Europe may have feared Ottoman domination, but they had no common view of how best to resist it, and were far more involved in conflicts nearer to home and interests which were more evident and direct. The Empire, and within it, Germany, remained deeply divided. The German princes did not really establish primogeniture until the sixteenth century. Only a few principalities were strongly organised. Branden-burg, and to a degree Saxony, were centralised, while Hesse became a wealthy and influential principality. Some princes sought to rule by employing professional administrators, notably Bavaria, and the new universities turned out more of these people and fostered the study of law. But for the most part these developments were at an early stage compared to France and England and the Hispanic states, let alone the fearsome Ottoman Empire. The nobilities, major and minor, of Central Europe could no longer expand as individuals and clans and they were enmeshed in the operations of the state as a way of maximising their status and power. There was, therefore, little likelihood of a response to papal appeals such as had greeted the First and occasionally later crusades. The crusade as a pan-European ideological instrument designed to forge unity behind papal leadership was, effectively, a dead letter. That does not mean that the crusade was dead – merely that it now had to be aimed at strong states like Spain, France, Portugal and Venice. This was not new – in a sense it had been clearly a growing development since the crusades of St Louis in the mid-thirteenth century. But these states were growing in competence and had their own view of crusading and their own priorities.

From the perspective of the papacy, the prospect of Europe at the end of the fifteenth century was discouraging because, effectively, the crusade, so long its deepest preoccupation, had fallen into the hands of secular rulers or ceased to be a real force. The extent of promise offered by the New World and the Portuguese expansion into the Indian Ocean was not yet evident, but what was clear was that most of the benefits would flow to the states which backed this process. The reduced status of the papacy in the emerging new world was underlined by the Italian wars and its total inability to exploit the problems of the Ottoman Empire. The death of Mehmed in 1481 was followed by violent convulsions in his dominions. The autocracy of the late ruler and his heavy taxes had offended many

310

forces within his lands, and his successor, Bayezid II (1481–1512), was obliged to bow to these. However, he faced a rival in his brother, Cem, who could play upon serious discontent. Eastern Asia Minor was restless because Ottoman policies threatened the traditional way of life of the Turkish tribes. Cem enlisted Mamluk aid in exploiting this situation and the result was a series of exhausting wars between the two great powers of the Muslim world which ended indecisively in 1491. By this time Cem had taken refuge with the Hospitallers on Rhodes to whom Bayezid paid 45,000 ducats annually if they would keep him in captivity. This tribute, paid latterly to the papacy, came to an end with Cem's death in 1495. In 1490 Bayezid even offered Charles VIII of France (1483–98) the crown of Jerusalem if he would guarantee to neutralise Cem. In 1490 Innocent VIII (1484–92) staged a great conference at Mantua at which crusading hopes were centred on support for Cem, but nothing came of it. However, the notion of a crusade served as a gloss to Charles VIII's invasion of Italy in 1494.

The main motive of this intervention was dynastic ambition. Italy was a divided land and the main forces in the peninsula were, in many cases, unstable. Sicily was firmly attached to the crown of Aragon, but was unfriendly to Naples, ruled by a bastard line of the same house. The regime in Naples was not especially popular and there was still sentiment in favour of the displaced Angevin line which resulted in a major uprising of the nobles against Ferrante I. Ultimately the Angevin claim passed to Charles VIII of France. The papal state was emerging as a powerful local entity in the centre of the peninsula. Further north, Florence was a strong city-state dominating its neighbours, but Pisa was restless while the Medici regime in the city was not universally popular and was weakened by the death of Lorenzo the Magnificent and the accession to power of Piero. Venice had become a powerful territorial state in the north-east of the Peninsula, but was distracted by its wide overseas interests. In Milan the ruling Sforza clan were divided and Naples were trying to undermine the regime of Lodovico Sforza who was Regent for his nephew, Gian Galeazzo. It was this pressure which prompted Lodovico to invite Charles VIII of France to intervene, but even he was really only seeking diplomatic support. In June 1494 Charles VIII invaded Italy with an army of about 30,000. He proclaimed that he had come to make good his rightful claim to Naples and to forward the crusade against the Turks. This, of course, reflected historical precedent in that Charles of Anjou had made similar protestations when he had conquered southern Italy in the thirteenth century.

This first phase of the Italian wars excited much contemporary comment because of the ease with which the French artillery could batter down the tall walls of Italian cities and castles. As a result historians have been so impressed that they have tended to see the Italian wars as a great turning point when a 'modern' style of war, dependent on gunpowder weapons, appeared. In fact, the French army was not so different from those of its enemies. At its core was the heavy cavalry, mostly hardened professionals retained in royal service. The most important element amongst the infantry were the Swiss mercenaries. However, the French had much more recent experience of large-scale siege warfare as a result of their long wars with England. The Italians had not absorbed the improved methods of defence which French cities had, perforce, learned, in particular the use of low walls of earth and timber or masonry to hold enemy canon out of range of vulnerable tall walls. At first the French, with their mobile artillery, were triumphant. However their forces were insufficient to maintain their conquests in the face of the coalition which the papacy created against them, this and they only narrowly escaped annihilation. This 'Holy League' was ostensibly formed to further the cause of crusade, but of course its real purpose was to resist the French in which they were successful. The Italians improved their fortifications by developing the celebrated *trace italienne*, a systematisation of methods using low earth and masonry walls designed to hold attacking artillery at bay. Though the *trace italienne* took time to perfect, effective improvisations were rapidly developed. As a result when Louis XII (1498–1515), the first of the Orleans kings of France, renewed the war to make good his inherited claim to Milan, resistance was stiffer. Having seized Milan, Charles then agreed a partition of Naples with Ferdinand of Aragon, Castile and Sicily, but again the French were unable to hold their gains whereas the Spanish did. In 1508 Louis attacked Venice. His diplomatic preparations again proclaimed his concern for the crusade, especially in the Treaty of Cambrai of 1508 signed with the Emperor and others and later supported by the pope. The reality was that Louis wanted to take advantage of the fact that the Venetians had alienated almost all their neighbours. But French success called into being another Holy League in 1511 and by 1513 the French had evacuated Italy. One important consequence of this French intervention was that Aragon acquired all of Naples which the French had never been strong enough to hold. Louis XII died in 1515 and Francis I (1515–47) reopened the war and secured Milan with a striking victory at Marignano. His apparent triumph was not to last long.

The Italian wars were a powerful distraction for the papacy in its concern with the crusade. In 1499 Bayezid attacked Venice and the republic found itself fighting virtually alone. Alexander VI (1492–1503) issued crusading indulgences and called upon the French to help but their aid was limited and Hungary did not join the Venetians till 1501. When peace was agreed in 1502, it registered Venetian losses, notably Lepanto, Modon, Coron, Navarino and Durazzo. The war clearly marked the emergence of the Ottomans as a first-class naval power, ending the long European maritime supremacy in the Eastern Mediterranean. A remarkable development in the Italian wars was that almost all the parties, when in difficulty, were willing to invoke Turkish aid. In particular, Milan and Naples became Turkish allies against Venice. This kind of accommodation was common enough in the Balkans, but its extension to Italy was, of course, detrimental to the whole spirit of crusade and it reflected the new political situation in the Mediterranean world in which Catholic Europe found itself sharply on the defensive. In the face of massive Ottoman power these alliances were signs of weakness which the Sultans, pledged to an ideological war (though one undertaken for more practical reasons also), could exploit. But they had their own problems. The

Turkish tribes of Asia Minor regarded the Ottomans with great suspicion and they rallied to the revolt of Ismail Safavi, a Shi'ite who had established himself on the throne of Iran. The revolt in Asia Minor was very threatening, but Bayezid had continued the modernisation of the army and when he was deposed as of infirm purpose his active son, Selim I (1512–20) crushed the rebels after a decisive victory over the Safavids in 1514. Selim proclaimed this campaign as a Sunni *jihad* against Shi'ite heresy, vesting the Ottoman Sultanate with a new religious authority. By this time the Portuguese incursion into the Indian Ocean was beginning to make a substantial impact on Islamic consciousness after the destruction of an Islamic fleet off Diu in 1509. The Ottomans sent naval aid to support the Mamluks and in the process obtained a foothold in Yemen. This made a considerable impression upon the Islamic world. The Mamluks felt threatened by Ottoman power and they were certainly in contact with the Safavids, but Selim struck quickly and defeated them, killing the Sultan of Cairo, at Marj Dabik near Aleppo on 24 August 1516. Selim then pressed on to Egypt where he destroyed the Mamluk Sultanate. His victories over the Mamluks were in part possible because they had declined to develop gunpowder weapons. Deep into the fourteenth century the Mamluks had been constantly reinforced by new recruits from the steppe and this had confirmed them in their attachment to traditional cavalry tactics, especially as they had proved very effective. However, the Ottomans were numerous enough to counter such methods and their infantry, equipped with handguns and employing armoured carts and canon in the style of the Hussites, could stand against Mamluk attack. Moreover, Ottoman artillery gave them a great advantage in sieges. Shortly after, the Sherif of Mecca announced his submission to the Ottomans, enhancing their prestige in the Muslim world. Only China, still essentially outside the European sphere of interest, exceeded the Ottoman state in power. Tax revenues increased enormously with Egypt and Syria contributing 100 million *aspers* and the new dominions provided *timars* and employment opportunities for the Ottoman elite. In the Islamic world its only rival was Safavid Persia which persistently looked to the west for support. The price of this glory was multiple and highly diverse interests, but of course Constantinople could now concentrate enormous resources for any expansionist plans.

But in Europe, too, political circumstances had radically changed. The Emperor Maximilian (1493–1519) was at first much concerned in various schemes to reform the Empire to which he had succeeded, and something of a framework of institutions was regularised, though it owed little to him. More importantly, he established total control of the Hapsburg lands which he proceeded to centralise so that they became a formidable state in their own right. After the death of Charles the Bold, duke of Burgundy in battle in 1477 Maximilian married the dead duke's daughter, Mary, and so gained control of the vast Burgundian lands in the name of his son Philip. After a series of wars in which the young prince played a notable part, Maximilian obtained Artois and Franche Comté from Charles VIII by the Treaty of Senlis of 1493 which opened the way for the French king's assault on Italy. In 1508 Maximilian agreed to the Treaty of Cambrai, cast in the form of an agreement to create a crusade, which opened the way for the renewed French intervention in Italy. Maximilian had championed the cause of crusade in Central Europe and sent real aid to the Hungarians. By the Treaty of Pressburg of 1515 he married his grandson Ferdinand and granddaughter Mary to the children of Ladislas of Bohemia and Hungary, establishing a Hapsburg claim to the throne of that divided country which became real in 1526. Pope Leo X (1513–21) called a Fifth Lateran Council in an effort to counter Selim's advances with a renewed crusade, and Maximilian, like Francis I of France, responded very positively, but nothing happened, although the Anglo-French Treaty of London of March 1518 paid lip-service to the idea. But it was the results of his death that caused a major change in the European political scene. Maximilian had clearly recognised that French power could dominate Europe and he had turned to a Spanish alliance to prevent this. His son by his marriage to Mary of Burgundy was Philip the Fair, who was married to Joanna the Mad, daughter of Ferdinand and Isabella. Philip died in 1506 and, there being no other heirs to the Spanish monarchy after Ferdinand died in 1516 or to the Hapsburg lands after Maximilian died in 1519, this vast inheritance was settled on Charles, Philip's eldest son, who was soon after elected as the Emperor Charles V (1519–56).

He was the ruler of a true world empire to rival that of the Ottomans now ruled by Suleyman I, 'The Magnificent' (1520–66) for whom he was clearly destined to be the enemy. The Hapsburg lands stood across the Danube, while as ruler of all Spain, much of Italy and the kingdom of Sicily-Naples, Charles represented Christian power in the Mediterranean. To support all this he enjoyed the fruits of the Spanish conquest of the New World whose silver was now beginning to flow in large quantities. To many in Europe, and especially in Germany and Central Europe, his accession seemed to offer a real prospect of relief from the growing Ottoman threat. On the other hand, the union of Spain, Italy and Austria was also threatening to some. The papacy always worked for a divided Italian peninsula and, in common with the minor powers of the area, resented the Hapsburg dominion. Above all, France felt surrounded and threatened. Charles' rival for the imperial throne had been Francis I of France. Both parties offered bribes and every kind of inducement to the Electors and both found it expedient to pose as champions of a new crusade against the Turks, and, indeed, Francis despatched a French fleet to the eastern Mediterranean. But once Charles was elected, reality intervened and war broke out in Italy. Undoubtedly Francis suffered from wounded *amour propre* and he was also, as the victor of Marignano, inspired by pride, though how far this can be weighed against real concerns that France was surrounded by the new power of Charles is uncertain. The result was that Francis struck into Italy, but in 1525 he was defeated and captured by Charles V at the battle of Pavia. In this moment of crisis France appealed to the Sultan for support, inaugurating a period of Franco-Ottoman friendship. In 1526 Suleyman crushed Hungary at Mohacs. Once he had been released from captivity by the Treaty of Madrid Francis renounced its terms and continued the war, only to be driven to the Treaty of Cambrai of 1529. Charles V was now established as master in Italy. All the efforts of the papacy to achieve a state of balance in the peninsula were in ruin and it was firmly tied to the Hapsburg cause. Francis renewed the war in Italy in 1536 and again in 1542, but his main hope rested in an alliance with the Ottomans. In 1536 he concluded a treaty with the Turks, though nothing came of it. In 1543 the Ottoman's army was on the offensive in the Danube valley and their fleet was active in the western Mediterranean. To the scandal of Europe, Francis allowed Barbarossa, Suleyman's commander in the naval war against Charles V to winter in Toulon whose inhabitants were forced to evacuate to allow for the billeting of the sailors. This was *realpolitik*, in painful contrast to the language of the Treaties of Madrid and Cambrai in which both Francis and Charles spoke of the need to advance the crusade against the Turks. Similar language had been used between Francis and Henry VIII of England (1509–47) at the 'Field of the Cloth of Gold' in 1520. The Anglo-French friendship, proclaimed there amidst scenes of chivalric splendour, was soon superseded by an Anglo-Spanish understanding couched in much the same language. Clearly new perspectives were emerging in the new political circumstances, even if the language of crusading and the symbolism of chivalry were still being used.

Papal propaganda and much popular converse continued to treat the Turks as a monolithic horror-state, an 'Evil Empire' whose only purpose was to destroy the true faith, but it was clearly possible to take a different view. The emergence of Charles V was a rather more proximate threat for many Europeans, and this was increasingly the case as Protestantism and protestant powers emerged and the Sultan's diplomacy made every effort to conciliate them. It is difficult to judge how far Suleyman was driven by ideology, by *jihad* against the infidel, and how far he was pursuing a pragmatic policy designed to strengthen his position. These are not, however, contradictory possibilities. His first major conquest was the capture of Belgrade in 1521, and it hard to see this as anything other than a step towards the destruction of Hungary. In 1522 his armies seized Rhodes, the seat of the Hospitallers. Their aggressive Christian ethos and their habit of preying upon Ottoman shipping were both spurs to decisive action. In the event they surrendered on terms and in 1530 rather unwillingly, accepted Malta from Charles V as their new base. In Hungary after Mohacs Suleyman tried to set up a vassal state governed by a Hungarian nobleman, John Zapolya, but many of the Hungarian nobles elected Charles V's brother, Ferdinand, as king. In 1529 Ferdinand's attempt to seize Hungary as a whole was repulsed and Zapolya was restored. Suleyman then raided into Austria, besieging Vienna for three weeks. Hungary continued to be disputed in 1531–32 and Ottoman attacks there were diverted by Charles V's naval assault in the Aegean. It is tempting to see the aggressive Ottoman policy in North Africa which followed in these years as merely a response to all this. However, they had already provocatively established a fleet based on Avlona in the Adriatic in 1518. Moreover, the Ottomans had been taking a strong interest in North Africa since the late fifteenth century, partly because of appeals from Spanish Muslims, and by 1512 were sponsoring the activities of the pirate brothers Oruc and Hayreddin Barbarossa. Again, this could be seen as an attempt to rescue an area where Muslim political authority had become weakened from the threat of the Spanish crusade which was picking off the important cities along the African littoral. Troubles with Safavid Persia led to a truce with Charles V in 1533 and to a campaign in Mesopotamia which resulted in the Ottoman conquest of Baghdad and Basra. Ottoman diplomacy skilfully called in the support of the Uzbeks against the Safavids. In 1534 Suleyman sponsored Hayreddin Barbarossa's capture of Tunis in 1534, but this city was recaptured and destroyed by Charles V in the following year, and a great naval war extended all over the Mediterranean. By 1540 Venice found it wise to accept the Ottoman presence in the Adriatic. Zapolya died in 1541 and Suleyman set out to conquer Hungary and reduce it to direct Ottoman rule, and at the same time despatched 110 galleys under Barbarossa to aid Francis I against the Hapsburgs. Charles V sacked Algiers in 1544 and Barbarossa's fleet wintered in Toulon and attacked imperial Nice in alliance with the French. A French artillery unit aided the Ottomans in Hungary. By 1547 Suleyman was distracted by war with Iran and signed a truce with Ferdinand and Charles V conceding the Hapsburg share of Hungary and it was Hapsburg aggression which renewed the war in 1552. Charles V also encouraged the Safavid Shah who opened a war with the Ottomans which lasted for seven years until a treaty of 1555 confirmed Ottoman domination of Baghdad. Henry II of France (1547–59) renewed the war against Charles V and the alliance with the Ottomans, encouraging Paul IV (1555–59) in his anti-Spanish instincts. However, in the end the French also had to acquiesce in the Hapsburg predominance, by the Treaty of Cateau-Cambrésis of 1559. Shortly after, France became racked by civil war between Protestants and Catholics. By this time, however, Charles V had abdicated, worn down by the task of governing his huge empire, and, in particular, by the war against the Protestants in Germany. His enormous inheritance was divided. Philip II of Spain (1556–98) inherited Spain, the Netherlands and Sicily along with the possessions in the New World, while Charles' brother, Ferdinand I, king of Hungary and Bohemia since 1526, became Emperor (1556–64) and ruler of northern Italy. Cateau-Cambrésis was actually concluded by Philip and made no mention of French gains at the expense of the Empire.

It is tempting to see in this pattern of events the Ottomans becoming caught up in a system of European alliances and essentially becoming part of the state-system of the west; in terms of resources a case could be made that they faced a very grave threat from that area. Charles V ruled about 14 million people directly and enjoyed some authority over about the same number in Germany, as opposed to the 13 million ruled by the Ottomans at the start of the sixteenth century, a figure which increased enormously by mid-century. In addition, the Hapsburgs could mobilise enormous wealth, much of its derived from the New World. But this ignores a great deal. Charles V could not raise money and troops at will. He had to treat separately with each of his lands where estates of one kind or another strongly resisted taxes and objected to expenditure for the benefit of other people within the Hapsburg lands. At the very start of his reign the revolt of the *Communeros*, an alliance of the nobles and cities, had threatened to tear the Hispanic peninsula from his grip. Even worse, the outbreak of the Protestant Reformation in Germany, created a block of hostile principalities there. By contrast, the Ottoman Sultans could mobilise their resources for war with much less resistance and they could count on large numbers of their subjects sharing the *ghazi* tradition which favoured aggressive war. In many ways this was reinforced by the Ottoman role as champions of Sunni Islam, which allowed fighting against the infidel to be presented as *jihad*. Of course there were disaffected elements within the Ottoman lands and the proclivity of the family for succession disputes could have had fatal results. But the prestige of success held the Ottoman lands together and this was reinforced by an effective administration which could appeal to Islamic solidarity to galvanise support. It is a mark of the wealth and effectiveness of the Ottoman state that at Constantinople they created the greatest shipyards in the world and were soon able to threaten the long-standing Christian naval domination of the Mediterranean. It is certainly true that Suleyman had to keep a wary eye on the Safavids of Iran, but he could in turn call upon the Uzbeks to neutralise them. By contrast, France was the greatest single western power and it formed a real threat to the Hapsburgs, especially as Charles had to deal with major problems in Germany. As a result the initiative in the Mediterranean rested with the Ottomans. In the eastern Mediterranean, Venetian Cyprus was isolated and Crete under threat, while effectively the republic had surrendered its domination of the Adriatic. North Africa had looked like a promising area for Spanish expansion, but the Ottomans were now on the march there. The Ottoman Sultans were as opportunist as any of the monarchs of the age, but underlying their policy was a strong religious current which enabled them to retain their hold over the diversity of Islamic peoples in their lands. No one should be too impressed by Suleyman's willingness to treat with France and others. The Ottomans had always sought their ends by whatever means came to hand and exploiting the divisions of their enemies was a favourite.

All in all it is hard to criticise those who proclaimed the danger to Christendom. Charles V was certainly a believer in the crusade and he seems to have dreamed of a universal monarchy which would crush the Ottomans and liberate Jerusalem. And this did influence his policies and acts. He poured a vast treasure into expeditions to North Africa, quite out of proportion to Spanish interests, and endured setbacks such as the capture of Tripoli by Barbarossa in 1551. Charles was very generous to Francis I after his defeat and capture at Pavia in 1525, and in 1544, by the Treaty of Crépy, he ceded most of his gains in the latest war to Francis in return for support for a projected crusade – fruitlessly in the event. The papacy was, as ever, anxious to support crusades. In 1536 as the Ottomans threatened to conquer the Dalmatian coast, Paul III (1534–49) gathered a naval league consisting of Venetian and papal ships together with the naval forces of Charles V under the command of a Genoese. This fleet was defeated by the Ottomans in September 1538 off Preveza. The Venetians made peace and, in effect, Europe was forced to acquiesce in an Ottoman advance into western waters. The Council of Trent (1545–63) was primarily called to settle the problem of the protestant movement in Germany, but it was also charged with the preparation of a crusade. But the two traditional powers of Christendom, Pope and Emperor, though they agreed in principle upon the need for crusade, were bitterly divided on other matters. In particular, the papacy had always sought to keep Italy a mosaic of competing powers because this was felt to guarantee the independence of the papal states and the papacy itself. When Charles VIII of France seized Naples in 1494–95, the papacy was one of the moving forces in the alliance which drove the French monarch out of Italy. In the complex diplomacy that accompanied the wars the papal objective was always to prevent any single power dominating the peninsula, so the Hapsburg ascendancy, which was the final outcome, was bitterly resented. In 1555 Paul IV allied with Henry II of France to overthrow Charles V's supremacy in Italy, and in 1557 this pope even spoke of calling in the Turks to defend the Holy See, though all this was cut short by the triumph of the Hapsburgs at Cateau-Cambrésis in 1559. But if the tensions between Pope and Emperor helped to fracture the crusade, it was undermined in a much more radical way by the rise of Protestantism.

The crusade was the occasion, though not the cause, of the Protestant Reformation. On All Saints Eve 1517 Martin Luther, an Augustinian priest and professor at the University of Wittenberg, pinned to the door of the Castle Chapel his famous '95 Theses'. These were an angry reaction to the arrival, in nearby Jüterbog, of Tetzel, a renowned seller of papal indulgences which offered men and women relief from the burden of sin in return for carefully graded payments, the money raised being supposedly dedicated to the crusade against the Turks. Pope Leo X (1513–21) had actually commissioned the archbishop of Mainz (who was granted a cut) to organise this preaching in conjunction with the Nuremberg banking house of Fugger in order to finance his lavish rebuilding of St Peter's at Rome. Luther was not the first to criticise this kind of mechanistic and materialistic approach to salvation: Chaucer, for example, had satirised it in his *Pardoner's Tale*. More importantly the 'Humanist' scholars of the fourteenth century had ventilated profound criticisms which, thanks to the printing press and improved communications, were circulated all over Europe. What distinguished Luther's attack was that it took place in Germany where it was widely felt that the weakness of the Empire enabled the papacy to milk the land of money. Luther's passionate denunciations, therefore, resonated with his German audience, especially as they were sustained by his stubborn and dominating personality. In reply to criticisms Luther chose to renounce the whole notion of salvation by good works and to uphold the doctrine of 'Justification by Faith alone'. When challenged upon this, he turned to the authority of the Bible, proclaiming the priesthood of all believers and denying that the papacy and the priesthood could stand as intermediaries between God and mankind. The late medieval Church had a remarkable vigour and had generated a ferment of ideas which focused on the need for reform. Christians were painfully aware of the shortcomings of the institution and the quest for reform had long been dominant. In this context Luther's ideas were dynamic, but what made them doubly dangerous was that Luther turned to the Elector of Saxony for protection. His original interest may have been intellectual, but it was not long before he and other princes realised that the adoption of the new religion brought with it power over the new Church and profit from the spurned aspects of the old, notably the dissolution of monasteries. For Charles V these new ideas were anathema, but he was much preoccupied, as has been seen here, by war in Italy and Germany and he had genuine scruples about using force, partly because he was aware of the depth of reformist feeling in Germany and partly because he needed German support in order to prevail against the Turks. But the new ideas spread, especially in North Germany, and rapidly developed into organised Churches rather than merely a reforming tendency. By 1530 the Protestant princes had gathered together to form the Schmalkaldic League. Charles' solution to the problem of religious dissent was to demand that the pope summon a General Council in order to reform the Church. But this was something the papacy, after its long struggle against the Councils of the fifteenth century, was loath to do. Only in 1544 was a promise extracted to convene the Council of Trent, but by that time Protestantism had become institutionalised, making reconciliation difficult. In addition, in the city of Geneva another brand of Protestantism, Calvinism, with its radical doctrine of predestination and its missionary zeal, had emerged. In three sittings, extending from 1545–63, the Council of Trent, dominated by the papacy, reasserted traditional beliefs and radically reorganised the Church as a militant organisation under papal leadership, but at the price of excluding the protestants. Charles V's dream of unity was shattered by militant Protestantism and the response to it, the creation of a reformed Catholicism whose intransigence was exemplified by the new Jesuit Order. By 1555 the protestant princes, who had allied with Henry II of France and opened discussions with the Ottomans, had driven the emperor to the Peace of Augsburg under which it was agreed that in Germany each prince would determine for himself whether to adopt Lutheranism or Catholicism. In 1556 Charles V abdicated, a broken man.

Charles V was a spectacular casualty of new circumstances. So too was the Teutonic Order. In 1511 the knights elected Margrave Albrecht of Hohenzollern-Ansbach as Master of the Prussian Order (1511–68). He had enjoyed a humanist education and was well aware of the ferment of ideas in Germany. It is a sign of the times that he was willing to ally with Basil III (1505–33) of Russia against Sigismund of Poland (1506–48) in order to find an escape from the obligations to Poland established by the Treaty of Thorn. In the event he was not successful and the war did little but further impoverish the Order. By 1522 Albrecht had come into contact with Lutheran ideas and he recognised immediately that adopting them offered a path to control the riches of the Church in his lands. Lutheran ideas and, to a degree, Church organisation, were already spreading in the *Ordenstaat*. In 1525 Albrecht took an oath of allegiance to Sigismund of Poland as duke of what later came to be East Prussia and a year later he married Dorothea, daughter of the king of Denmark. The Prussian branch of the Teutonic Order had vanished into a secular duchy which would later form the basis of the Prussian state. In Livonia the Order had defended the land against Russian attack and this had given it purpose and prestige. But its festering quarrel with the merchant community was given a new dimension as Lutheranism made headway amongst these people. Formidable attacks by Ivan IV 'the Terrible' (1533–84) made it apparent by 1559 that the Order could no longer defend Livonia which became the prey of Polish, Danish, Swedish and Russian armies. In 1561 the Livonian Grand Master, Gotthard Kettler, became Duke of Kurland, which was really the rump of the lands left to the Order, and a vassal of the Polish crown. The Livonian branch of the Teutonic Order had also vanished into a secular state. Ivan's determination meant that the war over Livonia went on but Poland and Sweden were strong enough to keep his armies from the Baltic and he needed to turn his forces on the Crimean Tartars. As a result he was forced to a peace in 1582. The lands and personnel of the Teutonic Order within Catholic South Germany were gathered under a Grand Master and its knights found a new purpose fighting for the Hapsburgs against the Ottomans, only to be dissolved by Napoleon.

The Order of St John was also dissolved by Napoleon but it achieved great glory before then. In 1530 Charles V had given them Malta as a replacement for Rhodes. The difference between the two places is not without interest. Rhodes stood at the junction of the Aegean and the eastern basin of the Mediterranean. It was a bone in the throat of Ottoman trade and could constitute a jumping off point for any crusade to the east. Malta was in the western basin of the Mediterranean and represented a defensive stance against Ottoman aggression. One of the conditions of the grant of Malta was that the knights would help in the defence of Tripoli, but in 1551 that fell to the Ottomans and in 1555 Bougie was captured by the brilliant Ottoman admiral, Dragut Reis. In 1558 a Spanish army was crushed at Mostaganem in North Africa and a heavy raid mounted upon Minorca. It seemed that the Ottomans, already firmly established in the Adriatic, would dominate the western basin of the Mediterranean. Pope Pius IV (1559–65) offered crusading privileges and support for a Spanish expedition to regain Tripoli but this force was destroyed in 1560 after capturing the island of Jerba. For Philip II North Africa was a matter of deep concern because in Ottoman hands it could be a threat to Sicily and Spain. Moreover, the Ottoman advance encouraged the Spanish Muslims who staged a mighty uprising in 1568–70, an unpleasant revelation of the limitations of the Spanish *reconquista*. After 1567 the Low Countries became the scene of a bitter war which consumed Spanish treasure and men on an enormous scale. The particularism of this part of Philip's lands was deeply offended by his autocratic rule and the objections of the local nobility to arbitrary rule from distant Spain were reinforced as Calvinism took root amongst them and the bourgeoisie. Philip was convinced of his sacred duty as the champion of Catholicism and he was reinforced in this by the emergence of a reformed and militant Catholicism emerging from the Council of Trent. In practice, he was juggling priorities between different parts of his empire.

In March 1565 Suleyman launched a huge army and fleet against Malta. The ferocity of the attack raised alarm bells across Europe and a significant number of nobles from various states, including France, went to strengthen the garrison. The failure of the siege was an enormous boost to Tridentine Catholicism and even convinced Protestants were disposed to admire the achievement. But the siege failed only because the besiegers were divided over policy and wasted the efforts of their army. Philip II understood that the fall of Malta would be a threat to his island of Sicily, and so raised a fleet whose arrival in September brought the siege to an end. But Ottoman power to wage offensive war was underlined the following year when they made significant gains in Hungary and a great naval expedition seized the Genoese island of Chios. Suleyman died in the camp at Chios, but he had secured the succession of his son, Selim II (1566–74) who was no less ambitious for conquest. The advance of Muscovy towards the Black Sea had become a matter of concern to the Ottomans and in 1569 they projected a canal between the Don and the Volga to oust the Russians from Astrakhan. This grand design would have blocked Russian expansion and opened a new front against Safavid Persia, but it failed because the canal was not technically feasible. However, in the same year Selim extinguished the Spanish hold on Tunis. Pope Gregory XIII (1572–85) tried to enlist Ivan of Moscow against the Ottomans, but the Tsar was happy to make peace once his hold on Astrakhan was consolidated and turned his attention to the war in the Baltic. Similarly, Gregory made fruitless overtures to the Safavids.

In 1570, fortified by yet another treaty of friendship with the French, Selim demanded that the Venetians evacuate Cyprus or face war. This forced the Venetians to seek allies. Pius V (1566–72) proclaimed a crusade and set about arranging a naval league between Philip and the Venetians. This was no easy task because Spain and Venice had very different interests. Moreover, the Venetians had stood aside from the earlier fighting because the Ottomans had respected their territories and they loathed the Genoese whose ships were an important element of the Spanish fleet. It says much for Philip's conviction of the need to support the crusade that in 1571 he undertook to pay for half of the great fleet which was raised for the 'Holy League' despite the war in the Low Countries and the revolt of the *Moriscos*. Papal galleys sailed with the fleet, but the Church's real contribution was financial support. Taxes raised on the Spanish Church may have paid for Philip's total contribution to the fleet. An allied fleet gathered late in 1570 to no effect, but in 1571 the forces of the League attacked an Ottoman fleet in the Gulf of Corinth and won the great victory of Lepanto which pitted approximately 208 Christian galleys against 275 Turkish ships. This was an enormous success but by the next year Selim could field a fleet as great if not greater than that lost at Lepanto. Moreover, the victory could not prevent the loss of Cyprus and as a result Venice came to terms with the Ottomans in 1573. The Spanish fought on, seizing Tunis again in 1573 but in 1574 an Ottoman fleet 300 strong recovered the city and went on to strengthen their hold on North Africa. In 1576 the new Sultan, Murad III (1574–95) seized Morocco. This provoked the intervention of the Portuguese king, Sebastian, who was killed at the battle of Alcazar-Kebir in 1578 which consolidated Ottoman power there. Sebastian's death enabled Philip II to absorb Portugal and in March 1580 a truce was agreed between Spain and the Ottomans which was to be regularly renewed. In effect the two powers disengaged on the basis of the status quo. Philip II went bankrupt three times during his reign, notably in 1575 after the Lepanto campaign and its sequel. He was the ruler of an empire upon which the sun never set because with the annexation of Portugal he had acquired the Portuguese empire in the Philipines and the Far East. Yet he had been forced to accept the Ottoman victory in North Africa. By contrast, the Ottomans were far from exhausted and in 1593 turned their attention to the Danube valley where they were determined to seize the rump of Hapsburg Hungary. The 'Long War' lasted until 1606 when the Sultan acknowledged the German Emperor as his equal by the Treaty of Zsitva-Torok which thereby laid the basis for the acceptance of the Sultan into the European balance of power. This Hapsburg success owed a great deal to papal support and diplomacy which stirred up Moldavia, Wallachia and Transylvania. But probably the crucial factor was the intervention of the Safavid Shah, Abbas. He suffered heavy losses against the Ottomans in 1590, but in 1599 sought his revenge by joining the Christian Emperor and the pope in an anti-Ottoman alliance which created a major war on both flanks of the Ottoman Empire. This dragged on until a peace of exhaustion overcame both sides in 1618. The Ottoman impulse to expansion was clearly checked, but they had time after time demonstrated enormous powers of recovery and every effort by Europeans to capitalise on their problems came to nothing in the seventeenth century.

There was certainly considerable unrest in the Ottoman Empire in the early seventeenth century; the deposition and murder of Osman II (1617–22) and Mustapha I (1622–23) are clear evidence of that. The decline of the janissary recruiting base and the consequent invasion of this privileged group by native Turks, together with banditry caused by inflation and heavy taxation caused severe disruption. But the empire was rejuvenated under Murad IV (1623–40), and in particular the army was reformed with forces chiefly recruited in Asia Minor. Intermittent war with the Safavids led to the reconquest of Baghdad in 1638. All this explains why the Ottomans failed to take advantage of the 'Thirty Years War' (1618–48). Ibrahim (1640–48) was governed by leading courtiers, but in his reign the Ottomans launched the conquest of Crete which ravaged that island from 1645–69. The chief reason why this took so long was the political disorder which characterised the reign of Mehmed IV (1648–87), but the rise of the Köprülü family (1656–83) established reform and a degree of stability within the empire. Venetian attacks on the Bosphorus were repelled and the conquest of Crete brought to a successful conclusion, while internal order was firmly established. Austrian attempts to improve their position in Hungary were repelled in 1660–01 and two years later the Turks captured important fortresses in Slovakia. In 1664 the Ottomans drove into Austria and were checked at Sankt Gotthard, which commanded the routs to Graz and Vienna. In a series of wars

Poland and Russia suffered defeats which expanded Ottoman territory. The appalling state of Hungary, allied to strong protestant influences, led to the rise of a movement to expel the Hapsburgs entirely and to establish local autonomy under Ottoman suzerainty. In 1682 the Sultan was able to conquer almost all of Hungary and to establish Thököly as king of Hungary. The great Ottoman general Kara Mustafa was persuaded by his French allies that this was the moment to strike and in 1683 prepared for an assault on Vienna. Pope Innocent XI (1676–89) appealed for a new crusade and this persuaded most of Catholic Europe to send help, though the main Hapsburg ally was John Sobieski of Poland (1674–96). Contemporaries were deeply impressed by the Ottoman siege of Vienna from June to September 1683. The Turks deployed the latest weapons in a systematic way and the discipline of their army excited favourable comment. It failed because the Turks were besieging a very strong modern fortification at the utmost reach of their logistical system, and because of the intervention of a Polish army under Sobieski. The skilful handling of Austrian forces meant that the retreat became a rout and the way was open for attacks on the Ottoman frontiers. Under papal aegis a Holy League, supported by Austria, Venice, Poland and even Russia, was formed to exploit the new situation and in the years 1684–99 a vigorous assault culminated in the Treaty of Carlowitz of 1699 by which the Ottomans evacuated almost all of Hungary, abandoning their allies to Hapsburg rule. In the Aegean the Venetians regained control of the Adriatic and much of its coast and reconquered the Morea (Peloponnese). It was while they were besieging Athens in 1687 that a Venetian shell exploded the Turkish magazine in the Parthenon. But these gains were all lost to the Ottomans in 1714. This was the last crusade, and it was appropriate that the Venetians, who had supported the First Crusade, were there at the end.

A series of developments within Catholic Europe combined to weaken papal leadership and the crusade with which it was inseparably connected. In Western Europe a series of very strong monarchies emerged and consolidated their power. There was nothing inevitable about this process, as the failure in Hungary indicates, because there were always strong countervailing forces. Amongst these aristocratic privilege was clearly the most important, but even where it was triumphant the elites continued to be absorbed in the new state structures which they did not abolish but tried to control. Kings and nobles patronised the new learning which increasingly legitimised secular power, and these novel habits of mind tended to undermine their responsiveness to papal appeals. Chivalry died hard because it was caught up in legitimising the position of the hereditary nobility of Western Europe, but increasingly service to the state, however conceived, was coming to prominence and displacing the old mind-set. The strong new states of the west enhanced their power by patronising this new secular learning and by opportunistic exploitation of exploration. This led to the rise of the Hapsburg super-state under Charles V and Philip II who were rulers on a world scale. Charles V was in the grip of an older mentality, in part because he was Emperor, but Philip was a king in a new mould with territories far beyond the jurisdiction of Rome and subjects obedient to a variety of faiths. The problems of the papacy were increased by the rise of protestantism which formally breached the unity of Christendom. The new religion had a particular appeal to rulers because it offered them control of the resources of the Church. In fact this intensified a long-standing trend to royal control where monarchies were strong, and in the course of the sixteenth century Catholic monarchs came to exercise just as much control as Protestant ones. Henry VIII of England (1509–47) was 'Head of the Church in England', but Philip II's authority was just as great, as a modern authority has remarked: 'Even in ecclesiastical affairs the Pope's writ hardly ran in Spain. The domination of the Church by the crown was probably more complete in Spain in the sixteenth century than in any other part of Europe, including Protestant countries with an Erastian system.' Moreover, secular rulers, whether Catholic or Protestant, in the course of the sixteenth century increasingly pursued self-interested policies without regard to religious end. As Sixtus V (1585–90) sourly remarked of Philip II, 'The king of Spain, as a temporal sovereign, is anxious above all to safeguard and increase his dominions . . . the preservation of the Catholic religion which is the principal aim of the Pope is only a pretext for His Majesty'.[5]

At the same time changes in the political context of Europe made appeals for a crusade ever more difficult. In the course of the sixteenth century the Ottoman state became the dominant military power in Europe and the Mediterranean. Since the fourteenth century the papacy had adapted its appeals for a crusade to defend against this menace. But the fact was that they had failed and the collapse of Hungary after 1526 set a seal upon this. The whole question of resisting the Turks became caught up in European rivalries. It was hardly surprising that Protestants were prepared to consider alliance with the Turks, but it was actually Catholic France which became its closest ally amongst the powers of Europe. Increasingly the Ottomans were seen less as a religious enemy than as a fact of political life which had to be dealt with pragmatically. Thus Philip II, for all his crusading rhetoric, withdrew from the confrontation in the Mediterranean in 1580, in order to focus upon more urgent priorities. Under Charles V the liberation of Jerusalem remained in men's minds, but by the later part of the sixteenth century it must have seemed increasingly remote. Only strong states could challenge the Ottomans, and they had priorities of their own which coincided only occasionally with those of the papacy. The sheer power of the Ottomans had imposed itself. Moreover, one of the oldest objectives of crusading, the acceptance of papal authority by the Orthodox, was even more distant. The Greek Church had become a *millet* insulated from contact with Rome, while in Russia a great empire had arisen whose myth proclaimed it to be the 'Third Rome'. Rome's alarm at this led to massive pressure upon the Orthodox population in

---

5 John Lynch, *Spain Under the Habsburgs. Empire and Absolutism 1516–1598*, 2 vols (Oxford: Blackwell, 1964), 1.369–70.

Poland-Lithuania, resulting in the formation of the Ukrainian Catholic Church under Roman authority, by the Union of Brest-Litovsk of 1595–96, but many of the Orthodox remained outside it.

Moreover, economic development militated against the crusading mentality. The Ottomans were happy to sanction trade with Christian peoples and penetration of their lands by western merchants proceeded apace. One of the nodes of this trade was Haleb in North Syria, and it is no accident that to this day we refer to it by its Italian form, Aleppo. There the Khan al-Gumruk, also known as the Great Khan, was built in 1574 and came to house French, Dutch, and English commercial firms. Similar European communities grew up in Constantinople, Alexandria and other places. But far more important was the enlargement of the world and the development of new trading systems as a result of the discoveries. The impulse to exploration owed much to the crusade and the search for new means of attacking Islam, but ultimately it created a new world with new economic relationships. Spain and Portugal had poorly developed economies and the wealth of their empires served to support state expenditures and the ostentation of their elites. Hard as they tried they could not entirely exclude other powers, the Dutch, French and English, from the commerce of their empires. At the end of the war with Spain in 1621 the Dutch established the Dutch West India Company which promoted trade and pillaging in the West Indies and in the consequent chaos the English and French also set up bases in the area. By the end of the sixteenth century the Dutch were making great inroads against the Portuguese into the Spice Islands and the English began the East India Company in 1600 to counter them. The British East India Company moved the focus of its work to India, where it faced French competition after the founding of the Compagnie des Indes Orientales in 1664. In the later sixteenth century there was great interest in founding colonies in North America, and as early as 1560 the French attempted a settlement in Florida. There were many more failed efforts before, in May 1607, the English planted their first enduring colony at Jamestown in Virginia. By 1613 this was strong enough to extinguish a French colony in Nova Scotia. In 1613 the Dutch secured a port at what is now Albany, New York, to tap the fur trade and by 1625–26 had acquired Manhattan. To the north, in what is now Canada, France tapped the rich fur trade with a series of settlements. Mediterranean commerce remained considerable and Venice continued to prosper from the spice trade, but increasingly it formed but a part of a much wider trading system, and by no means the most important part. For the aggressive powers of the Atlantic seaboard, the Mediterranean was no longer a great preoccupation, and in any case Protestant countries, unresponsive to papal priorities, enjoyed a disproportionate share of this new wealth.

What is striking is how skilfully the papacy adapted to this changing world. At the start of the period it had not recovered from the long 'Schism of the West' and it faced a bitter dispute with those who favoured the claims of a Council to rule the Church. Throughout the fifteenth and into the sixteenth century there was a rising demand for reform and much contempt for the perceived corruption of

Rome. But the Council of Trent restored its position and there emerged from that remarkable series of meetings a new, reformed and vigorous Church with an instructed priesthood and an energetic leadership. The inroads made by Protestantism were partly reversed and Rome learned to work in conjunction with the Catholic monarchies. But the claim to direct the world, though never abandoned, went into eclipse, because the achievement of Rome's ends clearly depended on those rulers feeling that their ends coincided with those of Rome. As far as the crusade was concerned this was becoming rarer and rarer because kings were preoccupied by the competition between Christian powers. Venice was intermittently a willing partner because it needed to defend its Mediterranean empire from the Ottomans, while the Hapsburgs of Central Europe collaborated when it suited them, because of their confrontation with the same enemy. But increasingly this was all a matter of power rivalries rather than ideological confrontation. The papacy had championed the crusade and even in this period had its triumphs. It was papal efforts which propped up Hungary and persuaded Spain, Venice, Genoa and others to make common cause, at least occasionally, against the Ottomans. Lepanto was at heart a papal victory, and it is at least arguable that without the tireless efforts of many popes, the Ottomans would have dominated the Mediterranean to an even greater extent than was the case. Perhaps most remarkably of all, the papacy organised a major missionary effort in South America, in the Philipines and elsewhere which was astonishingly successful. The authority of the Roman Church became a worldwide force, mirroring the superpower of Catholic Spain. But all this was at a price, and by the end of the seventeenth century the crusade had become an outmoded means of achieving political ends and recovery of Jerusalem had long faded from the political agenda. One of the powerhouses of the reformed Catholic Church was the French Congregation of St-Maur, founded in 1618, which undertook a series of intellectual tasks aimed at reinvigorating Benedictine monasticism. Its scholarly endeavour produced remarkable editions of documents and even earned the respect of learned Protestants. In the late eighteenth century the Congregation undertook to collect materials bearing on the history of the crusades. By that time the crusades were history. Unfortunately it was never realised because the French Revolutionary government dissolved the Congregation in 1790.

SELECTED READING

A number of works on the general history of Spain have been noted in earlier chapters, but C. A. Julien, *A History of North Africa* (London: Routledge, Kegan Paul, 1970) is useful for understanding the Islamic context for the conquest, and vital for the struggle between Spain and the Ottomans is A. C. Hess, *The Forgotten Frontier. A History of the Sixteenth-Century Ibero-African Frontier* (Chicago, IL: University of Chicago Press, 1978). For the history of Africa as a whole, see *Unesco General History of Africa*, 8 vols (London: Heinemann/Berkeley, 1981–99) or its abridged form, 8 vols (Berkeley, CA: J. Curry,

1988–97), 4. There is a vast literature on the age of discoveries. The biography of the enigmatic Henry the Navigator has been translated into English as Azurara, *Conquests and Discoveries of Henry the Navigator*, tr. B. Miall (London: Allen & Unwin, 1936). For the Portuguese expansion and the development of its maritime empire the authority is C. R. Boxer, *The Portuguese Seaborne Empire 1415–1825* (London: Hutchinson, 1969). On Columbus, see F. Fernández-Armesto, *Columbus* (London: Duckworth, 1996) and A. Hamdani, 'Columbus and the recovery of Jerusalem', *Journal of the American Oriental Society* 99 (1979), 39–48. F. Fernández-Armesto, *Before Columbus. Exploration and Colonisation from the Mediterranean to the Atlantic 1229–1492* (London: Macmillan, 1987) has argued that Portugal, and in particular Henry the Navigator, was much less interested in Africa than in the islands of the Atlantic, but this seems a little unlikely to the present writer, especially given the widespread interest at the time in the 'River of Gold' which was supposed to be the source of the West African gold-trade. For the notion of a 'Mediterranean Atlantic', see P. Chaunu, *European Expansion in the later Middle Ages*, tr. K. Bertram of a French original of 1969 (Amsterdam: North Holland, 1979). The splendid 'Catalan Atlas' has been edited by G. Grosjean, *Mapamundi. The Catalan Atlas of 1375* (Zurich: Urs Graf, 1978). For a very good popular treatment of the Spanish expansion in America, see M. Wood, *Conquistadors* (London: BBC Publications, 2000). There are very valuable studies of the nature and importance of gunpowder weapons in the early modern period by B. S. Hall, *Weapons and Warfare in Renaissance Europe* (Baltimore, MD: Johns Hopkins University Press, 1997) and K. Chase, *Firearms. A Global History to 1700* (Cambridge: Cambridge University Press, 2003). P. po-Chia Hsia, *The World of Catholic Renewal* (Cambridge: Cambridge University Press, 1998) is an excellent study of the process of renewal in the Roman Church, with interesting information about the New World. S. Runciman's *The Fall of Constantinople 1453* (Cambridge: Cambridge University Press, 1965) is an eminently readable account. There is a good treatment of Russian history by J. Martin, *Medieval Russia 980–1584* (Cambridge: Cambridge University Press, 1995), but it is helpful to use M. Gilbert, *The Routledge Atlas of Russian History* (London: Routledge, 3rd edition, 2003). A number of works on Ottoman history have been noted, to which should be added M. Kunt and C. Woodhead, *Suleyman the Magnificent and his Age* (London: Longman, 1995) and D. Goffman, *The Ottoman Empire and Early Modern Europe* (Cambridge: Cambridge, 2002). On the Ottoman military, see R. Murphey, *Ottoman Warfare 1500–1700* (London: UCL Press, 1999). W. Blockmans, *Emperor Charles V*, tr. I van den Hoven-Vardon (London: Arnold, 2002) is a useful recent attempt to set Charles in the context of his age. Traditionally historians have regarded the Church of the later Middle Ages as corrupt and at risk of losing its hold over its people. For a very traditional summary of this position, see V. H. H. Green, *Renaissance and Reformation* (London: Arnold, 1952), 111–30 and for a summary of new ideas R. MacKenny, *Sixteenth Century Europe. Expansion and Conflict* (Basingstoke: Macmillan, 1993), 129–48. The biography of Philip II is that of H. Kamen, *Philip of Spain* (New Haven, CT: Yale University Press, 1997). A useful summary is that of J. Woodward, *Philip II* (London: Longman, 1992). A good history of early modern Spain is that of J. Lynch, *Spain under the Hapsburgs. Empire and Absolutism 1516–98*, 2 vols (Oxford: Blackwell, 1981). The classic account of the siege of Malta is that of E. D. S. Bradford, *The Great Siege* (London: Hodder & Stoughton, 1961).

10

PERSPECTIVES

In many ways this book is a celebration of the diversity of Europe. In the Middle Ages Catholic Christendom grew because it was fragmented. As a result of bitter competition for limited resources, some of its competing forces extended their conflicts into the world beyond its frontiers. There was not one, but many expansions, and as a result little focus or control. The crusade was an attempt by the papacy, the only universally recognised authority in this area, to control the impulse to grow and conquer. It was not successful. Jerusalem was liberated and provided enormous prestige, but it could not be sustained as a Latin colony in a hostile environment. The papal project was possible because the antagonistic forces within Catholic Christendom had a substantial religious and cultural unity, and it failed because this could not be translated into a single political reality. There was nothing inevitable about the downfall of this idea of unity. Europe was no more diverse in terms of peoples and traditions than the Middle East. It looked back to the Roman Empire when all its peoples were ruled by a single emperor, and more recently the Carolingians had replicated this situation. But the papacy sought to achieve its leadership by ideological means – by developing a notion of spiritual dominion and by presenting Jerusalem as the golden key to heaven. This was quite effective, but ultimately not enough of the potentates of Europe developed a vested interest in the achievement of these ends. This book is largely, therefore, the history of a failure, but it is a failure with enormous consequences and vast achievements, so it is a story worth telling.

Towards the year 1000 the lands of what has here been called the 'Catholic core' occupied only a small part of what we now call Europe. Their sense of unity was largely based upon a common religion and culture and a shared historical experience. Their economies were dominated by cereal monoculture. Their ruling elites had seized governmental power and attached it to their private lands. This created rural lordships, highly efficient instruments of exploitation. But despite these unifying factors, the 'Catholic core' was politically divided. There were 'kings', but even they ruled through divided, quarrelsome aristocracies, who, in large parts of the area, were the only real authority. This was a region where a plethora of forces competed with one another for local supremacy. Some of the 'Catholic core' lay in what we call northern Europe; much of the rest bordered the Mediterranean, and for the whole area this sea was a focus, partly because the papacy was based in Rome and preoccupied by the politics of the inland sea. All around the Mediterranean were places mentioned daily in the liturgy of the Church, and above all, at its eastern end, lay Jerusalem, where Christ lived and died. This reinforced the belief of these peoples that they were the heirs of the Roman Empire. More prosaically, because of its position, the papacy was enmeshed in the politics of the Mediterranean as were the German kings, who ruled a vast area north of the Alps, but derived their title of 'Emperor' from rule over Italy. The Mediterranean was also a great economic focus because the luxury goods of the Far East, spices, silk, perfumes and dyes, reached the 'Catholic core' from its eastern shores. Of course, the north was itself a vigorous trading area and it had its own dynamic of economic growth, but for the powerful luxury items were a vital element in their way of life, distinguishing them from the bulk of the population.

The extent of this 'Catholic core', as it was about the year 1000, suggests that it would have been very vulnerable. It consisted of the lands around an axis drawn from Rome to the English Midlands. To the west and north were peoples who seemed likely to accept its culture and institutions, but to the east lived hostile pagan peoples. The whole southern flank was threatened by a belt of Islamic power whose frontier with the 'Catholic core' extended from the Pyrenees across the islands of the western basin of the Mediterranean to Sicily. South Italy was an outpost of another civilisation, that of the Greek-speaking remnant of the Roman Empire centred on Constantinople, usually called Byzantium. This powerful empire dominated the Balkans and the Adriatic coast and its influence reached deep into the Danube valley where its Orthodox Church competed with that of the Latins. Clearly, of the three great cultures which sat around the Mediterranean, that of the 'Catholic core' was by far the poorest. It was certainly the least unified. Byzantium was ruled by one emperor supported by a tax-collecting bureaucracy. Much of Islam had broken away from the domination of the Caliph at Baghdad, but the centres of power which emerged were, by western standards, immensely rich and powerful and enjoyed well articulated governmental structures. It is therefore extraordinary that by the end of the eleventh century this 'Catholic core', while continuing to be divided, had grown and some of its leading figures had become major players in the confrontation of three civilisations in the Mediterranean.

The basic drive to expand arose from developments within the 'Catholic core'. In the ninth century the Carolingian Empire, and with it the political unity of the 'Catholic core', had collapsed. It was succeeded by a mass of ferociously competing entities, many of them very small. Their struggles focused on possession of land and loot, the proceeds of raiding other people's territories. These sources of wealth also interested the elites of Byzantium and Islam, but great state structures mediated their ability to acquire them and offered other possibilities for enrichment, notably high office. Within the 'Catholic core' the absence of any unified authority with a strong governmental structure meant that the great fought among themselves, always for plunder but often in the hope of gaining land which was the premier and most stable form of wealth in their primitive

GREENLAND

ICELAND

Glasgow
London Amsterdam
Bristol Antwerp
St Malo Dunkirk
Brest Le Havre
Nantes Venice
La Rochelle Bordeaux Genoa
Marseilles Florence

CANADA
(NEW FRANCE)
F1634

NEWFOUNDLAND
E1480 (Cabot 1496)

MASS.
CONN. }
NEW ENGLAND
E1620

New York
OHIO
Philadelphia
PENNSYLVANIA
MARYLAND E1632
VIRGINIA E1607

Azores

Lisbon Seville
Cadiz

LOUISIANA
F1699

N. CAROLINA
S. CAROLINA
FLORIDA

North Atlantic
Ocean

Madeira Is.

Cueta
Mediterranean

MOROCCO

Sahara

Gulf of
Mexico

Canary Is.

MAURITANIA

CUBA HISPANIOLA

Caribbean Sea

Arguim
R. Senegal

Timbuktu

S1492

C. Verde Is.
Cape Verde
GAMBIA

VENEZUELA S1499

S1513

SIERRA LEONE
LOWER GUINEA
Axim
Mina

S1499

R. Niger

COLOMBIA

Equator

S. Tomé
R. Congo

R. Amazon

Belém

MARANHAÕ Pernambuco (Recife)

Luanda
ANGOLA

ANDES

PERU

R. São Francisco

Bahia

Benguela

Potosí
BRAZIL
Minas Gerais

Rio de Janeiro

CORDILLERA OF THE

Rio de la Plata

São Paulo

ARGENTINE

Pacific
Ocean

South Atlantic
Ocean

CHILE

Cape of
Good Hope
P1487

S1516

Key: D – Dutch
E – English
F – French
P – Portuguese
S – Spanish

Map 10.1 The European Reach by the end of the seventeenth century.

Source: based on a map in G. V. Scammell, *The First European Age* (London: Unwin Hyman, 1989),
xvii–xix.

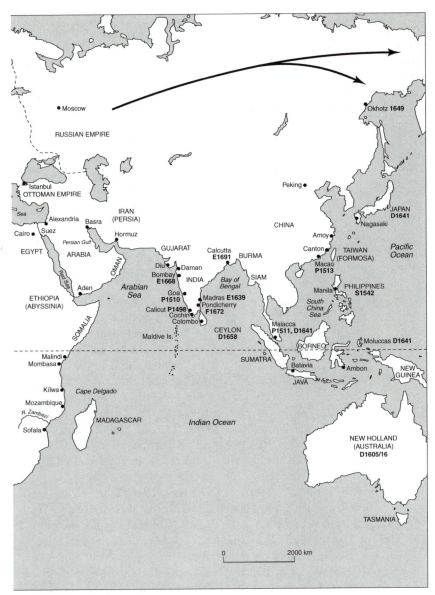

Landmarks: Treaty of Tordesillas 1494: gives Brazil to Portugal and the rest of the New World to Spain.

1522: First circumnavigation of the globe by Magellan's Spanish expedition.

1579: Drake circumnavigates the globe.

economies. On the peripheries of the 'Catholic core' the elites found they could prey upon their less developed neighbours and that this provided great opportunities for land-acquisition. Such areas became 'Marches' which protected the hinterlands and formed springboards for raiding and conquest, drawing upon the human and financial resources of larger areas. But the process of expansion which resulted was essentially localised because the ambitions of many of the elite were also caught up in their internecine struggles so that only a proportion of their energies and resources could be directed to the frontiers. Moreover, the growth of the 'Catholic core' was not merely a matter of military expansionism. For the elites of the peoples on its fringe, pagan and Christian, the settled society of the 'Catholic core' looked very attractive and inspired imitation. Intermarriage, trade and peaceful interaction drew them into its sphere. Of course, this was not unconnected to the use of force. Successful raiding was clear evidence of the value of the western model of organisation and encouraged emulation.

This kind of limited local expansionism had ebbed and flowed according to circumstances, notably in north-eastern Germany. Changes in the political environment of the 'Catholic core' in the late tenth and early eleventh centuries gave a new velocity to this hitherto sluggish process. In Central Europe missionaries sent from Byzantium and Germany, the threat of German power, admiration amongst their elites for western models and the processes of trade, brought about the conversions of Bohemia, Poland and Hungary to Catholic Christianity. This was an enormous addition to the 'Catholic core' and opened up additional prospects in Central Europe. It also created another frontier between the 'Catholic core' and the lands which had accepted the Orthodox faith, the 'Byzantine Commonwealth'. Much the same cocktail of long-term pressures, though without the element of competition with the Orthodox, led to the accession of the Scandinavian countries to the 'Catholic core'. This happened at the very moment when the other two great civilisations of the Mediterranean world weakened. In the Middle East the enormous empire ruled by the Caliph of Baghdad had long been breaking up; the most spectacular symptom of this decline was the rise of the Fatimid Caliphate of Cairo after 969. Of immense importance was the conquest of Baghdad in the mid-eleventh century by the Seljuk Turks. They gave a new vigour to the war of the Baghdad Caliphate against the Fatimids. The Turks also attacked the Byzantine Empire, where savage internal struggles amongst the greater aristocracy meant that the empire could not adopt a consistent policy of resistance. But the Turks were still a barbarian people and the Seljuk domination of the Arab Middle East broke up at the end of the eleventh century. These violent disruptions in the Islamic world were mirrored in *al-Andalus* which also began to fragment. This enabled the small Christian kingdoms of northern Spain, who had hitherto lived in effective subordination to *al-Andalus*, to expand at the expense of their Islamic neighbours, and to step up a process of border nibbling and raiding to one of major conquest.

It has been suggested that the 'Catholic core' was able to expand because its military technology was better than that of its neighbours. This idea reflects our recent experience that political ascendancy arises from the exploitation of technology for military purposes. But this was not the medieval situation and the technical advantages of the peoples of the 'Catholic core' over their neighbours were at best limited. The progressive agriculture of the west generated a demand for iron and as a result industries grew up to satisfy this demand. The western elites, therefore, were able to adopt a style of war which relied on iron production, notably for the mail shirt and the sword. European agriculture did not permit the raising of large numbers of light cavalry so breeds of heavy horses were developed which could support the heavily equipped knight. He was a well-protected all-purpose warrior who enjoyed the key advantage of mobility although in the wild peripheries of Europe, topography, weather and vegetation partly nullified these advantages. Infantry were important in western warfare because they could adapt to the fighting environment when it did not favour cavalry. An element amongst them was equipped with crossbows which could strike down the best protected of knights. However, the crossbow was slow to load and was at its best in defending and attacking fortifications, and it was so costly that it was never as widespread as the ordinary stave-bow. Other aspects of civilian technology had military applications. The boom in church-building as the economy developed in the eleventh century generalised the skills of building in timber and stone. The earth and timber blockhouse, even more the stone castle, originated from the quarrels of the elite and the consequent need for well-protected homes, but also had great value in extending authority in border areas whose native peoples lacked the skill and capital to create such strong-points. But none of this constituted a real technical advantage over the Muslims. They had access to the finest steels which is why the swords of Damascus and Toledo were so famous. The horse-archer, with his composite bow, was deadly in the field-warfare of the Middle East. The Muslims were just as good as the crusaders at constructing stone fortifications and in siege warfare were able to exploit 'Greek fire'. The roots of expansionism were social and political, not technical. It was the ambitions and quarrels of the divided and competing elite of the 'Catholic core' which drove them outwards in search of land. They were brave and adaptable soldiers who could use any military means which came to hand. In part they expanded because they were divided and needed new fields to satisfy their competitive culture.

This expansion posed threats and offered opportunities for the papacy. It was the sole authority recognised throughout the 'Catholic core' and to safeguard this position, which popes had always regarded as conferring a political leadership, they needed to control the process. The sanctification of wars, notably in Spain, was an effort by the popes to do just this. Far more ambitious was the attempt by Urban II to create an army of God at papal command. This had been tried before, but Urban eventually launched the First Crusade and its astonishing success forged a new weapon for the papacy in its effort to establish itself in a dominant position in Christendom. After the First Crusade the popes overshadowed all the rulers of what can be called Christendom, the enlarged 'Catholic core' now given a high degree of consciousness by its triumph in 1099. The Latin footholds in the

Holy Land needed to be sustained in the face of a hostile Turkish-led Islam and this task fell upon the papacy, acting for the rest of Christendom, further exalting its position. The crusade, however, was a papal instrument and Catholic Christendom accepted that it could be used for ends other than Jerusalem. In particular, the wars in Spain came to be regarded as crusades and this was accepted by the Spanish kingdoms because it brought support and finance. The fall of Jerusalem in 1187 marked a crucial stage in the revival of Islam in the Middle East. It also brought about a renewed surge in crusading, and the papacy of Innocent III gave the movement a new definition and an enhanced popularity. In the first half of the thirteenth century crusading and the papacy were at their zenith, and by then other aspects of Christian expansionism had been brought under the papal wing. The crusade made a major contribution to the Baltic expansion and this would continue through to the very end of the fourteenth century. The penetration of Livonia and Prussia took place away from the frontiers of the German realm; without the Teutonic Order and the frequent crusades to the area encouraged by the papacy it is difficult to see how this could have happened. The long resistance of Lithuania, which did not become Catholic until the very late fourteenth century, is clear evidence of the resilience of the native peoples and their dislike of external forces.

The papacy was always prepared to use the crusade as an instrument against its political enemies. Modern writers have called these 'political crusades', but this was a term unknown to medieval people. While those who suffered from such expeditions complained loudly, most contemporaries accepted that they were needed. However, timing was a different matter and the soundings of public opinion submitted to the Second Council of Lyon in 1274 suggest that proclaiming a crusade against the Hohenstaufen just as St Louis launched his crusade to Egypt was, at least in retrospect, seen as an error. Far more fundamental problems were now arising for the papal project. Kings were building governments which attracted the loyalty of the aristocracy. While buccaneering attitudes and actions continued, more and more lords were drawn into the service of the crown. This meant that for the purposes of the crusade the popes had to negotiate with powerful kings who controlled their noble subjects. The papacy was no longer the dominating force which it had been under Innocent III, though this had been something of an illusion because Innocent himself could not control crusades. The papacy had always shown itself remarkably flexible in its methods and approaches to crusading. The arrival of the Mongols in Catholic Christendom in 1241 was widely seen as a disaster, but the popes recognised that this was also an opportunity and embarked on a policy of diplomatic relations designed to enlist the Great Khans in the crusading cause. However, this flexibility deserted the popes when they allowed themselves to become dependent on France and its offshoot, the Angevin monarchy established at Naples. This proved to be a supreme misjudgement when the 'War of the Vespers' destroyed Angevin power and with it the whole papal strategy. Because the papacy and Christendom were enmeshed in the 'War of the Vespers' the Holy Land received relatively little help in the second half of the thirteenth century and the fall of Acre in 1291 did not give anything like the impulse to crusading which the loss of Jerusalem had produced in 1187. Shortly thereafter Pope Boniface VIII quarrelled with France, and the results of the conflict were disastrous for papal prestige. After 1337 France and England became involved in what we call the 'Hundred Years War', making it almost impossible for the papacy to call a new crusade.

But the more fundamental cause of the failures of the crusades to the Eastern Mediterranean was the change in the political environment. The union of Syria and Egypt under Saladin had destroyed the Latin Kingdom in 1187. Divisions amongst Saladin's successors reopened the breach between Syria and Egypt, providing the political environment for the zenith of crusading in the first half of the thirteenth century. But the vigour and military sophistication of the Mamluk regime which replaced the Ayyubids after 1250 created a different situation. The Mamluks fought off the Mongols, destroyed the crusader states and established themselves as the dominant power in the Middle East. Worse still, Byzantium had never managed to recover from the Latin conquest of 1204 and in the fourteenth century was paralysed by internal struggles. With amazing speed it was replaced by a new Muslim power, the Ottoman Turks, who quickly became a real threat to Christendom. This was possible because of the political fragmentation all around them extending from the Mamluk frontier in North Syria to the eastern borders of France. There were a number of Christian powers which had the potential to dominate this vast zone, notably Hungary and Poland-Lithuania, but their leaders proved incapable and their nobilities factious. By contrast, the Ottomans produced a series of Sultans who built an entirely new state drawing upon the traditions of both Byzantium and the Caliphate. The Ottomans reversed the tide of conquest which for so long had flowed from west to east, and by the fifteenth century were threatening Vienna and the Danube valley. In these circumstances the crusade became a defensive measure to protect Christendom. This proved to be very valuable and the late medieval papacy has, perhaps, not been given sufficient credit for its contribution. But by the sixteenth century the Ottoman Empire was the dominant military and naval power in the Mediterranean and any expansion there was, accordingly, very problematic. Moreover, in the fifteenth and sixteenth centuries the old principalities of Rus were absorbed into Muscovy. The rise of Orthodox Russia as the great power of the western steppelands barred any expansion of Catholic Christendom to the north-east.

But a new set of conditions was coming into existence in the western part of Catholic Christendom. One consequence of the divided state of Europe in the eleventh century was the rise of Italian merchant city-states, amongst which Venice and Genoa were pre-eminent. They discovered, rather to their surprise, that as a result of the crusader capture of the Palestinian littoral, their fleets were the dominant naval forces in the Mediterranean. This situation changed when the Ottomans grasped enough of the northern shore of the inland sea to make life very difficult for Christian shipping, and in the fifteenth and sixteenth centuries they created a great fleet which increasingly threatened the whole western basin of the Mediterranean. But by the end of the thirteenth century the northern and southern parts of Christendom were becoming economically integrated because the progress of the Spanish *reconquista* and the development of better ships made possible an active trade through the Gibraltar Strait. Symptomatic of this integration was the importance of Italian banking houses like the Bardi and Peruzzi who helped Edward III of England (1327–77) to finance his wars with France. The growth of trade through the Gibraltar strait increased western knowledge of the eastern Atlantic, and made accessible the riches of Africa hitherto known only through Arab traders. Furthermore, as a consequence of the Mongol dominion in Central Asia, westerners had reached China and India, enormously increasing their knowledge of the world beyond Islam; the growth of learning was, by the fourteenth century, attempting to systematise this knowledge. As a result Castile and Portugal were able to envisage a new expansion around Africa and across the Atlantic. This was partly motivated by traditional factors, aristocratic greed, the hope of outflanking Islam and finding allies to destroy her, but ultimately all other considerations were eclipsed by the possibilities of exploiting the wealth of the Indies and of the Americas. This expansion may have owed much to the same motives which had moved medieval people, but it was fundamentally different. There could be no Marches, for this was not a local conquest or assimilation. There was a place for brave young adventurers, but huge investment was needed and this could only be afforded by states; Cortes and his like were the creatures of state-sponsored expansionism.

The vital technology which made all this possible was maritime. The creation of a single trading zone in Catholic Christendom was the work of the thirteenth century and it brought together the expertise of Mediterranean and Atlantic sailors. Better ships became available. The voyages they were undertaking demanded systematic use of instruments and the development of charts, and the new literacy of the sea-lanes brought this kind of knowledge to the attention of intellectuals. Military technology also made a vital contribution. Gunpowder was a Chinese discovery but early guns were of limited use to the Chinese and their major enemies, the Mongol and Turkic tribes, who fought in an environment where speed of manoeuvre and the rapid fire of bows were crucial. Rather similar conditions of warfare prevailed in Iran and the Middle East. But in Europe, because of climate, topography and land use, the pace of war was much slower and fortifications were very common, so that the Ottomans and the powers of Catholic Christendom persisted with the clumsy and slow-firing gunpowder weapons. It gradually became apparent that these were highly effective when mounted on ships; this gave the Portuguese an enormous advantage when they penetrated the Indian Ocean and the Spice Islands, so that, despite the enormous distances involved, they were able to establish themselves in these areas in the sixteenth century. The Ottomans, of course, were just as effective as the Europeans in using gunpowder weapons, but the Indian Ocean was peripheral to their interests. In America, the Spanish brought the same advantages to bear upon more primitive peoples. The wealth the Spanish drew from this New World enabled them to build great fleets to fight off the encroachments of other European powers. Everywhere outside China, which was relatively little interested at this time in the world around it, the states of Europe discovered political fragmentation. They forced their way into these vacuums of power, not yet filling them as the British later did in India, but inserting themselves as new and potent factors which local authorities needed to consider.

In fact the new expansion gave rise to the first world-powers – the Hapsburg dominions of Charles V and the Spanish Empire of Philip II. These Catholic kings were nurtured in the spirit of crusade and both conceived of themselves as the champions of Christendom against the Turk and longed for the liberation of Jerusalem. But Christendom ceased to exist in the sixteenth century. The Protestant Reformation, instantly followed by the Counter-reformation, tore apart the old religious unity which had been the very bedrock of medieval thinking. The violent conflicts unleashed by the break-up of Catholic Christendom could not be controlled even by these superpowers. In addition, the rise of religious pluralism encouraged a new secular spirit in state policy-making, so that Catholic France, worried by the Hapsburg power, became the ally of the Ottomans. In these circumstances the Ottoman Empire continued to be the dominant military power in the Mediterranean and, right down to the late seventeenth century, a real threat to the Christian countries of the Danube valley. This effectively doomed the crusade. It had always been a papal instrument and never confined to the liberation of Jerusalem, but the particular glory of that city had always given impetus to the crusade. As its recovery became increasingly and self-evidently impossible, the whole idea fell into abeyance. The papacy adapted skilfully to the new world in which it found itself. A highly disciplined and educated Church was a powerful instrument of control for Catholic rulers who, accordingly, were minded to listen to its leaders.

Even more radically, the shape of the world had changed, creating a new identity for the people of what was once Catholic Christendom. Geographical knowledge had been growing rapidly since the thirteenth century. A New World across the Atlantic had been found and accurate knowledge of the lands and oceans beyond Islam became diffused. This coincided with the break-up of the old concept of Christendom. It was replaced with a geographic notion, Europe, which encompassed all the peoples who, to one degree or another, shared a common historical experience, including Roman Catholicism, the Protestant sects and the Orthodox. This was a new world. It owed much to its inheritance but the forces which controlled it and gave it shape were pre-eminently different from those of the medieval past. It is no accident that it was during the 'Age of Discoveries' that European savants invented the term 'Middle Ages', to describe what they saw as a static and lifeless era which had extended from the fall of Rome to the fifteenth century. In inventing such a pejorative term these scholars may have failed to recognise the vigour of the medieval centuries, or the degree to which their world had been shaped by the crusade, but they realised that, truly, they lived in a New World.

APPENDIX I

CHRONOLOGY OF EVENTS

955	Victory of Emperor Otto I over the Hungarians at the Lech
955	Victory of Emperor Otto I over the Slavs at Recknitz
969	Establishment of the Fatimid (Shi'ite) Caliphate at Cairo Byzantine recapture of Antioch
973	Saracens driven from their base at La Garde-Freinet in Southern France
988	St Vladimir, Prince of Kiev (980–1015), adopts Greek Orthodox Christianity
1000	The Millennium of the Birth of Christ
	St Stephen, King of Hungary adopts Latin Christianity
1002	Death of al-Mansur, the great military leader of the Muslims of Spain
	Spain fragments into the petty *Taifa* principalities
1009	The Fatimid Caliph, al-Hakim bi-Amr Allah (996–1021) destroys the Holy Sepulchre at Jerusalem
1017	Cnut of Denmark becomes king of England (1017–35)
	First appearance of the Normans in Southern Italy
1020	The Norman, Roger de Toeni, leads an expedition to Spain
1022	Major raid by the Muslims of Spain attacks Narbonne
1033	Millennium of the Passion of Christ
1044	Charles Martel, count of Anjou, captures Tours
1055	Lietbert, bishop of Cambrai, was turned back at Laodicaea, and was unable to complete his pilgrimage to Jerusalem
1055	Tughrul Bey establishes the Seljuk Sultanate at Baghdad
1059	Under Pope Nicholas II the Election Decree established new procedures for the selection of popes
	By the Treaty of Melfi Nicholas II invests Richard with the principality of Capua and Robert Guiscard with the duchies of Calabria, Apulia and perhaps Muslim Sicily
1064–65	The Great German Pilgrimage to Jerusalem
1066	William, duke of Normandy conquers England
	The Christian Prince of the Wends, Gottschalk of the Nakonid family, is overthrown by a pagan reaction
1069	Normans begin the conquest of Muslim Sicily with the seizure of Messina
1071	Victory of the Turks over the Byzantine Emperor Romanus IV at Manzikert
	Norman capture of Bari completes their control of southern Italy
1072	Norman capture of Palermo
1073	The Seljuks conquer Jerusalem from the Fatimids

1074	Pope Gregory VII appeals to the west in a series of letters to send a great military expedition against the Turks who were invading the Byzantine Empire – though with no practical result
1076	Outbreak of the Investiture Contest between Gregory VII and Henry IV Germany
1078	Gregory VII excommunicates the successors of the overthrown Byzantine Emperor, Michael VII
1081	Alexius Comnenus becomes Byzantine Emperor
	Robert Guiscard attempts the conquest of the Byzantine Empire
1082	Alexius Comnenus concedes substantial trading privileges to Venice by the 'Golden Bull'
1085	Alfonso VI of Léon-Castile captures Toledo
	Death of Robert Guiscard
	Death of Gregory VII
1086	Victory of the Almoravids over Alfonso VI at Sagrajas
1087	An army from Burgundy, Normandy, the Midi and northern France comes to Spain and campaigns with indifferent success in the Ebro valley
1087	A Pisan fleet attacks Mahdia in modern Tunisia
	Election of Urban II as pope
1089	Urban II lifts the excommunication of the Byzantine Emperor Alexius Comnenus at the Council of Melfi
	Urban II offers spiritual rewards comparable to those given to pilgrims to Jerusalem if they will aid the Spanish city of Tarragona
1090	Alexius Comnenus writes to Robert I, the Frisian, of Flanders, reminding him of his offer, made on pilgrimage, to send 500 knights to aid the emperor
1093	The Normans make major advances in Wales
	The Christian Nakonid ruler, Henry, in alliance with the Saxons, achieves a temporary leadership over the Wends
1095	Syria and Palestine fragment in the wake of succession disputes in the Seljuk family
	The kingdom of Aragon seizes Huesca
	Urban II launches the **First Crusade** at the Council of Clermont in November

The First Crusade

1095	
1–7 Mar.	Council of Piacenza
18–25 Nov.	Council of Clermont
27 Nov.	Raymond of Toulouse sends envoys to inform the Pope that he has taken the Cross
1096	
8 Mar.	Peter the Hermit leaves for Constantinople
1 Aug.	Peter the Hermit reaches Constantinople
11 Aug.	Peter and Walter at Civetot
Mid Aug.	Count Emicho's army massacred in Hungary
15 Aug.	Godfrey of Bouillon leaves for Constantinople
	Hugh of Vermandois writes to Alexius to announce his arrival
Sept./Oct.	Robert of Normandy, Robert of Flanders and Stephen of Blois leave France

Oct.	Hugh of Vermandois reaches Durazzo
21 Oct.	Turks destroy the 'Peoples Crusade' 26 Oct.
Nov.	Hugh of Vermandois reaches Constantinople
1 Nov.	Bohemond lands at Avlona
Late Nov. /early Dec.	Robert of Normandy, Stephen of Blois and Robert of Flanders reach Apulia. Robert of Flanders crosses to the Byzantine Empire
20 Dec.	The army of Raymond of Toulouse and Adhémar, the Papal Legate, enters Dalmatia
23 Dec.	Godfrey's army reaches Constantinople

1097

Early Feb.	The Army of Raymond of Toulouse enters Byzantine territory at Dyrrachium
Mid Feb.	Adhémar, Papal Legate, wounded in a skirmish with the Patzinaks, and rests at Thessalonica
5 Apr. (Easter Day)	Godfrey, Baldwin I and Robert of Flanders (?) take the oath to Alexius
9 Apr.	Robert of Normandy and Stephen of Blois land near Durazzo
10 Apr.	Bohemond reaches Constantinople ahead of his army and takes the oath
21 Apr.	Raymond of Toulouse reaches Constantinople ahead of his army
26 Apr.	Raymond takes a modified oath to Alexius
27 Apr.	Raymond's army reaches Constantinople
30 Apr.	Adhémar reaches Constantinople
4–6 May	Godfrey, Tancred, Robert of Flanders and Hugh of Vermandois march to Nicaea
14–28 May	Robert of Normandy and Stephen of Blois arrive and stay at Constantinople
14 May (Ascension)	Beginning of siege of Nicaea
16 May	Raymond arrives at Nicaea and defeats the army of Kilij Arslan
3 June	Robert of Normandy arrives at Nicaea
19 June	Nicaea surrenders to the Byzantines
22 June	Crusader leaders confer with Alexius at Pelecanum and shortly after, on 25 June, send an embassy to Cairo
1 July	Battle of Dorylaeum
14 Sept.	Tancred, nephew of Bohemond and Baldwin, brother of Godfrey, go to Cilicia
17 Oct.	Baldwin goes to Edessa
21 Oct.	Siege of Antioch begins
17 Nov.	Genoese fleet reaches Port S. Symeon
23 Nov.	Council of war: decision to build Malregard
28 Dec.– 1 Jan.	Expedition of Bohemond and Robert of Flanders to seek food in Syria. On 31 December they encounter the army of Damascus in a 'drawn battle' near al-Bara

1098

Early Feb.	The imperial representative on the crusade, Tatikios, leaves camp

9 Feb. (Shrove Tuesday)	Battle of the Lake Capture of Harenc Fatimid envoys reach crusader camp
4 Mar.	English fleet reaches Port S. Symeon
5 Mar.	Council of War: decision to build the Tower of La Mahommerie
9 Mar.	Baldwin I becomes Prince of Edessa, the first crusader state in the east
4–25 May	Kerbogah unsuccessfully besieges Edessa
29 May	Council of War: Bohemond conditionally granted Antioch
2 June	Stephen of Blois deserts
3 June	Antioch captured
4 June	Vanguard of Kerbogah's army reaches Antioch
14 June	Invention of the Holy Lance
20 June	Bohemond made Commander-in-Chief of the Crusader armies Stephen of Blois turns back the army of Alexius I at Philomelium
28 June	Kerbogah defeated and the Citadel surrenders
Early July	Hugh of Vermandois sent to inform Alexius of capture of Antioch
3 July	Council of Princes: march to Jerusalem deferred until All Saints
1 Aug.	Death of Adhémar
26 Aug.	Fatimids capture Jerusalem
11 Sept.	Letter of the Crusading Princes to Urban II shows great hostility towards the Byzantines
Mid Nov.	Violent disagreement in the Council of Princes in Antioch Cathedral
28 Nov.– 11 Dec.	Siege of Marra

1099

7 Jan.	Bohemond expels Provençal garrison from Antioch
13 Jan.	Raymond and Tancred leave for Jerusalem, later joined by Robert of Normandy
14 Feb.	Beginning of siege of Arqa
End Feb.	Godfrey, Bohemond and Robert of Flanders, under popular pressure, go to Laodicea where Bohemond deserts them
14 Mar.	Godfrey and Robert of Flanders reach Arqa
Early Apr.	Alexius' envoys reach crusader camp
8 Apr.	Peter Bartholemew undergoes ordeal by fire
Early May	Fatimid Embassy reaches crusader camp
13 May	End of siege of Arqa; march to Jerusalem resumed
6 June	Tancred takes Bethlehem
7 June	Siege of Jerusalem begins
13 June	First assault on Jerusalem
17 June	Latin fleet reaches Jaffa
15 July	Jerusalem captured
22 July	Godfrey elected *Advocatus Sancti Sepulchri*
29 July	Death of Urban II – succeeded by Paschal II (1099–1118)
1 Aug.	Arnulf elected Patriarch
12 Aug.	Battle of Ascalon
Late Summer	Pisan fleet arrives in the east

1100

18 July	Godfrey de Bouillon dies
15 Aug.	Bohemond captured by Danishmend Turks (until May 1103)
Autumn	Large armies of the 'Crusade of 1101' gather in the west: Lombards, William of Aquitane, Odo of Burgundy, William of Nevers, Welf IV of Bavaria. They march to Constantinople
11 Nov.	Baldwin of Edessa becomes king of Jerusalem. His cousin, Baldwin of Le Bourg is count of Edessa

1101 Tancred becomes Regent of Antioch

May The Lombards, some French and Germans accept Raymond of Toulouse as their leader and march into Asia Minor where they are destroyed by the coalition of Muslim armies at Merzifon in August

20 Aug. The Aquitanians and Bavarians crushed near Heraclea

26 Aug. The army of William of Nevers crushed near Heraclea

7 Sept. Baldwin defeats Egyptians at Ramla

1102

May Baldwin defeated by the Egyptians, but takes refuge at Arsug and is saved by the arrival of a pilgrim fleet whose troops enable him to defeat the Egyptians at the battle of Jaffa

1104

May The armies of Edessa and Antioch defeated at the battle of Harran which checked Frankish advance into the Jezireh

1105 Baldwin crushes an alliance of Damascus and Egypt at the battle of Ramla
Bohemond travels to the west to raise a crusade against Byzantium
Bohemond's crusade against Byzantium fails

1108 Appeal for a crusade against the Wends from Magdeburg
Chavli of Mosul and Baldwin II of Edessa fight Tancred and Ridwan of Aleppo

1109 Wizo establishes the castle of Wiston in Pembrokeshire
Tripoli captured

1110 Beirut captured

1112 Death of Tancred and accession of Roger of Salerno to Antioch

1114 Paschal II proclaims a crusade against the Muslims of the Balearics and eastern Spain

1115 Roger of Antioch defeats the Muslims at Tell Danith
About this time fief of *Oultrejourdain* established by Roman of Le Puy

1118 Gelasius II proclaims a crusade for the capture of Zaragoza
Baldwin I of Jerusalem succeeded by Baldwin II
Alexius Comnenus succeeded by his son, John

1119 Calixtus II proclaims crusades to Spain and to the Holy Land
Roger of Antioch defeated and killed at the 'Field of Blood'
Foundation of the Order of the Temple by Hugh of Payns

1120	The Canons of the Holy Sepulchre establish the village of Magna Mahomeria
1121	Last major Egyptian attack on Jerusalem
1122	Concordat of Worms ends the 'Investiture Contest'
1124	Tyre captured St Caradoc dies in Pembrokeshire after persecution by Flemish settlers
1125	Honorius II proclaims a crusade to Spain Alfonso I of Aragon attacks Granada
1126	Honorius II calls for a crusade against the Normans of South Italy
1128	Council of Troyes popularises the Order of the Temple Zengi becomes governor of Mosul and Aleppo
1129	Death of the last of the Nakonids results in a Danish king amongst the Wends Baldwin II attacks Damascus but fails
1130	Death of Bohemond II ushers in a succession crisis in Antioch
1131	Establishment of Segeberg by Lothar of Saxony Baldwin II of Jerusalem succeeded by Fulk of Anjou Alfonso I the Battler of Aragon bequeaths his kingdom to the Orders of the Temple and the Hospital
1132	Innocent II calls for a crusade against his rival, Anacletus II A last major naval raid by Egypt fails near Beirut
1135	Innocent's appeal for a crusade against Anacletus is supported by the Council of Pisa Fulk of Jerusalem gives the castle of Bethgibelin to the Order of the Hospital
1136	A Welsh army defeats the Normans at the battle of Crug Mawr Raymond of Poitiers becomes Prince of Antioch
1137	Adolf II of Holstein and Henry of Badwide annex many Wendish lands Emperor John Comnenus forces Raymond to do homage for Antioch
1143	Adolf of Holstein founds Lübeck Death of John Comnenus and succession of Manuel Fulk of Jerusalem is succeeded by a child Baldwin III, for whom his mother, Melisende, rules
1144	Zengi captures Edessa
1145	Eugenius III launches the Second Crusade with the Bull, *Quantum Praecedessores*
1146	March: Vézélay Court of Louis VII, St Bernard being present, launches the crusade
December:	Conrad III takes the cross at Speier
June:	Wendish Crusade gathers, but ends with nothing achieved in September
August:	Alfonso VII and Genoese seize Almeria
September:	Death of Zengi – he is succeeded by his son Nur ad-Din

1146–47   St Bernard of Clairvaux preaches the crusade in France, Germany and the Low Countries

1147   October: the Crusading fleet, in alliance with Afonso I of Portugal, captures Lisbon
November: German Crusade destroyed at Dorylaeum

1148   July: the crusader siege of Damascus fails
December: crusaders capture Tortosa in Spain

1149   Raymond of Antioch killed at the battle of 'Inab

1153   Baldwin III captures Ascalon

1154   Nur ad-Din becomes ruler of Damascus

1160   Henry the Lion of Saxony and his ally, Waldemar of Denmark, kill Nyklot

1163   Baldwin III of Jerusalem dies and is succeeded by his brother Amalric I
Manuel Comnenus establishes a protectorate in North Syria

1164   The Order of Calatrava founded in Spain

1168   Waldemar of Denmark seizes Rügen

1169   Shirkuh defeats a Franco-Byzantine invasion of Egypt

1171   Saladin suppresses the Fatimid Caliphate
Henry II invades Ireland

1172   Expulsion of the Venetians from Constantinople
Alexander III issues *Non parum animus noster* sanctioning the northern crusades
Henry II stabilises relations with the Welsh in agreement with the Lord Rhys

1174   Saladin seizes Damascus
Amalric I of Jerusalem dies and is succeeded by Baldwin IV, the Leper

1176   Manuel Comnenus defeated by the Seljuk Turks at the battle of Myriokephalon

1177   Baldwin IV defeats Saladin at the battle of Montgisard
Crusade of Philip of Flanders to the Holy Land

1179   Saladin destroys the new castle of Jacob's Ford

1180   Sybil, heiress of the kingdom of Jerusalem, marries Guy of Lusignan
Death of Manuel Comnenus ushers in a period of instability and uncertain succession at Constantinople

1182   Massacre of Latins at Constantinople under Andronicus II

1185   William II of Sicily attacks Byzantium, but his army is repulsed

1186   Guy and Sybil seize the crown of Jerusalem by a coup

1187   Third Crusade launched
July: Saladin defeats Guy at the battle of Hattin
October: Jerusalem falls to Saladin

Levon II the Magnificent establishes the Hetumid Kingdom of Cilician Armenia

1188   The Saladin tithe levied across Europe for the recovery of Jerusalem
        First meeting of the *Cortes* of Castile

1189   Guy of Lusignan begins siege of Acre

1190   Frederick I Barbarossa dies as his army completes the crossing of Asia Minor

1191   May: Richard I seizes Cyprus
        June: crusaders capture Acre
        September: Richard defeats Saladin at Arsuf

1192   Richard returns to the west

1193   Death of Saladin

1195   June: Almohad victory over Alfonso VIII of Castile

1197   Substantial German forces go to the east in anticipation of the crusade of Henry VI, who, however, dies before departing

1198   Accession of Pope Innocent III

1199   Albert of Buxtehude appointed bishop of Livonia, and moves his see to Riga
        Innocent III offers spiritual privileges to those who fight in Livonia
        Innocent III proclaims a crusade against Markward of Anweiler
        November: at a tournament at Ecry, the counts of Champagne and Blois take the cross, starting the Fourth Crusade

1201   April: the plenipotentiaries of the leaders conclude the Treaty of Venice to provide shipping for the Fourth Crusade

1202   The Fourth Crusade sacks Zara

1203   The Fourth Crusade installs Alexius IV on the Byzantine throne

1204   The Fourth Crusade sacks Constantinople

1208   The Albigensian Crusade is launched

1212   An alliance of Castile and Aragon defeats the Almodhads at Las Navas de Tolosa
        The 'Children's Crusade' agitates western Germany and northern France

1213   The Albigensian crusaders defeat and kill Peter I of Aragon at the battle of Muret

1215   Fourth Lateran Council imposes a tax of a twentieth for three years and proclaims a new crusade

1217   The Fifth Crusade is launched

1219   The Fifth Crusade captures Damietta

1221   The Fifth Crusade defeated

1225   Emperor Frederick II marries Isabel, heiress of Jerusalem

1226	The Golden Bull of Rimini establishes the Teutonic Order in Prussia
1227	Death of Chingis Khan (Temujin) – succeeded by Khan Ögödei
1229	Emperor Frederick II concludes a 10-year truce with Egypt which returns Jerusalem to Latin rule Frederick quarrels with the Ibelins precipitating a civil war for almost 20 years
1230	James I of Aragon seizes the Balearics
1236	Fernando III of Castile seizes Cordoba
1237	After the defeat of the 'Sword Brothers' the Teutonic Order are invited in to Livonia
1238	James I of Aragon captures Valencia
1239	Theobald of Champagne and Richard of Cornwall secure Jerusalem
1241	April: The Mongols destroy a Polish-German army at Leignitz (9th) and the kingdom of Hungary at Mohi (11th). The death of Khan Ögödei leads to the recall of the Mongol armies
1242	Alexander Nevsky defeats the Swedes, Finns and the Teutonic Order at the battle of Lake Peipus
1243	Frederick II's rule in Jerusalem effectively ends The Mongols conquer the Seljuk Sultanate of Rhum and reduce its rump and other principalities of Asia Minor to vassalage
1244	July: the Khorezmian horde sacks Jerusalem October: the Egyptians and Khorezmians defeat the army of Jerusalem at Harbiyah (La Forbie) Louis IX of France takes the cross
1245	Innocent IV launches his crusade against Emperor Frederick II during the First Council of Lyon
1248	September: Louis IX's army arrives in Cyprus November: Seville capitulates to Fernando III
1249	June: Louis IX captures Damietta
1250	February: Louis' advance to Cairo stalls after the battle of Mansourah April: Louis' army capitulates and he is captured May: St Louis freed and returns to the Holy Land December: Frederick II dies
1252	Florence issued the gold Florin
1253	William of Rubruck sent on a mission to the Mongol Khan
1254	St Louis returns to France
1256	Outbreak of the war of St Sabbas between Venice and Genoa lasting until 1270
1258	Mongol sack of Baghdad ends the Abassid Caliphate

1260 Mamluks defeat Mongols at Ain Jalut
The Prussians rebel against the Teutonic Order

1261 Michael VIII Palaeologus recaptures Constantinople

1264 Marinids of North Africa ally with Muslim Granada

1265 Mamluks capture Caesarea

1266 Charles of Anjou defeats Manfred at the battle of Benevento and becomes king of Naples

1267 Latins of Greece accept Charles of Anjou as their ruler

1268 Mamluks capture Antioch
Charles of Anjou defeats the Hohenstaufen Conradin at Tagliacozzo

1270 Louis IX dies on crusade in Tunisia

1271 Marco Polo leaves Acre for China, returning to Venice in 1295

1273 Election of Rudolf I of Hapsburg ends the great interregnum in Germany

1274 Crusading plans discussed at the Second Council of Lyon
The 'Union of Lyon' with the Greek Orthodox is proclaimed

1277 Charles of Anjou becomes ruler *in absentia* of Jerusalem

1282 The Sicilian Vespers overthrows Angevin rule and leads to Peter III of Aragon being asked to be its ruler
December: death of Llewellyn the Last, Prince of Wales

1283 Peter III of Aragon concedes the *Privilegio General* to the *Cortes* of Catalonia

1284 Venice issues the gold Ducat

1289 Mamluks capture Tripoli

1291 Acre falls to the Mamluks: extinction of the Latin Kingdom of Jerusalem
The Genoese Vivaldi brothers disappear leading an expedition down the west coast of Africa

1293 Instability in the Mamluk regime lasts until 1310
The Franciscan missionary, John of Monte Corvino, reaches Peking

1296 Boniface VIII issues *Clericis Laicos* and *Ineffabilis*

1298 Outbreak of quarrels between Riga and the Teutonic Order

1299 Il Khanid of Persia defeats Mamluks

1301 Deposition by Philip IV of Bernard bishop of Pamiers
Boniface VIII issues *Salvator Mundi* and *Ausculta Filii*

1302 Treaty of Caltabellotta ends the 'War of the Vespers'
July: French monarchy defeated by the Flemings at Courtrai
Philip IV calls the first Estates General and Boniface responds with *Unam Sanctam*

1303   Capture of Boniface by French agents at Anagni

1305   Clement V moves to Avignon

1306   Pierre Dubois writes his *On the Recovery of the Holy Land*

1307   October: Philip IV suppresses the Temple in France

1308   Teutonic Order seizes Danzig and Pomerelia precipitating a bitter quarrel with Poland

1309   Marienburg becomes the capital of the Teutonic Order

1310   Papacy inspires a naval league which captures Rhodes for the Hospital

1311   The Grand Catalan Company defeats the duke of Athens at Halmyros and create a Catalan duchy nominally subject to the kings of Aragon
        Council of Vienne sets up Chairs of Hebrew, Arabic, Greek and Syriac at western universities

1312   Revolt of the Pastoureaux calls for the liberation of Jerusalem

1313   Embassy from Ethiopia reaches the west

1314   Council of Vienne endorses Philip IV's suppression of the Templars

1320   Outbreak of a series of civil wars in the Byzantine Empire

1323   Gediminas of Lithuania becomes overlord of Kiev

1324   Mansa Musa, ruler of Mali goes on pilgrimage to Mecca

1326   Ottomans capture Bursa
        Viten of Lithuania allies with Poland against the Teutonic Order

1331   Accession of Stephen Dusan who creates a Serbian Empire
        Nicaea falls to the Ottomans

1336   Failure of the crusade projected by Philip VI of France

1337   Outbreak of the 'Hundred Years War' between England and France
        By the 'Declaration of Rense' the German Electors proclaim that they could elect without papal confirmation

1342   Catalan expedition to the Canaries fails

1343   By the 'peace of Kalish' Poland recognises the Teutonic Order's possession of Danzig and Pomerelia

1344   Alfonso XI of Castile conquers Algeciras
        A naval league promoted by the pope captures Smyrna

1344–45 Pope sponsors a crusade to the Canaries

1345   The Ottomans profit from civil war in Byzantium and are granted the fort of Jinbi in Gallipoli, their first foothold in Europe

1346   Teutonic Order buy Estonia from Denmark
        Stephen Dusan crowned 'Tsar of the Serbs and Romans'

Simone Vignoso of Genoa seizes Chios

1348	The 'Black Death' ravages Europe University of Prague, the first in central Europe, founded
1350	Failure of the Castilian siege of Gibraltar The rivalry over Black Sea trading rights between Genoa and Venice escalates into full-scale war until 1354
1356	By the 'Golden Bull' the Electors of the German Empire are fixed
1357–58	Revolution in Paris, the outcome of the horrors of war
1363	Ottomans seize Philippopolis Crusade of Amadeo VI of Savoy
1364	Foundation of the University of Cracow
1365	Peter I of Cyprus seizes Alexandria for 7 days
1367	Black Prince and his Castilian allies victorious over Aragon and its French allies at Najera
1369	Ottomans seize Adrianople
1371	Ottomans defeat the Serbs at Crnomen
1375	The 'Catalan Atlas' written
1378	Papal Schism breaks out, with rival lines of popes in Avignon and Rome The Venetian–Genoese quarrel over Tenedos becomes full-scale war ending only in exhaustion in 1380
1382	Re-imposition of Mongol ruler on Moscow
1383	Crusade of Henry Despenser bishop of Norwich to Flanders
1385	Portuguese, with English help, defeat a Castilian attempt to conquer them, supported by France, at Aljubarrota
1386	The Swiss establish their independence by defeating the Hapsburgs at Sempach 'Union of Krevo' by which Grand Duke Jogaila of Lithuania accepts Catholic Christianity and becomes ruler of Poland-Lithuania Ottomans seize Sofia and Nish
1388	Nerio Acciaioli becomes Duke of Athens, ending the rule of the Grand Catalan Company
1389	Ottomans crush Serbs and Bulgars at Kossovo
1390	Louis of Bourbon leads a successful French attack on Mahdiya in Tunisia
1390–91	Marshal Boucicaut and Henry Earl of Derby on *Reisen* with the Teutonic Knights in Prussia
1391	Great persecutions of the Jews of Christian Spain begin
1396	Defeat of a crusading army at Nicopolis

1401   After bitter factional fighting, France appoints Marshal Boucicaut to rule Genoa

1402   Tamerlane destroys an Ottoman army at Ankara, capturing Sultan Bayezid, and recaptures Smyrna for Islam
Jean de Bethencourt and Gadifer de la Salle lead a French expedition with Castilian backing to the Canaries

1405   Death of Tamerlane and break-up of his Mongol Empire

1409   All the German Professors secede from the University of Prague and found that of Leipzig

1410   July 15: The Poles defeat the Teutonic Order at the battle of Tannenberg
September: Henry of Trastamara captures Moorish Antequera

1414–18 Council of Constance condemns Hus, provoking rebellion in Bohemia. Its 'Union' with the Orthodox is highly unsatisfactory

1415   Portuguese capture Ceuta in Morocco

1420   Effective end of Marinid dominance in North Africa
Portuguese take Madeira

1425   Mamluks raid Cyprus and reduce it to a vassal state

1428   Ottomans conquer Wallachia

1432   Portuguese take the Azores

1434   The Utraquists of Bohemia crush the Taborites

1438–39 Council of Florence concludes a Union with the Orthodox

1439   Ottomans extinguish Serbia

1440–42 Ottoman attacks on Belgrade are repulsed and John Hunyadi is given much of the credit

1443–44 The Hungarians wage the successful 'Long Campaign' against the Ottomans

1444   Ladislas III and Cardinal Cesarini killed as the Ottomans defeat a crusader army at the battle of Varna

1450   Alfonso IV of Aragon concludes a Treaty with Mamluk Egypt to promote Catalan trade

1460   Civil war in Prussia as the Prussian League, in alliance with Poland, resist the Grand Master of the Teutonic Order

1466   By the Treaty of Thorn the Teutonic Order cedes Danzig and Pomerelia (West Prussia) to Poland

1448   The Russians elect a Patriarch of Moscow of their own; Iona is able to proclaim his orthodoxy after the fall of Constantinople in 1453, and his hatred of Latin Christendom with whom Constantinople had signed a 'Union'. This was the foundation of the notion of Moscow as the third and true Rome

1453	2 April: Ottomans conquer Constantinople French victory at Castillon brings the Hundred Years War to an end A conspiracy of Castilian nobles kills the king's minister, Alavaro de Luna
1454	By the Nieszawa Privileges Casimir IV makes sweeping concessions to the nobles of Poland
1456	Ottomans driven back from Belgrade by a crusade
1460	Portugal seizes the Cape Verde Islands Ottomans seize control of southern Greece
1462	Henry IV of Castile conquers Gibraltar Novgorod seized by the Grand Duke of Moscow
1468	Ottomans seize Albania
1470	Ottomans conquer the Venetian island of Negroponte, revealing the strength of their fleet
1474	Venice acquires Cyprus on the extinction of its Lusignan dynasty
1470–75	Portuguese explore the Gulf of Guinea
1479	Union of Isabella of Castile and Ferdinand of Aragon Castile dominant in the Canaries
1480	Ottomans conquer Otranto and hold it for a year
1481	Granada seizes Christian Zahara, triggering a Castilian assault
1483	A succession dispute in the Nasrid family of Granada facilitates the Castilian conquest Portuguese reach the Congo river
1485	Ladislas II of Poland guarantees religious freedom to Utraquits and Catholics at the Diet of Kutna Hora
1488	The Portuguese, Bartholemew Diaz, rounds the Cape of Good Hope
1492	Castilian conquest of Granada Expulsion of the Jews from Castile and Aragon Columbus sails to the West Indies
1494	Treaty of Tordesillas divides the New World between Spain and Portugal June: the French invade Italy in the first of a series of Italian wars
1496	John Cabot sails to Newfoundland
1497–99	Vasco da Gama sails to Calcutta
1501–02	*Moriscos* (Moors) of Castile given choice of conversion or expulsion
1502	After three years of war Venice loses most of its footholds in Greece to the Ottomans
1505	Castile conquers Mers-el-Kebir
1506	Death of Columbus

1509	Portuguese crush a Muslim fleet off Diu in Gujarat
1510	Castile conquers Tripoli (in modern Libya)
1513	First sighting of the Pacific by Spaniards
1514	Popular enthusiasm for the crusade in Hungary provokes the nobles to a civil war in which their enemies are crushed Vasily III of Moscow seizes Smolensk Ottomans crush the Safavid rebellion in Asia Minor
1515	Portuguese seize Ormuz in the Persian Gulf
1516	Spaniards reach the River Plate Ottomans conquer Mamluk Egypt
1517	Martin Luther posts his '95 Theses' at Wittenberg
1518	Ottomans establish a fleet at Avlona on the Adriatic
1519	Charles V inherits a world empire, as Emperor, heir to the Burgundian and Hapsburg lands and king of Spain with its domination in the New World Cortes overthrows the Aztec Empire Portuguese take Malacca
1519–22	First circumnavigation of the globe by Magellan's expedition
1520	Field of the Cloth of Gold between Henry VIII of England and Francis I of France
1521	Ottomans seize Belgrade
1522	Hospitallers driven by the Ottomans from their base at Rhodes
1525	Albrecht, Master of the Teutonic Order supports Lutheran ideas and becomes Duke of East Prussia, secularising the lands of the Order
1526	29 August: Ottomans crush Hungary at Mohacs and the kingdom ceases to have a separate existence
1530	Charles V gives Malta to the Hospitallers Protestant princes of Germany form the Schmalkaldic League
1536	Papacy inspires a naval league against the Ottomans in the Adriatic, but this was defeated by 1540
1539	Pizarro overthrows the Inca Empire of Peru
1543	Francis I of France allows an Ottoman fleet to use his bases against Charles V
1545–63	Council of Trent reforms and recasts Catholicism
1551	Ottomans reconquer Tripoli
1557	Portuguese establish Macao in China
1558	Spanish army defeated at Mostaganem in North Africa
1559	Abdication of Charles V

Philip inherits Spain, southern Italy, the Netherlands and the New World
Ferdinand inherits the Empire, Bohemia, a claim to Hungary and North Italy
Treaty of Cateau-Cambrésis confirms Hapsburg supremacy in Europe

1561	Gotthardt, Master of the Teutonic Order in Livonia, embraces Protestantism and becomes duke of Kurland, secularising the lands of the Order
1565	Ottoman expedition fails to take Malta
1566	Ottomans extinguish Genoese hold on Chios
1567	The Low Countries rebel against Philip II
1568–70	Rebellion of the Spanish *Moriscos*
1571	A Catholic League defeats the Ottoman fleet at Lepanto
1573	Venice accepts the loss of Cyprus to the Ottomans
1578	Sebastian King of Portugal killed in Morocco at Alcazar-Kebir
1600	English found the East India Company
1621	Dutch West India Company founded
1606	Treaty of Zsitva-Torok: Ottoman Sultan recognises the Emperor as his equal. A Safavid alliance helps to wear down the Ottomans
1607	English plant their first enduring colony in North America at Jamestown
1625–25	Dutch acquire Manhattan
1609–14	Expulsion of all *Moriscos* from Spain
1638	Ottoman conquest of Baghdad from the Safavids
1664	French Compagnie des Indes Orientales founded
1669	Venetian Crete conquered by the Ottomans after 20 years of war
1683	Ottoman assault on Vienna defeated with the aid of John Sobieski of Poland
1687	A shell from a Venetian ship explodes the Ottoman magazine in the Parthenon of Athens
1699	After a 15-year war waged by a Holy League organised by the papacy the Ottomans are driven from Hungary and make peace by the Treaty of Carlowitz
1714	Ottomans reconquer all the Venetian gains in southern Greece

APPENDIX II

LIST OF RULERS

Popes

First date is that of election. An. = antipope. For popes during the Great Schism (1378–1417), R. = Roman obedience, A. = Avignonese obedience, P. = Pisan obedience.

Sylvester II	999–1003	Innocent II	1130–43
John XVII	1003	Anacletus II An.	1130–38
John XVIII	1003–09	Victor III An.	1138
Sergius IV	1009–12	Celestine II	1143–44
Benedict VIII	1012–24	Lucius II	1144–45
John XIX	1024–33	Eugenius III	1145–53
Benedict IX	1033–46	Anastasius IV	1153–54
Sylvester III An.	1044–46	Adrian IV	1154–59
Gregory VI	1044–46	Alexander III	1159–81
Clement II	1046–47	Victor IV An.	1159–64
Damascus II	1048	Paschal III	1164–68
Leo IX	1048–54	Calixtus III	1168–78
Victor II	1055–57	Lucius III	1181–85
Stephen IX	1057–58	Urban III	1185–87
Benedict X	1058–59	Gregory VIII	1187
Nicholas II	1059–61	Clement III	1187–91
Alexander II	1061–73	Celestine III	1191–98
Honorius II An.	1061–64	Innocent III	1198–1216
Gregory VII	1073–85	Honorius III	1216–27
Clement III An.	1080–1100	Gregory IX	1227–41
Victor III	1086–87	Innocent IV	1243–54
Urban II	1088–99	Alexander IV	1254–61
Paschal II	1099–1118	Urban IV	1261–64
Theodoric An.	1100–01	Clement IV	1265–68
Albert An.	1102	Gregory X	1271–76
Sylvester IV An.	1106	Innocent V	1276
Gelasius II	1118–19	Adrian V	1276
Gregory VIII An.	1118–21	John XXI	1276–77
Calixtus II	1119–24	Nicholas III	1277–80
Honorius II	1124–30	Martin IV	1281–85

Honorius IV	1285–87	Alexander VI	1492–1503
Nicholas IV	1288–92	Pius III	1503
Celestine V	1294	Julius II	1503–13
Boniface VIII	1294–1303	Leo X	1513–21
Benedict XI	1303–04	Adrian VI	1522–23
Clement V	1305–14	Clement VII	1523–34
John XXII	1316–34	Paul III	1534–49
Nicholas V (An.)	1328–33	Julius III	1550–55
Benedict XII	1334–42	Marcellus II	1555
Clement VI	1342–52	Paul IV	1555–59
Innocent VI	1352–62	Pius IV	1559–65
Urban V	1362–70	Pius V	1566–72
Gregory XI	1370–78	Gregory XIII	1572–85
Urban VI (R.)	1378–89	Sixtus V	1585–90
Boniface IX (R.)	1389–1404	Urban VIII	1590
Innocent VII (R.)	1404–06	Gregory XIV	1590–91
Gregory XII (R.)	1406–15	Innocent IX	1591
Clement VII (A.)	1378–94	Clement VIII	1592–1605
Benedict XIII (A.)	1394–1423	Leo IX	1605
Alexander V (P.)	1409–10	Paul V	1605–21
John XXIII (P.)	1410–15	Gregory XV	1621–23
Martin V	1417–31	Urban VIII	1623–44
Eugenius IV	1431–47	Innocent X	1644–55
Felix V (An.)	1439–49	Alexander VII	1655–67
Nicholas V	1447–55	Clement IX	1667–69
Calixtus III	1455–58	Clement X	1670–76
Pius II	1458–64	Innocent XI	1676–89
Paul II	1464–71	Alexander VIII	1689–91
Sixtus IV	1471–84	Innocent XII	1691–1700
Innocent VIII	1484–92	Clement XI	1700–21

Ottoman sultans

Osman	d.1326	Mehmed III	1595–1603
Orhan	1326–62	Achmet I	1603–17
Murad I	1362–89	Mustapha I	1617
Bayezid I	1389–1403	Osman II	1617–22
Mehmed I	1413–21	Mustapha I	1622–23
Murad II	1421–51	Murad IV	1623–40
Mehmed II	1451–81	Ibrahim	1640–48
Bayezid II	1481–1512	Mehmed IV	1648–87
Selim I	1512–20	Suleyman II	1687–91
Suleyman I	1520–66	Achmet II	1691–95
Selim II	1566–74	Mustapaha II	1695–1703
Murad III	1574–95	Achmet III	1703–30

Byzantine emperors

Basil II, Bulgaroktonus	976–1025	Alexius V, Dukas	
Constantine VIII	1025–28	(Mourtzouphlus)	1204
Zoë	1028–50		
Romanus III, Argyrus	1028–34		
Michael IV, the Paphlagonian	1034–41	***Emperors of Nicaea***	
Michael V, Calaphates	1041–42	Theodore I Lascaris	1204–22
Constantine IX,		John III Vatatzes	1222–54
Monomachus	1042–54	Theodore II Lascaris	1254–58
Theodora	1054–56	John IV Lascaris	1258–61
Michael VI, Stratioticus	1056–57		
Isaac I, Comnenus	1057–59		
Constantine X, Dukas	1059–67	***Restored Byzantine emperors***	
Andronicus	1067	Michael VIII	1261–82
Constantine XI	1067	Andronicus II	1282–1328
Romanus IV, Diogenes	1067–71	Andronicus III	1328–41
Michael VII, Doukas	1071–78	John V	1341–47
Nicephorus III, Botaniates	1078–81	John VI (Cantacuzene)	1347–54
Alexius I, Comnenus	1081–1118	John V (restored)	1354–76
John II, Calus	1118–43	Andronikos IV	1376–79
Manuel I	1143–80	John V (restored)	1379–90
Alexius II	1180–83	John VII	1390
Andronicus II	1182–85	John V (restored)	1390–91
Isaac II, Angelus-Comnenus	1185–95	Manuel II	1391–1425
Alexius III, Angelus	1195–1203	John VIII	1425–48
Alexius IV	1203–04	Constantine XI Palaeologus	1449–53

German kings and Roman emperors

Otto III	983–1002	**Great Interregnum**	**1250–73**
Henry II	1002–24	Rudolf I of Hapsburg	1273–91
Conrad II	1024–39	Adolf of Nassau	1292–98
Henry III	1039–56	Albert I of Austria	1298–1308
Henry IV	1056–1106	Henry VII of Luxemburg	1308–13
Henry V	1106–25	Louis IV	1314–47
Lothar III	1125–38	Charles IV of Luxemburg	1347–78
Conrad III	1138–52	Wenceslas IV	1378–1419
Frederick I	1152–90	Sigismund I	1410–37
Henry VI	1190–97	Albert II of Hapsburg	1438–39
Frederick II	1197–1250	Frederick III	1440–93
Conrad IV	1250–54	Maximilian	1493–1519

Kings of Hungary

Stephen I	1000–38	Ladislas III	1204–1205
Peter	1038–41	Andrew II	1205–1235
Samuel	1041–44	Bela IV	1235–1270
Peter (again)	1044–46	Stephen V	1270–1272
Andrew I	1047–60	Ladislas IV	1272–90
Bela I	1060–63	Charles Martel	1290–95
Salamon	1063–74	Andrew III	1290–1301
Geza I	1074–77	Charles-Robert I	1301–42
Ladislas I	1077–95	Louis I	1342–82
Coloman	1095–1116	Sigismund	1387–1437
Stephen II	1116–31	Albert I	1438–39
Bela II	1131–41	Lazlo IV (Wladyslaw III	
Geza II	1141–62	of Poland)	1439–44
Ladislas II	1162–63	Ladislas V	1444–57
Stephen III	1163–72	Matthias Corvinus	1458–90
Stephen IV	1173–75	Lazlo VI	1490–1516
Bela III	1172–96	Louis II	1516–26
Emeric	1196–1204		

Lusignan kings and queens of Cyprus

Guy	1192–94	Peter I	1359–69
Amalric	1194–1205	Peter II	1369–82
Hugh I	1205–18	James I	1382–98
Henry I	1218–53	Janus	1398–1432
Hugh II	1253–67	John II	1432–58
Hugh III	1267–84	Charlotte	1458–64
John I	1284–85	James II	1464–73
Henry II	1285–1324	James III	1473–74
Hugh IV	1324–59	Catherine	1474–89

Grand Masters of the Temple

Hugh of Payns	1119–c.1136	Gilbert Erail	1194–1200
Robert of Craon	1136–49	Philip of Plessis	1201–09
Evrard des Barres	1149–52	William of Chartres	1210–18/19
Bernard of Tremelay	1153	Peter of Montaigu	1219–30/32
Andrew of Montbard	1154–56	Armand of Périgord	1232–44/46
Bertrand of Blancfort	1156–69	William of Sonnac	c.1247–50
Philip of Nablus	1169–71	Thomas Bérard	1256–73
Odo of Saint-Amand	c.1171–79	William of Beaujeu	1273–91
Arnold of Torroja	1181–84	Theobald Gaudin	1291–92/3
Gerard of Ridefort	1185–89	James of Molay	c.1293–1314
Robert of Sablé	1191–92/3		

Masters and Grand Masters of the Hospitallers

Peter Gerard	1070–1120	John of Lastic	1437–54
Raymond de Puy	1120–58/60	James of Milly	1454–61
Auger de Balben	1158/60–62/3	Peter Raymond Zacosta	1461–67
Arnaud de Comps	1162/3	Giovanni Battista Orsini	1467–76
Gilbert d'Assailly	1163–69/70	Peter of Aubusson	1476–1503
Gaston de Murols	c.1170–72	Emery of Amboise	1503–12
Joubert of Syria	c.1172–77	Guy of Blanchefort	1512–13
Roger des Moulins	1177–87	Fabrizio del Carretto	1513–21
Ermengard d'Asp	1188–c.90	Philip Villiers of L'Isle	
Garnier de Naplous	1189/90–92	Adam	1521–34
Geoffroy de Donjon	1189/90–1201	Pierino del Ponte	1534–35
Alphonse de Portugal	1202–06	Didiers of St Jalle	1535–36
Geoffrey Le Rat	1206–07	John of Omedes	1536–53
Garin de Montaigu	1207–27/8	Claude of La Sengle	1553–57
Bertrand de Thessy	1228–c.1231	John of La Valette	1557–68
Guerin Brooke	c.1231–36	Peter del Monte	1568–72
Bertrand de Comps	1236–39/40	John l'Aveque de la	
Pierre de Vieille-Bride	1239/40–42	Cassiere	1572–81
Guillaume de Chateauneuf	1242–58	Hugues Loubenx de	
Hugh Revel	1258–77	Verdale	1582–95
Nicholas Lorgne	1277–84	Martin Garzes	1595–1601
John of Villiers	1285–93	Alof de Wignacourt	1601–22
Odo of Pins	1294–96	Luis Mendes de	
William of Villaret	1296–1305	Vasconcellos	1622–23
Fulk of Villaret	1305–19	Antoine de Paule	1623–36
Hélion of Villeneuve	1319–46	Jean-Baptiste Lascaris de	
Dieudonné of Gozon	1346–53	Castellar	1636–57
Peter of Corneillan	1353–55	Martin de Redin y Cruzat	1657–60
Roger of Pins	1355–65	Anet de Clermont de	
Raymond Berenger	1365–74	Chattes Gessan	1660
Robert of Juilly	1374–77	Rafael Cotoner y de Oleza	1660–63
John Fernández of Heredia	1377–96	Nicolas Cotoner y de Oleza	1663–80
Philibert of Naillac	1396–1421	Adrien de Wignacourt	1690–97
Anton Fluvian	1421–37	Marcantonio Zondadari	1697–1720

Angevin kings of Naples

Charles I	1266–85	Louis II	1384–1417
Charles II	1285–1309	Ladislas	1386–1414
Robert I	1309–43	Joan II	1414–35
Joan I	1343–82	Louis III	1417–43
Charles III	1381–86	René of Anjou	1434–80
Louis I	1382–84		

Aragonese kings of Naples

Alfonso I	1442–58	**French Control**	**1495**
Ferdinand I	1458–94	Ferdinand II	1495–96
Alfonso II	1494–95	Frederick IV	1496–1500

Rulers of the Spanish kingdoms

Sancho the Great of Leon, Castile and Aragon (1000–35)

Rulers of Castile

Fernando I	1035–65	**Kings of Léon**	
Alfonso VI	1065–1109	Fernando II	1157–88
Alfonso I ofAragon	1109–26	Alfonso IX	1188–1230
Sancho III	1157–58		
Alfonso VII	1126–57	**Kings of Portugal**	
Alfonso VIII	1158–1214	Afonso I	1128–85
Henry I	1214–17	Sancho I	1185–1211
Fernando III	1217–52	Afonso II	1211–23
Alfonso X	1252–84	Sancho II	1223–48
Sancho IV	1284–95	Afonso III	1248–79
Ferdinand IV	1295–1312	Denis	1279–1325
Alfonso XI	1312–50	Afonso IV	1325–57
Peter I	1350–69	Pedro I	1357–67
Henry II	1369–79	Fernando	1367–83
John I	1379–90	Joao	1385–1433
Henry III	1390–1406	Duarte	1433–38
John II	1406–54	Afonso V	1438–81
Henry IV	1454–74	Joao II	1481–95
Isabella	1474–1504	Manuel I	1495–1521
Ferdinand V		Joao III	1521–57
(II of Aragon)	1475–1516	Sebastian I	1557–78
Philip II	1556–98	Henry	1578–80
Charles I (V of			
Germany)	1519–56	**Spanish Rule**	**1580–1640**
Phillip III	1598–1621	Joao IV	1640–56
Phillip IV	1621–65	Afonso VI	1656–67
Charles II	1665–1701	Pedro II	1667–1706

Kings of Aragon

Ramiro I	1035–63	Alfonso III	1285–91
Sancho Ramirez I	1063–94	James II	1291–1327
Peter I	1094–1104	Alfonso IV	1327–36
Alfonso I	1104–34	Peter IV	1336–87
Ramiro II	1134–37	John I	1387–96
Raymond Berengar IV		Martin I	1396–1410
of Barcelona	1137–62	Ferdinand I	
Alfonso II	1162–96	('of Antequera')	1412–16
Peter II	1196–1213	Alfonso V	1416–58
James I	1213–76	John II	1458–79
Peter III	1276–85	Ferdinand II (V of Castile)	1479–1516

Latin kings of Jerusalem

Godfrey de Bouillon	1099–1100	Baldwin IV the Leper	1174–85
Baldwin I	1100–18	Baldwin V	1185
Baldwin II	1118–31	Guy of Lusignan	1185–92
Fulk of Anjou	1131–43	Henry of Champagne	1192–97
Queen Melisende		Amalric II	1197–1205
(Regent and Co-Ruler)	1143–52	John of Brienne	1210–25
Baldwin III	1143–63	Frederick II of	
Amalric I	1163–74	Hohenstaufen	1225–43

The High Court of Jerusalem deposed Frederick's son, Conrad, and awarded the regency and later, in 1268, the crown, to the kings of Cyprus. However, Charles I of Anjou (1266–85) bought a claim to the kingdom and he and his successors regarded themselves as kings of Jerusalem. In practice the kings had no power and the monarchy was titular only.

Muslim dynasties in Spain

Sulayman (Last Ummayad)	1009, 1013–16	Yusuf I	1163–84
		Ya'qub	1184–99
		Muhammad II	1199–1213
		Yusuf II	1213–24
Almoravids		Abd al-Wahid	1224
Yusuf ibn Tashufin	1061–1106	Al-Adil	1224–27
Ali ibn Yusuf	1106–43	Abu'l Ula al-Mamun	1227–32
Tashufin ibn Ali	1143–45	Al-Rashid	1232–42
		Al-Sa'id	1242–48
		Al-Murtada	1248–66
Almohads			
Muhammad I	1163		

Nasrid Granada

Muhammad V	1354–59, 1362–91
Yusuf II ibn Muhammad	1391–92
Muhammad VII ibn Yusuf ibn Muhammad	1392–1408
Yusuf III ibn Yusuf ibn Muhammad	1408–17
Muhammad VIII ibn Yusuf ibn Yusuf ibn Muhammad	1417–19, 1427–29
Muhammad IX Uthman ibn Nasr ibn Muhammad	1419–27; 1430–31
Yusuf (not Nasrid)	1431–32, 1432–45, 1447–57
Muhammad X	1445–47
Muhammad XI ibn Muhammad ibn Yusuf ibn Yusuf ibn Muhammad	1448–54
Saad ibn Ali	1454–65
Abul Hasan	1465–82
Muhammad XII al Zagal	1482–87
Abu Abdullah	1487–92

Mamluk sultans of Egypt and Syria

Ezz Eddin Aybak	1250–57
Nur Eddin ben Aybak	1257–59
Zahir Rukn Eddin Bybars	1260–77
Said Nasser Eddin Baraka	1277–79
Adel Badr Eddin Salamish	1279
Mansour Seif Eddin Qalawoon	1279–90
Ashraf Salah Eddin Khalil	1290–93
Nasser Mohamed Ben Qalawoon (1st time)	1293–94
Adel Zeen Eddin Katubgha	1294–96
Mansour Hossam Eddin Lagin	1296–98
Nasser Mohamed Ben Qalawoon (2nd time)	1298–1309
Muzafar Rukn Eddin Bybars	1309
Nasser Mohamed Ben Qalawoon (3rd time)	1309–40
Mansour Seif Eddin Ben Mohamed	1340–41
Ashraf Alladin Ben Mohamed	1341–42
Nasser Shahab El-Dein Ben Mohamed	1342
Saleh Emad Eddin Ben Mohamed	1342–45
Kamil Seif Eddin Ben Mohamed	1345–46
Muzafar Zein Eddin Ben Mohamed	1346–47
Nasser Hassan Ben Mohamed (1st time)	1347–51
Salah Eddin Saleh Ben Mohamed	1351–54
Nasser Hassan Ben Mohamed (2nd time)	1354–61
Salah Eddin Mohamed Ben Hagi	1361–63
Ashraf Zeen Eddin Ben Hassan	1363–76
Mansour Aladin Ben Shaban	1376–81
Salih Zeen Edin Hagi	1381–82

Circassian Mamluks

Barquq al Yalburghawi	1382–88	Chaqmaq / Jaqmaq	1438–53
Hajji II	1389–90	Uthman	1453
Barquq al Yalburghawi	1390–99	Inal al Alai al Zahiri	1453–61
Faraj	1399–1405	Ahmad III	1461
Abd al Aziz	1405	Khushqadam	1461–67
Faraj	1405–12	Yalbay	1467
al Mustain	1412	Timurbugha	1467–68
Shaykh al Mahmudi		Qayit Bay al Zahiri	1468–96
(al Zahiri)	1412–21	Muhammad IV	1496–98
Ahmad II	1421	Qansawh I	1498–1500
Tatar	1421	Janbulat	1500–01
Muhammad III	1421–22	Tuman Bay I	1501
Barsbay	1422–38	Qansawh II al Ghawri	1501–16
Yusuf	1438	Tuman Bay II	1516–17

Muslim rulers in Egypt and Syria

Egypt

Saladin	1171–1193
Al-Aziz	1193–1198
Al-Mansur	1198–1200
Al-Adil I	1200–1218
Al-Kamil	1218–1238
Al-Adil II	1238–1240
As-Salih Ayyub	1240–1249
Turanshah	1249–1250
Al-Ashraf II	1250–1254

Syria

Saladin	1174–93
Al-Afdal	1193–96
Al-Adil I	1196–1218
Al-Mu'azzam	1218–27
An-Nasir Dawud	1227–29
Al-Ashraf	1229–37
As-Salih Ismail	1237
Al Kamil	1237–38
Al-Adil II	1238–39
As-Salih Ayyub	1239
As-Salih Ismail (2nd time)	1239–45
As-Salih Ayyub (2nd time)	1245–49
Turanshah	1249–50
An-Nasir Yusuf	1250–1260

Safavid rulers of Persia

Isma'il I	1501–24	Abbas II	1642–66
Tahmasp I	1524–76	Sulayman	1666–94
Isma'il II	1576–78	Sultan Husayn	1694–1722
Muhammad Khudabande	1578–88	Tahmasp II	1722–32
Abbas I	1588–1629	Nader	1732–36
Safi	1629–42		

Grand Masters of the Teutonic Order

Heinrich Walpot	1198–1200	Konrad Zöllner of Rotenstein	1382–90
Otto von Kerpen	1200–1208	Conrad of Wallenrode	1391–93
Heinrich Bart	1209–10?	Conrad of Jungingen	1393–1407
Hermann von Salza	1210–39	Ulrich of Jungingen	1407–10
Conrad von Thüringen	1239–40	Henry of Plauen	1410–13
Gerhard von Malberg	1241–44	Michael Küchmeister of	
Heinrich von Hohenlohe	1244–49	Sternberg	1414–22
Gunther von Wullersleben	1249–53	Paul of Rusdorf	1422–41
Poppo von Osterna	1253–57	Conrad of Erlichshausen	1441–49
Anno von Sangershausen	1257–73	Ludwig of Erlichhausen	1450–67
Hartmann of Heldrungen	1273–82	Henry Reuss of Plauen	1469–70
Burchard of Schwanden	1282–90	Henry Reffle of Richtenberg	1470–77
Conrad of Feuchtwangen	1291–96	Martin Truchsess of	
Gottfried of Hohenlohe	1297–1303	Wetzhausen	1477–89
Siegfried of Feuchtwangen	1303–11	John of Tiefen	1489–97
Charles of Trier	1311–24	Duke Frederick of Saxony	1498–1510
Werner of Orseln	1324–30	Margrave Albert of	
Luther of Brunswick	1331–35	Brandenburg-Ansbach	1511–25
Dietrich of Altenburg	1335–41	Walter of Kronberg	1527–43
Ludolf König	1342–45	Wolfgang Schutzbar	1543–66
Henry Dusemer	1345–51	George Hund of Wenckheim	1566–72
Winrich of Kniprode	1351–82	Henry of Bobenhausen	1572–90

Grand Princes and Grand Dukes of Lithuania

Traidenis	c.1270–82	Witold	1401–30
Pukuveras	c.1282–92	Switrigailo	1430–2
Vytenis	1293–1315	Sigismund	1432–40
Gediminas	1315–41	Casimir (IV)	1440–92
Algirdas	1342–77	Alexander (I)	1492–1506
Kenstutis	1377–82	Sigismund (I)	1506–48
Jogaila (Wladyslaw II		Sigismund (II)	1548–69*
of Poland)	1382–1401		

*The Grand Duchy was incorporated into the Polish Crown in 1569 by the Union of Lublin.

Rulers of Bohemia

Wratislaw II	1085–92	Charles I (IV)	1346–78
Wladislaw II (I)	1158–72	Wenzel (IV)	1378–1419
Premysl Ottokar I	1198–1230	Sigismund	1419–37
Wenceslas I	1230–53	Albrecht (II)	1437–39
Premysl Ottokar II	1253–78	Ladislas V	1440–57
Wenceslas II	1283–1305	George	1458–71
Wenceslas III	1305–06	Wladislaw II	1471–1516
Rudolf I (III)	1306–07	Louis II	1516–26
Heinrich	1307–10	Ferdinand I	1526–64
John	1310–46		

Kings of Poland

The Piast Dynasty

Boleslaw I the Brave	992–1025
Mieszko II	1025–34
Conflict	
Casimir I	1037–58
Conflict	
Boleslaw II	1076–79
Vladislav Herman	1079–1102
Zbigniev	1102–06
Boleslaw III Wrymouth	1106–38
Period of the Piast Dukes	**1138–1306**
Vladislav IV Lokietek (the Short)	1306–33
Casimir III	1333–70
Louis I	1370–82
Jadwiga	1384–99

Jagiellonian Dynasty

Wladyslaw II	1386–1434
Wladyslaw III	1434–44
Casimir IV	1446–92
John Albert	1492–1501

Alexander I	1501–06
Sigismund I	1506–48
Sigismund II	1548–72

Valois Dynasty

Henry of Valois	1573–74

House of Bathory

Stephen Bathory	1575–86

Polish Families

Sigismund III	1587–1632
Wladyslaw IV Vasa	1632–48
Jan Kazimierz Vasa	1648–68
Michał Korybut Wiśniowiecki	1669–73
John III Sobieski	1674–96

House of Wettin (Dukes of Saxony)

Augustus the Strong	1697–1706

Kings of France

Hugh Capet	987–96	John II	1350–64
Robert II	996–1031	Charles V	1364–80
Henry I	1031–60	Charles VI	1380–1422
Philip I	1060–1108	Charles VII	1422–61
Louis VI	1108–37	Louis XI	1461–83
Louis VII	1137–80	Charles VIII	1483–98
Philip II Augustus	1180–1223	Louis XII	1498–1515
Louis VIII	1223–26	Francis I	1515–47
Louis IX Saint	1226–70	Henry II	1547–59
Philip III	1270–85	Francis II	1559–60
Philip IV The Fair	1285–1314	Charles IX	1560–74
Louis X	1314–16	Henry III	1574–89
Philip V	1316–22	Henry IV Bourbon	1589–1610
Charles IV	1322–28	Louis XIII	1610–43
Philip VI of Valois	1328–1350	Louis XIV	1643–1715

Valois dukes of Burgundy

Philip the Bold	1363–1404	Philip the Good	1419–67
John Fearless	1404–19	Charles the Bold	1467–77

Mongol rulers

Grand khans/kaghans		*Il-khans of Persia*	
Chingiz Khan	1206–27	Hulagu	1256–65
Ögödei	1229–41	Abaqa	1265–82
Guyuk	1246–48	Ahmad	1282–84
Monke	1251–59	Arghun	1284–91
Kublah	1260–94	Gaykhatu	1291–95
		Baydu	1295
		Mahmud	1295–1304
		Oljaitu	1304–16
		Abu Said	1316–35

Princes of Moscow and tsars of Russia

Daniel	1276–1303	Vassily I	1389–1425
Yuri	1303–25	Vassily II	1425–62
Ivan I Kalita	1325–41	Ivan III	1462–1505
Simeon	1341–53	Vassily III	1503–33
Ivan II	1353–59	Ivan IV the Terrible	1533–84
Dmitri	1359–62	**Time of Troubles**	**1598–1682**
Dmitri Donskoy	1359–89	Peter the Great	1682–1725

Kings and queens of England

Alfred of Wessex	871–99	Edward 1	1272–1307
Cnut of Denmark	1017–35	Edward II	1307–27
Harold I	1035–40	Edward III	1327–77
Harthacnut	1040–42	Richard II	1377–99
Edward the Confessor	1042–66	Henry IV	1399–1413
Harold II	1066	Henry VIII	1509–47
William I	1066–87	Edward VI	1547–53
William II Rufus	1087–1100	Mary	1553–58
Henry I	1100–35	Elizabeth	1558–1603
Stephen	1135–54	James I	1603–25
Henry II	1154–89	Charles I	1625–49
Richard	1189–99	Protectorate	1649–59
John	1199–1216	Charles II	1660–85
Henry III	1216–72		

INDEX